Practical English Grammar & Composition

A Practical Approach to Grammatical Rules, their Usage & the Compositional English

SC Gupta
B.Sc, MA, LLB, DLL, M. Com, CAIIB

ARIHANT PUBLICATIONS (INDIA) LTD

ARIHANT PUBLICATIONS (INDIA) LIMITED

卐 Administrative & Production Offices

Corporate Office: 'Ramchhaya' 4577/15, Agarwal Road, Darya Ganj, New Delhi -110002
Tele: 011- 47630600, 43518550; Fax: 011- 23280316

Head Office: Kalindi, TP Nagar, Meerut (UP) - 250002
Tele: 0121-2401479, 2512970, 4004199; Fax: 0121-2401648

All disputes subject to Meerut (UP) jurisdiction only.

卐 Sales & Support Offices

Agra, Ahmedabad, Bengaluru, Bhubaneswar, Bareilly, Chennai, Delhi, Guwahati, Haldwani, Hyderabad, Jaipur Jalandhar, Jhansi, Kolkata, Kota, Lucknow, Meerut, Nagpur & Pune

卐 ISBN 978-81-8348-144-1

卐 Price : ₹ 275

Typeset by Arihant DTP Unit at Meerut

PO No. : TXT-59-T070829-5-26

PRINTED & BOUND BY ARIHANT PUBLICATIONS (I) LTD. (PRESS UNIT)

For further information about the products from Arihant log on to **www.arihantbooks.com** or email to **info@arihantbooks.com**

PREFACE

Most of the students find English, a language, difficult to understand. They found themselves incapable to understand and make the practical use of the grammatical rules. Most of them suffer from the phobia of English learning. I have kept these points in mind while writing this book. This is a practical hand book and an easy guide to the learning of English. This book is divided into three parts.

Part - I Practical Grammar   Part - II Essential Word Power   Part - III Composition

Part-I Comprises the basic rules of grammar along with illustrations and examples, denoting the applicability of the rules. A plenty of solved exercises are given on each chapter. These would be extremely helpful for the students in checking and testing their acquired knowledge. These exercises cover all types of questions usually asked about grammatical rules and their applicabilty in various academic and competitive examinations. In this way, students would become well conversant with the traditional and modern concepts of English Grammar.

Part-II Word Power is the most essential requirement of the students in writing and speaking English correctly. This part contains thousands of words, used in daily routine and asked about in various examinations. The part comprises the following segments of word power that would surely be much helpful for the students in improving their word power.

1. Synonyms
2. Antonyms
3. Paronyms
4. One Word Substitution
5. Homonyms
6. Idioms and Phrases
7. Animals: Males, Females, Youngs and Group Terms
8. Phrasal Verbs and Their Use
9. Sounds and Cries of Some Birds, Animals and Insects
10. Specific use of Words
11. Words Never used in Good Sense
12. Words Always Used in Good sense

Part-III This is a very important part, consists of various segments of compositional English. In this part valuable tips to attempt the comprehensions, writing precis and letters including essays, expansions, etc., have also been given. This part contains:

1. Paragraph Writing
2. Story Writing
3. Letter Writing
4. Invitations
5. Comprehensions
6. Precis Writing
7. Expansion Writing
8. Essay Writing
9. Report Writing
10. Autobiographies
11. Dialogue Writing
12. Figures of Speech
13. Appreciation of Poetry
14. Paraphrasing

It has been the utmost endeavour of the author to make the book really helpful for the students, studying in schools, colleges, universities and making preparations for various competitive examinations after completing their academic studies. Remember-

Something one finds difficult,
doesn't mean, one shouldn't try.
It means one should try harder.

Sagacious suggestions and constructive criticism are welcomed. I shall like to convey my sincere thanks to M/s Arihant Publications, especially to Mr. Deepesh Jain for bringing this book in the market, in the present shape and size.

SC Gupta
129-South West Block, Near Eidgah, Alwar (Rajasthan)
Ph : 0144-2700438

CONTENTS

1

Some Basic Terms of English

1. **Small and capital letters :** English language has 26 alphabets. Each letter of the English alphabet can be written as a 'small letter' or as a 'big letters'. Big letters are also called 'capital letters' or 'capitals'.

   A B C D E F G H I J K L M N O P Q R S T U V W X Y Z **—Capital letters**
   a b c d e f g h i j k l m n o p q r s t u v w x y z **—Small letters**

   Small letters are sometimes called 'lower case' and big letters 'upper case'.
2. **Sentence :** A sentence is a group of words that convey some meaning. It means, a sentence consists of words, but not every string of words constitute a sentence; as we can see in the following example :
   (a) To he market goes.
   A possible analysis is that if we look at this example we know the meaning of the individual words, but the sequence as a whole does not make sense or doesn't convey any meaning, so we cannot consider this structure, a sentence. Thus, we can affirm that if a sequence of words is to constitute a sentence, it must be meaningful; for instance :
   (a) He goes to market.
3. **Subject :** The subject is a person or thing 'performing' the action. In other words, subject is the noun, pronoun, or group of words acting as a noun, that performs the action indicated in the predicate of the sentence or clause.
4. **Predicate :** Basically, predicate is the rest of a sentence or clause other than the subject. It usually has a verb, and thus indicates some action, but may have other functions; such as modifying the subject. What is said about the subject is called predicate.
5. **Declarative sentence :** Declaration is a statement or observation. Narrative and descriptive passages are written using declarative sentences. As :
   (a) I did not abuse him. (b) We warned him.
6. **Interrogatives :** Questions are interrogative sentences. Grammarians like to use jargon, while telling writers to avoid it, so we have to deal with interrogative sentences.
   (a) Have you had your lunch?
   (b) Did you complete your work?
7. **Imperatives :** Imperative sentences convey commands, requests, advice or emergency pleas; for example:
   (a) It is imperative that you leave today.
   (b) Go there.
   (c) Please, open the door for me.

8. **Exclamations :** Most exclamations stand alone, making for very short sentences. Sentences can be exclamations, if they contain a strong emotion or opinion; for example :
   (a) Wah! (b) Wow! , (c) What a great fall!
9. **Sentence complements :** A sentence complement is a word or phrase adding meaning to the subject or verb. A complement clarifies the sentence. Complements usually appear after the simple predicate verb in a sentence, forming the complete predicate. Simply remember that complements complete predicates.
10. **Direct objects :** The objects , which receive directly the actions described by the verbs are called direct objects.
    A direct object answers the question "who or what?" and is being acted upon by the subject of a sentence.
11. **Indirect objects :** In addition to taking direct objects, some verbs also take indirect objects. In the following examples, the direct objects are printed in bold type, and the indirect objects are underlined.An indirect object answers "to/for whom/what?" Indirect objects usually refer to living things.
    (a) She gave the <u>child</u> a **pen**.
    (b) He sent the <u>man</u> the **information.**
12. **Clause :**Clause is such a group of words that forms part of a sentence and contains a subject and a finite verb. A clause contains both a subject and a predicate.
13. **Principal clause :** An independent clause has a subject and a finite verb. It can stand alone as a sentence.The independent clause is a short sentence.
14. **Subordinate clauses :** A subordinate clause modifies the sentence by acting as an adjective, adverb, or noun. Usually a dependent clause is introduced by a subordinate conjunction.
15. **Phrase :** A phrase is a group of words without a subject / verb or complete thought;e.g.-red tapism, ins and outs , hand in gloves etc.
16. **Simple sentence :**The most basic type of sentence is the simple sentence, which contains only one clause/ one finite verb. A simple sentence, contains a subject and a verb (finite), and it expresses a complete thought.
17. **Compound sentence :** A compound sentence is a sentence formed by two or more independent clauses.
18. **Complex sentence :** A complex sentence has an independent clause joined by one or more dependent clauses.Unlike a compound sentence, however, a complex sentence contains clauses which are not equal.
19. **Parts of speech :** Traditional grammar classifies words based on eight parts of speech. These are : verb, the noun, the pronoun, the adjective, the adverb, the preposition, the conjunction, and the interjection. Each part of speech explains not what the word is, but how the word is used. In fact, the same word can be a noun in one sentence and a verb or adjective in the next.
20. **Colloquial :** Means conversational, informal, everyday, casual , familiar, etc.
21. **Cognate object :** Some verbs take such an object after them that are similar in meaning to the verb. Such objects are called cognate objects.
    (a) He **sighed** a **deep sigh**. (b) Our army **fought** a **fierce fight**.
    In sentences (a) and (b), the verbs and the objects (cognate) are in bold type.

22. **Syllable** : A syllable is a part of a word that contains a single vowel sound and that is pronounced as a unit. So, for example, 'book' has one syllable, and 'reading' has two syllables.

One syllable words : run, sit, come, go, my, he etc.

Two syllable words : mon-day, four- teen, fa - ther, sun-day etc.

Words with more than two syllables : won-der-ful, beau-it-ful, de-mo-cra-cy, im-po-ssi-ble.

23. **Slang** : Slang consists of words, expressions and meanings that are informal and are used by the people who know each other very well and are quite familiar with one-another (generally abusive language).

24. **Tense** : Tense is that form of a verb which shows not only the time of an action but also the state of an action or event.

25. **Sequence of Tense** : The sequence of tenses are the principles which govern the tense of the verb in subordinate clause vis a vis the tense of the verb in principal clause.The rules which determine the tense of the subordinate clause if the tense of the principal clause is present or past or future, are studied under the heading sequence of tense.

26. **Noun** : A noun is a word used as name of a person, place or thing.

(i) **Proper noun** : Proper noun refers the name of a person, place or thing. e.g.Ram, Alwar, Jaipur etc.

(ii) **Common noun** : Common noun refers the name given to persons, things or places of the same kind or class, e.g. king, boy, girl,city etc.

(iii) **Collective noun** : Collective noun is the name of a group of persons or things taken together and spoken of as a whole, as unit; e.g. team, committee, army etc.

(iv) **Material noun** : A Material noun is the name of metal or substance, of which things are made of, e.g. silver, iron, wood etc.

(v) **Abstract noun** : Abstract noun in general refers to the name of quality, action or state; e.g.–honesty, bravery (quality), hatred, laughter (action), poverty, young(state), art etc.

27. **The Noun case** : The relation of noun with other words in a sentence is determined by its case :

(i) **Nominative case** : When a noun is used as subject of the verb in a sentence, it is in nominative case.

(ii) **Objective case** : When a noun is used as an object of the verb in a sentence, it is in objective case.

(iii) **Nominative of address** : When noun is used to address, it is nominative of address.
(a) Boys, don't make a noise. (b) Harish, wait for me.
'Boys' and 'Harish', are nominative of address.

(iv) **Case in apposition** : Two nouns referring to the same person or thing are in apposition, When one is placed immediately after the other, with no conjunction joining them; as in 'Her father,Naresh Chandra, left home three months ago.' Here, 'father and Naresh Chandra' refer to the same person.

28. **Conjunction** : A Conjunction is a word that joins words or sentences together.
A conjunction is also called a joiner, a word that connects (conjoins) parts of a sentence.

29. Adverb : An adverb is that word in a sentence which modifies the meaning of verb or adjective or another adverb or adverbial phrase.

30. Pronoun : Generally (but not always) pronouns stand for – 'pro + noun' or refer to a noun, an individual or individuals or thing or things (the pronoun's antecedent), whose identity is made clear earlier in the text.

31. Preposition : Preposition is a word placed before a noun or pronoun, denotes the relation, the person or thing referred by it, has with something else.

A preposition is followed by a 'noun'. It is never followed by a verb.

32. Subject-Verb Agreement : The verb must agree with its subject in number and person.

33. Weak Verbs : Verbs which require - ed, - d or - t to be added to their present tense form, to form the past are called weak verbs. These are also called Regular verbs. Examples :

Present	**Past**	**Past Participle**
Sell	Sold	Sold
Burn	Burnt	Burnt
Think	Thought	Thought
Lend	Lent	Lent
Talk	Talked	Talked
Live	Lived	Lived

34. Strong Verbs : Verbs that form their past tense by merely changing the vowel in their present form, without adding an ending, are called strong verbs. Examples :

Present	**Past**	**Past Participle**
Abide	Abode	Abode
Bear	Bore	Borne
Become	Became	Become
Find	Found	Found
See	Saw	Seen
Go	Went	Gone
Come	Came	Come

These are also called Irregular verbs.

35. Inchoative verbs : The term Inchoative verb is used for a verb that denotes the beginning, development or final stage, of a change of condition (***Guide to patterns and usage in English by* A S Hornby**). Examples :

Get, Became, Grow etc., as in following of sentences :

(a) My father is getting weaker.

(b) It is getting dark.

36. Transitive verb : Transitive verbs take objects. These verbs carry the action of a subject and apply it to an object. They tell us what the subject (agent) does, to something else (object).

37. Intransitive verbs : Intransitive verbs do not take an object; they express actions that do not require the agent's doing something to something else. Example :

38. **Linking verbs :** A linking verb connects a subject to a subject complement which identifies or describes the subject.

The following sentences are descriptive, using linking verbs :

(a) The house is green. (b) The house was white, until we painted it.

39. **Causative verbs :** Causative verbs show that somebody/something is indirectly responsible for an action. The subject doesn't perform the action itself, but causes someone/something else to do it instead. For example :

(a) I made her sing a song. (b) I made him polish my shoes.

40. **Modals :** Modal auxiliaries are special auxiliary verbs that express the degree of certainty of the action in the sentence, or the attitude or opinion of the writer/speaker concerning the action. These are verbs which 'help' other verbs to express a meaning : it is important to note that 'modal verbs' have no meaning by themselves.

41. **Non finites :** Non-finite verb forms are those that do not show number (they are not singular or plural) or tense (they do not make the sentence past or present.).

Non finites are of three kinds : 1. Infinitive, 2.Gerund, 3.Participle.

42. **Infinitive :** In grammar, the infinitive is the form of a verb that has no inflection to indicate person, number, mood or tense. Infinitives are also defined as 'to + base' form of the verb.

43. **Gerund :** Gerund is such a form of verb, that ends in 'ing'and has the force of a noun and a verb.

44. **Participle :** A participle is a non finite verb, called a 'verbal adjective,' which means that it has characteristics of both verbs and adjectives.Since they function as adjectives, participles modify nouns or pronouns. A participle most often ends in '-ing' or '-ed'.

45. **Unattached or dangling participle :** A participle is a verbal adjective , so it must be attached to some noun or pronoun. It means it must have a proper subject of reference.If the participle is not attached to some noun or pronoun, it is called dangling participle.

46. **Inversion :** Certain adverbs and adverb phrases, most with a restrictive or negative sense, can for emphasis be placed first in a sentence or clause and are then followed by the inverted (*i.e.*, interrogative) form of the verb. It is called Inversion.

47. **Synonym :** A synonym is a word or expression which means the same as another word or expression. For example :

The term 'industrial democracy' is often used as a synonym for 'worker participation'.

48. **Antonym :** The antonym of a word is a word which means the opposite. For example : day and night are antonyms.

49. **Heteronym :** A Heteronym is a word that has the same spelling as another word but with a different pronunciation and meaning. These words are sometimes also called homographs.

50. **Autograms :** A self-referencing sentence is a sentence that describes itself. For example: 'This sentence has five words.' An autogram is a self-referencing sentence that describes its letter content.

51. **Contronym :** The word contronym (also the synonym antagonym) is used to refer to words that, by some freak of language evolution, are their own antonyms. Both contronym and antagonym are relatively recent neologisms; however, there is no alternative term that is more established in the English language. Examples are :

(a) fast-quick, unmoving, (b) fix-restore, castrate.

52. Malapropism : A malapropism is the use of an incorrect word in place of a similarly sounding correct word; e.g. :

(a) Parents try to install these virtues in their children.

(b) He became affluent in French, Italian, Latin, and Greek.

53. Palindrome : A palindrome is a word or sentence that reads the same forward as it does backward. The words 'a' and 'I' are perhaps the simplest and least interesting palindromes; the word 'racecar' and the name 'Hannah' are more interesting and illustrative.

54. Palingram : A palingram is a sentence in which the letters, syllables, or words read the same backward as they do forward. The sentence, 'He was, was he?' is a word palingram, because the words can be placed in reverse order and still read the same. The sentence, 'I did, did I?' is not only a word palingram but a letter palingram(or palindrome) as well.

55. Pangram : A pangram is a sentence that contains all letters of the alphabet. Less frequently, such sentences are called holalphabetic sentences; e.g. :

The quick brown fox jumps over a lazy dog.

56. Eponym : An eponym is someone or something whose name is or is thought to be the source of something's name (such as a city, country, era, or product); e.g.—Xerox is a brand of photocopy machine; that word, too, has been since adopted to refer to any brand of photocopy machine and, moreover, also employed as a verb to describe the act of photocopying.

57. Adjunct : An adjunct is a word or group of words which indicates the circumstances of an action, event, or situation. An adjunct is usually a prepositional phrase or an adverb group.

58. Contraction : A contraction is a shortened form of a word or words :

(a) 'It's' (with an apostrophe) should be used only as a contraction for 'it is'.

(b) 'Can't' is the contracted form of 'cannot'.

59. Positive Degree : The positive degree of an adjective is the adjective in its general form.It denotes the mere existence of some quality.

60. Comparative Degree : The comparative degree denotes a higher degree of the quality than the positive .The comparative is used when two things are compared.

61. Superlative Degree : The Superlative degree denotes the highest degree of the quality. It is used when more than two things are compared.

Positive	**Comparative**	**Superlative**
Good	Better	Best
Strong	Stronger	Strongest
Tall	Taller	Tallest

2

Noun

Noun is a word used to name a person, animal, place, thing, and abstract idea. The **bold typed** words in the following sentences are nouns :

(a) Noun Last **year** our **neighbours** bought a **horse**.
(b) **Lata Mangeshkar** is a **singer**.
(c) The **inspector** looked at all the **passengers' tickets**.
(d) According to **Gandhi**, **honesty** is the best **policy**.

NOUN KINDS

There are five kinds of noun in English :

(1) Proper noun, (2) Common noun, (3) Collective noun,
(4) Material noun, (5) Abstract noun.

1. **Proper Noun :** Proper noun refers the name of a person, place or thing. For example : Ram, Alwar, Tom,France, Madrid, Mrs Smith etc.

   In each of the following sentences, the proper nouns are highlighted :

   (a) **Ram** is my friend. (b) I live at **Alwar.** (c) **Tom** is my friend **.**

2. **Common Noun :** A common noun is a noun referring to a person, place, or thing in a general way. Usually, one should write it with a capital letter only when it begins a sentence. For example : King, boy, girl, city, dog, man, table etc., are all common nouns.

   In each of the following sentences, the common nouns are highlighted :

   (a) According to this **board**, the nearest **town** is 80 kms. away from here.
   (b) All the **gardens** in the **neighbourhood** were invaded by **beetles** this **summer.**
   (c) The road **crew** was startled by the **sight** of three large **cats** crossing the **road.**

3. **Collective Noun :** A Collective noun is the name of a group of persons or things taken together and spoken of as a whole, as unit. For example : team, committee, army, crowd, flock, group, swarm etc.

   Collective noun takes singular verb in general.When it takes a plural verb, it is being used as a common noun.

   In each of the following sentences, the highlighted (bold type) words are collective nouns :

   (a) The **flock** of geese spends most of its time in the pasture.
   The collective noun 'geese' takes the singular verb 'spends.'
   (b) The **jury** is dining on take-out chicken tonight.
   In this example the collective noun 'jury' is the subject of the singular compound verb 'is dining.'

(c) The steering **committee** meets every Wednesday afternoon.

Here the collective noun 'committee' takes a singular verb, 'meets.'

4. **Material Noun :** A Material noun is the name of metal or substance, of which things are made of. As : silver, iron, wood etc.

The highlighted words in the following sentences are all material nouns :

(a) The necklace is made of **gold.**

(b) She has purchased a tea set of **silver.**

(c) He got his furniture made of teak **wood.**

Material nouns are uncountable.Material noun takes singular verb. One should not use article A /An before them.

5. **Abstract Noun :** An abstract noun is a noun which names anything which you can *not* perceive through your five physical senses. Abstract noun in general refers, the name of quality, action or state.

For example : Honesty, bravery, beauty (quality), joy, hatred, laughter (action), poverty, youth, disabled(state).

Abstract noun takes singular verb.

The highlighted words in the following sentences are all abstract nouns :

(a) Buying the emergency lights was an **afterthought.**

(b) **Honesty** is the best **policy**.

(c) **Justice** often seems to slip out of our **grasp**.

Countables and Non Countables

Noun is also classified as :

(A) Countable and (B) Non Countable noun.

(A) Countable Nouns : A countable noun is a noun with both a singular and a plural form, and it names anything (or anyone) that one can count.

In each of the following sentences, the highlighted words are countable nouns :

(a) We painted the **table** red and the **chairs** blue.

(b) She found six silver **dollars** in the **toe** of a **sock.**

(c) The oak **tree** lost three **branches** in the **hurricane**.

(B) Non-Countable Nouns : A non-countable noun is a noun which does not have a plural form, and which refers to something that one cannot usually count. A non-countable noun always takes a singular verb in a sentence. Non-countable nouns are similar to collective nouns, and are the opposite of countable nouns.

The highlighted words in the following sentences are non-countable nouns :

(a) J. Priestly discovered **oxygen.**

The word 'oxygen' cannot normally be made plural.

Since 'oxygen' is a non-countable noun, it takes the singular verb 'is' rather than the plural verb 'are.'

(b) They decided to sell the **furniture.**

We cannot make the noun 'furniture' plural.

(c) The **furniture** is heaped in the middle of the room.

Since 'furniture' is a non-countable noun, it takes a singular verb, 'is heaped.'

Some nouns are both noncountable and countable.

Sometimes a word that means one thing as a noncountable noun has a slightly different meaning as a countable noun. Remember, then, that the classifications, countable and noncountable, are not absolute.

Time is a good example :

(a) Time is money. (b) One should not waste the time on trifles.

Here use of '**Time**' is as noncountable noun.

See the following examples :

(a) When I was young I climbed this hill seven times.

(b) I have called her five times.

Here 'time' is used as countable noun.

NOUN RULES

Rule 1. **Some nouns always remain in plural form.They take plural verb. These nouns have no singular form.These are :**

Assets, alms, amends, annals, archives, ashes, arrears, athletics, auspices, species, scissors, trousers, pants, clippers, bellows, gallows, fangs, measles, eyeglasses, goggles, belongings, breeches, bowels, braces, binoculars, dregs, earnings, entrails, embers, fetters, fireworks, longings, lees, odds, outskirts, particulars, proceeds, proceedings, riches, remains, shambles, shears, spectacles, surroundings, tidings, tactics, tongs, vegetables, valuables, wages etc.

(a) Where are my pants.

(b) Where are the tongs.

(c) The proceeds were deposited in the court.

(d) All his assets were seized.

(e) He sees dissidents as the dregs of society.

(f) Alms were given to the beggars.

(g) The embers of the fire were still burning.

(h) He hated always to be the bearer of bad tidings.

NOTE *'Means' - In the sense of 'income' 'means' always takes a plural verb . In the sense of 'way to achieve some end' 'means' takes a singular verb . When 'a' or 'every' is used before 'means', it is singular.*

(a) My means were reduced substantially. (b) Every means is good if the end is good.

Rule 2. **Some nouns look plural in form but have singular meaning. Such nouns take singular verb. These are : News, Innings, Politics, Summons, Physics, Economics, Ethics, Mechanics, Mathematics,Measles, Mumps, Rickets, Billiards, Draughts, etc.**

(a) No news is good news. (b) Draughts is a good game.

(c) Economics is a good subject. (d) Ethics demands honesty in working.

Rule 3. **Some nouns look singular in form, but have plural meaning. Such nouns take plural verbs.These are : cattle, clergy, cavalry, infantry, poultry, peasantry, children, gentry, police etc.**

(a) Cattle are grazing in the field. (b) Our infantry have marched forward.

(c) There are no gentry in the colony. (d) Police have arrested the thieves.

Rule 4. **Some nouns are always used in singular form.These are uncountable nouns. We should not use article A/An with such nouns.These nouns are :**

Scenery, Poetry, Furniture, Advice, Information, Hair, Language, Business, Mischief, Bread, Stationery, Crockery, Luggage, Baggage, Postage, Knowledge, Wastage, Money, Jewelry, Breakage etc.

(a) The scenery of Darzeeling is very charming.
(b) I have no information about her residence.
(c) He transported his furniture by train.
(d) The mischief committed by him is unpardonable.
(e) His hair is black.
(f) He has no knowledge of grammar.

NOTE (i) *We cannot pluralise such nouns by adding 's' or 'es'. For example :It is incorrect to write sceneries, informations, furnitures, hairs.*

(ii) *We can make such nouns countables in the following way :*

(a) He gave me a piece of information.
(b) All pieces of information given by her were reliable.
(c) Many kinds of furniture are available in that shop.
(d) I want a few articles of Jewelry.
(e) He purchased some packets of bread.

(iii) *If hair is used as countable, it can be pluralised* : For example : one hair, two hairs.

(a) I need your two grey hairs. (b) I need three hairs of a black horse.

Rule 5. **Some nouns have the same form in singular as well as in plural form. For example : deer, fish, crew, family, team, jury, carp, pike, trout, aircraft, counsel,swine,vermin , etc.**

(a) Our team is the best.
(b) Our team are wearing their new uniform.
(c) The jury is considering its judgement.
(d) The jury are considering their verdict.
(e) One fish is there in the pond.
(f) There are many fish in the pond.

Rule 6. **Some nouns have plural meaning.If a definite numeral adjective is used before them, they are not pluralised. For example : pair, score, gross, stone, hundred, dozen, thousand, million, billion, etc.**

(a) I have two pair of shoes.
(b) I have two hundred rupees only.
(c) She purchased three dozen pencils.
(d) He has already donated five thousand rupees.
(e) It is a three feet wall.
(f) It is five feet in width.

Otherwise, in absence of a definite numeral adjective, these nouns can well be pluralised :

Dozens of women, hundreds of people, millions of dollars, scores of shops, many pairs of shoes, thousands, millions etc.

Rule 7. **If the same noun is repeated after preposition , the noun will be in singular form ; eg–**

(a) Town after town was devastated.
(b) Row upon row of pick marble looks beautiful.
(c) He enquired from door to door.
(d) Ship after ship is arriving.

Rule 8. **If a numeral adjective and a fraction are used with a noun ,the noun is used with the numeral and the noun will be in sigular form. For example :**

(a) He gave me one rupee and a half.
(b) She gave me two rupees and a quarter.

Avoid the following structure :

(a) He gave me one and a half rupees. *Incorrect.*
(b) She gave me two and a quarter rupees. *Incorrect.*

NOTE *If the numeral adjective and the fraction refer the multiplication, the noun will be placed in the end(after the fraction) and it must be plural.*

(a) Your deposits has grown two and a half **times** within two years.
(b) My salary has increased three and a quarter **times** within three years.

Rule 9. **Some nouns are known as common gender nouns. They can be used for either sex;Male or Female. These are called dual gender nouns. Such nouns are : teacher, student, child, clerk,candidate,advocate, worker, writer, author, leader, musician, politician,enemy, client, president, person, neighbour etc.When these nouns are used in singular form, use third person singular masculine (his) pronoun with them :**

(a) Every candidate should write his (not her) name.
(b) Every person should perform his (not her) duty.
(c) No one should abuse his (not her) neighbour.

Each , either , everyone, everybody, no one, nobody, neither , anybody are all **common gender pronouns.**

Rule 10. **Some nouns are used specifically for feminine gender only. Like : blonde, maid, mid wife, coquette, virgin etc.**

Nowadays nouns 'bachelor' and 'virgin' are being used for masculine and feminine gender as well .

(a) Ram is a bachelor . (b) Sita is a bachelor.
(c) Rahim is a virgin. (d) Rehana is a virgin.

NOUN GENDER

1. **Masculine Gender** : Tiger, Power, Violence, Father, Sun, Summer, Time, Thunder Men, Boys and Male animals (pronoun : he/ they).
2. **Feminine Gender** : Tigress, Woman, Lioness, Mother, Sister, Peace, Nature, Earth, Goddess etc. (pronoun : she/ they).
3. **Common Gender** : Teacher, Servant, Student, Cousin, Infant, Thief, Neighbour etc. (Pronoun : each, either, everbody etc.).
4. **Neuter** : Inanimate things; Copy, Book, Room, Paper, TV, Box, etc. (pronoun : it).

NOTE *Ships and sometimes cars and other vehicles when regarded with affection or respect are considered feminine. Countries when referred to by name , are also normally considered feminine.*

(a) The ship struck an iceberg, which tore a huge hole in her side.
(b) Scotland lost many of her bravest men in two great rebellions.

Personal masculine/ feminine nouns :different forms :

boy, girl
son, daughter
bridegroom, bride
father, mother
bachelor, spinster
husband, wife
man, woman
nephew,niece
gentleman, lady
uncle, aunt
widower, widow

Main exceptions : Following nouns have one form only :

baby
child
cousin
duke, duchess
earl, countess
infant
parent
relation
king, queen
lord, lady
relative
spouse
teenager
prince, princess

The majority of personal nouns have the same gender form :

artist
guide
doctor etc.
cook
assistant
driver
dancer

Main exceptions :

actor, actress
conductor, conductress
hero, heroine
host, hostess
manager, manageress
waiter, waitress

Also salesman, saleswoman, etc., but sometimes 'person' is used instead of 'man', 'woman'; as in- salesperson, spokesperson.

Domestic animals and many of the larger wild animals have different forms :

bull, cow
stallion, mare
stag, doe
lion, lioness
duck, drake
cock, hen
tiger, tigress
ram, ewe
gander, goose
dog, bitch

Others have the same form.

Rules of changing Masculine noun to Feminine noun

Rule 1. Some masculine form nouns can be changed to feminine form by adding 'ess' with the masculine form. For example :

Masculine	Feminine	Masculine	Feminine
Author	Authoress	Baron	Baroness
Count	Countess	Gaint	Gaintess
Host	Hostess	Heir	Heiress
Jew	Jewess	Lion	Lioness
Mayor	Mayoress	Manager	Manageress
Peer	Peeress	Patron	Patroness
Poet	Poetess	Priest	Priestess
Prophet	Prophetess	Tailor	Tailoress
Tutor	Tutoress	Steward	Stewardess
Shepherd	Shepherdess	Postmaster	Postmistress

Rule 2. **Some nouns can be changed to feminine form by removing the vowel and consonant from its masculine form and adding 'ess' as per following :**

Masculine	Feminine	Masculine	Feminine
Actor	Actress	Ambassador	Ambassadress
Benefactor	Benefactress	Director	Directress
Hunter	Huntress	Negro	Negress
Prince	Princess	Tiger	Tigress
Waiter	Waitress	Viscount	Viscountess

Rule 3. **In some cases, some masculine form nouns are changed to their feminine form by adding 'ess' as per following :**

Masculine	Feminine	Masculine	Feminine
Abbot	Abbess	Duke	Duchess
Emperor	Empress	God	Goddess
Governor	Governess	Master	Mistress
Marquis	Marchioness	Sorcer	Sorceress

Rule 4. **In case of compound masculine nouns some changes are made in first or second word :**

Masculine	Feminine	Masculine	Feminine
Man-servant	Maid-servant	Milk-man	Milk-maid
Doctor	Lady-doctor	Peacock	Peahen
Washerman	Washerwomen	Land-lord	Land-lady
Buck-rabbit	Doe-rabbit	Father-in-law	Mother-in-law
Brother-in-law	Sister-in-law	Step-father	Step-mother
He-bear	She-bear	He-goat	She-goat
Bull-calf	Cow-calf	Cock-sparrow	Hen-sparrow
Jack-ass	Jenny-ass	Dog-wolf	Bitch-wolf
Tomcat	She-cat	Step-brother	Step-sister
Head-master	Head-mistress	Grand-son	Grand-daughter

Rule 5. **Masculine and feminine genders of some important foreign words are given below. There is no rule for changing gender of such nouns :**

Masculine	Feminine	Masculine	Feminine
Administrator	Administratis	Shepherd	Shepherdess
Beau	Belle	Czar	Czarina
Executor	Executrix	Hero	Heroine
Lad	Lass	Monsieur	Madam
Prosecutor	Prosecutrix	Signor	Signora
Sultan	Sultana	Testator	Testatrix
Viceroy	Vicereine	Bachelor	Maid
Boar	Sow	Boy	Girl
Brother	Sister	Cock	Hen
Colt	Filly	Drake	Duck
Dog	Bitch	Drone	Bee
Buck	Doe	Bull	Cow
Earl	Countess	Father	Mother
Friar	Nun	Bridegroom	Bride

Gander	Goose	Gentleman	Lady
Hart	Roe	He	She
Horse	Mare	Husband	Wife
King	Queen	Lord	Lady
Lad	Lass	Man	Woman
Male	Female	Mister	Miss
Nephew	Niece	Ram	Ewe
Sir	Madam	Son	Daughter
Sire	Dame	Uncle	Aunt
Widower	Widow	Fox	Vixen
Wizard	Witch	Ox	Cow

NOUN NUMBER

Singular Noun : It refers 'one' (single) like; boy, girl, table, pen, man, woman etc.

Plural Noun : It refers more than one (not single), like ; cities, boys, girls, pens, men, women etc.

Changing Singular to Plural - Some Rules

(i) *The plural of a noun is usually made by adding 's' to the singular :*

day, days; dog, dogs; boy, boys; girl, girls ; kite,kites; telephone, telephones.

(ii) *Nouns ending in 'o or ch, sh, ss or x' , form their plural by adding es :*

Singular	Plural	Singular	Plural
Bus	Buses	Class	Classes
Fox	Foxes	Church	Churches
Watch	Watches	Mactch	Matches
Switch	Switches	Tax	Taxes
Ass	Asses	Dish	Dishes
Canvas	Canvases	Box	Boxes
Fix	Fixes	Coach	Coaches
Tomato	Tomatoes	Brush,	Brushes
Box,	Boxes	Church	Churches

Exceptions :

Dynamo, Dynamos	Kimono, Kimonos	Piano, Pianos
Kilo, Kilos	Photo, Photos	Soprano, Sopranos

(iii) *A few nouns form their plural by a vowel change :*

Foot, Feet	Louse, Lice	Mouse, Mice	Woman, women
Woman, Women	Goose, Geese	Man, Men	Goose, geese

(iv) *Nouns ending in 'double vowels' form their plural by adding 's' :*

Singular	Plural	Singular	Plural
Bee	Bees	Radio	Radios
Tree	Trees	Woe	Woes
Zoo	Zoos	Portfolio	Portfolios

(v) *Nouns ending in 'y' following a consonant, form their plural by adding 'ies' :*

Singular	Plural	Singular	Plural
Cry	Cries	City	Cities
Country	Countries	Dictionary	Dictionaries
Family	Families	Lorry	Lorries
Pony	Ponies	Reply	Replies

(vi) *There are twelve nouns, ending in 'f' or 'fe', drop the f or fe and add 'ves' :*

Singular	Plural	Singular	Plural
Calf	Calves	Life	Lives
Half	Halves	Leaf	Leaves
Wife	Wives	Self	Selves
Thief	Thieves	Knife	Knives
Wolf	Wolves	Shelf	Shelves
Loaf	Loaves	Sheaf	Sheaves

The nouns-hoof, scarf and wharf take either 's' or 'ves' in the plural :

hoofs or hooves scarfs or scarves wharfs or wharves

Exceptions

Singular	Plural	Singular	Plural
Belief	Beliefs	Proof	Proofs
Chief	Chiefs	Roof	Roofs
Cliff	Cliffs	Safe	Safes
Dwarf	Dwarfs	Scarf	Scarfs
Grief	Griefs	Strife	Strifes
Gulf	Gulfs	Turf	Turfs

(vii) *Compound nouns are pluralised by adding 's' with the main word* :

Singular	Plural
Brother-in-law	Brothers-in-law
Bed-room	Bed rooms
Commander in-chief	Commanders in chief
Step-daughter	Step-daughters
Maid-servant	Maid- servants
Peahen	Peahens
Peacock	Peacocks
Mother-in-law	Mothers-in-law
Sister-in-law	Sisters-in-law
Member of Parliament	Members of Parliament
Man servant	Men servants
Woman conductor	Women conductors
Man nurse	Men nurses
Woman engineer	Women engineers
Man hater	Man haters
Woman lover	Woman lovers
Man lover	Man lovers

(viii) *Following eight nouns are pluralised by changing inside vowels :*

Singular	Plural	Singular	Plural
Man	Men	Mouse	Mice
Woman	Women	Louse	Lice
Foot	Feet	Goose	Geese
Tooth	Teeth	Dormouse	Dormice

(ix) *Following nouns are pluralised by adding 'en' or 'ne' :*

Singular	Plural	Singular	Plural
Child	Children	Cow	Kine (Cows)
Ox	Oxen	Brother	Brethren

(x) *Some nouns have two plurals with different meanings :*

(1)	Brother	Brothers	Sons of the same parent.
		Brethren	Members of a society or community.
(2)	Cloth	Cloths	Unstitched cloth.
		Clothes	Stitched clothes (garments)
(3)	Die	Dies	Stamps used for printing and coining.
		Dice	Small cubes used in games.
(4)	Index	Indexes	Tables of contents in a book.
		Indices	Signs used in Algebra.

Some Typical Plural Nouns (Number)

1. ***Latin words** : Some Latin words ending in 'um' are pluralised by dropping 'um' and adding 'a' :*

Singular	Plural	Singular	Plural
Addendum	Addenda	Agendum	Agenda
Datum	Data	Dictum	Dicta
Ovum	Ova	Memorandum	Memoranda
Erratum	Errata	Stratum	Strata

NOTE *Agenda and Data are used in singular as well as in plural :*

(a) The agenda has been finalised.
(b) The agenda of the meeting are drawn to day.
(c) The data is incomplete.
(d) More data are required.

'Medium', when used in the sense of means or agency, its plural form is 'media'. When used in the sense of spiritual medium, its plural form is 'mediums'.

***Important** : Note the following Latin words , which are pluralised by adding 's' only :*

Singular	Plural	Singular	Plural
asylum	asylums	forum	forums
museum	museums	pendulum	pendulums
premium	premiums	quorum	quorums
petroleum	petroleums	formula	formulae / formulas

2. *Some Latin words ending in 'us' are pluralised by changing 'us' to 'i' :*

Singular	Plural	Singular	Plural
Radius	Radii	Locus	Loci
Syllabus	Syllabi	Genius	Genii

3. ***Greek words :*** *Some Greek words ending in 'is' are pluralised by changing 'is' to 'es' :*

Singular	Plural	Singular	Plural
Analysis	Analyses	Basis	Bases
Crisis	Crises	Thesis	Theses
Hypothesis	Hypotheses	Parenthesis	Parentheses.

4. *Some Greek words ending in 'on' are pluralised by changing 'on' to 'a' :*

Singular	Plural
Phenomenon	Phenomena
Criterion	Criteria

5. Various other nouns :Important

Singular	Plural	Singular	Plural
If	Ifs	But	Buts
I	I's	T	T's
5	5s	10	10s
P	P's	MP	MPs
BA	BAs	MA	MAs
ATM	ATMs	UPC	UPCs

USE OF APOSTROPHE WITH ' S

(A) You can form the possessive case of a singular noun that does not end in 's' by adding an apostrophe and 's'.We should use apostrophe in following situations only :

1. Living things :
(a) Mohan's book, (b) a cow's horn, (c) a woman's purse.

2. Thing personified :
(a) week's holiday, (b) earth's surface.

3. Space, time or weight :
(a) a day's leave, (b) a foot's length, (c) a pound's weight.

4. Certain dignified objects :
(a) the court's orders, (b) at duty's call,
(c) a razor's edge, (d) a needle's point.

5. Familiar phrases :
(a) at his wit's end, (b) at a stone's throw.

NOTE *If there are hissing sounds (sounds of 'sh' or 's') ending a word ,use apostrophe without 's' with such words.For example- for Jesus' sake, for conscience' sake, the roses' fragrance etc.(It can be noted that if we use apostrophe with 's' with such words, it couldn't be pronounced well).*

(B) You can form the possessive case of a singular noun that ends in 's', by adding an apostrophe alone or by adding an apostrophe and 's,' as in the following examples :

(a) The **bus's** seats are very comfortable.
(b) The **bus'** seats are very comfortable.
(c) The film crew accidentally crushed the **platypus's** eggs.
(d) The film crew accidentally crushed the **platypus'** eggs.

(C) You can form the possessive case of a plural noun that *does not* end in 's', by adding an apostrophe and a 's,' as in the following examples :

(a) The **children's** books were scattered on the floor of the porch.
(b) The **men's** cricket team will play as soon as the **women's** team is finished.

(D) You can form the possessive case of a plural noun that *does* end in 's' by adding an apostrophe :

(a) The concert was interrupted by the **dogs'** barking, the **ducks'** quacking, and the **babies'** squalling.
(b) The **janitors'** room is downstairs and to the left.
(c) My father spent many hours trying to locate the **squirrels'** nest.

(E) Do not use apostrophe with possessive pronouns like; his, hers, yours, mine, ours, its, theirs etc :

yours faithfully, yours truly, ours garden , his pen, hers purse, theirs room.
One should not write ''your's more's'', etc.

(F) Use apostrophe with the last word in following titles :

(a) Governor-general's instructions.
(b) Commander-in-chief's orders.
(c) My son in law's sister.
(d) Ram and Sons's shop.

(G) Do not use 'Double apostrophe' : Avoid double apostrophe in a sentence :

(a) My wife's secretary's mother has expired. *Incorrect*
The mother of my wife's secretary has expired. *Correct*

(b) Mrs. Kuwrani's now chairperson of society's proposal was rejected. *Incorrect*
The proposal of Mrs Kuwrani, now chairperson of society was rejected. *Correct*

(H) Apostrophe with 's' is used with ; Anybody/nobody/everybody/somebody/anyone/ some one/no one/every one.

(a) Everyone's concern is no one's concern.
(b) Every body's business is nobody's business.

NOTE *If 'else' is used after above said words, use apostrophe with 'else' as per following :*

(a) I can rely on your words, not somebody else's.
(b) I obey your orders and nobody else's.

NOUN CASE

1. Nominative case,
2. Objective case,
3. Possessive cases,
4. Case in apposition,
5. Nominative of address.

1. **Nominative case** : When a noun is used as subject of the verb in a sentence , it is in nominative case.

Read the following sentences :

(a) Ram writes an essay. (a) Sarla reads a novel.
(c) Rahim is playing chess. (d) The thief has ran away.

In above sentences nouns Ram, Sarla, Rahim and thief are in nominative case .

2. **Objective case :** When a noun is used as an object of the verb in a sentence, it is in objective case.

Read the following sentences :

(a) He eats an apple. (b) She plays football.
(c) I write a letter. (d) Shyam cooks food.

In above sentences all underlined words (nouns), are used in objective case.

3. **Possessive case :** In the possessive case, a noun changes its form to show that it owns or is closely related to something else. Usually, nouns become possessive by adding a combination of an apostrophe (') and the letter 's.' :

(a) Ramesh's wife. (b) Rahim's seat.
(c) Sarla's mother. (d) Mira's saree.

4. **Noun in apposition :** Apposition means-'having near'.Two nouns referring to the same person or thing are in apposition, if one is placed immediately after the other, with no conjunction joining them . For example :

Her father, Naresh Chandra, left home three months ago. Here, 'Her father' and 'Naresh Chandra' refer same man and have no conjunction joining them. They are nouns in apposition.

Read the following sentences :

(a) Ram, his brother, is an honest man. (b) Harish ,his son, is a naughty boy.
(c) Sita, her daughter, is a beautiful girl.

In above sentences nouns; father and Naresh , Ram and brother , Harish and son, and Sita and daughter, are in apposition.

5. **Nominative of address :** If a noun is used to address , such use of noun is called nominative of address.

Read the following sentences :

(a) Boys, don't make a noise. (b) Harish, wait for me.
(c) Suresh, go to Jaipur. (d) Rahul, come here.

In above sentences, Boys, Harish, Suresh and Rahul are nouns , used to address them.

CORRECT YOURSELF EXERCISE : NOUN

CYE : 01 Correct the sentence :

1. Her hairs are curly.
2. Our elders gave us many advices.
3. I have many work to do.
4. Sita has sold all her furnitures.
5. She gave me informations about this bank.
6. The sceneries of Himachal Pradesh are very charming.

7. The peoples are hard working.
8. The cattles are grazing in the field.
9. I want a paper.
10. I bring fruits and vegetables from the market.
11. You must continue your study.
12. These news are false.
13. They go to Agra during the summer vacations.
14. Her spectacle is very nice.
15. She has a twenty rupees note.

CYE : 02 Correct the sentence :

1. He got only passing marks.
2. Ram was true to his words
3. Ten miles are a long distance.
4. They want two dozens apple.
5. I want two pairs of white shoes.
6. Rahul has finished two third of his work.
7. The chair's legs are broken.
8. Good night , I am so glad to meet you.
9. There is no space in the car.
10. We should help the poors.
11. She left for Delhi by 8.30 O'clock bus.
12. One of his son is a teacher.
13. 'Amazing stories' are an interesting book.
14. This is my son's in law house.

CYE : 03 Correct the sentence :

1. I brought my furnitures by goods train
2. I saw two beautiful fishes in the pond.
3. Thomson's poetries are very charming
4. Is your scissors dull?
5. Light travel faster than sound.
6. All the furnitures of my house have stolen.
7. A poet and writer are dead.
8. The committee was divided on this issue.
9. Mathematics are not a dificult subject
10. My sympathies are always with the poor.
11. The mother both carried her son and daughter from the burning house .
12. My sister serves in boy's school.
13. Rohan's and Mohan's house is very far from here.
14. There are many news published in local paper.
15. The teacher has taught the alphabets.

CYE : 04 Correct the sentence :

1. Please reply, your's faithfully...
2. I go for a two miles walk daily.
3. She loves either you or I.
4. There are four breads in the kitchen.

5. One should not hate the poors.
6. The magistrate passed order of his release.
7. She has committed not one but many mischiefs.
8. The first inning is going to over now.
9. There is no place in this compartment.
10. He bought some stationeries.
11. My mother's brother's son has come.
12. There are a few peoples who are really honest.
13. Give me ten pices.
14. There were no gentries in that function.

CYE : 05 Correct the following sentences :

1. He is a sixty years old man.
2. A five men committee had a three hours meeting yesterday.
3. An all parties meeting was called to consider the drought situation in the country.
4. There is two ways traffic here, so no problem of traffic blockage.
5. How can our country accept the two nations theory?
6. He has gone to market to purchase vegetable.
7. He said, "Riches has wings".
8. I asked him where was his spectacles.
9. She said that she was suffering from measle.
10. She said, "Please give him an alm".

CYE : 06 Correct the following sentences :

1. Shelly's poetries are great.
2. I saw beautiful sceneries in Kashmir last year.
3. He has purchased new machineries.
4. He said, "He has purchased very costly crockeries".
5. There were very heavy traffics on the road.
6. She has bought very beautiful furnitures.
7. He gave me many informations.
8. I am going to purchase some stationeries.
9. Ram said, "The hair of Sita are black".
10. This house is made of bricks and stones.

CYE : 07 Correct the following sentences :

1. Cities after cities were destroyed by the army.
2. Hours after hours were passed,but she didn't turn up.
3. Ram said, "Ï beg from doors to doors daily".
4. Ships after ships were sailing by those days.
5. Rows upon rows of pink marble are soothing to the eyes.
6. I gave her three and a half apples.
7. The meeting was held for three and a quarter hours.
8. The length of this hall is three times and a half to that hall.
9. His salary is two times and a half to that of mine.
10. I have two and a half rupees only.

CYE : 08 Correct the following sentences :

1. What the peoples think, I can't say.
2. Who owns these poultries?
3. He is my cousin brother.
4. How many 3s are there in 31313.
5. How many cattles you have?
6. I have only ten five rupees's notes.
7. He has written a nice poetry.
8. Today I have received two month's wages.
9. What is this book's price.
10. There are only two females in the garden.

SOLUTIONS : CORRECT YOURSELF EXERCISE

Solutions CYE : 01

1. Her hair is curly
2. Our elders gave us many pieces of advice.
3. I have much work to do.
4. Sita has sold all her furniture.
5. She gave me information about this bank.
6. The seenery of Himachal Prardesh is very charming.
7. The people are hard working .
8. The cattle are grazing in the field.
9. I want a piece of paper.
10. I bring fruit and vegetables from the market.
11. You must continue your studies.
12. This news is false.
13. They go to Agra during the summer vacation.
14. Her spectacles are very nice.
15. She has a twenty rupee note.

Solutions CYE : 02

1. He got only pass marks .
2. Ram was true to his word.
3. Ten miles is long distance.
4. They want two dozen apples.
5. I want two pair of white shoes.
6. Rahul has finished two thirds of his work.
7. The legs of the chair are broken.
8. Good evening ,I am so glad to meet you.
9. There is no room in the car.
10. We should help the poor.
11. She left for Delhi by 8.30 bus.
12. One of his sons is a teacher.
13. 'Amazing stories' is an interesting book.
14. This is my son -in-law's house.

Solutions CYE : 03

1. I brought my furniture by goods train.
2. I saw two beautiful fish in the pond.
3. Thomson's poetry is very charming.
4. Are your scissors dull?
5. Light travels faster that sound.
6. All the furniture of my house have stolen.
7. A poet and writer is dead
8. The committee were divided on this issue.
9. Mathematics is not a dificult subject
10. My sympathy is always with the poor.
11. The mother carried both her son and daughter from the burning house.
12. My sister serves in boys' school.
13. Rohan and Mohan's house is very far from here.
14. There are many items of news published in the local paper.
15. The teacher has taught the letters of alphabet

Solutions CYE : 04

1. Please reply, yours faithfully
2. I go for a two mile walk daily.
3. She loves either you or me.
4. There are four pieces of bread in the kitchen.
5. One should not hate the poor.
6. The magistrate passed orders of his release.
7. She has committed not one but many acts of mischief.
8. The first innings is going to be over now.
9. There is no room in this compartment.
10. He bought some stationery.
11. The son of my mother's brother has come.
12. There are few people who are really honest.
13. Give me ten pice.
14. There were no gentry in that function.

Solutions CYE : 05

1. He is a sixty year old man.
2. A five man committee had a three hour meeting yesterday.
3. An all party meeting was called to consider the drought situation in the country.
4. There is two way traffic here so no problem of traffic blockage.
5. How can our country accept the two nation theory.
6. He has gone to market to purchase vegetables.
7. He said, "Riches have wings".
8. I asked him where were his spectacles.
9. She said that she was suffering from measles.
10. She said, "Please give him alms".

Solutions CYE : 06

1. Shelly's poetry is great.
2. I saw beautiful seenery in Kashmir last year.
3. He has purchased new machinery.
4. He said, "He has purchased very costly crockery".
5. There was very heavy traffic on the road.
6. She has bought very beautiful furniture.
7. He gave me a lot of information.
8. I am going to purchase some stationery.
9. Ram said, "The hair of Sita is black".
10. This house is made of brick and stone.

Solutions CYE : 07

1. City after city was destroyed by the army.
2. Hour after hour was passed but she didn't turn up.
3. Ram said , "I beg from door to door daily."
4. Ship after ship was sailing by those days.
5. Row upon row of pink marble is soothing to the eyes.
6. I gave her three apples and a half.
7. The meeting was held for three hours and a quarter.
8. The length of this hall is three and a half times to that of this hall.
9. His salary is two and a half times to that of mine.
10. I have two rupees and a half only.

Solutions CYE : 08

1. What the people think I can't say.
2. Who owns these poultry?
3. He is my cousin.
4. How many 3's are there in 31313?
5. How many cattle you have?
6. I have only ten five rupee notes.
7. He has written a nice poem.

   or

   He has written nice poetry.
8. Today I have received two months wages.
9. What is the price of this book?
10. There are only two women in the garden.

3

Adjective

DETERMINERS

The word-determiner is not found in traditional grammar books.Half of what we now call determiners used to be a separate class, the articles. The other half, even though they work in the same way as articles do, used to be lumped in with adjectives. So we had 'real' adjectives and also things called demonstrative adjectives, possessive adjectives, etc.

Modern grammarians and linguists make a clear distinction between adjectives and determiners, because they have different sorts of meanings and different uses. Adjectives tell us about the qualities of the thing referred to (*red* pens, a *black* dog , *beautiful* girls).

The most common determiners are as follows :

(i) Articles : *a, an, the.*
(ii) Quantifiers : *all, few, many, several, some.*
(iii) Possessives : *her, his, its, my, our, their, your.*
(iv) Demonstratives : *this, that, these, those .*
(v) Numerals : *one , three, hundred etc.*
(vi) Negative : *no.*

The determiner, along with the adjective, usually indicates whether a noun is singular or plural, masculine or feminine. In other words, it indicates Number and Gender. This means that most determiners have several different forms.

Determiners are words which quantify or identify nouns. Determiners are followed by a noun. Some categories of determiners are limited (there are only three articles, a handful of possessive pronouns, etc.), but the possessive nouns are as limitless as nouns themselves. This limited nature of most determiner categories, however, explains why determiners are grouped apart from adjectives even though both serve a modifying function. We can imagine that the language will never tire of inventing new adjectives; the determiners (except for those possessive nouns), on the other hand, are well established, and this class of words is not going to grow in number.

ADJECTIVES

An **adjective** modifies a noun or a pronoun by describing, identifying, or quantifying words. An adjective usually precedes the noun or the pronoun which it modifies.

Look at the following sentences :

(a) The **coal** mines are **dark** and **dank**
(b) **Many** stores have already begun to play **irritating Christmas** music.

(c) A **battered music** box sat on the **mahogany** sideboard.
(d) The **back** room was filed with **large, yellow rain** boots.
(e) She is a **good** girl.
(f) Alwar is a **small** city.
(g) He gave me **five** pencils.
(h) This is **my** pen.
All bold words in above sentences are adjectives.

Adjective clause : If a group of words containing a subject and verb acts as an adjective, it is called an **adjective clause**.

(a) My sister, who is much younger than I am, is a nurse.

Adjective phrase : If an adjective clause is stripped of its subject and verb, the resulting modifier becomes an **adjective phrase** : He is the man (who is) keeping his family in a hotel.

KINDS OF ADJECTIVES

1. **Proper Adjective :** Adjectives that are derived from proper nouns are called **proper adjectives**. Proper adjectives begin with a capital letter in English; Indian, African, American, European etc are proper adjectives.The proper adjectives in the following sentences are italicised :
   (a) This *Indian* town has an interesting history.
   (b) He is an *American*.
   (c) This building is a fine example of *Victorian* architecture.
   (d) I have many *German* friends.
2. **Attributive Adjectives :** Adjectives which precede the noun they modify are known as **attributive adjectives**. In the following examples, the attributive adjectives are italicised :
   (a) *Heavy* rain is expected. (b) We saw a *white* tiger in the zoo.
   In above examples, 'heavy' is an attributive adjective modifying the noun 'rain'; and 'white' is an attributive adjective modifying the noun 'tiger'.
   There are several types of attributive adjectives :
   (a) Adjectives indicating size e.g. **large, long, narrow , etc.**
   (b) Adjectives indicating weight e.g. **heavy, light , etc.**
   (c) Participles and other adjectives e.g. **clever, excited, interesting , etc.**
   (d) Adjectives indicating temperature e.g. **cold, hot, warm, etc.**
   (e) Adjectives indicating humidity e.g. **dry, damp, wet, etc.**
   (f) Adjectives indicating age e.g. **new, six-month-old, young, etc.**
   (g) Adjectives indicating shape e.g. **barrel-shaped, round, square, etc.**
   (h) Adjectives indicating colour e.g. **blue, grey, white, etc.**
   (i) Adjectives indicating materials e.g. **cloth, leather, metal, etc.**
   (j) Defining adjectives, usually indicating purpose, method of operation, location,time or categories of people etc .

(i) **Defining Adjectives :** When an attributive adjective preceding a noun not only describes the object being referred to, but also helps to define or identify the type of object meant, such adjective is called a **defining adjective**. The defining adjectives in the following examples are italicised :

(a) We had an enjoyable ***Eid*** party

(b) Ram is a fine ***young*** man

(c) I want to purchase a new ***telephone*** directory.

(ii) Ordinal adjectives : Attributive adjectives like; **next, last, first, second, third** etc., are sometimes referred to as **ordinal adjectives**. They indicate the order in which things occur.

3. Possessive Adjectives : Possessive adjectives ('my,' 'your,' 'his,' 'her,' 'its,' 'our,' 'their') are identical to possessive pronouns .A Possessive adjective modifies a noun or a noun phrase.

(a) This is ***my*** book.

(b) That is ***your*** almirah.

(c) What is ***your*** phone number.

In sentence (c) the possessive adjective 'your' modifies the noun phrase 'phone number'; the entire noun phrase 'your phone number' is a subject complement.

(d) They have lost **their** way in the forest.

In this sentence, the possessive adjective 'their' modifies 'way' and the noun phrase 'their way' is the direct object of the compound verb ''have lost''.

(e) The dog chased **its** ball down the stairs.

In this sentence, the possessive adjective 'its' modifies 'ball' and the noun phrase 'its ball' is the object of the verb 'chased.' Note that 'its' is the possessive adjective and 'it's' is a contraction for 'it is.'

4. Demonstrative Adjectives : The **demonstrative adjectives** ('this,' 'these,' 'that,' 'those,' and 'what' and 'such') are identical to the demonstrative pronouns.These are used to modify nouns or noun phrases.

Look at the following sentences :

(a) ***This*** girl is more intelligent than Sarla.

(b) ***That*** student is very honest.

(c) ***These*** apples are unripe.

(d) I don't like ***such*** jokes.

(e) ***Those*** thieves should be punished.

5. Interrogative Adjectives : An **interrogative adjective** ('which' , 'what' 'whose') is like an interrogative pronoun.These are used with nouns to introduce a question :

(a) **What** book are you reading?

(b) **Whose** pen is this?

(c) **Which** plants should be watered twice a week?

6. Indefinite Adjectives : An **indefinite adjective** is similar to an indefinite pronoun.An indefinite adjective modifies a noun, pronoun, or noun phrase.Such adjectives are ; all, any , many,several, few etc :

(a) Many people believe that corruption can't be eradicated.

The indefinite adjective 'many' modifies the noun 'people' and the noun phrase 'many people' is the subject of the sentence.

(b) I found a few goldfish floating belly up in the pound.

In this example the indefinite adjective 'few' modifies the noun 'goldfish' and the noun phrase is the direct object of the verb 'found' :

(c) All students went to Delhi.

Here the indefinite pronoun 'all' modifies 'students'.

7. **Emphasising Adjectives : Emphasising adjectives** are used to emphasise the nouns as per following :

   (a) Mind your **own** business.

   (b) I saw the witch by my **own** eyes.

   (c) This is the **very** book I wanted.

8. **Exclamatory Adjectives :** Look at the following sentences :

   (a) What a fall! (b) What an idea! (c) What a beauty!

   In these sentences 'what' is used as exclamatory adjective.

9. **Predicate Adjectives :** An **adjective** which is separated from the noun or pronoun (it modifies) by a verb is called a **predicate adjective**. The predicate adjectives in the following examples are underlined :

   (a) The dog is black. (b) The markets are long and wide.

   It should be understood well that some Attributive adjectives can also be used as predicate adjectives. In above examples, the adjective **'black'** modifies the noun **dog,** the adjectives **'long'** and **'wide'** modify the noun **'markets'.**

   Most general descriptive adjectives, as well as adjectives indicating colour, can also be used as **predicate adjectives**. In the following examples, the predicate adjectives are italicised.

   (a) The question was ***tough***. (b) The room was ***large***.

   (c) That girl is ***young***. (d) The cake is ***fresh***.

   But a few general descriptive adjectives cannot be used as predicate adjectives. For example, adjectives ;chief ,main ,principal ,sheer ,utter are normally used only as attributive adjectives. Proper adjectives are also sometimes used as predicate adjectives.

   (a) That car is ***Indian***. (b) This one is ***Japanese***.

   It should be also noted that hyphenated adjectives containing nouns normally are not used as predicate adjectives.In the following examples, the nouns contained in the hyphenated adjectives are italicised.

   (a) There was a two-***year***-old child (b) She bought forty-***dollar*** shoes

NOTE *Some adjectives with a prefix 'A' can be used as Predicate Adjectives not as attributive adjectives. Such adjectives are;afloat ,afraid,aglow,alive,alone,asleep.*

   (a) She is ***asleep***. (b) I found the child ***alive***.

10. **Interpolated Adjectives :** As well as being used as attributive or predicate adjectives, general descriptive adjectives and adjectives indicating colour can also be placed elsewhere in a sentence. When an adjective can be placed elsewhere in a sentence the adjective is called an **Interpolate Adjective**.Normally the general descriptive adjectives and the adjectives indicating colour are interpolated into a sentence. In the following sentences, the interpolated adjectives are italicised.

    (a) The child , *happy and excited*, ran behind the bus.

    (b) *Worried,entusiastic and alert,* we waited to see what would happen next.

    Since the use of interpolated adjectives is somewhat uncommon, the use of interpolation can serve to emphasize the adjectives. Interpolated adjectives are most often placed immediately after a noun, as shown in the first example; or before a noun or pronoun at the beginning of a sentence, as shown in the second example.

NOTE *When more than one adjective is used in a sentence, the last two adjectives are separated from one another by the word* ***and****, and previous adjectives are separated from one another by commas. The interpolated adjectives must also be separated from the rest of the sentence by commas. For instance, in the first example above, the interpolated adjectives* ***happy and excited*** *are separated from the rest of the sentence by a comma before the word* ***happy****, and a comma following the word* ***excited****. Likewise, in the second example, the interpolated adjective* ***worried, enthusiastic and alert*** *are separated from the rest of the sentence by a comma following the word* ***alert****. Further,* ***'Worried'*** *and* ***'enthusiastic'*** *are separated from each other by a comma, and the last two adjectives '****enthusiastic*** *and* ***'alert'*** *are separated by the word* ***'and'****.*
Interpolated adjectives are used more often in written English than in spoken English.

11. Participles used as Adjectives : Present and past participles of verbs can be used as adjectives.

(A) Present participles : Present participles used as adjectives refer to actions being performed **by** the things being described. In the following examples the present participles used as adjectives are italicised :

(a) I saw a ***falling*** star. (b) ***Barking*** dog seldom bites.

(B) Past participles : Past participles used as adjectives refer to actions which have been performed **on** the things being described. In the following examples, the past participles used as adjectives are italicised :

(a) She laid a blanket on ***scattered*** leaves. (b) I found there a ***broken*** drum.

Formation of Adjectives

1. *Some adjectives are formed by adding some words with the noun :*

Noun	Adjective	Noun	Adjective
Sick	Sicken	Glory	Glorious.
Gold	Golden	Boy	Boyish
Fool	Foolish	Laugh	Laughable
Play	Playful	Courage	Courageous
Care	Careful	Envy	Envious
Trouble	Troublesome	Man	Manly
Shame	Shameless	King	Kingly
Sense	Senseless	Woman	Womanish

2. *Some adjectives are formed by adding some words with verb :*

Verb	Adjective	Verb	Adjective
Tire	Tiring	Move	Movable
Talk	Talkative	Eat	Edible

3. *Some adjectives are formed from other adjectives :*

Adjective	Adjective	Adjective	Adjective
Colour	Colourful	Black	Blackish
Green	Greenish	Whole	Wholesome
Yellow	Yellowish	Three	Threesome

FORMATION OF COMPARATIVE AND SUPERLATIVE

Like adverbs there are three degrees of Adjectives : Positive, Comapraative and Superlative.

1. *The comparative degree of an adjective is normally formed by adding 'er' and the superlative is formed by adding 'est' to the positive :*

Positive	Comparative	Superlative
Sweet	Sweeter	Sweetest
Young	Younger	Youngest
High	Higher	Highest
Old	Older	Oldest

2. *When the positive ends in 'e' only 'r' and 'st' is usually added to make the compartive and superlative degrees:*

Positive	Comparative	Superlative
White	Whiter	Whitest
Noble	Nobler	Noblest
Wise	Wiser	Wisest
Large	Larger	Largest
Safe	Safer	Safest
Fine	Finer	Finest

3. *If the positive degree ends in 'y' and is preceded by a consonant, the 'y' is changed into 'i' before adding 'er' and 'est' to form comparative and superlative :*

Positive	Comparative	Superlative
Easy	Easier	Easiest
Lovely	Lovelier	Loveliest
Happy	Happier	Happiest
Heavy	Heavier	Heaviest
Healthy	Healthier	Healthiest
Pretty	Prettier	Prettiest
Merry	Merrier	Merriest

4. *If the positive is a word of one syllable and ends in a single consonant which is preceded by a short vowel, the consonant is doubled before adding 'er' or 'est' to form comparative and superlative degree :*

Positive	Comparative	Superlative
Wet	Wetter	Wettest
Big	Bigger	Biggest
Hot	Hotter	Hottest
Fat	Fatter	Fattest

5. *Some adjectives of two or more than two syllables form the comparative and superlative degrees by adding 'more' and 'most' before the positive form :*

Positive	Comparative	Superlative
Difficult	More difficult	Most difficult
Important	More important	Most important

Careless	More careless	Most careless
Beautiful	More beautiful	Most beautiful
Courageous	More courageous	Most Courageous
Useful	More useful	Most useful

6. *Some comparatives and superlatives are formed in an irregular manner :*

Positive	**Comparative**	**Superlative**
Ill,bad	Worse	Worst
Much	More	Most
Fore	Former	Foremost, First
Late	Later	Last
Good, Well	Better	Best

SOME IMPORTANT DETERMINERS AND ADJECTIVES

Farther/ Farthest and Further/ Furthest :

Both forms **(Farther/ Farthest and Further/ Furthest)** can be used *to express distances* :

(a) NewYork is farther/ further than Lincoln or Selby.

(b) NewYork is the farthest / furthest town .

(c) NewYork is the farthest / furthest of the three.

'Further' is usually used, with abstract nouns to mean additional / extra :

(a) No further action is needed in this matter.

(b) Further discussion would be pointless.

'Furthest' can also be used with abstract nouns.

(a) This was the furthest point they reached in their discussion.

(b) This was the furthest concession he would make.

Elder, Eldest ; Older, Oldest : 'Elder', 'eldest' are chiefly used for *comparisons within a family*. They imply seniority rather than age.Elder and eldest are used for persons, while older and oldest are used for persons as well as for things. Elder is not used with 'than' , it takes 'to'. 'Older / Oldest' is used for age.

(a) Ram is my elder brother.

(b) My mother is the eldest member of our family.

(c) Ram is older than Shyam.

(d) Sunder and Purinder are real brothers. Sunder is elder to Purinder.

(e) This is the oldest college in our city.

(f) The older people should be respected.

Later / Latest / Latter / Last : 'Later' and 'Latest' are used with reference to time. 'Latter' and 'last' are used with reference to order. 'Latest' refers to new(last up to now) or very recent things. 'Last' means final or no new after that.In talking about events , inventions , productions etc. , we use 'latest.' 'Latter' is used for comparison of two in order; for more than two we use 'last'.

Look at the following sentences :

(a) He came later than Ram.

(b) He came in the last.

(c) Between Ram and Shyam, the latter is more intelligent.

(d) Of iron and silver, the latter is known as white metal.

(e) This is the latest fashion.
(f) This is the latest technology.
(g) At last the chairman distributed the prizes.
(h) Lord Mountbatten was the last Governor General of India.

***Many and Much* (adjectives and pronouns) :**

'Many' (adjective) is used before *countable nouns. 'Much'* (adjective) is used before *uncountable nouns* :

(a) She didn't buy many books. (b) We haven't much sugar.

The comparative and superlative of **much** and **many** are same : **more** and **most; eg –** more books, more sugar, most men.

many, much, more, most can also be used as pronouns :

(a) He gets a lot of letters but she doesn't get many.
(b) You have a lot of free time but I haven't much.

'Much' and 'many' can be used quite freely with negative verbs, but with affirmative or interrogative verbs 'much' and 'many' have a restricted use :

(a) I haven't much patience. (b) She hasn't much money.

Use of many and much with affirmative verbs :

'Many' is used when it is modified by a good / a great. Both (much and many) can be used when modified by 'so/ as/ too' :

(a) Ram has made a good many friends there.
(b) She has had so many jobs that......
(c) He studied as much as he could.
(d) She drinks too much (wine).

We use 'a lot/ lots' of (+ noun) or 'a lot or lots' (pronouns) instead of 'many', when it is not modified and used as object or part of the object . 'Much' is also replaced by 'a great/ good deal of ' (+ noun) or 'a great/ good deal' (pronouns) as object or part of the object :

(a) I saw a lot/ lots of animals. I expect you saw a lot too.
(b) She spends a lot / lots of / a great deal of money on her new bungalow.
(c) I know many persons. *Incorrect*
(d) He bought much sugar. *Incorrect*

Use of 'much' and 'many' in affirmative sentence as object or part of object must be avoided.

Look at the following sentences : (negative and affirmative sentences)

(a) He hasn't won many competitions.
(b) You've won a lot/ lots of competitions. or You've won a lot. or
(c) You've won a great many competitions.
(d) She didn't eat much fruit.
(e) He ate a lot/ lots of fruit/ a great deal of fruit.
(f) He ate a lot/ a great deal.

Use of 'many' and 'much' in interrogative sentences :

Both can be used with 'how' : How many times? How much?

In questions where 'how' is not used, 'many' is possible but 'a lot' (of) is preferred when an affirmative answer is expected :

(a) Did you take a lot of photos? I expect you did.

We can use 'much' without 'how' but the other forms are a little more usual :

(b) Did you have a lot of rain/ much rain last year?

Less, Fewer and Lesser : When we talk about countable things, we use the word '*fewer*'; when we talk about uncountables we use the word '*less*'. She had fewer chores, but she also had less energy.' We do, however, definitely use '*less*' when referring to statistical or numerical expressions :

(a) It's less than fifty kilometres to Delhi.
(b) He's less than five feet tall.
(c) Your essay should be five hundred words or less.
(d) We spent less than two thousand rupees on this trip.
(e) The Nagar Parishad spent less than six percent of its budget on garbage removal.

'**Lesser**' means less important :

(a) Many lesser speakers also came to speak.
(b) Many lesser leaders were present in the function.

Taller than I / me , Which is correct?

(a) He is taller than I; or He is taller than me; Which one is correct ?

The correct answer is 'taller than I .' We are looking for the subject form : 'He is taller than I am' (Except we leave out the verb in the second clause, 'am') Some writers, however, will argue that the word 'than' should be allowed to function as a preposition. If we can say 'He is tall like me / her,' then (if 'than' could be prepositional like *like*) we should be able to say, 'He is taller than me / her.' It's an interesting argument, but — for now, anyway — in formal, academic prose, use the subject form in such comparisons.

More than / over : In the United States, we usually use 'more than' in countable numerical expressions meaning 'in excess of' or 'over.' In England, there is no such distinction. For instance, in the U.S., some editors would insist on 'more than 40,000 traffic deaths in one year,' whereas in the UK, 'over 40,000 traffic deaths' would be acceptable. Even in the U.S., however, you will commonly hear 'over' in numerical expressions of age, time, or height : (a)His sister is over forty. (b) She's over six feet tall. (c) We've been waiting well over two hours for her.

Good versus Well : In both casual speech and formal writing, we frequently have to choose between the **adjective** *good* and the **adverb** *well*. With most verbs, there is no contest : when modifying a verb, use the adverb :

(a) She swims well.
(b) She knows only too well who the thief is.

However, when using a **linking verb** or a verb that has to do with the five human senses, you want to use the adjective instead :

(a) How are you? I'm feeling good, thank you.
(b) After a bath, the baby smells so good.
(c) Even after my careful paint job, this room doesn't look good.

Many careful writers, however, will use '*well*' after linking verbs relating to health, and this is perfectly all right. In fact, to say that you are *good* or that you feel *good* usually implies not only that you're OK physically but also that your spirits are high.

(a) 'How are you?' (b) 'I am well, thank you.'

Bad versus Badly : We use **bad** to indicate that something is unpleasant or undesirable :

(a) He had a bad accident two years ago.

(b) We have been going through a bad time.

Badly : If something is done **badly** or goes **badly**, it is not very successful or effective :

(a) I was angry because I played so badly.

(b) The whole project was badly managed.

If someone or something is **badly** hurt or **badly** affected, it means they are severely hurt or affected :

(a) The bomb destroyed a police station and badly damaged a church.

(b) One man was killed and another badly injured.

(c) It was a gamble that went badly wrong.

If a person or his job is **badly** paid, it means he is not paid very much for what he does :

(a) You may have to work part-time, in a badly paid job with unsociable hours......

***Either* :**

1. We use '**either**' in front of the first of two or more alternatives, when we are stating the only possibilities or choices that are there. The other alternatives are introduced by 'or':

   (a) Sightseeing is best done either by tour bus or by bicycles :

   (b) The former President was demanding that he should be either put on trial or set free.

   (c) Either she goes or I go.

2. We use '**either**' in a negative statement in front of the first of two alternatives to indicate that the negative statement refers to both the alternatives :

   (a) There had been no indication of either breathlessness or any loss of mental faculties right until his death.

3. We can use '**either**' to refer to one of two things, people, or situations, when we want to say that they are both possible and it does not matter which one is chosen or considered :

   (a) There were glasses of champagne and cigars, but not many of either were consumed.

   '**Either**' is also a determiner :

   (a) I don't particularly agree with either group.

   (b) He sometimes couldn't remember either man's name.

   '**Either**' is also a quantifier :

   (a) There are no simple answers to either of those questions.

4. We can use '**either**' to introduce a noun that refers to each of two things when we are talking about both of them :

   (a) The basketball nets hung down from the ceiling at either end of the gymnasium.

   Both **:** We use '**both**' when we are referring to two people or things and saying that something is true about each of them.

   (a) She cried out in fear and flung both arms up to protect her face.

   (b) Put both vegetables into a bowl and crush with a potato masher.

   '**Both**' is also a predeterminer :

   (a) Both the band's writers are fascinating lyricists.

   (b) Both the horses were out, tacked up and ready to ride.

Verbal / Oral **: 'Oral'** communication is spoken rather than written :
(a) ...the written and oral traditions of ancient cultures.
(b) ...an oral agreement.

We use **'oral'** to indicate that something is done with a person's mouth or relates to a person's mouth :
(a) ...antibiotic tablets taken orally.

Verbal : We use **verbal** also to indicate that something is expressed in speech rather than in writing or action.
(a) They were jostled and subjected to a torrent of verbal abuse.
(b) We have a verbal agreement with her.
We use **'verbal'** to indicate that something is connected with words and the use of words :
(a) The test has scores for verbal skills, mathematical skills, and abstract reasoning skills.
In grammar, **'verbal'** means relating to a verb.
(a) ...a verbal noun.

Due to / Owing to : 'Due to' can be used as a complement of the verb. 'Due to' means– 'as a result of' while 'owing to' means–' because of'.

Look at the following sentences :
(a) He failed due to his negligency.
(b) Owing to his negligency he failed.
(c) The accident was due to carelessness.
(d) Owing to carelessness, there was an accident.

'Due to' is also used after a noun and to introduce an adjectival construction as per following :
(a) Mistakes due to carelessness may have serious consequences.
(b) A power failure due to a fault in the cable, brought all the machinery to standstill.

Near and Next **:** The adjective 'near' can be used like a preposition with or without to. 'To' is not normally used when we talk about physical closeness :
(a) He lives near the railway station.
When we talk about physical closeness , 'near to' is more usual :
Come and sit near to me.
'Next' is used to talk about time or series , it means– 'after this' :
(a) She got off at the next stop.
(b) I shall meet you at the next crossing.
(c) She lives at the next door.

Some and Any **:** 'Some' is used normally in affirmative with countables and uncountables as well.In interrogative sentences 'some' is used for making request or offer or command, for which answer in affirmation is expected :
(a) I shall buy some books. *Countables*
(b) They have purchased some fruit. *Uncountables*
(c) Will you give me some milk? *Request*
(d) Can you lend me some rupees? *Request*

Any : 'Any' is normally used in negative and interrogative sentences for countables and uncountables as well :

(a) I don't have any pen. (b) Have you any novel?
(c) He hasn't purchased any fruits. (d) Did anyone come here?
(e) They do not have any chair. (f) I haven't watched any serial today.

'Any' can also be used in affirmative sentences after 'if' :
(a) If you need any thing, call me.
(b) If you need any help, I will be at your service.

No any **:** 'No any' is no phrase . It is wrong to use this phrase :
(a) I have no any book. *Incorrect*
(b) I have no any pencil. *Incorrect*

'No' and 'Any', both are adjectives so both can't modify a noun as above.

Each / Every / Either / Neither : Each / Every / Either / Neither always takes singular noun and singular verb :
(a) Each student gets a prize. (b) Every seat was occupied.
(c) Either book is useful. (d) Neither book is useful.

If 'every' is followed by any plural adjective of number (two, three, four etc), then it takes plural noun :
(a) She takes medicine every three *hours*. (b) He visits here every two *months*.

Each / Every **:**

(A) 'Each' and 'Every' are similar in meaning. 'Each' is used for two and more than two, while 'every' is always used for more than two :
(a) Each of the two girls gets a prize.
(b) Each of the ten students gets a prize.
(c) Every student gets a prize.
(d) Every candidate was given a certificate.

Each	—	Two and more than two.
Every	—	More than two.

(B) 'Each' is used for more than two when it refers definite numbers. 'Every' refers indefinite numbers as shown in sentences (c) and (d). 'Each' refers individuality or action by individual, but 'every' refers action in a group :
(a) Each student was given a certificate by the Chief Guest one by one.
(b) Each student went to meet the Chairman in a queue.
(c) Every student has a book.
(d) Every student was happy.

(C) 'Each' is a pronoun and an adjective also , so we can use 'of' after 'each' but 'every' is an adjective so we can't use 'of' after it :
(a) Each of the teachers is doing his work. *Correct.*
(b) Every of the teachers is doing his work. *Incorrect.*

(D) 'Each and every' can be used jointly for 'more than two'(for two we use 'each') as per following :
(a) Each and every student received a prize.

Little / A little / The little **:** 'Little' is used for uncountables. 'Little' means– 'hardly any' .It has negative meaning(almost nothing). 'A little'–means 'some though not much'. It has positive meaning. 'The little' means–'not much 'but' all that is'.It also has positive meaning.

Use of little = 'hardly any' :

(a) He takes little interest in parental business. (He has hardly any or no interest.)

(b) We have little hope of his recovery.(We have almost no hope of his recovery.)

(c) He has little knowledge of computers. [He has no(almost nil) knowledge of computers.]

A little = Not much but some :

(a) We have a little hope of his recovery. (He may recover)

(b) A little knowledge is always dangerous. {Some (not full) knowledge}

(c) He takes a little interest in parental business.(He is not fully interested.)

The little = Not much but all there is :

(a) The little money she had, was also spent on medicines.(He had no money now.)

(b) Use the little time you have in a proper way now.(Whatever time left, use all.)

(c) He has wasted the little money he had in gambling.(All the money wasted.)

Few / A Few / The Few : 'Few' is used for countables. 'Few' means 'hardly any'.It has a negative meaning. 'A few' means 'not many'.It has a positive meaning. 'The few' means 'not many but all there are'. It also has positive meaning.

(A) Use of 'Few' : means – 'Hardly any' :

(a) Few people are fully happy. (Hardly any people)

(b) Few men are free from any disease. (Hardly any men)

(c) Few women can avoid talking.

(d) Few women can keep secrets.

(B) Use of 'A few' : means –'not many' :

(a) A few person can write correct English.

(b) He asked me a few questions.

(c) He died only a few months ago.

(d) A few students secured more than 80% marks in Physics.

(C) Use of 'The few'- means – 'not many but all there are' :

(a) The few utensils she had, all taken by the thief.(Now she has no utensils)

(b) The few clothes he had, all burnt in fire.(Now he has no clothes)

(c) The few members of the committee all took part in the demonstration.

(d) The few books he had, all taken by the thief.

Whole / All :

1. As adjective, 'whole' is preceded by 'the' :

(a) He wasted **the** whole day. (b) I worked the whole day.

2. When 'whole' is used before a proper noun, it is preceded by 'the' and followed by 'of' :

(a) **The** whole **of** India mourned the death of Gandhi.

(b) **The** whole **of** Rajasthan was in the grip of drought.

3. When 'all'is used with plural noun, it is followed by 'the'.With possessive noun or pronoun 'all' is placed before them :

(a) *All the* students were happy.

(b) *All the* girls were present.

(c) *All my friends* went to party.

(d) He spent *all his money*.

Another, Other, Others and Else :

The words '**another**', '**other**', '**others**' and '**else**' are used to indicate one or more additional or different things.

'**Another**' is formed from a combination of the words '**an**' and '**other**', and has a meaning similar to '**one other**'. See example (a) and (b) below–When used as an adjective, '**another**' can precede only a singular countable noun (knife). When used as a pronoun, **another** takes a singular verb (lives) :

(a) Please bring me **another** knife.
(b) **Another** of her uncles lives in Montreal.

In the first example, '**another**' modifies the singular noun '**knife**'. In the second example, the pronoun '**another**' is the subject of the singular verb '**lives**'.

'**Other**' can be used with singular countable, plural countable or uncountable nouns :

(a) The **other** door is open. (b) The **other** streets are paved.
(c) Do you have any **other** luggage?

In these examples, '**other**' modifies the singular countable noun '**door**', the plural countable noun '**streets**', and the uncountable noun '**luggage**'.

'**Another**' usually cannot be immediately preceded by a determiner. In contrast, when used before a singular countable noun, '**other**' usually must be preceded by a determiner :

(a) Please pass me the **other** cup.
(b) I do not know any **other** way to do it.
(c) There must be some **other** explanation.

In these examples, '**other**' is used with the singular countable nouns—'**cup**', '**way**' and '**explanation**', and is preceded by the determiners '**the**', '**any**' and '**some**'.

When '**other**' modifies a singular countable noun, the noun is sometimes omitted, particularly in the expression '**one ... the other**' :

(a) I have two pens. **One** is green and the **other** is blue.
(b) **One** of my parents is a teacher; the **other** is a doctor.

In these examples, the nouns following the word '**other**' are understood, rather than expressed. In the following sentences, the nouns which are understood are enclosed in square brackets :

(a) I have two pens. **One** is green and the **other** [pen] is blue.
(b) **One** of my parents is a teacher; the **other** [parent] is a doctor.

'**Others**' is a pronoun. '**Others**' can be used to take the place of the word '**other**', followed by a plural countable noun; e.g.—

(a) Those trees are hemlocks; the **others** are pines.
(b) Ten people belong to the group, and five **others** are planning to join.

In the first example, '**others**' takes the place of the words–'**other trees**'. In the second example, '**others**' takes the place of the words '**other people**'.

'**Others**' is often used in the expression–'**some ... others**'; e.g.—

(a) **Some** books are easy to read, but **others** are quite difficult.

(b) **Some** people like classical music, while **others** prefer jazz.

***Else* :** The word '**else**' has a meaning similar to '**other**'. However, rather than being used as an adjective preceding a noun, '**else**' usually follows interrogative pronouns such as '**who**' and '**what**', and indefinite pronouns such as '**anyone**' and '**someone**' :

(a) Who **else** was at the meeting? (b) What **else** is on the agenda?
(c) Has anyone **else** solved the problem? (d) Someone **else** may be able to help you.

First / Foremost :

'First' means that some thing (or some body) happens or comes before all the other. 'Foremost' means–'most important' or 'best' :

(a) Ram was the first to arrive here.
(b) Indira Gandhi was the foremost politician of her time.

'First and foremost' is used to emphasise the most important quality of something or someone :

(a) It is the first and foremost duty of an army personnel....
(b) It is first and foremost requirement of a sincere student....

RULES : USE OF ADJECTIVES

1. Positive forms of adjectives preceded and followed by 'as' :

(A) The positive forms of adjectives referring to qualities can be used in making certain types of comparisons. For example, in the following sentences, the positive forms of the adjectives 'proud' and 'intelligent' are combined with the word 'as' in order to make comparisons :

(a) She is as proud as a peacock. (b) They are as intelligent as I am.

The sentence '**She is as proud as a peacock**' gives an example of a traditional English saying which compares a person having a certain quality to an animal which is noted for possessing that quality :

(a) He is as clever as a monkey. (b) She is as wise as an owl.
(c) My sister looks as pretty as a princess.

Such type of comparison is known as a **simile.**

The expression using '**as**', followed by an adjective, followed by '**as**' can also be qualified by adverbs such as **not, almost, twice, three times, half, one-third** and so on.

Look at the following sentences :

(a) He is not as hard-working as his brother.
(b) She is almost as tall as he is.
(c) Her sister is twice as old as I am.
(d) A millimeter is one-tenth as long as a centimeter.

NOTE *In such a construction, the adverb is placed before the first occurrence of the word* '***as***'.

(B) The construction, 'as' followed by an adjective, followed by 'as', can also be combined with a noun, as shown in the following examples :

(a) Ram is as strong a swimmer as Shyam.
(b) Mohan is as clever an administrator as Rohan.
(c) The girls are as good students as the boys.

2. The comparative form of Adjectives are followed by 'than' :

(A) For the purpose of comparisons, the comparative forms of adjectives are usually followed by the word 'than' :

(a) Pawan is wiser than Ganesh.
(b) The tree is taller than this hotel.
(c) Jack is shorter than Mack.
(d) Ice feels colder than snow.
(e) Driving a car is easier than riding a horse.

(B) The comparative form of an adjective, followed by 'than' can also be combined with a noun :

(a) She is a better cook than her sister.
(b) He has wiser ideas than they do.

NOTE *When a singular countable noun is used after the adjective, the comparative form of the adjective follows the indefinite article* ***'a'*** *or* ***'an'*** *:*

(a) Jack is a braver person than you are.
(b) Steel is a stronger material than iron.

NOTE *In the case of nouns which are uncountable or plural, no article is required :*

(a) We produce sweeter honey than they do.
(b) They are better actors than we are.
(c) She has warmer gloves than her friend does.

(C) The comparative form of an adjective followed by 'than' can also be combined with longer phrases and clauses :

(a) The air is fresher in the mountains **than** in the valleys.
(b) The work seems easier once one becomes familiar with it **than** it does at first.

(D) The use of the subjective case :

In comparisons using 'than', personal pronouns following 'than' should be in the subjective case :

(a) I am taller than he is. (b) She is a better student than I am.

In formal English, the final verb of such sentences is sometimes omitted :

(a) I am taller than he. (b) She is a better student than I.

In informal English, the objective case of a personal pronoun is often used after **'than'**.

(a) I am taller than him. (b) She is a better student than me.

However, this use of the objective case is considered to be grammatically incorrect.

(E) Progressive comparisons: As well as being used in combination with 'than' to compare objects which differ in some respect, the comparative form of an adjective can also be used to describe a cFharacteristic which is becoming progressively more pronounced :

(a) The waves are growing rougher and rougher.
(b) The sounds became fainter and fainter.
(c) The noise is becoming louder and louder.

NOTE *In informal English, the verb* ***'to get'*** *is often used in this type of construction :*

(a) The noise is getting louder and louder.
(b) The lights got brighter and brighter.

3. While comparing an object with others , it is necessary to exclude it from the comparison :

(a) Iron is harder than any metal. *Incorrect*

Iron is harder than any other metal. *Correct*

(b) This building is larger than any building in the town. *Incorrect*

This building is larger than any other building in the town. *Correct*

(c) He is more intelligent than any student of his class. *Incorrect*

He is more intelligent than any other student of his class. *Correct*

(d) Ram is stronger than all students. *Incorrect*

Ram is stronger than any other student. *Correct*

4. Two comparative adjectives are not normally used in a sentence :

(a) He is more wiser than you. *Incorrect*

He is wiser than you. *Correct*

(b) I am comparatively better today. *Incorrect*

I am better today. *Correct*

I am comparatively well today. *Correct*

(c) I didn't find more costlier gift. *Incorrect*

I didn't find more costly gift. *Correct*

If one adjective is in comparative degree the other should be in positive.
We should also not use any comparative degree adjective with the word 'comparatively'.

NOTE *But we can use 'rather' with the adjective of comparative degree :*

(a) She is rather better today.

5. Some comparative degree adjectives, ending in 'or' are followed by the preposition 'to' instead of 'than' Such adjectives are ; senior, junior, posterior, superior, inferior, anterior . All these adjectives are borrowed from Latin. Likewise; elder, prefer and preferable also take preposition 'to' with them :

(a) He is superior to me. (b) She is junior to me.
(c) Ram is senior to Shyam. (d) He came prior to me.

NOTE *Major, minor, exterior, interior, outer, lower, ulterior, upper, former, inner are some words, that resemble with comparative degree adjectives, are no comparatives.*

6. When we compare two qualities in the same person or thing we should not use comparatives in 'er' form, instead we should use 'more'.

(a) Ram is more strong than intelligent.(not 'stronger')
(b) She is more clever than intelligent. (not 'cleverer')

7. **Superlative forms of adjectives :**

The superlative form of an adjective is used to describe something which possesses a characteristic in the greatest degree :

(a) Dhiraj is the youngest boy in our class.
(b) She is the best actress I have ever seen.

(A) The superlative form preceded by 'the' : The superlative forms of adjectives are usually preceded by **'the'**, and followed by the nouns they modify :

(a) Shyam is the tallest boy in the class. (b) Nisha is the fastest runner on the team.

The first example indicates that no other boy in the class is as tall as Shyam. The second example indicates that no one else on the team is as fast a runner as Nisha.

NOTE *The superlative forms of adjectives can be preceded by possessive adjectives, instead of by the definite article* ***'the'*** *:*

(a) This is my most beautiful painting.
(b) He promised to give it his closest attention.
(c) He is my best friend.

(B) The comparison of one or more things with a group :

When one or more things are compared with a group to which they do not belong, the comparative form of an adjective is normally used :

(a) The girls are cleverer than the boys.

The girls are being compared with **the boys**, a group to which they do not belong. Therefore, the comparative form **'cleverer'** is used.
In contrast, when one or more things are compared with members of a group to which they belong, the superlative form of an adjective is normally used :

(a) Ashok is the youngest of all the boys in the class.

In this example, Ashok is being compared with members of the group identified as **'all the boys'** in the class. This is a group to which he belongs. Therefore, the superlative form **'youngest'** is used.

8. Logical Comparison : While making comparisons, care must be taken, particularly in formal English, to ensure that the comparisons are logical and that the appropriate objects are in fact being compared.
For example :

(a) Life in the country is different from the city. *Incorrect*

The sentence is logically incorrect, because it compares **life in the country** to **the city**.In order to be logically correct, the sentence must be changed so that similar types of things are being compared :

(b) Life in the country is different from life in the city. *Correct.*

This sentence is logically correct, since it compares **life in the country** to **life in the city**.
Similarly :

(a) The vowel sounds of English are more numerous than Spanish. *Incorrect*

The sentence is logically incorrect, because it compares **'the vowel sounds' of English** to **Spanish** and not to the 'vowel sounds' of spanish.
In order to be logically correct, the sentence must be changed so that similar types of things are being compared. Thus, the sentence may be corrected as follows :

(b) The vowel sounds of English are more numerous than the vowel sounds of Spanish.

In such sentences, the noun or phrase which is repeated in the second part of the comparison may be replaced by **'that'** or **'those'**. **'That'** is used if the noun being replaced is singular, and **those** is used if the noun being replaced is plural :

(a) Life in the country is different from <u>that</u> in the city.
(b) The vowel sounds of English are more numerous than <u>those</u> of Spanish.

In the first example, '**that**' is used to replace the singular noun '**life**'. In the second example, '**those**' is used to replace the phrase '**the vowel sounds**'. The form '**those**' must be used, since the noun '**sounds**' is plural.

9. Comparative degree of adjectives is used for the comparison of two. For more than two, we should use the superlative. Like wise, we should not use superlative for comparing two objects :

(a) Which is better; Tea, coffee or milk? *Incorrect*
(b) Which is easier, Physics, Chemistry or Math? *Incorrect*
(c) He is the best of the two students. *Incorrect*
(d) Which is the cheapest; silver or gold? *Incorrect*

10. Normally two superlatives are not used in a sentence :

(a) He is the most strongest of all. *Incorrect*
He is the strongest of all. *Correct*
(b) The river is the most longest of all. *Incorrect*
The river is the longest of all. *Correct*

11. We should also not use 'other' or 'else' with superlatives :

(a) She is the most beautiful of all girls. (not 'all other girls')
(b) He is the strongest of all students. (not 'all other students')

12. We usually use 'of ' with superlative form but while referring 'place' we should use 'in' :

(a) Kolkata is the dirtiest city <u>in India</u>.
(b) Udaipur is the most beautiful city <u>in Rajasthan</u>.

13. The superlative with 'most' is sometimes used to denote the possession of a quality of a very high degree. In such cases no comparison is made :

(a) This is a most interesting book. (in the library).
(b) She is a most beautiful girl. (in the school).
(c) It was a most eloquent speech.

14. With 'like' we use superlative, 'best' and 'most'.In such case we do not use 'the' before the superlative :

(a) Which of the story do you like most? (b) Which of the magazine do you like best?

15. When more than one adjectives are connected with 'and' , they should be either in comparative or in superlative degree :

(a) Ram is wiser and stronger than Shyam. *Correct*
(b) Ram is wise and stronger than Shyam. *Incorrect*

16. Some adjectives expressing qualities of highest order or their extreme meanings, can't be compared. Such adjectives are : absolute, perfect, full, complete, entire, whole, chief, extreme, unique, universal, circular, square, round ,ideal, flat, impossible etc.

NOTE *A thing can't be more round,more square.*

Though we can find use of ; full, fuller, fullest ; perfect , more perfect , most perfect and also 'most impossible' , by some writers.

17. 'Kind' and 'sort' refer singular number.We can use 'this' and 'that' with them , but we can't use 'these' and 'those' with them :

(a) I don't like this kind of dresses. *Correct*

(b) He doesn't like that kind of shirts. *Correct*

(c) I don't like these kinds of shirts. *Incorrect*

(d) I don't like those kind of shirts. *Incorrect*

18. Note the structure of the following sentences :

One of ....if not ....Superlative....

(a) He is one of the greatest writers, if not the greatest writer.

(b) This is one of the largest buildings, if not the largest in the world.

(c) This is one of the longest rivers, if not the longest in the world.

NOTE *Use plural noun in first part and singular noun in second part of the sentence :*

One of the + superlative + plural noun...... if not the+ superlative + singular noun.

19. Note the following structure also :

(a) She runs as fast as, if not faster than Shyam.

(b) He is as good as if not better than you.

(c) The house is as large as if not larger than that.

POSITION OF ADJECTIVES

Adjectives usually appear immediately before the noun or noun phrase that they modify. Sometimes they appear in a string of adjectives, and when they do, they appear in a set order according to category. When indefinite pronouns, such as 'something', 'someone', 'anybody', are modified by an adjective, the adjective comes after the pronoun.

(a) Anyone capable of doing something horrible to someone nice should be punished.
And there are certain adjectives that, in combination with certain words, are always postpositive (coming after the thing they modify) :

(b) The president elect, heir apparent to the throne, lives in London proper.

Position of Attributive adjectives :

It is possible for a noun to be preceded by many different types of attributive adjective. In the following example, the attributive adjectives are underlined :

(a) Two small white cardboard sugar **cartons** placed on the table.

In this example, **'two'** is a cardinal number, **'small'** is an adjective indicating size, **'white'** is an adjective indicating color, **'cardboard'** is an adjective indicating a type of material, and **sugar** is a defining adjective indicating purpose.

When a noun is preceded by more than one type of attributive adjectives, the different types of adjectives are usually arranged in a certain order.

The different types of attributive adjectives are usually arranged as per the order shown in the following table :

Order of Attributive Adjectives

1. Certain determiners such as **all**, **both** and **half**,
2. Determiners including the articles **a**, **an** and **the**; possessive adjectives, e.g. **my**, **his**, **her**, **our** and **their**; demonstrative adjectives, e.g. **that**, **these**, **this**, and **those**; and certain other determiners such as **another**, **any**, **each**, **either**,**enough**, **every**, **neither**, **no**, **some**, **what** and **which**,

3. cardinal numbers e.g. **one, two, three**; and certain other determiners such as **few, many** and **several,**
4. determiners such as **fewer, fewest, least, less, more** and **most**;
5. general descriptive adjectives, often in the following order :
   (a) adjectives indicating size, e.g. **large, long, narrow**;
   (b) adjectives indicating weight, e.g. **heavy, light**;
   (c) participles and other adjectives, e.g. **clever, excited, interesting**;
   (d) adjectives indicating temperature, e.g. **cold, hot, warm**;
   (e) adjectives indicating humidity, e.g. **dry, damp, wet**;
   (f) adjectives indicating age, e.g. **new, six-month-old, young**;
   (g) adjectives indicating shape, e.g. **barrel-shaped, round, square**;
6. adjectives indicating color, e.g. **blue, grey, white**;
7. adjectives indicating materials, e.g. **cloth, leather, metal**;
8. proper adjectives, e.g. **Indian, Victorian**;
9. defining adjectives, usually indicating purpose, method of operation, location, time or categories of people.

NOTE *There are several types of general descriptive adjective, which often occur in a certain order. However, the order of different types of general descriptive adjective is more flexible than the order of other types of attributive adjective :*

(i) Attributive adjectives indicating size usually follow any determiners, but precede other types of attributive adjective. In the following phrases, the adjectives indicating size are underlined :
   (a) three <u>large</u>, level platforms,
   (b) that <u>enormous</u> Hindi-English dictionary.

(ii) Adjectives indicating weight usually follow adjectives indicating size, but precede other types of attributive adjective. In the following phrases, the adjectives indicating weight are underlined :
   (a) a small, <u>heavy</u> parcel,
   (b) two <u>light</u> nylon shoulder bags.

(iii) Participles and other general descriptive adjectives which do not fall into any of the other categories usually follow adjectives indicating size and weight, and precede other types of attributive adjective. In the following examples, the adjective '**alert**', and the participles '**twittering**' and '**excited**' are underlined :
   (a) two large, <u>alert</u> black dogs,
   (b) seven tiny, <u>twittering</u> birds,
   (c) many <u>excited</u> girls.

(iv) The order of *adjectives indicating temperature, humidity, age and shape* is not as predictable as the order of other attributive adjectives. For instance, adjectives indicating temperature occur sometimes before and sometimes after general descriptive adjectives; such as, '**clear**' and '**hard**'. Some other examples are :
   (a) clear, <u>cold</u> water,
   (b) <u>cold</u>, hard ice.

(v) It should be noted that the position of attributive adjectives indicating age may be altered to change the emphasis :

(a) a new, efficient method,
(b) an efficient, new method.

In the first example, the adjective '**new**' is emphasized. In the second example, the adjective '**efficient**' is emphasized.

The position of Adjectives indicating colour

Adjectives indicating colour usually precede adjectives indicating materials, proper adjectives, and defining adjectives, but follow other types of attributive adjective.
In the following examples, the adjectives indicating colour are underlined :

(a) threatening black clouds, (b) her new black leather coat,
(c) a square brown mahogany table.

The position of Adjectives indicating materials

Attributive adjectives indicating the materials usually follow any adjectives indicating colour and precede any proper or defining adjectives. In the following examples, adjectives indicating materials are underlined :

(a) a beautiful blue cotton scarf,
(b) six black iron coat hangers,
(c) the clean marble floor.

The position of Proper adjectives

Proper adjectives usually follow all other types of attributive adjective except defining adjectives.

It should be noted that proper adjectives may sometimes precede adjectives indicating materials, as in the following examples. This occurs when the adjective indicating a material is used as a type of defining adjective, to help identify what type of object is being described :

(a) Indian straw hats, (b) American pearl bangles.

The position of Defining adjectives

Defining adjectives usually immediately precede the nouns they modify. In the following examples, the defining adjectives are underlined :

(a) an egg carton, (b) a saree hanger.

An **egg carton** is a carton used for storing eggs, a **saree hanger** is an object used for hanging up sarees.

The position of Ordinal adjectives

Attributive adjectives; such as–**next**, **last**, **first**, **second**, **third** and so on, are sometimes referred to as **ordinal** adjectives, since they indicate the order in which things occur.

When they are not followed by commas, ordinal adjectives have the property of modifying any following attributive adjectives together with the accompanying noun. For this reason, the position of an ordinal adjective in relation with the other attributive adjectives can affect the meaning of a phrase; e.g. –

(a) the first reluctant girl. (b) the reluctant first girl.

These examples have different meanings. In the phrase–'**the first reluctant girl**', the adjective '**first**' modifies the following adjective '**reluctant**' together with the noun '**girl**'.
However, in the phrase '**the reluctant first girl**', the adjective '**first**' modifies only the noun 'girl'.

Both the above sentences have different meanings.
As such, the position of ordinal attributive adjectives varies depending upon what meaning is to be conveyed.

The position of Predicate adjectives

The order of predicate adjectives relative to one another is generally the same as the order of attributive adjectives relative to one another. The following examples illustrate the order of predicate adjectives :

(a) The box is small and light.
(b) The weather is clear, cold and dry.

In the first example, the adjective **small**, indicating size, precedes the adjective **'light'**, indicating weight. In the second example, the general descriptive adjective **'clear'** precedes the adjective **'cold'**, indicating temperature, which precedes the adjective **'dry'**, indicating humidity.

The position of Interpolated adjectives

The use of interpolated adjectives is somewhat uncommon; the use of interpolation can serve to emphasize the adjectives. Interpolated adjectives are most often placed immediately after a noun or before a noun or pronoun at the beginning of a sentence :

(a) The child , *happy and excited*, ran behind the bus.
(b) Worried; enthusiastic and *alert*, we waited to see what would happen next.

NOTE *When more than one adjective is used, the last two adjectives are separated from one another by the word* **'and'**, *and previous adjectives are separated from one another by commas.The interpolated adjectives must also be separated from the rest of the sentence by commas. For instance, in the first example above, the interpolated adjectives* **'happy and excited'** *are separated from the rest of the sentence by a comma before the word* **happy**, *and a comma following the word* **excited**. *Likewise, in the second example, the interpolated adjective* **worried, enthusiastic and alert** *are separated from the rest of the sentence by a comma, following the word* **'alert'**. *Further, interpolated adjectives* **'worried'** *and* **'enthusiastic'** *are separated from one another by a comma, and the last two adjectives–'enthusiastic' and 'alert' are separated from each other by the word* **'and'**.

Position of A-Adjectives : The most common of the so-called a- adjectives are; ablaze, afloat, afraid, aghast, alert, alike, alive, alone, aloof, ashamed, asleep, averse, awake, aware. These adjectives come after a linking verb as following :

(a) The boys were ashamed.
(b) The girls remained aloof.
(c) The trees were ablaze.
(d) Ram was asleep.

In some cases , however, you can find a- adjectives *before* the word they modify.When they are found before the word they modify, then they are themselves modified like – the nearly awake boy , the terribly alone girl. And a- adjectives are sometimes also modified by 'very much'; like – very much afraid, very much alone, very much ashamed, etc :

(a) She was very much afraid.
(b) After the death of his wife, Ram was very much alone.

CORRECT YOURSELF EXERCISE : ADJECTIVES

CYE : 01 Fill in the blanks with suitable determiners :

(i) Small cars are more economical than big..... .
(ii) I bought ..... mangoes.
(iii) Have you .... sugar ?
(iv) .... knowledge of English is essential for all of us.
(v) Clean .... floor properly.
(vi) .... room is airy.

CYE : 02 Fill in the blanks with suitable determiners :

(i) Will you have ...... cake ?
(ii) There isn't....... sugar in the bowl.
(iii) I'll have a cigarette; will you have ..... too ?

CYE : 03 Fill in the blanks with suitable determiners :

(i) Uneasy lies...... head that wears .... crown.
(ii) .... women of India are as beautiful as .... of Europe.
(iii) He got admission in .... university in.......... USA.
(iv) He started learning .... piano at .... age of ten.

CYE : 04 Fill in the blanks with appropriate determiners :

1. .... people have car. *a few/ a little*
2. Give me .... time to decided the matter. *a few/ a little*
3. He drank..........the water. *all/whole*
4. Delhi is .... from Alwar than Jaipur. *further/farther*
5. He is senior .... me. *than/to*
6. There are .... children outside the room. *some/any*
7. Have you .... question? *some/any*
8. Please give me .... water. *some/any*
9. Has he bought .... dress? *some/any*
10. He can't find .... banana tree? *some/any*
11. She has .... flowers of rose. *some/any*
12. I could not get .... note book there. *some/any*
13. Nisha did not eat .... mango. *some/any*
14. Will you please lend me .... money. *some/any*
15. She must give me .... time to finish this work. *some/any*
16. Is there .... money in your pocket. *some/any*
17. .... dreams are very romantic. *some/any*
18. Sorry, I am stranger here, I have .... knowledge about this place. *few/little*
19. She has .... clothes. *some/any*
20. He has not .... car. *some/any*

CYE : 05 Fill in the blanks with–'few/A few/the few'.

1. It is a work of .... months.
2. He will come back in .... days.

3. I have read all .... novels I had.
4. .... people can speak english correctly.
5. I have invited all .... friends I have.
6. .... day's rest is necessary for the patient.

CYE : 06 Fill in the blanks with–'little, A little, the little' :

1. I have .... influence in the political field now.
2. There is .... hope of his recovery, he is very serious.
3. She had donated .... property, she had.
4. He slept .... and felt better.
5. .... knowledge is a dangerous thing.
6. Please wait .... I am just coming.
7. I have no milk left with me. I have already given to cat .... milk, I had.

CYE : 07 Fill in the blanks with–'Near/ Next' :

1. Mr. Sharma lives .... to Ram's house.
2. Radhika will speak .... to Sarla.
3. The Railway station is .... to my school.
4. I will meet you at the .... crossing.
5. This matter will be discussed again in the .... meeting.

CYE : 08 Fill in the blanks with–'much/many' :

1. How .... students are there in the hostel
2. .... people comes to see this temple daily.
3. He doesn't have .... money to donate.
4. I love you very ....
5. There are .... balls in the store room.
6. I am .... obliged to you for your timely help.
7. .... girls were absent yesterday.

CYE : 09 Fill in the blanks with suitable determiners :

1. I haven't .... time.
2. There are not .... boys in the class.
3. There is .... food left,so you will not go hungry.
4............. good comes of impoliteness.
5. We must find an excuse; .... excuse will do.
6.Can I have............coffee?
7. Don't eat .... more of ice-cream.Leave............... of it for your brother.
8. Neither man could come,.............. men were ill.
9. .... trains are slow, others are fast.
10. Has he money .... to buy a car?
11. She went to market to buy .... things.
12. ....men here are expected to do their duty.
13. She gave ....child ..... ice-cream.
14. There was ....snow last winter.
15. Few people like cold weather, ... people like warm weather.
16. There were shady trees on ....side of the road.

17. .... man should do his best.
18. These flowers are pink, ... are yellow ones.
19. .... team could score a goal. So it was a drawn match.
20. .... children play in the park every day.

CYE : 10 Fill in the blanks in the following sentences with–'elder, eldest, older, oldest' :

1. Ram is .... than me.
2. My father is the .... member of our family.
3. My father is .... than your father.
4. My brother is .... to me.
5. This is the .... building in our village.
6. How .... are you ?
7. My ....brother is an IAS officer.
8. This building is .... than that.
9. We should respect to our ....
10. The .... he grew, the more demands he made.

CYE : 11 Fill in the blanks with–'last/later/latest/latter' :

1. At .... the president gave thanks to the audience.
2. Ram came .... than Shyam.
3. This is the .... technology in the field of computer science.
4. Between Ram and Shyam, the .... is more intelligent.
5. The .... half of the century saw many revolutions.
6. Ram was promoted as officer at a .... date.
7. The .... chapter of this book is very interesting.

CYE : 12 Correct the following sentences :

1. Whole girls were present in the function.
2. All the third books are in our course.
3. This is mine bed, which is your ?
4. None of these two books are useful.
5. A good deal of persons were present at the railway station.
6. All the sides of the coin are shining.
7. He alone lives in such a large house.
8. The both girls have arrived.
9. She is among the four first merit holders.
10. Lord Ram was an incarnate God.

C YE : 13 Correct the following sentences :

1. Our all members are very cooperative
2. His all books have been burnt in fire.
3. I bought tickets three for Delhi.
4. The Great Ashoka was a brave king.
5. This custom has been observed since immemorial time.
6. Have you new anything to tell me about the incident.?
7. Ram is as taller as his brother.
8. Sita is not more beautiful as Rita.

9. Gold is more precious than any metal.
10. She is not that all reliable.

CYE : 14 Correct the following sentences :

1. To drive is as difficult as fishing.
2. It is as difficult to swim as driving.
3. It is not as easy to write as reading.
4. They had better died than surrender before the enemy.
5. I had rather read than wasting my time here.
6. He is junior than me.
7. According to Ram, milk is preferable than tea.
8. She is more wiser than her brother.
9. My house is better than Ram.
10. The climate of Udaipur is better than Jaipur.

CYE : 15 Correct the following sentences :

1. There are lesser rooms in this hotel than that .
2. Take this tablet with a few milk.
3. Your problem is comparatively easier than that of mine.
4. The quality of this detergent powder is comparatively better .
5. He runs as faster, if not fast than you.
6. Sita is as beautiful as, if not beautiful than her sister.
7. The more you hide something, the most you expose your self.
8. This is all the more better.
9. The valley goes deep and deep after this point.
10. Ram said, 'I am very better now.'

CYE : 16 Correct the following sentences :

1. The cloth of this suit is very inferior.
2. This is longest river in the world.
3. He is the richest of all man in the city.
4. He is the strongest of all other students in the college.
5. Ramesh is one of the best student in the college.
6. He is my the best friend.
7. Ramesh is one of the strongest person, if not the strongest in the town.
8. I shall purchase the bigger of all these houses.
9. Mr. Sharma is the most ideal teacher.
10. This is more the best college in the city.

CYE : 17 Correct the following sentences :

1. I have the best and a cheaper magazine.
2. This is out and in the best hospital.
3. Which of these books do you like the most ?
4. I don't like these kind of apples.
5. I don't like these sort of men.
6. The poors should be helped.

7. That was a most excellent opportunity to earn good money.
8. She reached here the earliest of both girls.
9. This is the much best school.
10. She is getting weak and weaker.
11. He is braver than stronger.
12. The quality of this shirt is superior than yours.
13. Ram came prior than me .
14. The Ghee of Haryana is better than Rajasthan.
15. He is more intelligent than any student of his class.

SOLUTIONS : CORRECT YOURSELF EXERCISE

Solutions CYE : 01

1. (i) ones, (ii) some, (iii) any, (iv) A little/Some, (v) The, (vi) The.

Solutions CYE : 02

(i) a , (ii) any, (iii) one.

Solutions CYE : 03

(i) the, a (ii) the, those (iii) a, the (iv) the, the.

Solutions CYE : 04

1. A few, 2. A little, 3. all, 4. farther, 5. to, 6. some,
7. any, 8. some, 9. any, 10. any, 11. some, 12. any,
13. any, 14. some, 15. some, 16. any, 17. some, 18. little,
19. some, 20. any .

Solutions CYE : 05

1. A few, 2. a few, 3. the few, 4. a few, 5. the few, 6. a few.

Solutions CYE : 06

1. Little, 2. little, 3. the little, 4. a little, 5. a little, 6. a little,
7. the little.

Solutions CYE : 07

1. near, 2. next, 3. near, 4. next. 5. next.

Solutions CYE : 08

1. many, 2. many, 3. much, 4. much, 5. many, 6. much,
7. many.

Solutions CYE : 09

1. much/any, 2. many/any, 3. a little/some, 4. little/no, 5. any,
6. some, 7. any, some, 8. both, 9. some, 10. enough,
11. a few/many, 12. All, 13. each, some, 14. a lot of/much,
15. most, 16. either, 17. every, 18. those, 19. neither,
20. lots of /many.

Solutions CYE : 10

1. older , 2. eldest, 3. older, 4. elder, 5. oldest, 6. old, 7. elder,
8. older, 9, elders, 10. older.

Solutions CYE : 11

1. last, 2. later, 3. latest, 4. latter, 5. latter, 6. later, 7. last.

Solutions CYE : 12

1. All the girls were present in the function.
2. All the three books are in our course.
3. This is my bed, which is yours ?
4. Neither of these two books are useful.
5. A number of persons were present at the railway station.
6. Both the sides of the coin are shining.
7. He lives alone in such a large house.
8. Both the girls have arrived.
9. She is among the first four merit holders.
10. Lord Ram was God incarnate.

Solutions CYE : 13

1. All our members are very cooperative
2. All his books have been burnt in fire.
3. I bought three tickets for Delhi.
4. Ashoka the Great was a brave king.
5. This custom has been observed since time immemorial.
6. Have you anything new to tell me about the incident.?
7. Ram is as tall as his brother.
8. Sita is not as beautiful as Rita. or Sita is not more beautiful than Rita.
9. Gold is more precious than any other metal.
10. She is not all that reliable.

Solutions CYE : 14

1. Driving is as difficult as fishing.
2. It is as difficult to swim as drive.
3. It is not as easy to write as read.
4. They had better die than surrender before the enemy.
5. I had rather read than waste my time here.
6. He is junior to me.
7. According to Ram, milk is preferable to tea.
8. She is wiser than her brother.
9. My house is better than Ram's.
10. The climate of Udaipur is better than that of Jaipur.

Solutions CYE : 15

1. There are fewer rooms in this hotel than that .
2. Take this tablet with a little milk.

3. Your problem is comparatively easy than that of mine.
4. The quality of this detergent powder is comparatively good .
5. He runs as fast, if not faster than you.
6. Sita is as beautiful as, if not more beautiful than her sister.
7. The more you hide something, the more you expose yourself.
8. This is all the better.
9. The valley goes deeper and deeper after this point.
10. Ram said, "I am much better now."

Solutions CYE : 16

1. The cloth of this suit is much inferior.
2. This is the longest river in the world.
3. He is the richest of all men in the city.
4. He is the strongest of all students in the college.
5. Ramesh is one of the best students in the college.
6. He is my best friend.
7. Ramesh is one of the strongest persons, if not the strongest in the town.
8. I shall purchase the biggest of all these houses.
9. Mr. Sharma is an ideal teacher.
10. This is much the best college in the city.

Solutions CYE : 17

1. I have the best and the cheapest magazine.
2. This is out and out the best hospital.
3. Which of these books do you like most ?
4. I don't like this kind of apples.
5. I don't like this sort of men.
6. The poor should be helped.
7. That was an excellent opportunity to earn good money.
8. She reached here the earliest, of all girls.
9. This is the very best school. or This is much the best school.
10. She is getting weaker and weaker.
11. He is more brave than strong.
12. The quality of this shirt is superior to yours.
13. Ram came prior to me .
14. The Ghee of Haryana is better than that of Rajasthan.
15. He is more intelligent than any other student of his class.

4

Adverb

An adverb is that word in a sentence, which modifies the meaning of verb or adjective or another adverb or phrase or a clause.

Look at the following sentences :

(a) He ran fast. —*Modifies the verb ran.*

(b) These are very sweet magoes. —*Modifies the adjective, sweet.*

(c) She speaks very loudly. —*Modifies the adverb, loudly.*

(d) He was sitting close beside her —*Modifies the phrase, 'beside her'.*

If an adverb is used in the beginning of a sentence, it modifies the whole sentence.

For example :

(a) Unfortunately, the bank closed at two today.

(b) Certainly she is right.

(c) Fortunately we escaped unhurt.

In the above examples, the adverb modifies the entire sentence.

NOTE *As you will see, adverbs often tell when, where, why, or under what conditions some action takes place or took place. Adverbs usually end in -ly; however, many words and phrases not ending in -ly serve an adverbial function and an -ly ending is not a guarantee that a word is an adverb. The words; friendly, lovely, lonely, motherly, for instance, are adjectives.*

Adverb Clause : If a group of words containing a subject and verb acts as an adverb (modifying the verb of a sentence), it is called an **Adverb Clause :**

(a) When this class is over, we're going to market.

Adverbial Phrase : When a group of words not containing a subject and verb acts as an adverb, it is called an **Adverbial Phrase**. **Prepositional phrases** generally act as adverb (telling place and time, modifying the verb) :

(a) She went to the market.

(b) He works on holidays.

(c) They lived in USA during the war.

And **Infinitive phrases** can also act as adverbs (usually telling why) :

(a) She hurried to the railway station to see her mother.

(b) Ram ran to catch the train.

NOTE *Adverbs can modify **adjectives**, but an adjective cannot modify an adverb.*

KINDS OF ADVERB

Adverbs can be classified into following classes, depending on their meaning and function :

Simple, Relative and Interrogative Adverb

Simple Adverbs : Simple adverb simply modifies the words (Verb, Adverb, Adjective, Adverbial phrase) in a sentence.

Relative Adverbs : Relative Adverb not only modifies words but also refers back to the antecedent.

Interrogative Adverbs : Interrogative adverb not only modifies some word but also asks a question.

Detail description of these adverbs is as followes :

SIMPLE ADVERBS

Simple adverbs can be classified as follows :

1. **Adverb of time** : 'Daily, since, yesterday, soon, tomorrow, late' etc. are adverbs of time. These adverbs answer 'when' (the time of work) :

   (a) She comes here **daily.**
   (b) He went to Jaipur **yesterday.**
   (c) I will go to school **tomorrow.**
   (d) I have not seen him **since**.
   (e) He arrived **late** .

2. **Adverb of place** : 'Here, there, every where, in, away, up,out' etc. are the adverbs of place, which answer 'where'(the place of work) :

   (a) Come here.
   (b) Is Mr. gupta in?
   (c) The thief ran away.
   (d) Go there.
   (e) My wife is out.

3. **Adverb of Frequency or Number** : 'Frequently, again, often, seldom, once,twice,' etc. These adverbs answer 'how often'(the frequency of work) :

   (a) She often commits mistakes.
   (b) He telephoned again.
   (c) He frequently comes here.
   (d) I seldom go there.
   (e) I have reminded you twice.

4. **Adverb of manner** : Well, fast, swiftly, quickly, easily, slowly, loudly, so, bravely, hard etc. are adverbs of manner. These adverbs show 'in what manner'(the manner in which work is perfomed) :

   (a) This book is well written.
   (b) The child cried loudly.
   (c) Our army fought bravely.
   (d) Ram works hard .
   (e) Is that so?

5. **Adverb of degree or quantity** : Fully, very, rather, perfectly, pretty, almost, altogether, too, so, quite, rather, partly etc.These adverbs show 'how much' or in what degree or to what extent':

   (a) She is too careless.
   (b) The apples are almost ripe.
   (c) The sea is perfectly calm.
   (d) I am so glad to hear it.
   (e) He is altogether mistaken.

6. **Adverb of affirmation and negation :** Certainly, surely, seldom, never, always, definitely etc. These adverbs show ' positivity or negativity' :

(a) Surely you are wrong. (b) She certainly cooked.
(c) I certainly do not like her. (d) He never refuses.
(e) She will definitely help the poor.

7. **Adverb of Reasons :** 'Therefore', 'hence', 'on account of' etc. are adverbs of reason. These adverbs show 'reason or cause' :

(a) It is hence proved. (b) He therefore went to hospital.

8. **Adverb of contrast :** 'However', 'though', 'yet', 'even if', 'all the same' etc. are the examples. These adverbs refer the contrast or contradiction :

(a) He is poor though he is honest.
(b) She is very rich however she refused to donate anything.

9. **Adverb of condition :** 'Had, if, unless, provided that,as long as', so long as, etc. are the examples. These adverbs refer conditions :

(a) Had he come to me I would have helped him.
(b) If it rains we will go for a picnic.

10. **Adverb of extent :** 'So far as,as far as', etc. are adverbs of extent. These adverbs show the extent :

(a) So far as I could see there was nothing but dead bodies.
(b) As far as I can judge she is an intelligent girl.

11. **'Yes' and 'no', Adverbs :** When they(Yes or No) are used by themselves, they are equivalents of a sentence as shown below :

(a) Have you completed your work? Yes.
(Here 'yes' stands for the sentence–'I have completed my work'.)
(b) Are you going to market? No.
(Here 'no' means–'I am not going to market'.)

RELATIVE ADVERBS

Relative Adverb not only modifies verbs but also refers back to the antecedent.

Look at the following sentence :

(a) I remember the house, where he lived.

Here the word 'where' is a relative adverb, which modifies the verb 'lived' and refers back to the antecedent 'house'. Antecedent means–'which comes before.'

Such most commonly used adverbs are; What, When, Where, Why, How, Whatever, Whither, Wherever, Whence etc.

See more examples :

(b) I know the hotel where she lives.(Relative adverb - where, Antecedent -hotel)
(c) This is reason why she left. (Relative Adverb-why, Antecedent-reason)
(d) Tell me the time when the train will arrive.(Relative Adverb-when , Antecedent-time)

INTERROGATIVE ADVERBS

When Adverbs introduce a question, they are called **interrogative adverbs** .
Look at the following sentences :

1. When did he come? (Inter. adverb of time)
2. Why are you late? (Inter adverb of reason)
3. How many boys are there in your class? (Inter. adverb of number)
4. How high is Bhakra Nangal Dam? (Inter. adverb of degree)

NOTE *The forms of relative and interrogative adverb are identical .If there is no antecedent, the adverb is an interrogative adverb not a relative Adverb.*

CONJUNCTIVE ADVERBS

'Therefore, however, moreover, nevertheless, furthermore, consequently', etc. are **conjunctive adverbs**. This is a special kind of adverb , and plays the role of a conjunction also, between two independent clauses in a sentence . These adverbs serve as a transition between two independent clauses in a sentence.When using a conjunctive adverb at the beginning of the second independent clause, be sure to precede it with a semicolon not a comma :

(a) My classmate usually listens to classical music**;** however, he also likes jazz and rock music.

ADVERB/ADJECTIVE

Adverbs are words that modify verbs, adjectives, other adverbs, and sometimes clauses and whole sentences. Adjectives are words that modify nouns and pronouns. We must not use an adjective where we need an adverb.

Look at the following sentences :

1. Shalini walked **slow** out of the classroom. Incorrect
2. Shalini walked **slowly** out of the classroom.Correct
3. He tried **real** hard to secure the first position. Incorrect
4. He tried **really** hard to secure the first position. Correct

Some words have the same form as adverb and as adjective :

Adverb	**Adjective**
(a) He ran fast.	He is a fast runner.
(b) She has only two books.	She is the only daughter of her parents.
(c) Come back.	He entered from the back door.
(d) They work hard.	He is a hard worker.

Remember :

Most is an adjective, but ***almost*** is an adverb,
Easy is an adjective, but ***easily*** is an adverb,
Good is an adjective, but ***well*** is an adverb.

POSITION OF ADVERBS

Adverbs of manner

1. Generally 'adverb of manner' is placed after the verb :

(a) He played **beautifully.** (b) He wrote **quickly.**

If there is an object, the adverb is placed after it :

(c) She gave him a pen **reluctantly.**
(d) Ramesh speaks English and Hindi **well.**

Correct use	Incorrect use
(a) He talks well.	He well talks.
(b) He speaks English fluently.	He speaks fluently English.
(c) It is raining regularly.	It is regularly raining.
(d) I read my book carefully.	I carefully read my book.

2. If the structure of the sentence is " **Verb+ Preposition +Object**' , the adverb can be placed either before the prepostion or after the object :

(a) She looked at me surprisingly. or (b) She looked surprisingly at me.

In case the object contains a number of words, then put the adverb before the prepositon :

(a) She looked surprisingly at everyone who got off the car.

In case of sentence structure **"Verb + Object ",** if the object is long , put the adverb before the verb and for short object, the adverb should be placed after the object :

(a) He carefully picked up all the bits of broken mirror.
(b) She hastily denied that she had stolen the purse.
(c) She secretly decided to leave the city.

3. The adverb can be placed after the verb or after **verb + object**, but the meaning of the sentence is then changed.

Look at the following examples :

(a) She spoke kindly = 'His voice and words were kind' is not the same as,
'It was kind of her to speak to us'.

(b) He paid us generously = 'He paid more than the prevalent rate'. is not the same as,
'It was generous of him to pay us'.

(c) (i) He answered the questions stupidly (His answers were stupid), and
(ii) He stupidly answered the questions (Answering was stupid./ It was stupid of him to answer at all).

Adverbs of place : The most commonly used adverbs of place are;
'away, everywhere, here, nowhere, somewhere, there, abroad, upstairs' etc.

1. In sentences with object or object + preposition structure , adverb comes after :

(a) Ramesh sent his wife away. (b) I searched for her everywhere.

2. In sentences with no object adverbs are placed after the verb :

(a) The thief fled away. (b) He lives abroad. (c) Jack is upstairs.

3. 'There' and 'here' can be followed by **be / come / go** :

(a) Here's Ram. (b) There's Sita.
(c) Here comes the tram. (d) There goes our bus.

Adverbs of time

1. Adverbs of time; such as — **eventually,afterwards, lately, now, recently, soon, then, today, tomorrow** etc. , and adverb phrases of time; like — **at once, since then , till (6.00 O'clock etc.)** are usually placed at the very beginning or at the very end of the clause :

(a) Eventually she came . (b) She came eventually.
(c) Then they went home. (d) They went home then.
(e) Write now. (f) I shall wait till then.

2. Adverbs of time; such as;—**before, early, immediately and late** are usually placed at the end of the clause :

(a) Ram came late. (b) He will go early.

NOTE *If 'before' and 'immediately' are used as conjunctions, they are placed at the beginning of the clause :*

(a) Immediately the rain stops, we will go.
(b) I had left the house before he came .

3. Adverbs of time; such as — **since and ever since** are used with perfect tenses. 'Since' can be placed after the auxiliary verb or in the end after a negative or interrogative verb and 'ever since' (adverb) is usually placed in the end :

(a) He's been in bed since his accident .
(b) I have been working here since last January.
(c) She had an accident last mont hand has been on leave ever since.
(d) He hadn't turned up since.

Adverbs of frequency : The Adverbs of Frequency are divided in two groups to understand their use :

(a) always, continually, frequently, occasionally, often, once, twice, periodically, repeatedly, sometimes, usually etc.

(b) ever, hardly ever, never, rarely, scarcely ever, seldom etc.

1. All the above adverbs are placed after auxiliary **'is /am/are'** in simple sentences :

(a) He is always ready. (b) She is often late.
(c) He is occasionally late. (d) They are usually happy.

2. The same are placed before the verbs (if there is no auxiliary) :

(a) His mother never cooks food. (b) He always speaks the truth.
(c) He often comes late. (d) He has never advised me.
(e) We have never seen an aeroplane. (f) He can never understand.
(g) You have often been told not to do that.

NOTE *If the sentence contains auxiliary verbs 'has/have/can' etc. these adverbs of frequency are placed after first auxiliary; as in sentences—(d), (e), (f), (g) above.*
These adverbs are used after Auxiliary + subject in interrogative sentences :
(h) Have you ever taken meat? (i) Have you ever visited Agra?

Exceptions

(i) With 'used to' and 'have to', place the adverb before them :

(a) I hardly ever have to remind him; he always remembers.
(b) He is always used to smoke before going to bed.

(ii) Adverbs mentioned in group (a) above (except 'always' if not used with imperatives) can also be placed at the beginning or end of a sentence or clause.

The adverb 'often' if put at the end, normally requires the use of ' very' or 'quite' with it :

(a) Often he walked. (b) He walked quite often.
(c) She visits here very often. (d) She often visits here.

(iii) Adverbs mentioned in group (b) above; hardly ever, never, rarely etc. (but not 'ever' alone) can also be placed at the beginning of a sentence.

NOTE *If these are used at the beginning of the sentence , inversion of the verb is necessary.*

Negative verbs are not used with 'hardly/ scarcely ever, never, rarely and seldom', as these frequency adverbs are themselves negative in meanings :

(a) Hardly ever did we manage to meet unobserved.
(b) Never before had I been asked to do this work.
(c) I hardly ever go out.
(d) It hardly rained at all last summer.
(e) There were scarcely twenty girls present there.

Sentence adverbs : These adverbs normally modify the whole sentence or clause. These adverbs are divided in three groups as follows :

A Apparently,Actually, Clearly, Certainly, Evidently, Obviously, Presumably, Probably, Undoubtedly.

B Definitely.

C Surely, Perhaps, Possibly.

1. The adverbs in group (A) can be placed at the beginning or at the end of a sentence or clause :

(a) Apparently she knew this locality well. (b) She knew this locality well apparently.

2. Adverbs in group (A) can also be placed after 'be' form of verb :

(a) He is obviously clever. (b) She was actually present there.
(c) It is evidently clear now.

NOTE *(1) If the sentence contains auxiliary verbs : has/have/can(Compound verb) etc. these adverbs are placed after first auxiliary :*

(d) She has possibly sold her house.
(e) They have presumably shifted to some other location.

3. Adverbs in group (A)can be placed before verbs as well, if there is no auxiliary :

(a) Ramesh certainly works hard.
(b) Ramesh possibly lives near the railway station.

NOTE *(i) 'Perhaps' and 'Possibly' are usually placed in the beginning though they can be placed in the end also.*

(ii) 'Surely' is normally placed at the beginning or end, though it can also be placed next to the verb in interrogative sentences :

(a) Surely you could lift it . (b) You could lift it surely.

Adverbs of degree **:** The most commonly used adverbs of degree are :almost,absolutely, barely, completely, enough, entirely, extremely, fairly, far, hardly, just, much, nearly, only, quite, rather, really, scarcely, so, too, very etc.

1. **'Only :** The adverb **'only'** modifies verbs. Usually it is placed next to the word which it qualifies.It is placed before the verbs, adjectives and adverbs.It is also placed before and after the nouns and pronouns. The meaning of sentence changes with change of position of adverb 'only' :

(a) He had only four chairs. (not more than four)
(b) He only lent the umbrella. (He didn't sell it.)

(c) He gave the pen to me only. (not to anyone else)
(d) I believe only half of what he said.(not everything what he said)
Note the difference in meaning :
(a) Only she can speak.(She alone can speak)
(b) She can only speak.(She can't write or read)
(c) She can speak only.(She can't do any other work like cooking or washing)

2. The adverb **'just'** like 'only', should also be placed before the word it qualifies :
(a) I'll just buy one. (b) I had just enough money.
It can also be placed before the verb :
(c) I'll just buy one. (d) I just had enough money.
Note that the change of position of 'just' in a sentence would change the meaning :
(e) Just sign here; means –You are to sign only or This is all you have to do.
(f) Sign just here; means –Sign at this particular spot.

3. An adverb of degree usually modifies an adjective or another adverb. It is placed before the adjective or adverb it modefies :
(a) You are absolutely correct. (b) I was almost ruined.
Exception : The adverb 'enough' is placed after the adjective it modifies.
(a) The house isn't large enough.
(b) She didn't work quickly enough.
(c) He is tall enough to reach the fan.

4. Some adverbs of degree can also modify verbs. Adverbs; such as—almost, barely, enough, hardly, just, (a) little, much, nearly, quite, rather, really and scarcely are placed before the main verb it modifies like adverbs of frequency :
(a) She almost / nearly slipped. (b) He is just coming.

5. The adverb **'far'** usually needs a comparative degree modifier, or ' too + positive degree' :
(a) It is <u>far better</u> to keep mum. (b) She drives <u>far too</u> fast.

ORDER OF ADVERBS

If two or more adverbs are used in a sentence, then it becomes important to place them in a certain order.

1. When there are two **adverbs of time**, the adverbs indicating a point of time (e.g., three o'clock, 4 P.M.) or the shorter period of time is usually placed first.In some cases position can also be reversed :
(a) I saw the movie on Sunday evening last week.
(b) I'll meet you at four o'clock on Monday.
(c) She arrived at three o'clock yesterday evening.
(d) She was born at six o'clock in the evening on Sunday in 1987 .

NOTE *The adverb showing a period of time may have front position for emphasis, prominence or contrast :*
(a) Yesterday I went there at four o'clock, but tomorrow I'll go there at six o'clock.
(b) Yesterday evening she arrived at six o'clock, but tomorrow she'll arrive at seven o'clock.

NOTE *(i) when there are two such adverbs, one indicating point of time another indicating period of time ,the adverb showing point of time cannot have front position in isolation.*

(a) At four o'clock I'll meet you tomorrow. *Incorrect*

But if both are used combined , front position is possible :

(a) At four o' clock tomorrow I will meet you at the hotel. *Correct*

(ii) If, however, the larger unit of time is considered to be more important or for the sake of emphasis or if the smaller is an afterthought this order may be reversed :

(a) She arrived yesterday evening, at about six o'clock.

2. When there are two **adverbs of place**, the smaller unit is usually placed first. The order is often a matter of style and balance.It is not a mandatory rule :

(a) Ram lives in a small village in Rajasthan.
(b) We spent the holidays in a cottage in the mountains.
(c) We spent the holidays in the mountains in a small cottage we rented from a friend.

3. When a sentence contains both an **adverb of place** or **direction and** an **adverb of time**, the adverbial of time is usually placed last.

The examples below illustrates such combinations :

(a) We're going to Agra next month.
(b) I expect to be back home by Sunday.
(c) Meet me outside the church at six o'clock on Sunday.
(d) We went to a party last month.

NOTE *Variations in this order are possible. The adverbs of time may also have front position. The adverbs of place or direction are not placed normally in front position.*

(e) Last month we went to Kashmir ; next month we're going to Nainital.
(Adverbs of Time in front position)
(f) On Monday they sailed from Sri Lanka; on Saturday they landed in India.

4. **Adverbs of place and direction** usually precede the **adverbs of frequency**. Adverbs of frequency usually precede the adverbs of time :

(a) I have been to USA several times this year.
(b) He strolled round the park twice before supper.
(c) She gave lectures at the school, three days a week last term.
(d) I passed him in the street twice last month.
(e) She goes to USA every other year nowadays.

NOTE *Variations in this order are possible.We can place adverbs of time in front position for emphasis or contrast :*

(f) Before supper she strolled round the park twice.

(g) Last term she gave lectures at the school three days a week; this term she is lecturing there two days a week.

5. When **adverbs of manner**, **place and time** occur in one sentence-

(A) Adverb of manner usually precedes adverb of place :
(a) He climbed swiftly on the roof.
(b) He will stay happily there.

(B) But some adverbs like; away, back, down, forward, home, in, off, on, out, round and up usually precede adverbs of manner :

(c) He went back happily.
(d) She turned back anxiously.
(e) Ram went home sadly.
(f) She rode on confidently.

6. Adverbs of 'time'usually follow adverbs of manner and place :

(a) We worked hard in the office today.

(b) They lived there happily for two years.

But they can also be placed in front position for the sake of emphasis :

(c) Every day he queued silently at the railway station.

Look at the following sentences also :

(a) She spoke loudly at the meeting yesterday.
1 2 3

(b) He is crying loudly at the field now.
1 2 3

(c) He was going to Jaipur yesterday.
2 3

(d) She comes regularly at the ground daily.
1 2 3

1=Adverb of Manner, 2=Adverb of place, 3= Adverb of time

SOME IMPORTANT ADVERBS

1. Fairly and Rather

(i) 'Fairly' is used with favourable adjectives and adverbs while 'rather' is used before unfavourable adjectives and adverbs :

(a) Ram is fairly clever, but Ramesh is rather foolish.
(b) Ram walks fairly fast, but Anil walks rather slowly.
(c) Harish was fairly relaxed; Sita was rather tense.
(d) It was a fairly interesting film.
(e) It is rather a boring book.

NOTE *(i) With adjectives and adverbs like; fast, slow, thin, thick, hot, cold etc., which do not indicate in themselves either favourable or unfavourable sense, the use of 'fairly' reflects approval and use of 'rather', disapproval .*

(a) This coffee is fairly hot. (implies that the speaker likes hot coffee.)

(b) This coffee is rather hot. (implies that it is a little too hot for him.)

(ii) 'Rather' when used before; alike, like, similar, different etc. and before comparatives, means 'a little' or 'slightly' :

(a) These cats are rather like cubs in some ways.
(b) The weather was rather hot than we had expected.

(iii) 'Rather a' is possible with certain nouns like; disappointment, disadvantage, nuisance, pity, shame and sometimes joke :

(a) It's rather a nuisance (= a little inconvenient) that we can't play here.

(b) It's rather a disappointment (= a little unfortunate) that he failed again.

(iv) When 'rather' is used before favourable adjectives/adverbs like; clever, good, pretty, well, amusing etc. then its meaning changes; it becomes nearly equivalent to 'very' and expresses complimentary feelings :

(a) She is rather clever. (means—She is very clever.)

(b) It is rather a good movie. (means better than the perception about it, it is a recommendation)

(c) I rather like the smell of petrol.

(d) He rather enjoys queueing.

The use of 'rather'+ 'like/ enjoy' often expresses a liking.

2. Hard : The adverb 'hard' means hard as adjective .

(a) He works hard.

(b) She looked hard at me.

(c) He was running as hard as he could.

(d) She was working hard.

3. Hardly, Scarcely, Barely : The adverbs ; hardly, scarcely and barely are almost negative(almost not) in meaning. 'Hardly' is usually used with 'any', 'ever', 'at all', or the verb 'can' :

(a) She has hardly any money. (very little money)

(b) We hardly ever go out. (we very seldom go out.)

(c) It hardly rained at all summer, last year. (almost no rain)

(d) The bag is so heavy that he can hardly lift it. (unable to lift the bag)

'Hardly' can also be used with other verbs :

(a) I hardly know him. (I know him only very slightly.)

NOTE *One should not be confused with adverbs 'hard' and 'hardly' :*

(a) He looked hard at it. (He stared at it.)

(b) She hardly looked at me. (She gave me only a brief glance or didn't look .)

'Scarcely' means 'almost not' and can replace 'hardly' as used above.

But 'scarcely' is usually used to mean–not quite :

(a) There were scarcely ten people in the meeting. (probably fewer)

'Barely' means 'not more than' / 'only just' :

(a) His voice was barely audible. (it was only just audible)

(b) There were barely ten people in the meeting. (only just ten)

(c) I can barely see it. (I can only just see it.)

4. Yet and Still : Both are adverbs of time. 'Yet' means-up to the time of speaking. It is usually used with the negative or interrogative.

'Still' emphasises that the action continues. It is mainly used with the affirmative or interrogative .It can also be used with the negative to emphasize the continuance of an action :

(a) He hasn't completed (his work) yet.
(b) He hasn't yet applied for the licence I told him about.
(c) He is still in bed.
(d) Has she come? Not yet.
(e) The jeep hasn't arrived yet.
(f) Is lunch ready yet?
(g) Has the jeep arrived yet?
(h) It is still raining.
(i) She still doesn't understand. (Action of not understanding continues.)
(j) She doesn't understand yet. (The positive action of understanding hasn't yet started.)

NOTE *'Yet' is normally placed after verb or after verb + object.If the object consists of a large number of words 'yet' can be placed before the verb also.*

. 'Still' is placed after the verb 'be' but before other verbs :

5. **Since and Ever since :** 'Since' and 'ever since' are used with perfect tenses. 'Since' can be placed after the auxiliary or in end position after a negative or interrogative verb; 'ever since' (adverb) is usually placed in end position.

Phrases and clauses with 'since' and 'ever since' are usually placed in end position though front position is also possible :

(a) I first met her three years ago and have remembered her face ever since.
(b) I saw her five years ago and had been trying to meet her ever since.
(c) He's been in bed since his accident.
(d) It has been raining since I came.

6. **Somehow, Anyhow :** 'Somehow' (means-in some way or other) can be placed in the front position or after a verb without object or after the object :

(a) Somehow they managed.
(b) They managed somehow.
(c) They raised the money somehow.
(d) I wasn't qualified to apply for this job really but I got it anyhow .

'Anyhow' is an adverb of manner. It is often used to mean—'in any case'/ 'anyway'.

7. **Badly, Well :** 'Badly' and 'well' can be used as adverbs of manner or degree. As adverbs of manner, they come after an active verb, after the object or before the past participle in a passive verb :

(a) He behaved badly.
(b) He read well.
(c) He paid her badly.
(d) She speaks French well.
(e) She was badly paid.
(f) The trip was well organized.

'Badly' as an adverb of degree usually comes after the object or before the verb or past participle :

(a) The door needs a coat of paint badly/ The door badly needs a coat of paint.

(b) He was badly injured in the last match.

'Well' (degree) and 'well' (manner) have the same position rules :

(a) I'd like the steak well done.
(b) He knows the town well.

(c) Shake the bottle well.
(d) The children were well wrapped up.

The meaning of 'well' may depend on its position :

(a) You know that I can't drive well. (I'm not a good driver.)

'well' can be placed after 'may/might' and 'could', to emphasize the probability of an action :

(a) He may well refuse = It is quite likely that he will refuse.
(For may/ might as well)

8. Too : 'Too' is different from 'very'. 'Too' means 'excess' (more than enough or more than necessary or more than is wanted) :

(a) He is too weak to walk.
(b) She is too poor to pay her fee.
(c) It was too cold to go out, so we stayed at home.

(i) We can use an infinitive structure after 'too + adjective/adverb/determiner' :

(a) She is too old to work.
(b) It is far too cold to play tennis.
(c) We arrived too late to have lunch.

(ii) If the infinitive has its own subject, this is introduced by 'for' :

(a) It's too late for the shops to be open.
(b) The runway's too short for planes to land.
(c) There was too much mud for us to go walking.

(iii) The subject of a sentence with 'too' can also be the object of the following infintive. Object pronouns are not normally used after the infintive in such cases :

(a) The water is too hot to drink. *Correct*
The water is too hot to drink it. *Incorrect*

However, object pronouns are possible in this structures with 'for'.

(a) The water is too hot for us to drink (it).

NOTE *The two possible meanings of sentences like :*

(a) He's too stupid to teach (= He's too stupid to be a teacher.)
(b) He's too stupid for anyone to teach. (He can't be taught.)

(iv) 'Too' is not normally used before adjective + noun :

(a) I put down the bag because it was too heavy. *Correct*
I put down the too heavy bag. *Incorrect*
(b) She doesn't like men who are too tall. *Correct*
She doesn't like too tall men. *Incorrect*
(c) Let's forget this problem - it's too difficult. *Correct*
Let's forget this too difficult problem. *Incorrect*

In a rather formal style, 'too' can be used before adjective + a/ an + noun .

(d) It's too cold a day to go out.
(e) He was too clever a businessman to accept the offer initially.(It means -As a businessman, he was too clever to accept the offer initially.)

Note this structure also : **too + adverb + infinitive** :

(a) It is too soon (for me) to say whether the plan will succeed or not.

(b) She spoke too quickly for me to understand. ('for me' is necessary here.)

9. Too and Too much : Before adjectives without nouns and before adverbs we use 'too', not 'too much'.

(a) You're too kind to me.	*Correct*
You're too much kind to me.	*Incorrect*
(b) I arrived too early.	*Correct*
I arrived too much early.	*Incorrect*

10. Far, Farther, Farthest and Further, Furthest

'Far' is usually used in the comparative and superlative degrees :

(a) He travelled farther than we expected.

(b) He travelled the farthest of all and so got the first prize.

In negative and Interrogative sentence the positive form of 'Far'is more usual :

(a) How far can you see? I can't see far.

In the affirmative **'a long way'** is more usual than 'far' and a 'long way away' is more usual than 'far away' :

(a) They went a long way.

(b) Jack sailed a long way.

(c) Ram lives a long way away.

'Far' can be used in abstract terms also :

(a) The new law doesn't go far enough.

(b) You've gone too far! (You've been too insulting/ overbearing etc.)

NOTE *'Far' is also used with comparatives or with too/so + positive forms :*

(a) He explains far better than I do. (b) She eats far too much.

Further, Furthest : 'Further' and 'Furthest' can be used as adverbs of place/ distance :

(a) It doesn't appear safe to go any further / farther in this fog.
Further and Furthest can also be used in abstract terms :

(a) Ramesh said that these biting toys should not be on sale.

(b) Mahesh went further and said that no biting toy should be sold.

(c) Ganesh went furthest of all and said that no toys of any kind should be sold.

11. Much and Very much

(i) 'Much' (meaning—a lot) modifies comparative or superlative adjectives and adverbs :

(a) The dinner was much better.

(b) Nisha is much the best girl in the college.

(c) He completed the task much more quickly than we expected.

'Much too' can be used with positive forms :

(a) He spoke much too fast.

(ii) 'Much' also modifies negative verbs :

(a) He doesn't walk much nowadays.

In the interrogative sentences 'much' is mainly used with **'how'**. In questions without 'how', **much** can also be used but **'a lot'** is more common :

(a) How much has she walked? Has she walked a lot / much?

(iii) In affirmative sentences the construction **as/ so/ too + much** is possible, but 'a lot/a good deal/ a great deal' is preferable :

(a) He shouts so much that it causes irritation.
(b) He talks too much.
(c) She writes a lot/ a great deal.

(iv) 'Very much' (meaning—greatly)is used more widely in affirmative. It is used with; blame, praise, thank and with a number of verbs concerned with feelings like; admire, amuse, approve, dislike, distress, enjoy, impress, like, object, shock, surprise, etc. :

(a) Thank you very much.
(b) I admire her very much.
(c) They object very much to the noise we make.

'Much' (means—greatly), with or without 'very' can also be used with the participles like; admired,amused, disliked, distressed, impressed, liked, shocked, struck, upset :

(a) I was (very) much admired.
(b) He was (very) much impressed by her good manners.
(c) She was much shocked to hear the sad news.
(d) I was much upset to hear about the accident.

Much and Verh : Generally participles are modified by 'much' and adjectives by 'very'. Certain participles which have largely lost their verbal force and are felt to be adjectival, however , take 'very' :

(a) The law has been much abused. *Participle*
(b) Her dress was much admired. *Participle*
(c) It is a very good book. *Adjective*
(d) This is a very old building. *Adjective*
(e) She is a very clever girl. *Adjective*
(f) I was very interested in his story. *Adjectival*
(g) We are very worried about the position. *Adjectival*
(h) I feel very concerned about him. *Adjectival*

Conversely, participles used before a noun to make a compound adjective with a modifying adverb, take 'much' : a much abused privilege, a much travelled person, a much discussed question.

12. Quite :Quite has two meanings —

(i) It means 'completely' when it is used with a word or phrase which expresses the idea of completeness (such words or phrases are ;all right, certain, determined, empty, finished, full, ready, right, sure, wrong etc.) and also when it is used with a very strong adjective/ adverb like; amazing, extraordinary, horrible, perfect etc. :

(a) The container was quite empty.
(b) You're quite right.
(c) It was quite amazing. I can't believe it at all.

(ii) 'Quite' means—'slightly less' also, when it is used with other adjectives/ adverbs. It has a slightly weakening effect. 'Quite good' is normally less complimentary than 'good'. 'Quite' used in this way has approximately the same meaning as 'fairly' but its strength changes a lot according to the way it is stressed.For ***example :***

(a) quite good (weak quite, strong good) is slightly less than good.
(b) quite good (equal stress) means moderately good.
(c) quite good (strong quite, weak good) is much less than good.

Note the position of a/an with **'quite'** :

(a) We had quite a long walk.
(b) It is quite an old castle.

13. Seldom

(i) 'Seldom' is an adverb. We may say 'I seldom go to London', but not 'My visits to London are seldom', for here we are treating the word as a predicative adjective. 'Seldom' can be used after a verb in this way (and then as an adverb) only in the following types of construction :

(a) **After 'It is' :** After 'It is' (was), and followed by a 'that-clause' in apposition to the anticipatory pronoun 'it' :
(a) It is seldom that we get such an opportunity as this.
(b) **In a relative clause :** In a relative clause that refers back to the whole notion expressed in a preceding clause of time :
(a) When she lost her temper, which was seldom....
(b) Whenever I take a day off from work, which is seldom, ...
(c) **In a parenthetic clause :** In a parenthetic clause referring back to the entire notion expressed in a preceding adverb clause of time :
(a) Whenever I take a day off from work, which is seldom, ...

(ii) To modify 'seldom' : 'Seldom' is a negative word—meaning 'not often' and should not, therefore, be modified by another negative.

NOTE *The phrases 'seldom if ever' and 'seldom or never' are possible but not 'seldom or ever'.*

(a) She seldom or never tells lies.
(b) She seldom if ever asks the boys the reason of their absence.

14. Enough

(i) Adjective/ adverb + enough

When 'enough' modifies an adjective or adverb, it normally comes after the adjective/ adverb:

(a) Is that music loud enough?
(b) These shoes are not big enough.
(c) Is it warm enough for you? (NOT ..... enough warm ....)
(d) You're not driving fast enough.
(e) We haven't got a big enough house.
(f) We'll go swimming if we get warm enough weather.
(g) You could wear my shoes - you've got big enough feet.

(ii) Position with adjective + noun

'Enough' follows the adjective which it modifies (see paragraph I above). But when 'enough' modifies an adjective and noun together, it comes before the adjective.

Compare :

(a) We haven't got big enough nails.
(= We need bigger nails - enough modifies big.)

(b) We haven't got enough big nails.
(= We need more big nails – enough modifies big nails)

Enough + infinitive :

The adverb '*enough*' is often followed by an infinitive :

(a) She didn't run fast enough to win.

(b) She's old enough to do what she wants.

Infinitives can be introduced by for + noun/ pronoun. Object forms of pronouns are used.

(a) It's late enough for the staff to stop work.

(b) There was just enough light for us to see what we were doing.

(c) The radio's small enough to put in your pocket.

(d) Those tomatoes aren't ripe enough to eat. (NOT .... to eat them.)

15. Close and Closely

'Close' is used as an adverb meaning—'near' :

(a) Keep yourself close to me.

(b) He was following close behind.

'Closely' is used with other meanings; like—stirictly,carefully etc :

(a) The militants were closely (= strictly) guarded.

(b) Watch closely (= carefully) what she does.

(c) He explained the theory in six closely written pages. (i.e. with the words and lines close together.)

16. Dead and Deadly

'Dead' as an adverb means—'completely', 'absolutely'; e.g.— dead level; dead straight; going dead slow (almost stopped , very very slowly); dead certain ; dead drunk :

(a) I found him dead drunk.

(b) I am dead certain that Shyam has taken the purse.

(c) I am dead against the legalisation of prostitution.

(d) The wind was blowing dead against our desired direction.

'Deadly' is otherwise an adjective. It is used as an adverb, meaning–'like death' in deadly pale and (figuratively) deadly dull :

(a) The news was accurate and relible but deadly dull.

17. Direct and Directly

When used as adverb 'direct' means—'straight', 'without detours, intermediaries', etc.':

(a) This train goes direct to New Delhi.

(b) He went direct to the hospital.

(c) I shall communicate with you direct. (not through any intermediary)

Directly

'Directly' is used, meaning either 'at once', 'immediately, or 'after a short time', 'very soon':

(a) She left directly after lunch.
(b) I'll be with you directly.

Other meanings

(a) I am not directly affected by the changes in policy.
(b) He's directly descended from Indira Gandhi.

18. Easy and Easily

The use of 'Easy' as adverb is found in a few phrases only :

(a) Stand easy! (A military command)
(b) Take it easy. (Don't be worried about it or don't work too hard)
(c) Go easy with the cheese. (means 'use it with moderation')

'**Easily**' means—without difficulty or with ease :

(d) He solved the problem easily.
(e) She's not easily satisfied.
(f) He won the match easily.

19. High and Highly

'High' is used adverbially in a numer of phrases like; fly high, aim high, fix one's hopes high; dream high, play high :

(a) One should dream high.(have loftier aims)
(b) He aims high .

It is also used after 'run' in following kind of sentences :

(a) Feelings there have been running high , in the wake of last week's killings. (means, the people were angry or excited.)
(b) The sea was running high.(Sea was trubulent.)
(c) Passions were running high.(excitement)

Highly

'Highly' is used adverbially before participles like; highly interesting, highly paid, a highly educated ,highly qualified, highly amusing, highly intelligent , speak highly of someone, esteem someone highly, think highly of someone.

(a) He is highly educated . (b) She is a highly intelligent woman.
(c) I esteem my father highly.

20. Right and Rightly

'Right' has wide use as an adverb :

(a) It serves you right.(It is in your benefit.)
(b) She answered right.(correct)
(c) Nothing goes right with me.(I feel unlucky.)
(d) You will come right away (immediately or at once).

'**Rightly**' is usually meant 'correctly', and has mid position , with the verb :

(a) He rightly answered that question.
(b) I am unable to rightly recollect if she brought anything.
(c) The President rightly pointed out the mistake.

21. Round and Roundly

The adverb 'round' has different meanings with different verbs :

(a) He handed round the plate of sandwiches.(passed from person to person)
(b) She paused but did not turn round.(taking opposite direction)
(c) He is going to have a look round.(a cursory look of all surroundings)
(d) Christmas will soon be round again.
(e) Hand these leaflets round (= distribute them).
(f) The jeep will be round (= will be here) in a few minutes.

'Roundly' has a totally different meaning .It usually means 'pointedly', 'flatly', forcefully :

(a) I told her roundly that she was dismissed.
(b) He cursed me roundly.
(c) Political leaders have roundly condemned the killing of animals.

22. Just and Justly

The adverb 'just' is used in many phrases like; only just, just now/ then, just here/ there, just as you say, just so.It has no resemblance with the adjective 'just' and the noun 'justice' :

(a) We only just managed to catch the plane.
(b) He has arrived just now.
(c) They earn just enough for their needs.

Justly : The meaning of adverb 'justly' is linked with the adjective 'just' and the noun 'justice'.

'Justly' usually means—'rightly'or 'as per demand of justice' :

(a) As you justly (= rightly) notice .... (b) He was justly punished by the court.

23. Late and Lately

The meaning of adverb 'late' is the opposite of the adverb 'early' : go to bed late. get up late, stay up late; arrive late, marry late.

'Lately' means—'recently' :

(a) He came late today.
(b) I haven't seen her lately.(recently)
(c) She has finished her work lately.
(d) You are late.

DEGREES OF COMPARISON IN ADVERBS

Some adverbs have degrees of comparison like adjectives and these degrees are formed in the same way as in adjectives.

A. If the adverb is a word of one syllable , the comparative is formed by adding 'er' and the superlative by adding 'est' to the positive form :

Positive	Comparative	Superlative
1. Short	Shorter	Shortest.
2. Late	Later	Latest /Last
3. Hard	Harder	Hardest
4. Fast	Faster	Fastest

B. Some adverbs form the degrees of comparison in an irregular way :

Positive	Comparative	Superlative
1. Badly	Worse	Worst
2. Well	Better	Best
3. Little	Less	Least
4. Much	More	Most
5. Far	Farther	Farthest
6. Forth	Further	Furthest
7. Near	Nearer	Next

C. Adverbs ending in 'ly' form the comparative degree by adding 'more'and the superlative by adding 'most' :

Positive	Comparative	Superlative
1. Slowly	More slowly	Most slowly
2. Wisely	More wisely	Most wisely
3. Swiftly	More swiftly	Most swiftly
4. Skilfully	More skilfully	Most skilfully

(a) He ran swiftly.

(b) He ran more swiftly than Ramesh.

(c) He ran most swiftly of all students.

But note : 'Early, Earlier, Earliest' is an exception.

NOTE *Only the 'Adverbs of Manner', 'Adverbs of Degree' and 'Adverbs of Time' have the comparatives and superlatives .Many adverbs owing to their nature can't be compared . These are ; now , then ,where , there , once.*

CORRECT YOURSELF EXCERCISE : ADVERBS

CYE : 01 Correct the sentences :

1. She takes generally her breakfast at 8 AM.
2. Ram only came here last Saturday.
3. Ramesh was too tired when he came here.
4. Sita came quicker than I expected.
5. We wanted a better and efficient Office Assistant.
6. It was much cold last night.
7. I visited her frequently while in Newyork.
8. He will be quite sorry to know that.
9. The water of this tank is too cold.
10. He ran very fastly.

CYE : 02 Correct the sentences :

1. Hari was fortunately not available in the hostel.
2. It was nothing else than her arrogance.
3. He feels comparatively better today.
4. Come at 7 o'clock to my office.
5. I seldom or ever refused the leave.
6. He quickly ran away from the site.

7. Firstly you think over the words and then speak.
8. I go often to the Shani Temple.
9. No one hardly goes to church daily.
10. I care a straw for it.

CYE : 03 Correct the sentences

1. We were very delighted to get the news.
2. Call me anything else than a fraud.
3. They could not find her nowhere.
4. I only solved two sums.
5. She peacefully died yesterday.
6. Do you know to drive.
7. I went directly to Meerut.
8. It is very cold to go for a walk today.
9. Parul runs fastly than Nalini.
10. It you run fast, you would have won the race.

CYE : 04 Correct the sentences :

1. Hari speaks clear.
2. Sita writes neat.
3. Sarla hit the thief hardly on the head.
4. He is perfectly quite right.
5. The speaker spoke enough loud to be heard easily.
6. Ram is much old.
7. The story is much interesting.
8. Ram comes here seldom.
9. I am very satisfied with her conduct.
10. The train will arrive just now.
11. The film was mostly over when you entered.
12. He fared bad in the second innings.
13. Repeat again what you have said.
14. Breathe deeply when you walk.

CYE : 05 Correct the sentences :

1. He cautiously drives.
2. She heartily loves Ram.
3. There were every where flowers in the garden.
4. Ram comes at the field regularly every day.
5. She has been absenting herself frequently from the office.
6. Ram already has finished his work.
7. I see her frequently in the market.
8. She has often to go by tram.
9. He is intelligent wonderfully.
10. Sita regularly visits her friend Sarla.

CYE : 06 Correct the sentences :

1. I drive seldom after sunset.
2. He explained clearly the method of transplantation of the heart.
3. The parents heartily love their children.
4. Three passengers were unfortunately injured.
5. You are forbidden not to write on the table.
6. The day is hot too.
7. I was too tired after the swimming.
8. Sita loves her only daughter too much.
9. The new medicines have given her too much relief.
10. I met none else than your real brother.

CYE : 07 Correct the sentences :

1. She quickly writes.
2. Unless you do not work hard, you can't succeed.
3. The news is much interesting.
4. He seldom or ever refuses a genuine request.
5. You seldom or ever find a grammatical error in this book.
6. Ram ran very fastly.
7. They last evening, went to Jaipur.
8. I only solved two sums in an hour.
9. The matter has been very discussed.
10. I do not know to swim.

CYE : 08 Correct the sentences :

1. They have gone to Jaipur yesterday.
2. He has left this place five minutes ago.
3. Do you know him? Yes, I do not.
4. Do you know him? No, I do.
5. The teacher asked him to not sleep in the class.
6. Could you lend me your umbrella? Oh, no, I can.
7. She will today go to Mumbai.
8. With most humbly and respectfully, I beg to apprise.....
9. I have not pen with me.
10. There was no an intelligent student to solve that question.

SOLUTIONS : CORRECT YOURSELF EXERCISE

Solutions CYE : 01

1. Generally she takes her breakfast at 8 A.M..
2. Ram came here only last Saturday.
3. Ramesh was much tired when he came here.
4. Sita came quickly than I expected.
5. We wanted a better and more efficient Office Assistant.
6. It was very cold last night.
7. I frequently visited her while in Newyork.

8. He will be very sorry to know that.
9. The water of this tank is very cold.
10. He ran very fast.

Solutions CYE : 02

1. Fortunately Hari was not available in the hostel.
2. It was nothing else but her arrogance.
3. He feels better today.
4. Come to my office at 7 o'clock.
5. I seldom or never refused the leave.
6. He ran away quickly from the sight.
7. First you think over the words and then speak.
8. I often go to the Shani Temple.
9. Hardly any one goes to church daily.
10. I do not care a straw for it.

Solutions CYE : 03

1. We were much delightful to get the news.
2. Call me anything else but a fraud.
3. They could not find her anywhere.
4. I solved only two sums.
5. She died peacefully yesterday.
6. Do you know how to drive.
7. I went direct to Meerut.
8. It is too cold to go for a walk today.
9. Parul runs faster than Nalini.
10. Had you run fast, you would have won the race.

Solutions CYE : 04

1. Hari speaks clearly.
2. Sita writes neatly.
3. Sarla hit the thief hard on the head.
4. He is perfectly right.
5. The speaker spoke loud enough to be heard easily.
6. Ram is very old.
7. The story is very interesting.
8. Ram seldom comes here.
9. I am much satisfied with her conduct.
10. The train will arrive shortly.
11. The film was almost over when you entered.
12. He fared badly in the second innings.
13. Repeat what you have said.
14. Breathe deep when you walk.

Solutions CYE : 05

1. He drives cautiously .
2. She loves Ram heartily.

3. There were flowers every where in the garden.
4. Ram comes regularly at the field every day.
5. She has been frequently absenting herself from the office.
6. Ram has already finished his work.
7. I frequently see her in the market.
8. She often has to go by tram.
9. He is wonderfully intelligent .
10. Sita visits her friend Sarla regularly.

Solutions CYE : 06

1. I seldom drive after sunset.
2. He clearly explained the method of transplantation of the heart.
3. The parents love their children heartily.
4. Unfortunately, three passengers were injured.
5. You are forbidden to write on the table.
6. The day is too hot.
7. I was very tired after the swimming.
8. Sita loves her only daughter very much.
9. The new medicines have given her much relief.
10. I met none else but your real brother.

Solutions CYE : 07

1. She writes quickly.
2. Unless you work hard, you can't succeed.
3. The news is very interesting.
4. He seldom or never refuses a genuine request.
5. You seldom or never find a grammatical error in this book.
6. Ram ran very fast.
7. They went to Jaipur last evening.
8. I solved only two sums in an hour.
9. The matter has been much discussed.
10. I do not know how to swim.

Solutions CYE : 08

1. They went to Jaipur yesterday.
2. He left this place five minutes ago.
3. Do you know him? Yes, I do .
4. Do you know him? No, I don't.
5. The teacher asked him not to sleep in the class.
6. Could you lend me your umbrella? Oh no, I can't.
7. She will go to Mumbai today.
8. Most humbly and respectfully, I beg to apprise.....
9. I have no pen with me.
10. There was not an intelligent student to solve that question.

5

Article

Articles are members of determiner family. Articles are used before nouns.

'A (or An) and The'

There are two Articles- 'A' (or An) and 'The'. A (or An) is called- Indefinite Article.

'The' is called the Definite Article, because it refers some particular person or thing.

We use 'definite' to mean 'sure', 'certain'. 'Definite' is particular.We use 'indefinite' to mean not sure, not certain. 'Indefinite' is general. When we are talking about one thing in particular, we use '**the**'. When we are talking about one thing in general, we use **'A'** or **'An'**.

USE OF 'A' OR 'AN'

Article 'A' or 'An' is used before a singular noun. The choice between 'A' or 'An' is determined by **first sound of pronunciation** (not by the letter of alphabet even; it may be A, E, I, O,U of the noun.) If the first sound is vowel, **An**, is used :-

Look at the following sentences :

(a) He is an honest man. (b) He is a European.
(c) He is an M.L.A. (d) He is an S.D.O.

(e) He is a one eyed man.

In sentence (a), (c), (d), honest, M.L.A and S.D.O are nouns, that have first letter h, m, s, (none is a vowel) but the ***first sound of pronunciation*** of these nouns is vowel, **so 'An' is used**.

In sentence (b) & (e) 'European', and 'one', are nouns, that have first letter E and O (both are vowels) but the ***first sound of pronunciation***, is not vowel, **so 'A' is used**.

NOTE *The choice between 'A' or 'An' is also determined by the word which immediately follows 'A' or 'An'. If it is pronounced with vowel sound, use 'An' otherwise 'A' :*

(a) It was an extremely difficult situation. (b) I need an eighty feet long iron rod.

Please note the following words and the use of 'A' or 'An' before them. Students generally commit mistake using 'A' or 'An' before these words :

Note the correct use of Article : A or An

1. An hour.
2. An hourly meeting.
3. An hour's daybreak.

21. A one rupee note.
22. A one eyed man.
23. A uniform.

4. An honour.
5. An honorary post
6. An honourable person.
7. An honest man.
8. An heir
9. An honorarium.
10. A house
11. A historical fair.
12. A humble person.
13. A husband
14. A heinous crime.
15. A young man.
16. A ewe
17. A university
18. A unity
19. A union
20. A eulogy
24. A useful book .
25. A useful feature.
26. A unique decision.
27. A united front.
28. A unified plan.
29. A year.
30. A USA ally.
31. An FO.
32. A forest officer.
33. An MP/MLC.
34. A member of parliament.
35. An IAS / IPS / ILO.
36. An SP / SDO.
37. An M.A./M.Sc/M.Com..
38. An RTS / RTC / RO.
39. An RC worker.
40. A UK ship / European.

'A' or 'An' is used :

1. Before a singular noun which is countable ,when it is mentioned for the first time and represents no particular person or thing (with a particular noun 'the' is used.) :

(a) I need an umbrella .
(b) We live in a small house.
(c) He bought a briefcase.

2. Before a singular countable noun which represents a class of things :

(a) A vehicle must be insured. = (All vehicles /Any vehicle must be insured.)
(b) A child needs love. = (All children need/ Any child needs love.)

3. Before the name of a profession 'a' or 'an' is used :

(a) Rita is a nurse.
(b) She is a teacher.
(c) He is a doctor.
(d) He is an engineer.
(e) He is an M.P. / M.L.A.
(f) Mr. Srivastava is a doctor.

4. 'A' or 'an' is used with a noun complement :

(a) It was an earthquake.
(b) It was a tiger.
(c) It is a cat.

5. 'A' or 'an' is used with certain numbers :

For example : A hundred, A thousand, A million, A dozen, A couple; See the following sentences—

(a) I have a hundred pens.
(b) He has a thousand rupees.
(c) She has to walk two and a quarter kilometers daily.
(d) I have purchased a dozen eggs.

6. If a singular noun is placed after ; many / rather / quite / such , use 'a' or 'an' before the singular noun :
   (a) Many a woman would welcome such a chance.
   (b) It is rather a pity , I say.
   (c) It was quite an impossible task.
   (d) It was such a foolish argument.
7. 'A' or 'An' is used in expressions of price, speed, ratio, etc. :
   (a) She can run twelve kilometers an hour. (b) Rice sells fifty rupees a kilo.
   (c) I earn Rs twenty thousand a month. (d) This train runs seventy kms an hour.
8. 'A' or 'An' is used in exclamatory sentences before singular, countable nouns :
   (a) What a dog ! (b) Such a long queue!
   (c) What a pretty girl! (d) What a beautiful girl !
9. 'A' or 'An' is used in some phrases as :
   'In a fix', 'in a hurry', 'in a nutshell', 'make a noise', 'make a foot', 'keep a secret', 'as a rule', 'at a discount', 'at a stone's throw', 'a short while ago', at a loss', 'take a fancy to', 'take an interest in', 'to have a drink', 'go for a walk', 'have a good knowledge', 'make a foot', 'tell a lie', 'take a bath', 'half a kilo', 'a matter of chance' :
   (a) He has a good knowledge of English. (b) It is a matter of shame.
   (c) He is in a hurry. (d) He gave me a warning.
   (e) Do not make a noise. (f) It is a pity.
   (g) He has a headache. (h) Never tell a lie.
   (i) She comes here once a week. (j) Twelve inches make a foot.
10. Before a proper noun, when it is used as a common noun :
   (a) He is a Shakespeare.
   (b) You are a Hitler.
   (c) This man is a second Dara Singh.
11. When 'A' or 'An' is used before the name of a person (proper noun), it implies that person is not known to the speaker.
   (a) This poem is written by a Maneesh.
   (Maneesh is not known to the speaker, it means some person named Maneesh.)
   (b) This book is written by a Suresh .(Some person named Suresh)
   (As per rule, no article is used before the name of a person.)
12. When a verb 'a' or 'an' is used as a noun , 'a' or 'an' is used before it :
   (a) He goes for a <u>walk</u> daily. [Walk (verb) used as noun.]
   (b) He has gone for a <u>ride</u> . [Ride is a verb used as noun.]
   (c) Last Sunday, I had a long <u>talk</u> with my friend. [Talk is a verb used here as noun.]
   (d) I want to have a <u>rest</u> /a <u>drink</u> / a <u>bath</u>. [Rest/drink/bath are verbs used as noun.]

CAUTION

(a) 'A' or 'An' is not used before a plural noun.
(b) 'A' or 'An' is not used before a proper noun except in exceptional cases.
(c) 'A' or 'An' is not used before uncountable nouns in general.

Caution : Use of 'A' /'AN' and ONE

1. When counting or measuring—time, distance or weight etc. we can use either 'a'/ 'an' or one for the singular :

   $1 = a/one dollar, $1000000 = a/one million dollars.

But note that in,

'The rent is $100 a month.'

the **'a'** before month is not replaceable by 'one'.

In other types of statements, 'a/an' and 'one' are not normally interchangeable, because 'one' + noun normally means—one only, not more than one and a/an does not mean this :

(a) A pen is no good. [It the per is the wrong sort of thing.]

(b) One pen is no good. [I need two or three.]

2. **Special uses of 'ONE'**

(i) 'one' (adjective/pronoun) is used with **'another/others'** :

(a) One (girl) wanted to read, another/others wanted to watch TV.

(b) One day she wanted her lunch early, another day she wanted it late.

(ii) One can also be used before 'day / week / month / year/ summer/ winter' etc. or before the name of the day or month to denote a particular time when something happened :

(a) One night there was a terrible earthquake.

(b) One winter the snow fell heavily.

(c) One day a message arrived.

(iii) 'One day' can also be used to mean at some future time or date :

(a) One day you'll be sorry.

(b) One day you will realise your mistake.

3. **'A' / 'An' and 'One' (pronoun)**

'One' is the pronoun equivalent of 'A / An' :

(a) Did you get a ticket? Yes I managed to get one.

The plural of 'one' used in this way is 'some' :

(a) Did you get tickets? Yes I managed to get some.

'THE'-DEFINITE ARTICLE

The definite article 'The' is used in following cases :

1. While speaking of a particular person or thing or one already referred to :

Examples :

(a) She found a purse. **The** purse contained a Golden chain. **The** golden chain is very precious.

(b) **The** book you referred is out of print.

(c) I dislike **the** fellow who came here yesterday.

Exception : Important

(i) **First and subsequent reference** : When we first refer to something in written text, we often use an indefinite article to modify it.Read the following Example :

(a) "I'd like a glass of orange juice, please," John said. (first reference to 'glass' of juice)
(b) "I put the glass of juice on the counter already," Shilpa replied.
(Subsequent reference–'the is used')

Exception to the above rule :

(ii) When a modifier (adjective) appears between the article and the noun, **the subsequent article will continue to be indefinite :**

(a) "I'd like a big glass of orange juice, please," John said.
(b) "I put **a big glass** of juice on the counter already," Sheila replied.

2. When a singular noun is meant to represent a whole category/class, article 'the' is used :

Examples :

(a) The dog is a faithful animal. (Or we say, 'Dogs are faithful animals'.)
(b) The banyan is kind of fig tree.
(c) The cat loves comfort.

3. 'The' is used before superlatives :

(a) She is the most beautiful girl in our college.
(b) Ram is the best student in our school .
(c) The darkest cloud has a silver lining.

4. 'The' is used with the names of a **building, gulf, river, ocean, sea** etc :

The Taj Mahal, The Persian Gulf,
The Char Minar, The Pacific,
The Ganges, The Red Sea,
The Yamuna, The Thames.

5. 'The' is placed only before the **plural names of islands and the mountain rages, chains of mountains, plural names of countries; eg —**

The Netherlands, The Phillipines, The Bahamas,The Laccadives islands,
The Himalayas, the Alps, and before certain other names.

'The' is not used before the names of countries but if the names of countries contain words like;States, Kingdom, Republic, we use 'the' before them :

The USA, the USSR, the U.K., the Republic of Ireland, the Domonican Republic.

(a) He went to Mexico.
(b) He is from the United States.
(c) The USA and the U.K. both agreed on this point.

6. 'The' is used before names consisting of **adjective + noun** (provided the adjective is not 'east', 'west' etc.) : the Arabian Gulf, the New Forest, the High Street.

7. 'The' is also used before names consisting of **'noun + of + noun'** structure :
the Cape of Good Hope, the Bay of Biscay, the Gulf of Mexico.

8. 'The' is used before the adjectives **east/west etc. + noun in certain names :**

The East/ West End, the East/ West Indies,
the North/ South Pole.

9. 'The'is also used before the **name of directions :**
as : the East, the West, the North, the South.

(a) The sun rises in the east and sets in the west.

10. 'The' is used before the name of **persons(Family)in plural** :

The Raymonds, The Ambanis, The Birlas.

11. Before the names of important, renowned books, article 'the' is used :

(a) The Quran, (b) The Ramayana, (c) The Mahabharata.

But we say - Homer's Iliad, Valmiki's Ramayana, Jaidev's Geet Govind.

12. Before such common nouns that are names of things, unique of their kind :

The Sun, The Earth, The Sky,The Moon,The World,The Sea, The Environment—

(a) The sky is dark and the moon is shinning.

(b) The sea seems calm today.

(c) We must do something to protect the environment.

(d) The world is at the verge of destruction.

(i) In following case we do not use 'the' before 'sea'

(a) We go to sea as sailors.

(b) He is at sea now a days (on a voyage).

(ii) We can use 'the' before the word 'space' if it means place :

(a) He tried to park his car there but the space was too small.

But if 'space' means area beyond the earth's atmosphere , do not use 'the' before it.

(b) There are lacs of stars in space.

13. Before terms referring nationality, article 'the' is used :

The Indian, The French, The American,The English.

14. Before a proper noun, only when it is qualified by an adjective.

The great Caesar, The immortal Shakespeare, The brave Napolean.

15. 'The' is used with ordinals like :

(a) He was **the first** man to stand up.

(b) **The sixth** chapter of this book is very interesting.

(c) He was **the second** man to arrive.

First , second , third ..... are called ordinals.

One , Two , Three.........are called cardinals.

16. Before musical instruments and names of inventions :

(a) He can play the flute/the tabla / the harmonium well .

(b) Who invented the telephone?

17. Before an adjective, when the noun represents a class of persons :

(a) The young will support the motion.

(b) The poor can be trusted.

(c) The rich should help the poor.

(d) Three percent posts are reserved for the disabled.

18. Before a common noun, to give it the meaning of an abstract noun use 'the' :

(a) The moralist in Gandhi, revolted against the injustice.

(b) The judge in her prevailed upon the wife and she sentenced her husband to prison.

19. 'The' is used before name of newspaper, community, political party, historical event,train, ship, aeroplane etc
(a) The Hindus, the Muslims, the Sikhs.
(b) The B J P, the Congress, the Communist party.
(c) The French Revolution, the Quit India Movement.
(d) The Hindustan Times, The Indian Express.
(e) The Intercity, the Rajdhani express.
(f) The Boeing, the Vikrant.

20. When two or more nouns refer to one person, put 'the' before the first noun only .If both the nouns refer two differet persons or thing, 'the' is used before both of them :
(a) The producer and financier was present there.
(Producer and financier is one person.)
(b) The producer and the financier were present there.
(Producer and financier are two different persons.)

21. 'The' is used as an adverb with a comparative :
(a) The more she gets the more she demands.
(b) The sooner you complete the better it is.

22. 'The' is used before comparative degree being used for selection or comparison :
(a) He is the stronger of the two. (b) This is the better of the two novels.

23. When a person is being referred by his designation, 'the' is used; eg—
The Chairman, The Director, The President.
(a) All financial decisions will be taken by the chairman.
(b) It is the president who will take final decision in this case.

24. When the thing referred is understood 'the' is used :
(a) Kindly return the book. (That I gave you)
(b) Can you turn off the light? (The light in the room.)
(c) He has gone to the railway station. (The railway station of the town)
(d) I want to meet the manager. (The manager of the bank)
(e) Did you like the story? (That I told you yesterday)

25. 'The' is used in following phrases also :
(a) What is the matter? (b) Come to the point.
(c) She came to the rescue. (d) Keep to the left.
(e) The market is hot with the rumour. (f) He is in the wrong.
(g) Speak to the point,what is the problem.

26. In phrases ;Go to the cinema, Go to the theatre, 'the' is used :
(a) He went to the cinema yesterday. (b) She is going to the theatre.

27. Before names of ; committee, club, foundation and trust :
The Lions Club, The Rotary Club, The United Nation, The WHO, The Ford Foundation, The Rajiv Gandhi Trust etc.

28. Letters written to two or more unmarried sisters jointly may be addressed using 'the' :
The Misses + surname; eg—The Misses Smith.

ARTICLE IS OMITTED

Students should learn the following points carefully to avoid the wrong use of articles.

Article is omitted in following cases :

1. Before a proper noun; article is not used :

(a) Akbar was a great king. (b) Bombay is a beautiful city.

NOTE *When 'Article' is used before a proper noun, it becomes a common noun-Examples :*

(a) Mumbai is the Manchester of India.

(b) This man is a second Sachin.

2. Before a common noun, used in its widest sense, article is emitted :

(a) Man is mortal. (b) What kind of bird it is?

3. Before plural nouns referring a class in a general sense :

(a) Bankers are generally honest. (b) Lawyers are generally intelligent.

4. Article is omitted before abstract nouns that express qualities, state, feeling, actions :

(a) Honesty is the best policy. (b) Virtue is its own reward.

NOTE *When abstract nouns, instead of referring qualities, express person or things possessing such qualities or express qualities of definite objects, they are preceded by article.Example :*

(a) She possesses the cunningness of a fox.
(Here cunningness refers the quality of a definite object that is 'fox'.)

(b) He is a justice of peace ('Justice' stands for judge).

(c) He possesses the swiftness of a tiger.

5. Before material nouns, omit the article :

(a) Iron is a hard metal. (b) Silver is a semi precious metal.

NOTE *When material noun express things instead of matter of which they are made, they are representing 'common noun', so they can be preceded by the article :*

(a) He threw a stone on the cow.

(b) She threw a stick at the pig.

(c) She threw a chalk at the teacher.

6. Before names of diseases, like—fever, cholera, etc. no article is used :

(But if the names of diseases are plural in their form, the article is generally used as : the measles, the mumps.)

7. Article is omitted before names of regular meals, such as :

Breakfast, Lunch, Dinner :

(a) He was invited to dinner.

But if the meal becomes particular, article is used :

(b) The dinner hosted by the queen was superb.

8. Before names of things single in kind ;Hell, Heaven, God, Parliament,Paradise (But 'The Pope', 'The Devil' are exceptions) :

(a) He was condemned to hell. (b) The Pope delivered a religious speech.

(c) He raised the question in Parliament. (d) May God grant him success!

9. Before names of 'languages' and 'colours' the article is omitted :

(a) I do not know 'Hindi' but know 'English'.

(b) He is learning 'French'.

(c) He likes red and blue.

10. Before certain titles and names indicating the relationship; e.g.—

Emperor Ashoka,President Bush,Dewan Bahadur.

(a) Prince Charles is Queen Elizabeth's son.

(b) **President Kennedy** was assassinated in Dallas.

(c) **Dr. Watson** was Sherlock Holmes' friend.

(d) He is Duke of York.

(But : the Queen of England, the Pope are exceptions.)

11. Before a noun following the expression 'kind of' article is omitted :

(a) What kind of girl is she?

(b) What kind of boy is he?

12. In certain phrases, article to omitted :

To take breath, to set sail, to leave school, to lay seige, to catch fire, at home, in hand, at school, by water, at sunset, on earth, by land, by train,by car, on demand, in debt, in jest etc.

13. Before nouns, which are plural in their meanings , though singular in form; e.g.—

Cattle, gentry, furniture, scenery, advice, information.

14. Article is omitted before names of public institutions (church, school, university, prison, hospital,court, etc.) if they are used for the purpose they exist, rather than actual building :

(a) He went to church (It means he went to church for saying his prayer.)

He went to the church and from there he took a bus. (Use of 'the' before 'church' means that he went to the place where building of the church is situated, not to offer prayer.)

Like wise ;

(a) Ram goes to school daily at 10A.M.

(b) He goes to college at 8 A.M. daily.

(Here the purpose of going is for study.)

(c) I am going to the college, wherefrom I will catch the bus for Jaipur.(Here the purpose of going to college is not for the purpose the college is established.)

15. When two or more descriptive adjectives qualify the same noun and the said adjectives are connected by 'and', the article is used before the first adjective only :

This is a Hindi and English Dictionary. (Here dictionary is one.)

16. If two nouns refer to the same person or thing, article is used before the first noun only, but if they refer to different person or thing, the article must be used with each noun :

(a) He is a better soldier than statesman.

(b) He was a greater soldier than a statesman.

17. Article is omitted after the 's possessive case :

His brother's ***car***, Peter's ***house***.

18 Article is omitted with names of **professions** :

(a) **Engineering** is a useful career. (b) He'll probably go into **medicine**.

19 Article is omitted with ***years*** :

(a) 1947 was a wonderful year. (b) Do you remember 2000?

20. No article is used before name of games , sports :

(a) I am playing cricket. (b) He is fond of playing tennis.

21. No article is used before a noun when it is modified by either a possessive adjective or a demonstrative adjective.

(a) Do you like my shirt? (possessive adjective 'my')
(b) I like this pen. (demonstrative adjective 'this')

22. No article is used before a noun when it is preceded by a distributive adjective :

(a) Every student got a prize. (distributive adjective 'every')
(b) Each student was present in the hall. (distributive adjective 'each')

23. No article is used before 'number + noun' :

(a) The train arrives at platform 7. (b) I want shoes in size 10.

24. Work (= place of work) is used without definite article 'the' :

(a) He is on his way to work. (b) She is at work.
(c) They haven't back from work yet.

25. Office (= place of work) needs 'the' : He is at/in the office.

'To be in office' (without 'the') means—to hold an official (usually political) position.

'To be out of office' = to be no longer in power.

26 Definite article 'the' is omitted when speaking of the subject's or speaker's own town :

(a) We go to town sometimes to meet our mother.
(b) We went to town last year and remained there for a week.

27. 'Nature' when means environment , do not use article before it :

(a) If you interfere with nature you will suffer for it.

28. No article is used before name of 'Season':

(a) In spring we like to clean the house.
(b) She is planning to visit her parents in winter.

29. Definite article 'the' is not used before 'Time of day' :

(a) We travelled mostly by night. (b) We'll be there around midnight.

30. **Sea :** We can use definite article 'the' before 'sea' in following cases :

We go **to sea** as sailors. To be **at sea** = to be on a voyage (as passengers or crew).
But, to be **at the** sea = to be at the seaside. We can also live **'by/ near' the sea.**

31. Names without 'the' :

Names of many places, especially names of important buildings and institutions consist of two words.First word is usually the name of a person or a place , we do not use 'the' before such names usually.

For example : Delhi airport, Victoria Station, London Zoo, Jaisingh Palace, Indira Gandhi Airport, Edinburgh Castle, Jaipur Place , etc.

32. Usually no article is used with the names of Airlines, Companies : British Airways, Sony, IBM, KODAK, Indian Airlines, etc.

CORRECT YOURSELF EXERCISE : ARTICLE

CYE : 01 Fill in the blanks with articles, where necessary.

1. He went to .... college to meet .... class teacher.
2. I will take .... tram from ....church.
3. He came and sat on .... bed.
4. He has already gone to .... bed.
5. Ram was appointed .... clerk.
6. Suresh was declared .... captain of our team.
7. Ramesh invited Sarla for .... dinner yesterday.
8. He organised .... nice lunch in honour of .... President.
9. .... dinner hosted by Ram was superb.
10. .... measles is .... contagious disease.
11. He died of .... cholera.
12. She has been suffering from .... fever for three days.
13. He can speak .... Hindi, but I can't speak .... English.
14. I like .... blue colour.
15. When I went to .... home, Raja was watching .... TV.
16. I heard .... news on .... radio.
17. He is .... rich man, he always go by .... car.
18. Three percent posts are reserved for .... disabled and two percent for...........ex-servicemen.
19. He went first to .... Mexico and then to .... USA.
20. Ram took .... action with ....swiftness of .... tiger.

CYE : 02 Rewrite the following sentences after filling up the blanks with suitable articles, where necessary :

During .... first two years .... village project had .... awful time. .... Mission had accepted .... use of .... farm from .... affluent landowner, and ....natives believed .... story that this land would be returned to ....owner after ten years. .... project never started.

CYE : 03 Insert suitable articles, wherever they are missing :

1. Pt. Jawahar Lal Nehru was.......... first Prime minister of free India.
2. Indian Government wants to build......... strong India.
3. She has never touched.......... onion.
4. After discussing this matter for hour or two we are sure to arrive at ....decision.
5. Pt. Nehru was..............great man .He struggled hard to attain ....freedom from ..... Britishers.

CYE : 04 Rewrite the following sentences after filling up the blanks with suitable articles , where necessary :

Once there were elections . ... entire polling station seemed to be .... huge mass of humanity. Men and women all seemed to be quite conscious of their votes.I had seen .... old man insisting on the polling officer and he would not even return .... identity slip. Women had come in groups and were putting on colourful clothes. .... polling stations assumed .... shape of .... fair and .... crowd also behaved likewise. It was really .... pleasure to see them in such .... jolly mood. It was ..... nice scene.

CYE : 05 Insert suitable articles, wherever necessary :

1. Will you like to have .... cup of tea?
2. .... room is airy.
3. .... dog is a faithful animal.
4. Will you go to .... hospital to see your friend?
5. There are sixty seconds in .... minute.
6. Take ....umbrella with you.
7. I have made................. mistake.
8. I saw .... old man yesterday.
9. This poem is written by .... foreign writer.
10. I found .... book last night. ....book is very useful.
11. He is .... able man.
12. He has applied for .... post of an officer.
13. .... camel is ....ship of ... desert.
14. ....earth revolves round ....sun.
15. Kalidas is .... Shakespeare of .... India.

CYE : 06 Rewrite the following sentences after filling up the blanks with suitable articles , where necessary :

Once .... businessman of ....colony was shot dead by ....armed intruder on Sunday night . ... dead man's wife also received .... gunshot, but she is said to be progressing in .... Civil Hospital . ... murder is said to be .... result of .... old dispute over financial matters between killer and his victim.After three days .... killer surrendered before ....police.

CYE : 07 Fill in the blanks with a, an or the :

1. Ram gave me .... one-rupee note.
2. She bought .... ink-pot,............. bag and...........umbrella yesterday.
3. Has .... postman brought any letter for me today?
4. .... camel can go .... long distance without water.
5. This is one of .... most interesting books I have ever read.
6. ......Kashmir is .... Switzerland of India.
7. .... teachers of this school are very liberal and intelligent.
8. Let us discuss .... matter seriously.

9. He is .... honour to his profession.
10. .... scheme failed for want of sufficient funds.
11. I ordered .... servant to leave .... room.
12. Italy is .... European country.
13. There is .... hourly tram service on this route.
14. God made .... country and man made................. town.
15. Kalidas is .... Shakespeare of India.
16. Do you know ....way to .... railway station ?
17. You cannot doubt .... honesty of these men.
18. .... friend in need is .... friend indeed.
19. May we have .... pleasure of your company for lunch?
20. We should always follow .... good and love.................. beautiful.

CYE : 08

A Put appropriate articles in the blanks :

India is one of .... very big countries in the world. If a man takes ..... quickest train, he will take nearly...........week to go from one end of India to the other. One who leaves Ramnad in ...... South on .... first day of .... month will perhaps get to Srinagar in .... North only about .... sixth of .... same month.

B Fill in the blanks with appropriate articles. :

Number..... hundred and two, ... house next door to us, is for sale, It's quite .... nice house with .... big rooms........ back windows look out on ....park. I don't know what......... price .... owners are asking . You could give them ....call and make them .... offer.

SOLUTIONS : CORRECT YOURSELF EXERCISE

Solutions CYE : 01

1. the, the	2. a, the	3. the	4. x	5. x	6. x
7. x	8. a, the	9. the	10. the, a	11. x	12. x
13. x, x	14. x	15. x, x	16. the, the	17. a, x	18. the, the
19. x, the	20. the, the, a				

Solutions CYE : 02

During the first two years the village project had an awful time.The Mission had accepted the use of a farm from an affluent landowner, and the natives believed the story that this land would be returned to the owner after ten years.The project never started.

Solutions CYE : 03

1. Pt. Jawahar Lal Nehru was the first Prime minister of free India.
2. Indian Government wants to build a strong India.
3. She has never touched an onion.
4. After discussing this matter for an hour or two we are sure to arrive at a decision.
5. Pt. Nehru was a great man .He struggled hard to attain freedom from the Britishers.

Solutions CYE : 04

Once there were elections. The entire polling station seemed to be a huge mass of humanity. Men and women all seemed to be quite conscious of their votes.I had seen an old man insisting on the polling officer and he would not even return the identity slip. Women had come in groups and were putting on colourful clothes .The polling stations assumed the shape of a fair and the crowd also behaved likewise. It was really a pleasure to see them in such a jolly mood.It was a nice scene.

Solutions CYE : 05

1. a, 2. the, 3. the, 4. the, 5. a, 6. an,
7. a, 8. an, 9. a, 10. a, the, 11. an, 12. the,
13. the, the, the, 14. the, the, 15. the, x

Solutions CYE : 06

Once a businessman of the colony was shot dead by an armed intruder on Sunday night . The dead man's wife also received a gunshot, but she is said to be progressing in the Eivil Hospital. The murder is said to be the result of an old dispute over financial matters between the killer and his victim.After three days the killer surrendered before the police.

Solutions CYE : 07

1. a, 2. an, a, an, 3. the 4. A, a , 5. the
6. x., the 7. The 8. the 9. an 10. The
11. the, the, 12. a 13. an 14. the, the 15. the
16. the, the 17. the 18. A, a 19. the 20. the, the

Solutions CYE : 08

(a). the, the, a, the, the, a, the, the, the.
(b). x, the, a, x, the the/a, x, the, a, an.

6

Tense

In English, there are three basic tenses : **present, past, and future**. Each has a *perfect form*, indicating completed action; each has a *progressive form*, indicating ongoing action; and each has a *perfect progressive form*, indicating ongoing action that will be completed at some definite time.

Read the following sentences :

I. I **write** a letter.
II. I **wrote** a letter.
III. I **shall write** a letter.
All underlined words in above sentences are the verbs.
In sentence I, the verb, 'write' refers to **present time**.
In sentence II, the verb 'wrote' refers to **past time**.
In sentence III, the verb 'shall write' refers to **future time**.

A verb that refers to present time is said to be in ***present tense****. Similarly a verb that refers to past or future time is said to be in* ***past or future tense****.*

TENSE AND TIME

Tense is a grammatical concept. It indicates time of an action/state. Present tense usually refers to present time, past tense refers to past time. Time, unlike tense is not a grammatical concept. It is a natural thing. Tense is related to the language (English). Time doesn't have any relation as such. Hence, tense and time are different things. There are many sentences of present or past tense that may indicate future time actions. Many sentences of future tense may denote present time action.

Look at the following examples :

1. He leaves for USA next month.
   (Sentence of simple present, refers to future time.)
2. She is comming on next sunday.
   (Sentence of present progressive, indicating future time.)
3. I wish I knew his address.
   (Sentence of past tense, indicates present time.)
4. Will you have a cup of tea?
   (Sentence of future simple, indicates present time.)

FORMS OF VERBS

Verb is also classified as Regular and Irregular Verbs :

Regular Verbs : Those verbs which form their past tense and past participle by adding 'ed' are called Regular verbs.

Irregular Verbs : Those verbs which form their past tense and past participle in a different way are called irregular verbs.

We are giving below three lists of Irregular Verbs :

List I : Verbs which have all the three forms same.

List II : Verbs which have two forms same.

List III : Verbs which have all the three forms different.

List (I), All three forms are the same (Irregular verbs) :

Base form	Past Tense	Past Participle
bet	bet	bet
burst	burst	burst
cast	cast	cast
cost	cost	cost
cut	cut	cut
hit	hit	hit
hurt	hurt	hurt
let	let	let
put	put	put
read	read	read
rid	rid	rid
set	set	set
shut	shut	shut
split	split	split
spread	spread	spread

List (II), Two of the forms are the same (Irregular verbs) :

Base Form	Past Tense	Past Participle
abide	abode	abode
awake	awoke	awoke
beat	beaten	beaten
become	became	become
bend	bent	bent
bleed	bled	bled
breed	bred	bred
bring	brought	brought
build	built	built
burn	burnt/ burned	burnt/ burned
buy	bought	bought
catch	caught	caught
come	came	come
creep	crept	crept
deal	dug	dug
dream	dreamt/ dreamed	dreamt/ dreamed
feed	fed	fed
feel	felt	felt
fight	fought	fought
find	found	found

fling	flung	flung
get	got	got
hang	hung	hung
have	had	had
hear	heard	heard
hold	held	held
keep	kept	kept
lay	laid	laid
lead	led	led
lean	lent/ leaned	lent/ leaned
learn	learnt/ learned	learnt/ learned
leap	leapt/ leaped	leapt/ leaped
leave	left	left
lend	lent	lent
light	lit	lit
lose	lost	lost
make	made	made
mean	meant	meant
meet	met	met
pay	paid	paid
run	ran	ran
say	said	said
sell	sold	sold
send	sent	sent
shine	shone	shone
shoot	shot	shot
sit	sat	sat
sleep	slept	slept
smell	smelt/ smelled	smelt/ smelled
spell	spelt	spelt
spend	spent	spent
spill	spilt/ spilled	spilt/ spilled
spit	spat	spat
spoil	spoilt/ spoiled	spoilt/ spoiled
stand	stood	stood
stick	stuck	stuck
strike	struck	struck
sting	stung	stung
sweep	swept	swept
swing	swung	swung
teach	taught	taught
tell	told	told
think	thought	thought
understand	understood	understood
win	won	won
wind	wound	wound

List (III), All three forms are different (Irregular verbes) :

Base Form	Past Tense	Past Participle
arise	arose	arisen
be	was/ were	been
bear	bore	born
begin	began	begun
bite	bit	bitten
blow	blew	blown
break	broke	broken
choose	chose	chosen
do	did	done
draw	drew	drawn
drink	drank	drunk
drive	drove	driven
eat	ate	eaten
fall	fell	fallen
fly	flew	flown
forbid	forbade	forbidden
forget	forgot	forgotten
forgive	forgave	forgiven
freeze	froze	frozen
give	gave	given
go	went	gone
grow	grew	grown
hide	hid	hidden
know	knew	known
lie	lay	lain
mistake	mistook	mistaken
ride	rode	ridden
ring	rang	rung
rise	rose	risen
see	saw	seen
shake	shook	shaken
sew	sewed	sewn/ sewed
show	showed	shown
shrink	shrank	shrunk
sing	sang	sung
sink	sank	sunk
speak	spoke	spoken
spring	sprang	sprung
steal	stole	stolen
swear	swore	sworn
swim	swam	swum
take	took	taken
tear	tore	torn
throw	threw	thrown

wake	woke	woken
wear	wore	worn
write	wrote	written
weave	wove	woven

1. **Adjectival past participle** : Following verbs also have a different past participle(**Adjectival**) form , which can only be used as adjective .

Verb	**Normal Past**	**Adjectival**.
Participle	Past	Participle
drink	drunk	drunken
melt	melted	molten
prove	proved	proven
shave	shaved	shaven
shear	sheared	shorn
shrink	shrunk	shrunken
sink	sunk	sunken
strike	struck	stricken

For the sake of convenience, two more forms of verbs are in use these days. These are :

2. **Present participle form (V-4)** :Base form (V-I)+ ing .For example ; going , playing , writing etc.

3. **Infinitive (V-5)** : To + Base form (V-I) .For example; to play , to go , to write etc.

TENSES

There are three main **tenses :**

1. The Present Tense.
2. The Past Tense.
3. The Future Tense.

The tense of a verb in a sentence shows time of action.

PRESENT TENSE

Look at the following sentences :

1. I play.	Simple Present.
2. I am playing.	Present Continuous.
3. I have played.	Present Perfect.
4. I have been playing.	Present Perfect Continuous.

All the above sentences show action in present time.

In above sentence (1) the verb 'play' shows that the action takes place, but we do not know about the completeness or incompleteness of the action.In sentence (2), the verb 'playing' shows that the action is continue or taking place at the time of speaking ,but not completed so far. The action is still going on.In sentence (3), the verb 'have played' shows that the action is finished, completed or perfect.In sentence (4) the verb 'have been playing' shows that the action started in past and is going on continuously and not completed up to the present moment.

As such, we see that the tense of a verb shows not only the time of an action, but also the state of an action, whether continuous, completed, or going on for some period.

The **present tense** is further classified in four forms :

1. Simple Present or Present Indefinite,
2. Present Continuous or Present Progressive,
3. Present Perfect, and
4. Present Perfect Continuous.

SIMPLE PRESENT TENSE

Usual structure of sentences :

Subject + I form of verb (s or es) + object.

Look at the following sentences :

	Subject	I form of Verb	Object
1.	I	play	football.
2.	They	play	football.
3.	He	plays	football.
4.	She	catches	the train.
5.	Ram	goes	to market.
6.	She	verifies	the bills.

Use of 's' or 'es' with the verbs in present indefinite tense :

Look at the following sentences :

1. I write a letter.
2. They play football.
3. He plays.
4. She writes a letter.
5. We go to market.
6. Hari goes to market.
7. I pass the ball to Hari
8. He passes the ball to Hari.
9. They cry.
10. She cries.
11. She clarifies her stand.
12. Sita loves Ram.

In sentence 3, 4, 6, 8,12 you see that, 's' or 'es' is affixed to the verb. *Do you note anything important about the subject?*

Here the subject is **'Singular Number, Third Person'**, so **'s'** or **'es'** is used with the verb.

Rules (Learn well) :

Rule 1. ***If the subject is singular number third person, affix 's' or 'es' to the verb.***

If the verb ends with any of the following :

ss, o, x, z, sh, ch,

add, **'es'** instead of **'s'** with the verb.

Like : Pass, Miss, Do, Mix, Fix, Whiz, buzz, Catch, Fetch, Clash, Rush etc. (See sentences 6 and 8.)

Rule 2. ***If the verb ends with the alphabet 'y', and 'y' is preceded by a consonant, change 'y' to 'ies', with subject-singular number third person.See sentences10 and 11.***

Like : verify, clarify, cry, try.

If 'y' is preceded by a vowel , put 's' with the verb.

Like : play, say etc.

NOTE *In present indefinite sentences, the number and person of the subject play an important role. Singular number means, 'One' (not plural), third person means, about which we talk, which is not 'first' or 'second' person.*

I Person	II Person	III Person
I	You	They, Friends
We	You	He, She,It, Students, Name of any Person.

As such, with subject singular number third person (He, She, It, Name) we are to affix 's' or 'es' to the verb.

NEGATIVE (PRESENT INDEFINITE)

Present indefinite negative sentences, have usually the following structure :

Subject + do not or does not + V-1 (i, e, first form of the verb) + object.

1. Use **'do not'** with; **I, We, You, They**, or **any plural noun**.
2. Use **'does not'** with; **He, She, it, name,or any** singular number third person subject.

Look at the following Sentences :

1. I play football. *Affirmative*
   I do not play football. *Negative*
2. They go to market. *Affirmative*
   They do not go to market. *Negative*
3. She sings a song. *Affirmative*
   She does not sing a song. *Negative*
4. He goes to market. *Affirmative*
   He does not go to market. *Negative*
5. We learn our lesson. *Affirmative*
   We do not learn our lesson. *Negative*
6. You write a letter. *Affirmative*
   You do not write a letter. *Negative*
7. Sita drives a car. *Affirmative*
   Sita does not drive a car. *Negative*
8. It rains. *Affirmative*
   It does not rain. *Negative*
9. Ram verifies the bills. *Affirmative*
   Ram does not verify the bills. *Negative*
10. My father comes home at 8 P.M. *Affirmative*
    My father does not come home at 8 P.M. *Negative*

NOTE *(i) See above sentences number (1), (2), (5), (6). You find that with 'I', 'They', 'We' , 'You' or 'any plural' subject, while transforming an affirmative sentence into negative, we use 'do not' after the subject and there is no change in the form of verb.*

(ii) See sentences 3, 4, 7, 8, 9 & 10, you find that, with 'He', 'She' 'It' 'name',or any singular number third person, while transforming affirmative into negative, we use 'does not' after the subject, and 's' or 'es' affixed to the verb is removed.

INTERROGATIVE (PRESENT INDEFINITE)

Present indefinite interrogative sentences, have usually the following structure :

Do or Does + Subject + First form of verb + object ?

Look at the following sentences

1. I eat an apple. *Affirmative*
   Do I eat an apple? *Interrogative*
2. We go to market. *Affirmative*
   Do we go to market ? *Interrogative*
3. You play cricket. *Affirmative*
   Do you play cricket ? *Interrogative*
4. They learn their lessons. *Affirmative*
   Do they learn their lessons ? *Interrogative*
5. He writes a letter. *Affirmative*
   Does he write a letter ? *Interrogative*
6. She sings a song. *Affirmative*
   Does she sing a song ? *Interrogative*
7. Sita dances. *Affirmative*
   Does Sita dance ? *Interrogative*
8. It rains. *Affirmative*
   Does it rain? *Interrogative*
9. Ram cries. *Affirmative*
   Does Ram cry ? *Interrogative*
10. My brother goes to college. *Affirmative*
    Does my brother go to college? *Interrogative*

NOTE *1. With ; I, you, we, they or any plural subject, put 'Do' before the subject .*
2. With;He, She, It, name or any singular number third person, put 'Does' before the subject.

INTERROGATIVE NEGATIVE : PRESENT INDEFINITE

Usual structure of sentences :

Do/Does + Subject + not + V-I + Object. ...(I)
or Don't/Doesn't + Subject + V-I + Object. ...(II)

(a) He goes to market. *Affirmative*
    Does he not go to market? *Interrogative Negative*
    Doesn't he go to market? *Interrogative Negative*

(b) I play football. *Affirmative*
    Do I not play football ? *Interrogative Negative*
    Don't I play football? *Interrogative Negative*

Use of simple present tense in different situations :

1. **To denote a habitual action** (Any work which we do in normal course or as a habit. :
   (a) I get up early in the morning. (b) He drinks tea at 6 A.M. every day.
   (c) She takes exercises in the morning. (d) I go to school at 10 AM.

2. **To denote a universal /eternal truth, scientific theory simple present tense is used :**
(a) The sun rises in the east.
(b) The earth revolves round the sun.
(c) Birds fly.
(d) The sun sets in the west.
(e) Light travels faster than sound.
(f) Water boils at 100 degree celsius.

3. **In exclamatory sentences, beginning with 'here' or 'there' simple present tense is used :**
(a) Here, comes the tram!
(b) There, she works!
(c) Here, lives Hari!
(d) There, she goes!

4. **To denote a future event, that is part of a plan or arrangement :**
(a) The school opens in the month of July.
(b) They leave for Jaipur by next bus.
(c) We go to Agra next Monday.
(d) Mr. Sharma retires on 31st December.

5. **Present indefinite tense is also used to introduce quotations :**
(a) He says, "Truth always triumphs".
(b) She says, "Honesty is the best policy."
(c) Shakespeare says, "Frailty, thy name is woman."

6. **In broadcasting live description of sports events or commentaries, simple present tense is used :**
Raju passes the ball to Saluja, Saluja passes it to Somu, who heads it past the goalkeeper and scores!

7. Simple present tense is used **in newspaper headlines :**
Prime Minister visits Goa.
Peace talks fail.

8. When the main verb is in future, *use present simple in clauses beginning with ; if, till, as soon as, when, unless, before, until, even if, in case and as :*
(a) We shall wait till she arrives.
(b) I shall not go there even if it rains.
(c) I shall go to market, if it rains.
(d) I shall go to Jaipur in case she asks me.
(e) We shall move as soon as the taxi arrives.
(f) I shall start my work as he comes.
(g) Unless he works hard, he will not pass.
(h) I shall wait until it strikes seven.
(i) When he comes, I shall give him a gift.
(j) Before he comes, I shall finish my work.
This is very important point. Students should learn it properly.

9. Present simple must be used *instead of the present continuous* with verbs related to perception (feel, hear, smell etc.), verbs of cognition (believe, know, think, etc.), verbs expressing emotion (hope, love, hate etc), which cannot be used normally in continuous form :
Detail description of such verbs of perception, cognition and emotion is given in the heading Present Continuous Tense :

I am seeing you .	*Incorrect*
I see you.	*Correct*
I am loving you .	*Incorrect*
I love you.	*Correct*

10. Simple present tense is also used in proverbs :

(a) A stitch in time saves nine.

(b)A bad workman quarrels with his tools.

11. Simple present tense is also used with; always, never, occasionally, often , usually etc.

(a) He always speaks the truth.

(b) She usually comes late.

(c) She never misses the train.

(d) I often go there.

12. See the use of simple present with 'when' and 'whenever' :

(a)Whenever it rains the roof leaks.

(b) When you close the door, a light goes on.

PRESENT CONTINUOUS TENSE

Present Continuous Tense is also known as **Present Progressive Tense.**

Usual structure of sentences (Present Continuous) :

Subject + is / am /are + V- IV *(V-I + ing)* + object.

Look at the following sentences :

1. I am going to market.
2. She is singing a song.
3. You are playing football.
4. They are arriving by train.
5. Ram is writing a lesson.
6. We are writing a lesson.
7. He is reading a book.
8. It is hailing.
9. Students are creating problems.
10. My friend Ashok is coming today.

NOTE *Auxiliary 'is / am / are' is used with the subjects as per following :*

Subject	**Auxiliary**
I	am
You, we, they, or any plural noun	are
He, she, it, name or any singular noun except 'I'	is

NEGATIVE (PRESENT CONTINUOUS)

Present continuous negative sentences, have usually the following structure :

Subject + is / am /are+ not + V- IV (V-I+ing) + object.

Look at the following sentences :

1. I am playing football. *Affirmative*
   I am not playing football. *Negative*
2. She is writing a letter. *Affirmative*
   She is not writing a letter. *Negative*
3. Ram is going to Jaipur *Affirmative*
   Ram is not going to Jaipur. *Negative*
4. It is raining. *Affirmative*
   It is not raining. *Negative*
5. You are playing. *Affirmative*
   You are not playing. *Negative*

In negative present continuous sentences, we use, 'not' after the auxiliary verb, as above.

INTERROGATIVE (PRESENT CONTINUOUS)

Interrogative present continuous sentences, have usually the following structure :

Is / Am /Are + Subject + V- IV + object ?

Look at the following sentences :

1. I am going to market. *Affirmative*
   Am I going to market? *Interrogative*
2. She is writing a letter. *Affirmative*
   Is she writing a letter? *Interrogative*
3. Ramesh is going to Jaipur. *Affirmative*
   Is Ramesh going to Jaipur? *Interrogative*
4. It is hailing. *Affirmative*
   Is it hailing? *Interrogative*
5. You are drinking milk. *Affirmative*
   Are you drinking milk? *Interrogative*

In interrogative sentences, we put auxiliary, is/ am/ are, before the subject, as above.

Interrogative Negative Sentences :

Usual structure of Interrogative negative sentences :

Is/are/am + Subject + not + V-IV + Object ?

or Isn't/Aren't + Subject + V-IV + Object ?

Affirmative	**Interrogative Negative**
(a) I am going to hospital.	Am I not going to hospital? Aren't I going to hospital?
(b) It is raining.	Is it not raining? Isn't it raining?

NOTE *the use of Aren't (Amn't is no word in English) in sentence (a) above.*

Use of present continuous in different situations :

1. To denote an action, going on at the time of speaking, present continous tense is used :

(a) He is writing. (b) She is reading.
(c) I am playing. (d) You are preparing tea.

(The action is continue or going on at the time of speaking.)

2. To denote an action, which may not be going on, at the time of speaking, but is going on in a regular process :

(a) He is writing a book.
(b) I am nowadays, learning English grammar.
(c) She is nowadays teaching in our school.

(At the time of speaking, the action is not actually going on, but action is in regular process.)

3. To denote an action, that is planned or arranged to take place in near future, present continuous tense is used :

(a) She is going to Jaipur tonight.
(b) My wife is arriving tomorrow.
(c) We are meeting tomorrow at 8 p.m.

(The action is planned or arranged, to take place in near future.)

4. Present continuous is **used with ; 'always'** *for repeated actions usually* **when the frequency annoys the speaker** or **it seems unreasonable to him** :
   (a) She is always complaining.
   (b) You are always finding faults with others.
   (c) She is always losing her purse.
   (d) He is always making that mistake.

STATIVE AND DYNAMIC VERBS IN CONTINUOUS TENSE

Verbs can be classified into two categories : *stative* verbs and *dynamic* verbs. **Dynamic verbs** (sometimes referred to as 'action verbs') *usually describe actions we can take, or things that happen; STATIVE VERBS usually refer to a state or condition which is not changing or likely to change.* The difference is important, because **stative verbs cannot normally be used in the continuous forms**.

Dynamic verbs : There are many types of dynamic verbs, but **most of them describe activities or events which can begin and finish**. Here are some examples :

Dynamic	Verb Type	Example
Play	activity	She plays chess every Friday. She is playing chess right now.
Melt	process	The snow melts every spring. The snow is melting right now.
Hit	momentary action	When one boxer hits another, brain damage can result. (This suggests only 'one' punch.)

Dynamic verbs, as you **can see as above, can be used in the simple and perfect forms** (*plays, played, has played, had played*) **as well as the continuous or progressive forms** (*is playing, was playing, has been playing, had been playing*).

Stative verbs : Stative verbs usually **refer to a state or condition which is quite static** or **unchanging**. They can be divided into **verbs** of **perception or cognition** (which refer to things in the mind), or **verbs of relation** (which describe the relationships between things). Here are some examples :

Stative verbs	Verb Type	Example
hate	perception	I hate chocolate.
believe	perception	She believes in rebirth.
contain	relation	The box contains ten books.
own	relation	He owns two houses.

Note that **we cannot use** ***stative verbs*** **in the continuous** (progressive) **forms**; you can't say : 'He is owning two houses.'

'*Owning*' is a state, not an action, so it is always in the simple form.

Stative verbs can be classified in followng categories :

1. **Verb of Perception :** See, hear, smell, taste, feel are called the verbs of perception.Verbs notice and recognise are also included in this category.
2. **Verb of appearance :** Look, resemble, seem, appear etc.

3. **Verbs of emotions :** Want, desire, wish, hate, hope, like, refuse, hope, believe, doubt, loathe, mind, care, detest, adore, appreciate, admire, fear, expect etc.
4. **Verbs of thinking :** Think, suppose, agree, consider, trust, remember, forget, know, understand, perceive, realise, recollect etc.
5. **Verbs of possession :** Belong, owe, own, possess, contain, have etc.

Note the use of these verbs :

Incorrect	Correct
1. We are seeing with our eyes.	1. We see with our eyes.
2. Are you hearing a strange noise?	2. Do you hear a strange noise?
3. We are smelling with our nose.	3. We smell with our nose.
4. I am feeling you are worng.	4. I feel you are wrong.
5. The water is feeling cold.	5. The water feels cold.
6. The coffee is tasting bitter.	6. The coffee tastes bitter.
7. How much am I owing you?	7. How much do I owe you?
8. I am hating it.	8. I hate it.
9. I am having a car.	9. I have a car.
10. I am thinking.	10. I think.
11. I am understanding.	11. I understand.
12. The book is belonging to me.	12. The book belongs to me.
13. He is resembling his brother.	13. He resembles his brother.
14. I am believing in God.	14. I believe in God.
15. I am loving her.	15. I love her.
16. I am remembering him.	16. I remember him.
17. Are you smelling some thing burning?	17. Do you smell something burning?
18. The milk is tasting sour.	18. The milk tastes sour.
19. This is feeling like silk.	19. This feels like silk.
20. I am differing from you on this point.	20. I differ from you on this point.

But these stative verbs can be used in progressive form in following cases :

1. The Session Judge is *hearing* our case.
2. We are *thinking* of going to USA next year.
3. He is *minding* (looking after) the children, while his wife is away.
4. I am *seeing* my lawyer today.
5. I am *having* some difficulties with this puzzle.
6. Are you *forgetting* your manners? (A reminder)
7. The dog is *smelling* the packet of food.
8. She is *tasting* the sauce to find out whether it is tasteful or not.
9. The doctor is *feeling* the pulse of the patient.
10. He is *looking* for his glasses.

Important

When used in progressive form, to state a temporary action, stative verbs become Dynamic Verbs :

1. We see with our eyes. (Permanent-Stative Verb ; see.)
2. I am seeing the teacher tomorrow. (Temporary- Dynamic Verb)

3. I have a Maruti car. (Permanent- Stative verb ; have)
4. I am having a nice time. (Temporary- Dynamic verb)
5. This apple tastes sweet. (Permanent- Stative verb taste)
6. She is tasting an apple. (Temporary- Dynamic verb)
7. We smell with our nose. (Permanent-Stative verb ; smell)
8. He is smelling flower. (Temporary- Dynamic verb)
9. I forget what she said. (Permanent-Stative verb ; forget)
10. I am forgetting her name. (Temporary- Dynamic verb)

PRESENT PERFECT TENSE

Usual structure of sentences (Present perfect) :

Subject + has or have +V- III + object.

Look at the following sentences :

1. He has written a letter.
2. Suresh has just arrived.
3. She has completed her work.
4. We have already visited Taj.
5. It has just struck seven.
6. He has eaten all the apples .

NOTE ***'Has' is used with 'He', 'She', 'it', name and any singular noun, while 'have' is used with 'I', 'we', 'you', 'they' and any plural noun.***

NEGATIVE (PRESENT PERFECT)

Present perfect negative sentences, have usually the following structure :

Subject + has or have + not +V- III + object.

Look at the following sentences :

1. I have completed my work. *Affirmative*
   I have not completed my work. *Negative*
2. He has written a book. *Affirmative*
   He has not written a book. *Negative*
3. She has already cooked. *Affirmative*
   She has not already cooked. *Negative*
4. They have gone to market. *Affirmative*
   They have not gone to market. *Negative*
5. You have already taken food. *Affirmative*
   You have not already taken food. *Negative*

In Negative : Put, 'not' after 'has' or 'have' as shown above No change in form of verb is required.

INTERROGATIVE (PRESENT PERFECT)

Present perfect interrogative sentences, have usually the following structure :

Has or Have + Subject +V-III + object?

Look at the following sentences :

1. She has taken breakfast. *Affirmative*
   Has she taken breakfast? *Interrogative*

2. He has eaten an apple. *Affirmative*
Has he eaten an apple? *Interrogative*
3. She has learnt her lesson. *Affirmative*
Has she learnt her lesson? *Interrogative*
4. They have gone out. *Affirmative*
Have they gone out? *Interrogative*
5. Ramesh has written a poem. *Affirmative*
Has Ramesh written a poem? *Interrogative*

In interrogative : Put 'has' or 'have', before the subject as shown above. No change in form of verb is required.

INTERROGATIVE NEGATIVE : PRESENT PERFECT

Usual structure of Interrogative negative sentences :

Has/Have + Subject + not + V-III + Object ?
or **Hasn't/Haven't + Subject + V-III + Object ?**

Affirmative	**Interrogative Negative**
1. He has taken food.	Has he not taken food? Hasn't he taken food?
2. I have done my work.	Have I not done my work? Haven't I done my work?

Use of present perfect tense in different situations :

1. The present prefect is **used for a recently completed action with 'just'**; e.g.—
(a) She has just gone out.
(b) It has just struck five.
(c) He has just arrived.
(d) Ram has just gone out. = Ram went out a few minutes ago.

NOTE *'Just' must be placed between the auxiliary and the main verb.*

It is not normally used in the negative. This combination is used chiefly in the affirmative, though the interrogative form is also possible : Has he just gone out?

2. The present perfect tense is **used for 'past actions' where time is not known** :

(i) The present perfect tense is used for recent actions when the time is not mentioned :
(a) I have read the notice but I don't understand it.
(b) Have you had lunch? - No, I haven't had it yet.

(ii) Possible answers to questions in the present perfect is used in questions and answers for past actions : For example :
(a) Have you seen my book? - Yes, I have/ No, I haven't .
(b) Have you had breakfast? - Yes, I have or No, I haven't had it yet.

3. Present perfect tense is used to describe a completed action, the effect of which is being felt in the present :
(a) Ramesh has eaten all the apples. (Now no more available for you)
(b) He has cut his finger. (And it requires treatment.)

(c) I have completed my work. (Now I am free.)
(d) I've washed the car. (Now you can use it.)
(e) The lift has broken down. (You have to use the stairs.)

NOTE *The use of 'present perfect + yet' usually have results in the present :*

He hasn't come yet. (so we are also waiting for him.)

4. Present perfect is **used** for **describing actions which occured farther back in the past,** provided their relation with the present is still maintained and it is expected that the action could be repeated in the present :
   (a) I have seen tigers in that forest.
   It implies that it is still possible to see them.
   (b) Thomas has written a number of short poems.
   It implies that Thomas is still alive and can write more.

5. **To express an action, beginning at sometimes in the past and continuing up to the present moment :**
   (a) She has been ill since last Monday. (She is still ill.)
   (b) We haven't seen Rani for two months. (We haven't seen her so far.)
   (c) I have known her for five years. (I know her today also.)
   (d) They have lived here for three years. (They are living here at present also.)

6. The Present perfect is **used for actions occurring in an incomplete period** ;
   An incomplete period may be indicated by 'today or this morning/ afternoon/ evening/ week/ month/ year' etc.
   It should be well undersood that the present perfect can be used with 'this morning' only up to about 12 O'clock because after that 'this morning' becomes a completed period (past) and actions occurring in it must be put into the simple past instead of present perfect :
   (a) (at 11 a.m.) Sita has rung up three times this morning already.
   (at 2 p.m.) Sita rang up three times this morning.
   Similarly, this afternoon will end at about 5 O'clock :
   (b) (at 4 p.m.) I haven't seen Ram this afternoon.
   (at 6 p.m.) I didn't see Ram this afternoon.
   (d) Have you seen him today? (at any time today) - Yes, I have./
   Yes, I've seen him today. (at some time during the day)

NOTE **(i)** *If we know that an action usually happens at a certain time or in a certain part of incomplete period we use the simple past tense.*

Imagine that the milkman normally comes between six and seven. *Form six till seven* we will use present perfect tense and say :

Has the milkman come yet / this morning?

But after seven we will say (use past tense) :

Did the milkman come this morning? (Past tense)

(ii) *Present perfect Tense is used with ; lately, recently, also. They indicate an incomplete period of time* :

(a) Has he been here lately/ recently? (b) He hasn't been here lately /recently.

Here, lately/ recently means–at any time during the last week/ month etc.; 'lately' is not usually used with the affirmative, except for actions covering recent period of time :

(c) There have been some changes lately/ recently.

7. The present perfect can also be, **used with; yet, ever, never, occasionally,often, so far,** several times,already, upto now, etc. :

(a) Have the children gone to school yet?
(b) Has Ramesh left yet?
(c) I have already visited Agra.
(d) I have already seen this film.
(e) Have you ever been to Russia?
(f) I have never been down a mine.
(g) I have often been there.
(h) I have read this novel several times.
(i) Have you done much work this week?
(j) Yes I have visited Agra several times.
(k) Hari hasn't come to college this morning.
(l) Have you ever visited Shimla?
(m) Upto now every thing has been okay.
(n) We have no trouble so far.
(o) Have you ever fallen off horse?
(p) I have never been late for work.

8. The present perfect can also **be used with ; since + a point in time, since + clause, or since, as adverb** etc. :

(a) It is three years since I have seen her.
(b) It is two months since I have smoked a cigarette.
(c) I haven't seen him since January.
(d) Has she written since she left home?

9. We can also **use present perfect with "for + a period of time" :**

(a) I've used my left hand for a year now.
(b) I've not smoked for ten years.

10. We can also **use present perfect in following type of sentences :**

This / It / That is the first /second/ third / only / best /worst etc...

(a) This is the best whisky, I have ever drunk.
(b) This is the easiest job, I have ever had.
(c) This is the worst novel, I have ever read.
(d) This is the only book, he has written.
(e) This is the first time that I have heard her sing.
(f) This is the third time, you have asked me the same question.
(g) That is the fifth banana you have eaten so far.

10. **For past actions, conversation is begun with present perfect tense** :

(a) Where have you been? — I've been to the cinema.
(b) What have you bought? — I have bought one saree only.

11. The present perfect tense may also **indicate future time in conditional clauses :**

(a) I can't decide until I've discussed the matter with my wife.

(b) I will come as soon as I've finished writing this letter.

The present and present perfect tenses may indicate future time in temporal and conditional clauses : *Guide to patterns and usage in English page 98 - A.S. Hornby*

12. The present perfect tense is also **used in letters** :

(a) We have carefully considered your request and have decided to take the action as per following.

(b) I am sorry, I haven't written you before, as I have been very busy lately, as my father has been away.

13. The present perfect tense is often **used in newspapers reports** and live **broadcasts** :

(a) Five millions rupees worth of heroin has been seized from the smugglers.

(b) Ten thousand pounds worth of jewellery has been stolen from 'Jack and John', the jewellers.

14. The present perfect tense is also **used in following sentence structure with *'It's'*** :

(a) It is three years since I have seen her.

(b) It is two months since I have smoked a cigarette.

15. The present perfect tense can also be ***used for habitual actions :***

(a) They've always answered my letters.

(b) I've never been late for office.

IMPORTANT

We must not use adverbs of past time like; yesterday, last year, last month,ago,short while ago etc.in present perfect tense.

He has gone to Delhi yesterday. *Incorrect.*
He went to Delhi yesterday. *Correct.*
He has completed his book yesterday. *Incorrect.*
He completed his book yesterday. *Correct.*
I have met her three days ago. *Incorrect*
I met her three days ago. *Correct*

PRESENT PERFECT CONTINUOUS

Usual structure of sentences (present perfect continuous) :

Subject + have been/ has been+ V-IV +...+ since or for+...

1. 'have been' is used with; I, we, you, they or any plural noun.
2. 'has been' is used with; He, she, it, name or any singular noun.

Use of Since or For :

Students commit mistake in using 'since' or 'for' in such sentences. **Please note,** 'for' is used to express **'period of time'** and ***'since'* is used** to denote 'point of time'. With morning, evening etc., use 'since' and with 'some time', 'hours', 'months', etc. use 'for'.

NEGATIVE (PRESENT PERFECT CONTINUOUS)

Negative sentences, have usually the following structure :

Subject + have/ has +not + been + V-IV +...+ since / for +... .

Look at the following sentences :

1. I have been living here since 1997. *Affirmative*
   I have not been living here since 1997. *Negative*
2. She has been sleeping for two hours. *Affirmative*
   She has not been sleeping for two hours. *Negative*
3. They have been playing since evening. *Affirmative*
   They have not been playing since evening. *Negative*
4. Ram has been working on this project for six months. *Affirmative*
   Ram has not been working on this project for six months. *Negative*
5. He has been watching TV since 10 A.M. *Affirmative*
   He has not been watching TV since 10 A.M. *Negative*

NOTE *In negative put 'not' after 'have' or 'has' as shown above.*

INTERROGATIVE (PRESENT PERFECT CONTINUOUS)

Interrogative sentences, have usually the following structure :

Have/ Has+Subject + been + V-IV +...+ since / for +... ?

Look at the following sentences :

1. We have been playing for two hours. *Affirmative*
   Have we been playing for two hours? *Interrogative*
2. She has been sleeping since 12 p.m. *Affirmative*
   Has she been sleeping since 12 p.m? *Interrogative*
3. They have been watching TV for three hours. *Affirmative*
   Have they been watching TV for three hours? *Interrogative*
4. My friend has been waiting for two hours. *Affirmative*
   Has my friend been waiting for two hours? *Interrogative*
5. I have been studying since one p.m. *Affirmative*
   Have I been studying since one p.m.? *Interrogative*

NOTE *In interrogative, put 'Have' or 'Has' before the subject, as shown above. No change in verb or structure of the sentence is required.*

INTERROGATIVE NEGATIVE SENTENCES

Usual structures of interrogative negative sentences :

Has/Have + Subject + not + been + V-IV +...+ since/for + ...?

or, **Hasn't/Haven't + Subject + been + V-IV+... + since/for +...?**

Affirmative Interrogative Negative

1. He has been playing for two hours. *Affirmative*
   Has he not been playing for two hours? *Inrerrogative negative*
   Hasn't he been playing for two hours? *Interrogative negative*

2. They have been making a noise since morning. *Affirmative*
Have they not been making a noise since morning? *Interrogative Negative*
Haven't they been making a noise since morning? *Interrogaive Negative*

The present perfect continuous is used :

To denote an action, which began some time in the past and is still continuing.

Look at the following sentences :

1. He has been playing for two hours.
2. She has been studying since 2 O'clock.
3. I have been playing chess for three hours.
4. They have been building this house for six months.
5. I have been living here since 1997.
6. We have been watching TV since morning.
7. He has been sleeping for two hours.

DIFFERENCE BETWEEN PRESENT CONTINUOUS AND PRESENT PERFECT CONTINUOUS

Look at the following sentences :

1. I am playing. *Present Continuous*
   I have been playing for two hours. *Present Perfect Continuous*
2. He is watching TV. *Present Continuous*
   He has been watching TV since morning. *Presen Perfect Continuous*
3. We are living here. *Present Continuous*
   We have been living here since January. *Present Perfect Continuous*

NOTE *In the above pair of sentences when the action began some time in the past and is still continuing, we use present perfect continuous. But when there is no reference of any, 'point to time' or 'period of time' or the reference of the sentence does not show the continuation of work for a period or point of time , we use present continuous tense.*

COMPARISON OF THE PRESENT PERFECT AND THE PRESENT PERFECT CONTINUOUS

1 With verbs ; **'expect, hope, learn, lie, live, look, rain, sleep, sit, snow, stand, stay, study, teach, wait, want, work'**, an action which began in the past and is still continuing or has just completed can well be expressed either by the present perfect or the present perfect continuous :

(a) How long have you learnt English? *Present perfect*
(b) How long have you been learning English? *Present perfect continuous*
(c) He has slept for ten hours. *Present Perfect*
(d) He has been sleeping for ten hours. *Present perfect continuous*
(e) It has rained for a long time. *Present perfect*
(f) It has been raining for a long time. *Present perfect continuous*

Please note that such construction is not possible with verbs which can't be used in continuous form; like–have, know, etc.

2. **A repeated action in the present perfect** can also be expressed as a continuous action by the present perfect continuous :

(a) I've written many letters since morning.
I've been writing letters since morning.

(b) I have knocked many times. I don't think anyone's in.
I've been knocking. I don't think anyone's in.

TEST YOUR KNOWLEDGE

(A)

Incorrect	**Correct**
1. I writes a letter.	write a letter.
2. He go to temple daily.	He goes to temple daily.
3. Sita crys.	Sita cries.
4. He flys kites.	He flies kites.
5. He do not play.	He does not play.
6. Does I write a letter?	Do I write a letter?
7. Do she swims?	Does she swim?
8. Does she goes to school?	Does she go to school?
9. Ram does not tells a lie.	Ram does not tell a lie.
10. He never verifys the bills.	He never verifies the bills.

(B)

Incorrect	**Correct**
1. You is playing	You are playing.
2. I is reading	I am reading.
3. They are read.	They are reading.
4. She does not swimming.	She is not swimming.
5. Is it rains?	Is it raining?
6. Are she cooking?	Is she cooking?
7. Am he playing?	Is he playing?
8. Is you coming?	Are you coming?
9. I is going to play.	I am going to play.
10. She are speaking.	She is speaking.
11. I am seeing.	I see.
12. I am having a car.	I have a car.
13. I am understanding.	I understand.
14. He is knowing me.	He knows me.
15. He is resembling his brother.	He resembles his brother.

(C)

Incorrect	**Correct**
1. He have gone to Jaipur.	He has gone to Jaipur.
2. I has played.	I have played.
3. They have arrived yesterday.	They arrived yesterday.
4. Have he played a match?	Has he played a match?
5. Ram has gone two minutes ago.	Ram has just gone.
6. He not has taken food.	He has not taken food.
7. He was ill since Monday.	He has been ill since Monday.
8. I have been playing since two hours.	I have been playing for two hours.
9. He has been swimming for 2'O clock.	He has been swimming since 2 O'clock.
10. Has she cooking for two hours?	Has she been cooking for two hours?

11. Have I been not playing for one hour? — Have I not been playing for an hour?
12. She have just arrive. — She has just arrived.
13. Raju is playing for three hours. — Raju has been playing for three hours.

CORRECT YOURSELF EXERCISE : PRESENT TENSE

CYE : 01 Correct the following sentences

1. Sarita go to office at 10 A.M.daily
2. She has been cooking meal from 7 A.M.
3. Nisha is playing tabla for 2 hours.
4. Rani have just come from college.
5. They have been residing here since four years.
6. They goes to field at 5 A.M.
7. Ram do his work in time.
8. He drink coffee in the morning.
9. Mr Sharma teachs us English grammar.
10. Sakshi catchs the train at 8 O'clock.
11. He flys kite on Sunday.
12. We takes bath together in the river .
13. We have been playing for 12 O'clock.
14. Raheja has been singing since one hour.
15. He pass all the tests without fail.

Solutions CYE : 01

1. change 'go' to 'goes'
2. change 'from' to 'since'
3. change 'is' to 'has been'
4. change 'have' to 'has'
5. change 'since' to 'for'
6. change ' goes' to 'go'
7. change 'do' to 'does'
8. change 'drink' to 'drinks'
9. change 'teachs' to 'teaches'
10. change 'catchs' to 'catches'
11. change ' flys' to 'flies'
12. change 'takes' to 'take'
13. change ' for' to 'since'
14. change 'since' to 'for'
15. change 'pass' to 'passes

PAST TENSE

Past tense also has four forms :

1. Simple Past or Past Indefinite Tense.
2. Past Continuous Tense.
3. Past Perfect.
4. Past Perfect Continuous.

Look at the following sentences :

1. I wrote a letter. — Simple Past.
2. I was writing a letter. — Past Continuous.
3. I had written a letter. — Past Perfect.
4. I had been writing a letter. — Past Perfect Continuous.

SIMPLE PAST Or PAST INDEFINITE

Usual structure of sentence *(Past Indefinite)*

Subject + V-II + Object.

1. He went to Jaipur yesterday.
2. I wrote her a letter two days ago.
3. India defeated Pakistan.
4. He wrote a book.
5. Ramesh studied four hours per day.
6. She often carried her purse.

All the above sentences are in Simple Past tense.

NEGATIVE (PAST INDEFINITE TENSE)

Negative sentences have usually the following structure :

Subject + did not + V-I + object.

1. I wrote a letter. *Affirmative*
   I did not write a letter. *Negative.*
2. She sang a song. *Affirmative*
   She did not sing a song. *Negative*
3. He played a match yesterday. *Affirmative*
   He did not play a match yesterday *Negative*
4. They went to market. *Affirmative*
   They did not go to market. *Negative*
5. We went for a picnic last month. *Affirmative*
   We did not go for a picnic last month. *Negative*

In negative, use **'did not'** in past indefinite tense, after subject and change II form of verb to I form of the verb as shown above.

INTERROGATIVE (PAST INDEFINITE)

Interrogative sentences have usually the following structure :

Did + Subject + V-I + Object ?

1. I wrote a letter. *Affirmative*
   Did I write a letter ? *Interrogative*
2. She sang a song. *Affirmative*
   Did she sing a song? *Interrogative*
3. He played a match yesterday. *Affirmative*
   Did he play a match yesterday? *Interrogative*
4. They went to market. *Affirmative*
   Did they go to market? *Interrogative*
5. He went for a picnic last month. *Affirmative*
   Did he go for a picnic last month. *Interrogative*

Remember, in negative and interrogative sentences of past indefinite tense, we should use 'I form of the verb'.

INTERROGATIVE NEGATIVE SENTENCES

Usual structure of Interrogative negative sentences (Past tense) :

Did + Subject + not + V-I + Object ?

or, **Didn't + Subject + V-I + Object ?**

Affirmative	Interrogative Negative
1. He watched TV.	Did he not watch TV? Didn't he watch TV?
2. He went to market.	Did he not go to market? Didn't he go to market?

Use of simple past tense in different situations :

Simple past tense is used for actions completed in the past, as follows :

1. **When the time of a past action is given**, simple past tense is used :
   (a) I met him yesterday. (b) Jackie died in 2001.
2. **When time of a past action is not given**, simple past tense is used :
   (a) He worked in that office for two years. (He does not work there now.)
   (b) She lived in USA for many years. (She is not living there now.)
   (c) My grandmother once saw Abraham Lincoln.
   (d) Did you ever visit Kolkata?
3. **When the time** of past action is **asked about** :
   (a) When did you meet her? (b) When did you finish your work?
4. The simple past tense is also **used is reference to a past habit** :
   (a) He always carried a stick.
   (b) They never ate meat.
   (c) She always scolded her husband.
5. If **two or more actions** took place in sequence, we **use simple past tense to denote the actions**. (Otherwise past perfect is used to denote the earlier action.) This is usually used with conjunction 'before' :
   (a) He switched on the light before he opened the door.
   (b) The train started just before I reached the station.
   (c) He changed his dress before he went to bed.
   (d) She switched off the light before he locked the door.
6. **When two events took place at the same time** in past, simple past is used to describe them:
   (a) When the queen entered the hall, the orchestra played the National Anthem.
   (b) When the P.M. entered the meeting room, all congratulated him.
7. **The simple past is also used in following type of conditional sentences :**
   (a) If I had a map I would give it to her.
   [But I haven't a map. The meaning is 'present' (*i.e.*, It means I don't have a map)]
   (b) If he tried to blackmail me, I would inform you.
   (But I don't expect that he will try to blackmail me. The meaning here is future.)

8. **The use of simple past tense with ; 'wish' and 'if only' shows 'unreal past' and present state of things :**

(a) I wish I were a millionaire. (I am not a millionaire.)
(b) I wish I knew her. (I don't know her.)
(c) If only I knew her. (I don't know her.)
(d) If only he allowed me to deliver a lecture. (He doesn't allow me.)

9. In following structure the **use of simple past denotes 'unreal past' and present time situation :**

(a) It is time we went home. (It is time for us to go home.)
(b) It is time you finished. (It is time for you to finish.)
(c) It is high time we left. (It is proper time for us to leave.)
(d) 11 O'clock ! it is time you went home. (It is time for you to go home.)

PAST CONTINUOUS

The past continuous is used to express an action that was going on at some time in the past. The time of action may or may not be indicated.

Usual structure of sentences (Past Continuous)

Subject + Was / Were + IV form of the verb + Object.

'Was' is used with singular nouns and 'were' is used with plural subjects :

1. He was reading a book in the morning.
2. When I saw her, she was going to market.
3. They were playing cricket.
4. It was getting darker.
5. Ram was writing a letter.

NEGATIVE (PAST CONTINUOUS)

Negative sentences have usually the following structure :

Subject + was / were + not +V- IV + object.

1. My friends were waiting for me. *Affirmative*
   My friends were not waiting for me. *Negative*
2. She was reading a novel. *Affirmative*
   She was not reading a novel. *Negative*
3. When I saw her, she was singing a song. *Affirmative*
   When I saw her, she was not singing a song. *Negative*
4. It was thundering. *Affirmative*
   It was not thundering. *Negative*
5. Ram was playing chess. *Affirmative*
   Ram was not playing chess. *Negative*

NOTE *Use 'not' after 'was' or 'were' in negative sentences, as shown above.*

INTERROGATIVE (PAST CONTINUOUS)

Interrogative sentences have usually the following structure :

Was / Were +Subject + V- IV + Object?

1. She was cooking lunch.	*Affirmative*
Was she cooking lunch?	*Interrogative*
2. It was raining.	*Affirmative*
Was it raining?	*Interrogative*
3. I was playing cricket.	*Affirmative*
Was I playing cricket?	*Interrogative*
4. They were going to Jaipur.	*Affirmative*
Were they going to Jaipur?	*Interrogative*
5. You were writing a letter.	*Affirmative*
Were you writing a letter?	*Interrogative*

INTERROGATIVE NEGATIVE SENTENCES

Usual structure of Interrogative negative sentences, past continuous :

Was/Were +Subject + not + V-IV + Object ?

or

Wasn't/Weren't +Subject + V-IV+ Object ?

Affirmative	**Interrogative negative**
1. He was going to market.	Was he not going to market? Wasn't he going to market?
2. They were playing cards.	Were they not playing cards? Weren't they playing cards?

Use of Past continuous tense in different situations :

1. The past continuous tense is used to describe **such past actions, which continued for some time** .It indicates uncertainly about times of starting or finishing of such actions :

(a) He was playing cricket.
(b) They were watching TV.
(c) She was swimming in the river.
(d) Rahim was repairing the car.

2. Past Continuous tense is also **used without a time expression, indicating gradual development :**

(a) It was getting darker.
(b) The wind was rising.

3. Past continuous tense is **used with a point of time. It refers an action which began before that time and probably continued after it also.**

(a) At seven he was having breakfast. This implies that he was in the middle of breakfast at seven.
(b) At six in the morning Ramesh was reading newspaper.This implies that Ramesh had not finished reading the newspaper at six.

4. Use of past continuous tense with 'when' and 'while' :

'When' is usually used in past continuous tense, when one action was completed and another action was going on :

(a) When he arrived, his wife was washing her clothes.
(b) Where were you living, when the war broke out?

'While' is used when two actions were going on at a time :
(a) While she was cooking, I was washing the clothes.
(b) While I was singing, Ramesh was reading.

5. Past continuous tense is **used with; always, continually, constantly. Here it denotes the actions which were usually being done more frequently or habitually in past :**
(a) He was always abusing others. (b) She was constantly crying those days.
(c) They were continually threatening us. (d) She was always grumbling.

PAST PERFECT TENSE

Usual Structure of Sentences (Past Perfect)

Subject + had +V- III + object.

Look at the following sentences :

1. The train had arrived before he reached the station.
2. The patient had died before the doctor reached there.
3. The bell had rung before the teacher entered the class.
4. She had lived in India for ten years when I met her.
5. I had hoped that she would come here.
6. When the teachers had left the class the boys made a noise.
7. It was something that I had not expected.
8. Ram had gone before Sita came.
9. I had met her several times before she left for London.
10. Sita had finished her work when the guest came.

Past Perfect is used :

1. **To describe one event or happening following another in the past**, the 'Past perfect tense' is used. Past perfect tense is used to describe the earlier event and Past indefinite tense is used for the event, that took place later on.
2. Past perfect tense is also **used with such verbs as hope, expect, think etc. to indicate that a past hope, expectation, desire etc was fulfilled**. See sentences (5) and (7) above.

Negative (Past Perfect)

Negative sentences have usually the following structure :

Subject + had + not +V- III + object.

Affirmative	**Negative**
1. She had written a novel.	She had not written a novel.
2. Ram had gone to Agra.	Ram had not gone to Agra.
3. I had played a match.	I had not played a match.
4. She had advised Sita.	She had not advised Sita.
5. She had warned you.	She had not warned you.

INTERROGATIVE (PAST PERFECT)

Interrogative sentences in past perfect tense have usually the following structure :

Had +Subject + V-III from + Object ?

Affirmative	**Interrogative**
1. She had written a novel.	Had she written a novel?
2. Ram had gone to Agra.	Had Ram gone to Agra?
3. I had played a match.	Had I played a match?
4. She had advised Sita.	Had she advised Sita?
5. She had warned you.	Had she warned you?

INTERROGATIVE NEGATIVE SENTENCES

Usual structure of Past perfect interrogative negative sentences :

Had +Subject + not + V-III form + Object ?

or, **Hadn't +Subject + V-III form + Object ?**

Affirmative	**Interrogative negative**
1. I had already visited Agra.	Had I not already visited Agra? Hadn't I already visited Agra?
2. The train had departed before I reached there	Had the train not departed before I reached there? Hadn't the train departed before I reached there?

Use of past perfect tense in different situations :

1. The past perfect is **used for an action which began before the time of speaking in the past and was still continuing at that time :**
   (a) He had been a captain for ten years.(He was captain on the date of speech.)
   (b) He had been a soldier since he was only eighteen.(He was a soldier as on date.)
   (c) Ram had lived in this house for twenty years.(He lived in that house as on date.)

NOTE *In above construction (c) past perfect continuous; 'had been living' would also be possible.)*

2. The Past Perfect is also used to describe **an action which began before the time of speaking in the past and had stopped at that time or just before that time :**
   (a) The old Peepal tree, which had stood in the ground for 70 years before our house was built, suddenly crashed to the ground.

NOTE *Here the past perfect continuous tense; 'had been standing' would also be possible.*

   (b) Prakash , who had waited for two hours, was very angry with his friend, when he at last turned up. ('had been waiting' would also be possible here.)

3. The past perfect is also used **to describe an action which began before the time of speaking in the past and which stopped some time before the time of speaking.**
   (a) He had served in a bank for twenty years; then he retired and established his business. His children were now well settled.

NOTE *Here we cannot use either 'since' or the past perfect continuous.*

4. The past perfect is also **used when we look back on earlier action from a certain point in the past :**

(a) I had just poured myself a glass of milk when the phone rang.
(b) She had completed her work, before I reached there.
(c) The chief guest had arrived before we reached there.
(d) Ram had slept before it struck seven.
(e) I met her in Mumbai in 1995. I had last seen her ten years before.

NOTE *But if we merely give the events in the order in which they took place, use of past perfect tense is not necessary :*

(a) Ram's father died when Ram was eight. Before he died he advised Ram not to marry till he was 21, and Ram at 20 still intended to follow his advice.

5. The past perfect tense is **used after 'when' to describe the first action** : *when the first action was completed before the second one started* :

(a) When Ram had shut the window, we opened the door of the cage. (We waited for the window to be quite shut before opening the cage.)
(b) When she had completed her work, she went to market.

The past perfect **can also be used with 'as soon as'**, *denoting the moment, immediately* :

(c) She went to market as soon as she had completed her work.

6. The past perfect tense can also be **used with 'till/ until' and 'before'**. *It refers the completion or expected completion of an action* :

(a) She refused to leave till she had checked all the vouchers.
(b) She did not wait till we had finished our lunch.
(c) Before we had finished our lunch she ordered us back to work.
(d) Before we had walked three kilometers she complained of pain in her stomach.

7. In past perfect **'after' is normally followed by a past perfect tense** instead of simple past :

(a) After the will had been read there were joyous exclamations.
(b) We reached the station after the train had departed.

8. It should be well understood that the **actions viewed in retrospect from a point of time in the past should be expressed by the past perfect tense** :

(a) She had been to school but she had learnt nothing there, so she was now illiterate.
(b) When she had been at school she had learnt nothing, so she was now illiterate.

In sentence (b) the verb in the time clause can also be put in simple past as following.

(c) When she <u>was at school</u> she had learnt nothing , so she was now illiterate.

9. **While transforming Direct narration to Indirect narration** the past simple and present perfect tenses are changed into past perfect tense (when Reporting verb is in the past) :

(a) She said to me, 'I have already read that novel.'
She told me that she had already read that novel.

(b) He said to me, 'Tony died two days ago.'
He told me that Tony had died two days before.

10. Past perfect is also *used in conditional sentences*, as following :

(a) If he had met me, I would have helped him.

(b) If he had informed me, I would have gone there positively.

(c) If she had come to me, I would have given her a gift.

NOTE *This is an important structure, students should learn it well :*

If +Subject + had + V-III +....+ would have +V-III +... .

(a) If he had come to me, I would have helped him. or,

(b) Had he come to me, I would have helped him.

Both these sentences have the same meaning.

PAST PERFECT CONTINUOUS

Past perfect continuous tense is used to denote an action that began before a certain point in the past and has continued up to the time of speaking.

Look at the following sentences :

1. He had been playing cricket for two hours.
2. The teacher had been teaching us for two months.
3. At that time, she had been writing a book for three months.
4. When I joined the school, she had already been teaching there for two years.
5. I had been waiting for him for two hours.

In past perfect continuous tense, action had already begun sometime ago and continued up to the time of speech, as shown in above sentences.

Usual Structure of Sentences

Subject + had been + IV form of verb +....+ since or for +... .

NOTE *As discussed earlier also, 'since' is used to denote 'point of time' and 'for' is used to denote 'period of time'. 'Since' is used with , morning , evening etc. and 'for', is used with 'sometime', period of time.*

NEGATIVE (PAST PERFECT CONTINUOUS)

Negative sentences have usually the following structure :

Subject + had+not+ been + IV form of verb +....+ since / for +... .

Look the following sentences :

1. He had been playing cricket for two hours. *Affirmative*
   He had not been playing cricket for two hours. *Negative*
2. I had been waiting for her since Monday. *Affirmative*
   I had not been waiting for her since Monday. *Negative*
3. The teacher had been teaching us since January. *Affirmative*
   The teacher had not been teaching us since January. *Negative*

NOTE *Put 'not' after had and before 'been'. No change in form of verb or in structure of the sentence is required.*

INTERROGATIVE(PAST PERFECT CONTINUOUS)

Interrogative sentences have usually the following structures :

Had +Subject + been + IV form of verb +....+ since / for +...?

Look at the following sentences :

1. He had been playing cricket for two hours. *Affirmative*
   Had he been playing cricket for two hours? *Interrogative*
2. I had been waiting for her since Monday. *Affirmative*
   Had I been waiting for her since Monday? *Interrogative*
3. The teacher had been teaching us since January. *Affirmative*
   Had the teacher been teaching us since January? *Interrogative*

INTERROGATIVE NEGATIVE SENTENCES

Usual structure of Interrogative negative sentences in past perfect continuous tense :

Had +Subject + not + been + V-IV form +... since/for +...

or, Hadn't + Subject + been + V-IV form + ... since/for + ...

1. I had been flying kites since morning. *Affirmative*
   Had I not been flying kites since morning? *Interrogative negative*
   Hadn't I been flying kites since morning? *Interrogative negative*
2. She had been waiting for me for an hour. *Affirmative*
   Had she not been waiting for me for an hour? *Interrogative negative*
   Hadn't she been waiting for me for an hour? *Interrogative negative*

Use of past perfect continuous tense in different situations :

The past perfect continuous bears the same relation to the past perfect as the present perfect continuous bears to the present perfect.

1. Past perfect continuous is **used when the action began before the time of speaking in the past, and continued up to that time** :

(a) It was now eight and she was tired because she had been cleaning the house since dawn.

2. Past perfect continuous is also used when the action began before the time of speaking in the past, and **stopped just before the time of speech.**

(a) I was very tired when I arrived home . I had been working all the day.

3. A repeated action in the past perfect can also be expressed as a continuous action by the past perfect continuous tense :

(a) She had tried many times to get him on the mobile.

(b) She had been trying to get him on the mobile.

NOTE *(i) There is a difference between an action in the past perfect and an action in the past perfect continuous :*

(a) By eight O'clock he had repaired the car. (The job had been completed.)

(b) He had been repairing the car . (It denotes how he had spent the previous one or two hours etc. It does not tell us whether or not the job was completed.)

(ii) Another difference is that an action in the past perfect continuous continues up to, or even after the time of speaking in the past. Past Perfect denotes that the action may occur shortly before the time of speaking, but there should be interval between them (*i.e.,* speech and action). :

(a) Ramesh had been painting the house. (The paint was probably still wet.)

(b) But Ramesh had painted the house. (perhaps recently or perhaps some time ago.)

Compare present perfect continuous and past perfect continuous

(a) We hope the tram comes soon. We have been waiting for half an hour. (It denotes that we have been waiting before now) (Present Perfect Continuous)

(b) At last the tram came. We had been waiting for half an hour. (It denotes that we had been waiting for half an hour before the tram came.) (Past Perfect Continuous)

TEST YOUR KNOWLEDGE

(A)

Incorrect	Correct
1. He gone to Jaipur.	He went to Jaipur.
2. He just went to Jaipur.	He went to Jaipur a short while ago.
3. He did not went to Jaipur.	He did not go to Jaipur.
4. Did he came yesterday?	Did he come yesterday?
5. He did not opened the door.	He did not open the door.
6. He were not going.	He was not going.
7. I were not doing that.	I was not doing that.
8. You was making a noise.	You were making a noise.
9. She did not asked me.	She did not ask me.
10. Did he not reminded you?	Did he not remind you?
11. Was you not playing?	Were you not playing?
12. Were not you writing?	Weren't you writing?
13. Was not I watching movie?	Wasn't I watching movie?
14. Were she not cooking?	Was she not cooking?
15. Were they playing not football?	Were they not playing football?

(B)

1. I had knew her for five years. *Incorrect*
   I had known her for five years. *Correct*
2. If he has come to me, I would have help him. *Incorrect*
   If he had come to me, I would have helped him. *Correct*
3. If I had a pen, I will give you. *Incorrect*
   If I had a pen, I would give you. *Correct*
4. She had not play. *Incorrect*
   She had not played. *Correct*
5. Ram told Sita that he have seen her photos. *Incorrect*
   Ram told Sita that he had seen her photos. *Correct*
6. The train had departed before I reach. *Incorrect*
   The train had departed before I reached the station. *Correct*
7. Had she warn you before. *Incorrect*
   Had she warned you before. *Correct*
8. Ram had been waiting for me since two hours. *Incorrect*
   Ram had been waiting for me for two hours. *Correct*
9. Had Sita been not cooking since morning? *Incorrect*
   Had Sita not been cooking since morning? *Correct*

10. Suresh had been writing a book since three months. *Incorrect*
Suresh had been writing a book for three months. *Correct*
11. It had been raining for last evening. *Incorrect*
It had been raining since last evening. *Correct*
12. He told that he has been writing a letter the last one hour. *Incorrect*
He told that he had been writing a letter for the last one hour. *Correct*
13. Had not he waiting for you for two hours? *Incorrect*
Hadn't he been waiting for you for two hours? *Correct*
14. Maya had already inform me. *Incorrect*
Maya had already informed me. *Correct*
15. Gita not had been waiting for you since. *Incorrect*
Gita had not been waiting for you since January. *Correct*

CORRECT YOUR SELF EXERCISE : PAST TENSE

CYE : 01 Correct the following sentences :

1. Tejpal and his friends were playing chess for two hours.
2. Sita had been cooking for 2 0'clock.
3. Rahim gone to market.
4. The teacher was taught us Hindi at that time.
5. Ramesh had took your purse.
6. The girl had been crying since an hour.
7. We had been playing chess since two hours.
8. The train arrived before we reached there.
9. The patient had fainted than the doctor came.
10. My friends was comming by bus.

CYE : 02 Fill in the blanks with correct form of the verbs (present & past) given in brackets in the space given.

1. It is already four p.m. They..........(not arrive) yet.
2. Rashmi is not in the hostel. She.....(go) out.
3. Sita........(hurt) her leg. She can't walk fast.
4. Suresh has no more books to sell. He ....(sell) all the books.
5. They ....(play) the second match in the morning.
6. Shilpa.......(reach) home last evening.
7. They ....(complete) their project just now.
8. Ramesh.........(finish) his work before Rakhi came.
9. The girl ....(fall) from the roof while......(fly) a kite.
10. It..........(rain) heavily since Monday.
11. Raksha ....(fall) down while she..........(walk) in the gallery.
12. Ranu.........(slip) while she.........(climb) up the roof.
13. The light.........(go) out while we..........(have) drinks in the hotel.
14. Swami ......(ring) the bell at 4 p.m. daily.
15. We ....(live) in this country since India attained freedom.
16. We..........(wait) for the train for last three hours.
17. Ankita.........(read) the 'Ramayana' daily in the morning.
18. A dog...........(bite) him, while she.......(pass) through the forest last week.

19. Smrita..........(write) an story when Rahul.........(enter) the room.
20. They.............(climb) up the ladder when they ....(hear) a loud sound.
21. When seema arrived, they ....(take) them lunch.
22. They ....(play) football for half an hour when it started to rain.
23. We.............(try) hard for ten weeks when we succeeded in sloving the puzzle.
24. He............(put) hard to secure first rank for three years, he finaly achived the succes.
25. She...........(suffer) from fever for more than five days, when she received the appointment letter.

Solutions CYE : 01

1. change 'were' to 'had been'
2. change 'for' to 'since'
3. change 'gone' to 'went'
4. change 'taught' to 'teaching'
5. change 'took' to 'taken'
6. change 'since' to 'for'
7. change 'since' to 'for'
8. insert 'had' before 'arrived'
9. change 'than' to 'before'
10. change 'was' to 'were'

Solutions CYE : 02

1. have not arrived
2. has gone
3. has hurt
4. has sold
5. have played
6. reached
7. have completed
8. have finished
9. fell,flying.
10. has been raining
11. fell, was walking
12. slipped, was climbing
13. went, were having
14. rings
15. have been living
16. have been waiting
17. reads
18. bit, was passing
19. was writing, entered
20. climbed, heard
21. had been taking
22. had been playing
23. had been trying
24. had been putting
25. had been suffering.

FUTURE TENSE

Future tense also has four forms :

1. Simple Future or Future Indefinite,
2. Future Continuous
3. Future Perfect,
4. Future Perfect Continuous.

Look at the following sentences :

1. I shall write a letter. — Simple Future
2. I shall be writing a letter. — Future Continuous
3. I shall have written a letter. — Future Perfect
4. I shall have been writing a letter. — Future Perfect Continuous

Simple future or future indefinite tense

Usual structure of sentences (Simple future)

Subject + will/shall + V-I + Object.

NOTE *In general, 'shall' is used with first person and 'will' is used with the II and III person. Use I form of verb as shown above.*

Look at the following sentences :

1. He will go to Delhi on Saturday.
2. I shall visit her on Monday.
3. They will do this work tomorrow.
4. We shall play cricket match on Sunday.

5. He will come tomorrow.
6. I shall go to Jaipur on next Monday.
7. He will complete his work by tomorrow.
8. It will rain today.
9. She will go by train.
10. Ram will write a poem.

NEGATIVE(SIMPLE FUTURE)

Negative sentences of simple future tense have usually the following structure :

Subject + will / shall + not + V-1 + Object.

Look at the following sentences :

1. He will go to market at 5 p.m. *Affirmative*
   He will not go to market at 5 p.m.. *Negative*
2. I shall write a letter tomorrow. *Affirmative*
   I shall not write a letter tomorrow. *Negative*
3. It will rain. *Affirmative*
   It will not rain. *Negative*
4. Ram will come by night train. *Affirmative*
   Ram will not come by night train. *Negative*

NOTE *In negative, put 'not' after 'shall/will'. No change in form of verb or structure of sentence is required, as shown above.*

INTERROGATIVE (SIMPLE FUTURE)

Interrogative sentences have usually the following structure :

Will/Shall + Subject + V-I + Object ?

Look at the following sentences :

1. She will wait for me. *Affirmative*
   Will she wait for me? *Interrogative*
2. Hari will come tomorrow. *Affirmative*
   Will Hari come tomorrow? *Interrogative*
3. They will go to college tomorrow. *Affirmative*
   Will they go to college tomorrow? *Interrogative*
4. I shall buy a car on Monday. *Affirmative*
   Shall I buy a car on Monday? *Interrogative*
5. We shall go to temple tomorrow. *Affirmative*
   Shall we go to temple tomorrow? *Interrogative*

NOTE *In interrogative, put 'will, shall, may' etc. before the subject. No more change in verb or structure of the sentences in Simple Future is required, as shown above.*

INTERROGATIVE NEGATIVE SENTENCES

Interrogative negative sentences in simple future tense have usually the following structure :

Will / Shall + Subject + not + V-1 + Object ?

or Won't / Shan't + Subject + V-1 + Object ?

(a) I shall buy a TV. *Affirmative*
Shall I not buy a TV? or Shan't I buy a TV? *Interrogative Negative*

(b) He will go to market. *Affirmative*

Will he not go to market? or Won't he go to market? *Interrogative Negative*

Won't = Will not and Shan't = Shall not (contracted form)

Use of simple future tense in different situations :

1. The simple future tense is used to describe an action that will take place in future :
   (a) I shall write a letter. (b) He will go to Delhi on next Monday.
   (c) We may play a match. (d) She will buy a pen.
2. The future simple tense is used to describe such habitual actions that will take place in usual course :
   (a)Winter will come again. (b)Birds will build nests.
   (c)Everyone will die one day. (d)The girls will talk .
3. The future simple is also used in sentences containing clauses of condition and time :
   (a) I shall go to market, if it does not rain.
   (b) I shall go to Jaipur in case she asks me.
   (c) We shall move as soon as the taxi arrives.
   (d) I shall start my work as he comes.
4. With verbs that are not normally used in the continuous tenses,(for example verbs of the senses, of emotion, thinking, possessing etc.), we usually express the future using the future simple tense :
   (a) She will be here at seven. (b) You will surely have time for lunch.
   (c) She will wonder where you are. (d) He will know everything tonight.
5. The future simple tense is also used in newspapers and news broadcasts, for formal announcement of future plans and for giving weather forecasts :
   NEWSPAPER : The President will inaugurate the Seminar tomorrow.
   : The fog will persist in the city.

VARIOUS WAYS TO DENOTE FUTURE ACTIONS

1. **Use of 'going to' form for future actions :** The 'going to' form expresses the subject's intention to perform an action certainly. This intention is generally premeditated and that some preparation for the action has already been made. Actions expressed by the 'going to' form are, therefore, usually considered very likely to be performed.

   Note the following points :

   (i) The 'going to' form can be used to refer the near future with a time expression as an alternative to the present continuous :
   (a) I am meeting Ram at the park at ten.
   (b) I am going to meet Ram at the park at ten.
   But note that 'I am meting Ram' implies an arrangement with Ram. 'I am going to meet Ram' denotes : Ram may get a surprise.

   (ii) We use 'going to' form with time clauses when we wish to emphasize the subject's intention :
   (a) He is going to be an engineer when he grows up.
   (b) What are you going to do, when you pass your graduation?

(iii) The 'going to' form can also be used without a time expression :

(a) He is going to lend me his bicycle.

(b) She is going to let out her house.

It then usually denotes the immediate or near future.

2. Use of 'about to' for future actions :

(a) The train is about to start.

(b) The shop is about to close.

(c) The Chief Guest is about to arrive.

3. Use of simple present tense for future actions (for planned future actions) :

(a) Mr. Sharma retires on 31st December. (b) The President visits Gujarat tomorrow.

4. Use of present continuous tense for future actions (for planned future actions) :

(a) We are meeting today in the evening. (b) The wedding is on Sunday next.

5. Use of 'to be' form of verb for future actions :

(a) I am to go there.

(b) He is to complete his work.

(c) They are to come here tomorrow.

(d) She is to sing a song.

(e) I have to go to hospital.

FUTURE CONTINUOUS

Future Continuous Tense denotes an action, imagined to be going on at some future time.

Usual structure of Sentences (Future Continuous)

Subject + shall be / will be +V- IV + object +..

Look at the following sentences :

1. I shall be writing a letter then.
2. When she gets home, her husband will be watching T.V.
3. I shall be visiting her next week.
4. She will be staying here till Monday.
5. When I reach home, she will be cooking dinner.

In all above sentences, the action is not taking place at the moment, but action will be taking place at sometime in future.

NEGATIVE (FUTURE CONTINUOUS)

Usual structure of future continuous negative sentences :

Subject + will / shall + not + be + V-IV + Object.

1. I shall be writing a letter. *Affirmative*
   I shall not be writing a letter. *Negative*
2. He will be playing in the field. *Affirmative*
   He will not be playing in the field. *Negative*
3. She will be cooking food. *Affirmative*
   She will not be cooking food. *Negative*
4. He will be learning his lesson . *Affirmative*
   He will not be learning his lesson. *Negative*
5. Ram will be coming by evening train. *Affirmative*
   Ram will not be coming by evening train. *Negative*

In Negative sentences, put 'not' after—'will, shall, may, must' as shown above. No more change in form of verb or in structure of the sentence is required.

INTERROGATIVE (FUTURE CONTINUOUS)

Usual structure of Interrogative sentences :

Will / Shall + subject + be + V-IV + Object ?

1. I shall be playing football. *Affirmative*
   Shall I be playing football? *Interrogative*
2. He will be going to market. *Affirmative*
   Will he be going to market? *Interrogative*
3. He will be learning a poem. *Affirmative*
   Will he be learning a poem. *Interrogative*
4. She will be cooking food. *Affirmative*
   Will she be cooking food? *Interrogative*
5. They will be coming tomorrow. *Affirmative*
   Will they be coming tomorrow? *Interrogative*

In interrogative, put 'shall' or'will' or 'may' etc before the subject , as shown above,and no further change in the structure is required.

INTERROGATIVE NEGATIVE SENTENCES

Usual structure of the sentences :

Will/Shall + Subject +not + be + V-IV + Object ?

or, **Won't /Shan't + Subject + be + V-IV + Object ?**

Affirmative	**Interrogative Negative**
1. I shall be playing cricket tomorrow.	Shall I not be playing cricket tomorrow? Shan't I be playing cricket tomorrow?
2. They will be washing their clothes.	Will they not be washing their clothes? Won't they be washing their clothes?

Use of Future Continuous tense in different situations :

1. The Future continuous tense is used as an ordinary continuous tense :

Future continuous : It is used with a point in time, and expresses an action which begins before that time and may continues after it. This use is best seen by following example :

(a) Imagine a class of students at 10.30 a.m. ;

We may say : Now the students are sitting in their classroom. They are listening to a tape. On Sunday there is no class. So on Sunday *they will not be sitting* in the classroom. They *will be doing* other things. Ramesh *will be playing* chess. Anil *will be shopping*. Sakshi *will be washing* her clothes.

2. The future continuous tense is used to express future without intention :

(a) I will be helping my mother tomorrow.
(This does not imply that the speaker has arranged to help her. It merely states that this action will happen.)

(b) I will be meeting him on Sunday. (No prior appointment or arrangement)

(c) He will be working in this office tomorrow. (As usual)

FUTURE PERFECT TENSE

The future perfect tense denotes imaginary completion of an action by a certain future time. When an action is to be completed on some future date or time, we use future perfect tense.

Usual structure of the sentences (Future Perfect) :

Subject + will have or shall have + V -III + Object.

As shown above, in future perfect tense, III form of the verb is used with 'shall have/will have' etc.

Look at the following sentences :

1. I shall have completed this work by next Monday.
2. He will have gone to market before you reach there.
3. The train will have departed before he reaches station.
4. He will have written all the lessons before 8 P.M.
5. They will have cleaned the room, before Miss Mary arrives.
6. The patient will have died before the doctor reaches.
7. She will have left India before sunset.
8. Students will have broken the gate before the principal comes.
9. She will have finished the work before her husband arrives.
10. The peon will have rung the bell before the teacher enters the class.

You see, here the action is neither completed, not going on at this moment, but as per the imaginations, the action will be completed at some future time.

Important

1. It is important to note that in one clause of the sentence, future perfect is used and in another clause, present indefinite is used.
2. To describe the action, which is to be completed first, use future perfect and to describe the action which is to be completed afterwards, use present indefinite tense, as shown above in sentences 2, 3, 5, 6, 8, 9, 10.It is important.

NEGATIVE (FUTURE PERFECT)

Usual structure of negative sentences :

Subject + shall / will + not + have + V-III + Object.

Look at the following sentences :

1. I shall have completed this work by next Monday. *Affirmative*
   I shall not have completed this work by next Monday. *Negative*
2. The patient will have died before the doctor reaches there. *Affirmative*
   The patient will not have died before the doctor reaches there. *Negative*
3. She will have left India by Sunset. *Affirmative*
   She will not have left India by Sunset. *Negative*
4. He will have gone to market by 5 p.m. *Affirmative*
   He will not have gone to market by 5 p.m. *Negative*
5. The teacher will have taught the grammar by next week. *Affirmative*
   The teacher will not have taught the grammar by next week. *Negative*

In negative sentences put 'not' after 'will/shall/may/must' etc. No change in form of verb or in structure of sentence is required as shown above.

INTERROGATIVE (FUTURE PERFECT)

Usual structure of interrogative sentences :

Shall / Will + Subject + have + V-III + Object ?

Look at the following sentences :

1. I shall have gone to market by 5 P.M. *Affirmative*
   Shall I have gone to market by 5 P.M ? *Interrogative*
2. She will have left India by sunset. *Affirmative*
   Will she have left India by sunset ? *Interrogative*
3. The patient will have died before the doctor reaches. *Affirmative*
   Will the patient have died before the doctor reaches ? *Interrogative*

In interrogative sentences, we put 'will / shall' etc., before the subject. No change in form of verb or in structure of sentence is required as shown above.

INTERROGATIVE NEGATIVE SENTENCES

Usual structure of sentences :

Shall / Will + Subject + have + not + V-III + Object?

or, Won't /Shan't + Subject + have + V-III + Object?

	Affirmative	Interrogative Negative
1.	He will have repaired the car by 5 P.M.	Will he not have repaired the car by 5 P.M.? Won't he have repaired the car by 5 P.M.?
2.	I shall have informed her by tomorrow.	Shall I not have informed her by tomorrow? Shan't I have informed her by tomorrow?

Use of Future Perfect Tense in different situations :

1. Future perfect tense is used **to describe the actions which are going to be completed on some future date or time :**

(a) I shall have passed my graduation by next year.
(b) He will have completed his work by tomorrow.
(c) The mechanic will have repaired the car by 7 P.M.
(d) By the end of this year I shall have saved Rs.one lac.
(e) By the end of next month he will have been here for ten years.

NOTE *We use 'by'('by then', 'by that time', 'by the 15th') for time expression .*

2. Future perfect is also **used to describe an action which at a given future time will be in the past or will just have finished**. For example :

(a) Imagine that it is 2nd July and Rina is much worried about an examination that she is taking on 31st July.

Someone planning a function might say, "We'd better wait till 31st July. *Rina will have taken her exam by then*, so she will be able to enjoy herself."

(b) I save Rs500/- a month and I started saving in January. So *by the end of the year I will / shall have saved Rs. 6000/-.*

3. **When two actions** are to be taken on some future time, **we use future perfect tense for the action completed first** and present simple for the action to be completed afterwards :

(a) The student will have left the class before the teacher comes.
(b) The show will have started before I reach there.
(c) The function will have started before we reach there.
(d) The mechanic will have repaired the TV before it strikes eight.

4. Future perfect tense is also used to express **such future incidents/actions about which we presume that another person already had the knowledge** of that incident or **the action is already completed** by that time :

(a) You will have heard about Mother Teressa .
(b) You will have heard about our plans of investment.
(c) He will have read the newspaper so far.
(d) They will have heard about the accident by this time.

FUTURE PERFECT CONTINUOUS

Future perfect continuous tense denotes an action which is in progress over a period of time and that will be completed at sometime in future.

Usual structure of sentences :

Subject + will have been/shall have been + V- IV +.... + for/ Since +

In Future perfect continuous tense, 'IV form' of the verb(V-I + ing) is used with, 'shall have been/ will have been'. As already discussed earlier, **'for' is used** to denote **'period of time'** and **'since` is used to express 'point of time'**.

Look at the following sentences :

1. We shall have been residing here for six years by the year 2006.
2. I shall have been studying in this college for 3 year by next January.
3. Maneesh will have been serving in this company for five year by July 2005.
4. I shall have been reading for six hours by 2 O'clock.
5. Sita may have been waiting for me since 5 O'clock on next Monday.
6. By the end of this year he'll have been acting for thirty years.

NOTE *Like the future perfect tense, it is also used with a time expression beginning with 'by'.*

The future perfect continuous bears the same relationship to the future perfect as the present perfect continuous bears to the present perfect.It means the **future perfect continuous tense can also be used instead of the future perfect tense :**

1. When the action is in progress future perfect continuous tense :
   (a) By the end of the month she will have been working here for seven years.
2. **When the action is expressed as a continuous action :**
   (a) By the end of this month he will have been training horses for seven years.
   But if we mention the number of horses and divide this action in any way, it is necessary to use the future perfect tense :
   (b) By the end of this month he will have trained 300 horses.

NEGATIVE (FUTURE PERFECT CONTINUOUS)

Usual structure of negative sentences :

Subject + shall /will +not + have been + V-IV + ...

Look at the following sentences :

1. We shall have been residing here for 6 years by the year 2006. *Affirmative*
   We shall not have been residing here for 6 years by the year 2006. *Negative*
2. I shall have been studying in this college for five years. *Affirmative*
   I shall not have been studying in this college for five years. *Negative*
3. Maneesh will have been serving in the firm for last five years. *Affirmative*
   Maneesh will not have been serving in the firm for last five years. *Negative*

In negative, put 'not' after 'will/shall/may/must' etc. as shown above. No change in form of verb or in structure of sentences is required.

INTERROGATIVE (FUTURE PERFECT CONTINUOUS)

Usual structure of interrogative sentences :

Shall / Will + Subject + have been + V-IV +....?

Look at the following sentences :

1. We shall have been residing here for six years by this year 2006. *Affirmative*
   Shall we have been residing here for six years by this year 2006? *Interrogative*
2. I shall have been studing in this college for five years. *Affirmative*
   Shall I have been studing in this college for five years ? *Interrogative*
3. Maneesh will have been serving in this firm for last five years. *Affirmative*
   Will Maneesh have been serving in this firm for last five years? *Interrogative*

In interrogative, put 'shall/ will' etc., before the subject as shown above. No change in the form of verb or in structure of the sentence is required.

INTERROGATIVE NEGATIVE SENTENCES

Usual structure of the sentences :

Will / Shall + Subject + not + have been + V-IV +... + since/for +... +...?

or, Won't / Shan't +Subject + have been + V-IV + ... + since/for +... + ...?

1. I shall have been playing match since morning. *Affirmative*
   Shall I not have been playing match since morning? *Interrogative negative*
   or Shan't I have been playing match since morning? *Interrogative negative*
2. He will have been watching TV for two hours. *Affirmative*
   Will he not have been watching TV for two hours? *Interrogative negative*
   or Won't he have been watching T.V. for two hours? *Interrogative negative*

Test Your Knowledge (A)

Incorrect	**Correct**
1. Let I go there.	Let me go there.
2. We will play a match.	We shall play a match.
3. Will he not played?	Will he not play?
4. If he will come, I shall go.	If he comes, I shall go.
5. He will be play tomorrow.	He will be playing tomorrow.

6. He will be staying here yesterday.	He will be staying here tomorrow.
7. Ram shall not be playing football.	Ram will not be playing football.
8. Will not he be going to market.	Won't he be going to market?
9. Suchi will about to come.	Suchi is about to come.
10. Will not you play?	Won't you play?

Test Your Knowledge (B)

1. The students will have left the school before the principal came. *Incorrect*
   The students will have left the school before the principal comes. *Correct*
2. The train will have arrived before I reaches the station. *Incorrect*
   The train will have arrived before I reach the station. *Correct*
3. He would have reached here before the sun set. *Incorrect*
   He will have reached here before the sun sets. *Correct*
4. Will he has completed his work by tomorrow? *Incorrect*
   Will he have completed his work by tomorrow? *Correct*
5. Will he have not repaired the car by 7 P.M.? *Incorrect*
   Will he not have repaired the car by 7 P.M.? *Correct*
6. He will has been waiting for you for three days. *Incorrect*
   He will have been waiting for you for three days. *Correct*
7. Will not he have been waiting for you since morning? *Incorrect*
   Won't he have been waiting for you since morning? *Correct*
8. Ram will have not been playing at this time tomorrow. *Incorrect*
   Ram will not have been playing at this time tomorrow. *Correct*
9. Will the girls have played the game at 7 P.M? *Incorrect*
   Will the girls have played the game by 7 P.M? *Correct*
10. He will have finish the work by 8 P.M. *Incorrect*
    He will have finished the work by 8 P.M. *Correct*

CORRECT YOURSELF EXERCISE : FUTURE TENSE

CYE : 01 Correct the following (Future Tense) :

1. They will be playing cricket for two hours.
2. Let I play tabla.
3. We should obeyed our elders.
4. She will be gone to market at this time .
5. The patient will die before the doctor reaches here.
6. I shall be living in Alwar for 8 years by the year 2010.
7. He will waiting for you.
8. Let the students played.
9. He must be coming by Rajdhani Express.
10. He should be completd his work by next Monday.

Solutions CYE : 01

1. change 'will be' to 'will have been',	2. change 'I' to 'us',
3. change 'obeyed' to 'obey',	4. change 'gone' to 'going',
5. change 'will die' 'will have died',	6. change 'shall be' to 'shall have been',
7. insert 'be' to after 'will',	8. change 'played' to 'play',
9. no change,	10. change 'should be' to 'will have' .

CYE : 02 Fill in the blanks with the future continuous /perfect/perfect continuous form of the verbs, given in the brackets :

1. ....she..........(go) home after Holi ?
2. The students ....(works) on their project next year.
3. The gardener ....(water) the plants at 7 pm. in the evening tomorrow.
4. Ramesh ....(repair) his bicycle all the day tomorrow.
5. Her brother..........(study) in this college next year positively.
6. You........(complete) your work by the end of this month.
7. By the end of next year I..........(finish) my project positively.
8. The farmers..........(plough) all their fields before the monsoon reaches.
9. We.............(manufacture) remote controlled planes by the end of the next year.
10. By next month, you............(visit) all the famous places of Udaipur.
11. Rahul ....(practise) it for two months by January next.
12. Sangita.......(teach) English for two years by March, 2006.
13. Mr. Prassana.....(work) in this hospital for three years by Dec.2006.
14. We.........(serve) in this firm for three years by Jan.2007.
15. I........(live) here for twenty years by Nov.2003

Solutions CYE : 02

1. will, be going,
2. will be working,
3. will be watering,
4. will be repairing,
5. will be studying,
6. will have completed,
7. will have finished,
8. will have ploughed,
9. will have manufactured,
10. shall have visited,
11. will have been practising,
12. will have been teaching,
13. will have been working,
14. shall have been serving,
15. shall have been living.

CYE : 03 (A) Supply the correct tense forms of the verbs given in brackets :

(a) When we (take) our exams, we'll have a holiday ?
(b) I (leave) these flowers at the hospital for you. I (go) there anyway to visit my cousin.
(c) When I reached the school, the first bell (already go).
(d) Only the wearer (know) where the shoe (pinch).
(e) He (play) the Guitar outside her house when someone opened the window and (throw) out a bucket of water.
(f) I wish you (tell) me you arleady (buy) the book.

(B) Supply the correct tense forms of the verbs given in brackets :

(a) I (not like) the dance last night.
(b) Please sit here until my husband (come).
(c) She (play) tennis since 4 o'clock.
(d) My friend (not see) me for many years when I met him last week.

(C) Supply the correct tense forms of the verbs given in brackets.

(a) They (build) that bridge when I (be) here last year. They (not finish) it yet.
(b) Lend me your rubber. I (make) a mistake and (wish) to rub it out.
(c) I wish I (know) his name.
(d) When the aeroplane landed, the pilot (find) that one of the wings (be damaged) by a shell.
(e) Look, a man (run) after the bus. He (want) to catch it.

(D) Supply the correct tense.

(a) If I (be) a ghost. I (try) to frighten all the people I dislike.
(b) He (know) her a long time before he finally (get) married to her.
(c) What you (do) just now while I (wash) the dishes ?
(d) I always (tell) you to comb your hair, but your never (do) what I say.
(e) I hope it (not rain) when the bride (leave) the church.

Solutions CYE : 03

(A) (a) have taken, (b) left, had gone,
(c) had already gone, (d) knows, pinches,
(e) was playing, threw, (f) told, had already bought.

(B) (a) did not like, (b) comes,
(c) has been playing, (d) had not seen .

(C) (a) were building, was, have not finished (b) have made, wish,
(c) knew (d) found, had been damaged,
(e) is running, wants.

(D) (a) were, would try, (b) had known, got,
(c) were you doing, was washing, (d) tell, do,
(e) won't rain, leaves.

CYE : 04 Fill in blanks

(A) Supply correct tense form of the verbs given in brackets

The city of Katagum .... (build) in the form of an oblong with the chief's house in the centre .... (look) like an old English castle. There .... (be) a high clay tower, with a wall around it about twenty feet high; inside the courtyard ....(be) small houses for women and servants. The chief himself and his soldiers .... (occupy) the upper part of the three storied tower in times of alarm and danger. All round the tower walls, small holes .... (cut), through which archers could fire their arrows at an attacking enemy.

(B) Supply correct tense form of the verbs given in brackets

'The fire........... (look) very serious',............. (say) a young soldier, "but I wonder why they .... (not order) everyone to leave the building till the fire .... (to be extinguished)." Suddenly a great tongue of flame .... (shoot) out of a window on the fourth floor and the broken glass......(begin) to fall. I ....(look) at the soldier and he (look) at me. "Come on", he said, "We ......(go) to see what ....(happen) there".

(C) Fill in the blanks

When I .... home yesterday, I .... the noise of a fire engine, and when I .... up, I .... that smoke was .... out of the fourth floor of a high rise building. I .... over to the place and .... a small group of people who all were ...... at the smoke and ...... together in serious tones as if something really serious .... happened.

Solutions CYE : 04

(A) was built, looking, was, were, occupied, (would occupy), were cut.
(B) is looking, said, are not ordering, is extinguished, shot, began, looked, looked, shall go, has happened (is happening).
(C) reached, heard, went, saw, coming, went, saw, gazing, talking, had.

SEQUENCE OF TENSE

Sequence of Tense : The Sequence of Tenses are **the principles which govern the tense of the verb in subordinate clause vis a vis the tense of the verb in principal clause.** *The rules which determine the tense of the subordinate clause if the tense of the principal clause is present or past or future, are studied under the heading,* ***Sequence of Tense.***

Rules

1. **If the principal clause is in the past tense, the subordinate clause should also be in the past.** For example :

    (a) My father assured me that he would buy a bike for me.
    (b) He failed because he didn't work hard.
    (c) He asked me what she was reading.
    (d) I thought that I could win the race.
    (e) Ram said that he would come on Monday.

Exceptions

(i) ***A Past tense in the principal clause may be followed by a Present tense in the subordinate clause when the subordinate clause expresses a universal truth, mathematical calculation, historical fact, moral guideline, habitual fact or something that has not yet changed.*** In such cases, the tense of the subordinate clause is not governed by the tense of principal clause(The subordinate clause is usually in present tense in such cases).For example :

(a) He said that the earth revolves round the sun.
(b) We learnt at school that the truth always triumphs.
(c) He said that two and two is four.
(d) Krishna told in Geeta that life is not victory but battle.
(e) Ram said that man is mortal.
(f) I was happy to note that India is progressing.
(g) Newton discovered that the apple falls because of gravitational pull of earth.

(ii) **If the subordinate clause is introduced by a conjunction of comparison** such as ; 'than', 'as well as' etc., in such case, a past tense in the principal clause may be followed by any tense in the subordinate clause as per the sense of the statement.Furthermore, any tense in principal clause can be followed by any tense in the subordinate clause.For example :

(a) He loved me more than he loved you.
(b) He loved me more than he loves you.
(c) He loved me more than he will love you.
(d) He will love you more than he loved me.
(e) He has loved you more than he loved me.
(f) He will love you more than he loves me.
(g) She helps you as well as she helped me.
(h) She will help you as well as she has helped me.

(iii) **If the subordinate clause is an adjective clause**, in that case, it may be in any tense even if the principal clause is in past tense.

(a) I visited the place where accident took place.
(b) I visited the village where he lives.
(c) I visited the hotel where she will stay.

2. **A present or future tense in the principal clause** *may be followed by any tense in the subordinate clause :*

   1. He says that she passed the examination.
   2. He says that she will come tomorrow.
   3. Ram says that he likes that girl.
   4. Ram will say that Sita is a beautiful girl.
   5. Ram will say that he didn't like that girl.
   6. He will say that he will pass the examination positively.

Exception

If the subordinate clause is introduced by; 'if, till, as soon as, when, unless, before, until, even if, as', etc. and the principal clause is in simple future , in that case the verb in subordinate clause must be in present simple form. For example :

1. We shall not go to market if it rains.
2. He will wait till she comes.
3. We will start as soon as the taxi arrives.
4. I shall ask him, when he meets me.
5. I shall not go before he comes.
6. I shall not help him unless he asks me.
7. I shall help him even if he doesn't ask me.
8. He will start as the taxi arrives.

7

The Verb

Importance of Verb : We cannot frame a sentence without a verb. Verbs indicate thoughts and actions. We need nouns to name things and verbs to express what those things do. Verbs do more than show action : they indicate when the action happened, how many things were acting, and can describe the action.

The **tense** of a verb indicates time. The use of **sigular** and **plural** forms indicates the quantity of things 'acting' in a sentence. Most **verbs** make a statement, ask a question, or give a command. Some verbs connect a description to a sentence's subject. It is often told that verbs are 'action words' because they do frequently indicate an action. Verbs indicate what the subject of a sentence is doing, thinking, or being at a given moment in time.

KINDS OF VERB

Verb can be classified as following :

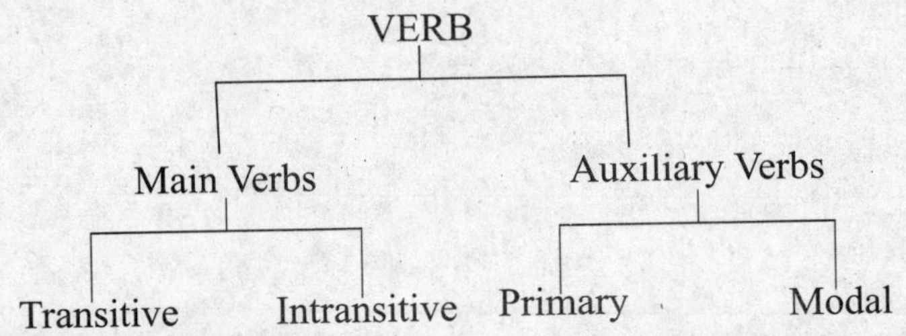

Look at the following sentences :

(a) I am playing - am (auxiliary verb), play (main verb)
(b) He is writing -is (auxiliary verb), write (main verb)
(c) They are reading - are (auxiliary verb), read (main verb)

TRANSITIVE AND INTRANSITIVE VERB

Verbs can be divided into two categories, *transitive* and *intransitive*.

Transitive Verb : Transitive verbs take objects. That is, these verbs carry the action of a subject and apply it to an object. They tell us what the subject (agent) does to something else (object).

Examples :

(a)	He	bought	a pen.
	agent	did something **(action)**	**object**- answers the question 'what?'
(b)	She	brushes	her hair every hour.
(c)	Marina	will lose	the race.

NOTE *A transitive verb can take any tense.*

Intransitive verbs : ***Intransitive verbs do not take an object***; they express actions that do not require the agent's doing something to something else.

Examples :

(a) *Sita danced.*

The intransitive verb 'danced' is a complete action by itself and does not require a direct object to receive the action.

(b) *They ran down the road.*

They ran, but they did not run 'something' in this sentence. The sentence contains no object.

(c) The boy ***ran*** away as fast as he could.

(d) I must ***lie*** down.

RULES : TRANSITIVE AND INTRANSITIVE VERBS

1. Verbs can be used both transitively and intransitively :

Some verbs can function both transitively and intransitively. So it is not reasonable to classify a verb as ***transitive*** *or* ***intransitive****, instead we should say that the verb is used transitively or intransitively.*

Verbs used transitively	**Verbs used intransitively**
(a) He **speaks** the truth.	(a) Sita **speaks** slowly.
(b) The students **rang** the ball	(b) The bell **rang** loudly.
(c) He **flies** kites.	(c) A bird **flies**.

Burn, stop, break, and open are other verbs which can be used both-intransitively and transitively :

Transitive	**Intransitive**
She **burnt** her hand.	She **burnt** with guilt.
He **stops** the car.	The car **stops**.
She **broke** a bottle.	The bottle **broke.**
Open all the gates.	The office **opens** at ten o' clock.

2. **Passive voice is possible only with transitive verbs.**
3. **Some verbs** like 'come, go, fall, die, sleep, lie' **refer actions that can't be done to anything or can't be passed over to any object**. These verbs are, therefore, not used transitively.
4. **Some intransitive verbs can be made transitive by adding a preposition with them :**

(a) He *looks* **after** his parents.

(b) They *laughed* **at** me.

(c) The committee has *gone* **through** your proposal.

(d) I will *look* **into** your matter.

(e) The TTE *asked* **for** his ticket.

(f) We have *talked* **about** this matter earlier also.

The words in bold type are prepositions added to the intransitive verbs, thus making them transitive.

NOTE *In some cases the preposition is prefixed to the verbs as following :*

(a) A dizziness *overcame* him. (b) She *overcame* the thief.
(c) Our army bravely *withstood* the attack. (d) The river *overflew* its bank.

5. **Some intransitive verbs take an object after them that are similar in meaning to the verb**. Such objects are called **Cognate objects** :

(a) He **sighed** a deep **sigh**. (b) Our army **fought** a fierce **fight.**
(c) I **dreamt** a sweet **dream**. (d) She **sang** a melodious **song**.
(e) She **slept** a deep **sleep**. (f) She **smiled** a mysterious **smile.**

In above sentence the verbs and the objects (**Cognate**) are in bold type.

6. **Some verbs are used reflexively**. A verb is said to be used reflexively when the verb and the object both refer to the same person :

(a) The girl killed herself. (b) The man killed himself.

Some verbs though used reflexively but the reflexive pronoun is not used with them. Such verbs are pure intransitive in nature :

(a) The tube **burst** (itself) .
(b) The girls **made**(themselves) merry.
(c) The foreigners **feed** (themselves) on meat.
(d) Please **keep** (yourself) quiet.

Some verbs can be used as ordinary transitive verb as well as reflexively.Look at the following ***examples :***

(a) I Enjoy myself reading novels.
(b) I enjoy good health.
(c) She interested herself in her parents, welfare.
(d) Her habits does not interest me.

VERBS OF INCOMPLETE PREDICATION

Look at the following sentences :

(a) He **laughs.** (b) The girl **sleeps.**
(c) She **seems** sad. (d) Ram **became** a teacher.

The verbs in all the above sentences are **used intransitively**. Sentence (a) and (b) make a sense, but sentence (c)without 'sad' (She seems) does not make any sense. **To complete the meaning or to make the sentence meaningful we are to use some complement**. *The word* **'sad'** *in sentence(c) and words* **'a teacher'** *in sentence* (d) are **complements of the verbs** *'seems'* and '*became*' respectively.These verbs are called **Verbs of incomplete predication.**

Such a verb which requires a word to make its sense complete is called a verb of incomplete predication.

Subjective and Objective Complements **:** A complement is usually a noun or an adjective or an adjective + noun. **When the complement modifies**(describes) **a subject , it is called** a **Subjective complement** and **when the complement modifies or describes an object**, it is called **Objective complement :**

(a) Pusy is a **cat**. (b) Ram is a **teacher.**
(c) He appears **pleased.** (d) Sweets taste **sweet.**

(e) You look **tired.** (f) He became a **minister.**
(g) The flowers smell **sweet.** (h) The building is to **let.**

All the bold typed words in above sentences are **subjective complements** , describing the subjects.

NOTE *When the Subjective complement is a noun it should be in nominative case.*

Look at the following sentences :

(a) We made Ram **monitor.** (b) I consider the man **honest.**
(c) The judge found him **guilty**. (d) He called his father a **rustic.**
(e) His wife named him **Lovy**. (f) I thought him **trustworthy.**
(g) He called his wife a **pros.** (h) The teacher considers Ram **intelligent**.

In above sentences, all the bold typed words are **Objective complements** , modifying or describing the objects.

NOTE *When the objective complement is a noun it should be in objective case.*

8. **Ditransitive verbs : Some verbs take two objects, *one direct* and the other *indirect object.*** Such commonly used verbs are; give, ask, tell, offer , promise, send, etc.These verbs are called **Ditransitive verbs ; eg—**

(a) He gave me a pen.
(b) Ram asked her a personal question.
(c) She told me a story.

Direct and Indirect Objects of the verb

Direct Objects : When a verb is in the Active Voice, the subject of the verb refers to the person or thing performing the action described by the verb; and the **object** of the verb refers to the person or thing receiving the action described by the verb.

In the following examples, the objects of the verbs are printed in bold type.

(a) She read the **magazine**.
(b) I did not see the **car**.
(c) He ate the **apples** quickly.

In these sentences, the verbs; **read, did, see** and **ate**, are verbs in the Active Voice; and the words; **magazine**, **car**,and **apples**, are the objects of the verbs. These objects are said to be **direct objects**, because they refer to things which receive directly the actions described by the verbs.

Indirect objects : In addition to taking direct objects, some verbs also take **indirect** objects. In the following examples, the direct objects are printed in bold type, and the **indirect objects** are underlined.

She gave the child a **pen**.
He sent the man the **information**.

In above examples, the words **'child'** and **'man'** are said to be the indirect objects of the verbs **'gave'** and **'sent'**. Indirect objects refer to things which receive indirectly the actions described by the verbs. In the above examples, the words **'pen'** and **'information'** are the direct objects of the verbs. **Indirect objects usually refer to living things.**

It is possible for a sentence containing an indirect object to be rewritten by placing a preposition before the indirect object. When this is done, **the original indirect object can be regarded either as the indirect object of the verb**, or *as the object of the preposition.*

For example, the sentence **'We gave the child a pen'**, can be rewritten as follows :

We gave a **pen** to the child.

In the rewritten sentence, **'child'** can be regarded either as the indirect object of the verb **'gave'**, or as the object of the preposition **'to'**.

Linking verbs : A linking verb connects a subject to a subject complement which identifies or describes the subject. Linking verbs are :

(i) *forms of 'to be'* when followed by a description or definition,
(ii) sensory verbs, including synonyms for *look, smell, taste, feel, and sound,*
(iii) empathic verbs, including *seem, feel* (emotion), and *appear,*
(iv) tranformation verbs, including *become, evolve, grow, keep, and remain.*

The following sentences are descriptive, using ***linking verbs*** :

1. The house **is** green.
2. The house **was** white, until we painted it.
3. It **looks** beautiful.
4. His cooking **tasted** like charcoal.
5. They **seem** quite in love.

A **predicate** is the part of a sentence, following the simple verb. If an intransitive sentence renames or defines the subject using a noun or pronoun, the predicate is known as a **predicate nominative** form. If the predicate describes the subject using an adjective, it is in the **predicate adjective** form.

Many linking verbs (with the significant exception of 'be') can also be used as transitive or intransitive verbs :

(a) He says that the water in Mumbai **tastes** terrible.(Linking verb **taste:** intransitive use.)
(b) I **tasted** the soup before adding more salt. (transitive use of 'taste')

11. *Important*

We should not be confused with the verbs 'to lay' and **'to lie'**, since, the Simple Past of the verb **'to lie'** has the same form as the bare infinitive of the verb **'to lay'**. Likewise **'to raise'**, **'to rise'**; **'to set, to sit'** should also not confuse you. See the following table :

	Infinitive	**Simple Past**	**PastParticiple**
Transitive :	to lay	laid	laid
Intransitive :	to lie	lay	lain
Transitive :	to raise	raised	raised
Intransitive :	to rise	rose	risen
Transitive :	to set	set	set
Intransitive :	to sit	sat	sat

A. To Lay and To Lie : **To lay is a transitive verb**, which takes an object. The following examples illustrate the use of the present continuous, simple past, and present perfect tenses of the verb **'to lay'**. The verbs are underlined, and the objects of the verbs are printed in bold type :

(a) He is laying the **table**.
(b) He laid a **bet** on the white horse.
(c) The hen has laid an **egg**.

'To lie' is an intransitive verb, which do not take an object. The following examples illustrate the use of the present continuous, simple past, and present perfect tense forms of the verb **'to lie'** :

(a) **He** is lying on the sofa.

(b) They lay on the beach in the sun.

(c) She has lain in bed for a week.

In these examples, it might appear that the words **'sofa, beach**, and **bed'** act as objects of the verb **to lie**. However, this is not true.

In the examples above, **'sofa'**, and **'beach'** are objects of the preposition **'on'**; and **'bed'** is the object of the preposition **in**.

(B) To Raise and To Rise

'To raise' is a transitive verb, which takes an object. The following examples illustrate the use of the present continuous, simple past, and present perfect tense forms of the verb **'to raise'**. The verbs are underlined, and the objects of the verbs are printed in bold type :

(a) The government is raising **taxes**.

(b) He raised the **glass**.

(c) They have raised a **crop** of barley.

'To rise' is an intransitive verb, which does not take an object. The following examples illustrate the use of the present continuous, simple past, and present perfect tense forms of the verb **'to rise'**.

(a) The sun is rising in the east.

(b) She rose to the occasion.

(c) The temperature has risen by ten degrees.

In these sentences, the verbs have no objects. The words **'east, occasion** and **degrees'** are the objects of the prepositions **'in, to** and **by'**.

(C) To Set and To Sit

'To set' is a transitive verb, which takes an object. The following examples illustrate the use of the present continuous, simple past, and present perfect tense forms of the verb **'to set'**. The verbs are underlined, and the objects of the verbs are printed in bold type.

(a) He is setting a **record.**

(b) We set the **pots** on a shelf.

(c) Have you set the **alarm** for the morning?

'To sit' is an intransitive verb, which does not take an object. The following examples illustrate the use of the Present Continuous, Simple Past, and Present Perfect tense forms of the verb **'to sit'**.

(a) He is sitting on the **table**.

(b) I sat at my **desk** for two hours.

(c) They have sat on the **couch** all afternoon.

In these sentences, the verbs have no objects. The words **table, desk**, and **couch** are the objects of the prepositions **on, at** and **on**.

CAUSATIVE VERBS

12. Causative verbs show that somebody/something is *indirectly* responsible for an action. *The subject doesn't perform the action itself*, **but causes someone/something else to do it instead**. For example :

Yesterday I had my hair cut.

(I didn't cut my own hair, but I made someone else do it for me instead; I 'caused' him to cut my hair.)

Look at the following sentences :

(a) I made her sing a song. (b) I made him polish my shoes.
(c) I got my clothes washed by him. (d) I got my thesis written by him.

Such commonly used causative verbs are ; *get, make, have, keep* etc. :

(a) I made him laugh.
(b) I made him write a letter.
(c) He made me polish his shoes.
(d) I kept her waiting.
(e) He keeps me away from the office.
(f) I shall make him complete the project today.

The causative verbs 'make, keep' are used in active voice, while 'have, get' are used in passive voice :

(a) I got my shoes polished by him.
(b) I got my car repaired by the mechanic.
(c) I got my clothes washed by her.
(d) I had a song sung by her.
(e) I had the thesis written by him.
(f) I had my clothes washed by her.
(g) I shall get the project completed by him today.

Some more causative verbs :

Let :

'Let' can be **used as a causative verb.**

'Let' is used when, a **person gives permission** to **another person to do something.**

See the following examples :

(a) I should let this car cool. (b) Would you let me join your party?

Help :

Help can also be **used as a causative**. It means—**a person assists another person to do something.**

See the following examples :

(a) I helped her to pack the luggage. (b) Would you help me deliver this box?

The most common error with causatives is using 'to' unnecessarily. For example :

(a) We made Jack <u>to</u> finish his supper. *Incorrect*
We made Jack finish his supper. *Correct*

(b) I let Jim <u>to</u> clean up the mess. *Incorrect*
I let Jim clean up the mess. *Correct*

AUXILIARY VERBS

Auxiliary verbs can be divided in **Primary** and **Modal auxiliary verbs**. In this chapter only *primary auxiliary verbs are described. Modal auxiliary verbs are described in a separte chapter* in this book. Primary auxiliary verbs can be further divided as following :

1. Verbs 'to be ' :- is, am , are ,was , were
2. Verbs 'to have' :- have, has ,had
3. Verbs 'to do' :- do, does, did.

1. Auxiliary Verb 'To be' (Is/ Am/ Are/ Was/ Were)

'Is /Am/ Are', *are used in present tense while* **'was / were'** *are used in past tense.* **'Am'** *is used with I only*, while **'is'** *is used with other singulars.* **'Are/were'** *are used with plurals.* **'Was'** *is used in past tense with singular subject.*

'to be' form of verbs are also used in continuous tense and in Active/ Passive structures. Please refer the corresponding chapters for the deatils.

Uses of auxiliary 'to be' :

(A) The **'be + infinitive'** structure is used in following ways :

(i) To tell about a plan or scheduled arrangement :

(a) The Prime Minister is to make a statement tomorrow.
(b) He is to marry next week.
(c) I am to go to USA next month.
(d) He was to go to the hospital.

(ii) To convey instructions / orders/ commands :

(a) You are to wait here till we return.
(b) No one is to leave this place without our permission.
(c) Stay here till she sleeps.

(B) 'be' about + infinitive *expresses an idea of immediate future action* :

(a) The train is about to start.
(b) He is just about to leave.
(c) She was just about to dive when she saw a whale in the sea.
(d) They were just to leave by car.

(C) 'To be' form of verbs as *ordinary verbs :*

(i) As ordinary verb 'be' form of verbs are used **to give information about a person or thing** :

(a) Ram is a teacher.
(b) She is a girl.
(c) The dog is in the room.
(d) Silver is a white metal.
(e) The road was rough and muddy.

(ii) 'To be' is also used **to denote mental and physical condition** as following :

(a) She was angry/ excited.
(b) They were happy.
(c) I was calm.
(d) He is wise.

(iii) 'To be' is also used **to denote age/size and weight** .

(a) She is twenty five years old.
(b) She is twenty five.

(c) It is 200 hundred years old.
(d) I am 165 cms.
(e) I am 67 kilos.
(f) She is 45 kilos only.

(iv) **With some adjectives**, such as; stupid, difficult, funny, polite, etc. the use of 'to be' form of verb in continuous form implies that the subject is deliberately acting in the manner described by the said adjective :
(a) She is being difficult .(She is creating unnecessary fuss).
(b) He is being funny. (He is only jocking.)
(c) You are being stupid.(You are knowingly not trying to understand.)

(D) Use of 'to be' form with '*there*' :

When a noun represents an indefinite person or thing and it acts as subject of the verb 'to be' we normally use **there+ be** structure :
(a) There is a cow in the field.
(b) There are four girls in the room.
(c) There is a mistake in the sentence.
(d) There is someone on the phone for you.
(e) There is nothing to do.
(f) There was a boy in the room.
(g) There were several girls in the hostel.

2. Auxiliary Verb 'to have' (Have/ Has/ Had)

'Have / Has/ Had' are used in continuous form in perfect structures. **'Have/ Has / Had'** are also used to show possession / ownership. **'Have'** is used with plural and **'Has'** is used with singular subject. With pronoun 'I' , use of **'have'**. **'Have'** and **'Has'** refer present tense while use of **'Had'** refers past tense :

(a) I have a car.
(b) I have got a car
(c) He has a book.
(d) He has got a book.
(e) He had a beautiful house.
(f) He had got several good opportunities.
(g) I have two sisters.
(h) She has two sons.
(i) I have five friends.
(j) They have two brothers.
(k) I had two sons.
(l) He had one daughter.
(m) A man has two legs.
(n) A cow has four legs.
(o) The room has four walls.
(p) A chair has four legs.

The use of 'got' with 'have' merely emphasise the point.

(A) Have/had are also used to mean; take,receive,experience :
(a) I have my dinner at 9 PM.(take)
(b) I have my bath in the morning (take).
(c) I had no problem in searching his house (experience).
(d) I had many messages from my past employer. (receive)

As main verbs, '*have*' and '*be*' can come before '*not*' in negative sentences (*We haven't any pickles; He is not there*). They can also appear before the subject in questions (*Is anybody home; Have you no shame?*). It just goes to show that even the most basic words can turn out to be quite complex, once you examine how they are used.

(B) Note the negative and interrogative structures with 'have / has / had' :

	Affirmative	Negative	Interrogative
(a)	I have a pen.	I have no pen.	Have I a pen?
	I don't have a pen.	Do I have a pen?	
(b)	She has a car.	She has no car.	Has she a car?
		She hasn't any car.	Does she have a car ?
		She doesn't have a car.	
(c)	He had a house.	He had no house.	Had he a house?
		He hadn't any house.	Did he have a house?
		He did not have a house.	

(C) 'Have' is often combined with an infinitive to form an auxiliary whose meaning is similar to 'must' :

(a) I have to have a car like that!

(b) She has to pay her own tuition fee at college.

(c) He has to have been the first student to try that.

3. Auxiliary Verb 'to do' (Do/ Does/ Did)

(A) Do/does/did are used in framing negative and interrogative questions in present and past tenses.See the chapter on tenses.

(B) Emphatic 'Do' :

The so-called emphatic 'do' has many uses in English :

(i) To add emphasis to an entire sentence, emphatic 'do' is used :

(a) He does like eggs. He really does!

(ii) **To add emphasis to an imperative**, 'do' is used emphatically :

(a) Do come in. (actually softens the command)

(iii) **To add emphasis to a frequency adverb** 'do' and its forms are used emphatically :

(a) He never did understand his mother.

(b) She always does manage to hurt her mother's feelings.

(iv) **To contradict a negative statement** :

(a) You didn't do your homework, did you? Oh, but I did finish it.

(v) **To ask a clarifying question about a previous negative statement** :

(a) Raju didn't take the purse. Then who did take the purse ?

(vi) **To indicate a strong concession** 'do' and its forms are used emphatically :

(a) Although Jack denied any wrong-doing, he did return some of the presents.

(C) 'Do' is also used to show suitability or adequacy :

(a) Have you a torch?
I haven't got a torch.
Will a match box do?(Whether the matchbox will be suitable?)
No a matchbox won't do.(No matchbox won't be suitable.)
I am trying to find out the gas leak.

(b) Could you lend me rupees one thousand ?
Would Rs. 100/- do? (= be adequate?)
No it wouldn't. I need Rs.1000 to deposit my annual fees.

D. 'to do with' is also used to refer the 'concern':

(a) It is nothing to do with you. (It doesn't concern you.)
(b) It was nothing to do with me (It didn't concern me.)

E. Forms of 'do' are useful in expressing similarity and differences in conjunction with 'so' and 'neither' :

(a) My wife hates eggs and so does my son.
(b) My wife doesn't like eggs ; neither do I.

F. 'Do' is also used to avoid the repetition of the verb :

(a) Shalini excelled in language studies; **so did** his brother.
(b) Rahul studies as hard as his sister **does.**

4. One Principal Verb + Two Auxiliaries

When two auxiliaries are used with a principal verb , the principal verb need not be repeated if the same form (of principal verb) serves the purpose with both the auxiliaries.But if the same verb does not serve the purpose with both the auxiliaries, we must use different forms of the principal verb with each auxiliary as shown in sentences (e) & (f) below .

Look at the following examples :

(a) She neither **can** nor **will** *help* him. (b) He **did** not and **should** not *talk* to him.
(c) He neither **will** nor **can** *solve* it. (d) They **did** not and **will** not *help* you.

Words in bold type are auxiliaries and words in italicized type are principal verbs.

Look at the following sentences also :

(e) He neither has **talked** nor will **talk** to me.
(f) They have not **helped** and will not **help** you.

In above sentences (e) and (f) different forms of principal verb are used with each auxiliary.These sentence must not be written in following way :

(a) He neither has nor will talk to me *(Incorrect)*
(b) They have not and will not help you. *(Incorrect)*

INCHOATIVE VERBS

The term 'Inchoative verb' is used for a verb that denotes the beginning ,development or final stage, of a change of condition.- ***Guide to patterns and usage in English by AS Hornby.***

Get, Become, Grow etc.are some commonly used inchoative verbs :

(a) My father is getting weaker.
(b) He has become the richest man in the town.
(c) It is growing dark.
(d) It is getting dark.

Other such verbs are ;come, go, turn, fall, run, wear :

(a) The paper of the book turn yellow. (b) Will his dream come true?
(c) Ram soon fell asleep. (d) The carpet is wearing thin.
(e) The supply of water is running low now-a-days.

(A) **Get** : Inchoative verb - 'get' is used most extensively. **'Get' is normally used in continuous form.** 'Get' is used **with positive and comparative degrees of adjectives**. It is also used with participles as adjectives.

(a) Sugar is getting scarcer.
(b) It is getting dark.
(c) He is getting weaker.
(d) She is getting older.
(e) Ramesh often gets quarrelsome when he's been drinking.

'Get' is also used with 'to' infinitives.In continuous structures it usually means—'become':

(f) He is getting to be (= becoming) a good pianist.
(g) He got to be (became) my best friend.
(h) They got to words and then to blows (i.e. began arguing and then fighting).

'Get' is also used in phrases as; get rid of, get clear of, get out of.

(B) **Become** : Like 'get', 'become' is also used widely. 'Become' is used with positive and comparatives and with participles as adjectives :

(a) How did you become acquainted with her ?
(b) He became suspicious.
(c) The leaves became red in autumn.
(d) The child became pale and thin.

'Become' is also used with nouns as following :

(a) On leaving school she became an actress.
(b) He soon became the richest man in the town.
(c) Are you likely ever to become a principal.
(d) He became Chairman of the Municipal council last year.

(C) **Grow** : grow is used with positive and comparative degrees of adjectives and as participles as adjectives :

(a) Time is growing short. (Time is getting short)
(b) It is growing dark. (or It is getting dark or It is becoming dark.)
(c) The sea is growing calm.
(d) The child is growing slimmer. (The child is getting slimmer.)
(e) He is growing to be more and more like his father.

(D) **Come** : 'Come' is used with positive and comparative degrees of adjectives.It is also used with past participle adjectives in **'un' form** (undone, unstitched, untied etc.)that refer an undesirable situation :

(a) My dreams have come true.
(b) The hinge has come loose.
(c) The knot came untied.
(d) My shoe laees have come undone.
(e) The seam came unstitched.

'Come' is also used with 'to' infinitives as following :

(f) How did she come to hear the news?
(g) She came to know that......
(h) When I came to know them better....
(i) Now-a-days this park has come to be used as a parking place for vehicles.

(E) **'Go'** : 'Go' is used **with adjectives to refer a definite or ultimate change** :

(a) His hair has gone white.
(b) He went mad.
(c) She is going bald.
(d) Her cheeks went a very pretty pink.
(e) My telephone has gone dead.
(f) The milk went sour.

'Go' is also used **with prepositional phrases**, such as; ***go to bed, go to pieces*** etc. :

(g) They started to go off the idea.(go off = not like)
(h) He went to sleep.(fell asleep)
(i) She nearly went to pieces when has father died. (fell to pieces = lost her control)

(F) **'Turn'** : 'Turn' is also **used with positive and comparative degrees of adjectives :**

(a) The weather has turned much colder.
(b) The bananas are turning black.
(c) The ink turns pink when it dries.

'Turn' is also used with nouns :

(d) I believe you'll never turn traitor
(e) Is it wise for a great General to turn politician?
(f) When her servant left, she had to turn cook. (become cook for the household)

NOTE *Here the noun is used without the indefinite article 'a/an'.*

(G) **Run** : 'Run' is usually **used with adjectives; *dry, low*** and ***short*** and denotes a change in the condition :

(a) The well has run dry.(No water)
(b) The cows are running dry. (not giving milk)
(c) Gas supply is running short now a days.

(H) **'Fall'** is used with positive degree of adjectives (**not with comparatives**) :

(a) He fell sick / ill. (b) When do the returns fall due ?
(c) The post of manager fell vacant. (d) She soon fell asleep.

'Fall' is used with some prepositional phrases as 'fall out of favour', 'fall behind the time', 'fall to pieces'.

CORRECT YOURSEFF EXERCISE : THE VERB

CYE : 01 Identify the underlined part of speech.Choose the correct answer :

1. The burglar **disappeared** with the cash.
   (a) transitive verb, (b) intransitive verb,
   (c) linking verb, (d) auxiliary verb.
2. The director **told** the actors, 'Do your best, and we'll be a hit.'
   (a) transitive verb, (b) intransitive verb,
   (c) linking verb, (d) auxiliary verb.
3. He **would** tell me if he thought we were in danger.
   (a) transitive verb, (b) intransitive verb,
   (c) linking verb, (d) auxiliary verb.

4. His ability to concentrate **is** legendary.
(a) transitive verb, (b) intransitive verb,
(c) linking verb, (d) auxiliary verb.

5. The campers **hid** inside the cabin when they saw the bear.
(a) transitive verb, (b) intransitive verb,
(c) linking verb, (d) auxiliary verb.

6. Alexis **is** swimming in the state championship contest next week.
(a) transitive verb, (b) intransitive verb,
(c) linking verb, (d) auxiliary verb.

7. Frustrated with the official's call, Ethan **kicked** the bench.
(a) transitive verb, (b) intransitive verb,
(c) linking verb, (d) auxiliary verb.

8. The student **procrastinated** too long and failed to finish the project.
(a) transitive verb, (b) intransitive verb,
(c) linking verb, (d) auxiliary verb.

9. The vegetarian burger **tasted** like salted cardboard.
(a) transitive verb, (b) intransitive verb,
(c) linking verb, (d) auxiliary verb.

10. Ellen **nodded** to the audience and sang her song.
(a) transitive verb, (b) intransitive verb,
(c) linking verb, (d) auxiliary verb.

11. Her brother **likes** bananas, but she likes peaches.
(a) transitive verb, (b) intransitive verb,
(c) linking verb, (d) auxiliary verb.

12. Adjunct faculty **are teaching** in several of the lower division courses.
(a) transitive verb, (b) intransitive verb,
(c) linking verb, (d) auxiliary verb.

13. The director told the actors, '**Do** your best, and we'll be a hit.'
(a) transitive verb, (b) intransitive verb,
(c) linking verb, (d) auxiliary verb.

14. Regis Philbin, the host of 'Who Wants to be a Millionaire,' **smiled** at her answer.
(a) transitive verb, (b) intransitive verb,
(c) linking verb, (d) auxiliary verb.

15. When the contestant **completed** the first test, she received another clue.
(a) transitive verb, (b) intransitive verb,
(c) linking verb, (d) auxiliary verb.

16. Dennis **became** impatient when Thomas took so long choosing a movie.
(a) transitive verb, (b) intransitive verb,
(c) linking verb, (d) auxiliary verb.

17. President Clinton **pushed** into the crowd and shook her hand.
(a) transitive verb, (b) intransitive verb,
(c) linking verb, (d) auxiliary verb.

18. The hiker **turned** quickly toward the noise behind him.
(a) transitive verb, (b) intransitive verb,
(c) linking verb, (d) auxiliary verb.

19. Our teacher **gave** each of us another chance to take the exam.
(a) transitive verb, (b) intransitive verb,
(c) linking verb, (d) auxiliary verb.

20. After the chef **completed** the demonstration, she left the students to clean the kitchen.
(a) transitive verb, (b) intransitive verb,
(c) linking verb, (d) auxiliary verb.

Solutions CYE : 01

1.b, 2.a, 3.d , 4. c, 5.b, 6.d, 7.a, 8.b, 9.c, 10.b,
11.a, 12.b, 13.a, 14.b, 15.a, 16.c, 17. b, 18.b, 19.a, 20.a.

CYE : 02 Use the following verbs because answers are not in appropriate tense to fill in the blanks :

let, make, have, get .

1. Sam really wanted a dog, but his parents wouldn't --------- him have a pet.
2. I can't believe she--------- you look at her vacation pictures again last night. We have to look at those stupid pictures every time we go to her house.
3. I don't know how you convince your children to clean up their rooms. I couldn't --------- my children to clean up their rooms if my life depended on it.
4. Professor Yu --------- each of her students write an essay describing their future goals in life.
5. Professor Yu --------- her students use a dictionary while they were taking the test.
6. Debbie's husband hates the opera. But after days of nagging, she finally --------- him to go see the new production of La Boheme.
7. Sally --------- me take off my shoes before I went into her house. She said she wanted to keep the carpet clean.
8. Rebecca Smith requested a copy of that expense report, so I --------- the courier take one over to her last week.
9. Diane thinks television is a waste of time, so she won't ---------her children watch TV.
10. Susie --------- her son take out the trash before he went to the park to play soccer.
11. Marcus ---------me drive his new BMW. I couldn't believe how quickly it picked up speed.
12. How did you --------- the doctor to make a house call? I haven't heard of a doctor actually going to a patient's house in years.
13. My boss ---------me get him coffee, pick up his dry cleaning and buy presents for his wife. He can't do anything by himself!
14. Tommy didn't want to go to his cousin's birthday party, but his mom --------- him go.
15. I can't believe the zoo keeper --------- you feed the snake. That was so cool!

16. The contract was very detailed, and it was essential that the wording be absolutely correct.
   Therefore, I --------- the translator recheck his work several times to make sure there would be no misunderstandings.
17. Cheryl didn't want to wash her car, so with a little smooth talk she --------- her boyfriend to wash it for her.
18. If you ask me nicely, I'll --------- you lick the bowl after I make the cookies.
19. Jack found a fly floating in his coffee, so he --------- the waiter bring him a new cup.
20. The news coverage of the recent tornado was incredibly moving. The interview with the little boy who lost his family in the tragedy --------- everyone cry.

Solutions CYE : 02

1. let,	2. make,	3. get,	4. have,	5. let,
6. get,	7. make,	8. have,	9. let ,	10. have
11 let,	12. get,	13. make,	14. make,	15. let,
16 . have,	17 get,	18. let,	19. have,	20. make.

CYE : 03 Underline the verb in each sentence and indicate whether it is being used as a transitive verb or an intransitive verb :

1. Many contemporary television programmes expose children to violence and vulgar language.
2. My exam grade will exclude me from the soccer game.
3. Alice imagined a world full of fascinating creatures.
4. James ran in the park every afternoon.
5. The tornado destroyed entire buildings when it struck.
6. I raked the yard on Saturday.
7. The boiling water scalded my hand.
8. We talked about the news all evening.
9. My mother washes clothes every Saturday.
10. I opened the door for the lady with the stroller.

Solutions CYE : 03

T - Transitive , I Intransitive

1. Many contemporary television programmes expose children to violence and vulgar language. T
2. My exam grade will exclude me from the soccer game. T
3. Alice imagined a world full of fascinating creatures. T
4. James ran in the park every afternoon. I
5. The tornado destroyed entire buildings when it struck. (destroyed T ; *Struck- I*)
6. I raked the yard on Saturday. T
7. The boiling water scalded my hand. T
8. We talked about the news all evening. I
9. My mother washes clothes every Saturday. T
10. I opened the door for the lady with the stroller. T

SUBJECT : VERB AGREEMENT

- **If the subject is singular, the verb must be singular.**
- **If the subject is plural, the verb must also be plural.**

The subject of a sentence must agree with the verb of the sentence. They must agree in two ways:

(A) In Number : Singular *vs* Plural

(B) In Person: First, Second, or Third Person

Look at the following sentences :

(a) I am reading.
(b) They are dancing.
(c) You are doing your work.
(d) We are swimming.
(e) Ram plays football.
(f) They play football.
(g) Sita sings a song.
(h) We go to see movie.

In sentences (a), (b), (c), (d) each, the verb agrees with the person of the subject. With first person use 'am', while with second person use 'are' and with third person singular use 'is'. In sentences (e), (f), (g), (h) each, the verb agrees with the subject in number. Use singular verb with singular subject.

Exceptions to the rule (Subject singular/ plural-verb singular/plural)

A) In sentences expressing some imaginary wish, supposition, the verb used in plural as following:

(a) I wish I were the Prime Minister.
(b) I wish I were a bird.
(c) Were he a king!
(d) Were she an eagle, she would fly to me.
(e) She ordered as if she were my mother.
(f) If I were you, I would kill him.

B) Verbs; bless, save, help, live, when used to express good wishes, desire, blessings etc., always used in plural.

(a) God save (not saves) the queen.
(b) God help (not helps) you.
(c) Long live (not lives) the king.
(d) God bless (not blesses) you with a son!

C) When 'Dare and Need' are used as 'modal' (in negative and interrogative) these are not made singular by adding 's'(dares or needs).

(a) He need not to go there. (not needs)
(b) She dare not oppose your proposal.
(c) Need he go there?
(d) One need not write anything to him.
(e) Dare she oppose you?(not dares)
(f) He dare not speak like this.

RULES OF CORRECT USE OF VERBS

Rule-(1) If the two subjects are joined by 'and' the verb will be plural.

(a) He and she were present in the function.
(b) Ram and Rahim are friends.

Rule-(2) When two nouns refer to the same person or thing, take singular verb.

(a) The poet and painter has died.
(b) The Project Director and Additional Collector is on tour.
(c) 'The clerk and counsellor was present in the meeting.

Please note in such case, article is used with the first noun only.

Rule-(3) When two nouns almost identical in meaning used in a sentence, just for the sake of emphasis, we use singular verb.

(a) The scheme and plan of my life differs from that of yours.
(b) His authority and command is indeed great.
(c) The benefit and advantage from this business is enormous.

Rule-(4) When two nouns are not identical in meaning but part of the same idea and used as a phrase, the verb used is singular.

(a) Bread and butter is a good breakfast.
(b) Slow and steady wins the race.
(c) 'Early to bed, early to rise' is a good habit.
(d) Pen and ink is needed by me.

Rule-(5) When two subjects are connected by; or, either ... or, neither ... nor, and not only ... but also, the' subject which is closest to the verb determines whether the verb is singular or plural. Usually the plural subject is placed near the verb (it means if one subject is singular and the other is plural, the plural subject will be placed near the verb and the verb will be plural).

(a) Neither the principal nor the teachers were present in the function.
(b) Either Ramesh or his friends have stolen the watch.
(c) Ramesh or his friends are abusing him.
(d) Not only the principal but also the teachers were playing the match.
(e) Either you or I am to go there.
(f) Neither he nor you are to attend them.
(g) You or Ramesh is responsible for the loss.
(h) He or I am to go there.

Rule-(6) With collective nouns like; team, family, jury, crowd, class, committee, army, assembly, fleet, majority, mob, government, parliament council, staff, etc., the verb used can be singular or plural. If the collective noun functions as a unit the verb will be singular, but ifthe collective noun functions dividedly or not in' unison, the verb used will be plural.

(a) The Parliament has passed the bill.
(b) Army was deployed at the border.
(c) The fleet has reached the port .

(d) The Assembly is in session now-a-days.
(e) The mob moves towards Parliament.
(f) The jury has taken a unanimous decision.
(g) The committee are divided our proposal.
(h) The team have arrived.
(i) The jury are divided in opinion.
(j) The audience were getting bored.
(k) The commitee's meeting is on Sunday.
(I) The jury are coming out of the jury room now.

Rule-(7) Some nouns ends with 's', look like plurals, but actually singular in meaning take singular verbs. Such commonly used nouns are; *Physics, Mathematics, Economics, News, Gallows, Billiards, Innings, Wages, Alms, Politics, Measles, Mumps etc.*

(a) No news is good news.
(b) Physics/Economics/Maths is a good subject.
(c) Billiards is a good game.
(d) First innings was spoiled due to rain.
(e) Measles is a dangerous disease in older people, so is mumps.

Rule-(8) A plural noun denoting quantity or measurements of time, money, distance and weight as a unit takes singular verb.

(a) Five kilograms is not a heavy weight.
(b) Hundered rupees is a big amount for him.
(c) Six miles is not a long distance.
(d) Eight hours of sleep is enough.

Rule-(9) Some nouns appear, singular but are plural in meaning take plural verbs. Such commonly used nouns are; *Dozen, Hundred, Million, Cattle, People. Score, Thousand, Gentry, Police, Peasantry, Company, Alphabet, Progeny, Offspring. Clergy, Infantry etc.*

(a) The cattle are grazing in the field.
(b) A score were saved by him.
(c) Not less than a dozen were injured.
(d) The people were fully satisfied.

Rule-(10) Sometimes a word that is actually an adjective is used as a noun. It is preceded by the and means 'people'. the poor = people who are poor, the old = people who are old, the young = people who are young.

(a) The poor are trustworthy.
(b) The rich are generally unkind to the poor.

Rule-(11) Each and every take singular noun and singular verb.

(a) Each boy and girl has to attend the function.
(b) Every man, women and child was happy to meet with the President.
(c) Each minute and each second is precious.
(d) Each male and every female was protesting against that law.

Rule-(12) Usually singular verb is used in sentences showing arithmetical calculations. Also note the following views* of Norman Lewis.

* Five and Five is ten :- Right --- But don't jump to the conclusion that 'five and five are ten' is wrong both verbs are equally acceptance.(Norman Lewis)

(a) Four and four is eight.
(b) Four and four are eight.
(c) Three plus three equals six.
(d) Three plus three equal six.
(e) Two times six is twelve.
(f) Three substracted from seven is four.

Rule-(13) One of, Either of, Neither of, None of always take plural noun and singular verb. Note the construction:

One of/None of/Either of/Neither of /None of + plural noun + singular verb.

(a) One of my friends needs some help.
(b) None of those reasons is valid.
(c) Either of those books is adequate.
(d) Neither of the girls is here.

Rule-(14) Some nouns uncountable in nature like; *furniture, luggage, information, advice, work, knowledge, equipment, behaviour, scenery, traffic, fruit, electricity, music, progress, weather, nonsense, sense, etc.,* **can't be pluralised by adding's'. Uncountable noun, take singular verbs.**

(a) Work is worship.
(b) Knowledge is power.
(c) His behaviour was not proper.
(d) His advice in the matter is trustworthy.
(e) The scenery of Kashmir is indeed beautiful.
(f) His behaviour is indeed praiseworthy.

Rule-(15) When two nouns joined together by; *besides, as well as, and not, in addition to, like, with, together with, including, accompanied by,* **the verb is governed by the former noun.**

(a) Ram and not his friends was present there.
(b) The house with all its belongings was sold.
(c) The President as well as the members has come.
(d) The pigeon like other birds has wings.
(e) Four questions in addition to the first question have to be answered.
(f) The President accompanied by his wife is travelling to India.
(g) All the books including yours are in that rack.

Rule-(16) Hair is used in singular and usually takes singular verb. But if hair is used as countable, use plural verb as following:

(a) His hair is black.
(b) Five hairs of the horse are needed by him.

Rule-(17) If a countable noun follows 'all' or 'some' in a sentence the noun as well as the verb used will be plural. But if the noun following is uncountable, the verb used will be singular.

(a) All the tigers are wild animals.
(b) All the money was taken away by the thief.
(c) Some animals are faithful.
(d) Some milk is needed.

Note : If the use of all denotes a 'unit' the verb used will be singular.

(a) He informed the police all that happened last night.
(b) I would inform you all that was discussed in the meeting.

Rule-(18) When used in sentences, the titles of books, plays, poems movies, and so on are singular and so take singular verb.

(a) Salman Rushdie's 'Midnight's Children' is my favourite novel.

The Untouchables **was a very violent movie.**

The X-files **is re-screening this evening.**

Rule-(19) The verb used after 'there' will be singular or plural depends upon the subject follows. If it is singular, use singular verb, if plural use plural verb.

(a) There is a girl in the room.
(b) There are ten students in the class.
(c) There was a queen.
(d) There were several ministers in the party.

Rule-(20) Some nouns consist of two parts, take plural verbs. Such commonly used nouns are; *scissors, paints, trousers, binoculars, tongs, spectacles, shorts, breeches, shoes, scales, glasses, googles etc.*

(a) My shoes are new.
(b) The scissors are blunt.
(c) His paints are tight.
(d) Her spectacles are beautiful.

Note : If' a pair' is used with such nouns, the verb used in singular.

(a) Only a pair of shoes is required. .
(b) A pair of scissors was purchased by me.

Rule-(21) Some sentences have following constructions:

Singular noun+ Preposition + Singular noun .... Singular verb

Use singular verb in such constructions. It is important.

(a) Man after man was coming there.
(b) One month after another has passed.
(c) Ship after ship is arriving regularly.
(d) He begs from door to door.

Rule-(22) Some nouns have the same form in singular as well as in plural. The verb is used according to what we mean to refer. Such nouns are; sheep, fish, deer, pice etc.

(a) A sheep is a beautiful animal.
(b) Many sheep are grazing there.
(c) I found a pice.
(d) I found five pice.
(e) There are many fishes in the pond. (Incorrect)
There are many fish in the pond. (Correct)

Rule-(23) If in a sentence; infinitive, gerund, phrase, or a clause, functions as subject. Use singular verb.

(a) Swimming is a good exercise. —Gerund
(b) To swim is good for you. — Infinitive
(c) How to start it is a big question. —Phrase
(d) That she is poor is known to me.—Clause

Rule-(24) If phrase; *a number of / lots of / a lot of / plenty of / a quarter of / part of / per cent of proportion of / none of / remainder of / two third of / most of / some of / majority of much of / many of / a good deal of / a great deal of / heaps of, etc.,* **is followed by a countable noun, it will be plural and the verb used will also be plural. If the noun followed is uncountable the verb used will be singular.**

(a) Most of the persons are dishonest.
(b) Most of people like the goverment jobs.
(c) Most of the milk was impure.
(d) Most of the sugar was wet with water.
(a) About half of the students were present there.
(b) He said that half of the hostlers were absent.
(c) Half of the milk was spoiled.
(d) Half of the land was cultivable and half was uncultivable.
(a) Plenty of sugar is required.
(b) Plenty of chairs have been purchased.
(c) A lot of books were destroyed in fire.
(d) Lot of milk was sent there.

Some more sentences are following:

(a) A large proportion of the Northern army was British.—H.G. Wells
(b) The rest of the prose of the age is too voluminous.—1. Evans
(c) Most of those who use it are probably unaware that assets is itself a singular. Fowler
(d) There were a number of such little reasons.—A. Huxley
(e) The majority of writers never pass that stage .—E. Pound
(f) Much of time is lost.
(g) Much of the sugar is impure.

Rul-(25) A number/the number

A number means many, always takes plural verb.

The number means a definite number, acts as collective noun, takes singular verb.

(a) The number of students opted English in Administrative services is generally small.
(b) The number of candidates appeared in SSC this year was very large.
(c) A number of English books are available in library.
(d) There were a number of students waiting for their turn.

Rule-(26) 'None' usually takes singular verb, but some renowned Grammarians also use plural verbs with none.

(a) It is mistake to suppose that the pronoun 'none' is singular only and must at all costs be followed by singular verb.-Fowler
(b) None was originally used only as singular but it has also acquired a plural meaning. —Nesfield
(c) None is an abbreviated form of not one or no one and would therefore seem to be singular, but in its context it usually has a plural sense.-Vallins

As such none can be used in singular as well as in plural.
(a) None but the brave deserves the reward. (Singular)
(b) None were injured. (Plural)
(c) None of the minor characters were present on the day of rehersal. (Plural)
(d) None of his works shows his capabilities and his calibre. (Singular)

Rule-(27) The ·phrase 'Nothing but' is treated as singular, so it takes singular verb, irrespective of the noun following it, is singular or plural.

(a) Nothing but hill is seen.
(b) Nothing but birds is' seen.
(c) Nothing but girls is there.
(d) Nothing but a student is there.

Rule-(28) If 'no' precedes each of the two singular nouns in a sentence as following, singular verb is used.

(a) No boy and no girl was present in the party.
(b) No man and no woman was swimming at that time.

Rule-(29) Following indefinite words require singular verbs; anybody, anyone, each, every, everyone, everybody, much, no one, one, other, someone, something, somebody.

Has <u>anybody</u> seen my purse?

<u>Anyone</u> is welcome.

<u>Each</u> child gets a prize.

<u>Every</u> dog has its day.

<u>Everyone</u> is welcome.

<u>Everybody</u> is welcome.

<u>Much</u> has been made of his new book.

<u>No one</u> was willing to try.

<u>One</u> of them is lying.

This is my painting. The other is my sister's.

<u>Somebody</u> has stolen my car.

<u>Someone</u> is waiting for you.

<u>Something</u> is worrying Pluto.

Rule-(30) Following indefinite words can have singular or plural verb. If the subject is singular verb will also be singular, if the subject is plural verb will be plural. Such commonly used words are; all, any, enough, most, some.

All she wants is to be happy.

All her dreams have come true.

Any friend of yours is a friend of mine.

Any friends he had were few and far between.

Enough has been said about that already.

Enough people have been hurt already.

Most of his day is spent reading.

Most boys in New Zealand play rugby.

Some fool is firing a rifle in the woodshed.

Some girls play rugby, too.

Rule-(31) Wben the subject and verb are separated, find the subject and verb and make sure they agree. Ignore the words in-between because they do not affect agreement.

(a) The <u>quality</u> of these goods is well known.
(b) Financial help from all the countries <u>was</u> received.
(c) The <u>colour</u> of this shirt is liked by all.
(d) Your <u>view</u> son this matter <u>are</u> supported by all.
(e) The <u>details</u> of the accident <u>were</u> not received by us so far.
(f) The <u>cost</u> of production of steel goods is increasing.
(g) Economic <u>co-operation</u> between India and Pakistan <u>is</u> increasing.
(h) The <u>smell</u> of these flowers is liked by all.
(i) The manager‘s <u>remarks</u> in a newspaper about the conduct of the player <u>were</u> not appreciated by anyone. —(1)
(j) The <u>characters</u> in Shakespeare's *Twelfth Night* <u>lives</u> in a world that has been turned upside-down. Incorrect
(k) The characters in Shakespeare‘s Twelfth Night live in a world that has "been turned upside-down. Correct

Rule-(32) In some sentences the apposition is placed between subject and predicate, the verb will be governed, in number and person by the subject's number and person.

(a) You, my friend, are not guilty of misconduct.
(b) I, manager of this company, am responsible for the loss.
(c) She, his wife, was asking for the address of Rahim.
(d) They, your students, have created a fuss in the ground .

Rule-(33) The relative pronouns (who, whom, which, and that) are either singular or plural, depending on the words they refer to. If the word referred is singular, verb will also be singular, otherwise plural.

(a) It is I who am responsible for the loss.
(b) It is he who is responsible for this loss.
(c) The book that is here is mine.
(d) The books that are here are mine.
(e) The woman who is in black saree is my wife.
(t) The women who are standing there are my sister.

In the above sentences the verb is governed by the antecedent (that comes before the relative pronoun).

Read the following sentences carefully :

(a) He is one of those, who do not attend the meeting. (who refers those)
(b) It is one of the problems that hamper the work. (that refers problems)

Rule-(34) If a sentence compounds a positive and a negative subject and one is plural, the other singular, the verb should agree with the positive subject.

(a) The staff members but not the' principal have decided not to teach on Independence Day.
(b) It is not the teachers but the principal who decides this issue.
(c) It was the speaker, not his ideas, that has provoked the students to riot.

Rule-(35) Many a is distributive in nature and effect, so requires a sigular verb.

(a) Many a man has failed to do his duty.
(b) Many a girl has come to visit the temple today.

Rule-(36) Some verbs are followed by 'as'.These are; regard, describe, represent, portray, depict, mention, define, treat.

(a) You ought to have regarded him as your brother.
(b) He was described by his wife as the most harmless man.
(c) He portrayed him as a typical country farmer.
(d) Someone has defined genius as an infinite capacity for learning.
(e) You should have treated him as your brother.

Rule-(37) Verbs such as ; name, call, term, think, consider, nominate, appoint are not . followed by 'as' :

(a) The chairman nominated Hari secretary of the society.
(b) Ram called him a fool, a rogue and a crook.

(c) Ram calls his wife 'Situ'.
(d) I think him an intelligent man.
(e) I consider it a badly managed organisation.
(f) He acted as principal.
(g) He passed as a gentleman.

Note : Verb 'act'and pass are followed by 'as' ,in following constructions .

Rule-(38) More than one, though its sense is necessarily plural, is treated as a sort of compound of 'one', following its construction, and agrees with a singular noun and takes a singular verb. —Fowler

(a) More than one worker was absent.
(b) More than one student was killed.
(c) More than one workman was killed, not 'workmen' or 'were'. -Fowler

Rule-(39) Note: the construction 'more + noun + than one +...'

Plural verb is used in following constructions.

(a) More books than one have been purchased by her
(b) More girls than one were present in the party.
(c) More students than one have attended the class.
(d) More workmen than one are not traceable.

Rule-(40) 'The following' and 'the undersigned' if used for singular subject/noun the verb will be singular otherwise plural.

(a) The following are the new prices of the items.
(b) Undersigned has taken a decision S.K. Jain.
(c) We the undersigned request the pleasure of your company. S.K. Jain and P.K. Jain.
(d) The following is the summary of the discussions held in the meeting.

Rule-(41) Note : LANGUAGE v/s. PEOPLE

(a) Chinese <u>is</u> a difficult language.
(b) The Chinese <u>are</u> friendly.
(c) French <u>is</u> spoken in many countries.
(d) The French <u>make</u> good wines.
(e) English <u>is</u> easy to learn, isn't it?
(f) The English <u>drink</u> more tea that Americans do.

In (a) Chinese = language takes singular verb. In (b): The Chinese = people of China takes plural verb

INVERSION

In normal english sentences, subject comes before the verb with following constructions :

Subject + Verb + ...

In some situations, like in questions, the order is reversed with following constructions :

Verb + Subject + ...

Such type of constructions, wherein verb comes before the subject, are known as **inversion** .

Inversion of the Verb : *'Certain adverbs and adverb phrases, most with a restrictive or negative sense, can for emphasis be placed first in a sentence or clause and are then followed by the inverted (i.e. interrogative) form of the verb.'* (**Thomson and Martinet**).

Inversion can be of two types.

1. **When 'Auxiliary' comes before the subject** but main verb comes after the subject :
   (a) Never does he go to temple. (b) Hardly does he come here.
2. **When main verb comes before the subject :**
   (a) Round the corner went *Jacob.* (Main verb + subject.)
   (b) Under a tree was sitting an old lady. (Auxiliary+ Main Verb + Subject.)

When to use 'Inversion'?

1. **When a sentence begins with ;hardly, rarely, scarcely, seldom, never, little etc. :**
   (a) Hardly does she go to church.
   (b) Seldom had I seen such a healthy baby.
   (c) Never does she go to temple.
   (d) Scarcely ever did they manage to meet the deadline.
   (e) Rarely is she absent from duty.
   (f) Little do you know how much trouble you are in.
2. **Use of conjuction 'Not only .... but also', inversion is used in such cases :**
   (a) Not only did she watch TV but she also cooked meal.
   (b) Not only does he rob her but he also smashes everything.
3. **Inversion of the verb takes place with 'No sooner' :**
   (a) No sooner had she seen her husband than she hugged him.
   (b) No sooner did he see the dead body of his wife, than he burst into tears.
4. **Inversion of the verb takes place in sentences beginning with following phrases :** ***'Under no circumstances', 'In no way', 'On no account', 'On no condition', 'At no time'***—
   (a) Under no circumstances shall I accept this proposal.
   (b) On no condition will she sell the house.
   (c) In no way will I forgive her.
   (d) On no account must this button be pushed.
5. **With adverbial expressions beginning with 'only'**, such as ; *only yesterday, only the day before yesterday, only last month, only last fortnight, only after a month/ year, only then, only in this way, only when, only by doing this thing, only in a few schools/colleges/countries/continents* etc. :

(a) Only yesterday did he buy that car.
(b) Only by taking risk did he save the life of the minister.
(c) Only by accepting the condition, did he join this job.
(d) Only by shouting was she able to make herself heard.

6. **With adverbial expressions showing place, such as**; *outside the gate, under the table, in the valley, along the border, round the corner, on a hill* etc., inversion of verb takes place :
   (a) In the valley did I see a strange man.
   (b) Out side the gate did he notice something moving.
   (c) On a hill did he find a new revolver.

   With adverbial expressions like; *under a tree, on the bed, ten/five miles beyond the school/college/city, nowhere else* etc., inversion is used :
   (a) Under a tree was sleeping an old lady.
   (b) On the bed was sitting her friend.
   (c) Five miles beyond the city was a mysterious palace.

7. In sentences beginning with; Here/There/Away/Out/Up/Indoor/Out doors/In/down, inversion of verb takes place :
   (a) Down fell a dozen apples. (b) In came the child weeping.
   (c) Here comes the train. (d) There goes Sita.
   (e) Away went Ram.

NOTE *When a pronoun is used as subject , no inversion takes place in such sentences :*

(a) There she goes. (b) Away he went. (c) Here she comes.

8. Sentences beginning with 'so + adverb of manner', show inversion :
   (a) So well did he organise the function, that everyone started praising him.
   (b) So absurdly did he speak that everyone was offended.
   (c) So suspicious did he become that he couldn't talk to her properly.

9. **Sentences beginning with** ; *to such a degree/to such an extent/ to such a point/to such a length, show inversion :*
   (a) To such an extent he made the investment that people started trusting him.
   (b) To such a degree they made a noise that Principal had to call the police.

10. **The most common use of inversion is in the forming of questions.** We use the auxiliary verbs 'be' (for progressive and passive forms), 'have' (for perfect forms) and 'do' (for most other forms). Modal verbs can also be inverted to form questions :
    (a) **Were** they ready when you arrived? (b) Where **was** it made?
    (c) **Have** you ever visited France? (d) Where **do** you live?
    (e) What **should** we do now?

11. **When we are making wishes**, we can use inversion :
    (a) May you both live happily ever after! (b) May you live long!

12. **In question tags inversion takes place** :
    (a) Tomorrow is Sunday, isn't it ? (b) She left yesterday, didn't she?

13. **In following type of sentences inversion of the verb is used** :
    (a) Were I a bird! (Imaginary hope/ wish)

(b) Had he come to me, I would have helped him.(conditional sentence)
(If he had come to me, I would have helped him.)
(c) Sonia went to church, so did I.
(d) She did not visit the Agra, neither did I .
(e) He did not go there, nor did I.

NOTE *The inversion takes place with 'so, neither, nor', when there is similarity of action, as in sentences (c), (d), (e) above.*

(f) ''Let us play cricket'', proposed Ram.
''Let us go to market'', said Sita.
(g) ''Do it for me'', said Krishna.
''Go there'', instructed Rahim.

NOTE *When reporting verb is placed after the reported speech, inversion takes place as in sentences (f) s (g) above. But if a pronoun is used as subject as in following sentences ,no inversion takes place :*

(h) 'Do it for me', she said (i) 'Go there', he instructed.

CORRECT YOURSELF EXERCISE : THE VERB

CYE : 01 Spotting the error (Inversion) :

1. "Under no circumstances (A) I can help you in (B) this venture", (C) said Sita. (D)
2. "I don't like (A) such a bright (B) colour nor she does", (C) he said to Ram. (D)
3. Every member of his family is (A) addicted to (B) gambling (C) and so John is. (D)
4. Never before (A) I had been asked (B) to go there (C) by bus. (D)
5. On no account (A) this switch must (B) be touched. (C)
6. "Seldom I had (A) seen such a (B) beautiful girl'', (C) said Mohanti. (D)
7. Under a tree (A) was sleeping an (B) old lady (C) with her young child. (D)
8. To such a (A) degree he created (B) the problems that (C) people thrashed him. (D)
9. Not only (A) she watched the news (B) but she also (C) cooked food. (D)

10. No sooner the plane landed at the airport than a group of armed
A B C
commandos surrounded it.
D

CYE : 02 Fill in the blanks with suitable forms of verbs given in brackets :

1. He (live) in Kolkata for five years.
2. At the moment he (play) in the park.
3. I (wish) I knew the girl's name.
4. She(take) a bath when the telephone rang.
5. I (tell) already you that you should work hard.
6. Ram always (remember) that honesty is the best policy.
7. Ramesh (leave) his house before I called on him.
8. They always (believe) that love is stronger than hate.
9. She told me that her mother (go) to the doctor half an hour before.
10. I (wash) my hands when he came.
11. I (tell)already you what to do under these circumstances.
12. It is high time you (start) working with full zeal.

CYE : 03 Fill in the blanks with suitable forms of the verbs given in brackets :

1. Ramesh (pass) the post-office on his way to office every day.
2. He (watch) television when Ramesh came in.
3. He (tell) me that she had never met you.
4. He (read) since 2 O' clock.
5. If you promise to work hard I (allow) you to go on leave.
6. The doctor (arrive) just before Sita went away.
7. The sun (shine) by day and the moon by night.
8. She (attend) college since May last.
9. You (receive) your award tomorrow.
10. I (have) dinner last night at 9 O'clock.
11. I (write) a letter before I went to play.
12. He (read) the newspaper when Ram came in.

CYE : 04 Supply the correct tense form of the verbs given in brakets :

(A) A farmer was very fond of the two animals.When he (come) out for a stroll, these two creatures (amuse) him. One day as the farmer (walk) in the garden, these pets (run) away from him.He.... (search) for them but of no avail.

(B) He (be) a black man. One winter morning he (look) out of his window as he (dress) . He (not hate) the winter now, for he (know) that it (be) merely the spring asleep and that the flowers (rest).

CYE : 05 Rewrite the following sentences using suitable forms of the verbs given in brakets, to fill in the blanks :

1. When they left this morning, the sun................ (shine)
2. The Chairman cannot see anybody as he .... some letters. (dictate)
3. If it is possible, we .... to Chennai tomorrow. (go)
4. Ram .... from fever since yesterday night. (suffer)
5. We .... nothing to eat for three days. (have)
6. He said that he .... for a walk today in the evening. (go)
7. If I were you I .... to accept the bribe. (refuse)
8. We .... at the news of his defeat. (surprise)
9. He.................. while stealing the jewels. (catch)
10. The children ....(please)at the prospect of going for a picnic.
11. She .... of herself. (ashamed)
12. Ravi Shankar .... by the Music Society. (honour)
13. .... you .... playing cricket? (like)
14. .... the doctor .... to see you yesterday? (come)
15. .... it .... all the year round here? (rain)

CYE : 06 Fill in the blanks with suitable forms of the verbs given in brakets. Rewrite the sentences :

1. She saw that the clock.............. (to stop)
2. He replied that he .... better. (to feel)
3. Ramesh .... so hard that he is certain to succeed. (to work)
4. He speaks as one who. .... (to know)
5. So long as the rain .... I stayed in office. (to continue)
6. If I go to market I .... a pen for you. (to bring)
7. A child always....................magazines about ghosts. (to enjoy)
8. He .... to Delhi last week. (to go)
9. They .... in Jaipur for three years. (to stay)
10. They............. here for the last two hours. (to wait)
11. I .... to her day before yesterday. (to write)
12. These students .... cricket next Sunday. (to play)
13. It .... when they went out. (to rain)
14. Cow .... grass. (to eat)
15. We .... to the pictures yesterday. (go)

CYE : 07 Fill in the blanks with suitable forms of the verbs given in brakets. Rewrite the sentences :

1. She .... letters yesterday. (write)
2. The construction of new hotel .... stopped. (be)
3. I .... English for three years now. (study)
4. I .... her for a very long time. (know)
5. He................ away last week (go)
6. We.................. tennis together last June. (play)
7. I enjoy .... a good social film. (watch)

8. The little boy admitted that he .... the glass. (break)
9. She forgot .... the door when she went to market. (lock)
10. As she .... there, someone bumped into her. (wait)
11. He will unlock the door when he ....here. (get)
12. He would have done it if you .... him so. (tell)
13. He is used to .... on a hard bed so he does not mind. (sleep)
14. He managed to avoid ....hit by the bat. (be)

CYE : 08 Rewrite the following with the correct forms of the verbs given within the brackets :

1. I (sleep) soundly and (dream) that a dog (enter) the room. I (spring) off the bed.
2. The shot (wound) the elephant. It (rush) back into the forest.
3. We (plan) to go to a hill station. Last year we (go) to Shimla. We (decide) to go somewhere else this time.
4. Railways (connect) almost all the big cities and towns. In olden days people (use) to travel on horse-back or bullock carts. Travelling (become) easy now. We can imagine the difficulty the people (face)in the past.

CYE : 09 Rewrite the following sentences with the correct tense forms of the verbs given in brackets :

(A) Yesterday I (go) to the market to buy a pen. I ought to have(purchase) a good one but I (choose) a cheap one with the result that it (do) not write smoothly now.

(B) I (wake) up early in the morning. I (go) out for a walk. Suddenly the wind (blow) violently. Many trees were (bring) down.

(C) The next morning his landlord (bring) him two pieces of news with his breakfast. One was that someone had (plant) a most beautiful climbing rose in the lane , the other was that Mr. Ramesh couldn't be (find) anywhere in the village. Everyone was (worry) about him.

(D) A walk through a garden ..(be) good for health and mind.We (go) for stroll in the Company Garden last Sunday. The flowers (present) a scene of colourfulness and we (feel) very happy.

CYE : 10 Rewrite the following sentences, using correct forms of the verbs given in brackets :

1. His mother (die) three months ago.
2. We were taught at school that water (boil) at 212'F.
3. He knew that I had (pass).
4. I should be pleased if he (not come).
5. When Sahani (be) on his way to the railway station it (begin) to rain.
6. Bakani (collect) stamps since childhood.
7. Now tests (carry) on to find out the reaction of the new medicines on animals.
8. I (go) for a walk daily in the evening. Last evening I (come) back from office rather late.Even though it (be) 7 p.m., I still (go), for my walk as usual. On (return) home I (find) that my little son (injure) his arm seriously. I (rush) to the nearby doctor for first-aid.

CYE : 11 Fill in the blanks with suitable verbs in agreement with the subjects. Select one from those given in bracket :

(a) Either the mother or the daughter .... made this pudding. (have, has)
(b) A sum of fifty thousand rupees .... paid to him for this piece of land. (were, was)
(c) A variety of subjects .... taught in this school. (is, are)
(d) The father and his daughter .... coming to us today. (is, are)

CYE : 12 Fill in the blanks with the correct forms of the verbs :

(A) I love nature.The spring season (be) the best of all seasons.There (be) freshness all around. Nature (breath) a new life and (look) colourful like a bride. Beautiful flowers (dance) merrily.

(B) The Taj Mahal (be) beautiful building.The Taj (stand) on the bank of the river Yamuna.It is (make) of white marble. It (have) four marble minarets on which the great dome (stand).Shah Jahan (build) it in memory of his beloved queen, Mumtaz, and it (cost) over three crore of rupees.

CYE : 13 Fill in the blanks with the correct forms of the verbs :

1. Sound sleep (be) necessary for good health. Every body(dream) during sleep. Sometimes the dreams (be) pleasant and at others, unpleasant. Last week I (have) a very bad dream. I (dream) that my class, accompanied by our teachers,(go) to Shimla for the weekend.
2. Last Sunday (be) a bad day for me as I (spend) the whole of it in bed. When I (get) up at 7 O'clock, I (have) a severe headache and (perspire). My mother (take) my temperature I (consult) a doctor .He(check)me thoroughly.

CYE : 14 Fill in the blanks with correct forms of the verbs given in the brackets :

1. A flock of sheep_____grazing in the ground. (is/are)
2. Time and tide _____for none. (wait/waits)
3. More than five persons____signed the complaint. (have/has)
4. One third of the work______left incomplete. (was/were)
5. Neither he nor his sister_____invited. (was/were)
6. Sachin is one of the players who _____been selected for the match. (have/has)
7. One of the students of our class______selected. (was/were)
8. Age and experience_____a man wise. (make/makes)
9. Ten times fifty______five hundred. (is/are)
10. It is I who ____ to answer him. (is/am)
11. The sun_____in the east. (rise)
12. I_____her last weak at her residence . (meet)

CYE : 15 Fill in the blanks with correct forms of the verbs given in the brackets :

1. What ______ the latest news (is/are)
2. Fifty rupees ______ not a big amount. (is/are)
3. The United States ______ a powerful nation. (is/are)
4. Economics ______ an interesting subject. (is/are)
5. Cattle ______ grazing in the field. (is/are)
6. Neither of us ______ ready to go there (is/are)
7. Billiards ______ my favourite game. (is/are)
8. What I say and what I think ______ my personal matters. (are/is)
9. Both of them ______ good friends. (is/are)
10. What ______ the news. (is/are)
11. Honesty ______ the best policy. (be)
12. She ______ a letter now. (write)

CYE : 16 Fill in the blanks with suitable Verbs :

1. Half of the apples ______ ripe. (is/are)
2. Half of the land ______ uncultivated. (is /are)
3. Barking dogs never ______ . (bite/bites)
4. A lot of food ______ still lying on the table. (is/are)
5. Fifty rupees ______ not a big sum for him. (is/are)
6. The Himalayas ______ a range of mountains. (is/are)
7. Neither she nor her son ______ arrived so far. (has/have)
8. It is I who ______ to bear the loss. (is/am)
9. I wish I ______ a writer. (was/were)
10. Your trousers ______ very tight. (is/are)
11. She ______ a letter to me last month. (write)
12. I wish I ______ a queen. (be)

CYE : 17 Fill in the blanks with correct forms of the verbs given in the brackets :

1. Suraj, rather than his friends ______ guilty. (is/are)
2. Quarters of this type ______ three bed rooms. (has/have)
3. Oil and water ______ not mix fully. (do/does)
4. A bunch of keys ______ found by her. (was/were)
5. His trousers ______ not clean . (is/are)
6. A flock of sheep ______ grazing in the field. (is/are)
7. Time and tide ______ for none. (wait/waits)
8. Everyone of the students ______ present in function. (was/were)
9. I wish I ______ a beautiful girl. (was/were)
10. A set of combs ______ been lost. (has/have)
11. I ______ cricket, when she came. (play)
12. We ______ that she would visit the college soon . (expect)

CYE : 18 Fill in the blanks with suitable forms of the verb :

1. I_____ Sita for a long time. (not see)
2. Who_____the Taj Mahal? (build)
3. Did you____the poem ? (learn)
4. Ram_____here at 5 p.m daily. (come)
5. I _____here for three years. (live)
6. She will come here if you ____ him. (invite)
7. I_____her letter two days ago. (receive)
8. Sita will assist you if you _____her. (ask)
9. She_____come till now. (not)
10. He_______here for the last five years. (work)
11. Had she worked hard she_____. (pass)
12. He said earth_____round the sun. (move)

CYE : 19 Correct the following sentences :

1. Rahul as well as his sisters were present in the party.
2. Suresh and not his relatives were arrested.
3. The Principal and the Warden was against the proposal.
4. Either Ram or his friends was guilty.
5. Neither Ram nor his friend Shyam were present in the party.
6. The horse and carriage are at the gate.
7. His kindness and benevolence are well known to everyone.
8. His friend and benefactor were present there to protect him.
9. The jury was divided in their opinion in that case.
10. The wages of sin are death.
11. Three parts of the house were left for me to live.
12. Rahul together with his elder brother were present in the meeting.
13. Neither of these questions are right.
14. He qualified himself as an engineer.
15. She has enlisted herself in the nursing college.

CYE : 20 Correct the following sentences :

1. Either he or I is to represent the school.
2. Neither you nor he are to go now.
3. The mob move towards the collectorate.
4. The second innings were spoiled due to fire.
5. Each hour and each minute are to be utilised by you.
6. Every young and every old were happy to receive a gift.
7. Not only the Tajmahal but also other monuments is worth seeing.
8. The house with all its furniture were auctioned at a very low bid.
9. The peacock like other birds have wings to fly.
10. There is another schools better than this.
11. The poors are never reliable.

12. All the milk were used in the preparation of sweets.
13. All the animal were given the proper diet.
14. She apprised the inspector all that have happened yesterday night.
15. Most of the person are reliable.

CYE : 21 Correct the following sentences :

1. About half of the girls was present in the hall.,
2. Half of the sugar were spoiled due to heavy rains.
3. The apparatus purchased by the Nagar Parishad were very old.
4. The advice of his friend are indeed valuable.
5. Men after men were coming to visit the art gallery.
6. One month after another have passed.
7. His shoes is shining.
8. Approximately ten sheeps were grazing in the college ground.
9. A pair of shoes are purchased by her for her husband.
10. There are many fishes in the aquarium.
11. Each of the sports women were given a certificate.
12. I wish I will be the minister.
13. She ordered as if she is my elder sister.
14. God saves our queen!
15. He needs not go to market.

CYE : 22 Correct the following sentences :

1. More than one girl were killed in the accident.
2. God blesses you with success!
3. Financial help from all the quarters were received.
4. The quality of these items are appreciated by everyone.
5. The fragrance of these beautiful flowers are liked by all.
6. More workman than one are not traceable.
7. He said, 'Plenty of milk are required for the party.'
8. A lot of books and magazines was destroyed by the fire.
9. The number of students opted Hindi in RAS are generally large.
10. A number of English magazines is available in the college library.

CYE : 23 Correct the following sentences :

1. It is I who is responsible for the loss in the business.
2. The women who is standing there are my sisters.
3. He is one of those who does know anything about the incident.
4. It is one of the problems that was taken care of by the civil administration.
5. Nothing but monkeys are seen.
6. No man and no woman were allowed to enter without payment.
7. Much of the time were wasted by the students.
8. More than one man were killed there.

9. Economic cooperation between India and China are decreasing day by day.
10. More students than one has solutions in the annual function.

Solutions CYE : 01

1. (B), 2. (C), 3. (D), 4. (B), 5. (B)
6. (A), 7. (E) Correct sentence, 8. (B), 9. (B)
10. (A)

Solutions CYE : 02

1. He has been living in Kolkata for five years .
2. At the moment he is playing in the park.
3. I wish I knew the girl's name.
4. She was taking a bath when the telephone rang.
5. I have already told you that you should work hard.
6. Ram always remembers that honesty is the best policy.
7. Ramesh had left his house before I called on him.
8. They always believe that love is stronger than hate.
9. She told me that her mother had gone to the doctor half an hour before.
10. I was washing my hands when he came.
11. I have already told you what to do under these circumstances.
12. It is high time you started working with full zeal.

Solutions CYE : 03

1. Ramesh passes the post-office on his way to office every day.
2. He was watching television when Ramesh came in.
3. He told me that she had never met you.
4. He has been reading since 2 O' clock.
5. If you promise to work hard I shall allow you to go on leave.
6. The doctor arrived just before Sita went away.
7. The sun shines by day and the moon by night.
8. She has been attending college since May last.
9. You will receive your award tomorrow.
10. I had dinner last night at 9 O'clock.
11. I had written a letter before I went to play.
12. He was reading the newspaper when Ram came in.

Solutions CYE : 04

(A) A farmer was very fond of the two animals.When he came out for a stroll, these two creatures amused him. One day as the farmer was walking in the garden, these pets ran away from him.He searched for them but of no avail.

(B) was, looked , was dressing, did not hate, knew, was, were resting.

Solutions CYE : 05

1. When they left this morning, the sun was shining.
2. The Chairman cannot see anybody as he is dictating some letters.
3. If it is possible, we shall go to Chennai tomorrow.
4. Ram has been suffering from fever since yesterday night.

5. We have / had nothing to eat for three days.
6. He said that he would go for a walk today in the evening.
7. If I were you I would refuse to accept the bribe.
8. We were surprised at the news of his defeat.
9. He was caught while stealing the jewels.
10. The children were pleased at the prospect of going for a picnic.
11. She was ashamed of herself.
12. Ravi Shankar was honoured by the Music Society.
13. Do you like playing cricket?
14. Did the doctor come to see you yesterday?
15. Does it rain all the year round here?

Solutions CYE : 06

1. She saw that the clock had stopped
2. He replied that he was feeling better.
3. Ramesh is working so hard that he is certain to succeed.
4. He speaks as one who knows.
5. So long as the rain continued I stayed in office.
6. If I go to market I shall bring a pen for you.
7. A child always enjoys magazines about ghosts.
8. He went to Delhi last week.
9. They have been staying in Jaipur for three years.
10. They have been waiting here for the last two hours.
11. I wrote to her day before yesterday.
12. These students will play cricket next Sunday.
13. It was raining when they went out.
14. Cow eats grass.
15. We went to the pictures yesterday..

Solutions CYE : 07

1. She wrote letters yesterday.
2. The construction of new hotel was stopped.
3. I have studied English for three years now.
4. I have known her for a very long time.
5. He went away last week.
6. We played tennis together last June.
7. I enjoy watching a good social film.
8. The little boy admitted that he had broken the glass.
9. She forgot to lock the door when she went to market.
10. As she was waiting there, someone bumped into her.
11. He will unlock the door when he gets here.
12. He would have done it if you had told him so.
13. He is used to sleeping on a hard bed so he does not mind.
14. He managed to avoid being hit by the bat.

Solutions CYE : 08

1. I was sleeping soundly and dreamt that a dog had entered the room. I sprang off the bed.
2. The shot wounded the elephant. It rushed back into the forest.
3. We are planning to go to a hill station. Last year we went to Shimla. We have decided to go somewhere else this time.
4. Railways connect almost all the big cities and towns. In olden days people used to travel on horse-back or bullock carts. Travelling has become easy now. We can imagine the difficulty the people faced in the past.

Solutions CYE : 09

(A) Yesterday I went to market to buy a pen. I ought to have purchased a good one but I chose a cheap one with the result that it does not write smoothly now.

(B) I woke up early in the morning. I went out for a walk. Suddenly the wind blew violently. Many trees were brought down.

(C) The next morning his landlord brought him two pieces of news with his breakfast. One was that someone had planted a most beautiful climbing rose in the lane, the other was that Mr. Ramesh couldn't be found anywhere in the village. Everyone was worried about him.

(D) A walk through a garden is good for health and mind.We went for stroll in the Company Garden last Sunday. The flowers presented a scene of colourfulness and we felt very happy.

Solutions CYE : 10

1. His mother died three months ago.
2. We were taught at school that water boils at 212'F.
3. He knew that I had passed.
4. I should be pleased if he does not come.
5. When Sahani was on his way to the railway station it began to rain.
6. Bakani has been collecting stamps since childhood.
7. Now tests are being carried on to find out the reaction of the new medicines on animals.
8. I go for a walk daily in the evening. Last evening I came back from office rather late.Even though it was 7 p.m., I still went, for my walk as usual. On returning home I found that my little son had injured his arm seriously. I rushed to the nearby doctor for first aid.

Solutions CYE : 11

(a) Either the mother or the daughter has made this pudding.

(b) A sum of fifty thousand rupees was paid to him for this piece of land.

(c) A variety of subjects is taught in this school.

(d) The father and his daughter are coming to us today.

Solutions CYE : 12

(A) . is, is , breathes, looks, dance.

(B) . is, stands,made,has , stands , built, cost.

Solutions CYE : 13

1. is, dreams,are, had, dreamed, had gone.
2. was,spent, got, had, was perspiring,took, consulted, checked.

Solutions CYE : 14

1. is, 2. wait, 3. have, 4.was, 5. was, 6. have,
7. was, 8. makes, 9. is, 10. am, 11. rises , 12. met.

Solutions CYE : 15

1. is, 2. is, 3. is, 4. is, 5. are, 6. is,
7. is, 8. are, 9. are, 10. is, 11. is, 12. is writing.

Solutions CYE : 16

1. are, 2. is, 3. bite, 4. is, 5. is, 6. are,
7. has, 8. am, 9. were, 10. are, 11.wrote, 12. were.

Solutions CYE : 17

1. Is, 2. Have, 3. Do, 4. Is, 5. Are, 6. Is,
7. Wait, 8. Was, 9. Were, 10. Has, 11. was playing,
12. had expected.

Solutions CYE : 18

1. have not seen, 2. built, 3. learn, 4. comes, 5. have been living,
6. invite, 7. received, 8. ask, 9. has not, 10. has been working,
11. would have been passed, 12. moves.

Solutions CYE : 19

1. Rahul as well as his sisters was present in the party.
2. Suresh and not his relatives was arrested.
3. The Principal and the Warden were against the proposal.
4. Either Ram or his friends were guilty.
5. Neither Ram nor his friend Shyam was present in the party.
6. The horse and carriage is at the gate.
7. His kindness and benevolence is well known to everyone.
8. His friend and benefactor was present there to protect him.
9. The jury were divided in their opinion in that case.
10. The wages of sin is death.
11. Three parts of the house was left for me to live.
12. Rahul together with his elder brother was present in the meeting.
13. Neither of these questions is right.
14. He qualified as an engineer.
15. She has enlisted in the nursing college.

Solutions CYE : 20

1. Either he or I am to represent the school.
2. Neither you nor he is to go now.
3. The mob moves towards the collectorate.
4. The second innings was spoiled due to fire.
5. Each hour and each minute is to be utilised by you.
6. Every young and every old was happy to receive a gift.

7. Not only the Tajmahal but also other monuments are worth seeing.
8. The house with all its furniture was auctioned at a very low bid.
9. The peacock like other birds has wings to fly.
10. There is another school better than this.
11. The poor are never reliable.
12. All the milk was used in the preparation of sweets.
13. All the animals were given the proper diet.
14. She apprised the inspector all that has happened yesterday night.
15. Most of the persons are reliable.

Solutions CYE : 21

1. About half of the girls were present in the hall.
2. Half of the sugar was spoiled due to heavy rains.
3. The apparatus purchased by the Nager fouished was very old.
4. The advice of his friend was indeed valuable.
5. Man after man was coming to visit the art gallery.
6. One month after another has passed.
7. His shoes are shining.
8. Approximately ten sheep were grazing in the college ground.
9. A pair of shoes is purchased by her for her husband.
10. There are many fish in the aquarium.
11. Each of the sports women was given a certificate.
12. I wish I were the minister.
13. She ordered as if she were my elder sister.
14. God save our queen!
15. He need not go to market.

Solutions CYE : 22

1. More than one girl was killed in the accident.
2. God bless you with success!
3. Financial help from all the quarters was received.
4. The quality of these items is appreciated by everyone.
5. The fragrance of these beautiful flowers is liked by all.
6. More workman than one is not traceable.
7. He said, 'Plenty of milk is required for the party.'
8. A lot of books and magazines were destroyed by the fire.
9. The number of students opted Hindi in RAS is generally large.
10. A number of English magazines are available in the college library.

Solutions CYE : 23

1. It is I who am responsible for the loss in the business.
2. The women who are standing there are my sisters.
3. He is one of those who do know anything about the incident.
4. It is one of the problems that were taken care of by the civil administration.
5. Nothing but monkeys is seen.
6. No man and no woman was allowed to enter without payment.
7. Much of the time was wasted by the students.
8. More than one man was killed there.
9. Economic cooperation between India and China is decreasing day by day.
10. More students than one have participated in the annual function.

8

Modals

Modal auxiliaries are special *auxiliary verbs* that express the degree of certainty of the action in the sentence, or **the attitude or opinion of the writer /speaker** concerning the action. Some common modal auxiliaries are ***may, might, can , could,will, shall, would, should ,must,need, dare , ought to, used to*.('Need,dare, used to' are called Semi Modals.)**

Modals are verbs which 'help' other verbs to express a meaning : it is important to note that 'modal verbs' convey no meaning by themselves.

Special features of modal auxiliaries.

(i) **Modal verbs are NEVER used with other auxiliary verbs** such as ***do, does, did* etc.** The negative is formed simply by adding 'not' after the verb; questions are formed by inversion of the verb and subject :
(a) You should not do that.
(b) Could you pick me up when I've finished?

(ii) Modal verbs **NEVER change form** ; you can never add an '-s' or '-ed' with modals, for example.

(iii) **Modal verbs are NEVER followed by *'to'*, with the exception of *'ought to'*.**

(iv) They do **not** have **infinitive form,** modal verbs do not take 'to' before them.

(v) **Two modals can never go together**.

(vi) We always use base(V-1)form of the verbs with Modals.

(vii) What sort of meanings do modals give to other verbs :

The meaning are usually connected with ideas of DOUBT, CERTAINTY, POSSIBILITY, PROBABILITY, OBLIGATION and PERMISSION (or lack of these). You will see that modal verbs are not used to talk about things that definitely exist, or events that definitely happened.

A LIST OF MODAL VERBS AND THEIR FUNCTIONS

Let's look at each modal verb separately, and the functions they help to express :

A. May/might :

I. Use of May :

1. *To show or ask for permission 'may' is used* :

(a) May I go now? (Seeking permission)
Yes you may. (Giving permission)

(b) May I borrow two books from the library? (Seeking permission)
You may borrow one book at a time. (Giving permission)

(c) May I come in? (Seeking permission)
Yes you may. (Giving permission)

(d) May I watch television tonight ? (Seeking permission)
Yes, you may. (Giving permission)

2. *'May' is also used for making informal request :*

(a) May I have the salt please?
(b) May I borrow your pen?

3. 'May' and 'Might' are used in case the sentence expresses *present or future possibility* :

We can use either of 'may' or 'might' to express present or future possibility , but use of 'might' slightly increases the element of doubt or uncertainty :

(a) The sky is cloudy, it may rain today.
(b) The sky is not cloudy but a change in weather is always possible; it might rain today (remote possibility).
(c) He has purchased hundred tickets of lottery, he may win a prize (possibility).
He might win the first prize. (remote possibility)

The use of 'may' shows possibility while use of 'might' shows remote possibility.

4. *'May' is used* for *expressing good wishes, desires in formal english :*

(a) May God bless you ! (b) May you live long !

5. *'May / Might' is also used for expressing 'purpose'.*

(a) We eat so that we may live.
(b) He works hard so that he may earn good livelihood.
(c) I play so that I may have good health.
(d) They died so that we might live.

6. 'May' can also be used *to show astonishment* and *for seeking the knowledge of a thing* :

(a) Who may be my friend here? (Astonishment)
(b) How old she may be? (Knowledge)
(c) When may we expect you? (Knowledge)

7. *'May' is not used in the interrogative sentences* **unless it occurs after a 'Wh'- word** :

(a) When may we expect you? (= When are you likely to arrive?)
(b) What may be the result of the new taxation policy?

But a construction with 'be + likely or think' is more usual :

(a) When are you likely to arrive?
(b) What do you think the result will be?

II Use of Might :

1. The use of 'might' for making request **expresses more politeness, hesitation or lack of confidence** of the speaker :

(a) Might I borrow your golden necklace?
(b) Might I talk to the P.M.?
(c) Might I borrow your car?

2. ***'Might' is past eqivalent of 'may'***. While transforming a sentence from direct to indirect narration, 'may' is changed to 'might' if the reporting verbs are in 'past'.

(a) He asked if he might come in.
(b) He said that it might rain that day

3. *Use of 'May and might' in perfect tense :*

'May' is used in perfect tense when you are not certain about a past action. When the uncertainty no longer exists in the present (*i.e.* something did not happen but it was possible) then only 'might' is used in perfect tense.

(a) He may have been wounded.

(We do not know so far, but he is perhaps injured, possibility exists.)

(b) He has not arrived so far. He may have taken a wrong way. (We don't know the actual position, but as he has not arrived so far, so the prossibility is that he may have taken a wrong way.)

(c) He might have been wounded. [that was a possibility in the past. (but he was not wounded.)

(d) You might have invited me to your wedding (but you didn't invite me).

(e) She might have come, if we asked her. (but we didn't ask her)

4. ***Use of 'Might' in conditional sentences*** :

'Might' (not may) is used in conditional sentences when the expression is introduced by a verb in the past tense :

(a) If you invited her she might attend the party.

(b) If he came he might sing a song.

B. Can

1. *'Can' is used to express* ***physical or mental ability/capacity/capability :***

(a) I can solve this puzzle. (b) Can you lift this suitcase?
(c) He can read without glasses. (d) Can you speak French?

2. 'Can' is also used *to denote ability arising out of the circumstances*. It is usually meant to express **'are you in a position to do** so?' :

(a) Can you lend me ten lacs rupees?

(Are you in a position to do so ? Are you having this much amount surplus?)

(b) Can you attend the meeting tomorrow? (Are you free tomorrow?)

3. ***In questions with 'Wh' words*** *'can' denotes puzzleness / impatience/ anger of the speaker :*

(a) What can he do ? (b) What can she say, I wonder?
(c) Where can he go? (d) How can she resign?

4. 'Can' also *shows the* ***'circumstantial possibility' :***

(a) You can ski on the hills now a days. (As there is enough snow)

(b) You can go there by road now. (As the road is repaired now)

I. May and Can

'May' and 'Can' are used *for seeking or granting permission in present and future* :

1. *With first person :*

(a) I can meet the chairman whenever I want.

(It means, I have already been granted permission.)

(b) I can purchase stationary items whenever I need.

(It means, I have alreay been given authority.)

We can also use **'may'** in above construction but the use of **'can'** is more common :

(a) I may purchase stationery items whenever I need.

(b) I may meet the chairman whenever I want.

2. *With second person* : 'May' is usually used **when the permission is being given** by the speaker :

(a) You may park your vehicle here.

(It means : I give you permission to park your vehicle here.It does not mean that you have authority to park your vehicle here.)

The use of 'can' refers the authority / right of the person :

(a) You can park your vehicle here.(You have authority to park your vehicle here.)

(b) You can take rest in library room.

It means :You have an authority. / The competent authority has allowed you.

3. *With third person* : The use of 'may' refers the permission given by the speaker, as above :

(a) He may take my umbrella. (b) He may take my scooter.

(c) I give him permission ....

We can also use '**can**' in such sentences :

(d) He can take my car. (e) He can use my phone.

The use of 'can' denotes the right or authority of the subject or it denotes that the relations between speaker and listner are so informal that he doesn't need any permission (example (d), (e) above), while the use of 'may' usually denotes the permission granted by somebody else (sentences (a), (b) above).

Note the difference in the following sentences :

(a) In certain circumstances an officer may ask a driver to take a vision test.

(b) An officer can ask a driver to take a vision test.

(c) If allowed, an accused person may appeal against the judgement of High Court.

(d) An accused person can appeal against the judgement of High court in criminal cases.

'May' shows the authority given by someone else. 'Can' shows authority lying with the subject.

II. 'May not' and 'Cannot'

The use of ***'may not'*** *denotes* ***improbability/uncertainty***, while ***'cannot'*** *denotes* ***impossibility*** :

(a) The news may not be true. (may or may not be true)

(b) The news cannot be true. (There is no possibility of its come out to be true)

(c) You may go from A to B, by changing train at C or you may go by way of D, but you cannot go direct. (As there is no direct route from A to B.)

(d) You cannot go there by water. (As there is no water route.)

III. Can/Could

1. 'Could you?' is a very good way of making a request.It denotes more politeness and courteousness :

(a) Could you lend me your car for a day?

(b) Could you lend me your Sofaset?

(c) Could you please send me an application form?

2. The use of ***'could' refers past ability***. It then means–'was able to' :

(a) When I was young, I could climb any tree.

(b) When Ram was young, he could swim across this river.

3. ***'Could' is used in present context with conditions :***

(a) Could you operate the machine by yourself? (if it becomes necessary)

(b) Could you get another job? (if you lose this)

(c) I could get you a ballpen. (if you want one)

In the first two examples 'could' can be replaced by 'would be able'.

4. *The use of 'could' in perfect tense* shows **such a past possibility that didn't take place or the action was actually not performed :**

(a) He could have caught the train, if he had hurried. (But he didn't catch the train.)

(b) He could have done it with out much problem. (But he didn't do it.)

(c) He could have sent a message. (But he didn't send.)

(d) I could have lent you the money. Why didn't you ask me?

The use of 'could' in above construction can also express irritation at or reproach for the non performance of an action :

(e) You could have informed me...(means—I am annoyed/ disappointed that you didn't inform me.)

NOTE ***'Could /might' in perfect tense can also be used to express possibility :***

(a) I wonder how Sarla knew about Anita's engagement.

She could /might have heard it from Sunita. (Perhaps she heard it from Sunita.)

We can use might or could in interrogative also :

(b) Could/ Might the bank have made a mistake? (Do you think it is possible that the bank (has) made a mistake?)

But in the negative sentences the meanings are different :

(c) Anita might not have seen Ram yesterday. (perhaps she didn't see him)

(d) Anita couldn't have seen Ram yesterday. (Anita and Ram were in different towns yesterday.)

5. **'Could' is also used as *past tense form of 'can'*** in indirect narrations or otherwise :

(a) Ramesh told me that he could lend me his umbrella.

(b) I did all that I could.

6. *'Could' is also used in **unreal conditions :***

(a) If I had ten crores of rupees, I could build a temple.(I don't have ten crores.)

(b) If I had wings, I could fly to Himalayas.(I don't have wings , neither I could have.)

7. 'Could' is also used to **express general permission in the past :**

(a) On Sundays we could (were allowed to) stay up late.

(b) On holidays I could use company's car.

8. 'Could' is also used *to express **presumption or probability :***

(a) I wonder where Shyam is. He could be in the club. (Perhaps he is in the club.)

(b) I wonder why Sita isn't here so far? She could still be waiting for a taxi.

(Perhaps she is still waiting for a taxi.)

In the interrogative we can use either 'could or might' :

(a) Might/ Could she be waiting for us at the railway station?

(Do you think she is waiting .....?)

But in the negative there is a difference of meaning between 'could' and 'might' :

(a) She might not be driving the car herself.

(Perhaps she isn't driving the car herself.)

(b) She couldn't be driving the car herself.

(It means—'This is impossible. She can't drive.')

9. Use of the negative interrogative form, ***'Couldn't I?'* shows that the speaker expects an affirmative answer :**

(a) Couldn't I pay by cheque? (b) Couldn't I pay in cash ?

C. Shall /Will

As per traditional grammar '**shall**' is used with first person(I /we)and '**will**' is used with second and third person to ***denote pure future actions***. As modals, when '**shall**' is used with second and third person and '**will**' is used with first person, they ***denote determination, threat,*** warning or promise.

I. Shall

1. *The use of* ***'shall' in first person*** *denotes a* ***pure future action****, while use of 'shall' in* ***second and third person*** *denotes,* ***promise, determination, threat or warning*** *:*

(a) I shall go to market tomorrow. (Future action)
(b) He shall pay you on Monday. (Promise)
(c) He shall work hard to achieve success. (Determination)
(d) Anyone find involved shall be punished. (Warning / threat)
(e) You shall be transferred it you don't work properly. (Warning / threat)
(f) We shall play a hockey match tomorrow. (Future action)

2. The use of **'shall'** ***with second and third person*** also *expresses* ***compulsion, bindings,or an idea of a force :***

(a) You shall go to meet him tomorrow. (You are instructed to go and meet him.)
(b) She shall complete her work by tommorrow. (She has to complete her work by tomorrow.)

3. *The use of* ***'shall not'*** in **second and third person** denotes **prohibition or a negative *command :***

(a) You shall not meet him.
(b) Nobody shall write on the table.
(c) She shall not attend the night party.

4. The use of 'shall' with first person in interrogative form *expresses the idea of* ***knowing the willingness*** *of the other person :*

(a) Shall I open the door for you?
(b) Shall I carry this box into the room for you?

(c) Shall I thread the needle for you?
(d) Shall I assist you?

5. The use of 'shall' in third person also *expresses an idea of* ***working as per the wish of the others :***

(a) Shall Rahim wait for you ?
(Do you want him to wait for you?)
(b) Shall the messenger wait out side?
(Do you want the messenger to wait out side?)

II. Will

1. *The use of* ***'will'*** *in* ***second and third person*** *denotes pure* ***future actions.*** *With first person 'will' denotes, threat, warning, promise or determination :*

(a) He will go tomorrow. (b) You will work here.
(c) I will see you. (threat, warning) (d) I will pay you on Monday. (promise)
(e) I will achieve my goal. (determination) (f) I will never speak to him.(determination)

2. *'Will' is also used for making* ***formal request :***

(a) Will you close the door?
(b) Will you bring me a glass of water?

3. *'Will' also* ***expresses probability*** in combination with all the persons.The negative form 'will not' (won't) denotes refusal :

(a) I won't go there. (b) He will not sanction your leave.
(c) He will be in the park. (d) Today is 15th Aug, schools will be closed.

4. *'Won't'* (will not) ***in interrogative sentence denotes 'invitation'*** :

(a) Won't you have a cup of tea?(invitation , I want you to have a cup of tea.)
(b) Won't you meet her?
(c) Won't you stay for a day?

5. *'Will' is also used for* ***commands and instructions*** *:*

(a) All the cadets will attend the parade. (Instruction, command)
(b) The girls will not wear the shorts. (Instruction, command)
(c) You will deliver the welcome speech. (Instruction, command)

6. *'Will' in third person denotes a* ***general habit*** *:*

(a) The women will not keep mum. (habit) (b) The girls will talk. (habit)
(c) He will smoke. (habit) (d) The minister will come late. (habit)

III. Should

1. *'Should' can be used to express;* **duty, responsibility, advice, probability, expectation, presumption, moral obligation and mild command :**

(a) One should obey one's elders. (Duty)
(b) You should obey your parents. (Moral obligation)
(c) The rich should help the poor. (Expectation)
(d) You should work hard. (Advice)
(e) You should find her in the play-ground. (Probability)

(f) You should take care of your health. (Advice)
(g) You should take care of your briefcase. (Responsibilily)
(h) You should complete your work everyday. (Mild command)
(i) He should be reading now. (Probability)
(j) He should be worried about me. (Presumption)
(k) They should be anxious about us. (Presumption)

2. 'Should' is also *used for expressing purpose* like 'may and might' :
(a) I taught her so that she should pass. (she might pass.)
(b) I scolded him so that he should work hard. (he might work hard.)

3. *The use of 'should' in perfect tense* denotes an **obligation that was not fulfilled :**
(a) He should have gone by morning bus. (but he didn't go)
(b) She should have informed me about the incident. (but she didn't inform me)
(c) Ramesh should have submitted the bills. (but he didn't submit)

4 *'Should' is also used with 'lest'* in following type of **conditional sentences. 'Lest' means—'in case' or 'so that...not'**
(a) Move fast lest you should miss the bus. (b) Work hard lest you should fail.

IV. Would

1. *For making request use* of 'would' ***shows more politeness in comparison to 'will'***. 'Would' is more commonly used for requests. Would is also used to know the wishes of the others.
(a) Would you accompany me to the railway station? (Polite request)
(b) Would you send me an application form? (Polite request)
(c) Would you sing at the concert tomorrow? (Willingness querry)

2. 'Would' is also used *to express, **likelihood, presumption and probability :***
(a) He would be in the field now. (likelihood)
(b) She would be in the club at this time (probability)
(c) She would be cooking now. (likelihood)
(d) She would be about 80 now. (presumption)

3. *The use of 'would' **with 'rather' shows preference** :*
(a) I would rather rest now.
(b) I would rather study than see a movie.
(c) I would rather play than rest now.

4. The use of 'would' ***in following construction shows strong desire / willingness :***
(a) I wish, you would fight this election.
(b) I wish you would support her fully.
(c) I wish they would agree to this proprosal.

5 *'Would' is also used in **conditional sentences*** for **showing unreal imaginations :**
(a) If I had one crore rupees, I would donate fifty lacs to the trust.
(b) If I had wings I would fly to Europe.
(c) If I were the king, I would make you my chief adviser
(d) If a tiger came into the room, what would you do?

6. The **use of 'would'** in following type of conditional sentences *denotes the* ***action which did not take place :***

(a) If he had come to me I would have given him a job. (He didn't come.)

(b) If she had asked me I would have helped her. (But she didn't ask me)

7. ***'Would' is the past tense form of 'will'***, it is used in indirect narrations too :

(a) He told me that he would go to Jaipur the next day.

(b) He told me that she would not agree to the proposal.

8. ***'Would you like....?' expresses invitation :***

(a) Would you like a cup of tea? (b) Would you like to come in?

D. Must

'Must' is a ***defective verb . It has no past form.*** It is used to ***express present or future obligation***. In reported speech 'must' is used for past time. Except in reported speech 'must' is not used to express past obligations normally.In some circumstances 'must' is changed to 'had to' in indirect narrations.

1. *'Must' is used to express* ***commands , compulsion, order :***

(a) Soldiers must obey orders without any question.

(b) All the girls must attend the function.

(c) You must do as you are told.

2. 'Must' is also used *to express,* ***moral duty/obligation :***

(a) We must respect our elders. (b) You must help your friends in need.

3. 'Must' also expresses—***necessity, urgency, circumstancial compulsion :***

(a) I must leave now, otherwise I may miss the train.

(b) The electricity will be cut off at 8 A.M. so I must complete my work before.

4. The use of ***'must not' expresses—prohibition, emphatic advice :***

(a) Students must not resort to copying. (Prohibition)

(b) You must not miss the classes. (Emphatic advice)

(c) You must not talk to that fellow. (Prohibition)

(d) Visitors must not feed the animals. (Prohibition)

5. 'Must' ***expresses—strong probability / likelihood or logical presumption :***

(a) She must be eighty now.

(b) They have not arrived so far. They must have taken a wrong turn.

6. **In questions introduced with 'must'**, *if answered in affirmative*, we use 'must', otherwise (in negative answer) 'need not' :

(a) Must I attend the meeteing ?

Yes, you must.

No, you needn't.

(b) Must I raise the issue in the board meeting?

Yes, you must.

No, you need not.

7. The use of **'must' with ' have + past participle of the main verb'**, *shows a logical conclusion about a past event :*

(a) The roads are wet. It must have rained last night.

(b) You must have heard about the robbery in the bank in our locality.

(c) They must have reached there in time.

(d) She must have taken sleeping pills last night.She didn't wake up till 11 am.

8. The use of **'must + have been'** *shows certainty of a happening :*

(a) He must have been living here.

(b) She delivered her speech quite fluently. She must have been a debater.

E. NEED and **DARE**

'Need' *and* ***'dare'*** *are considered semi-modals* because ***they can be used either as modal auxiliaries or as main verbs*** . The modal verb construction is restricted to non-assertive contexts (i.e. mainly negative and interrogative sentences), whereas the main verb construction can always be used and is in fact the more common.

I. Need

As a Modal **auxiliary verb** in negative terms *it indicates absence of obligation. It expresses the speaker's authority or advise* and it is used for the present and the future :

(a) You needn't type this letter. (The speaker is the authority, it could be his boss.)

But 'need' can also take 'do' (auxiliary) and in this case it expresses absence of obligation as well but in this case the speaker is not the authority : *You don't need to type this letter* (here it could be a conversation among colleagues), as main verb 'need' means 'require'.

1. As Modal, the forms of 'need' are 'needn't' or 'need' and is used in negative and interrogative for all persons in present and future tenses. 'Need' in such construction takes a bare infinitive :

(a) He need not talk to her. (b) Need he talk to her?

(c) You needn't wear a tie. (d) Need I wear a tie?

'Need' is sometimes used in formal English **with 'hardly/ scarcely or only' :**

(a) I need hardly say how pleased we are to welcome Mrs Sonia Gandhi here.
(I needn't say....)

(b) You need only touch one of the buttons for all the alarm bells to start buzzing.
(If you even touch one of the buttons all the bells will start buzzing.)

As already stated, **'need not' expresses the speaker's authority or advice :**

(a) You needn't remind me again. Just set the alarm on.

(b) I'm in no hurry. He needn't send it by speed post . He can send it by ordinary post.

2. The use of 'needn't' in perfect tense ***denotes an unnecessary action which was nevertheless performed :***

(a) He needn't have written such a detailed essay. (The essay was to be written is 300 words only.)

(b) You needn't have bought such a costly gift. (waste of money)

(c) You needn't have written to him, as he phoned me shortly. (but you had written, thus wasted time)
(d) They needn't have left home at 8.00, the train doesn't arrive till 10.00. (So they will have two hours to wait.)

3. 'Needn't' in direct speech can be reported unchanged in indirect speech :
(a) 'You needn't pay till the 30th' she says/ said =
(b) She says/ said I needn't pay till the 30th.

4. ***'Need'*** *when used as ordinary verb in negative* ***takes auxiliary 'do'***. 'Need', conjugated with will/ shall, do/ does/ did etc. takes the full infintive.It sometimes occurs in affirmative also :
(a) I do not need to write him anything.
(b) He won't need to attend the court.
(c) She didn't need to remind me.
(d) She needs to be careful.

5. As main verb,'need' takes 's' with subject 'singular number third person' in present tense and in past it takes 'ed' :
(a) He needs my assistance.
(b) I need your help.
(c) He needed my help.
(d) They needed a sofaset.

II. Dare

'Dare' is also called semi modal as it can be used as main verb as well as a modal verb.

Use of Dare as Modal

1. ***In the affirmative 'dare' is used like a main verb,*** *i.e.,* ***'dare/ dares'*** in the present, ***'dared'*** in the past. But in the negative and interrogative it can be used either like a main verb or like a modal auxiliary, *i.e.* it is a semi modal :
(a) He dares to oppose you .
(b) He does not dare to oppose you.
(c) Does he dare to oppose you?
(d) Do you dare to speak against him?
(e) You do not dare to speak against him.
(f) We do not dare to talk to the president.

In above constructions 'Dare' is used as an ordinary verb.

Use of dare as modal :
(a) He dare not say like this.
(b) I dare not talk to the chairman.
(c) Dare he not say like this ?
(d) Dare I talk to the chairman?
(e) He dare not oppose you.
(f) Dare he oppose you?
(g) Dare she complain against you?
(h) She dare not complain against you.

The ordinary verb construction is more commonly used.

2. The constructions ; ***'how dare (d) you?*** how dare(d) ***he/ they?' express indignation :***
(a) How dare you speak like this ? (I am indignant because you spoke like this.)
(b) How dare my wife leave without my permission?
(c) How dare you act in this manner?
(d) How dare he say so ?

3. ***Infinitives after 'Dare'***. In theory the negative and interrogative forms of 'dare' with 'do/ did' are followed by the infintive 'to' but in practice the ***'to' is often omitted*** :

(a) He doesn't dare (to) say anything. (b) Did he dare (to) say anything.

Dare I/ he/ you/ they/we? etc. and 'dare not' constructions take the infinitive without 'to' :

(a) Dare we disturb you ? (b) They dared not go.

When 'dare' is preceded by nobody, anybody etc, the 'to' is optional :

(a) Nobody dare to comment like that.
(b) Nobody dare comment like that.
(c) Some body dare complain in the matter.
(d) Somebody dare to complain in the matter.

4. 'Dare' is not often used in affirmative except in the construction 'I daresay'. 'Daresay' has two meanings; *(i). I suppose, and (ii). I accept what you say (but it doesn't make any difference) :*

(i) *Dare = I suppose*

(a) I daresay he will come. (I suppose)
(b) I dare say they will be happy to get this news. (I suppose)

(ii) *Dare = I accept what you say :*

Indian Tourist : But I drive on the left in India!
Swiss Policeman : I daresay you do, but we drive on the right here.
Traveller : But the watch was gifted to me; I didn't buy it.
Customs officer : I daresay you didn't but you'll have to pay duty on it .

NOTE *'Daresay' is used in this way with the first person singular only.*

F. 'Used to' :

'Used' has no present tense. 'Used' is followed by the full infinitive 'to'.

1. To *express a* ***discontinued habit or a past situation*** **which is no more in the present :**

(a) He used to drink daily. (Now he does not drink.)
(b) I used to smoke one packet of cigarettes. (Now I do not smoke.)
(c) He used to go for a walk. (Now he does not go for a walk)

2. *'Used' is also used* ***as an adjective meaning—'accustomed'***. It is then preceded by 'be' form of verb or become or get in any tense and followed by the preposition 'to' :

(a) I am used to take tea in the morning.
(b) He is used to read newspaper with morning tea.
(c) He would soon used to live at Mumbai.
(d) I am used to the cooler's noise.
(e) I am used to working in a noisy room.
(f) You will soon get used to the electric typewriters.
(g) They soon get used to the traffic regulations.

3. Note the use of *'Used to' in negative and interrogative sentences* :

(a) I used not to smoke daily *Negative*
or I did not use to smoke earlier? *Negative*
(b) He used to play chess at college. *Affirmative*
He didn't use to play chess at college. *Negative*

Used he to play chess at college? *Interrogative*
Did he use to play chess at college? *Interrogative*

For making negative of such sentences we can use either 'used not to' or 'did not use to'.In interrogative sentences we can use either 'Used + subject + to' or 'Did + subject + use + to' structure as shown above.

G. Ought to : 'Ought' is also a modal verb.The same form of 'ought' is used for present and future. It is also used in past when preceded by a verb in past tense or followed by a perfect infintive.

Ought is always followed by full infinitive 'to' :

(a) I ought to write to her today/ tomorrow.
(b) I knew I ought to write to her.
(c) He said I ought to write.
(d) I know/ knew that I ought to have written.

The negative form of 'ought' is : 'ought not' / 'oughtn't'
and the interrogative form is : ought I / he / you ? etc.
Negative interrogative form is : ought I not / oughtn't I? etc.

1. *'Ought' is used for* ***advice , moral obligation, duty :***

(a) You ought to consult a physician. (Advice)
(b) We ought to respect our parents (Moral duty)
(c) We ought to help our friends (Moral obligation)
(d) You ought to follow the advice of the doctor (Advice)
(e) You ought not to smoke so much. (Advice)
(f) Children ought not to watch T.V. so long. (Advice)

2. *The use of 'ought' in perfect tense* denotes an **unfulfilled obligation or an action that didn't take place :**

(a) She ought to have invited him in the function. (But she didn't invite him)
(b) He ought to have helped him in that matter. (But he didn't help him)
(c) He ought to have opposed the move. (But he didn't oppose)
(d) They ought to have come in time. (But they didn't come in time)
(e) You ought to have stopped at the traffic light. (But you didn't stop)

3. It is generally assumed that *'ought to'* and *'should'* have similar uses. But **in formal notices or for information** etc., **'should'** (but not **'ought') is used**.

(a) Students should be prepared to donate the blood.
(b) Travellers should be in possession of the following documents.
(c) On hearing the alarm bell, the students should leave their rooms immediately .

We can't use ought in above sentences.

CORRECT YOURSELF EXERCISE : MODALS

CYE : 01 Correct the following sentences :

1. I possess two brothers.
2. She possesses three sisters.
3. I have not books.
4. He has his book write by Ramesh.
5. He was a earlier banker.
6. She have been to London.
7. I have have my lunch.
8. I had have my work completed by him.

9. Do has a cup of coffee.
10. I do went to meet her.
11. She does learns her lessons well.
12. He did came here yesterday.
13. I received a song sung by her.
14. I found my clothes washed by him.
15. She neither talked nor will speak to him.

CYE : 02 Fill in the blanks with 'can, could, may, might' :

1. .... you live long!
2. .... you read when you were five?
3. My father .... speak and write five languages.
4. You .... write on both sides of the paper.
5. We thought it .... rain.
6. He said he .... always come when called.
7. .... you ride your bicycle up to that hill?
8. I ran fast so that I .... catch the train.
9. He tried to solve the sum but he ....not.
10. Do not put off till tomorrow what you .... do today.

CYE : 03 Fill in the blanks with 'shall, will, should, would' :

1. .... you do me a favour?
2. When................ I see you again?
3. ....we go to the pictures today ?
4. His daughter .... be sixteen next month.
5. The wound ....not heal in spite of all the treatment he had.
6. ....that I were rich!
7. Had you worked hard, you................. have passed the examination.
8. As you sow, so............. you reap.
9. Those who live in glass houses .... not throw stones at others.
10. If you .... see him, give him my regards.

CYE : 04 Fill in the blanks with appropriate forms of 'must , need, dare, ought to, used to' :

1. The door .... painting.
2. I .... smoking but I gave it up last year.
3. You ....come and have dinner with me.
4. He has lost your book and he .... not tell you.
5. You...................have written to him yesterday.
6. .... he wait any longer ?
7. He .... pay you the loan he owes you.
8. .... you speak rudely to your father?
9. I .... be a clerk, but now I am an officer.
10. What cannot be cured............... be endured.

CYE : 05 Use appropriate modal to fill in the blanks :

1. .... you, please, stop talking?
2. You ....go only when you have finished your work.
3. .... you rather have tea or coffee?
4. I........................ try again if you wish.
5. You .... not hurry, there is plenty of time.

6. I .... like you to do as I tell you.
7. If only they .... keep quiet for a moment.
8. .... God bless you!
9. You .... be mad to do this.
10. I......................... learn English, and none shall stop me.
11. I .... prefer not to give any explanation.

CYE : 06 Use appropriate modals to fill in the blanks :

1. One .... obey one's parents.
2. You......................... go home whenever you like.
3. I .... like you to answer my question properly.
4. My father says we .... buy some sweets.
5. .... God give you courage to face it!
6. .... you like to have lunch now?
7. .... you please tell me where the Cinema House is?
8. It ....rain, it is so sultry.
9. The doctor said that the patient .... recover. (The doctor was not very sure about it.)
10. You .... insist on being given your share. (Note the stress on the word 'insist'.)
11. .....God bless you!

CYE : 07 Use appropriate modals to fill in the blanks :

1. You .... have given me a helping hand. It was your moral duty.
2. I .... try to get you a job. I promise.
3. Arun is not a weak student. He is also not a very good student. He .... however, pass.
4. The student politely said to the teacher, '............ I have a word with you?'
5. You .... go now. (Permission)
6. ....you please close the door ? (A polite request in the form of a question)
7. It ....rain soon. (It is likely to happen)
8. You ....see a doctor at once. (It is an advice)
9. We .... hurry. We are very late.
10. I'm afraid I .... tell you that .It is a secret.

CYE : 08 Identify the notion/concept expressed by each of the following sentences by choosing one of the three alternatives mentioned against each sentence :

1. No smoking ! (Advice/prohibition/threat)
2. I wish you'd be quiet. (Request /wish/suggestion)
3. I'm seeing the Principal this afternoon. (Likelihood/ determination/ arrangement)
4. You needn't have hurried. (Absence of necessity/ prohibition/ suggestion of hesitation)
5. It might rain before evening. (Possibility/ strong possibility/ remote possibility)

CYE : 09 Restructure the following sentences using 'may, might, must, ought to, wish, only'.

1. Candidates are required to answer at least five out of ten questions.
2. He was not careful enough.
3. Perhaps he was hurt.

4. Please make a little less noise. (you can make it less if you wish to.)
5. Please be quiet. (request)

CYE : 10 Fill in the blanks supplying the appropriate modals :

1. You .... have watered the flowers, for it is going to rain.
2. If we had taken the other road we ...... have arrived earlier.
3. The bank closes at two but the manager.... allow you to get in. (remote possibility)
4. .... you please send me an application form ? (request)
5. As John was the only person who visited us yesterday. It ...... be he who left the main gate open. (probability)
6. You ...... read his latest book.
7. She .... speak three languages when she was twelve.
8. I .... see quite clearly what the children are doing in the garden.
9. He ...... be at least sixty.
10. Your job .... be very demanding, but at least it isn't boring.

CYE : 11 Fill in the blanks with the appropriate modals :

1. Usha ...... run a hundred yards in ten seconds.
2. .... his soul rest in peace !
3. The baby is crying, he .... be hungry.
4. .... you tell me the way to the post-office, please ?
5. You ...... keep your scooter locked.
6. .... I bring you a cup of coffee ?
7. When I was a boy, I ...... walk forty miles in a day.
8. I have come to ask if Ram....... use your bicycle tomorrow.
9. .... you have another cup of tea ?
10. All of us .... die.
11. Drivers know that they .... stop when they come to the main road. (obligation)
12. If you have a bad throat, you ...... smoke. (prohibition)

SOLUTIONS : CORRECT YOURSELF EXERCISE

Solutions CYE : 01

1. I have two brothers.
2. She has three sisters.
3. I have no books.
4. He has his book written by Ramesh.
5. He has been a banker.
6. She has been to London.
7. I have had my lunch.
8. I had had my work completed by him.
9. Do have a cup of coffee.
10. I did go to meet her.
11. She does learn her lessons well.
12. He did come here yesterday.
13. I had a song sung by her.
14. I had my clothes washed by him.
15. She neither has talked nor will speak to him.

Solutions CYE : 02

1. may, 2. could, 3. can, 4. may, 5. might,
6. could, 7. can, 8. might, 9. could, 10. can.

Solutions CYE : 03

1. will, 2. shall, 3. shall, 4. will, 5. would,
6. would, 7. would, 8. shall, 9. should, 10. should.

Solutions CYE 04 :

1. needs. 2. used to, 3. must, 4. dare, 5. ought to,
6. need, 7. ought to, 8. dare, 9. used to, 10. must.

Solutions CYE : 05

1. Will you, please, stop talking?
2. You can (or should) go only when you have finished your work.
3. Would you rather have tea or coffee?
4. I will try again if you wish.
5. You need not hurry, there is plenty of time.
6. I should like you to do as I tell you.
7. If only they would keep quiet for a moment.
8. May God bless you!
9. You should be mad to do this.
10. I will learn English, and none shall stop me.
11. I should prefer not to give any explanation.

Solutions CYE : 06

1. One should obey one's parents.
2. You may go home whenever you like.
3. I should like you to answer my question properly.
4. My father says we shall buy some sweets.
5. May God give you courage to face it!
6. Would you like to have lunch now?
7. Will you please tell me where the Cinema House is?
8. It may rain, it is so sultry.
9. The doctor said that the patient might recover.
10. You must insist on being given your share.
11. May God bless you!

Solutions CYE : 07

1. You should have given me a helping hand. It was your moral duty.
2. I will try to get you a job. I promise.
3. Arun is not a weak student. He is also not a very good student. He can however , pass.
4. The student politely said to the teacher, "Could I have a word with you?"
5. You can go now.
6. Would you please close the door ?
7. It may rain soon.
8. You should see a doctor at once.
9. We must hurry. We are very late.
10. I'm afraid I cannot tell you that .It is a secret.

Solutions CYE : 08

1. Prohibition, 2. request, 3. arrangement,
4. absence of necessity, 5. remote possibility.

Solutions CYE : 09

1. Candidates must answer at least five out of the ten questions.
2. He ought to have been more careful.
3. He may have been hurt.
4. You might make a little less noise.
5. I wish you would be quiet.

Solutions CYE : 10

1. need not, 2. would, 3. might, 4. would, 5. might,
6. should, 7. could, 8. can, 9. must, 10. may.

Solutions CYE : 11

1. can, 2. may, 3. must, 4. will, 5. should/must,
6. shall, 7. could, 8. may, 9. will, 10. will,
11. must, 12. must not.

9

Non Finites

Verb can also be classified as Finite and Non finite verbs :

Non Finite verb : The *non-finite* forms of a verb have no tense, person or singular/plural.

Look at the following sentences :

(a) I like to play.
(b) He likes to play.
(c) They like to play.
(d) He liked to play.
(e) She liked to play.
(f) They liked to play.

In above sentences **'to play'** is a non finite verb which has same form with all persons, numbers and in all tenses, while **like** is a finite verb as its form changes with the number and person of the subject and it has different forms in different tenses.

NOTE *Non-finite verb forms are those that do not show number (they are not singular or plural) or tense (they do not make the sentence past or present).*

NON FINITE : KINDS

Non finites are of three kinds :

NON FINITES

- INFINITIVE (With or with out 'to')
- GERUND (Verb+ing Verbal noun)
- PARTICIPLE (Verb+ing verbal adjective)

INFINITIVE

In grammar, the **infinitive** is the form of a verb that has *no inflection to indicate person, number, mood or tense*. It is called the 'infinitive' because the verb is usually not made 'finite', or limited by inflection.By far the **most common form of an infinitive in English language is with the particle 'to'**, such as in **'to walk', 'to cry', 'to eat', 'to fear'. This is known as the *'to'-infinitive***.*Infinitives* are also defined as ***to + base form** of the verb*. It can function as a subject, direct object, subject complement, adjective, or adverb in a sentence.

'TO' INFINITIVES

Infinitives have several functions :

1. ***As subject*** :

(a) To err is human. (b) To live peacefully is not easy.
(c) To find fault is very easy.

2. As object of a *verb* :

(a) I love to play. (b) I want to write. (c) I wish to wait there.

3. As object of a *preposition* :

(a) The bus is about to start. (b) I have no choice but to go.
(c) The match is yet to finish.

4. As *complement of a verb* :

(a) He only wishes to be an IAS officer.
(b) His ambition is to build a temple.
(c) Her dream is to purchase the whole city.

5. As an objective complement :

(a) I saw her go. (b) I bade him go.
(c) I shall have you realise your mistake.
(Underlined infinitives are bare infinitives)

6. (i) As *adverb* (modifying a verb) :

(a) He came to meet her. (b) We earn to live happily.
(c) We went there to learn.

(ii) As *adverb* (modifying an adjective) :

(a) I am happy to meet you. (b) These fruit are delicious to eat.
(c) I was worried to know it.

(iii) As *adverb*(modifyng the whole sentence) :

(a) To tell the truth, I forgot what I said.
(b) To be honest, I indeed didn't recognise her.
(c) To swim in sea water is very easy.

7. As *adjective* (modifying a noun)

(a) There is no chair to sit. (b) I have no money to waste.
(c) I have no magazine to read.

BARE INFINITIVE OR INFINITIVE WITHOUT 'TO'

In English, a verb's infinitive is its unmarked form, such as 'be,' 'do,' 'have,' or 'sit,' often introduced by the particle 'to.' When this particle is absent, the infinitive is said to be a '*bare infinitive*'. The bare infinitive and the 'to-infinitive' are not generally interchangeable, but the distinction does not generally affect the meaning of a sentence.

Use of Bare Infinitive :

1. After following modal auxiliaries, infinitive comes without 'to'.

These modals are ; 'shall, will, should, do, did , may, might, must, can, could, need' :

(a) I shall play .
(b) He will come.
(c) I should write.
(d) He would write.
(e) I may go.
(f) He might come.
(g) They must play.
(h) He can say.
(i) I could talk.
(j) He need not come here.

2. **Following verbs** when used in active voice, take infinitive without 'to';

Bid, let, make, feel, watch, behold, hear, overhear, notice, observe, see, know :

(a) She bade me go.
(b) Let her sing.
(c) I made him sing.
(d) I didn't notice him go.
(e) I feel her touch me.
(f) I observed him play.

In passive these verbs take infinitive with 'to' :

(a) He was made to sing .
(b) I was bidden to go.

But 'let' always takes infinitive without 'to'; e.g.—She was let sing.

3. **Following words** take bare infinitive after them ;

'had better, would rather, would sooner, sooner than, rather than, had sooner' :

(a) He had better withdraw.
(b) You had better resign.
(c) He would sooner resign than fight with the boss.
(d) I would go rather than waste my time here.

4. 'Bare infinitive' is ***used after the conjunction 'than'*** :

(a) She is better able to speak than write. (b) He is stronger than me.

5. **Have / has / had + noun / pronoun**, is followed by a bare infinitive :

(a) I will have him realise his mistake.
(b) I had him know his mistakes.
(c) They will have you accept your fault.

6. ***'But'* and *'except'* take the bare infinitive** when they follow **'do+nothing /anything/everything'** :

(a) I can do nothing but protest.
(b) He did nothing but cry.
(c) They did nothing but weep.
(d) The dog does nothing except bark.

7. **'Why + bare infinitive ....?'** is *used to question a foolish or illogical action* :

(a) Why hire a taxi? (When we have sufficient room to accommodate you.)
(b) Why talk to him? (When he has openly criticized you.)

'Why not +bare infinitive' ...? is used to advise or suggest :

(a) Why not consult a doctor?
(b) Why not write to your father?
(c) Why not inform your parents?

Specific use of Infinitives : Rules.

1. ***Following verbs are followed directly by the Infinitive (With 'to')*** :

agree	appear	aim	arrange	target
attempt	ask	guarantee	bother	claim
happen	care	decide	learn	choose

demand	pretend	condescend	determine	promise
consent	resolve	prove	decline	be determined
seem	fail	swear	hesitate	threaten
hope	undertake	long	manage	neglect
offer	plan	prepare	be prepared	proceed
refuse	tend	trouble(negative)	volunteer	vow

(a) He agreed to pay Rs. 250 only.
(b) They are preparing to evacuate the colony.
(c) He refused to surrender.
(d) I volunteered to help with bread and money.
(e) They can't afford to live in this posh area.
(f) I don't bother to answer any question.
(g) We failed to contact her in time.

2. **Verbs**; ***'ask, beg, expect, would hate, help, intend, like, would like, would love, mean, prefer, want, wish'***, can be used in either of the **following constructions** :

Verb + Object + Infinitive or Verb + Infinitive

(a) He likes to take tea.
(b) He likes his friends to drink well.
(c) I want to go.
(d) I want you to go.
(e) I asked him to come here.
(f) I asked him to speak to Mrs. James.
(g) I begged to go. (Please let me go.)
(h) I begged him to go. (Please go.)
(i) I expect her to arrive tomorrow.
(j) I expect to arrive tomorrow.

3. **Following verbs are used in construction :**

Verb + Object + Infinitive

advise	forbid	entitle	allow
oblige	teach	bribe	order
tell	command	implore	permit
tempt	compel	induce	persuade
instruct	remind	urge	encourage
invite	request	train	enable
warn	force	make*	hear*
let*	see*	watch*	feel*
help*	notice*	observe*	look at*

NOTE *Verbs ; 'advise, allow, permit' can also be used with gerunds.*

(*) Single starred verbs in the above table take infinitive without 'to' (Bare infinitive). See following examples :

(a) He persuaded me to go with her.
(b) I have trained these dogs to sniff out drugs.
(c) He encouraged me to try again.
(d) They forbade us to pluck the flowers.
(e) These goggles will enable you to see in dim light.
(f) We watched him clear the table.
(g) They heard the thief crash through the door.
(h) She made me do it.
(i) We helped her finish the homework.

NOTE *Verbs; 'show, teach, tell' take 'how' after them in following constructons :*

(a) He showed me how to operate the machine.
(b) He told me how to replace a fuse.
(c) He taught me how to light a cigarette without a match box.

NOTE *If the skill is very common we can drop 'how' after 'teach'.*

(a) He taught me to ride.
(b) He taught me to write my name.

4. Verb + how/what/when/where/which/why + infinitive

The verbs; *ask, decide, discover, find out, forget, know, learn, remember, see (= understand, perceive), think,understand, want to know, wonder etc.* are usually used in above construction.We can also use **'how + object + 'wh' word + infinitive'** in the above construction:

(a) He knows how to swim.
(b) He discovered how to operate the machine.
(c) I asked him, where to buy fruits at reasonable rate.
(d) I remember when to switch off the machine.
(e) Tell me what to do.
(f) He wants to know how to write a good letter.
(g) I learned how to write a good precis.
(h) I showed him which button to press.
(i) I remembered to get a ticket.
(j) I decided to do it.

NOTE ***Verbs; 'ask, decide, forget, learn, remember', can also be followed directly by the infinitive.In such case the meaning will be different*.***

(a) She learnt to drive a car.
(b) She decided to go to Jaipur.
(c) She asked to bring a copy.
(d) I remembered to get a ticket.

Note the difference* :

I *decided* **to cut** it = I myself decided to cut it.
I *decided how* **to cut** it = I myself decided the way to cut it .
I *remembered* **to get** a ticket. (I *got a ticket.*)
I remembered where **to get** a ticket. (I remembered that the *tickets could be obtained* from the Association's office.)

5. *'Whether + infinitive'* can be used similarly *after* ***'want to know'***, ***'wonder'*** as following :

(a) I wonder whether to write or not.
(b) I wanted to know *whether to protest* or keep silence.

6. The Infinitive is also *used after* ; ***'the first'***, ***'the second'***, ...etc., ***'the last', the only*** and also *after superlative degree of adjectives :*

(a) Sita loves parties, she is always *the first* **to arrive** and *the last* **to leave.**

(the first who comes and the last who leaves)

(b) He was the only one to survive the train accident.

(the only one who survived)

(c) It was the best play to be performed that year.

(means the best play that was performed that year)

7. *Verbs*; ***'assume, believe, feel, suppose, consider, understand'***, are used in the following construction :

Verb + object + to be +...

(a) I *assume him to be* the best athlete .

(b) I *consider him to be* an honest person.

(c) I *thought her to be* a dedicated teacher.

(d) He is *supposed to be* washing the car.

8. Following ***nouns take infinitive directly*** :

ability	decision	effort	promise	willingness
ambition	demand	failure	refusal	wish
anxiety	determination	offer	request	desire
attempt	eagerness	plan	scheme	

(a) He made an *attempt to walk* without support .

(b) His *ability to get* the work done is his main assets.

(c) *Failure to find* the fault may result in termination.

(d) Their *'offer/plan/promise' to rebuild* the house was not taken seriously.

(e) His *unwillingness to do* his work may result in his dismissal.

(f) She made an *effort to solve* the problem.

9. ***Infinitive after 'too'***,

(I) ... + too + adjective + infinitive

(a) He is *too weak* to walk. (He is so weak that he cannot walk.)

(b) He was *too young* to get married .(He is so young that he cannot get married.)

(c) The box was too heavy to be carried by me.

(d) The grass was too wet to sit on.

(e) The light is too dim to read by.

(II) ...+ too + adjective +a + noun + infinitive

(a) He is *too shrewd a man* to rely on anybody.

(b) He is *too experienced a driver* to mind what anybody says.

(III) ...+ too + adverb + infinitive.

(a) It is *too soon* to say whether the plan will run or not.

(b) He cried *too loudly* to be understood by any one.

(c) He works too slowly to be of much use to her.

10. ***Infinitive after enough*** :

(I) ...+ adjective + enough + infinitive

(a) He is *matured enough* to take decisions.

(b) She is *bold enough* to travel by herself.

(c) He is intelligent enough to solve the question.
(d) The ice was thick enough to walk on.

(II)... + adverb + enough + infinitive

(a) He jumped *high enough* to win the first prize.
(b) He spoke *loudly enough* to be understood by all.
(c) He walked *quickly enough* to catch the train.
(d) She ran fast enough to catch the bus.

11. ***So .... as + infinitive*** **:**

(a) He was *so foolish as* to leave his car unlocked.
(b) He was *so intelligent* as to argue without any difficulty.
(c) Would you be *so kind* as to forward my request?

12. To avoid repetition 'to' can also be used as following :

(a) Would you like to accompany me? Yes, *I love to*. ('accompany you'-avoided.)
(b) Did you get a book ? No, *I tried to* (get a book), but there weren't left any.
(c) Why did you hire a taxi? I *had to* (hire a taxi), I was very late.
(d) Does he swim? Not now but he used to (swim).

13. ***Use of 'only' before the infinitive shows disappointment / frustration of the subject*** :

(a) He hurried to his house *only to find* his wife dead.
(b) He survived the crash *only to die* in the hills.
(c) He hurried to the house *only to find* that it was looted by the thieves.

14. ***If two infinitives are joined by 'and'*, the 'to' of the second infinitive is usually dropped :**

(a) I intend to sit in my room *and read* novels. (not—'and *to* clean')
(b) I want you to assist me and clean the room. (not—'and *to* clean')

15. ***'Be + infinitive'* is used to convey orders/ instructions /commands :**

(a) No one is to leave the hotel without the permission of the inspector.
(b) You are to stay here till I return.

16. ***'Be about + infinitive'* conveys the immediate future :**

(a) The bus *is about* to start. (b) They *are just about* to leave.

17. ***Infinitive is also used to express purpose*.** Purpose can be expressed by the infinitive alone or with the use of following construction :

in order / so as + infinitive......

(a) He went to Jaipur to meet Ramesh.
(b) He attended the coaching to learn English.
(c) She is learning English in *order / so as to qualify* for a better job.
(d) She learnt computers in *order / so as to help* her father with his work.

SPLIT INFINITIVE

The general rule is that **no word should separate the *'to' of an infinitive from the simple form of the verb that follows*. If a word does come between these two components, a split infinitive results.** It used to be seen as a **grammatical crime to split an infinitive**, although the *rationale for this view is not clear*.

Henry Fowler, in *A Dictionary of Modern English Usage*, refers to "*Those who do not know but do care [about a split infinitive] would as soon be caught putting their knives in their mouths as splitting an infinitive, but have only hazy notions of what constitutes that deplorable breach of etiquette ...*"

A split infinitive has another word placed between the 'to' and the 'base verb', such as 'to sometimes fight' and 'to never yield' or 'to boldly go' where no man has ever gone before.

This ban on the split infinitive was misguided. There are many adverbs that need to be placed immediately before the verb :

(a) I ought to flatly refuse. (b) We have to always be careful.

If you put the adverb somewhere else, you change the emphasis, and the sentence is awkward;

I ought flatly to refuse. I ought to refuse flatly.

You have always to be careful. You have to be careful always.

Whether you put an adverb between the to and the verb is a matter of style and meaning. We have to sometimes revise old grammatical terminology.

CONTINUOUS INFINITIVE

The Continuous Infinitive has the form- **to be+ Present Participle :**

(a) Ram may be watching TV at this time.

Use of Continuous Infinitive :

(A) After the auxiliary verbs;'will/shall/may/might/can/could/must/would/should', continuous infinitive (be + present participle) is used :

(a) They'll be playing now.
(b) He might/may be watching TV.
(c) He can't /could't be playing. (The field is occupied by the election team.)
(d) He can't /couldn't be watching TV. (Because the cable operators are on strike.)
(e) She must be coming by morning train.
(f) She shouldn't be reading a magazine.
(g) She should be reading her text books.
(h) They would be waiting for us.

(B) After verbs; 'appear, happen, pretend, seem', continuous infinitive (to be + present participle) is used :

(a) I happened *to be looking* towards the road when their car stopped.
(b) She seems *to be following* us.
(c) He appears *to be living* in that area.
(d) He pretended *to be looking* for a magazine.

NOTE *Continuous infinitive can also be used after the verbs; 'agree, arrange, decide, determine, hope, manage, plan' :*

(a) I hope *to be earning* my livings in a year's time.

(b) I determined *to be waiting* at the door.

(c) I agreed *to be standing* near the tree.

(C) After the verbs ; 'believe, consider, suppose, think', etc. continuous infinitive is used in passive structure :

(a) She is believed *to be living* in France.

(b) He is considered *to be supporting* the Liberals.

PERFECT INFINITIVE

Perfect Infinitive form - **to have+ Past Participle** e.g. 'to have gone', 'to have completed' etc.

Use of Perfect Infinitive :

1. It is used after auxiliary verbs.

The use of perfect infinitive ***with 'was/were' denotes an unfulfilled plan or arrangement*** :

(a) The house *was to have been ready* so far. (But it is not ready)

(b) She *was to have gone*. (But she has not gone.)

2. *Perfect infinitive is normally used with ;* ***'should/would/might/could' in conditional sentences*** :

(a) If I had seen him, I *would have invited* him.

(b) If he had come to me, I *might have helped* him.

(c) If she had informed, I *could have helped* her.

3. The use of perfect infinitive with *'may/might' denotes the probability of completing of action in past* :

(a) He *'may/might' have heard* the news so far.

(It is possible that he has heard the news by now.)

4. The use of perfect infinitive *with 'must' denotes the certainty* :

(a) The thief must have entered through this gate. (Here are his footprints.)

5. The use of perfect infinitive with ***'needn't' denotes an unnecessary past action :***

(a) He needn't have watered the plants. (As it rained a day before)

(b) You needn't have written him. (As I had telephonic discussions with him yesterday).

NOTE ***Verbs; 'appear, hope, pretend, seem' are used with perfect infinitives as following :***

(a) He *pretended to have learned* the lesson.

(b) He seemed to have been a great sportsman.

(c) I happened to have driven that kind of jeep before.

(d) He hopes that he will have finished his project by January.

NOTE ***Verbs; 'acknowledge, believe, consider, find, how, know, report, say, suppose, think, understand', are used with perfect infinitive in passive structure :***

(a) They are *understood to have left* the village.

(b) He was believed to have been a great artist.

(c) She is thought to have information which will be useful to the police.

(d) She is known to have been a great leader.

PERFECT CONTINUOUS INFINITIVE

Perfect continuous infinitive form— **to have been + present participle** +...

Use :

(A) The perfect continuous infinitive is used mainly after auxiliaries and after the verbs; 'appear, seem, happen, pretend' :

(a) He seems to have been standing there since morning.
(b) She appears to have been waiting a long time.
(c) He pretended to have been studying.

(B) The perfect continuous infinitive is also used after the verbs; 'believe, know, report' and 'understand' in passive structure :

He is believed to have been mobilising the militants those days.

CORRECT YOURSELF EXERCISE : NON FINITIVE

CYE : 01 Correct the following sentences :

1. English is difficult to be learnt.
2. Do you dare refuse me?
3. I watched her to cross the road.
4. The act is easy to be performed.
5. He is better able to act than to sing.
6. She can do nothing but to abuse him.
7. Stop to write.
8. I had sooner run than to walk.
9. I have decided helping her.
10. Better to reign in hell than to serve in heaven.
11. I made him to polish my shoes.
12. She avoids to do her duties seriously.
13. I am looking forward to meet you soon.
14. I got a mechanic repairing my car.
15. A brave man does not fear dying.
16. The river is very deep to be crossed by the army.

CYE : 02 Correct the following sentences :

1. Please tell me to close it.
2. I know swim.
3. I can't decide to get out of this trouble.
4. I chanced meeting her in the art gallery.
5. She appears recognising me.
6. Could you tell me to explain the situation?
7. There was no board to write.
8. She hopes of passing with distinction.
9. She is eager to meeting me.
10. He went to Jaipur seeing the Jantar Mantar.
11. She failed winning the prize.
12. I shall be glad meeting you.

CYE : 03 Correct the following sentences :

1. I have no pen to write.
2. She has a house for furnishing.
3. I have no house to live.
4. He requested me going to Jaipur.
5. He did nothing but to talk and to laugh.
6. I will have you to remember me.
7. She was known having hidden the jewellery box.
8. I would study rather than to waste my time.
9. They bade me to go.
10. Let I sing a song.
11. I observed him to play.
12. We had him to know his mistakes.

CYE : 04 Correct the following sentences :

1. He learned to operate the machine.
2. I asked him from where to buy shirts at reasonable rates.
3. I wonder whether go or not.
4. She pretended to look for some eatables.
5. Ramesh seems to follow us in his car.
6. He seemed to be a great musician.
7. His plan of rebuild the building was not approved by the municipality.
8. He made an effort to getting pass without copying.
9. She is too weak that she cannot walk.
10. She is enough matured to go alone.
11. She ran enough fast to catch the train.
12. He was so foolish as left his car unlocked.
13. Will you be so kind as sanction my leave?
14. She is the only one secure 95% marks.
15. She likes to completely change the colour.

CYE : 05 Underline the infinitive phrase and label the way it is used in the sentence, adding any punctuation as needed :

1. I want to go.
2. I want you to go home.
3. We want to see the play.
4. To see a shooting star is good luck.
5. To fight against those odds would be ridiculous.
6. To design a new building for them would be challenging.
7. I want him to be my bodyguard.
8. Jim is expected to program computers at his new job.
9. They will try to build a new stadium in ten years.
10. To distill a quart of moonshine takes two hours.
11. The president wants to use nuclear energy for peaceful purposes.
12. She has the money to buy it.

13. We demonstrated to attract attention to our agenda.
14. I do not like to give poor grades.
15. The dogs were taught to stand, to sit, and to bark on command.
16. To be great is to be true to yourself and to the highest principles of honour.
17. To see is to believe.

SOLUTIONS : CORRECT YOURSELF EXERCISE

Solutions CYE : 01

1. English is difficult to learn.
2. Do you dare to refuse me?
3. I watched her cross the road.
4. The act is easy to perform.
5. He is better able to act than sing.
6. She can do nothing but abuse him.
7. Stop writing.
8. I had sooner run than walk.
9. I have decided to help her.
10. Better reign in hell than serve in heaven.
11. I made him polish my shoes.
12. She avoids doing her duties seriously.
13. I am looking forward to meeting you soon.
14. I got a mechanic to repair my car.
15. A brave man does not fear to die.
16. The river is very deep to cross by the army.

Solutions CYE : 02

1. Please tell me how to close it.
2. I know how to swim.
3. I can't decide how to get out of this trouble.
4. I chanced to meet her in the art gallery.
5. She appears to recognise me.
6. Could you tell me how to explain the situation?
7. There was no board to write on.
8. She hopes to pass with distinction.
9. She is eager to meet me.
10. He went to Jaipur to see the Jantar Mantar.
11. She failed to win the prize.
12. I shall be glad to meet you.

Solutions CYE : 03

1. I have no pen to write with.
2. She has a house to furnish.
3. I have no house to live in.
4. He requested me to go to Jaipur.
5. He did nothing but talk and laugh.

6. I will have you remember me.
7. She was known to have hidden the jewellery box.
8. I would study rather than waste my time.
9. They bade me go.
10. Let me sing a song.
11. I observed him playing.
12. We had him know his mistakes.

Solutions CYE : 04

1. He learned how to operate the machine.
2. I asked him where to buy shirts at reasonable rates.
3. I wonder whether to go or not.
4. She pretended to be looking for some eatables.
5. Ramesh seems to be following us in his car.
6. He seemed to have been a great musician.
7. His plan to rebuild the building was not approved by the municipality.
8. He made an effort to get pass without copying.
9. She is too weak to walk.
10. She is matured enough to go alone.
11. She ran fast enough to catch the train.
12. He was so foolish as to leave his car unlocked.
13. Will you be so kind as to sanction my leave?
14. She is the only one to secure 95% marks.
15. She likes to change the colour completely.

Solutions CYE : 05

1. I want to go. [noun/direct object]
2. I want you to go home. [noun/direct object]
3. We want to see the play. [noun/direct object]
4. To see a shooting star is good luck. [noun/subject]
5. To fight against those odds would be ridiculous. [noun/subject]
6. To design a new building for them would be challenging. [noun/subject]
7. I want him to be my bodyguard. [noun/direct object]
8. Jim is expected to program computers at his new job. [noun/direct object]
9. They will try to build a new stadium in ten years. [noun/direct object]
10. To distill a quart of moonshine takes two hours. [noun/subject]
11. The president wants to use nuclear energy for peaceful purposes. [noun/direct object]
12. She has the money to buy it. [adjective, modifying '*money*']
13. We demonstrated to attract attention to our agenda. [adverb, modifying *demonstrated*; note that '*to our agenda*' is a prepositional phrase, not an infinitive phrase.]
14. I do not like to give poor grades. [noun/direct object]
15. The dogs were taught to stand, to sit, and to bark on command. [nouns/direct objects]
16. To be great is to be true to yourself and to the highest principles of honour. [nouns : 1. subject; 2. subject complement; note that *to yourself* and *to the highest principles of honour* are both prepositional phrases, not infinitive phrases]
17. To see is to believe. [nouns : 1. subject; 2. subject complement.]

10

Gerund

Gerund is defined as the '–ing' form of a verb and has the characteristics of a noun also; e.g.—walking, running, reading, writing, etc.

PRESENT PARTICIPLE V/S GERUND

Every gerund, without exception, ends in -ing. Gerunds are not, however, all that easy to find out. The problem is that all present participles also *end in -ing*. What is the difference? **Gerunds function as nouns**. Gerunds are called verbal nouns. ***Present participles*, on the other hand act as modifiers**. Present participles are also called **verbal adjectives**.

Use of Gerund

1. ***As subject*** :
   (a) Swimming is good for health.
   (b) Seeing is believing.
   (c) Fishing is a good profession.
2. ***As object to the verb :***
   (a) I love fishing. (b) He loves telling stories. (c) Stop shouting.
3. ***As object to the preposition*** :
   (a) He is fond of writing letters.
   (b) We are tired of waiting.
   (c) I am against speaking ill of others.
4. ***As complement of a verb :***
   (a) What I love is making friends !
   (b) His weakness is writing slowly.
   (c) What I hate is abusing others !
5. ***As an objective complement :***
   (a) It is foolish of him crying now.
   (b) It is worthless requesting to him.
   (c) It is no use running after her.

GERUND V/S SIMPLE INFINITIVE

Gerunds and infinitives are forms of verbs that act like nouns.

A **gerund** is a verb + -ing.
An **infinitive** is to + the verb.

In both the examples above, the **gerund and the infinitive are the *objects of the verbs*** in the sentence. However, as noun substitutes, **gerunds and infinitives can also be *the subject of a sentence.* We can use either gerund or infinitive with following verbs** :

advise	hate	propose	used to
agree	intend	recommend	want
allow	like	regret	be ashamed
being	love	remember	afraid
can /could bear	mean	require	sorry
cease	need	start	go on
continue	permit	stop	prefer
forget	try	care	

GERUND	INFINITIVE
(a) They began playing.	(a) They began to play.
(b) We prefer taking tea.	(b) We prefer to take tea.
(c) He never ceased complaining	(c) He never ceased to complain about quality.
(d) I can't bear waiting so long.	(d) I can't bear to wait so long.
(e) I intend buying it.	(e) I intend to buy it.
(f) He advised me writing today.	(f) He advised me to write today.
(g) He doesn't allow parking here.	(g) He doesn't allow us to park here.

Specific use of Gerund - Rules

1. ***A preposition is always followed by a gerund, and not by an infinitive.*** This is a good rule. It has no exceptions.If we want to use a verb after a preposition, it must be a gerund. It is impossible to use an infinitive after a preposition :
   (a) He is fond *of fishing.*
   (b) She is good *at swimming.*
   (c) He is too afraid *of losing.*
   (d) I am tired *of arguing.*
   (e) I felt cold *after swimming.*
   (f) I am sorry *for telling* you all this.
   (g) There is no point *in arguing* now.
   (h) Are you not interested *in making* money?
2. ***Some verbs followed by prepostion /adverb take the gerund.*** The most common of such are; be for/ against, care for, give up, keep on, leave off, look forward to, put off, see about, take to' etc. :
   (a) We do not *care for standing* in queues.
   (b) We are *looking forward to meeting* you in the party.
   (c) He has given up smoking since long.
   (d) At last the lion left off roaring.
3. **The word 'to'often causes confusion.It is either a part of an infinitive, or a preposition.** When 'to' is followed by a noun/ pronoun or gerund it is a preposition.When 'to' is used as preposition it is always followed by gerund :
   (a) I am looking forward *to meeting* you. ('To' used as preposition)
   (b) I am accustomed *to smoking.* ('To' used as preposition)
   (c) I want *to go* there. ('To' used as part of infinitive)
   (d) Will you like *to come* in? ('To' used as part of infinitive)
4. ***Following verbs are followed by gerund*** :

admit	keep (= continues)	anticipate	loathe
appreciate	mean (= involve)	consider	miss
avoid	mind (= object)	defer	pardon

dislike	propose (= suggest)	delay	postpone
enjoy	remember (= recollect)	deny	practise
detest	prevent	dread	recollect
escape	resent	excuse	resist
risk	fancy (= imagine)	imagine	suggest
finish	save	involve	understand
forgive	stop (= cease)		

(a) He *admitted taking* the bribe .
(b) You should *avoid overeating*.
(c) He *detests waiting.*
(d) I *dislike standing* here.
(e) We dread getting old.
(f) I do not enjoy teaching.
(g) He kept crying.
(h) I do not want to risk getting wet.
(i) We couldn't help laughing.
(j) I don't find there anything worth buying.

5. **(A) 'Verb+ possessive adjective / pronoun object'** ***is followed by*** **gerund** and this gerund refers the person denoted by the possessive adjective or pronoun .
(a) He insisted on my reading the letter.
(b) He resented on my refusing the entry.

(B) If the 'verb or verb + preposition' is ***followed directly by the gerund,*** **the gerund refers to the subject of the verb**.
(a) Sarla insisted on reading the letter. (Sarla read it.)
Following verbs can take either of the constructions :

dislike	propose	understand
dread	recollect	approve/ disapprove of
fancy	remember	insist on
involve	resent	it's no good/ use
like (negative)	save	object to
mean	stop	there's no point in
mind	suggest	what's the point of

(a) She disliked working late.
(b) She disliked me/ my working late.
(c) I object to paying twice for the same thing.
(d) I object to his/ him making private calls on this phone.

6. ***Forgive, excuse, pardon and prevent' are not followed directly by the gerund***. These take either possessive adjective /pronoun + gerund or pronoun +preposition + gerund :
(a) Please forgive my / me calling you so early.
(b) We can't prevent him wasting his own money.
(c) I indeed appreciate your giving me so much of your time.

7. ***To refer a past action*** *perfect gerund* **(having worked, having spoken** etc.) *is used* :
(a) He was accused of having deserted his ship.
(b) He denied having been involved in the murder.

8. ***Gerund used after the verbs 'need, require and want' has a passive sense :***
(a) I have three shirts that *need* **washing**. (need to be washed)
(b) This letter *requires* **signing**. (needs to be signed)
(c) The house *wants* **repainting**. (needs to be repainted)

USING POSSESSIVES WITH GERUNDS : A NOTE

Do we say ***"I can't stand him singing in the shower,"*** or do we say ***"I can't stand his singing in the shower"***? Well, you have to decide **what you find objectionable** : is it him, **the fact that he is singing in the shower,** or **is it the singing** that is being done by him that you can't stand? Chances are, it's the latter, it's the singing that belongs to him that bugs you. So we would say, ***"I can't stand his singing in the shower."***

On the other hand, do we say ***"I noticed your standing in the alley last night"***? Probably not, because it's not the action that we noticed; it's the person. So we'd say and write, instead, ***"I noticed you standing in the alley last night."*** Usually, however, **when a noun** or **pronoun precedes a gerund, that noun or pronoun takes a possessive form**. This is especially true of formal, academic writing.

There are exceptions to this rule :

(a) ***When the noun preceding the gerund is modified by other words*****, use the common form of that noun, not the possessive** : for example
Federico was pleased by Carlos's making the Dean's List for the first time. ***but***
Federico was pleased by Carlos, his oldest son, making the Dean's List for the first time.

(b) ***When the noun preceding the gerund is plural, collective, or abstract***, use the common form of that noun, not the possessive :
Professor Villa was amazed by her students working as hard as they did.
The class working collaboratively was somebody else's idea.
It was a case of old age getting the better of them.

(c) There are certain situations in which the *possessive and the gerund create an awkward combination*. This seems to be particularly true when indefinite pronouns are involved.
'I was shocked by *somebody's making* that remark'.
The above sentence would be greatly improved by saying, instead;
'I was shocked that somebody would make that remark'.

(d) This is also true ***when the 'owner' of the gerund comes wrapped in a noun phrase :***
I was thankful for the guy next door shoveling snow from my driveway.

The above note has been adopted from "Grammar Dimensions" : *Form Meaning, and Use by Jan Frodesen & Janet Eyring.*

CORRECT YOURSELF EXERCISE : GERUND

CYE : 01 Correct the following sentences :

1. She is good at write.
2. He is afraid to lose the game.
3. I cannot forget you for you helping me.
4. It is totally useless to cry over the past misdeeds.
5. He said, 'Don't give up to try again.'
6. Would you mind to work with me?
7. She is fond of being admire.
8. I am sorry for me getting late.
9. I am happy at your arrival at schedule time.
10. To drink being his habit, we didn't go with him.

CYE : 02 Correct the following sentences :

1. I enjoy to travel.
2. Check the air before to start the generator.
3. It is no good to work with him.
4. Some people prefer to spend money to earn it.
5. I am thinking to leave my job and going back to my native place.
6. She said to me, 'Don't forget to lock the door before go to bed.'
7. I heard someone crying but I failed seeing anyone.
8. She has finished to wash the clothes.
9. I prefer to play football to reading my course books.
10. A novice can't learnt to spelling without being help.

CYE : 03 Fill in the blanks with appropriate words :

1. Try .... being late for office. (to avoid/avoiding)
2. We have nothing to do but .... for her. (waiting/to wait/wait)
3. Does your wife object .... on holidays. (to work/to working/have worked)
4. Sita was charged and fined for .... without lights. (driving/have driven/drove)
5. When he spoke, it was very difficult for me .... (to understood/to understand/ understanding)
6. .... an aim, the hunter shot the lion. (took/ to take/ taking)
7. .... his work, he went to market. (completing/having completed/after complete)
8. .... inside a bus is prohibited. (to smoke/smoking/have smoking)
9. The students refused .... the hostel. (leaving/to leave/lefting)
10. I had sooner .... than walk. (ran/run/to run/running)
11. Tell me .... this typical machine. (operation/how to operate/operating system)
12. Most of the students like .... cricket. (to play/playing/have playing)
13. He is too young .... this movie. (watching/watch/to watch)
14. He advised me 'You had better .... now.' (leaving/leave/left)
15. The office needs proper .... (cleanliness/cleaning/to clean)

CYE : 04 Underline the gerunds or gerund phrases in the following sentences and label how they function in the sentence (subject, direct object, subject complement, object of preposition).

1. Swimming keeps me in shape.
2. Swimming in your pool is always fun.
3. Telling your father was a mistake.
4. The college recommends sending applications early.
5. He won the game by scoring during the overtime period.
6. Her most important achievement was winning the national championship.
7. Going to work today took all my energy.
8. Fighting for a losing cause made them depressed.

SOLUTIONS : CORRECT YOURSELF EXERCISE

Solutions CYE : 01

1. She is good at writing.
2. He is afraid of losing the game.
3. I cannot forget you for your helping me.
4. It is totally useless crying over the past misdeeds.
5. He said, 'Don't give up trying again.'
6. Would you mind working with me?
7. She is fond of being admired.
8. I am sorry for my getting late.
9. I am happy at your arriving at schedule time.
10. Drinking being his habit, we didn't go with him.

Solutions CYE : 02

1. I enjoy travelling.
2. Check the air before starting the generator.
3. It is no good working with him.
4. Some people prefer spending money to earning it.
5. I am thinking of leaving my job and going back to my native place.
6. She said to me, 'Don't forget to lock the door before going to bed.'
7. I heard someone cry but I failed to see anyone.
8. She has finished washing the clothes.
9. I prefer playing football to reading my course books.
10. A novice can't learn to spell without being helped.

Solutions CYE : 03

1. to avoid, 2. wait, 3. to working, 4. driving,
5. to understand, 6. taking, 7. having completed, 8. smoking,
9. to leave, 10. run, 11. how to operate, 12. playing,
13. to watch, 14. leave, 15. cleaning.

Solutions CYE : 04

1. Swimming keeps me in shape. [subject]
2. Swimming in your pool is always fun. [subject]
3. Telling your father was a mistake. [subject]
4. The college recommends sending applications early. [direct object]
5. He won the game by scoring during the overtime period. [object of preposition]
6. Her most important achievement was winning the national championship. [subject complement]
7. Going to work today took all my energy. [subject]
8. Fighting for a losing cause made them depressed. [subject]

11

Participle

A participle is a non finite verb, called a 'verbal adjective,' *which means that* **it has characteristics of both verbs and adjectives.** The term 'verbal' indicates that a participle is based on a verb and therefore expresses action or a state of being. However, since **participles function as adjectives, they modify nouns or pronouns. A participle most often ends in '-ing'** or **'-ed'.**

There are three types of participles : present participle, past participle and perfect participle.

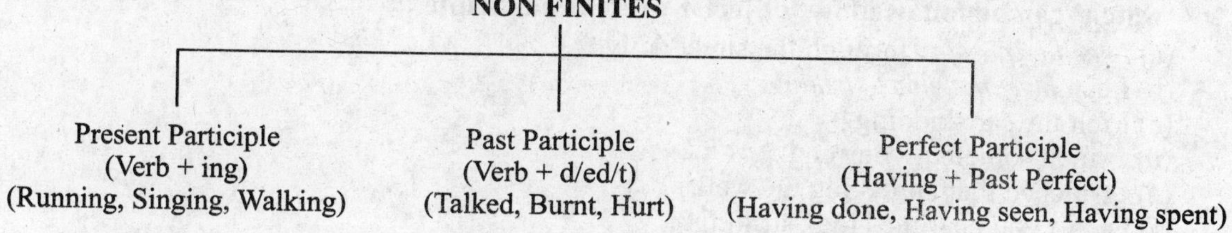

PRESENT PARTICIPLE

The ***present participle*** *is the 'ing' form of a verb*, used as a modifier :

(a) This is an **interesting** novel .

(b) He jumped from the **running** train

(c) It was a **tiring** journey.

Present Participle : USE

(A) Present participle is used to form continuous tenses :

(a) He is *playing* football.

(b) They have been *reading* for an hour.

(c) Sita was *watching* TV.

(B) Present participle is used as adjective :

(i) It was a ***tiring journey***.

(ii) I read an ***interesting novel***.

(C) After 'have + Object' :

(a) I will *have you swimming* within a week.
(As a result of my efforts you will be swimming within a week.)

(b) We *had them all dancing*.
(We persuaded them to dance.)

(c) I *have them both speaking* to one another.
(I persuaded or encouraged them to speak to one another.)
(d) If you give such cocktail parties, you will *have the neighbours complaining.*
(e) If celebrities put their numbers in telephone directories,they'd *have everyone ringing* them up.

(D) 'I won't + have + Object + Present Participle', expresses the meaning 'I won't / don't allow this'...
(a) I won't have them playing cricket in my garden.
(b) I won't have him cleaning his vehicles in the corridor.
(I won't / don't allow him to clean his vehicles in the corridor.)

(E) Present Participle can also replace 'Relative Pronoun + Verb'
(a) There are many people who wish to visit the temple.
There are many people wishing to visit the temple. ('wishing' replaces 'who wish')
(b) Please segregate the children who need immediate medical assistance.
Please segregate the children needing immediate medical assistance.

(F) The verbs of perception; 'see, hear, feel, smell', and the verbs—'listen' (to), 'notice' and 'watch' can be followed by 'object + present participle' :
(a) *I see her passing* through the street daily.
(b) I can *hear the clock striking.*
(c) I felt the car skidding.
(d) I smelt something burning.
(e) I watched them breaking the wall.
(f) Didn't you hear the clock striking?

NOTE *Verbs; 'see, hear, feel' and sometimes 'listen' (to), 'notice' and 'watch' can also be followed by* ***'object + bare infintive' :***
(a) *I saw her leave* the college.
(b) *I saw him repair* the car.
(c) I saw him change the wheel. (It means that I saw the whole action.)

The use of **infinitive implies that the action is complete** (as in above sentences), or the infinitive is used when we want **to emphasize that the action is complete**, while the use of **participle can express both complete and incomplete action :**
(a) I saw her repairing the car.
It could mean that I watched the whole action or that I saw only part of it.

(G) Catch/find/leave + Object + Present Participle
(i) The use of 'catch' **denotes an unpleasant action** while the use of **'find' doesn't reflect any such feelings :**
(a) I caught him stealing the purse. (stealing—unpleasant action)
(b) If he catches you using his computer, he will be furious.
(c) I found her waiting for me.
(d) I found him standing at the gate.
(e) We found a man lying on the road.

(ii) 'Leave' can also be used in above constructions :

(a) I left her working in the office.
(She was working in the office when I left.)

(b) I left him talking on phone.
(He was talking on phone when I left.)

(H) Present participle is normally used with; 'come / go / spend / waste / be busy', in following situations :

(a) We are going shopping today afternoon.
(b) They are going sailing.
(c) Come dancing.
(d) They are going skiing..
(e) He spent a huge amount modernizing his old house.
(f) They wasted five hours trying to find the solution to this problem.
(g) I spend four hours a day travelling.
(h) She doesn't spend much time cooking her meal.
(i) She was busy writing lessons.
(j) She was busy packing.

(I) Other uses of Present Participle :

(i) ***When two actions are done simultaneously*** by the same subject ,one of them can well be expressed by the present participle. The participle can be placed before or after the finite verb as following :

(a) She went away.
(a. 1) She cried as she went.
(a. 2) She *went away crying.*
(b) She holds the rope with one hand and stretches out the other to the man in the river :
Holding the rope with one hand she stretches out the other to the man in the river.

(ii) ***If one action is immediately followed by another***, by the same subject, the first action can also be denoted by a present participle :

(a) He opened the almirah. He took out a file.
Opening the almirah he took out a file.
(b) He takes off his clothes and creeps cautiously into the water.
Taking off his clothes he creeps cautiously into the water.

NOTE *In above sentences we can also use perfect participle and say 'Having opened ...., Having taken off'...., but this is not necessary except when the use of the present participle leads to ambiguity.*

(iii) ***When the second action (mentioned latter) is the part or a result of the first action*** (mentioned earlier), we can express the second action by a present participle :

(a) He went out slamming the iron gate.
(b) He fired, wounding several persons in the crowd.
In the above sentence (b) the *second action*, **'wounding several persons'**, is expressed by a present participle ***'wound + ing'*** as per above rule; as this *second action 'wounding* is result of the *first action*, **'fired'**.
(c) I fell, striking my head against the wall and cutting it.
(Here are three actions, the last two expressed by participles.)

(iv) ***The present participle can replace 'as/ since/ because' + subject + verb***, as following :

(a) As he was a student he was interested in books.
Being a student he was interested in books. ('*As he was*' is replaced by—'*Being*')

(b) Because he was ill he didn't go to Jaipur
Being ill he didn't go to Jaipur.

(c) *Since he knew* that he wouldn't be able to recognize her,he used an addressed plate.
Knowing that he wouldn't be able to recognize her, he used an addressed plate.

(v) ***Two or more participles can also be used in a sentence*, one after the other** :

(a) Realizing that he hadn't enough money and not wanting to borrow from his friends, he decided to sell his chain.

(b) Not knowing the language and having no friends in the city, he found it hard to get a room on rent.

NOTE *We should not use a present participle to express an action which is not consistent with the action of the principal clause :*

He sailed for Srilanka on Tuesday and arriving their on Saturday. *Incorrect.*
He sailed for Srilanka on Tuesday and arrived their on Saturday. *Correct.*

Here 'sailed' is used in principal clause so we cannot use 'arriving' in subordinating clause.We should use 'arrived'.

PAST PARTICIPLE

Most of the Past participles end in *-ed, -en, -d, -t,* or *-n*, as in the words *walked*, *eaten*,gone, *saved*, *dealt*, and *seen*.

1. As Adjective :

(a) This is a *fried* fish.
(b) A burnt child dreads the fire.
(c) I need a *boiled* egg.
(d) Police wanted a written statement.

2. Past participle is used to form perfect tense :

(a) Ram has *arrived.*
(b) They have *completed* the work.
(c) I have *finished* my work.
(d) He had *gone* to Jaipur.

3. Past participle is used in Passive structures :

(a) This is the book written by me.
(b) Learn the lessons taught by her.
(c) He can't forget the favour shown to him.

4. *Past participles can replace passive verbs* as following :

(a) She was aroused by the noise and leapt to her feet.
Aroused by the noise she leapt to her feet.

(b) He enters. He is accompanied by his sister.
He enters, accompanied by his sister.

(c) The railway bridge had been weakened by successive storms and was no longer safe.
Weakened by successive storms, the railway bridge was no longer safe.

PERFECT PARTICIPLE : USE

(A) As mentioned on the preceeding page, under the heading Present participle (I-B), *if one action is immediately followed by another, by the same subject the first action can also be denoted by a Perfect participle* :

(i) Opening the almirah, he took out a file. *Present Participle*
Having opened the almirah, he took out a life. *Perfect Participle*

(ii) Taking off his clothes, he creeps cautiously into the water. *Present Participle*
Having taken off his clothes, he creeps into the water. *Perfect Participle*

(B) The perfect participle is used ***when there is an interval of time between the two actions :***

(a) Having failed thrice, she didn't want to apply again.

(b) Having passed his M.A, he enrolled for Ph.D.

(C) Perfect participle is also used **when the first action covered a period of time :**

(a) Having been his own boss for many years, he found it unusual to accept orders from others.

(b) Having been a boxer for six years ,he knew where to punch.

(D) The perfect participle passive structure **(having been + past participle)** is used when it is necessary **to clarify that the action expressed by the participle happened before** the action expressed by the another verb :

(a) Having been warned about the bandits they deposited the valuables in the lockers.

(b) Having been bitten twice, the courier man refused to deliver the goods, unless the dog is chained up.

UNATTACHED OR DANGLING PARTICIPLE

A participle is a verbal adjective , so it must be attached to some noun or pronoun. It means it must have a proper subject of reference. **If the participle is not attached to some noun or pronoun it is** *called dangling participle.*

Look at the following sentence :

Waiting for the train, a brick fell on my feet. *Incorrect*

It appears that the brick was waiting for the train, which is nonsense.

A participle linked in this way to the wrong noun / pronoun is said to be **misrelated** or the participle 'waiting' has no noun or pronoun to which it is attached.

The above sentence should have been written as following :

While I was waiting for the train, a brick fell on my feet. *Correct*

See more such examples :

(a) Standing near the gate, a dog caught her. *Incorrect*
While she was standing near the gate, a dog caught her. *Correct*

(b) When using this machine it must be remembered to unlock it first. *Incorrect*
When using this machine, you must remember to unlock it first. *Correct*

(c) Deciding to join the navy, the recruiter happily pumped Jack's hand. *Incorrect*
(The recruiter is not deciding to join the navy; Jack is.)

The recruiter happily pumped Jack's hand after learning that Jack had decided to join the navy. *Correct*

(d) When watching films, commercials are especially irritating. *Incorrect*

How to correct the above sentence?

(i) One option would be *to change the subject* so that it names the actor that the modifier implies :

When watching films, I find commercials especially irritating. *Correct*

(ii) Another option would be *to turn the modifier into a word group that includes the actor:*

When I am watching films, commercials are especially irritating. *Correct*

(e) Being a cold morning I didn't go to office. *Incorrect*

It being a cold morning I didn't go to office. or, *Correct*

The morning being cold, I didn't go to office. *Correct*

(f) Being a rainy day, the school remained closed. *Incorrect*

It being a rainy day, the school remained closed. or, *Correct*

The day being rainy, the school remained closed. *Correct*

As you can see, a dangling participle is one that either has no noun or pronoun to modify or else is not close enough to the word it is supposed to modify, to prevent it from attaching to another element. In either case, the sentence is both ambiguous and nonsensical. Even if a sentence is not rendered nonsense by a dangling participle, it will still be ambiguous, and that is almost as bad. **Dangling participles are not considered acceptable in standard English, so they should be avoided in writing.**

NOTE *However, some participles as 'considering, regarding, concerning, taking, speaking, touching', etc. do not need to agree with the subject of the sentence :*

(a) Considering the price, the quality of the cloth is good.
(b) Speaking roughly, the distance between Delhi and Alwar is 150 Kms.
(c) Taking every point into consideration, the proposal is very attractive.

CORRECT YOURSELF EXERCISE : PARTICIPLE

CYE : 01 Correct the following sentences :

1. Being Sunday, I am thinking to go to a movie.
2. Remember the lessons teach by the teacher.
3. Where is the book wrote by Mr. Gupta?
4. Ploughing his fields some old statues were found.
5. I want a wrote complaint.
6. There is no drink water in the office.
7. Having satisfied with his reply, I didn't take any action.
8. Tired, I couldn't work any more.
9. Left from hand to month, he yet maintains his standard of living.
10. Having referred to your application, I beg to write...

CYE : 02 Correct the following sentences :

1. In regard to my qualification I beg to submit...
2. Sleeping in the house, a thief entered their house.
3. Having injured he went to hospital.

4. Turn to the left you can see the palace.
5. Walking in the forest a lion was seen.
6. Don't get off a ran bus.
7. The ship has sunken.
8. Having been worked hard he got tired.
9. Having opened the drawer she took out a knife.
10. We must provide good education to grow children.

CYE : 03 Fill in the blanks with correct form of non-finite verbs :

(Infinitive/Gerund/Participle)

1. His speech left me .... (to think/thought/thinking)
2. Some boys like .... the TV. (to watch/watch)
3. Sita is good at .... (swim/swimming/to swim)
4. I had an aversion .... meet. (to eat/ to eating)
5. It is wrong .... a lie before the judge at least. (to tell/telling/have told)
6. He had rather .... than beg. (to starve/starve/starved)
7. My greatest pleasure is .... while alone. (singing/to sing/sung)
8. He wears a .... look today. (worrying/worried/to worry)
9. You had better .... nothing. (to say/saying/say/said)
10. .... is a good exercise for the young. (to swim/swimming)

CYE : 04 Fill in the blanks with correct form of non-finite verbs :

(Infinitive/Gerund/Participle)

1. I watched her .... and come often. (going/go /to go)
2. .... is easier than reading. (to play/having played/playing)
3. I found his daughter .... (to cry/crying/have cried)
4. She denied .... any force to get him accept his fault. (used/to use/using)
5. I hate .... and cheating. (to lie/lying)
6. He said, "He has given up ...." (to smoke/smoking/have smoked)
7. I remember .... her in the park. (seeing/to see)
8. She stopped .... others. (to advise/advising/had advised)
9. They want us .... for the girls to arrive. (waiting/to wait)
10. .... many times, he doesn't want to try again now. (failing/failed/having failed)
11. .... that she was early, she went to meet her friends. (to know/having know/knowing)
12. The book .... on the chair is mine. (lye/lying)
13. Please excuse my .... early today. (leave/left/leaving)
14. She disliked my .... on Sunday. (work/working).
15. .... out of the window, she saw a strange creature. (looked/looking/having looked)

CYE : 05 Underline the participial phrase(s) in each of the following sentences, and mention the noun or pronoun modified.

1. Getting up at five, we got an early start.
2. Facing college standards, the students realized that they hadn't worked hard enough in high school.

3. Statistics reported by the National Education Association revealed that seventy percent of American colleges offer remedial English classes emphasizing composition.
4. The overloaded car gathered speed slowly.
5. Gathering my courage, I asked for a temporary loan.
6. Starting out as an army officer, Karen's father was frequently transferred.
7. Mrs. Sears showing more bravery than wisdom invited thirty boys and girls to a party.
8. The student, left in charge of the class, was unable to keep order.
9. Applicants must investigate various colleges learning as much as possible about them before applying for admission.
10. The crying boy, angered by the bully, began to fight.

Rewrite the following sentences (you may need to reword them slightly) with the correct placement and punctuation of the participial phrases :

11. Espousing a conservative point of view, the proposal for more spending on federal social programmes bothered him.
12. Absorbed in an interesting conversation, my scheduled appointment time passed unnoticed.

SOLUTIONS : TEST YOURSELF EXERCISE

Solutions CYE : 01

1. It being Sunday, I am thinking to go to a movie.
2. Remember the lessons taught by the teacher.
3. Where is the book written by Mr. Gupta?
4. While ploughing his fields he found some old statues .
5. I want a written complaint.
6. There is no drinking water in the office.
7. Having been satisfied with his reply, I didn't take any action.
8. Being tired, I couldn't work any more.
9. Living from hand to month, he yet maintains his standard of living.
10. Referring to your application, I beg to write....

Solutions CYE : 02

1. Regarding my qualification I beg to submit...
2. While they were sleeping in the house, a thief entered their house.
3. Having been injured he went to hospital.
4. Turning to the left you can see the palace.
5. While I was walking in the forest I saw a lion.
6. Don't get off a running bus.
7. The ship has sunk.
8. Having worked hard he got tired.
9. Opening the drawer she took out a knife.
10. We must provide good education to growing children.

Solutions CYE : 03

1. thinking, 2. to watch, 3. swimming, 4. to eating, 5. to tell,
6. starve, 7. to sing, 8. worried, 9. say, 10. swimming.

Solutions CYE : 04

1. go, 2. playing, 3. crying, 4. using, 5. lying, 6. smoking, 7. seeing, 8. advising, 9. to wait, 10. Having failed, 11. knowing, 12. lying, 13. leaving, 14. working, 15. looking.

Solutions CYE : 05

1. Getting up at five, we got an early start. [modifies *we*]
2. Facing college standards, the students realized that they hadn't worked hard enough in high school. [modifies *the students*]
3. Statistics reported by the National Education Association revealed that seventy percent of American colleges offer remedial English classes emphasizing composition. [1. modifies *statistics*; 2. modifies *classes*]
4. The overloaded car gathered speed slowly. [modifies *car*]
5. Gathering my courage, I asked for a temporary loan. [modifies *I*]
6. Starting out as an army officer, Karen's father was frequently transferred. [modifies *Karen's father*]
7. Mrs. Sears, showing more bravery than wisdom, invited thirty boys and girls to a party. [modifies *Mrs. Sears*]
8. The student left in charge of the class was unable to keep order. [modifies *student*]
9. Applicants must investigate various colleges, learning as much as possible about them before applying for admission.
   [modifies *applicants*; note that *applying for admission* is a gerund phrase, not a participial phrase.]
10. The crying boy, angered by the bully, began to fight. [both modify *boy*]
11. Espousing a conservative point of view the proposal for more spending on federal social programs bothered him.

The opening participial phrase is misplaced because it is intended to modify '*him*', not '*the proposal*'. A possible revision would be : Espousing a conservative point of view, he was bothered by the proposal for more spending on federal social programs.

12. Absorbed in an interesting conversation my scheduled appointment time passed unnoticed.

The opening participial phrase is dangling because it modifies a term that doesn't appear in the sentence : '*I*', that is, the person having the conversation. The 'scheduled appointment time' couldn't have been 'absorbed in an interesting conversation.' A possible revision would be : Absorbed in an interesting conversation, I allowed my scheduled appointment time to pass unnoticed.

12

Active Voice-Passive Voice

Verbs are also said to be either '*active*' or '*passive*' in voice. In the active voice, the subject and verb relationship is straightforward : the subject is a doer and the verb moves the sentence along. In the **passive voice**, the subject of the sentence is not a doer but is acted upon by some other **agent** or by something unnamed.

What is Voice ?

***The voice of a verb* tells whether the subject of the sentence performs or receives the action.**

Active Voice : In active voice, the **subject performs the action** *expressed by the verb.*

Passive Voice : In passive voice, the **subject receives the action** *expressed by the* verb :

(a) He sings a song *Active voice*

(b) A song is sung by him. *Passive voice*

(b) Active Verb : A verb is 'Active' when its form shows (as in sentence -a) that the subject does some work or subject is Active.

(c) Passive verb : A verb is 'Passive' when its form shows (as in sentence -b) that some thing is done to the subject (of sentence a) or subject is not Active, but Passive.

WHY AND WHEN TO USE PASSIVE STRUCTURE ?

1. ***When subject is not known*** *or it is not necessary to tell about the subject :*

(a) This mosque was built years ago.

(b) The mirror was broken yesterday.

(c) The shop was looted and three persons were arrested.

(d) A bomb was exploded.

2. *When it is necessary to give importance to the object :*

(a) The letter was written by Mr. Ganesh.

(b) The white tiger was killed by the hunter.

3. The passive voice is especially helpful (and even regarded as mandatory) ***in scientific or technical writing or lab reports***, where the subject is not really important but the process or principle being described is of ultimate importance.

(a) Hydrochloric acid is produced when hydrozen and chlorine are mixed.

(b) Telephone was invented by Grahambell.

4. We use the passive voice ***to avoid responsibility for actions taken.***

Thus 'Wine ads are designed to appeal especially to students'.----- places the burden on the ads — as opposed to burden on the designer/advertiser.

'We designed the wine ads to appeal especially to students,' in which 'we' accepts responsibility.

GENERAL RULES TO CHANGE THE VOICE

If you want to change an active-voice sentence to passive voice, consider carefully who or what(subject) is performing the action expressed by the verb, and then make that agent (who or what) the object of a 'by the...' phrase. Make what is acted upon, the 'subject' of the sentence, and change the verb to a form of *'be* + past participle'. Including an explicit 'by the...' phrase is optional. 'By' is used when the subject of active sentence is important .

NOTE *the following points carefully :*

1. **Make the *'object'* of the active sentence - *'subject'* of the passive sentence.**
   (a) I write a letter. *Active Voice*
   Object of Active sentence is 'a letter' . It becomes subject of the passive sentence as follows :
   (a) A letter (is writtenj by me.)
2. **Make the *'subject'* of the active sentence- *'agent'* of the passive sentence**. The agent will be in objective form.Use 'by' before it.'By' is used when the subject of active sentence is important to mention .
   Subject of the above active sentence is 'I'; Its objective form is 'me'. So we write 'by me'
3. Always ***use third form of the verb* (past participle) in passive structures**.The past participle (V–III) will be preceded by 'to be' form of verb, as per the tense of the sentence.
4. Please take care that the *'to be' form of verb is governed by the new subject* (subject of the passive sentence) .
   Look at the following examples :
   (a) I write a letter. *Active*
   A letter is written by me. *Passive*
   (b) She is helping the students . *Active*
   The students are being helped by her. *Passive*
   Here in sentence (b), plural verb - 'are' is used as per the new subject - 'students'.
5. ***Change of Subject of Active sentence in to Object of Passive is done as per following table :***

Active Voice	Passive Voice	Active Voice	Passive Voice
I	Me	She	Her
He	Him	They	Them
You	You	It	It
We	Us	Who	Whom

6. ***Only transitive verbs*** (those that take objects) ***can be transformed into passive constructions.*** Furthermore, active sentences containing **certain verbs cannot be transformed into passive structures.** '*To have*' is the most important of these verbs. We can say "He has a new cycle ," but we cannot say "A new cycle is had by him." Here is a brief list of such verbs : **'resemble, look like, equal ,agree with ,mean,contain ,hold ,comprise ,lack,suit,fit,become' etc.** These verbs are intransitive in nature.

7. Sentences in 'present perfect continuous', 'past perfect continuous', 'future perfect continuous' and 'future continuous' can't be **transformed into Passive.**

The change of verbs *(tensewise)* takes place as per following table :

Tense	Verb (Active)	Verb (Passive)To be form + VIII
1. Simple Present	write / writes	am / is / are written
2. Simple Past	wrote	was / were written
3. Simple Future	shall / will write	shall / will be written
4. Present Continuous	is / am / are writing	is / am / are being written
5. Past Continuous	was / were writing	was / were being written
6. Present Perfect	has / have written	has / have been written
7. Past Perfect	had written	had been written
8. Future Perfect	will / shall have written	will / shall have been written

VARIOUS TENSES AND CHANGE OF VOICE

VOICE CHANGE : PRESENT TENSE

1. **Present Indefinite :** In Active voice , sentences have the following structure usually :

(a) He writes a letter. *Active voice*

(Subject + V-I + Object.)

*While changing it into **passive**, it becoms :* *Passive voice*

(a) A letter is written by him.

Subject + is + V-3 + by + Agent (in objective form).

More examples :

Active

(a) I love you.

(b) She washes the clothes in the evening.

Passive

(a) You are loved by me.

(b) The clothes are washed by her in the evening.

2. **Present Continuous :** In Active voice , sentences have the following structure usually :

(a) He is writing a letter.

(Subject + is / am / are + verb + ing + Object)

*While **changing it into passive**, it becomes :*

(a) A letter is being written by him.

Subject + is + being + V-3 + by Agent. (in objective form)

More examples :

Active	Passive
(a) We are playing football.	Football is being played by us.
(b) She is making tea.	Tea is being made by her.

3. **Present Perfect :** In Active voice , sentences have the following structure usually :

(a) I have written a letter.

(Subject + have / has +V-III + Object)

*While **changing it into passive** it becomes :*

A letter has been written by me.

Subject + has been + V -3 + by + Agent. (in objective form)

More examples :

Active.	**Passive**
(a) He has bought a scooter.	A scooter has been bought by him.
(b) He has repaired the car.	The car has been repaired by him.

VOICE CHANGE : PAST TENSE

1. **Past Indefinite :** In Active voice , sentences have the following structure usually :

(a) I wrote a letter.

Subject + V- II + Object

*While **changing it into passive** it becomes :*

(a) A letter was written by me.

Subject + was + V-3 + by + Agent (in objective form)

Active	**Passive**
(a) We won the match.	The match was won by us.
(b) I purchased a pen.	A pen was purchased by me.

2. **Past Continuous :** In Active voice , sentences have the following structure usually:

(a) He was writing a letter.

(Subject + was / were + verb + ing + object)

*While **changing it into passive**, it becomes :*

(a) A letter was being written by him.

Subject + was + being + V-III + by + Agent (in objective form)

Active	**Passive**
(a) Ram was driving a car.	A car was being driven by Ram.
(b) They were flying the kites.	The kites were being flown by them.

3. **Past Perfect :** In Active voice , sentences have the following structure usually :

(a) He had written a letter.

(Subject + had + V -III + object)

*While **changing it into passive**, it becomes :*

(a) A letter had been written by him.

Subject + had been + V-3 + by + Agent (in objective form)

Active	**Passive**
(a) He had killed a dog.	A dog had been killed by him.
(b) They had completed the project.	The project had been completed by them.

VOICE CHANGE : FUTURE TENSE

1. **Future Indefinite :** In Active voice , sentences have the following structure usually :

(a) I shall write a letter.

(Subject + shall / will + V - 1 + Object)

While changing it into passive, it becomes :

(a) A letter will be written by me.

(Subject + will be + V- 3 + by + Agent (in objective form)

Active	**Passive**
(a) He will give you a gift.	A gift will be given to you by him.
(b) He will phone you.	You will be phoned by him.

2. Future Perfect : In Active voice , sentences have the following structure usually :

(a) I shall have bought a pen.

(Subject + will / shall have +V-3 + Object.)

*While **changing it into passive**, it becomes :*

(a) A pen will have been bought by me.

(Subject + will have been + V- 3 + by + agent)

Active

(a) She will have written a thesis.

(b) Ramesh will have completed the project.

Passive

A thesis will have been written by her.

The project will have been completed by Ramesh.

PASSIVE OF INTERROGATIVE SENTENCES

Interrogative sentences are normally of two types :

(a) 'Yes / No' questions. (b) 'Wh' questions.

1. 'Yes / No' questions

'Yes/No' questions are those questions which begin with an auxiliary :

(A) Questions beginning with is / am / are. ***The passive structure*** of such questions will be as per following :

Is / am / are / + subject + being + V -III + by + agent ?

Active	**Passive**
(a) Is he writing a letter?	Is a letter being written by him ?
(b) Are they ploughing the field?	Is the field being ploughed by them ?
(c) Am I catching the thief?	Is the thief being caught by me ?

(B) Questions beginning with 'do / does': ***The passive structure*** of such questions will be as per following :

Is / am / are / + subject + V-III + by + agent ?

Active	**Passive**
(a) Does he need a pen?	Is a pen needed by him?
(b) Do you like the rooms?	Are the rooms liked by you?
(c) Do you write a lesson?	Is a lesson written by you?

(C) Questions beginning with 'Did' : ***The Passive structure*** of such questions will be as per following :

Was / Were + subject + V -III + by + agent ?

Active	Passive
(a) Did he write a letter?	Was a letter written by him?
(b) Did she help you?	Were you helped by him?
(c) Did he phone you?	Were you phoned by him?

(D) Questions beginning with ' was / were'. ***The passive structure*** of such questions will be as per following :

Was/Were + subject + being + V -III + by + agent ?

Active	Passive
(a) Was she cooking food?	Was food being cooked by her?
(b) Were they playing chess?	Was the chess being played by them?
(c) Was he washing the clothes?	Were the clothes being washed by him?
(d) Were you serving your parents?	Were your parents being served by you?

(E) Questions beginning with Have / has / had : ***The Passive structure*** of such questions will be as per following :

Has/Have/Had + subject + been+ V -3 + by + agent ?

Active	Passive
(a) Has he written a book?	Has A book been written by him?
(b) Have they played a match?	Have a match been played by them?
(c) Had she written a letter?	Had a letter been written by her?

(F) Questions beginning with modal auxiliary verbs. The passive structure of such questions will be as per following :

Modal Auxiliary + Subject + be + V -III + by + agent ?

Active	Passive
(a) Can she control the situation ?	Can the situation be controlled by her ?
(b) May he cross the river?	May the river be crossed by him?
(c) Should he cut the wood ?	Should the wood be cut by him?
(d) Will you steal the book ?	Will the book be stolen by you?
(e) Will they win the match?	Will the match be won by them?
(f) Would you repair the car?	Would the car be repaired by you?

2. 'Wh' words

Questions beginning with ; what, why, when, where, who etc : The structure of many 'Wh' questions in active voice is as following :

'Wh' word + auxiliary +subject + main verb + object?

The Passive structure of such Wh questions in passive is as following :

Wh word + auxiliary +Subject(object of active)+ V-III + by + agent ?

Active	Passive
(a) Why have you broken the mirror?	Why has the mirror been broken by you?
(b) Why do you write a letter?	Why is a letter written by you?
(c) When will you return my pen?	When will my pen be returned by you?
(d) Why are you laughing at her?	Why is she being laughed at by you?
(e) Where did he put the things?	Where were the things put by him?
(f) What did he break?	What was broken by him?

(g) When do you write the lesson?	When is the lesson written by you?
(h) Why does he kick the ball ?	Why is the ball kicked by him?
(i) When do they send the parcel?	When is the parcel sent by them?
(j) Where did she buy the books?	Where were the books bought by her?

Questions beginning with 'who' : Here 'who' acts as subject. The passive of such questions is made as following.

Active	Passive
(a) Who broke this beautiful glass?	By whom was this beautiful glass broken?
(b) Who solved that problem?	By whom was that problem solved?
(c) Who can break this stick?	By whom can this stick be broken?
(d) Who will help her in difficulty?	By whom will she be helped in difficulty?
(e) Who wrote the Ramayana?	By whom was the Ramayana written?
(f) Who has deceived you?	By whom have you been deceived?

Questions begin with 'whom' : The passive of such questions is made as following :

Active	Passive
(a) Whom have you invited?	Who has been invited by you?
(b) Whom has he abused?	Who has been abused by him?
(c) Whom has she reported?	Who has been reported by her?

PASSIVE WITHOUT AGENT

In passive structures we should not use 'by + agent' when the subject is understood or vague or unimportant to mention.For example **if the subject in active voice is - 'someone, somebody, nobody, people', etc.**

	Active	Passive
(a)	People speak English all over the world.	English is spoken all over the world.
(b)	Police arrested the thieves.	The thieves were arrested.(Subject is understood.)
(c)	Someone has stolen my watch.	My watch has been stolen.
(d)	We execute all instructions without delay	All instructions are executed without delay.
(e)	Robbers looted the shop.	The shop was looted.

NOTE *'In all passive voice exercises the use of 'by' with an agent must be rigorously suppressed, except in those examples where our interest in the predicate has led us to use the passive voice - we should omit the agent where the agent is vague or unknown.'* ***W.S. Allen (Living English Structure)***

SENTENCES WITH MODALS

Look at the following sentences with modals :

Active	Passive
(a) Sita could help him.	He could be helped by Sita.
(b) I will write a letter by me.	A letter will be written by me.
(c) You must write a book.	A book must be written by you.
(d) She should obey your parents.	Your parents should be obeyed by her.
(e) I may purchase a pen.	A pen may be purchased by me.

PASSIVE VOICE : IMPERATIVE SENTENCES

Imperative sentences are such sentences that contain expression of 'order, request, advise, suggestions' etc :

(A) Sentences with order !, Command :

Active	Passive
(a) Shut the window.	Let the window be shut.
(b) Bring a glass of water.	Let a glass of water be brought.
(c) Finish this work.	Let this work be finished.
(d) Switch off the light.	Let the light be switched off.
(e) Inform the police.	Let the police be informed.
(f) Search the briefcase.	Let the briefcase be searched.
(g) Turn him out.	Let him be turned out.

The Passive structure is usually as following :

Let + Subject + be +V- III +... .

NOTE *Sentences containing express command of order can be changed into passive as following :*

(a) Get out of this office. *Active*
You are ordered to get out of this office. *Passive*
(b) Bring some glasses of water for them. *Active*
You are ordered to bring some glasses of water for them. *Passive*

The Passive structure will be as following :

You are ordered to + verb I + ...

(B) Sentences containing request :

Active	Passive
(a) Please open the door.	You are requested to open the door
(b) Please help that old lady.	You are requested to help that old lady.
(c) Take this seat please.	You are requested to take this seat.
(d) Please give me a book.	You are requested to give me a book.
(e) Do it for me please.	You are requested to do it for me.
(f) Please don't disturb me.	You are requested not to disturb me.

The Passive structure will be as following :

You are requested to +V- I ...

(C) Sentences with suggestion :

Active	Passive
(a) Help the disabled.	The disabled should be helped.
(b) Listen to me.	I should be listened to.
(c) Help the needy and poor.	The needy and poor should be helped.
(d) Always speak the truth.	The truth should always be spoken.
(e) Love the kids.	The kids should be loved.
(f) Hear him now.	He should be heard now.
(g) Help your dear and near.	Your dear andnear should be helped.
(h) Love your country.	Your country should be loved.

The Passive structure will be as following :

Subject + should be +V- III +... .

(D) Sentences with Advice :

Active	Passive
(a) Work hard.	You are advised to work hard.
(b) Get up early.	You are advised to get up early.
(c) Do not smoke.	You are advised not to smoke.
(d) Be careful.	You are advised to be careful.
(e) Think before you speak.	You are advised to think before you speak.

The Passive structure will be as following :

You are advised to + V- I +... .

PASSIVE OF INFINITIVE

Sentences with infinitive in ***active voice*** *have following structures :*

Subject + is / am / are / was / were/ have / has / had + to + verb -I + object .

The ***passive structure*** *is as following :*

Subject + is / am / are / was / were / have / has / had + to be + V-3 + by + agent.

Look at the following solved examples :

Active	Passive
(a) I am to finish this work.	This work is to be finished by me.
(b) You are to write an essay.	An essay is to be written by you.
(c) They are to buy a TV.	A TV is to be bought by them.
(d) He was to sell this freeze.	This freeze was to be sold by him.
(e) We were to buy a car.	A car was to be bought by us.
(f) I am to assist him.	He is to be assisted by me.
(g) She has to help him.	He has to be helped by her.
(h) You were to bring him here.	He was to be brought here by you.
(i) The students have to write notes.	Notes have to be written by the students.
(j) Harish had to complete this work.	This work had to be completed by Harish.
(k) Ramesh has to repair this car.	This car has to be repaired by Ramesh.
(l) I have to purchase a pen.	A pen has to be purchased by me.
(m) You have to choose a house.	A house has to be chosen by you.

MISCELLANEOUS STRUCTURES

(A) It is time to + V-1 + noun .... —*Active structure*

The passive structure is :**It is time + for + noun + to be + V-3 ..... .**

Active	Passive
1. It is time to close the office.	It is time for the office to be closed.
2. It is time to supply food.	It is time for food to be supplied.
3. It is time to stop writing.	It time for the writing to be stopped.
4. It is time to give the final warning.	It is time for the final warning to be given.

(B) Sentences beginning with 'there'

There +be form of verb + noun + infinitive. *Active structure*

PASSIVE STRUCTURE

There + be form of verb + noun + to be + V-III. ***Passive structure***

	Active	Passive
1.	There is a lot of work to complete.	There is a lot of work to be completed.
2.	There are six letters to write	here are six letters to be written.
3.	There is no time to lose.	There is no time to be lost.
4.	There is no money to donate.	There is no money to be donated.
5.	There is no milk to waste.	There is no milk to be wasted.
6.	There is no work to do.	There is no work to be done.

(C) Passive of verbs showing state of mind or feelings : Some verbs do not express any action but simply express—state of mind or feelings.We should not use 'by' in passive structures of sentences heaving such verbs, instead an appropriate preposition should be used :

	Active	Passive
1.	I know her.	She is known to me. (Preposition - 'to')
2.	He annoyed her.	She was annoyed with him.(Preposition - 'with')
3.	Her behavior annoyed him.	He was annoyed at her behavior. (Prep.-'at')
4.	The news surprised all.	All were surprised at the news.(Prep. - 'at')
5.	The result amazed me.	I was amazed at the result. (Prep. -'at')
6.	She annoyed me.	I was annoyed with her. (Prep.-'with')
7.	Her conduct shocked me.	I was shocked at her conduct.(Prep.-'at')
8.	He satisfied everybody.	Everybody was satisfied with him.(Prep.-'with')
9.	This magazine has greatly interested me.	I have been greatly interested in this magazine. (Prep.-'in')
10.	The news pleased her.	She was pleased with the news. (Prep.-'with')

(D) Passive voice of verbs with appropriate prepositions :

Some verbs take preposition before an object .The preposition remains intact even in passive construction :

	Active	Passive
1.	He laughed at me.	I was laughed at by him.
2.	The police is enquiring into the matter.	The matter is being enquired into by the police.
3.	Sita smiled at Ram.	Ram was smiled at by Sita.
4.	He looks after his parents.	His parents are looked after by him
5.	Rahim mocked at our class teacher.	Our class teacher was mocked at by Rahim.

Such commonly used verbs are; 'look at', 'look after', 'laugh at', 'smile at', 'deride at', 'mock at' etc.

(E) Some sentences have following constructions in active voice :

Subject + ask + object + if / whether + clause.

	Active	Passive
1.	I asked Rani, if she went to Jaipur.	Rani was asked if she went to Jaipur.
2.	He asked me, when I would completle my work.	I was asked when I would complete my work.
3.	They asked me, if I knew his address.	I was asked if I knew his address.
4.	Rajesh asked me, when I would return.	I was asked by Rajesh when I would return.

(F) Gerund Constructions :

Verbs such as ; **'recommend , suggest , propose, insist, advise' + gerund + object** are converted into passive as following :

Active	Passive
1. She insisted using steel mugs.	She insisted that steel mugs should be used.
2. He recommended using knife.	He recommended that knife should be used.

Other gerund constructions are expressed in passive as following :

1. I remember them taking me to the club. *Active*
I remember being taken to the club. *Passive*

(G) Causative Verbs :

Active	Passive
1. I made him polish my shoes.	He was made to polish my shoes.
2. He made me sing a song.	I was made to sing a song.
3. I saw her go.	She was seen to go.
4. I let him go.	He was let go.

NOTE ***'to' is not used with 'let' even in passive constructions.***

Active	Passive
5. They made him king.	He was made king.
6. We elected him monitor.	He was elected monitor.
7. I found her crossing the road.	She was found crossing the road.
8. We saw her sing a song.	She was seen to sing a song.

(H) Sentences of the type ; They believed..., People think..., People say..., We know...,Everyone knows.. etc. have two possible passive forms :

1. It was/is/.. believed that.............
2. He is/ was/.. known / said / believed to be.........

Look at the following examples :

	Active	Passive
1.	They believed that Mr Shukla was very rich.	Mr Shukla was believed to be very rich. or It was believed that Mr. Shukla was very rich.
2.	We know that some children go wise early.	It is known that some children go wise early. Some children are known to go wise early.
3.	People consider that she is intelligent.	She is considered to be intelligent. or, It is considered that she is intelligent.

4. People say that he is a thief.	It is said that he is a thief. or, He is said to be a thief.
5. Everyone knows that he is a gangster.	It is known that he is a gangster or, He is known to be a gangster.

(I) Double Passive

1. They looted the shop and took away the money. *Active*
   The shop was looted and the money was taken away. *Passive*
2. She wrote the book and got published. *Active*
   The book was written and got published by her. *Passive*
3. The police arrested the thieves and sent them to jail. *Active*
   The thieves were arrested and sent to jail. *Passive*

(J) Verbs with two objects : Some sentences have two objects ;**(i) Direct(non living),** and **(ii) Indirect (living).We can use any of the object while converting these into passive : Generally indirect object is used.**

Active	Passive
1. He gave me a purse.	I was given a purse by him. or A purse was given to me by him.
2. Rahim teaches us English.	English is taught us by Rahim. or We are taught English by Rahim.
3. The principal asked him a question.	A question was asked him by the principal. or, He was asked a question by the principal.
4. Rani gave him a letter.	A letter was given to him by Rani. or, He was given a letter by Rani.

MISCELLANEOUS SENTENCES

1. He likes people to call him, 'Don'. *Active*
   He likes to be called 'Don'. *Passive*
2. Someone will serve lunch. *Active*
   Lunch will be served. *Passive*
3. None must leave bicycles and scooters unlocked. *Active*
   Bicycles and scooters must not be left unlocked. *Passive*
4. Students may keep the library books for two weeks only. After that they must return them, otherwise they have to pay fine. *Active*
   The library books may be kept for two weeks only. After that they must be returned otherwise fine has to be paid. *Passive*
5. No one can do any thing unless someone gives us accurate information. *Active*
   Nothing can be done unless we are given accurate information. *Passive*
6. They threw him out. *Active*
   He was thrown out (by them). *Passive*
7. One must do one's duty. *Active*
   Duty must be done. *Passive*
8. The officer wants his subordinates to obey him. *Active*
   The officer wants to be obeyed by his subordinates. *Passive*
9. He wants that he should be treated as king. *Active*
   He wants to be treated as king. *Passive*

10. Ram desires his wife to respect his parents. *Active*
Ram desires his parents to be respected by his wife. *Passive*
11. He wants someone to take photographs. *Active*
He wants photographs to be taken. *Passive*
12. He recommended using the bullet proof car. *Active*
He recommended that the bullet proof car should be used. *Passive*
13. I remember them taking me to library. *Active*
I remember being taken to library. *Passive*
14. We saw them go out. *Active*
They were seen go out. *Passive*
15. They let us go. *Active*
We were let go. *Passive*
16. When he arrived home, police arrested him. *Active*
When he arrived home he was arrested. *Passive*
17. I saw her sing a song. *Active*
She was seen to sing a song. *Passive*
18. Brutus accused Caesar of ambition. *Active*
Caesar was accused of ambition by Brutus. *Passive*
19. We elected him secretary of the society. *Active*
He was elected secretary of the society. *Passive*
20. Her reply shocked me. *Active*
I was shocked at her reply. *Passive*
21. Honey tastes sweet. *Active*
Honey is sweet when (it is) tasted. *Passive*
22. Thank God! *Active*
God be thanked. *Passive*
23. These oranges taste sour. *Active*
These oranges are sour when they are tasted. *Passive*
24. The biscuits eat short and crisp. *Active*
The biscuits are short and crisp when they are eaten. *Passive*
25. The flower smells sweet. *Active*
The flower is sweet when it is smelt. *Passive*

TEST YOUR KNOWLEDGE : ACTIVE-PASSIVE VOICE

Change the following sentences into Passive Voice :

Simple present :

1.The movie fascinates me.

2.The movie bores Jack.

3.The movie surprises them.

Simple past :

4.The movie bored me.

5.The movie fascinated Janu.

6.The movie surprised them.

Present continuous

7. I am helping Shanu.
8. Jane is helping Suresh and Lily.
9. I am cleaning the bathroom.

Past continuous

10. They were cleaning the bedroom.
11. Surabhi was cleaning the kitchen and gallery.

Present perfect :

12. I have mailed the gift.
13. Janu has mailed the gifts.

Past perfect :

14. Jack had directed the movie.
15. Prem had directed those movies.

Future perfect :

16. Johny will have finished the project next month.
17. They will have finished the projects before then.

Future tense with 'will' :

18. I will mail the gift.
19. Janu will mail the gifts.

Future tense with 'going to' :

20. I am going to make the cake.
21. Surabhi is going to make two cakes.

Future tonse with : 'will / won't' (will not) :

22. Shanu will invite Toni to the party.
23. Shanu won't invite Jack to the party.
    (Shanu will not invite Jack to the party.)

Active voice sentences with 'can / can't' : change to passive voice :

24. Mata can foretell the future.
25. Toni can't foretell the future.
    (Toni can not foretell the future.)

Active voice sentences with may / may not : change to passive voice :

26. Her company may give Kashyap a new office.
27. The lazy students may not do the homework.

Active voice sentences with might/ might not : change to passive voice

28. Her company might give Kashyap new office.
29. The lazy students might not do the homework.

Active voice sentences with should / should not : change to passive voice

30. Students should memorize English verbs.

31. Children shouldn't smoke cigarettes.

Active voice sentences with Ought to, : change to passive voice :

32. Students ought to learn English verbs.
(Negative ought to is rarely used)

Active voice sentences with Had better / had better not : change to passive voice :

33. Students had better practice English every day.

34. Children had better not drink whiskey.

Active voice sentences with must/must not, change to passive voice :

35. Tourists must apply for a passport to travel abroad.

36. Customers must not use that door.

Active voice sentences with has to / have to : change to passive voice :

37. She has to practise English every day.

38. Sarala and Mira have to wash the dishes every day.

Active voice sentences with doesn't have to / don't have to : change to passive voice :

39. Mira doesn't have to clean her bedroom every day.

40. The children don't have to clean their bedrooms every day

Active voice sentences with be supposed to / not supposed to : change to passive voice :

41. I am supposed to type the composition.

42. I am not supposed to copy the stories in the book.

43. Jackii is supposed to clean the living room.

44. She isn't supposed to eat candy and gum.

45. They are supposed to make dinner for the family.

46. They aren't supposed to make dessert.

Active voice sentences with should / shouldn't have : Change to passive choice :

47. The students should have learned the verbs.

48. The children shouldn't have broken the window.

Active voice sentences with ought to have : change to passive choice :

49. Students ought to have learned the verbs.
(Negative ought to is rarely used)

Active voice sentences with supposed to (Past) : change to passive voice :

50. I was supposed to type the composition.

51. I wasn't supposed to copy the story in the book.

52. Jackii was supposed to clean the living room.

53. She wasn't supposed to eat candy and gum.

54. Frank and Jane were supposed to make dinner.

55. They weren't supposed to make dessert.

Active voice sentences with may have / may not have : change to passive voice :

56. That firm may have offered Kakitana a new job.
57. The students may not have written the paper.

Active voice sentences with might have /might not have : change to passive voice :

58. That firm might have offered Kakitana a new job.
59. The students might not have written the paper.

SOLUTIONS : TEST YOUR KNOWLEDGE

1. I am fascinated by the movie.
2. Jack is bored by the movie.
3. They are surprised by the movie.
4. I was bored by the movie.
5. Janu was fascinated by the movie.
6. They were surprised by the movie.
7. Shanu is being helped by me.
8. Suresh and Lily are being helped by Jane.
9. The bathroom is being cleaned by me.
10. The bedroom was being cleaned by them.
11. The kitchen and gallery were being cleaned by Surabhi.
12. The gift has been mailed by me.
13. The gifts have been mailed by Janu.
14. The movie had been directed by Jack.
15. Those movies had been directed by Prem.
16. The project will have been finished by next month by Johny.
17. The projects will have been finished before then.
18. The gift will be mailed by me.
19. The gifts will be mailed by Janu.
20. The cake is going to be made by me.
21. Two cakes are going to be made by Surabhi.
22. Toni will be invited to the party by Shanu.
23. Jack won't be invited to the party by Shanu.
    (Jack will not be invited to the party by Shanu.)
24. The future can be foretold by Mata.
25. The future can't be foretold by Toni.
    (The future can not be foretold by Toni.)
26. Kashyap may be given a new office by her company.
27. The homework may not be done by the lazy students.
28. Kashyap might be given new office by her company.
29. The homework might not be done by the lazy students.
30. English verbs should be memorized.
31. Cigarettes shouldn't be smoken by children.

32. English verbs ought to be learnt by students.
33. English had better be practised by students every day.
34. Whiskey had better not be drunk by children.
35. A passport must be applied for by tourists to travel abroad.
36. That door must not be used by customers.
37. English has to be practised by her every day.
38. The dishes have to be washed by Sarla and Mira every day.
39. Her bedroom doesn't have to be cleaned by Mira every day.
40. Their bedrooms don't have to be cleaned by the children every day.
41. The composition is supposed to be typed by me.
42. The stories in the book are not supposed to be copied by me.
43. The living room is supposed to be cleaned by Jackii.
44. Candy and gum aren't supposed to be eaten by her.
45. Dinner for the family is supposed to be made by them.
46. Dessert isn't supposed to be made by them.

Passive : should have / shouldn't have

47. The verbs should have been learned by the students.
48. The window shouldn't have been broken by the children.

Passive : ought to

49. The verbs ought to have been learned by the students,

Passive : (be supposed to) (past tense)

50. The composition was supposed to be typed by me.
51. The story in the book wasn't supposed to be copied.
52. The living room was supposed to be cleaned by Jackii.
53. Candy and gum weren't supposed to be eaten by her.
54. Dinner was supposed to be made by them.
55. Dessert wasn't supposed to be made by them.

Passive : may / may not

56. Kakitana may have been offered a new job by that firm.
57. The paper may not have been written by the students.

Passive : might / might not

58. Kakitana might have been offered a new job by that firm.
59. The paper might not have been written by the students.

CORRECT YOURSELF EXERCISE : ACTIVE–PASSIVE

CYE : 01 : Change the following into passive voice :

1. You should switch off the electricity when changing a fuse.

2. The Government is spending too much money on Operation Pink.
3. They have built six new helipads at Naila.
4. She always gives me calendars and diaries at new year.
5. You will have to amuse him with riddles and bed-time stories.
6. They discovered a new pill to stimulate the appetite.
7. It fascinated me.
8. A duke of the sixteenth century had killed his wife in this room.
9. He performed his symphony for the first time last week.
10. The owner himself showed them the house.
11. Have they carried out his instructions ?
12. We have to pick the fruit very early in the morning.
13. They allowed Harry to go but they did not allow Dick.
14. Fear of death oppresses some old people.
15. The judge advised me to the settle the matter out of court.
16. Rajeev chose his words with care.
17. If in the sixteenth century they could make history by building monuments,in the twentieth century they can make it by selling and reselling them.
18. They promised Mary a new doll for her birthday.
19. No one ever taught me the rudiments of music.
20. They have proved all his calculations wrong.
21. No one has climbed this mountain before.
22. Did you grow these vegetables in your own garden ?
23. They answered me most rudely in the shop.

CYE : 02

1. Rewrite the following sentences in the passive voice :

1. They rejected his proposal and laughed at him.
2. Who is bothering you ?
3. One must do one's duty.

2. Rewrite the following sentences in the passive voice :

4. Two oxen pull the plough.
5. The murderer hid the knife in the grass.
6. Anyone will rob you if you are not careful.

3. Rewrite the following sentences into the passive voice :

7. He asked me to wait.
8. She is running a school these days.
9. Let them do it now.
10. Everyone knows that Mr.A is gang leader.
11. Has someone told you about your result?

4. Put the following sentences into the passive voice :

12. Please sit here and wait till I return.
13. Has someone made all the necessary arrangements ?
14. It was clear that the parents had brought the child up well.
15. They can't put you in prison if they haven't tried you.
16. People say that tortoises live longer than elephants.

5. **Put the following sentences into the passive voice :**

17. They did not tell me the truth about the situation.
18. They will look after you well.
19. Did they not tell you to he here by six O'clock?
20. It surprised me to hear someone had robbed you.

6. **Change the voice of the following :**

21. Did you paint these pictures in your own studio?
22. They have decided to increase the school fees this year.
23. Anger provokes many people to take hasty decisions which they later regret very much.
24. You must understand clearly that this is the last time I shall allow it.
25. You can not expect children to understand these problems.

CYE : 03 Change the following sentences into passive voice :

1. He will have closed his shop by 8 O'clock.
2. They will have finished the paper by 11 O'clock.
3. I shall have saved enough money to buy a house by 1990.
4. He will have advised me.
5. He can help you.
6. The child could not climb the tree.
7. You may return the book next week.
8. They might win the match.
9. We should obey our parents.
10. He would make no promise.
11. We ought to respect our teachers.
12. You must do your duty.
13. You could have solved the sum.
14. He should have helped his friend.
15. I would have attended the meeting but for the rain.
16. Father must have taken away the purse.

CYE : 04 Change the following sentences into passive voice :

1. Post this letter.
2. Never tell a lie.
3. Tell him to go.
4. Do not pluck flowers.
5. Cut your coat according to your cloth.
6. Let him sing a song.
7. Please shut the door.
8. Kindly grant me leave.
9. Hurry up,please.
10. Work hard.
11 Do not smoke.
12. Stand up on the bench.

CYE : 05 Change the following sentences into passive voice :

1. Do they like their teachers?
2. Does this shopkeeper sell grocery?
3. Did they win the match?
4. Did you grow vegetables?
5. Is he running a race?
6. Were they singing songs?
7. What does this word mean?
8. Why do you blame us?
9. Who teaches you English?
10. Can you solve this sum?

CYE : 06 Change the following sentences into passive voice :

1. This bottle contains milk.
2. I know his father.
3. The report alarmed us.
4. My progress satisfied my teachers.
5. You cannot please everybody.
6. Satish married Kanika.
7. Her failure surprised us.
8. Stamp collection interested the boy.
9. His death shocked us.
10. His servant has offended him.
11. I want to buy a house.
12. Women like men to flatter them.
13. It is time to take tea.
14. It is now time to close the shop.
15. He ran fast to win the race.
16. Let me play now.

CYE : 07 Change the following sentences into passive voice :

1. Honey tastes sweet.
2. The rose smells sweet.
3. He hopes to win a prize.
4. Thank God!
5. May you live long!
6. People take rice all over the world.
7. One should keep one's promise.
8. One must endure what one cannot cure.
9. God helps those who help themselves.
10. Those who live in glass houses should not throw stones at others.

CYE : 08 Change into active voice from the passive :

1. The plants are being watered by the gardener.
2. He is not hated by me.
3. Were you consulted by him?
4. Your kindness will never be forgotten by me.
5. The room is being swept by the sweeper.
6. Good news was being expected by us.
7. We have been insulted by her.
8. The clerk had been bribed by them.
9. Will the lesson have been taught by the teacher?
10. The poor must be helped by the rich.
11. Let the poor not be teased.
12. He was offered a good job by the management.
13. The matter is being looked into by the judge.
14. The minister was being waited for by the people.
15. We were shocked at the news of his death.
16. By whom were you insulted?

CYE : 09 Change the following sentences into passive voice :

1. She has invited me.
2. He has insulted you.
3. We have painted the doors.
4. They have won the match.
5. The peon has posted the letter.
6. The servant had already cooked food.
7. He had not seen the Taj before.
8. I had sold the old newspapers.
9. They had prepared many plans.
10. I had never seen such a lovely sight before.

CYE : 10 Change the following sentences into passive voice :

1. Should we not obey our parents?
2. Must I help him?
3. How can I serve my country?
4. Could you have done it?
5. Have you finished the assignment?
6. Has he returned the books?
7. Had he obtained leave?
8. Will you have read the book by tomorrow?
9. What have you drawn?
10. Who has broken the bottle?

CYE :11 Change the following sentences into passive voice :

1. My friends helped me.
2. She did not like the sari.
3. They wrote letters.
4. The teacher corrected our notebooks.
5. A large crowd cheered the players.
6. The teacher will teach a new lesson today.
7. The labourers will repair the road.
8. We shall serve our country.
9. She will help us.
10. They will not disobey me.

CYE : 12 Change the following sentences into passive voice :

1. It is time to say prayers.
2. It is necessary to write this essay.
3. She told me a wonderful story.
4. Somebody gave her a box of chocolates on her birthday.
5. They laughed at the blind man.
6. A car ran over a child.
7. I am listening to you.
8. We must obey the laws of the land.
9. They are watching the sports.
10. Did you make a noise ?
11. Shalini threw the ball.
12. Shall I ever forget those happy days ?

CYE : 13 Change the following sentences into passive voice :

1. The farmer will not have watered the fields.
2. Get out of my sight.
3. We shall no more hear his voice .
4. People will remember him.
5. A child cannot lift it .
6. He might solve it.
7. We can buy gold but we cannot buy sympathy.

8. You might have heard the name of Gandhijee.
9. There is no money to waste.
10. The policeman shot down the criminal with a revolver.
11. You must write your answer on both sides.
12. They don't allow smoking here.

CYE : 14 Change the following sentences into passive voice :

1. The fruit-seller sells fruit.
2. The teacher calls the roll.
3. My friends help me.
4. The doctor treats the patients.
5. Children like sweets.
6. He writes poems.
7. Everybody worships the rising sun.
8. I do not understand this question.
9. He does not obey his parents.
10. He sang a song.

CYE : 15 Change the following sentences into passive voice :

1. The boy is flying a kite.
2. You are reading this lesson.
3. We are not wasting our time.
4. The farmers are reaping the crops.
5. The girls are drawing the pictures.
6. He is deceiving me.
7. The grandmother was telling a story.
8. We were expecting good news.
9. The magician was showing tricks.
10. The students were solving the sums.

SOLUTIONS : CORRECT YOURSELF EXERCISE

Solutions CYE : 01

1. The electricity should be switched off when changing a fuse.
2. Too much money is being spent on Operation Pink.
3. Six new helipads have been built at Naila.
4. I am always given calendars and diaries at new year by her.
5. He will have to be amused with riddles and bed time stories.
6. A new pill to stimulate the appetite was discovered.
7. I was fascinated by it.
8. The wife of a duke of the sixteenth century was killed by him in this room.
9. His symphony was performed for the first time last week.
10. They were shown the house by the owner himself.
11. Have his instructions been carried out by them ?
12. The fruit have to be picked very early in the morning.
13. Harry was allowed to go but Dick was not (allowed to go).
14. Some old people are oppressed with the fear of death.

15. I was advised to settle the matter out of court by the judge.
16. Words were chosen with care by Rajiv.
17. It history could be made by building monuments in the 16th century it can be made by selling and reselling them in the twentieth century.
18. Mary was promised a new doll on her birthday.
19. I was never taught the rudiments of music.
20. All his calculations have been proved wrong.
21. This mountain hasn't been climbed before.
22. Were these vegetables grown in your own garden ?
23. I was most rudely answered in the shop.

Solutions CYE : 02

1. His proposal was rejected and he was laughed at.
2. By whom are you being bothered?
3. Duty must be done.
4. The plough is pulled by two oxen.
5. The knife was hidden in the grass by the murderer.
6. You will be robbed if you are not careful.
7. I was asked to wait.
8. A school is being run by her these days.
9. Let it be done by them now.
10. Mr. A is known to be a gang leader.
11. Have you been told about your result ?
12. You are requested to sit here and wait till I return.
13. Have all the necessary arrangements been made ?
14. It was clear that the child had been well brought up.
15. You can't be put in prison if you haven't been tried.
16. Tortoises are said to live longer than elephants.
17. I was not told the truth about the situation.
18. You will be well looked after be them.
19. Were you not told to be here by six O'clock?
20. I was surprised to hear you had been robbed.
21. Were these pictures painted by you in your own studio ?
22. It has been decided to increase the school fees this year.
23. Many people are provoked by anger to take hasty decisions which are very much regretted later.
24. It must be understood clearly by you that this is the last time it will be allowed by me.
25. The children cannot be expected to understand these problems.

Solutions CYE : 03

1. His shop will have been closed by him by 8 O'clock.
2. The paper will have been finished by them by 11 O'clock.
3. Enough money will have been saved by me to buy a house by 1990.
4. I shall have been advised by him.
5. You can be helped by him.
6. The tree could not be climbed by the child.

7. The book may be returned by you next week.
8. The match might be won by them.
9. Our parents should be obeyed by us.
10. No promise would be made by him.
11. Our teachers ought to be respected by us.
12. Your duty must be done by you.
13. The sum could have been solved by you.
14. His friend should have been helped by him.
15. The meeting would have been attended by me but for the rain.
16. The purse must have been taken away by father.

Solutions CYE : 04

1. Let this letter be posted.
2. Let a lie never be told.
3. Let him be told to go.
4. Let flowers not be plucked.
5. Let your coat be cut according to your cloth.
6. Let a song be sung by him.
7. You are requested to shut the door.
8. You are requested to grant me leave.
9. You are requested to hurry up.
10. You are advised to work hard.
11. You are advised not to smoke.
12. You are ordered to stand up on the bench.

Solutions CYE : 05

1. Are their teachers liked by them?
2. Is grocery sold by this shopkeeper?
3. Was the match won by them?
4. Were vegetables grown by you?
5. Is a race being run by him?
6. Were songs being sung by them?
7. What is meant by this word?
8. Why are we blamed by you?
9. By whom are you taught English?
10. Can this sum be solved by you?

Solutions CYE : 06

1. Milk is contained in this bottle.
2. His father is known to me.
3. We were alarmed at the report.
4. My teachers were satisfied with my progress.
5. Everybody cannot be pleased with you.
6. Kanika was married to Satish.
7. We were surprised at her failure.
8. The boy was interested in stamp collection.
9. We were shocked at his death.
10. He has been offended with his servant.

11. I want a house to be bought.
12. Women like to be flattered by men.
13. It is time for tea to be taken.
14. It is now time for the shop to be closed.
15. He ran fast for the race to be won.
16. You are requested to let me play now.

Solutions CYE : 07

1. Honey is sweet when (it is) tasted
2. The rose is sweet when (it is) smelt.
3. It is hoped that he will win a prize.
4. God be thanked.
5. It is prayed that you may live long.
6. Rice is taken all over the world.
7. Promise should be kept.
8. What cannot be cured must be endured.
9. Those who help themselves are helped by God.
10. Stones should not be thrown at others by those who live in glass houses.

Solutions CYE : 08

1. The gardener is watering the plants.
2. I do not hate him.
3. Did he consult you?
4. I shall never forget your kindness.
5. The sweeper is sweeping the room.
6. We were expecting good news.
7. She has insulted us.
8. They had bribed the clerk.
9. Will the teacher have taught the lesson.
10. The rich must help the poor.
11. Do not tease the poor.
12. The management offered him a good job.
13. The judge is looking into the matter.
14. The people were waiting for the minister.
15. The news of his death shocked us.
16. Who insulted you?

Solutions CYE : 09

1. I have been invited by her.
2. You have been insulted by him.
3. The doors have been painted by us.
4. The match has been won by them.
5. The letter has been posted by the peon.
6. Food had already been cooked by the servant.
7. The Taj had not been seen by him before.
8. The old newspapers had been sold by me.
9. Many plans had been prepared by them.
10. Such a lovely sight had never been seen by me before.

Solutions CYE : 10

1. Should our parents not be obeyed by us?
2. Must he be helped by me?
3. How can my country be served by me?
4. Could it have been done by you?
5. Has the assignment been finished by you?
6. Have the books been returned by him?
7. Has leave been obtained by him?
8. Will the book have been read by you by tomorrow?
9. What has been drawn by you?
10. By whom has the bottle been broken?

Solutions CYE : 11

1. I was helped by my friends.
2. The sari was not liked by her.
3. Letters were written by them.
4. Our notebooks were corrected by the teacher.
5. The players were cheered by a large crowd.
6. A new lesson will be taught by the teacher today.
7. The road will be repaired by the labourers.
8. Our country will be served by us.
9. We shall be helped by her.
10. I shall not be disobeyed by them.

Solutions CYE :12

1. It is time for prayers to be said.'
2. It is necessary for this essay to be written.
3. A wonderful story was told to me.
   Or I was told a wonderful story by her.
4. A box of chocolates was given to her on her birthday.
   Or She was given a box of chocolates on her birthday.
5. The blind man was laughed at by them.
6. A child was run over by a car.
7. You are being listened to by me.
8. The laws of the land must be obeyed.
9. The sports are being watched by them.
10. Was a noise made by you ?
11. The ball was thrown by Shalini.
12. Will those happy days ever be forgotten by me ?

Solutions CYE : 13

1. The fields will not have been watered by the farmers.
2. You are ordered to get out of my sight.
3. His voice will be heard no more.
4. He will be remembered .
5. It cannot be lifted by a child.

6. It might be solved by him.
7. Gold can be bought but sympathy cannot be bought.
8. The name of Gandhijee might have been heard by you.
9. There is no money to be wasted.
10. The criminal was shot down by the policeman with a revolver.
11. Your answer must be written on both sides.
12. Smoking is not allowed here.

Solution CYE : 14

1. Fruit is sold by the fruit-seller.
2. The roll is called by the teacher.
3. I am helped by my friends.
4. The patients are treated by the doctor.
5. Sweets are liked by children.
6. Poems are written by him.
7. The rising sun is worshipped by every body.
8. This question is not understood by me.
9. His parents are not obeyed by him.
10. A song was sung by him.

Solution CYE : 15

1. A kite is being flown by the boy.
2. This lesson is being read by you.
3. Our time is not being wasted by us.
4. The crops are being reaped by the farmers.
5. The pictures are being drawn by the girls.
6. I am being deceived by him.
7. A story was being told by the grandmother.
8. Good news was being expected by us.
9. Tricks were being shown by the magician.
10. The sums were being solved by the students.

13

Reported Speech
(DIRECT-INDIRECT NARRATIONS)

In English, there are two ways of telling someone, what someone else has said. Often we may choose to repeat their actual words using a **quoted speech** or **direct speech.** *Reporting exactly what someone has said is called direct speech or quoted speech.*

Here, what a person says appears within quotation marks ('...') and should be word for word.

For example :

She said, "I am watching T.V.."

Indirect speech (also called reported speech), doesn't use quotation marks to enclose what the person said and it doesn't have to be word for word.

However, when the information that someone conveys is more important than the actual words, we may want to explain what they have said using our own words, e.g :

1. She said that she was getting married on Saturday.
2. Joe asked whether she was going to invite her father to the wedding.

Examples like these are sometimes referred to as **indirect speech** or **reported speech**. Sentences in reported speech contain a **reporting clause** with a **reporting verb**; like- *say* or *ask*, e.g :

She said...
Joe asked...

This is followed by a **reported clause** showing someone's original statement, question or thought, e.g :

...(that) she was getting married on Saturday
...whether she was going to invite her father to the wedding

We often have to give information about what people say or think. In order to do this we can use 'direct or quoted' speech, or 'indirect or reported' speech.

DIRECT SPEECH

Reporting exactly what someone has said is called 'direct speech' (sometimes called **'quoted'** speech.)

Here what a person says, appears within quotation marks ("...") and should be *word* for *word*.

For example :

1. She said, "Today's lesson is on presentations."

or

"Today's lesson is on presentations," she said.

INDIRECT SPEECH

Indirect speech (sometimes called reported speech), **doesn't use quotation marks** to enclose what the person said and **it doesn't have to be word for word.**

When 'reporting verb' is in past tense, the tense of the 'reported speech' usually changes. This is because when we use reported speech, we are usually talking about a time in the past (because obviously the person who spoke originally spoke in the past). The verbs therefore usually have to be in the past too.

Example :

Direct speech	**Indirect speech**
'I'm going to the cinema', he said.	He said he was going to the cinema.

REPORTER/REPORTING VERB/REPORTED SPEECH

Reporter : The speaker or narrator is called the 'Reporter'.

Reporting Verb : The verb used by the 'Reporter' is called Reporting verb.

Reported Speech : Sentence enclosed within the inverted commas ("....")is called Reported Speech.

Look at the following sentence :

She said to me, "I am going to Jaipur"

In this sentence : 'She'- **Reporter** , 'said' - **Reporting verb** and 'I am going to Jaipur'- **Reported Speech** .

NOTE

1. Reported Speech always begins with a **capital letter** and enclosed within the **inverted commas (" ")** .
2. While we change a narration from direct to indirect , **the inverted commas are removed.**

RULES OF CHANGING DIRECT SPEECH INTO INDIRECT SPEECH

For the sake of understanding vividly, we may divide the rules of changing direct speech into indirect speech broadly into two parts :

1. General rules applicable to all kinds of sentences.

2. Specific rules applicable to specific kind of sentences.

General Rules and Method of transforming a sentence into indirect narration :

Rule 1. First of all, ascertain the *tense* of the *'reporting verb'*.

(a) If the reporting verb is in present or future tense, the tense of reported speech remains unchanged.

(b) If the reporting verb is in past , see the rules in next pages.

Rule 2. **The reporting verb changes as following :**

Reporting verb in Direct speech	Reporting verb in Indirect speech
say	say
says	says
say to	tell
says to	tells
will say	will say
will say to	will tell
said	said
said to	told/asked

NOTE *An object must follow 'tell' or 'told'' :*

He tells, "Ram is playing" (he tells whom?). *Incorrect*
He told, "I am going". *Incorrect*
He told that he was going. *Incorrect*

Rule 3. **While changing into indirect speech the *personal pronouns* of the reported speech are changed as per following :**

(a) First person pronoun — According to subject of reporting verb.
(b) Second person pronoun — According to object of reporting verb.
(c) Third person pronoun — No change.

NOTE *The 'number' and 'case' of the 'person' do not change .Learn well the following table to understand the change of personal pronouns :*

FORMS OF PERSONAL PRONOUNS

Person	Nominative Case	Objective Case	Possessive Case	
			Possessive Adjective	Possessive Pronoun
I Person	I	me	my	mine
	We	us	our	ours
II Person	You	You	Your	Yours
III Person	he	him	his	his
	She	her	her	hers
	it	it	its	X
	they	them	their	theirs

Rule 4. ***Conjunction 'that'* is commonly used while changing into indirect speech :**

Examples :

(a) He says, "I am going to Jaipur". *Direct*
He says *that* he is going to Jaipur. *Indirect*
(b) She says to me, "You are writing a letter to him." *Direct*
She tells me *that* I am writing a letter to him . *Indirect*
(c) They say to Ram, "We will go to Jaipur." *Direct*
They tell Ram *that* they will go to Jaipur. *Indirect*

Look at the methodology of transformation into indirect speech.

Sentence (a)

(i) Ascertain the tense of the reporting verb 'says'. It is present tense.

So there will be no change in the tense of the reported speech.

(ii) Reporting verb, 'says' will remain unchanged .

(iii) The personal pronoun 'I' (first person)will change according to subject of the reporting verb 'he'. So in indirect narration the pronoun will be 'he' instead of 'I' and the verb will be 'is'.

Sentence (b) :

(i) Ascertain the tense of the reporting verb. It is present tense.

So there will be no change in the tense of the reported speech.

(ii) The reporting verb, 'says to' changes to 'tells'.

(iii) The personal pronoun 'you' (II person)will change according to the object of the reporting verb ('me') so it will change into 'I', and the objective pronoun 'him' (III person) will remain unchanged.

See more solved examples

(a) Ramesh says to me, "I am your fast friend". *Direct*
Ramesh tells me that he is my fast friend. *Indirect*

(b) I say to her, "I will not talk to you". *Direct*
I tell her that I will not talk to her. *Indirect*

(c) He says to me, "I can teach you." *Direct*
He tells me that he can teach me. *Indirect*

(d) Hari says to Shalu, "I am your brother and you are my sister." *Direct*
Hari tells Shalu that he is her brother and she is his sister. *Indirect*

(e) He will say to Shalu , "I love you" *Direct*
He will tell Shalu that he loves her. *Indirect*

(f) I say to Shyam, "I will help you". *Direct*
I tell Shyam that I will help him. *Indirect*

REPORTING VERB IN THE PAST

Rule 6. **If the reporting verb is in 'past' , the tense of *the reported speech changes* as following :**

Direct Narration	Indirect Narration
1. Prsent Indefinite	Past Indefinite
2. Present Continuous	Past Continuous
3. Present Perfect	Past Perfect
4. Present Perfect Continuous	Past Perfect Continuous
5. Past Indefinite	Past Perfect
6. Past Continuous	Past Perfect Continuous
7. Past Perfect	No change of tense
8. Past Perfect Continuous	No chanege of tense

Change in "future tense sentences" (reported speech)

1. Will / shall	Would / should
2. Can	Could
3. May	Might
4. Could /should /would /might	No change

Rule 7. **When the reporting verb is in 'past', *words denoting time or place* in reported speech change as following :**

Direct Narration	Indirect Narration
1. This	That
2. These	Those
3. Here	There
4. Hence	Thence
5. Hither	Thither
6. Now	Then
7. Ago	Before
8. Thus	So
9. Today	That day
10. Tomorrow	The next day / the following day
11. Yesterday	The previous day
12. Last week / month / year	The previous week / month / year
13. The last fortnight	The previous fortnight
14. The day before yesterday	The day before the previous day

Look at the solved examples :

CHANGE IN NARRATION TENSE WISE

Present Indefinite

1. He said to me, ''I never eat sweets''. *Direct*
   He told me that he never ate sweets. *Indirect*
2. He said to Hina, "I love you". *Direct*
   He told Hina that he loved her. *Indirect*

Present Continuous

1. Ram said to Shyam, "I am watching T.V." *Direct*
   Ram told Shyam that he was watching T.V. *Indirect*
2. They said to Rahim, ''They are playing football''. *Direct*
   They told Rahim that they were playing football. *Indirect*

Present Perfect

1. Sita said, "I have already cooked". *Direct*
   Sita said that she had already cooked. *Indirect*
2. Ram said to Shyam, ' I have seen her today'. *Direct*
   Ram told Shyam that he had seen her that day. *Indirect*

Present Perfect Continuous

1. Sonu said to me, "I have been reading for an hour". *Direct*
   Sonu told me that he had been reading for an hour. *Indirect*
2. Shyam said to Ram, "Sita has been playing since morning". *Direct*
   Shyam told Ram that Sita had been playing since morning. *Indirect*

Past Indefinite

1. She said to Ram, "I went to Jaipur last week" *Direct*
   She told Ram that she had gone to Jaipur the previous week. *Indirect*

2. Ramesh said to me, "I telephoned you yesterday". *Direct*
Ramesh told me that he had telephoned me the previous day. *Indirect*

Past Continuous

1. She said to me, "I was waiting for you". *Direct*
She told me that she had been waiting for me. *Indirect*
2. Shyam said to Sita , "You were playing tennis". *Direct*
Shyam told Sita that she had been playing tennis. *Indirect*

Past Perfect

1. He said to me, "I had completed my project". *Direct*
He told me that he had completed his project. *Indirect*
2. She said to Meena, "Ram had already visited Agra". *Direct*
She told Meena that Ram had already visited Agra. *Indirect*

Past Perfect Continuous

1. He said , "I had been playing chess for two hours". *Direct*
He said that he had been playing chess for two hours. *Indirect*
2. I said to you, "Ram had been waiting for you since 2 O'clock". *Direct*
I told you that Ram had been waiting for you since 2 O' clock. *Indirect*

Future Indefinite

1. Ram said to Meena, "I shall write a letter." *Direct*
Ram told Meena that he would write a letter. *Indirect*
2. Sita said to Kuku , "You will attend the party tomorrow." *Direct*
Sita told Kuku that she (kuku) would attend the party the next day. *Indirect*

Future Continuous

1. Rahim said to Ram, "Sita will be waiting for you". *Direct*
Rahim told Ram that Sita would be waiting for him (Ram). *Indirect*
2. I said to her, "I shall be writing an essay". *Direct*
I told her that I should be writing an essay. *Indirect*

Future Perfect

1. Sita said to Ram, "I will have completed my work". *Direct*
Sita told Ram that she would have completed her work. *Indirect*
2. She said to me, "Ram will have vacated the room". *Direct*
She told me that Ram would have vacated the room. *Indirect*

Future Perfect Continuous

1. Nisha said to me, "I shall have been reading the book." *Direct*
Nisha told me that she would have been reading the book. *Indirect*
2. Chanchal said to Ekta, "We shall have been visiting the fair tomorrow". *Direct*
Chanchal told Ekta that we would have been visiting the fair the next day. *Indirect*

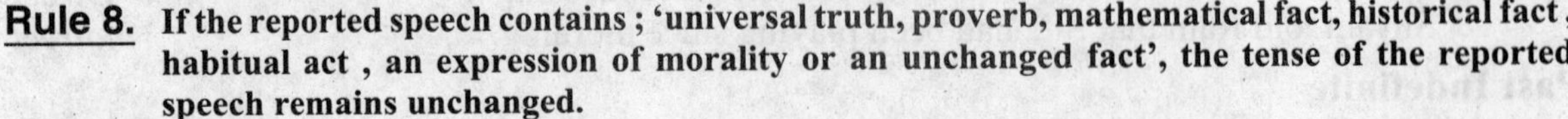

Rule 8. **If the reported speech contains ; 'universal truth, proverb, mathematical fact, historical fact, habitual act , an expression of morality or an unchanged fact', the tense of the reported speech remains unchanged.**

Look at the following Sentences :

1. He said, "The sun sets in the west.'' (universal truth) *Direct*
   He said that the sun sets in the west. *Indirect*
2. He said, "Man is Mortal.'' (universal truth) *Direct*
   He said that the man is mortal. *Indirect*
3. The teacher said, "India became Republic on 26th Jan 1950".(historical fact) *Direct*
   The teacher said that India became Republic on 26th Jan 1950. *Indirect*
4. She said to me, "Honesty is the best policy. (expression of morality) *Direct*
   She told me that honesty is the best policy. *Indirect*
5. She said, "Two and two is four.'' (mathematical fact) *Direct*
   She said that two and two is four. *Indirect*
6. He said, "London is the capital of U.K."(unchanged fact) *Direct*
   He said that London is the capital of U.K. *Indirect*
7. He said, "Mr. ManMohan Singh is the P.M. of India". (unchanged fact) *Direct*
   He said that Mr. ManMohan Singh is the P.M. of India. *Indirect*
8. He said, "Kashmir is in the north of India". (unchanged fact) *Direct*
   He said that Kashmir is in the north of India. *Indirect*
9. He said to me, "I go for a walk daily." (habitual act) *Direct*
   He told me that he goes for a walk daily. *Indirect*
10. Ram said to me, "I get up early in the morning daily.'' (habitual act). *Direct*
    Ram told me that he gets up early in the morning daily. *Indirect*
11. Radha said to her, "I go to office at 10 O'clock.'' (habit) *Direct*
    Radha told her that she goes to office at 10 O' clock. *Indirect*
12. The saint said , "Man proposes and God disposes.'' (proverb) *Direct*
    The saint said that man proposes and God disposes. *Indirect*
13. The teacher said, "Something is better than nothing.'' (proverb) *Direct*
    The teacher said that something is better than nothing. *Indirect*
14. The teacher said , "A stitch in time saves nine.'' (proverb) *Direct*
    The teacher said that a stitch in time saves nine. *Indirect*

CHANGE IN NARRATION SPECIFIC RULES
INTERROGATIVE SENTENCES

Interrogative sentences can be classified in two types :

1. 'Yes / No' questions : These can be answered in 'yes' or 'no' :

(a) Are you happy? Yes or No.
(b) Do you know me? Yes or No.
(c) Will you accompany me? Yes or No.

2. 'Wh' questions : Questions beginning with 'Wh' words; What, Where, Which, Who, How, etc. :

(a) Where do you live?
(b) What is your name?
(c) How are you?

'Yes / No' questions : Rules

Rule 1. **Use conjunction 'if' or 'whether' in place of 'that'. 'Whether' is used when the question expresses an alternative.**

(a) She said to me, 'Do you like tea or coffee?' *Direct*
She asked me whether I liked tea or coffee. *Indirect*

Rule 2. **Remove the question mark(?) and the interrogative sentence(the question) is changed to assertive sentence (Subject + verb +...).**

Rule 3. **Reporting verb ; 'ask, asks, asked' is used in indirect narrations.We can also use 'inquire' or 'enquire of'. 'Enquire of' is used when an object follows it.For example : He enquired of me .**

Rule 4. **Other rules in respect to the change of pronouns and change of tense are also to be followed.**

Look at the following solved examples :

(a) She said to me , "Are you going to college?" *Direct*
She asked me if I was going to college. *Indirect*
(b) She said to Shyam, "Have you an extra copy?" *Direct*
She asked Shyam if he had an extra copy. *Indirect*
(c) He said , "Am I looking smart?" *Direct*
He asked if he was looking smart. *Indirect*
(d) He said to me , "Can you write a letter?" *Direct*
He asked me if I could write a letter. *Indirect*
(e) She said to me, "Will you help me?" *Direct*
She asked me if I would help her. *Indirect*

CHANGING REPORTED SPEECH : INTERROGATIVE TO ASSERTIVE

Interrogative sentence	Assertive sentence
(a) Are you going ?	I was going. [example (a) above]
(b) Have you an extra copy ?	he had an extra copy. [example (b) above]
(c) Am I looking smart ?	he was looking smart [example (c) above]

NOTE *Sometimes answer is also attached with the main question.In that case 'yes' is changed into affirmation and 'no' into negation.*

(a) She said to me , "Can you solve this question?" "No", I said.
She asked me if I could solve that question, I said , I couldn't or I replied in negative.
(b) He said to me , "Do you knew me ?" I said, "Yes".
He asked me if I knew him, I said, I did or I replied in affirmative.

2. Questions beginning with 'Wh' words : Rules

Rule 5. **In questions beginning with 'Wh' words, no conjunction (that, if, whether) is used, instead the 'wh' word itself functions as conjunction.**

Rule 6. **The interrogative sentence is changed into assertive (subject+ verb+...)**

Look at the following solved examples :

1. He said to her , "What do you want?" *Direct*
He asked her what she wanted. *Indirect*
2. He said to me , "Why are you happy?" *Direct*
He asked me why I was happy. *Indirect*

3. Ram said to Hari, "Where do you live?" *Direct*
Ram asked Hari where he lived. *Indirect*

4. She said to Hari, "When will you come?" *Direct*
She asked Hari when he would come. *Indirect*

5. Ram said to Sita, "Who are you?" *Direct*
Ram asked Sita who she was. *Indirect*

6. Sita said to Mohan, "How many cars have you?" *Direct*
Sita asked Mohan how many cars he had. *Indirect*

7. I said to Shyam, "Which class do you read in?" *Direct*
I asked Shyam which class he read in. *Indirect*

8. I said to the teacher, "How many students are there in the school?" *Direct*
I asked the teacher how many students there were in the school. *Indirect*

9. He said to me, "Which team won the match?" *Direct*
He asked me which team had won the match. *Indirect*

10. He said to me, "What is your father ?" *Direct*
He asked me what my father was. *Indirect*

Rule 7. **Questions :Shall I / We + ... ?**

Such questions can denote; speculation/request/advice/offer of service / suggestion.

Read the following examples :

(A) When a speculation is expressed or an information is sought :

(a) "Shall I ever see her again ?", he said .(Speculation) *Direct*
He wondered if he would ever see her again. *Indirect*

(b) "When shall I know the result of the election?", Ram asked. *Direct*
Ram asked when he would know the result of the election. *Indirect*

Shall is as usual changed to would.Speculations are ordinarily introduced by "wonder".

(B) In case of request or advice :

(a) He said to the customer, "Shall we dispatch these letters?" *Direct*
He asked the customer if they should dispatch those letters. *Indirect*

(b) "What shall I say father ?", he said. *Direct*
He asked his father what he should say. *Indirect*

Request and advice are expressed in indirect speech by 'ask, inquire' etc. Requests or advice are normally reported by 'should' :

When a choice is required we normally use 'whether' in indirect speech.
'Whether + infinitive' is also sometimes possible :

(a) "Shall I lock the room or leave it unlocked ?," Rajesh said. *Direct*
Rajesh asked whether he should lock the room or leave it unlocked. *Indirect*

(C) When an offer is made :

(i) "Shall I bring you something to eat?," she said to me. *Direct*
(i) She offered to bring me something to eat. *Indirect*

(D) When suggestion is made :

(i) "Shall we meet again tomorrow?," he said. *Direct*

(i) He suggested to meet again the next day. *Indirect*

Rule 8. Questions beginning 'will you/ would you/ could you': Such questions may express invitations,commands, requests or may also be an ordinary question.The reporting verb is used according to the tenor/ theme of the statement :

(a) He said, "Will you be there on Monday ?" (Ordinary question.) *Direct*
He asked if I would be there on Monday. *Indirect*

(b) He shouted, "Will you keep silence?" *Direct*
He shouted at me to keep silence. or He ordered me to keep silence. *Indirect*

(c) He asked, "Would you like to do job in USA?" *Direct*
He asked if I would like to do job in USA. *Indirect*

(d) He said, "Would you like a lift?" *Direct*
He offered me a lift". *Indirect*

(e) He said, "Would you like to have a drink?" *Direct*
He invited me for a drink.or He offered me a drink. *Indirect*

CHANGING NARRATION : IMPERATIVES

Sentences expressing; command,order, advice, request etc.are usually called imperative sentences.Imperative sentences have two characteristics :

First, imperative sentences make a command or request.

Second, imperative sentences do not end with a question mark or mark of exclamation etc. Rather, they end with a period (full stop)

Rules for changing imperative sentences into indirect speech :

Rule 1. Use conjunction 'to' instead of 'that'. Negative commands, requests etc.are reported by 'not + infinitive' (example 4, below).

Rule 2. In indirect speech expressions of commands, requests, advice are usually expressed by a **verb of command / request/ advice + object + infinitive** (examples 5, 6, etc. below). Verbs : 'advise, ask, beg, command, encourage, entreat, forbid, implore, invite, order, recommend, remind, request, tell, urge, warn etc.' are normally used to express the notions of command /order/request/advice.(We do not use 'say' or 'said' in such sentences.)

Rule 3. If a sentence contains words like ; **please , kindly ,etc. these are not mentioned in the indirect speech** (example 1. below), as the notion is well expressed by the reporting verb 'request' in such case.

Look at the following solved examples :

1. She said to Ramu, "Please bring my book." *Direct*
She requested Ramu **to** bring her book. (conjunction–'to') *Indirect*
2. She said to me , "Have a glass of milk". *Direct*
She asked me **to** have a glass of milk. *Indirect*
3. Ram said to Sita , "Take medicines regularly." *Direct*
Ram advised Sita to take medicines regularly. *Indirect*

4. I said to Hari, "Don't pluck the flowers". *Direct*
I ordered Hari not to pluck the flowers. *Indirect*
5. The SP said to the SHO, "Shoot the robber". *Direct*
The SP ordered the SHO to shoot the robber. *Indirect*
6. The Principal said to the students, "Get out from my office". *Direct*
The Principal ordered the students to get out from his office. *Indirect*
7. He said, "Follow my instructions". *Direct*
He ordered me to follow his instructions. *Indirect*
8. He said to Sarla, "Please lend me your Physics book". *Direct*
He requested Sarla to lend him her Physics book. *Indirect*

CHANGING NARRATION : NEGATIVE IMPERATIVES

Negative commands, requests etc.are usually reported by **'not + infinitive', or 'forbid'** can also be used for prohibitions, but 'forbade' is more common in the passive than in the active.

1. The teacher said to Hari, "Don't write on the table". *Direct*
The teacher forbade Hari to write on the table. *Indirect*
The teacher instructed Hari not to write ('not + infinitive') on the table. *Indirect*
2. The Principal said, "Don't make a noise students". *Direct*
The Principal forbade the students to make a noise. *Indirect*
The Principal instructed the students not to make a noise. *Indirect*
3. She said to me, "Don't park your car here". *Direct*
She forbade me to park my car there. *Indirect*
She asked me not to park my car there. *Indirect*
Remember : When use 'forbid, never use 'not' as both have negative meanings.

NOTE *Verbs ; **advise, ask, beg, command, encourage, entreat,forbid, implore, invite, order, recommend, remind, request, tell, urge, warn** , require object + infinitive, i.e. they are required to be followed directly by the object (person addressed) without preposition . The person addressed is often not mentioned in direct speech.*

He said, "Get out." *Direct*
He told "me/ him/ her/ us/ them/ the children" to get out. *Indirect*

Verb - 'ask'.

The verb 'ask' can also be followed directly by the infintive of some specific verbs, e.g. see, speak to, talk to :

(a) He said, "Could I see Rita, please?" *Direct*
He asked to see Rita. *Indirect*
(b) He said, "could I speak to Ram?" *Direct*
He asked to speak to Ram. *Indirect*

Both 'ask' and 'beg' can also be followed by the passive infinitive :
"Please, send me to a hilly area," he asked/ begged. *Direct*
He asked/ begged us to send him to a hilly area. *Indirect*
He asked/ begged to be sent to a warm climate. *Indirect*

DIRECT-INDIRECT : EMPHATIC IMPERATIVE (USE OF 'DO')

Look at the following sentences, where 'Do' is used to make the request more emphatic, more polite or courteous :

1. He said to me, "Do have a cup of coffee please". *Direct*
   He requested me to have a cup of coffee. *Indirect*
2. She said to me , "Do come again" *Direct*
   She requested me to come again. *Indirect*
3. Rahim said to her, "Do have a seat please" *Direct*
   Rahim requested her to have a seat. *Indirect*

DIRECT-INDIRECT : IMPERATIVE AND TAG QUESTION

Sometimes tag questions are attached to the imperatives to make them more emphatic.Look at the following examples :

1. He said to me, 'Open the door, *will you* ? *Direct*
   He asked me to open the door. *Indirect*
2. She Said to Ram , 'Bring me a glass of water, *won't you*? *Direct*
   She asked Ram to bring her a glass of water. *Indirect*
3. The leader said to us, 'Caste your votes, *will you*? *Direct*
   The leader advised us to caste our votes. *Indirect*

NOTE ***A question tag at the end of an imperative sentence is left out in indirect narrations.***

Sometimes question tag is more important than the statement .
Look at the following sentences :

1. He said, ' You don't love her, do you?' *Direct*
   He asked me if I loved her. *Indirect*
2. She said to me , 'Do you like coffee, don't you?' *Direct*
   She asked me whether I liked coffee. *Indirect*

DIRECT-INDIRECT : IMPERATIVES WITH 'LET'

Sentences with 'Let' can be used to express ; suggestion, order, request and wish.

(A) 'Let's / Let us' for suggestions :

(a) He said, "Let's leave the bag at the hotel" *Direct*
He suggested leaving the bag at the hotel. *Indirect*
He suggested that they/ we should leave the bag at the hotel. *Indirect*

(b) She said, "Let's stop now and finish it afterwards" *Direct*
She suggested stopping then and finishing it afterwards. *Indirect*
She suggested that we should stop then and finish it afterwards. *Indirect*

Negative sentences

(c) He said, "Let's not do anything about it till we know the facts". *Direct*
He suggested not doing anything about it till they knew the facts. *Indirect*
He suggested doing nothing about it till they knew the facts. *Indirect*
He suggested that they shouldn't do anything about it till they knew the facts. *Indirect*

NOTE ***'Let's not', can also be reported in indirect speech by some phrases, such as; against / objected / opposed the idea etc.***

(d) "Let's purchase this T.V.," said Ramesh. "Let's not," said Anita. *Direct*
Ramesh suggested purchasing the T.V. but Anita was against it. *Indirect*

'Let's/ let us' sometimes expresses a call for an action. In that case reporting verb 'urge' or 'advise' is used and the *construction of the indirect speech will be* :

urge/ advise + object + infintive

(e) The leader said, "Let's show the owner that we can face the lockout well". *Direct*
The leader urged the workers to show the owner that they could face the lockout well. *Indirect*

(B) 'Let him/ them' for expressing command / order :

(a) "Let the boys clean the ground," said the principal.
The principal said that the boys were to clean the ground.

(b) The principal said to the peon, "Let the students come in".
The principal ordered the peon to allow the students come in.

(c) "Let the workers be given bonus," he ordered.
He ordered that the workers should be given bonus.

NOTE *Very often the speaker has no authority over the person who is to obey the command* :

(d) "It's not my job," said the clerk. "Let the manager do something about it." *Direct*
Here, the speaker has no authority but expressing an obligation. Sentences of this type are, therefore, usually reported by 'ought / should' :

The clerk said that it wasn't his job and that the manager ought to/should do something about it. *Indirect*

Sometimes 'let him/ them' is used to express a suggestion . In such cases it is reported by **'suggest, or say' + should :**

(e) He said, "Let them go to their advocate". *Direct*
He suggested them going to their advocate. *Indirect*
He said that they should go to their advocate. *Indirect*

'Let him/ them' is also used to express an indifferent attitude :

(f) "Ramesh will complain," said Anita."Let him (complain)," said Tina *Direct*
Tina expressed indifference. *Indirect*
Tina said she didn't mind (if he complained). *Indirect*

(C) "Let there be' construction is used to order,advise,urge or beg :

(a) "Let there be no further action," said the union leader. *Direct*
The union leader urged/ begged that there should be no further action. *Indirect*

(D) 'Let' can also be used to express 'wish' :

(a) The student said, "Let me take food". *Direct*
The student wished that he should take food. *Indirect*

(b) The lady said, "Let me have an ice cream pack". *Direct*
The lady wished that she should have an ice cream pack. *Indirect*

(c) She said, "Let him be my friend". *Direct*
She wished that he should be her friend. *Indirect*

(E) 'Let' for request : In such cases conjunction 'to' is used :

(a) The boy said to the teacher, "Let me go home now." *Direct*
The boy requested the teacher to allow him to go home then. *Indirect*

(b) The student said to the teacher, "Let me complete this assignment". *Direct*
The student requested the teacher to allow him to complete that assignment. *Indirect*

CHANGE IN NARRATION : OPTATIVE SENTENCES

(A) Sentences containing expressions of good wishes,prayer for someone or desires are called optative sentences.

Rule 1. The reporting verb is changed according to the mood of the expression.Usually 'that' conjunction is used in such cases and the reported speech is changed into assertive :

1. My mother said to my friend, "May you live long !" *Direct*
My mother wished my friend *that* he might live long. *Indirect*
2. She said to Sita, "May God bless you with a son !" *Direct*
She prayed *that* God might bless Sita with a son. *Indirect*
3. She said, "God grant you success !" (May God grant you success! 'May is' hidden.) *Direct*
She prayed /wished that God might grant me success. *Indirect*

(B) Expressions of salutations :

1. He said to the teacher, "Good morning !" *Direct*
He wished the teacher good morning. *Indirect*
2. She said, "Good morning, sir !" *Direct*
She wished the sir good morning. *Indirect*
3. I said, "Good afternoon, father !" *Direct*
I wished my father good afternoon. *Indirect*

(C) Expressions of farewell; Reporting verb 'bid / bade' is used :

1. She said to me, "Good bye". *Direct*
She bade me good bye. *Indirect*
2. The leader said, "Farewell my friends". *Direct*
The leader bade his friends farewell. *Indirect*

CHANGE IN NARRATION : EXCLAMATORY SENTENCES

Sentences containing sudden expressions of joy, sorrow, anger, applause, surprise, contempt are called exclamatory sentences.

Rules
(a) **Reporting verb**; exclaimed with joy, exclaimed with sorrow, exclaimed with surprise, exclaimed with applause, exclaimed with anger, exclaimed with contempt, etc. **is used according to the tenor of the sentence.**
(b) **Conjunction 'that'** *is used as usual.*
(c) **Words such as ; Alas, Bravo, Oh, Wow, Wah, Hurrah, used in direct speech are left out in indirect narration**. (See examples 3, 4, 9, 10 below.)
(d) Exclamatory sentence is transformed into Assertive .
(e) *For any wish* like; If I were a bird, If I were the P.M., etc. **reporting verb 'wish' is used** (See examples 1, 2 bellow.).
(f) All other rules regarding change of pronoun and change of tense also apply.

Look at the following solved examples :

1. She said, "If I were a bird !" *Direct*
   She wished *that* she would be a bird. *Indirect*
2. He said, "If I were young again !" *Direct*
   He wished that he would be young again !' *Indirect*
3. Ram said, "Alas ! I have been ruined". Direct
   Ram exclaimed with sorrow that he had been ruined. *Indirect*
4. The lady said, "Oh ! My dog is dead". *Direct*
   The lady exclaimed with sorrow that her dog was dead. *Indirect*
5. He said, "What a beautiful girl Sita is !" *Direct*
   He exclaimed with praise that Sita was a beautiful girl. *Indirect*
6. We said, "What a nice place it is !" *Direct*
   We exclaimed with surprise that it was a nice place. *Indirect*
7. They said, "What a great fall!" *Direct*
   They exclaimed with aplause that it was a great fall. *Indirect*
8. The captain said, "Well done! My friends". *Direct*
   The captain exclaimed with applause that his friends had done well. *Indirect*
9. The player said, "Hurrah ! We have won". *Direct*
   The player exclaimed with joy that they had won. *Indirect*
10. He said, "Wow ! What a pleasant weather it is !" *Direct*
    He exclaimed with joy that it was a very pleasant weather. *Indirect*

Change of reported speech : exclamatory into assertive :

Exclamatory	**Assertive**
1. What a beautiful girl she is !	She is a beautiful girl.
1. What a nice place it is !	It is a very nice place.
3. What a great fall !	It is a great fall.
4. What an idea !	It is a great idea.
5. What a fool you are !	You are a great fool.
6. How dark the night is !	It is a very dark night.

Note the change into indirect narrations in following sentences :

Direct	**Indirect**
1. He said to me, "Congratulations !"	He congratulated me.
2. The teacher said to the student, "stupid!"	The teacher called the student, stupid.
3. She said, "Thank you !	She thanked me.
4. They said to us, "Welcome !"	They welcomed us.
5. I said to her, "Happy Christmas !"	I wished her happy Christmas.
6. The notice said, "Welcome to Rajasthan!"	The notice welcomed visitors to Rajasthan.

CHANGING NARRATION : MISCELLANEOUS SENTENCES

(A) When name of a person / sir/ madam , is inside the inverted commas :

1. He said, "Rajeev, I am waiting for you." *Direct*
   He told Rajeev that he is waiting for him (Rajeev).
2. She said, "Take your purse, Tony"
   She asked Tony to take his purse.

3. Sheela said, "Brother please help me." *Direct*
Sheela requested her brother to help her. *Indirect*
4. He said, "Kuku what are you doing." *Direct*
He asked Kuku what she was doing. *Indirect*
5. He said, "May I leave now Madam ?" *Direct*
He asked the Madam if he might leave then. *Indirect*
6. She said, "May I attend the class, Sir ?" *Direct*
She asked respectfully if she might attend the class. *Indirect*

(B) Some sentences with ; 'Well, Okay, You see, You know etc'. are changed into indirect narration as following :

1. The receptionist said, "Well, what can I do for you ?" *Direct*
The receptionist asked politely what she could do for me. *Indirect*
2. 'Okay', She said, "I will consider your proposal." *Direct*
She said that she would consider my proposal. *Indirect*

(C) (i) Must : 'Must' used for conclusion /deduction /command /prohibition and to express intention remains unchanged.

1. She said, "I usually meet him here ; he must live near here."(Deductions) *Direct*
She said that she usually met him there, he must live in that area. *Indirect*
2. She said, "This room must be kept locked". (Command) *Direct*
She said that the room must be kept locked. *Indirect*
3. She said, "We must have a party to celebrate this".(Intention) *Direct*
She said that they must have a party to celebrate it. *Indirect*

(ii) 'Must' used to express obligation usually changes to 'would have to' or 'had to' :

'Would have to' is used when the obligation depends on some future action or when the fulfillment of the obligation is not certain or appears remote or uncertain i.e. when 'must' means 'will have to' :

1. Sarpanch said, "If the floods get worse we must (will have to) leave this place". *Direct*
Sarpanch said that if the floods got worse they would have to leave that place. *Indirect*
2. I said, "When it stops drizzling we must start digging again". *Direct*
I said that when it stopped drizzling we would have to start digging again. *Indirect*
3. She said, "We must call the mechanic tomorrow". *Direct*
She said that they would have to call the mechanic the next day. *Indirect*
4. "I have just received a letter," she said. "I must leave for Jaipur". *Direct*
She said that she had just received a letter and would have to leave for Jaipur. *Indirect*

NOTE *'had to', would be more usual here if she left at once, i.e. had to would imply that she left at once.*

(iii) *'Must'*changes to *' had to'* where times for **fulfillments of the obligation** either have been fixed or the obligation is fulfilled fairly promptly or at least by the time the speech is reported :

1. She said, "I must take a quick bath."(and presumably did so.) *Direct*
She said that she had to take a quick bath . *Indirect*
2. Harish said, "I must be there by six tomorrow morning". *Direct*
Harish said that he had to be there by six the next morning. *Indirect*

(iv) 'Must I/ you/ he?' can also change similarly but as 'must' in the interrogative usually concerns the present or immediate future so **it changes to 'had to'** :

1. I said, "Must you go today?" *Direct*
   I asked him if he had to go that day. *Indirect*

(v) 'Must not' : *'I must not'* and *'You must not'* usually **remain unchanged** :

1. She said to me, "You mustn't talk anyone about it." *Direct*
   She told me that I mustn't talk to anyone about that . *Indirect*

(D) Needn't

'Needn't' usually remains unchanged. It can be changed to 'didn't have to/ wouldn't have to' just as 'must' changes to 'had to/ would have to' :

1. Ram said to me, "You needn't wait". *Direct*
   Ram told me that I needn't wait. *Indirect*
2. I said, 'If you can lend me the rupees five thousand I needn't go to the bank . *Direct*
   I said that if he could lend me rupees five thousand I needn't / wouldn't have to go to the bank. *Indirect*
3. He said, "I needn't be in office till next Monday". *Direct*
   He said that he needn't / didn't have to be in office till next Monday. *Indirct*
4. He said, "You must not speak to anyone". *Direct*
   He said that I must not speak to anyone. *Indirect*
5. She said, "You need not purchase this book". *Direct*
   She said that I need not purchase that book. *Indirect*

"Need I/ you/ he?" normally becomes had to :

1. "Need I finish my homework?,"asked the little baby. *Direct*
   The little baby asked if she had to finish her homework. *Indiret*

(E) Sometimes when the direct speech consists of 'statement + question' or 'question + command' or command + statement, or all three together, normally each requires its own reporting verb.

1. He said, "I don't know the way. Do you?" *Direct*
   He said he didn't know the way and asked me if I did. *Indirect*
2. 'A stranger is coming,' he said, "Get behind the wall". *Direct*
   He said that a stranger was coming and told me to get behind the wall. *Indirect*
3. "I'm going shopping. May I get you anything?" he said. *Direct*
   He said he was going shopping and asked if he might get me anything. *Indirect*
4. "I can hardly hear the T.V.," he said, "Could you high the volume ?" *Direct*
   He said he could hardly hear the T.V. and asked her to high the volume. *Indirect*

NOTE *In some cases, we use 'as' when the last clause is a statement, which explains the first clause.*

5. He said , "You'd better wear a woolen shirt. It's cold today". *Direct*
   He advised me to wear a woolen shirt as it was cold that day. *Indirect*
6. Hari said to her, "You'd better not walk across the lane alone. People have been mugged there." *Direct*
   Hari warned her not to walk across the lane alone as people had been mugged there. *Indirect*

In some cases the second reporting verb can be a participle :

7. Sarla said to her husband, "Please, please, don't drink to much! Remember that you'll have to drive home". *Direct*
   Sarla begged her husband not to drink too much, reminding him that he'd have to drive home. *Indirect*
8. He said to his wife , "Let's shop on Monday. The shopping mall will be very crowded on Sunday". *Direct*

He suggested shopping on Monday, pointing out that the shopping mall would be very crowded on Sunday. *Indirect*

(F) 'Would / Should / Could / Might', remains unchanged usually in indirect speech :

He said, "She would / should / could / might attend the party". *Direct*
He said that she would / should / could / might attend the party. *Indirect*

(G) 'Had to' changes into ' had had to' in indirect speech :

The poet said, "After the function, I had to rush to my house". *Direct*
The poet said that after the function he had had to rush to his house. *Indirect*

(H) Indirect Commands

Look at the following sentences :

1. She said, "If I were you, I'd stop smoking." *Direct*
   She advised me to stop smoking. *Indirect*
2. He said, "Why don't you change your clothes ?" *Direct*
   He advised me to change my clothes. *Indirect*
3. "Would / could you show me your ticket, please ?", the TC said. *Direct*
   The TC asked me to show him my ticket. *Indirect*
4. The receptionist said, "If you'd just sign the application form". *Direct*
   The receptionist asked him to sign the application form. *Indirect*
5. His wife said, "Please, please don't take risk". *Direct*
   His wife begged / implored him not to take risk. *Indired*
6. Mrs Jacob said, "Don't forget to order the whisky". *Direct*
   Mrs Jacob reminded him to order the whisky. *Indirect*
7. He said to me , "If your brakes are bad don't drive so fast". *Direct*
   He told me that if my brakes were bad I shouldn't drive so fast. or, *Indirect*
   He advised me not to drive so fast if my brakes were bad . *Indirect*
8. He said to me, "If she leaves the house follow her". *Direct*
   He instructed me that if she left the house I was to follow her. *Indirect*

(I) Joint Sentences :

1. She said, "I am a girl. I cannot stay here in night". *Direct*
   She said that she was a girl and added that she could not stay there in night. *Indirect*
2. Ramesh said, "Sita is going to Jaipur tomorrow. I can also go with her." *Direct*
   Ramesh said that Sita was going to Jaipur next day and he could also go with her. *Indirect*
3. Payal said, "I will not marry this year. I am preparing for IAS examinations". *Direct*
   Payal said that she would not marry that year and further added that she was preparing for IAS examinations. *Indirect*
4. He said, "Do you know who is he ?" *Direct*
   He asked me if I knew who he was. *Indirect*

5. She said, "Can you find, where are the keys? *Direct*
She asked me if I could find where the keys were. *Indirect*
6. He said, "Sarla is coming, wait here." *Direct*
He said that Sarla was coming and asked me to wait there. *Indirect*
7. He said, "Where is your purse, I have lost mine." *Direct*
He asked me where my purse was and added that he had lost his. *Indirect*
8. My father said, "I am going to office, where are you going?" *Direct*
My father said that he was going to his office and wanted to know where I was going. *Indirect*
9. The leader said, "Friends, my country men, lend me your support. I will take care of your problems." *Direct*
The leader addressed the people as friends, my country men and requested them to lend him their support. He further added that he would take care of their problems. *Indirect*
10. "Where are you going Sheela ? Come here and we will talk about our marriage", said he. *Direct*
He asked Sheela where she was going and added that they would talk about their marriage. *Indirect*
11. Sita said to Ram, "No, No, I can't play with you. My father has, forbidden me to play with you. *Direct*
Sita told Ram that she could not play with him as her father had forbidden her to play with him. *Indirect*

(J) 'Accuse ...of/admit/apologise for/deny/insist on' + gerund construction can sometimes be used instead of 'say (that)' :

1. She said , "You took the money". *Direct*
She accused me of taking the money.
2. He said,"I didn't steal the purse". *Direct*
He denied stealing the purse.
3. Ram said , "I'm sorry I'm late." *Direct*
Ram apologized for being late. *Indirect*

(K) In some sentences we do not see object with the reporting verb.In such cases we can also choose an object .

(i) Direct : Sita said, "I am waiting for you."
Indirect : Sita told me that she was waiting for me.
Sita told him that she was waiting for him

(ii) Direct : My mother said, "You should take proper diet".
Indirect : My mother told me that I should take proper diet.
My mother told her that she should take proper diet.

(iii) Direct : He said, "I do not like to talk to any of you".
Indirect : He told us that he did not like to talk to any of us.
He told them that he did not like to talk to any of them

(iv) Direct : The teacher said, "You should learn the lessons well".
Indirect : The teacher told the students/me/him/her that they / I/he/she should learn the lessons well.

Some specific points about reported speech

(A) As per the rules we have learnt so far, the **past continuous tense changes to the past perfect continuous but in practice usually remains unchanged** except when it refers to a completed action. For example :

1. He said, "When I saw her, she was playing football." *Direct*
   He said that when he saw her, she was playing football. *Indirect*
2. She said, "When I saw them, they were swimming in the river." *Direct*
   She said that when she saw them, they were swimming in the river. *Indirect*
3. He said, "When we were living in London we often saw Mr. James. *Direct*
   He said that when they were living in London they often saw/had often seen Mr. James. *Indirect*

(B) **If the past tense describes a situation which still exists** (unchanged) when the speech is reported, tense of the reported speech remains unchanged :

1. He said, "I decided not to purchase the house, because it was near the railway track."
   He said that he had decided not to purchase the house because it was near the railway track.
2. They said, "We decided not to buy the house as it was on the main road."
   They said that they had decided not to buy the house as it was on the main road.

(In above sentences 'it was near the railway track', 'it was on the main road ', show that the situation did not change.)

(C) **Unreal past tenses** after **'wish, would rather/ sooner'** and **'it is time' do not change** :

1. He said, "I wish I didn"t have to take examination,"
   He said he wished he didn't have to take examination.
2. "It is time we began planning for our examinations,"he said.
   He said that it was time they began planning for their examinations.
3. 'Kate wants to go alone,' said Amar, "but I'd rather she went with her sister".
   Amar said that Kate wanted to go alone but that he'd rather she went with her sister.

(D) Usually **the construction 'I/ he/ she/ we/ they had better' remains unchanged. 'You had better' can remain unchanged** or can be reported by 'advise + object + infinitive **:**

1. "The children had better go to bed early", said Ram. *Direct*
   Ram said that the children had better go to bed early. *Indirect*
2. Sita said, "You had better give up smoking." *Direct*
   Sita said that *you had better* give up smoking. *Indirect*
   Sita *advised me to give up* smoking. *Indirect*
3. She said, "The old had better go for a walk daily. *Direct*
   She said that the old had better go for a walk daily. *Indirect*
4. He said, "You had better not drink the tea." *Direct*
   He advised me not to drink the tea. *Indirect*
   He said that I had better not drink the tea. *Indirect*

(E) In following type of **conditional sentences, no change of tense is needed :**

1. He said, "If I had a permit I could get this job".
   He said that if he had a permit he could get that job.
2. He sad, "If she had come to me, I would have helped her."
   He said that if she had come to him, he would have helped her.

3. He said, "If I had the tools I could mend the car".
He said that if he had the tools he could mend the car.
4. She boasted, "I could read when I was there."
She boasted that she could read when she was there.
5. He said, "When I was a boy, I could stay up as long as I liked".
He said that when he was a boy he could stay up as long as he liked.
6. He said, "If my children were older I would leave India".
He said that if his children were older he would leave India.

REPORTED SPEECH

CORRECT YOURSELF EXERCISES

CYE : 01 Change the following sentences into indirect narrations :

1. He says, "Ram is a good player."
2. Rita says, "Kishore sang a song."
3. You will say, "Ganesh works hard."
4. Kali will say, "Mira will swim in the river."
5. He said, "Kalu reads well."
6. He said, "The birds are flying."
7. The servant said, "The guest has arrived."
8. The washerman said, "It has been raining since morning."
9. The boys said, "The teacher did not come."
10. I said, "Ganesh was playing."
11. You said, "Kalu can lift the box."
12. The teacher said, "Mala may go."
13. I said, "I shall work hard."
14. He said, "The boys will write lessons."

CYE : 02 Change the following sentences into indirect narrations :

1. Sheela said, "The earth moves round the sun."
2. The saint said, "Man is mortal."
3. The teacher said, "India became free in 1947."
4. Mohan said, "Babar won the first battle of Panipat."
5. Mohan said, "Two and two make four."
6. Sheela said, "Truth always triumphs"
7. He said, "Mohan could solve the sum."
8. She said, "It might happen."

CYE : 03 Change the following sentences into indirect narrations :

1. I said, "I am happy."
2. You said, "We are learning our lesson."
3. He said, "I am not to blame."
4. She said, "I do not care for him."
5. They said, "We trust in God."
6. I said to him, "You are always late."
7. You said to me, "You may go."

8. Sheela said to us, "You must work hard."
9. Ram said to me, "Sita does not like meat."
10. I said to him, "He must not tell lies."
11. He said to me, "Let us go for a walk."
12. You said to me, "Let us play now."
13. She said, "I am going now."
14. I said, "I know this man."
15. They said, "We are leaving tonight."
16. He said to me, "I shall see you tomorrow."
17. She said, "My uncle came yesterday."
18. I said, "I bought the book last week."
19. Mother said, "It will rain next month."
20. She said, "I went to Jaipur a week ago."

CYE : 04 Change the following sentences into indirect narrations :

1. He said to me, "You have made a mistake."
2. The students said, "We shall play a match tomorrow."
3. Harish said, "I am going now, Mother."
4. The teacher said, "Honesty is the best policy."
5. He said to his parents, "I have done my best and can do no more."
6. The dying man said, "My sons, I am leaving you a treasure buried in my fields."
7. The Principal said, "Harish is very intelligent."
8. The Principal said, "Tomorrow will be a holiday."
9. The Prime Minister said, "National integrity will be preserved at all costs."
10. The Minister said, "The prices have started falling."
11. He said to me, "My father went to Mumbai last week."
12. I said to her, "I may come tomorrow."
13. The officer said to him, "You will be dismissed if you do not attend the office in time."
14. The doctor said to him, "You have fallen ill because you over-ate yesterday."

CYE : 05 Change the following sentences into indirect narrations :

1. He said to me, "Do you play hockey?"
2. I said to her, "Are you leaving tonight?"
3. He said to his friend, "Will you lend me fifty rupees?"
4. He said to his son, "Have you seen the Tajmahal?"
5. "Haven"t you got a television set ?" , he asked me.
6. The servant said, "Shall I lay the table now?"
7. "Shall I ever get married?"she said.
8. Ram said to me, "What are you doing?"
9. She said to the stranger, "Who are you?"
10. The teacher said to me, "Which is your pen?"

CYE : 06 Change the following sentences into indirect narrations :

1. His father said to him, "Why did you misbehave?"
2. I said to Sita, "Where are you going?"
3. Ram's mother said to him, "How have you fared in the examination?"
4. The madam said to the boys, "Whose book is this?"

5. She said to me, “How many boys are there in your school?”
6. My father said to me, “Are you feeling well?”
7. He said to her, “Can you lend me your umbrella?”
8. I said to Harish, “Do you want to settle at Kanpur?”
9. I said to the servant, “Where is my camera?”
10. The teacher said to Ganesh, “Why are you not taking the examination?”

CYE : 07 Change the following sentences into indirect narration :

1. The teacher said, “Never make mischief again.”
2. I said to Sita, “Can you keep it for me till tomorrow?”
3. She told Ram, “Leave it with me but don’t come back.”
4. The retailer said, “Where can you find such variety of cloths?”
5. “My advice,” said our madam, “Is that you should go home now?”
6. The girl shouted, “What a funny man you are !”
7. The old man said to his son, “What have you learnt at school?”
8. The assistant said, “Sir, give me the list of the dealers.”
9. Sohani said, “Rajesh, who has taken away my bike?”
10. The child said to his mother,“Are you going to office today?”

CYE : 08 Change the following sentences into indirect narration :

1. “Good morning, sir”, said Shyam to his teacher.
2. “Thank you child, for showing me the way to the hospital,” said the old lady.
3. “Wish you a happy journey,” said my wife.
4. “Hello, Ramesh, how are you doing these days?” said Ashok.
5. “Alas!,” she said, “We have lost badly in the match.”
6. “May you live long, my son,” said my mother.
7. “This book is full of errors,” shouted Mr. Janardhan.
8. The thief said to the judge, “Please pardon me, sir.”
9. The priest said to her, “May God help you!”
10. The stranger said, “Good Heavens! What do I see before me !”

CYE : 09 Change the following sentences into indirect narration :

1. He said, “ Two and two make four.”
2. She said, “ I saw a tiger here.”
3. Maneesh said, “I may go to Delhi tomorrow.”
4. He asked me, “Where has he gone?”
5. Sita said to me, “Is it still raining.”
6. He said to me, “When will she come?”
7. She said to me, “Is Raju your friend?”
8. She said to me, “Have you a car?”
9. She said, “Do they play chess?”
10. Rahim said, “Who are they?”

CYE : 10 Change the following sentences into indirect narration :

1. Kanika said to Suresh, “Is the tea ready?”
2. She said to me, “Is it my book?”
3. Tarmesh said to me, “Will you keep shut?.”

4. Chinkoo said to him, "Get out?"
5. The teacher said, "Hurry up, students ."
6. He said to the president, "Please give me one chance."
7. She said to him, "Please cooperate me."
8. The teacher said to the girls, "Keep away from the wall!"
9. She said, "What a pitiful scene!"
10. He said, "Hurrah! I am the first"

CYE : 11 Change the following sentences into indirect narration :

1. The queen said, "O, I were young again !"
2. The Principal said, "Well done! my boys."
3. He said, "God save the King".
4. The mother said, "Long live my son."
5. She said to me, "Do have some drinks?"
6. Rahul said to him, "Will you go to Jaipur?"
7. The boy said, "Sir, may I come in?"
8. Hari said to Rahim, "You must obey your parents."
9. He said, "I must go to Jaipur next week."
10. She said, "You need not talk to me."

CYE : 12 Change the following sentences into indirect narration :

1. He said to me, "Let us go to hospital."
2. She said, "Let them play."
3. Ramesh said, "Sarla will not dance."
4. The professor said, "Alas! I am undone."
5. He said to me, "Do you know who is there?"
6. He said, "Thanks for reminding me."
7. He said, "Hello, what are you doing? "
8. She said, "Congratulations."
9. She said, "Farewell my dear friends ."
10. He said to her, "Good morning !"

CYE : 13 Change the following sentences into indirect narration :

1. He says, "Mohan will write a letter."
2. He says to me, "I will go to Mumbai tomorrow."
3. He said to me, "I am reading a book."
4. Ram said to me, "I can teach you".
5. He said, "Mohan has been living here since 2000."
6. He said, "The sun rises in the east."
7. He said, "The moon revolves round the earth".
8. I said to her, "I wrote a letter."
9. I said to her, "Have you learned your lesson ?"
10. Ram says to me, "You are smart."
11. He said to me, "Are you going to Jaipur?"
12. I said to him, "Who teach you English?"
13. I said to Harsh, "Please help me."
14. Mohan said to me, " Do not tell a lie."
15. She said, "Good bye Ramesh."

CYE : 14 Change the following sentences into indirect narration :

1. My mother said to me, "May you live long!"
2. I said to Ram, "Let me go there."
3. He said, "If I were the King!"
4. He said, "How intelligent Ravi is!"
5. She said, "Keep this room open."
6. The captain said, "Well done! my boys."
7. Ram said, "You need not talk to me."
8. He said, "What a beautiful picture?"
9. He said, "I must go to Jaipur next month."
10. The teacher said, "Hurry up."
11. She said to me, "Is it still drizzling?"
12. She said, "I saw a lion here."
13. He said to me, "What is your father's name?"
14. Ram said to the servant, "Clean up the house."
15. She said, "How old are you?"

CYE : 15 Change the following sentences into indirect narration :

1. He says, "I am ill."
2. Mohan said to me, "I am doing my work."
3. I said to him, "I went there on Tuesday."
4. The teacher said to us, "The earth is round."
5. The boy said, "I saw him while I was running.
6. She said, "You need not wail."
7. I said to him, "Your brother has passed."
8. I said to him, "Where do you live?"
9. He said to me, "Work hard if you want to pass."
10. He said to me, "Do not go there."
11. He said, "What a pitiful scene?"
12. She said, "Where is the hospital."
13. The big man said, "Quite right."
14. "We'll wait for you if you're late",they said.
15. Ram asked Mohan, "What is the time?"
16. The saint said to her, "May God help you."
17. "Wish you a happy journey," said Harsh.
18. The boy said, " Hurrah! we have won the match."
19. Sarla said, "Alas! I have failed."
20. My mother said to me, "Don't jump on my bed."

CYE : 16 Change the following sentences into indirect narration :

1. Sumit said, "Father, I want to go abroad after I finish my studies here."
2. I said to Sumit,"Why do you want to go abroad ? Where actually do you want to go?"
3. "Don't go home yet," I told my colleague, " Remember you promised to finish your work before leaving."
4. "Please listen to me," he answered, "I must go now because my son is very ill."
5. "What a relief to know that the girl has passed !" I exclaimed, "now she can get a job."

6. The station master said to me, “You are very late; it is one full hour since the train left.”
7. Nitin said to me, “Why don’t you come with us ? Why do you wnat to be so unsocial ?”
8. The gang leader shouted, “Keep together and run, the police are after us.”
9. I said to my companions, “Let them not come with us if they don’t want to, let’s not wait for them any longer.”
10. “What a pleasant surprise !’ I exclaimed on seeing John in the room, “I never expected to find you here.”
11. I said to Harish, “The man who came to meet you asked if we could see his boss tomorrow.”
12. He said to his secretary, “Why don’t you carry out orders exactly ? Remember if you don’t, you will be punished.”
13. I said to the boy, “You have no ticket, get out before you are driven out.”
14. The lecturer paused and said, “Those who are tired of listening to me can go. I shall not mind it.”
15. They said, “How very awkward ! What shall we say to him?

CYE : 17 Change the following sentences into indirect narration :

1. Madhur said to his sister, “Before I go to Delhi, I shall meet Sushila.”
2. Govind said to Mohit, “Do not come here again or you will get a beating.”
3. John said to James, “Have you come here just to see me or are there some other reasons.”
4. Abdul said, “What a lovely morning for tennis” ?
5. The teacher said to the boy, “Since it is so warm let us go swimming.”
6. They said, “Mother, we are not hungry; we shall eat later.”
7. He said angrily to his brother, “Why don’t you do as you are told.”
8. I said to the visitor, “Don’t sit on that chair, it is broken.”
9. My little brother said, “I wish it rains hard, so I don’t have to go to school.”
10. “How steep the path is !” they said, “we are quite tired.”
11. “Neither a borrower, nor a lender be,” said the father to son.
12. “And remember always that true education means the training of the mind,” said the V.C. addressing students.
13. The teacher said to his students , “Ever in your life and conversation prove worthy of your glorious Alma Mater.”
14. The son said to his father reverently, “Do you expect me to have ever done this sort of a mean thing.”
15. “Don’t hang upon me ,young man, I do not like flatterers”, said the officer to his secretary.

CYE : 18 Choose the best alternative to complete the sentences below :

1. Please tell me ......

(a) where is the bus stop. (b) where the bus stop be.
(c) where stops the bus . (d) where the bus stop is.

2. I told him ......

(a) what the homework was. (b) what was the homework.
(c) what was to be the homework. (d) what is the homework.

3. I think .....

(a) will be the plane on time. (b) the plane will be on time.
(c) the plane to be on time. (d) it will be on time the plane.

4. I didn't know ...

(a) what he mean. (b) what did he mean.
(c) what did he meant. (d) what he meant.

5. He said ....

(a) that the weather colder than usual. (b) the weather be colder than usual.
(c) the weather was colder than usual. (c) the weather it is colder than usual.

6. I think ....

(a) today it is Wednesday. (b) that is today Wednesday.
(c) today is Wednesday. (d) today be Wednesday.

7. He said ....

(a) that yesterday he gone downtown. (b) he goes downtown yesterday.
(c) he go downtown yesterday. (d) he went downtown yesterday.

8. I believe ......

(a) him he is right. (b) he is right.
(c) he be right. (d) that he right.

9. She said .....

(a) that she was hungry. (b) she hungry.
(c) she be hungry. (d) her was hungry.

10. He told us .....

(a) that he enjoy the movie. (b) he enjoyed the movie.
(c) he be enjoying the movie. (d) that enjoyed the movie.

SOLUTIONS : CORRECT YOURSELF EXERCISE

Solutions CYE : 01

1. He says that Ram is a good player.
2. Rita says that Kishore sang a song.
3. You will say that Ganesh works hard.
4. Kali will say that Mira will swim in the river.
5. He said that Kalu read well.
6. He said that the birds were flying.
7. The servant said that the guest had arrived.
8. The washerman said that it had been raining since morning.
9. The boys said that the teacher had not come.
10. I said that Ganesh had been playing.
11. You said that Kalu could lift the box.
12. The teacher said that Mala might go.
13. I said that I should work hard.
14. He said that the boys would write lessons.

Solutions CYE : 02

1. Sheela said that the earth moves round the sun.
2. The saint said that man is mortal.
3. The teacher said that India became free in 1947.
4. Mohan said that Babar won the first battle of Panipat.
5. Mohan said that two and two make four.
6. Sheela said that truth always triumphs.
7. He said that Mohan could solve the sum.
8. She said that it might happen.

Solutions CYE : 03

1. I said that I was happy.
2. You said that you were learning your lesson.
3. He said that he was not to blame.
4. She said that she did not care for him.
5. They said that they trusted in God.
6. I told him that he was always late.
7. You told me that I might go.
8. Sheela told us that we must work hard.
9. Ram told me that Sita did not like meat.
10. I told him that he must not tell lies.
11. He proposed to me that we should go for a walk.
12. You proposed to me that we should play now.
13. She said that she was going then.
14. I said that I knew that man.
15. They said that they were leaving that night.
16. He told me that he would see me the next day.
17. She said that her uncle had come the previous day .
18. I said that I had bought the book the previous week.
19. Mother said that it would rain the following month.
20. She said that she had gone to Jaipur a week before.

Solutions CYE : 04

1. He told me that I had made a mistake.
2. The students said that they would play a match the next day.
3. Harish told his mother that he was going then.
4. The teacher said that honesty is the best policy.
5. He told his parents that he had done his best and could do no more.
6. The dying man told his sons that he was leaving them a treasure buried in his fields.
7. The Principal remarked that Harish was very intelligent.
8. The Principal announced that the next day would be a holiday.
9. The Prime Minister declared that national integrity would be preserved at all costs.
10. The Minister informed that the prices had started falling.
11. He told me that his father had gone to Mumbai the previous week.
12. I told her that I might come the next day.

13. The officer warned him that he would be dismissed if he did not attend the office in time.
14. The doctor apprised him that he had fallen ill because he had over-eaten the previous day.

Solutions CYE : 05

1. He asked me if I played hockey.
2. I asked her if she was leaving that night.
3. He asked his friend if he would lend him fifty rupees.
4. He asked his son if he had seen the Tajmahal.
5. He asked me if I hadn't got a television set.
6. The servant wanted to know if he should lay the table then.
7. She wondered if she would ever get married.
8. Ram asked me what I was doing.
9. She asked the stranger who he was.
10. The teacher asked me which my pen was.

Solutions CYE : 06

1. His father asked him why he had misbehaved.
2. I asked Sita where she was going.
3. Ram's mother asked him how he had fared in the examination.
4. The Madam asked the boys whose book that was.
5. She asked me how many boys there were in my school.
6. My father asked me whether I was feeling well.
7. He enquired of her if she could lend him her umbrella.
8. I enquire of Harish whether he wanted to settle at Kanpur.
9. I asked the servant where my camera was.
10. The teacher asked Ganesh why he was not taking the examaination.

Solutions CYE : 07

1. The teacher warned me never to make mischief again.
2. I asked Sita if she could keep it for me till the next day.
3. She asked Ram to leave it with her but not to come back.
4. The retailer asked me where I could find such variety of cloths.
5. Our madam advised us to go home then.
6. The girl exclaimed that I was a very funny man.
7. The old man asked his son what he (the son) had learnt at school.
8. The assistant requested him to give the list of the dealers.
9. Sohani asked Rajesh who had taken away her (Sohani's) bike.
10. The child asked his mother whether she was going to office that day.

Solutions CYE : 08

1. Shyam respectfully wished his teacher good morning.
2. The old lady thanked the child for showing her the way to the hospital.
3. My wife wished me a happy journey.
4. Ashok greeted Ramesh and asked how he was doing those days.
5. She exclaimed with sorrow that they had lost badly in the match.

6. My mother wished me that I might live long.
7. Mr. Janardhan shouted that, that book was full of errors.
8. The thief respectfully requested the judge to pardon him.
9. The priest blessed her that God might help her.
10. The stranger exclaimed with surprise what he saw before him.

Solutions CYE : 09

1. He said that two and two make four.
2. She said that she had seen a tiger there.
3. Maneesh said that he might go to Delhi the next day.
4. He asked me where he had gone
5. Sita asked me if it was raining till then.
6. He asked me when she would come.
7. She asked me if Raju was my friend.
8. She asked me if I had a car.
9. She asked me if they played chess.
10. Rahim asked who they were.

Solutions CYE : 10

1. Kanika asked Suresh if the tea was ready.
2. She asked me whether it was her book.
3. Tarmesh asked me if I would keep shut.
4. Chinkoo ordered him to get out.
5. The teacher asked the students to hurry up.
6. He requested the president to give him one chance.
7. She requested him to cooperate her.
8. The teacher instructed the girls to keep away from the wall.
9. She exclaimed that it was a pitiful scene.
10. He exclaimed with joy that he was the first.

Solutions CYE : 11

1. The queen eagerly wished that she were young again.
2. The Principal exclaimed with applause that the boys had done well.
3. He prayed that God might save the King.
4. The mother wished that his son should live long.
5. She requested me to have some drinks.
6. Rahul asked him if he would go to Jaipur .
7. The boy respectfully asked whether he could come in.
8. Hari told Rahim that he must obey his parents.
9. He said that he had to go to Jaipur the following week.
10. She said that I need not talk to her.

Solutions CYE : 12

1. He suggested to me that we should go to the hospital.
2. She advised that they should be allowed to play.
3. Ramesh said that Sarla would not dance.
4. The professor exclaimed with sorrow that he was undone.

5. He asked me if I knew who was there.
6. He thanked me for reminding him.
7. He greeted and asked me what I was doing.
8. She congratulated me.
9. She bade farewell to her friends.
10. He wished her good morning.

Solutions CYE : 13

1. He says that Mohan will write a letter.
2. He tells me that he will go to Mumbai tomorrow.
3. He told me that he was reading a book.
4. Ram told me that he could teach me.
5. He said that Mohan had been living there since 2000.
6. He said that the sun rises in the east.
7. He said that the moon revolves round the earth.
8. I told her that I had written a letter.
9. I asked her whether she had learnt her lesson.
10. Ram tells me that I am smart.
11. He asked me if I was going to Jaipur.
12. I asked him who taught him English.
13. I requested Harsh to help me.
14. Mohan advised me not to tell a lie.
15. She bade Ramesh good bye.

Solutions CYE : 14

1. My mother prayed that I might live long.
2. I requested Ram to let me go there.
3. He wished that he would be the king.
4. He exclaimed that Ravi was very intelligent.
5. She ordered to keep that room open.
6. The captain shouted with applause that his boys had done well.
7. Ram said that I need not talk to him.
8. He exclaimed that it was a beautiful picture.
9. He said that he would have to go to Jaipur the following month.
10. The teacher asked to hurry up.
11. She asked me if it was drizzling till then.
12. She said that she had seen a lion there.
13. He asked me what my father's name is.
14. Ram ordered the servant to clean up the house.
15. She asked me how old I was.

Solutions CYE : 15

1. He says that he is ill.
2. Mohn told me that he was doing his work.
3. I told him that I had gone there on Tuesday.
4. The teacher told us that the earth is round.
5. The boy said that he had seen him while he (the boy) was running.

6. She said that I need not wait.
7. I told him that his brother had passed.
8. I asked him where he lived.
9. He advised me to work hard if I wanted to pass.
10. He forbade me to go there.
11. He exclaimed that it was a pitiful scene.
12. She asked where the hospital was.
13. The big man said that it was quite right.
14. They told me that they would wait for me if I was late.
15. Ram asked Mohan what the time was.
16. The saint wished that God might help her.
17. Harsh wished me a happy journey.
18. The boy exclaimed with joy that they had won the match.
19. Sarla exclaimed with sorrow that she had failed.
20. My mother asked me not to jump on her bed.

Solutions CYE : 16

1. Sumit told his father that he wanted to go abroad after he finished his studies here.
2. I asked Sumit why he wanted to go abroad and where he actually wanted to go.
3. I requested my colleague not to go home yet and to remember that he promised to finish his work before leaving.
4. He asnwered politely to listen to him and that he must go then because his son was very ill.
5. I exclaimed with joy that it was a great relief to know that the girl had passed and then she would get a job.
6. The station master told me that I was very late and it was one full hour since the train had left.
7. Nitin asked me why I did not come with them. He further asked why I wanted to be so unsocial.
8. The gang leader shouted to his followers to keep together and run because the police were after them.
9. I told the companions that they need not come with them if they didn't want to, I suggested that they (the companions) should not wait for them any longer.
10. I exclaimed on seeing John in the room that it was a very pleasanst surprise, and I had never accepted to find him there.
11. I told Harish that the man who had come to meet him, had asked if we would see his boss the following day.
12. He asked his secretary why he did not carry out orders exactly, he warned him that if he did not (carry out orders) he would be punished.
13. I ordered the boy to get out (as he had no ticket) before he was driven out.
14. The lecturer paused and said that those who were tired of listening to him could go and that he would not mind that.
15. They cried out with contempt what they would tell him (by way of explanation), exclaimed that it was very awkward.

Solutions CYE : 17

1. Madhur told his sister that before going to Delhi, he would meet Sushila.
2. Govind told Mohit not to come there again or he would get a beating.
3. John asked James if he had come there just to see him or there were some other reasons.
4. Abdul exclaimed that was a lovely morning for tennis.
5. The teacher suggested the boys that they should go swimming since it was so warm.
6. They told their mother that they were not hungry, they would eat later.
7. He angrily asked his brother why he did not do as he was told.
8. I cautioned the visitor against sitting on that chair, (as) it was broken.
9. My little brother earnestly wished that it (should) rain so hard that he would not have to go to school.
10. They exclaimed that the path was very steep and they were quite tired.
11. The father advised his son neither to be a borrower, nor to be a lender.
12. Addressing the new graduates the Vice-Chancellor exhorted them to remember always that true education means the training of the mind.
13. The teacher exhorted his students, ever in their life and conversation, to prove worthy of their glorious Alma Mater.
14. The son asked his father respectfully if he expected him to have ever done that sort of a mean thing.
15. Addressing the secretary as young man, the officer advised him not to hang upon him, as he (the officer) did'nt like flatterers.

Solutions CYE :18

1. (d), 2. (a), 3. (b), 4. (d), 5. (c),
6. (c), 7. (d), 8. (b), 9. (a), 10. (b).

14

Preposition

Preposition is a word placed before a noun or pronoun or gerund, and it **denotes the relation**, the **person or thing referred by it, has with something else.**

A word such as a noun, pronoun or gerund **following a preposition is said to be the *object of the preposition***. It should be noted that a personal pronoun following a preposition must be in the objective case.

There is one very simple rule about prepositions. And, unlike most rules, this rule has no exceptions :

A preposition is followed by a 'noun'. It is never followed by a verb.

By 'noun' we include : (a) common noun (cat, money, love), (b)proper noun (names-India, Mira), (c) pronoun (him, you, her, us), (d) noun group (my first job) and (e) gerund (swimming , playing).

A preposition cannot be followed by a verb. If we want to follow a preposition by a verb, we must use the '-ing' form which is really **a gerund or verb in noun form**.

Read the following sentences :

In the following sentences, why is 'to' followed by a verb? That should be impossible, according to the above rule :

(a) I would like *to move* now.
(b)He used *to smoke*.

NOTE *In these sentences, 'to' is not a preposition. It is part of the infinitive ('to move', 'to smoke').*

Read the following examples :

(a) The food is on the **table**.
(b) She lives in **China.**
(c) Mira is looking for **you.**
(d) The letter is under **your black book**.
(e) I ate before **coming.**
(f) He is swimming in the **river.**

In above sentences, all underlined words are **prepositions** and the words in bold type are **objects**.

A preposition serves to connect its object with the rest of a sentence. In doing so, a preposition indicates the relationship of the idea expressed in the prepositional phrase to the ideas expressed in the rest of the sentence.

POSITION OF PREPOSITION

Prepositions normally precede nouns or pronouns. However in certain cases it is possible to move the preposition to the end of the sentence :

1. **When 'object' of the preposition is an interrogative pronoun**; what, who, whom, which, where' etc., the preposition takes **end or front position :**

   (a) What are you thinking of ? (b) Who were you talking to?
   (c) What are you staring at? (d) Which of these chairs did you sit on?

   It used to be thought ungrammatical to end a sentence with a preposition, but it is now accepted.

2. **When 'object' of the preposition is relative pronoun** 'that', the preposition takes **end position:**

   (a) Here is the magazine that you asked for. (b) This is the dish that she is fond of.
   (c) This is the girl that I told you of . (d) I know the colony that he lives in.

3. **When 'object' of the preposition is infinitive**(to + verb), the preposition is placed after infinitive :

   (a) This is a good hotel *to stay* at. (b) I need a pencil *to write* with .
   (c) It is a beautiful house *to live* in . (d) This is the ball *to play* with.

4. In some sentences **relative pronoun is hidden :**

   (a) This is the house(where) I lived in.
   (b) This is the girl (that) I told you of.

5. In some miscellaneous sentences , where **preposition is attached with the verb** :

   (a) I hate being *laughed* at. (b) This I *insist* on.
   (c) He likes being *looked* at. (d) He is *known* all the world over.

6. In some cases the **preposition comes in the beginning**.These are usually **interrogative sentences :**

   (a) By which train did you come ? (b) For whom was instruction given ?
   (c) In which class do you read? (d) To whom were you talking?

KINDS OF PREPOSITION

Preposition can be classified in following categories :

1. **Simple prepositions :** ***At,in,for,from,of, off,on,out,till,to,up,with,through,down,by,***etc.are some of the prepositions that are included in this category.These are most commonly used prepositions.

2. **Compound prepositions :** These are usually **formed by prefixing a preposition** ('a' or 'be') to a noun , an adjective or an adverb :

about	beside	inside
along	below	outside
amidst	beneath	within
among	between	without
aloud	beyond	underneath

3. **Phrasal prepositions :** These are **formed by joining two or more words** and function as a preposition :

along with	in addition to	in place of
because of	in case of	in spite of
by means of	in course of	owing to
for the sake of	with reference to	in comparison to
in favour of	with regard to	instead of
in accordance	with respect to	according to
in lieu of	in front of	in consequence of

4. **Participial prepositions :** When **present participles** are **used without any noun or pronoun attached to them**, these **are called participial prepositions.** Such most commonly used present participles are : ***concerning, pending, regarding, considering, touching, during, notwithstanding*** etc :
   (a) Pending enquiry into the matter, he was transferred from the office.
   (b) Considering the quality, the prices are reasonable.
   (c) Notwithstanding the protest made by the people , he was arrested by the police.
   (d) Regarding your suggestions, we are to inform you that we cannot allow any relaxation further.

Prepositional phrase

A phrase beginning with a preposition can be referred to as a **prepositional phrase**. The prepositional phrases in the following examples are underlined :

(a) He owns the hotel on the corner. (b) We are waiting for her.
(c) She has read many books about flying.

In the first example, the noun **corner** is the object of the preposition **on**. In the second example, the personal pronoun **her** is the object of the preposition **for**. It can be seen that the personal pronoun **her** is in the objective case. In the third example, the gerund **flying** is the object of the preposition **about**.

A preposition serves to connect its object with the rest of a sentence. In doing so, a preposition indicates the relationship of the idea expressed in the prepositional phrase to the ideas expressed in the rest of the sentence.

SOME IMPORTANT PREPOSITIONS

1. **At / In / On :**

These are very commonly used prepositions.

Note the use of these prepositions in reference of 'Time' :

(i) 'At' is used for a PRECISE TIME,
(ii) 'In' is used for MONTHS, YEARS, CENTURIES and LONG PERIODS,
(iii) 'On' is used for DAYS and DATES.

AT	IN	ON
Precise Time	Months, Years, Centuries and Long Periods	Days , Dates
at 3 o'clock	in May	on Sunday
at 10.30am	in summer	on Tuesdays
at noon	in the summer	on 6 March

at dinner time	in 1990	on 25th Jan.2007.
at bedtime	in the 1990s	on Christmas Day
at sunrise	in the next century	on Independence Day
at sunset	in the Ice Age	on my birthday
at the moment	in the past/future	on New Year's Eve

Look at the following examples :

(a) I have a meeting at 10 am.
(b) That shop closes at midnight.
(c) Richa went home at lunchtime.
(d) Where will you be on Independence Day?
(e) Do you think we will go to Saturn in the future?
(f) There should be a lot of progress in the next century.
(g) Do you work on Sundays?
(h) Her birthday is on 26April.

Note the use of the preposition of time 'At' , in the following expressions :

Expression	**Example**
at night	The stars shine at night.
at the weekend	I don't usually work at the weekend.
at Christmas/Easter	I stay with my family at Christmas.
at the same time	We finished the test at the same time.
at present	He's not home at present. Try later.

Note the use of the prepositions of time 'in' and 'on' in these common expressions :

IN	**ON**
in the morning	on Tuesday morning
in the mornings	on Saturday mornings
in the afternoon(s)	on Sunday afternoons
in the evening(s)	on Monday evening

Important : We should not use ; 'at , in ,on' with 'last, next, every' :

(a) I went to Mexico last May. (not in last May)
(b) He's coming back next Sunday. (not on next Sunday)
(c) I go home every Easter. (not at every Easter)
(d) We'll call you this evening. (not in this evening)

Note the use of these prepositions in reference of 'Place' :

(a) 'At' is used for a POINT,
(b) 'In' is used for an ENCLOSED SPACE,
(c) 'On' is used for a SURFACE.

AT **POINT**	**IN** **ENCLOSED SPACE**	**ON** **SURFACE**
at the corner	in the garden	on the wall
at the bus stop	in Delhi	on the ceiling
at the door	in India	on the door
at the top of the page	in a box	on the cover
at the end of the road	in my pocket	on the floor
at the entrance	in my wallet	on the carpet
at the crossroads	in a building	on the menu
at the altar	in a car	on a page

Look at the following examples :

(a) Rima is waiting for you at the bus stop.
(b) The shop is at the end of the lane.
(c) I live on the 4th floor at 21 Diamond Street in Kolkata.
(d) When will you arrive at the school?
(e) Do you work in a company?
(f) I have a meeting in Delhi .
(g) Do you live in India ?
(h) Saturn is in the Solar system.
(i) The author's name is on the cover of the book.
(j) There are no prices on this menu.
(k) You are standing on my foot.
(l) There was a 'no smoking' sign on the wall.

Please note that these three prepositions are most commonly used, in writing and speaking , so the students must learn the use of these preposition well.

Comparing At, In, To, Into :

(A) 'At' shows stationery position or existing state while 'in' shows movement :

(a) She is at home. (b) The train is in motion.

(B) 'At' for small place, town etc. while **'in' for big place** , town ,city, country etc. :

(a) He lives at Alwar in Rajasthan. (b) A temple is situated at Madurai in Tamilnadu.

(C) 'At' is used **for point of time** and **'in'** is used **for period of time :**

(a) The train will arrive at six in the morning.
(b) He will meet you in the morning.

(D) In/Into : 'In' shows existing state of things while **'into' shows movement :**

(a) He jumped into the river. (b) There are three students in the class.
(c)They climbed into the lorry. (d) He is swimming in the river.

'In' can also be used as an adverb :

Come in = Enter; eg – Get in (into the train).

(E) To/Into : 'To' and 'Into' are used as following :

To

(a) In the direction of : Turn **to** the right.
(b) Destination : I am going **to** Jaipur.
(c) Until : from Monday **to** Friday; five minutes **to** ten.
(d) Compared with : They prefer hockey **to** soccer. (Hockey and soccer compared.)
(e) With indirect object : Please give it **to** me.
(f) As part of infinitive : I like **to ski**; he wants **to help**.
(g) In order to : We went to the store (in order) **to** buy soap.

Into

(a) To the inside of : We stepped **into the room.**
(b) Change of condition : The boy changed **into a man.**

2. On/Onto :

'On' can be used for both existing position and movement :

(a) He was sitting on his bag. (b) Snow fell on the hills.
(c) His number is on the gate. (d) He went on board ship.

'On' can also be used as an adverb :

(a) Go on. (b) Come on.

'Onto' is used when there is movement involving a change of level :

(a) People climbed onto their roofs. (b) He lifted her onto the table.

3. With/ By :

'With' is used for instruments and 'by' is used for agents.

(a) The snake was killed by him with a stick.
(b) The letter was written by Suresh with a pencil.

4. Since/ For/ From :

'Since' is often used with period of time present perfect or past perfect tense. **'Since' is used to denote point of time** and **never for period of time**, as; *Since 6 O'Clock/last night/last Monday/since morning/ evening/ Monday/January/2005 etc :*

(a) It has been raining since two O'Clock. (b) He had been ill since Monday.

NOTE *'Since' can also be used as an adverb :*

(a) He left school in 1983. I haven't seen him since.
(b) It is two years since I last saw Tom.

'For' is used to express period of time : two hours/two days/two years/a long time/some time/for ever etc. :

(a) Boil it for two hours. (b) He lived in this house for six months.

For is also used with present perfect tense or past perfect tense **for an action which extends up to the time of speaking :**

(a) He has worked here for a year. (b) It has been raining for two hours.
(c) He worked for three hours.

'From' is normally **used with 'to or till / until' :**

(a) Most people work from eight to six.

'From' can also be used of place :

(a) He is from Mumbai. (b) Where do you come from ?

5. For/ During : 'During' is used with known periods of time, i.e. periods known by name, such as Christmas, Easter or periods which have been already defined :

1. during the Middle ages,
2. during the summer,
3. during his childhood.

(a) It rained all Sunday but stopped raining during the night.
(b) She was ill for a week, and during that week she ate nothing.

'For' **may be used to denote purpose and may also be used before known periods :**

(a) I went there for the summer. (b) I rented my house for my holidays.
(c) I rented my car for the summer only.

'For' has various other uses :

(a) He asked for ten.I paid six for it. (b) I bought one for Kuku.

(c) He has been ill for three days.

6. **Below / Under / Beneath :** 'Below' and 'under' both mean–lower than(in level) and sometimes either can be used. But **'under' usually denotes physical contact and 'below' denotes space between the things :**

(a) He put the books under the pillow.

(b) He placed the lamp below the Almirah.

(c) They live below us. (We live at the second floor while they live at the first floor.)

(d) I was wearing a sweater also under the jacket.

'Below' and 'under' may also mean junior in rank :

(e) He is under me; means that I am superior to him.

(f) He is working under me.

'Below' is used meaning—opposite to 'above'.

(g) The temperature can fall below 15 degree Celsius.

(h) Rainfall has been below average this year.

Beneath : *Something that is* **beneath** *another thing is* **under the other thing :**

(i) I could see the muscles of his shoulders beneath his T-shirt...

(j) I found pleasure in sitting beneath the trees...

(k) ...the frozen grass crunching beneath his feet.

'Beneath' could also mean 'unworthy as per status' or 'in lower strata in social class' :

(l) It is beneath his dignity to beg for money. (unworthy of him)

(m) She married beneath her. (into a lower social class)

7. **In/ Within :**

'In' means the maximum time limit, while **'within' denotes the period upto which the work will be completed**. 'Within a particular length of time' means before that length of time, while 'in' refers the maximum time required for the completion of the job :

(a) I will complete the work in a month.

(b) I can repair the car within two hours.

(c) He will write a book in three months.

(d) He can solve this question within an hour.

8. **Ago and Before :**

'Ago' is used for past events while **'before' is used in reference to two events :**

(a) He came three days ago.

(b) The train had left before he reached the station .

9. **Beside/Besides :**

Beside and Besides have altogether different meanings. Don't confuse beside with besides ;
beside = at the side of :

(a) He was sitting beside Sarla. (b)We camped beside a lake.

besides = in addition to / as well as :

(a) He has a car besides a motor cycle.

(b) Besides doing the cooking I help Ram.

10. Between/ Among :

'Between' is **normally used for ' two' things or persons**, but it can also be used for more than 'two', when we have a definite number in mind and there is a close relationship/association within them :

(a) He distributed his property between his *two* sons.
(b) Luxembourg lies between Belgium, Germany and France.
(c) A treaty was signed between *three* parties.
(d) He inserted a needle between the close petals of a flower.

'Among' is usually **used for more than two persons or things** *when we have no definite number in mind :*

(e) He was happy to be among friends again.
(f) He distributed his property among the poor.

11. Among/ Amongst :

Both have same meaning.Either of them can be used if **followed by 'the'**. *If followed by a word, beginning with a vowel, 'amongst' is used.* The use of amongst is usually found in literary writings.

(a) He distributed the toffees among/amongst *the* poor.
(b) He distributed the toffees amongst *us*. ('us' begins with vowel 'u'.)

12. Of/ Off :

'Of' and 'Off' are used in following situations referring :

1. **Location :** east **of** here; the middle **of** the road,
2. **Possession :** a friend **of** mine; the sound **of** music,
3. **Part of a group :** one **of** us; a member **of** the team,
4. **Measurement :** a cup **of** milk; two metres **of** snow.
5. Not on; away from ;eg– Please keep **off** the grass.
6. At some distance from ; eg– There are islands **off** the coast.

(a) He is a member of our family.
(b) She is a member of our society.
(c) She parked her car in the middle of the road.
(d) He is off duty now.
(e) He jumped off the tower.

13. Above/ Over :

Above and **over both mean—'higher than'** and sometimes either can be used :

(a) The helicopter hovered above/ over us.
(b) White flags were waved above/ over the buildings.

But **'over'** also means—**'covering' / 'on the other side of '/ 'across' :**

(a) I put a cloth over her. (covering)
(b) He lives over this mountain. (on the other side of)
(c) There is a bridge over the railway line. (across)
(d) He put a blanket over the dead body.

'**Above**' can have none of these meanings.

'Over' can mean higher in rank :

(e) He is over me.(means ; He is my immediate boss.)

'Over' is also **used with meals/ food/ drink :**
(a) We had a chat over a cup of tea. (while drinking tea)
(b) The matter was decided over the lunch.
'Above' is also used **meaning 'earlier'or 'previous':**
(a) He lives at the above address. (Previously mentioned)
(b) For details please see (P-1) above. (Previously mentioned)

14. Make of / Make from :

Both refer material used

'Make' of is used **when the shape of the material is not changed (only physical change) :**
(a) A note book is made of papers. (b) A house is made of bricks.
'Make from' is used when shape of the material has undergone a total change (Chemical change) :
(a) Butter is made from milk (b) Paper is made from grass.

15. In/ With :

'In' is used in following situations :
1. Place thought of as an area : **in** London; **in** Europe
2. Within a location : **in** the room; **in** the building
3. Large units of time : That happened **in** March, **in** 1992.
4. Within a certain time : I will return **in** an hour.
5. By means of : write **in** pencil; speak in English
6. Condition : **in** doubt; **in** a hurry; **in** secret
7. A member of : He is **in** the orchestra; **in** the navy
8. Wearing : the boy **in** the blue shirt
9. With reference to : lacking **in** ideas; rich **in** oil.

'With' is used in following situations :
1. Accompanying : He came **with** her; I have my keys **with** me.
2. Having; containing : Here is a book **with** a map of the island.
3. By means of; using : I repaired the shoes **with** glue.
4. Manner : **with** pleasure; **with** ease; **with** difficulty.
5. Because of : We were paralyzed **with** fear.
6. Agreement : I agree **with** you.

16. Opposite / In front of :

'Opposite' is used **meaning-'antonym' and ' position in front'. 'Infront of'always means front position**. See the following example :

Ram and Shyam are having a meal. Ram is sitting at one side of the table and Shyam at the other side.We will say :
(a) Ram is sitting opposite Shyam.(Ram is facing Shyam).
(b) People living on one side of a street will talk of the houses on the other side, as the houses *opposite* rather than the houses *in front of* us.
(c) His house is opposite to ours

'Infront of' is used in following ways :
(a) He parked the car in front of the hotel.
(b) He put the plates on the table in front of us.

17. By and Before :

'By a time/by a date' usually implies before that time or date :

(a) The train starts at 7.15, so you had better be at the station by 7.00 ('by 7.00' implies—'before 7.00'.)

By + a time expression structure is **often used with future perfect tense :**

(b) By the end of July I'll have read all those books.

'Before' can be **used as a preposition** or as a **conjunction** or **as an adverb :**

(c) Before signing this agreement let us discuss each and every point thread bare. (preposition)

(d) Before you sign this you can discuss it with your father. (conjunction)

(e) I've seen her somewhere before. (adverb)

18. After and Afterwards :

'After' must be followed by a noun, pronoun or gerund :

(a) After *breakfast* he ordered a taxi. (breakfast-noun)

(b) Don't run immediately after a meal / after *eating*. (eating–gerund)

(c) Don't have a meal and run immediately after *it*. (it–pronoun)

If we do not like to use a noun/ pronoun or gerund, we cannot use 'after', but we can use 'afterwards' or 'then' :

(a) Don't have a meal and run immediately afterwards.

(b) They bathed and afterwards played games.

'Afterwards' can be used **at either end of the clause** and *can be modified* by **'soon, immediately, not long,'** etc. :

(a) Soon afterwards I got a call. (b) I got a call not long afterwards.

19. But and Except :

Both have the same meaning and **are usually interchangeable.**

After 'nobody/ none/ nothing/ nowhere' etc. usually 'but' is used :

(a) Nobody but Shyam knew the way. (b) Nothing but the best is sold in our shop.

'Except' is used when the prepositional phrase comes later in a sentence.
Look at the following example :

(a) Nobody knew the way except Shyam.

NOTE *After 'but' and 'except' bare infinitive (infinitive without 'to') is used.*

20. To and Towards :

The preposition **'to' indicates movement with the aim of a specific destination, which can be a place or an event**, e.g :

(a) I'm going **to** USA tomorrow. (b) I need to go **to** the bank.

(c) Can you tell me the way **to** the station? (d) Are you going **to** the party?

(e) I've never been **to** a cricket match. (f) What time did you go **to** work?

NOTE *that **'up to'** is often used to express movement to a person, e.g :*

(a) She came **up to** me and asked me what the time was.

The preposition **'to'** is sometimes used to indicate a specific position, especially if a person or object is facing something, e.g :

(a) There's a door **to** your left. (b) He stood with his back **to** the window.

Towards :

The preposition **towards indicates movement in a particular direction,** e.g :

(a) She was carrying a suitcase and walking **towards** the railway station.

(b) He hit the ball **towards** the goal.

(c) She pointed **towards** the door.

(d) Everyone sitting in the room turned **towards** me.

NOTE ***the contrast in the following two examples :***

(a) I'm going **to** Newyork for a meeting.

(b) I think we're heading **towards** Newyork now, we must have gone wrong.

In the first example, **'to' refers a specific destination.** In the second example with ***towards***, the **direction of movement is more importantly indicated.**

NOTE *that occasionally,* ***'towards'*** *is also used to indicate position, but this is a position in relation to a particular direction from the point of view of the speaker, e.g :*

(a) She was sitting **towards** the back of the room.

(b) Tom stood with his back **towards** the door.

21. Through and Into :

The preposition **'through' refers to movement within a space** *which can be thought of as three-dimensional*, e.g :

(a) We couldn't get the new sofa **through** the door.

(b) They drove **through** some spectacular countryside.

(c) The canal flows **through** the city centre.

(d) You won't be able to see it unless you look **through** the binoculars.

'Through' *usually* **suggests movement across an entire space**, from one side of something to another, e.g :

(a) He cut **through** the wire.

The preposition **'into'** *refers to* **movement from the outside to the inside of** *a three dimensional space, e.g* :

(a) We got **into** the back of the car.

(b) She reached **into** her bag and found the keys.

With certain verbs **'into'** can be used *to express the idea of movement in the direction of something, often resulting in actually hitting it*, as in the example (b) below :

(a) He looked straight into her eyes.

(b) She swerved and crashed into the fence.

22. Across, over and along :

The prepositions **'across'** and **'over'** are used **to talk about movement from one side of a place to another**. They usually refer to movement in relation to places which can be thought of as *two-dimensional*, such as-surfaces (e.g : a lawn) or lines (e.g : a river), for example :

(a) I'll jump **over** the wall and open the gate.

(b) The aircraft flew low **over** the lake.

(c) How are we going to get **across** the stream?

(d) It's the first time I've flown **across** the Atlantic.

'**Over**' also functions as a preposition **expressing position**. It often *has a similar meaning to the preposition* **'above'**, e.g :

(a) There was a mirror **above/over** the sink.

One of its core uses however is to express position in relation to a two-dimensional surface, e.g :

(b) A white tablecloth was spread **over** the table.

Or to show when something is positioned on the opposite side of a 'line', e.g : road, bridge, etc.

(c) The hotel is **over** the bridge.

'**Across**' is sometimes used to **express position in relation to something which stretches from one side of a place to another**, e.g :

(a) There was a barrier **across** the road.

And like '**over**' 'across' is also used to show when something is positioned on the opposite side of a place in relation to the speaker, e.g :

(a) The bank is **across** the street.

The preposition **along** is **used to show movement following a line,** e.g :

(a) We walked **along** the river.
(b) I followed Mr Jackson **along** the corridor.
(c) Well-wishers began placing flowers **along** the railings.

It is also sometimes used to show a specific position in relation to a line, e.g :

(d) Somewhere **along** the path there's a signpost.

Or to show position when a group of things are positioned in a line next to something, e.g :

(e) There were plenty of restaurants **along** the river front.

PREPOSITIONS WITH NOUNS, ADJECTIVES AND VERBS

Prepositions are sometimes so firmly attached to other words that they have practically become one word.

NOUNS FOLLOWED BY PREPOSITIONS

The following are examples of nouns which are usually followed by certain prepositions. In the case of phrases which are idioms, the meanings of the phrases are indicated in brackets.

Against :
take precautions against

For :
have affection for
have compassion for
a reason for
have respect for
have a talent for
pave the way for (prepare for)
make allowances for
an excuse for
have a reputation for
have sympathy for
lie in wait for (ambush)

From :
absence from

In :

have confidence in
have faith in
have an interest in
taking part in
make progress in

Into :

have insight into

Of :

have an abhorrence of
an acknowledgment of
take advantage of
take care of
take command of
evidence of
an example of
an excess of
make a fool of
make fun of (ridicule)
have an impression of
a lack of
neglect of
a number of
a pair of
be part of
a possibility of
make a practice of (do often)
a proof of
a quantity of
recognition of
a recollection of
a result of
run the risk of (risk)
catch sight of (see suddenly)
a sign of
a survey of
a symbol of
a symptom of
a token of
make use of
a way of
wash one's hands of (stop caring about and dealing with)

On

an attack on
dependence on
make an impression on
play a joke on
shed light on (explain)
have pity on

To

have access to
pay attention to
an objection to
a reply to
a response to
lay siege to (besiege)
shut one's eyes to (deliberately ignore a problem)

Toward or **Towards**

animosity toward(s)
an attitude toward(s)

With

have a connection with
find fault with (criticize)
fall in love with
change places with

ADJECTIVES AND VERBS IN THE PASSIVE VOICE FOLLOWED BY PREPOSITIONS

In some cases, different prepositions can be used without causing a change in meaning. For instance, both the following examples have the same meaning :

(a) I was angry **at** them.
(b) I was angry **with** them.

However, in many cases, the use of different prepositions causes a change in meaning. For instance, the past participle '**protected**' is typically followed by the preposition '**from**'. However, like many other past participles, '**protected**' may also be followed by the preposition '**by**', where '**by**' serves to introduce the performer of the action expressed by the past participle.

(a) The city is *protected* **from** the soldiers.

(a 1.) The city is *protected* **by** the soldiers.

The first example indicates that the soldiers are a threat to the city; whereas the second example indicates that the soldiers are protecting the city.

The following are examples of **predicate adjectives and past participles of verbs** in the passive voice which are usually **followed by certain prepositions**. In addition, it should be kept in mind that most verbs in the passive voice can be followed by a phrase beginning with the preposition '**by**'.

About

anxious about	concerned about	curious about	depressed about
doubtful about	enthusiastic about	excited about	happy about
pleased about	wrong about	worried about	

At

adept at	alarmed at	amazed at	overjoyed at
shocked at	surprised at		

Between

torn between

By

accompanied by	caused by	guided by	manufactured by
obsessed by	written by		

For

blamed for	eligible for	famous for	fit for
known for	late for	noted for	praised for
punished for	qualified for	ready for	responsible for
ripe for	sorry for	suitable for	

From

absent from	apart from	derived from	descended from
detached from	different from	distinct from	exempt from
far from	isolated from	omitted from	protected from
removed from	safe from	separated from	

In

absorbed in	disappointed in	engaged in	immersed in
interested in	involved in		

Of

accused of	afraid of	ashamed of	aware of
capable of	certain of	composed of	conscious of
convinced of	deprived of	devoid of	fond of
ignorant of	independent of	jealous of	proud of

regardless of	reminded of	sure of	suspicious of
suspected of	terrified of	tired of	worthy of

On

based on	dependent on	intent on

To

acceptable to	accessible to	accustomed to	adapted to
addicted to	adjacent to	attached to	attributable to
close to	committed to	comparable to	dedicated to
detrimental to	devoted to	due to	equal to
equivalent to	essential to	exposed to	faithful to
favorable to	foreign to	impervious to	indifferent to
indispensable to	inferior to	kind to	loyal to
next to	obedient to	obliged to	oblivious to
parallel to	partial to	peculiar to	preferable to
prior to	proportional to	reconciled to	reduced to
related to	relative to	relevant to	resigned to
resistant to	restricted to	senior to	sensitive to
similar to	subject to	subordinate to	suited to
superior to	susceptible to	tied to	opposed to

Toward or **Towards**

protective toward(s)

With

acquainted with	affiliated with	associated with	besieged with
compared with	compatible with	confronted with	consistent with
covered with	cursed with	exasperated with	familiar with
finished with	identified with	infatuated with	patient with
pleased with	satisfied with	synonymous with	threatened with

VERBS FOLLOWED BY PREPOSITIONS

The following are examples of verbs which are often followed by certain prepositions :

About

care about	complain about	forget about	lie about (tell a lie)
reminisce about	talk about	think about	wonder about
worry about			

Against

discriminate against protest against react against rebel against turn against

At

aim at	bark at	connive at	frown at
gaze at	glare at	growl at	hint at
look at	point at	shoot at	smile at
snap at	sneer at	stare at	wave at wink at

For

apply for	apologize for	beg for	blame for
budget for	hope for	long for	look for

mourn for pay for plead for pose for
pray for prepare for press for register for
search for shop for substitute for vouch for
wait for wish for

From

abstain from benefit from deduct from derive from
desist from deter from detract from deviate from
differ from divert from escape from extricate from
flee from infer from profit from protect from
quote from radiate from recoil from recover from
refrain from shrink from stem from suffer from

In

believe in engage in indulge in intervene in
invest in participate in persist in succeed in

Into

change into convert into delve into dip into
develop into divide into fall into merge into
plunge into pry into sink into transform into

Of

approve of beware of conceive of consist of
deprive of die of disapprove of smell of

On

blame on concentrate on depend on impinge on
impose on insist on intrude on pounce on
reflect on rely on report on spy on
subsist on thrive on

Over

preside over trip over

To

adapt to adhere to adjust to amount to
belong to conform to contribute to correspond to
listen to object to pertain to prefer to
refer to relate to respond to resort to
revert to submit to subscribe to succumb to
surrender to yield to

With

agree with associate with collaborate with combine with
communicate with comply with concur with consort with
contend with cooperate with cope with correspond with
flirt with mingle with share with sympathize with

PREPOSITIONS USED IN IDIOMS

Below are examples of **idioms consisting of prepositional phrases**. The meaning of each idiom is indicated after the colon :

At

not **at** all : not in any way
at all times : always
at any rate : whatever happens
keep someone **at** arm's length : avoid becoming closely involved with someone
at close quarters : very near
at one's disposal : to be used as one wishes
at a distance : not near
at fault : causing something wrong, on the wrong side
at first : at the beginning
see **at** a glance : see immediately
at hand : near; readily available
at last : finally, after some delay
at a loss : uncertain what to do or say
at the mercy of : without defense against
at the moment : now
at once : immediately
at present : now
at rest : not moving
at risk : threatened by danger or loss
at short notice : with little warning
at stake : to be won or lost
at a stretch : continuously
at that rate : under those circumstances
at this point : at this place; at this moment
at the wheel : in control

Behind

behind the scene : (of persons) influencing events secretly; (in a theater) behind the stage
behind schedule : not on time

Beside

be **beside** oneself : lose one's self-control
beside the point : irrelevant

Between

read **between** the lines : deduce a meaning that is not actually expressed (but might be inferred)

Beyond

beyond help : unable to be helped
beyond a joke : too annoying to be amusing
beyond reproach : perfect; blameless

By

by accident : not deliberately
by all means : by any possible method
bit **by** bit : gradually
by chance : by accident; without planning, by coincidence
by courtesy of : with the help or permission of
win **by** default : win because of lack of competition
by degrees : gradually
perform **by** ear : perform (music) by listening to the sound, without referring to written music
by hand : without the use of machinery, manually
by heart : from memory
little **by** little : gradually
by means of : by using
by mistake : accidentally
by no means : not at all
one **by** one : one at a time
by oneself : alone
side **by** side : beside one another
by the way : incidentally (used to introduce an unrelated topic of conversation)
by word of mouth : orally

For

once and **for** all : for the last time (e.g. used when giving someone a final warning)
for certain : definitely; without doubt
for a change : for the sake of variety
for example : as an illustration
for fun : for the sake of enjoyment
for good : permanently
for good measure : in addition to the necessary amount
for instance : for example; as an illustration
for keeps : (colloquial) permanently
for a living : as a profession
for now : temporarily
run **for** office : compete for an elected position
for one thing : because of one reason (out of several)
for the sake of : for the benefit of; for the purpose of
for sale : intended to be sold
for sure : definitely (more colloquial than 'for certain')
food **for** thought : something which makes one think
play **for** time : delay doing something in the hope that the situation will improve
for the time being : until some other arrangement is made
ask **for** trouble : act in a dangerous or foolish way (which may result in trouble)
for a while : for a period of time
word **for** word : exactly as said or written

From

from afar : from a distance
from all sides : from all directions
from head to foot : (of a person) completely; all over
from scratch : from the beginning
from time to time : occasionally

In

in addition to : as well as
in advance : before
be **in** agreement with : have the same opinion as
in any case : whatever happens
in brief : in a few words
in bulk : (of goods) in large amounts; not in packages
be **in** charge of : have responsibility for
in common : shared by all members of a group
in control : having the power to direct something
in the course of : during
in danger : iikely to be harmed
in a daze : unable to think clearly; confused
in debt : owing money
in demand : (of goods or persons) desired by many people
in depth : (investigate something) thoroughly
in detail : (explain something) thoroughly
in disgrace : regarded with disapproval because of having done something wrong
in the distance : far away
in doubt : uncertain
in duplicate : so that there are two identical copies (of a document)
in earnest : seriously; in a determined way
in effect : (of rules) operating
in the end : finally
in fact : in reality; really
in fashion : fashionable; accepted as being the most desirable and up to date
in favour of : supporting (an idea), in support of
in flames : burning with visible flames
in a flash : very quickly; suddenly
in full : without omitting anything
in general : usually; as a whole
hand **in** hand : (of persons) holding hands; (of related situations) occurring together
in a hurry : trying to accomplish something quickly
in jest : as a joke
in kind : (payment) in goods rather than in money
in itself : without reference to anything else
in league with : (of persons) joined together with (usually for a dishonest purpose)
be **in** the limelight : be the focus of attention; receive great publicity
in the long run : in the end; eventually

in the long term : looking ahead to the distant future
leave someone **in** the lurch : abandon someone who is in a difficult situation
be **in** the minority : be in the smaller of two groups
in mint condition : (of manufactured goods) perfect; brand-new
in a minute : soon
in a moment : soon; quickly
set something **in** motion : start something going
nip something **in** the bud : put an end to something before it gets properly started
in no time : very soon; very quickly
in order of : arranged according to
in order to : for the purpose of
in part : to some degree
in particular : especially
in power : (of a political party) holding office
in practice : able to do something well because of recent practice; in reality (opposite of **in** theory), also customs *in practice (observed)*
in print : (of a book) printed and available from the publisher
in private : not in front of other people
in public : openly; not in private
in reality : really
in reserve : saved for later use
in retrospect : looking back over past events
in return for : as repayment for
be **in** the right : be correct
in season : (of fruit or vegetables) readily available at that time of year
in a second : soon; quickly
in short supply : scarce; not easily obtainable
in sight : able to be seen
in stock : (of goods at a store) present and available
in that case : if that is true
in theory : ideally; according to theoretical considerations
be **in** time : not be late
in touch with : in communication with; informed about
in triplicate : so that there are three identical copies (of a document)
be **in** trouble : be in a difficult situation; be blamed or punished for doing something wrong
in tune : at the correct pitch
act **in** unison : act together
in vain : without success
in the vicinity of : near
once **in** a while : occasionally
in words of one syllable : (explain something) clearly and simply
in working order : able to function properly
in the wrong : responsible for an error; guilty

Inside

inside out : with the inner side out; thoroughly

Into

paint oneself **into** a corner : take a course of action which greatly narrows one's future choices of action, limit one's options
go **into** hiding : hide oneself
get **into** a rut : get into a fixed and uninteresting way of life
get **into** trouble : get into a difficult situation; do something deserving blame or punishment

Of

of course : certainly; as one would expect; as everyone knows
hard **of** hearing : somewhat deaf
next **of** kin : nearest relative or relatives
of one's own accord : voluntarily; on one's own initiative
of one's own free will : voluntarily; by choice
one's point **of** view : one's opinion about something
right **of** way : public right to use a path or road; (of road traffic) right to proceed before others
rule **of** thumb : a simple way to calculate what procedure to follow, based on extensive experience, rather than on theoretical considerations

Off

go **off** the air : (of radio or television) stop broadcasting
off duty : not engaged in one's regular work
off one's hands : no longer one's responsibility
off and on : from time to time
off the record : say something privately, that is not to be officially recorded
off the track : following a wrong line of thought or action

On

on account of : because of
be **on** the air : (of radio or television) be in the process of broadcasting
on the alert : ready to act
be **on** all fours : (of a person) be on hands and knees
on the average : usually; normally
on behalf of : for; in the interests of
on board : on a ship or airplane
on business : as part of one's work
on condition that : only if; provided that
on demand : when asked for
on display : being exhibited
on duty : engaged in one's regular work
on fire : burning
to go **on** foot : to walk
be **on** one's guard : be alert and ready to meet an attack
on hand : available

on loan : lent and not yet returned
shoot **on** location : (of a movie) film in natural surroundings, not in a studio
on the lookout : watchful
put something **on** the map : cause something to become well-known
get **on** one's nerves : annoy; irritate
on no account : absolutely not
on the one hand : (used to introduce one side of an argument)
on one's own : alone; without help
act **on** one's own initiative : act independently, without orders from anyone else
on order : requested but not yet delivered
on the other hand : (used to introduce a contrasting side of an argument)
act **on** principle : do something to support a policy
on purpose : deliberately
go **on** record : say something which is to be officially recorded
on sale : being sold at a lower price than usual
on schedule : at the correct time; as planned or predicted
on second thoughts : after thinking further about something
on a shoestring : with a very small amount of money
be **on** the spot : be where important events are taking place; be placed in an awkward situation
on the spur of the moment : on a sudden impulse
go off **on** a tangent : change suddenly to a new line of thought or action
on time : at the correct time
walk **on** tiptoe : walk on the toes and balls of the feet
accept something **on** trust : accept something without proof, in good faith
on the verge of : very close to; about to
on the whole : taking everything into consideration

Out of

out of the blue : unexpectedly
out of breath : (after running) panting from a shortage of oxygen
out of character : unlike a person's known character
out of control : not able to be regulated or guided
out of danger : safe
out of date : no longer used; old-fashioned; (of news) no longer true
out of debt : having paid one's debts
be **out of** one's depth : be unable to handle a situation because of lack of experience
out-doors : in the open air; not in a building
out of fashion : not fashionable; not presently in common use
out of hand : not under control
out of harm's way : safe
out of line with : in disagreement with
be **out of** one's mind : be insane
out of order : not functioning properly; (at a formal meeting) not behaving according to the rules
out of the ordinary : unusual
out of place : unsuitable

out of practice : unable to do something as well as one has (done) in past, because of lack of recent practice
out of print : (of a book) no longer available from the publisher
out of proportion : too big or too small; not having the appropriate relationship to something
out of the question : impossible; not to be considered
out of season : (of fruit or vegetables) not readily available at that time of year
out of shape : (of persons) not in top condition because of lack of exercise
out of sight : hidden, not able to be seen
out of stock : (of goods at a store) temporarily unavailable
out of style : not fashionable
out of touch : with not in communication with; not informed about
out of town : having temporarily left town
out of trouble : not in trouble
out of tune : not at the correct pitch
out of work : no longer having employment

To

to all intents and purposes : in all important ways
to a certain extent : partly
to date : so far; until now
up **to** date : current; modern
see eye **to** eye with : agree entirely with
take something **to** heart : be much affected by something
made **to** measure : exactly suitable; (of clothes) made for a certain person
keep something **to** oneself : not tell anyone
to the point : relevant

Under

under age : below the age of being legally permitted to do something
be **under** arrest : be held prisoner and charged with wrongdoing
under the auspices of : with the patronage of; supported by
under one's breath : in a whisper
under the circumstances : in existing situation or in present state of things
under consideration : in the process of being thought about
under control : able to be regulated or guided
under cover of : protected by; undetected because of
under fire : being shot at; being criticized
under the impression that : having the idea that
be **under** the influence of : be affected by
be **under** oath : have sworn to tell the truth
under observation : being watched carefully
under restraint : prevented from doing something

Up

have something **up** one's sleeve : have a secret idea or plan in reserve

With

with impunity : without risk of injury or punishment
with the naked eye : without using a magnifying lens
with no strings attached : (of help given) with no conditions; to be used freely
take **with** a pinch of salt : not believe completely
with regard to : concerning; about
with respect to : concerning; about
tarred **with** the same brush : having the same faults
with a vengeance : very much; more than usual

Within

within limits : to a certain extent; not too much
within living memory : within the memory of people now alive

Without

go **without** saying : be obvious

UNNECESSARY PREPOSITIONS

In everyday speech, we fall into some bad habits, ***using prepositions where they are not required.*** It would be a good idea to eliminate these words altogether, but we must be especially careful not to use them in formal, academic prose :

(a) She met ~~**up with**~~ the new coach on the ground.
(b) The glass fell off ~~**of**~~ the desk.
(c) He threw the glass out ~~**of**~~ the window.
(d) He wouldn't let the cat inside ~~**of**~~ the house. [or use "in"]
(e) Where did they go ~~**to**~~?
(f) Where is your college ~~**at**~~?

(A) Ellipsis in preposition

When two words or phrases are used in parallel and require the *same preposition* to be idiomatically correct, the **preposition does not have to be used twice :**

(a) You can wear that outfit *in* summer and ~~**in**~~ winter.
(b) The female was both attracted ~~**by**~~ and distracted *by* the male's dance.

However, **when the idiomatic use of phrases calls for *different prepositions*, we must be careful not to omit one of them :**

(a) The children were *interested in* and *disgusted by* the movie.
(b) It was clear that this player could both *contribute to* and *learn from* every game he played.
(c) He was *fascinated by* and *enamored of* this beguiling woman.
(d) We should prevent damage and theft of public property. *Incorrect*
We should prevent damage to and theft of public property. *Correct*
(e) He is neither ashamed nor sorry for his misdeeds. *Incorrect*
He is neither ashamed of nor sorry for his misdeeds. *Correct*
(f) The design of this house is different and inferior to that of other house. *Incorrect*
The design of this house in different from and inferior to that of other house. *Correct*

(B) Preposition Omitted

1. **Some transitive verbs do not take prepositions with them**. Such commonly used verbs are; ***Reach, Resist, Resemble, Afford, Accompany, Attack, Assist, Pick, Pervade, Precede, Obey, Order, Combat, Benefit, Inform, Violate etc.***

   (a) He ordered for a cup of tea. *Incorrect*
   He ordered a cup of tea. *Correct*
   (b) India attacked on Pakistan. *Incorrect*
   India attacked Pakistan. *Correct*
   (c) He informed to me yesterday. *Incorrect*
   He informed me yesterday. *Correct*

2. In case of nouns denoting time (morning, evening, day, night, month,week, year), **if such nouns are preceded by objectives like ; this, that, next, every, last etc.we should not use preposition with such words.**

   (a) She is going to Jaipur next morning. (on next morning–incorrect)
   (b) I met her last evening. (on last evening–incorrect)
   (c) Ram is coming here next month.

3. **Nouns; 'yesterday, today, tomorrow,** are also **used without preposition :**

   (a) Please meet me tomorrow. (not-'on tomorrow')
   (b) He is arriving today. (not 'on today')
   (c) He went yesterday.

4. **Words denoting time and place like**; ***'last week, last month, abroad, minute, bit, inside, outside',*** etc. are also used **without preposition :**

   (a) He came here last month. (not-*in* last month)
   (b) Sita is going abroad next week.
   (c) Please wait a minute / bit.
   (d) Please come inside.
   (e) Why are you standing outside?

5. **Home** : *If verbs showing movement like,* go, get etc **are used with home, we should not use any preposition** before home :

   (a) It took them three hours to get home.
   (b) I went home by bus. not–'to home'

NOTE *If any pronoun / adjective /phrase is used immediately before 'home', the use of preposition is necessary :*

(a) She returned *to her husband's home.* (b) I went *to his home.*

The preposition 'at' is also used with home as following :

(a) You can do this work at home.
(b) We can stay at home.
(c) He is at home.

NOTE ***We can't use 'in' immediately before 'home' :***

(a) You can do this job in your own home.
(b) We can live in our home.
(c) He is in home. **Incorrect**

6. Verbs denoting ; **command, request, invitation and advice; e.g.-advise; ask, beg, command, encourage, implore, invite, order, recommend, remind, request, tell, urge, warn**, *can be followed directly by the person addressed* **without the use of preposition 'to'**.

Look at the following examples :

(a) I advised her to wait. (not—'advised *to* her')
(b) We urged him to try again. ('urged on him'–incorrect)
(c) I reminded them that there were no trains after 8 PM.
(d) She warned him that the ice was thin .

But note that 'recommend' (means advise) when used with other constructions needs **'to'** before the person addressed :

(a) He recommended me to buy it.
(b) He recommended it to me. (In this construction 'to' is required)
(c) He recommended me. (It would mean that, he said, "I was suitable".)

When 'ask' is used in following construction the preposition 'to' is never used here :

He asked* (me) about his health. ('asked *to* me' is in correct.)
He asked* (me) if I liked that job.
She asked* (her employer) for an hour leave.

NOTE * *'to' is never used after ask in above constructions.*

PREPOSITION + GERUND

It should be understood well that **verbs placed immediately after preposition must be in gerund form :**

(a) He prevented me from drinking cold water.
(b) He insist on trying again.
(c) He was debarred from taking examination.
(d) He succeeded in achieving his goal.
(e) They are afraid of loosing the match.
(f) Ram is angry about walking in the rain.
(g) Prakash is good at working in the garden.
(h) I'm worried about making mistakes.
(i) This girl is crazy about playing tennis.
(j) He is disappointed about seeing such a bad report.
(k) We are excited about making our own film.
(l) Sunder is famous for singing songs.
(m) I'm fed up with being treated as a child.
(n) Hina is fond of going to parties.
(o) She is glad about getting married again.
(p) The children are not happy about seeing a doctor.
(q) Are you interested in writing poems?
(r) Joe is keen on drawing.
(s) She is proud of riding a snowboard.
(t) We're sick of sitting around like this.
(u) He's sorry for eating in the class.
(v) I'm tired of waiting for you.
(w) She is used to smoking
(x) He is clever at skateboarding.

PREPOSITIONS AND ADVERBS

Many words can be used as either prepositions or adverbs. A word functions as preposition when it governs a noun or pronoun. When a word does not govern a noun or pronoun it is an adverb. (See the chapter of Adverb to know its characteristics in detail.)

(a) He was here *before* seven. (preposition)
(b) He has done this kind of work *before*. (adverb)
(c) Ramesh is *behind* us. (preposition)
(d) He's a long way *behind*. (adverb)
(e) He ran *up* the stairs. (preposition)
(f) He went *up* in the lift. (adverb)
(g) He has been ill since Monday. (preposition)
(h) I haven't seen her since. (adverb)

USE OF SOME PREPOSITIONS

A

1. **Abide at (place) :** I will abide at the *railway station* till the train arrives.
   Abide in (house) : She has been abiding in my house for the last three months.
   Abide by (decision) : She will abide by my decision positively.
   Abide with (person) : He will abide with his friend Suresh in all circumstances.
2. **Angry at (thing):** He is angry at your *way of questioning*.
   Angry with (person) : Sita is angry with *Ram*.
   Angry for (action) : He is angry for your *laughing* at her wife.
3. **Arrive at (place) :** The train is going to arrive at the *station* within ten minutes.
   Arrive in (country) : He is scheduled to arrive in *India* on next Monday.
4. **Alight on (ground, thing) :** A large number of birds alight on the roof of my house.
   Alight at (a place) : The groom alighted from the elephant at her gate.
5. **Appeal to (person) :** I earnestly appealed to the principal to consider the matter again.
   Appeal against (decision) : He appealed against the decision of the lower court.
6. **Amuse at (thing) :** He is greatly amused at the indifferent attitude of his father.
   Amused with (action) : The boys amused themselves with throwing flowers at the girls.
7. **Ask for (a thing) :** He asked me for some help.
   Ask from (person) : He asked some help from me.
8. **Affiliated to (University, Board) :** Our college is affiliated to the University of Punjab.
   Affiliated with (a party) : Bajrang Dal is affiliated with BJP indirectly.
9. **Annoyed at (thing) :** He became annoyed at my *laughing*.
   Annoyed with (person) : He is annoyed with *you*.
10. **Antipathy to (thing) :** He has a great antipathy to *wine*.
    Antipathy against (person) :You should not have any antipathy against *your friend Jack*.
11. **Answer to (person) :** You have to answer to *me* for your conduct.
    Answer for (action) : He was asked to answer for the *misbehaviour*.

12. **Arm against (danger) :** We must arm ourselves against the danger of chemical weapons.
Arm with (weapon) : He armed himself with a revolver and a knife.

13. **Atone to (person) :** I tried to atone to *him* by offering market price of the land.
Atone for (action) : He tried to atone for the *mischief he had committed*.

14. **Award for (action) :** He was awarded a gold medal for winning 100 *metre race*.
Awarded to (person) : A silver medal will be awarded to the best *sports girl*.

15. **Antidote to (medicine) :** Diamond is regarded as an antidote to the venom of the snake.
Antidote against (infection) : Quinine is an antidote against Malaria.

16. **Argue against or about (a matter) :** He went to argue against the topic of debate.
He argued well about the newly introduced bill.
Argue with (person) : Don't argue with me unnecessarily.

17. **Agree in (opinion) :** Ganesh agrees with Ram in opinion expressed by him (Ram).
Agree to (proposal) : I cannot agree to his proposal of dividing the property.
Agree with (person) : I fully agree with you on this issue .
Agree on (subject) : After a lot of discussion all agreed on the terms of agreement.

18. **Accomplice with (person) :** Her wife was an accomplice with the *murderer*.
Accomplice in (act): His wife was an accomplice in the *murder*.

19. **Authority for (action) :** You have no authority for instructing me as such.
Authority on (subject) : She is indeed an unquestionable authority on Physics.
Authority over (person) : He has no authority over me officially.

20. **Accused of (a crime) :** He is an accused of murder.

21. **Accused by (a person) :** He was accused by his wife .

B

1. **Blush for (fault) :** She blushed for the misbehaviour of her husband.
Blush at (praise) : She blushed at the comments of her husband.

2. **Blind to (deeds, action) :** He should not be blind to the misdeeds of his son Rakesh.
Blind in (one eye) : His husband is blind in the right eye.

3. **Born of (parents) :** He was born of an orthodox mother.
Born at, in (place) : He was born at general hospital at Alwar in Rajasthan.

4. **Buy from (shop) :** You can buy this item from any grocery shop.
Buy for (person) : I bought this ball pen for my son.

5. **Beg of/from (person) :** I begged of him to give me some time to pay.
I begged some rice from him.
Beg for (person) : I begged him for some rice.

C

1. **Close to (adjective) :** His house is very close to the railway station.
Close with (= shut) : She closed the door with a bang.

Close down (= to terminate the operation) : He closed down his shop within six months.
Close out (= to reduce the price) He closed out the price of sugar to increase sales.

2. **Confer about (= consult on a matter) :** Ram and Rahim confer together about nominating the secretary.
   Confer with (= consult with a person) : I will confer with my father in this matter.
3. **Contend for (thing) :** Mr.S. S. Shekhawat will contend for a seat in Vidhan Sabha.
   Contend with (person) You should not contend with a person like Lalu Singh.
4. **Consist in (= remain in) :** The beauty of this building consist in its style and grandeur.
   Consist of (= composed of) : Our body consists of flesh, bone and blood.
5. **Condemn to (punishment) :** He was condemned to death by the judge.
   Condemn for (crime) : He was condemned for murder by the court.
6. **Compare to (comparing two different kind of things) :** Don't compare water to milk.
   Compare with (comparing two things of same class) : Kalidas was compared with Shakespeare by several renowned scholars.
7. **Care for (= like) :** I do not care for drinks.
   Care about (thing) : She takes full care about her sarees and makeup.
8. **Consult on (matter) :** We were not consulted on the new issue of debentures.
   Consult with (person) : You should consult with some expert before taking a final decision.
9. **Controversy on (matter) :** A lot of controversy was raised on this issue.
   Controversy with (person) : I do not have any controversy with any of the members on this matter.
10. **Confide to (= to tell) :** You should not confide your secrets to anybody.
    Confide in (= to pose confidence) : I confided in him, but he deceived me.
11. **Complain of (a thing) :** I complained of his misconduct to the boss.
    Complain to (person) : I complained to his father of his misbehaviour.
12. **Compete with(person) :** Can you compete with him ?
    Compete for (job) : I will try my best to compete for the job.
13. **Cause of (problem) :** He is the main cause of all the trouble.
    Cause for (anxiety) : I do not have any cause for anxiety.
14. **Clothed in (dressing) :** She was clothed in a silken dress.
    Clothed with (some quality) : She was clothed with modesty.
15. **Connect to (= join) :** Connect the end of this rod to the other.
    Connect with (= relation) : I have no connection with her for the last three years.

D

1. **Displeased at (thing) :** She is not displeased at such humorous jokes.
   Displeased with (person) : Ram is greatly displeased with Sita.
2. **Disqualified for (post) :** She was declared disqualified for the election .
   Disqualified from (competing) : He was disqualified from taking part in the competition.

3. **Dwell upon (= to speak) :**The Chairman dwelt upon the importance of truth and honesty.
Dwell in (country) : The French dwell in France.
Dwell at (place) : These days Ram is dwelling at his friend's hotel.
Dwell among (people) : He is dwelling among the tribals.

4. **Disgusted at (thing) :** She became disgusted at your silly joke.
Disgusted with (person or life) : I am very much disgusted with him .

5. **Deal with (= to do with the matter) :** This book deals with the population problem in India .
Deal in (trade) : He deals in iron scrap.
Deal out (= distribute) : The principal should deal out equal treatment to all the teachers.

6. **Differ on (point) :** I totally differ on this point.
Differ with (person) : I differ with you on this point.
Differ from (thing) : Your views entirely differ from that of mine.

7. **Die of (a disease) :** He died of hunger.
Die from (some cause) : He died from hard labour.

8. **Destined for (= created for) :** God had destined him for the post of President of India.
Destined to (subject) : He is destined to such a pitiable condition.

9. **Dine with (person) :** I am scheduled to dine with him to night.
Dine on (thing) : I can't dine on same kind of menu daily.

10. **Dispense with (= do with out) :** Jack can't easily dispense with her .
Dispense to (= distribute) : A judge must dispense equal justice to all.

11. **Dispose of (= to sell) :** She wants to dispose of all the goods at the earliest .
Dispose to (state of things) : The news of his father's death disposed him to a deep sorrow.

12. **Dispute with (person) :** Why are you disputing with your friends on such a trifle matter.
Dispute about (thing) : There was a great dispute about the nomination of chairman.

E

1. **Embark on (a vessel) :** She embarked on the ship for Srilanka.
Embark in (new business) : He has embarked in the new business with full fervour.

2. **Enter into (thing) :** They have entered into an agreement with Ramesh.
Enter upon (new course) : After marriage I entered upon a new way of life.

3. **Exchange for (thing) :** She exchanged a book for a piece of art.
Exchange with (person) : I want to exchange my views with you.

4. **Exult at (success) :** She was exulted at her brilliant success.
Exult over (an enemy) : Our army exulted over the enemy's force.
Exult in (misery) One should not be exulted in the misery of others.

5. **Eager for (fame) :** She is very much eager for making a name in society.
Eager in (to find) He has involved himself eagerly in pursuit of finding the cause of miseries in life.

6. **Equivalent for (word) :** Write a word equivalent for 'fear'.
   Equivalent to (money, thing) : One million is equivalent to ten lacs.
7. **Exact from (person) :** Heavy fines were exacted from the unruly students.
   Exact in (adjective) : He is not exact in repayment.
8. **Expert in (doing) :** He is expert in repairing automobiles.
   Expert at (thing) : He is expert at English Grammar.
9. **Enquire of (person) :** I enquired of him the secret of his happiness.
   Enquire into (a matter) : The police enquired into the case of bank robbery.
10. **Entrust with (a thing) :** I entrusted him with my camera.
    Entrust to (person) : I entrusted my camera to him.

F

1. **Fit out (= equip) :** The ship was fitted out for Srilanka.
   Fit up (furnishing) : He fitted up his house with all necessary furniture.
2. **Fascinated with (person) :** I was fascinated with Rekha.
   Fascinated by (thing) : I was fascinated by her manners and looks.
3. **False to (person) :** One should not be false to one's friends.
   False of (thing, heart) : He is not false of heart.
4. **Fight for (= defend) :** Our army is ready to fight for the country.
   Fight with (together) : We must not fight with our friends.
   Fight against (thing) : We must fight against the evil of illiteracy.
5. **Familiar to (thing) :** Your looks are quite familiar to that of Sachin.
   Familiar with (person) I am familiar with him.

G

1. **Gaze at (= look attentively) :** Don't gaze at these girls, they are the cops .
   Gaze on (= look strangely) : He stood gazing on the pathetic scene of accident.
2. **Grieve for (person) :** She was extremely grieved for him.
   Grieve at (event) : Everyone was grieved at the death of Rajeev Gandhi.
   Grieve over (thing) : She grieved over my unfortunate loss.
3. **Good for (nothing) :** He is a good for nothing fellow.
   Good at (something) : She is good at swimming.

H

1. **Held by (person) :** A condolence meeting was held by the staff yesterday.
   Held in (esteem or contempt) : In the heart of every Indian, Gandhiji is held in great respect.
   Held at (place) : A meeting was held at Hope Circus yesterday.

2. **Hear of (something) :** I heard of this robbery from Sarla.
Hear from (person) : I heard of this robbery from Sarla.
Hear by (post) : I hear by this letter about your promotion.

3. **Happen to (person) :** Please tell me what happened to you in Newyork.
Happen at (place) : This event happened at Red Square.
Happen on (come across) : While returning from market I happened on a gang of thieves.

4. **Hidden from (view) :** The Neem tree has hidden your house from direct view.
Hidden by (person, thing) : My shoes were hidden by his sister.

I

1. **Introduce to (person) :** Let me first introduce my friend to you.
Introduce into (= make modifications) : The UPSC has introduced many changes into the syllabus of IAS .

2. **Invest with (authority) :** The President invested him with the honour of Bharat Ratna.
Invest in (business) I am ready to invest Rs. fifty lacs in this business.

3. **Inquire for (a thing) :** I went there to inquire for my lost brief case.
Inquire into (matter) The police will inquire into the cause of death.
Inquire about (concern) She came here to inquire about the health of her son.
Inquire of (asking) First inquire of the way, then move.

4. **Involve in (thing) :** She seems to be involved in some serious trouble.
Involve with (person) Don't involve yourself with such unruly persons.

5. **Irritated at (thing) :** I was greatly irritated at his unruly behaviour.
Irritated against (person) : She was extremely irritated against her husband.

6. **Impatient at (unexpected thing) :** He became impatient at the unexpected delay.
Impatient for (expected thing) : She is very much impatient for the arrival of her husband.

7. **Indebted for (thing) :** I am indebted for your timely help.
Indebted to (person) He is greatly indebted to Rani for her timely help.

J

1. **Jest at (person) :** I don't like to jest at a lunatic person.
Jest with (thing) : We should not jest with the communal thing.

2. **Judge of (= give opinion) :** Without going in details, how can you judge of this matter.
Judge by (observing) : Judging by her qualifications, I think she is not fit for this job.

K

1. **Know by (= recognize) :** A man is known by his actions.
Know for (quality) : He is known for his foolish decisions.

L

1. **Live at (a small town) :** He lives at Alwar in Rajasthan.
   Live in (in country, big place) : He is living at Alwar in Rajasthan.
   Live on (food) : He lives entirely on breads.
   Live for (devote) : We must live and die for the cause of truth.
   Live with(a person) : I live here with my parents.
2. **Liable for (crime) :** You are liable for the death of your wife.
   Liable to (punishment) : He was held liable to imprisonment for three years.
3. **Listen for (sound) :** I am listening for the voice of Lata Mangeshkar.
   Listen to (= hear attentively) : We should listen to the advice of our elders.
4. **Laugh at (= make fun) :** We must not laugh at our friends.
   Laugh with (= indulge with) : Better to laugh with disabled than to laugh at disabled.

M

1. **Married to (a woman) :** Ramesh was married to Sarla.
   Married with (a man) : Sarla was married with Ramesh.
2. **Moved with (sorrow) :** He was actually moved with a feeling of sorrow.
   Moved to (tears) : On hearing the news of sudden death of his wife, he moved to tears.
   Moved from (one's determination) : You can't move me from my decision with your logics.
   Moved at (a scene) : He was greatly moved at the sight of her mother's dead body.

O

1. **Obliged to (person) :** I am very much obliged to you.
   Obliged at (thing) : I am obliged for your timely help.
2. **Occupied in (doing a job) :** He is fully occupied in writing a book.
   Occupied by (thing) : That house is occupied by a marriage party.
3. **Originate with (person) :** All the planning were originated with him.
   Originate in (place, cause) : A fierce fire was originated in connaught place yesterday.

P

1. **Part from (person) :** I parted from my wife in Kumbh.
   Part with (thing) : He is not ready to part with his furniture at any cost.
2. **Prepare for (be ready) :** I am preparing for the IAS examination this year.
   Prepare against (danger) : We must prepare ourselves against the danger of water pollution.
3. **Pray for (thing) :** My wife prayed for my success .
   Pray to (= make prayer) : I prayed to God to help me in facing the unwarranted problems.
4. **Perish by (famine) :** Our district was perished by the drought last year.
   Perish with (hunger) : During drought the cattle are perishing with starvation.

5. **Plead with (person) :** He pleaded with the Principal for mercy.
   Plead for (thing) : He pleaded with the king for mercy.
6. **Play at (cards) :** They were playing at cards.
   Play upon (musical instrument) : Harish played upon the violin in the party.

Q

1. **Quick in (doing) :** He is quick in solving reasoning questions .
   Quick of (understanding) : Ramesh is quick of understanding the questions.
2. **Quarrel over (thing) :** You must not quarrel over the parental property.
   Quarrel with (person) : We must not quarrel with our friends.

R

1. **Responsible to (person) :** An MLA is responsible to the Legislative Assembly.
   Responsible for (action) : She is responsible for the loss caused due to her negligence.
2. **Reason with (person) :** I reasoned with him on each and every point in this matter.
   Reason about (thing) : You can't reason about the importance of self respect .
3. **Ready for (action) :** I am ready for the match.
   Ready with (something) : I was totally ready with my arguments on that day .
   Ready in (replying) : I always found her ready in her reply.
4. **Revenge on (person) :** He revenged himself on his enemy.
   Revenge for (action) : I will positively revenge for the insult inflicted on me by her.
5. **Reduce to (= to decrease) :** His salary was reduced to Rs four thousands only.
   Reduce by (= decrease by an amount) : His salary was reduced by three hundred rupees per month.

S

1. **Share of (thing) :** I must be paid my share of profit.
   Share with (person) : I do not share my lunch with anybody.
2. **Skilful at (thing) :** He is skilful at numbers.
   Skilful in (doing a thing) : He is skilful in mathematical calculations.
3. **Succeed to (property) :** He succeeded to his uncle's empire.
   Succeed in (doing) : This time she succeeded in IAS examination.
4. **Start at (time) :** I started at 10 O'clock in the morning.
   Start from (place) : I started at 10 O'clock in the morning from Delhi.
   Started for (place) : I started at 7 O'clock in the morning for Delhi.
5. **Struggle for (thing) :** We have to struggle hard for keeping peace in the country.
   Struggle with (person) : We should not struggle with our neighbours; the fighter struggled with the opponent and over-powered him.
6. **Serve out (= distribute) :** Sweets were served out to the audience.
   Serve up (= to give food) : A nice lunch was served up there in the function.

7. **Speak for (person) :** You go there, I have already spoken for you to the secretary.
   Speak about (thing) : He is speaking about 'Unemployment Problem'.
8. **Starved to (death) :** She was starved to death by her husband.
   Starved with (hunger) : He starved with hunger.
9. **Suited for (action) :** She is not suited for the role of vamp.
   Suited to (occasion) : Sad song does not suit to such a merry occasion.
10. **Supply to (person) :** The municipality is supplying water to all the colonies in the city.
    Supply with (thing) : Govt must supply poor with food and clothing.

T

1. **Thankful for (thing) :** I am really thankful for your timely help.
   Thankful to (person) : I am very much thankful to you for your kind favour.
2. **Think over (= to consider) :** The society agreed to think over the case in the next meeting.
   Think on (= meditate) : I have been thinking on this matter for the last many days.
3. **Trust in (person) :** Trust in God and work hard.
   Trust to (thing) I trusted to his words, and he was right.
4. **Tired of (= disgusted) :** I am tired of your daily excuses.
   Tired with (= exhausted) You seems to be tired with the long run.
5. **Talk with (person) :** I will talk with my father on this matter.
   Talk about (thing) : I will talk about this matter with my parents.
   Talk over (= discuss) : All the members of the society talked over the issue for many hours.

U

1. **Useful for (thing) :** The bag is very much useful for picnic parties.
   Useful to (person) : I found that these directives are useful to me for success in exam.

V

1. **Vote for (person) :** Vote for me please.
   Vote on (a resolution) : After having cast votes on the resolution , all took lunch.
2. **Vexed with (person) :** Why are you vexed with your wife ?
   Vexed at (thing) : He is vexed at my jokes.

W

1. **Wait at (place) :** I will wait at church near the hospital.
   Wait for (person) : I will wait for you up to tomorrow.
2. **Wake up (= to get up) :** She wakes up at 6 AM daily.
   Wake from (to be awaken) : She waked from slumber and decided to take action.
3. **Warn against (an action) :** I have already warned you, against your such negligence.
   Warn of (danger) : I have already warned you of the risk involved .

Z

1. **Zealous for (a thing) :** A dedicated worker is always zealous for achieving the target.
   Zealous in (a cause) : We must be zealous in the cause of humanity.

APPROPRIATE PREPOSITIONS

1. Abundance of (wealth)
2. Assent to (a proposal)
3. Accustomed to (work)
4. Avail ourselves of (an opportunity)
5. Attain to (a position)
6. Addicted to (drinking wine etc.)
7. Accede to (a request)
8. Abstain from (food, indulgence etc.)
9. Absolved from (a promise, a sin)
10. Acquiesce (an opinion, in proposal)
11. Adhere to (principles)
12. Afraid of (a ghost)
13. Abhorrent to (good nature)
14. Accession to (throne)
15. Assure of (a thing)
16. Absorbed in (study)
17. Acquit (someone) of a charge
18. Acquaintance with (a person)
19. Beware of (cheating)
20. Comply with (one's wishes)
21. Condemn to (death)
22. Cured of (a disease)
23. Comply with (wishes)
24. Conducive to (health)
25. Despair of (success)
26. Desirous of (doing some thing)
27. Deprive of (something)
28. Devoid of (quality)
29. Duty of (the country)
30. Eligible for (a post)
31. Exception to (a rule)
32. Excuse for (a fault)
33. Envious of (a person or a thing)
34. Exchange (a thing) with (a person)
35. Elder to (some family member)
36. Fatal to (one's cause)
37. Fearful of (death)
38. Furnish with (clothes)
39. Greedy of (money)
40. Heir to (ancestral property)
41. Healed of (a disease)
42. Hopeful of (success)
43. Hostile to (a person)
44. Hunger after (fame)
45. Innocent of (a crime)
46. Intimate with (a person)
47. Invite to (dinner)
48. Insist on a (thing)
49. Intimate with (person)
50. Impertinent to (elders)
51. Invite to (dinner)
52. Insight into(a matter or thing)
53. Jealous of (a person)
54. Keep to (the left, the point)
55. Knock at (the door)
56. Match for (a person)
57. Key to (success)
58. Mourn for (the dead)
59. Match for (a person)
60. Mad with (anger)
61. Motive for (an action)
62. Need for (help)
63. Need of (a thing)
64. Notorious for (drinking, bad habits etc.)
65. Occur to (mind)
66. Overwhelmed with (sorrow, grief)
67. Pay for (one's mistakes)
68. Passion for (study)
69. Peculiar to (a person or a thing)
70. Persist in (doing)
71. Pity for (poor, downtrodden)
72. Pleased with (a person)
73. Preface to (a book)
74. Proud of (a thing)
75. Pride (on a thing)
76. Prefer to (a thing)
77. Refrain from (doing some wrong)
78. Repent of (a mistake)
79. Respectful to (a person)
80. Rob (a person) of (a thing)
81. Sentence to (punishment)
82. Short of (money)

83. Side with (a person)
84. Shocked at (a loss)
85. Superior to (a thing)
86. Sure of (some fact)
87. Search for (a thing)
88. Sacred to (a cause)
89. Triumph over (difficulties)
90. Trouble to (person)
91. Vain of (beauty)
92. Want of (money)
93. Wanting in (wisdom)
94. Worthy of (a reward)
95. Yield to (an enemy)
96. Search for (a thing)
97. Sacred to (a cause)
98. Work at (subject)
99. Surrender to (enemy)
100. Stick to (point)
101. Suspect of (something)
102. Translate into (English, a language)
103. Touch upon (subject)
104. Slur on (character)

CORRECT YOURSELF EXERCISE : PREPOSITION

CYE : 01 Fill in the blanks with appropriate prepositions :

1. Ram killed the snake .... a stick.
2. He lives .... Alwar.
3. Rice is selling .... five rupees a kilo.
4. His car ran .... a dog.
5. He assured to stand .... me in all circumstances.
6. I will stand .... for my rights.
7. He put .... a coat of red colour.
8. He is proud .... his riches.
9. He lives .... Mumbai.
10. In general, acids act .... metals.
11. Ram was beaten .... by Mohan for no reason.
12. He sat .... the ground.
13. He fell the tree .... an axe.
14. An epidemic broke .... in the town last year.
15. I called .... her from a distant place.

CYE : 02 Fill in the blanks with appropriate prepositions :

1. He finished the work .... four hours.
2. I took him .... a thief.
3. Mahesh is now rid .... all his troubles.
4. He sat .... me.
5. He agreed .... my plan.
6. The cat ran .... the mouse.
7. He died .... heart failure.
8. He fell .... the bed.
9. They were walking .... the road.
10. He rushed .... the pathway.
11. He acted according .... my desire.
12. We did it ....you.

13. Anil goes to office .... car.
14. Look .... the picture.
15. He ran .... the room and sat .... his father.

CYE : 03 Correct the sentence :

1. You cannot prevent me to go to the market.
2. She refrains to do this work.
3. I insisted him to attend the class.
4. He has a passion to learn English grammar.
5. She is negligent to attend the meetings.
6. She persisted to write again.
7. He is bent to fight again.
8. I am confident to win the match.
9. He succeeded to pass the examination this time.
10. I am proud to have a friend like Ram.
11. I cannot hinder her to enter the temple.
12. She is desirous to leave the place.
13. Ram was disqualified to compete in this tournament.
14. I cannot think to oppose him.
15. He was prohibited to enter the temple.
16. You should abstain to drink now.
17. He intends to go to Jaipur.
18. It is very difficult to dissuade him to go there.
19. He is fortunate to get a ticket.
20. I am hopeful to achieve success.

CYE : 04 Correct the sentence :

1. She was neither ashamed nor sorry for her misbehaviour.
2. She neither objected nor approved of it.
3. Ram has no interest and passion for cricket.
4. We must prevent damage and theft of public property.
5. Please listen and reflect on this topic afterwards.
6. He asked from her a silly question.
7. The police investigated into the case.
8. Ram resembles to his father.
9. She resigned from his post.
10. Ram signed to the agreement.
11. The poet described about the nature
12. She must love to her children.
13. We have discussed on the merits of the issue.
14. In this article the author has described about poverty.
15. She criticised upon my action without logic.

CYE : 05 Fill in the blanks with appropriate prepositions :

1. Morning walk is beneficial .... health.
2. You are not eligible .... this post.
3. I find no exception .... this rule of grammar.
4. She has a great passion .... natural beauty.

5. You are very much weak .... mathematics .
6. Suitable reward is an important incentive....... hard work.
7. I am sick..................... the whole episode.
8. He insisted .... complaining against the officer.
9. You are to conform .... the rules of the institute.
10. Your views don't accord .... mine.
11. She comes .... a very noble family.
12. His path is beset .... many difficulties.
13. You are addicted .... gambling.
14. Your scheme is adverse .... my career.
15. The court has restored the property .... its true owner.

CYE : 06 Fill in the blanks with appropriate prepositions :

1. This is subsequent .... my application dated 5th July.
2. This is consequent .... your application dated 5th July.
3. I am fond .... reading newspaper.
4. You have made all preparations .... the marriage.
5. I am proud .... my heritage.
6. He is a descendant .... king.
7. I have no trust .... him.
8. She has distrust..................... you.
9. I feel shame .... her conduct.
10. I am much ashamed .... my son.
11. We must provide .... the bad days.
12. God will provide .... our necessities.
13. It is expected .... you to find the solution.
14. Such rude behaviour was not expected .... you.
15. I am disappointed ....you.

CYE : 07 Fill in the blanks with appropriate prepositions :

1. She jumped .... the well.
2. There was no student .... the class.
3. I have no idea how he got………… Iraq.
4. Ram is sitting .... the kitchen.
5. He lives .... Delhi.
6. Please close your office.................... 9.30 pm positively.
7. She goes for a walk .... the morning daily.
8. He is .... the top.
9. Please sit .... the green chair.
10. The dog jumped .... the cat.
11. She is sitting .... the roof.
12. The letter was written ....Shyam.
13. He wrote a letter .... a pen.
14. A Banyan tree stands .... the Yamuna river.
15. He has a car .... a scooter.

16. I will go to school .... next Monday.
17. I know Hindi, ... Punjabi.
18. I haven't seen her .... the last three days.
19. I haven't seen her .... January.
20. She turned pale .... fear.

CYE : 08 Put 'for' or 'during' or 'while :

1. What did Ram say about me .... I was out of the room ?
2. Rahim read a number of books and magazines .... he was ill.
3. I went out for dinner last night. Unfortunately, I began to feel ill .... the meal and had to go home.
4. Please don't interrupt me .... I am speaking.
5. There were many interruptions .... the Chairman's speech.
6. Can you lay the table .... I get the dinner ready?
7. They hadn't had anything to eat..................... they were travelling.
8. Manisha was very angry with me. She didn't speak to me...........a week.
9. We usually go out at weekend, but we don't often go out..........the week.
10. Kamlesh started a new job a few weeks ago. Before that he was out of work...........six month.
11. I need a change. I think I'll go away..........a few days.
12. The Chairman delivered a long speech. He spoke..........three hours.
13. We were hungry when we came. We hadn't had anything to eat...........the journey.
14. We were hungry when we came. We hadn't had anything to eat...........eight hours.
15. We met a lot of people..................we were on holiday.
16. We met a lot of people...................our holiday.
17. I met Manisha.....................I was shopping.
18. ....we were in Agra, we stayed at a very comfortable hotel.
19. ....our stay in Agra, we visited a lot of museums and galleries.
20. The phone rang three times...................... they were having dinner.
21. The phone range many times .... the night.
22. I had been away for many years. ....that period, many things had changed.

CYE : 09 Put in 'by' or 'until' in the following sentences :

1. I'm moving into my new house next month. I'm staying with a friend..................then.
2. Sorry, but I must go. I have to be at home latest ....9 O'clock .
3. I've been offered a lucrative job ...... my friend. I haven't decided yet whether to accept it or not. I have to decided ....next Monday.
4. I think I'll wait .... Sunday before making a final decision.
5. It's too late to go shopping. The shops are only open .... 9.30. They'll be closed .... now.
6. I'd better pay the electricity bill. It has to be paid .... tomorrow positively.
7. Don't pay the bill today, wait ....next Monday, you can get some relief.
8. A : Have you finished redecorating your house?
   B : Not yet. We hope to finish .... the end of this fortnight.
9. A : I'm going out now. I'll be back at 7.30. Will you still be there?
   B : I don't think so. I'll probably have gone out .... then.
10. Suresh has gone away. He'll be away ....Saturday.

CYE : 10 Put in 'at', 'on' or 'in' in the following sentences :

1. The telephone and the doorbell rang.................. the same time.
2. Harish and Sarla always go out for a meal .... their wedding anniversary.
3. Ramu is 58. He'll be retiring from his job..................... two years' time.
4. I've been invited to a wedding .... 15th August.
5. Hurry up! We've got to go .... five minutes.
6. I'm busy just now but I'll be with you .... a moment.
7. Ram's brother is a banker but he's out of work.......... the moment.
8. There are usually a lot of parties .... New Year's Eve.
9. I hope the weather will be nice................the weakened.
10. We travelled overnight to London and arrived.........5 O'clock...............the morning.
11. The course begins..................... 27th June and ends sometime..................... August.
12. It was quite a short novel and easy to read. I read it .... a day.
13. He might not be at home .....Tuesday morning but he'll probably be there ...... the afternoon.
14. My jeep is being repaired at the garage. It will be ready .... two hours.

CYE :11

1. The poor have to work .... morning to evening.
(a) in, (b) to, (c) from, (d) before. ( )

2. I go .... swim every morning.
(a) to, (b) for, (c) at, (d) in. ( )

3. Never laugh .... the disabled.
(a) on, (b) from, (c) to, (d) at. ( )

4. Please wait .... me, I am coming within five minutes.
(a) for, (b) by, (c) from, (d) to. ( )

5. He fell .... love with Sakshi.
(a) by, (b) for, (c) in, (d) with. ( )

6. I got your parcel .... Tuesday.
(a) since, (b) for, (c) to, (d) on. ( )

7. She was married .... an early age.
(a) for, (b) of, (c) at, (d) in. ( )

8. His father died .... the age of sixty three.
(a) at, (b) in, (c) for, (d) of. ( )

9. They will go to Bangalore ....plane .
(a) on, (b) in, (c) by, (d) from. ( )

10. The man .... a beard is my brother.
(a) in, (b) of, (c) for, (d) with. ( )

11. I am grateful .... my friends for their moral support.
(a) for, (b) to, (c) of, (d) with. ( )

12. Gandhiji fought .... the freedom of our country.
(a) by, (b) in, (c) of, (d) for. ( )

13. This watch is a gift .... my uncle.
(a) by, (b) from, (c) of, (d) in. ( )

14. He spoke .... the subject for two hours regularly.
(a) in, (b) on, (c) of, (d) with. ( )

15. They will leave the place ....10 P.M.
(a) on, (b) since, (c) for, (d) at. ( )

CYE :12

1. She was punished .... stealing a saree.
(a) for, (b) by, (c) with, (d) from. ( )

2. The box belonged .... the landlord.
(a) of, (b) with, (c) to, (d) for. ( )

3. You must finish your project .... 5 O'clock positively.
(a) in, (b) for, (c) till, (d) to. ( )

4. Children are fond .... chocolates and computer games.
(a) for, (b) of, (c) with, (d) in. ( )

5. We get rains .... July every year.
(a) for, (b) to, (c) on, (d) in. ( )

6. His father died .... cancer.
(a) in, (b) of, (c) by, (d) for. ( )

7. He is not popular .... the students.
(a) by, (b) among, (c) with, (d) at. ( )

8. She has great love .... her children.
(a) for, (b) of, (c) by, (d) with. ( )

9. He was prevented .... going to college.
(a) to, (b) of, (c) by, (d) from. ( )

10. Listen .... what your teachers say.
(a) at, (b) in, (c) to, (d) for. ( )

11. Please beware .... the dog.
(a) of, (b) with, (c) to, (d) for. ( )

12. This book is a collection .... Shakespeare's poem.
(a) for, (b) of, (c) with, (d) by. ( )

13. They have quarrelled .... a piece of land.
(a) at, (b) on, (c) for, (d) over. ( )

CYE : 13

1. She wants to get rid ....the brown fox.
(a) for, (b) to, (c) with, (d) of. ( )

2. I was invited .... tea by his mother.
(a) for, (b) to, (c) with, (d) in. ( )

3. You cannot see germs .... naked eyes.
(a) by, (b) with, (c) for, (d) in. ( )

4. He is not interested .... playing and skiing.
(a) in, (b) for, (c) by, (d) of. ( )

5. He was fast asleep .... his bed.
(a) into, (b) in, (c) by, (d) for. ( )

6. We have a very good news .... him.
(a) for, (b) of, (c) to, (d) with. ( )

7. They have been reading .... 7 O'clock.
(a) for, (b) in, (c) since, (d) at. ( )

8. Never quarrel .... your friends.
(a) to, (b) with, (c) by, (d) over. ( )

9. The four brothers always quarrelled .... themselves.
(a) to, (b) between, (c) for, (d) among. ( )

10. There were several policemen .... duty on Republic Day.
(a) to, (b) on, (c) for, (d) at. ( )

11. These boys go to college .... college bus.
(a) by, (b) on, (c) to, (d) for. ( )

12. He is not an honest man. You cannot rely .... him.
(a) to, (b) for, (c) at, (d) on. ( )

13. He was fined .... driving negligently.
(a) to, (b) of, (c) by, (d) for. ( )

14. He is often late .... his dinner.
(a) for, (b) at, (c) to, (d) in. ( )

15. Try to reach the village .... the sunset.
(a) before, (b) by, (c) from, (d) of. ( )

CYE : 14

1. In the month of December the temperature falls .... 4^0 C.
(a) from, (b) below, (c) at, (d) into. ( )

2. A jeep hit him while he was going .... the main road.
(a) on, (b) across, (c) behind, (d) through. ( )

3. She is .... a noble family of Rajputs.
(a) from, (b) of, (c) among, (d) at. ( )

4. The case was put .... the judge and the judge decided it within an year.
(a) at, (b) from, (c) before, (d) of. ( )

5. The bridge .... this river was built in the year 1995.
(a) at, (b) over, (c) above, (d) on. ( )

6. She is suffering ....fever.
(a) with, (b) of, (c) through, (d) from. ( )

7. We saw a wounded tiger while passing .... the forest.
(a) from, (b) through, (c) along, (d) among. ( )

8. Chairs are made .... wood.
(a) of, (b) from, (c) on, (d) through. ( )

9. There are tall beautiful coconut trees .... the river.
(a) along, (b) at, (c) into, (d) over. ( )

10. We are proud .... our children.
(a) on, (b) at, (c) after, (d) of. ( )

11. Mt. Abu is about five thousand feet .... the sea-level.
(a) above, (b) along, (c) after, (d) behind. ( )

12. His birthday is .... next Sunday.
(a) in, (b) at, (c) on, (d) for. ( )

13. Ramesh fell down while he was running .... a bus.
(a) into, (b) after, (c) over, (d) through. ( )

14. Ramesh is the best .... all the other players.
(a) into, (b) among, (c) above, (d) between. ( )

CYE : 15 Fill in the blanks with appropriate preposition :

1. The meeting took place _____ the company's corporate office. at / to / on /by
2. It was a very long voyage. We were _____ sea for 50 days. in/ at /on/by/to
3. I was _____ Peter's last night. in/on/at/by/for
4. The train called _____ Kolkata main station. in/on/to/at/by
5. I lost my passport _____ the way to India. in/at/by/to/on
6. He is a genius. He is _____ the black lists of many casinos. on/in/with/by/at
7. We reached late at the cinema so we had to sit _____ the back row. on/in/at/to/by
8. Is there anything interesting _____ the paper today? on/by/in/at/from/
9. Have you ever been _____ Mexico? in/on/by/to/
10. These books are _____ Rs150/- each. in/on/with/at
11. Some people are _____ prison for crimes they have not committed . in/on/at/by/to
12. I am really sorry but you are standing _____ my way. on/in/at/with/behind
13. There was a very serious accident _____ the roundabout. in/at/to/from
14. In many countries people drive _____ the left. in/at/by/on/to
15. I forgot my umbrella _____ the bus. in/into/by/onto/on
16. I am _____ love with her. in/on/with/from/
17. We are offering solutions _____ a price almost anyone can afford. in/at/on/by/through
18. He behaves just like his father. He really takes _____ him. to/from/after/by/at
19. That old house is being offered _____ sale. in/at/on/for/by
20. It is very difficult to enter _____ partnership with a person you do not know very well. to/on/by/with/into

SOLUTIONS CORRECT YOURSELF EXERCISE

Solutions CYE : 01

1. with,	2. at,	3. at,	4. over,	5. by,
6. up,	7. on,	8. of,	9. in,	10. on,
11. up,	12. on,	13. with,	14. out,	15. out.

Solutions CYE : 02

1. in,	2. for,	3. of,	4. beside,	5. to
6. after,	7. of,	8. upon,	9. along,	10. into,
11. to,	12. for,	13. by,	14. at,	15. into, beside.

Solutions CYE : 03

1. You cannot prevent me from going to the market.
2. She refrains from doing this work.
3. I insisted him on attending the class.
4. He has a passion for learning English grammar.
5. She is negligent in attending the meeting.
6. She persisted in writing again.
7. He is bent on fighting again.
8. I am confident of winning the match.
9. He succeeded in passing the examination this time.
10. I am proud of having a friend like Ram.
11. I cannot hinder her from entering the temple.
12. She is desirous of leaving the place.
13. Ram was disqualified from competing in this tournament.
14. I cannot think of opposing him.
15. He was prohibited from entering the temple.
16. You should abstain from drinking now.
17. He intends going to Jaipur.
18. It is very difficult to dissuade him from going there.
19. He is fortunate in getting a ticket.
20. I am hopeful of achieving success.

Solutions CYE : 04

1. She was neither ashamed of nor sorry for her misbehaviour.
2. She neither objected to nor approved of it.
3. Ram has no interest in and passion for cricket.
4. We must prevent damage to and theft of public property.
5. Please listen to and reflect on this topic afterwards.
6. He asked her a silly question.
7. The police investigated the case.
8. Ram resembles his father.
9. She resigned his post.
10. Ram signed the agreement.
11. The poet described the nature.
12. She must love her children.

13. We have discussed the merits of the issue.
14. In this article the author has described poverty.
15. She criticised my action without logic.

Solutions CYE : 05

1. to, 2. for, 3. to, 4. for, 5. in, 6. to,
7. of, 8. on, 9. to, 10. with, 11. from, 12. with,
13. to, 14. to, 15. to .

Solutions CYE : 06

1. to, 2. upon, 3. of, 4. for, 5. of, 6. of,
7. in, 8. of, 9. at, 10. of, 11. against, 12. for,
13. of, 14. from, 15. in.

Solutions CYE : 07

1. into, 2. in, 3. into, 4. in, 5. in, 6. at,
7. in, 8. at, 9. on, 10. upon, 11. on, 12. by,
13. with, 14. beside, 15. besides. 16. from, 17. besides, 18. for,
19. since, 20. with.

Solutions CYE : 08

1. while, 2. while, 3. during, 4. while, 5. during,
6. while, 7. while 8. for, 9. during, 10. for,
11. for, 12. for, 13. during, 14. for, 15. while,
16. during, 17. while, 18. while, 19. during, 20. while,
21. during, 22. during.

Solutions CYE : 09

1. until, 2. by, 3. by, by, 4. until, 5. until, by,
6. by, 7. until, 8. by, 9. by, 10. until.

Solutions CYE : 10

1. at, 2. on, 3. in, 4. on, 5. in,
6. in, 7. at, 8. on, 9. at, 10. at , in,
11. On, in, 12. in, 13. on, in, 14. in.

Solutions CYE 11

1. (c), 2. (b), 3. (d), 4. (a), 5. (c),
6. (d), 7. (c), 8. (a), 9. (c), 10. (d),
11. (b), 12. (d), 13. (b), 14. (b), 15. (d).

Solutions CYE : 12

1. (a), 2. (c), 3. (c), 4. (b), 5. (d),
6. (b), 7. (c), 8. (a), 9. (d), 10. (c),
11. (a), 12. (b), 13. (d).

Solutions CYE :13

1. (d),	2. (b),	3. (b),	4. (a),	5. (b),
6. (a),	7. (c),	8. (b),	9. (d),	10. (b),
11. (b),	12. (d),	13. (d),	14. (a),	15. (a).

Solutions CYE : 14

1. (b),	2. (b),	3. (a),	4. (c),	5. (b),
6. (d),	7. (b),	8. (a),	9. (a),	10. (d),
11. (a),	12. (c),	13. (b),	14. (b).	

Solutions CYE : 15

1. at,	2. at,	3. at,	4. at,	5. on,
6. on,	7. in,	8. in,	9. to,	10. No preposition,
11. in,	12. in,	13. at,	14. on,	15. on
16. in,	17. at,	18. after,	19. for,	20. into.

15

Conjunction

A conjunction is a word that joins words, phrases, clauses or sentences .

Conjunction can also be defined as a word that joins clauses together to make sentence , and shows how the meanings of the clauses relate to each other.A conjunction is also called a **joiner , connector or sentence linker.**

KINDS OF CONJUNCTION

There are three types of conjunction :

(a) Coordinating Conjunction,

(b) Subordinating Conjunction,

(c) Correlative Conjunction.

(A) Coordinating Conjunctions : Coordinating conjunctions may join single words, or they may join groups of words, but **they always join elements of same kind** : *either subject and subject*, or *verb phrase and verb phrase*,or *sentence and sentence.*

The most commonly used coordinating conjunctions are : **For, And, Nor, But, Or, Yet, So** . Remember the acronym **FANBOYS.**Each of the letters in this word is the first letter of one of the coordinating conjunctions. **For-And-Nor-But-Or-Yet-So.** When a coordinating conjunction connects two **independent clauses**, it is often (but not always) accompanied by a comma.

(B) Subordinating Conjunctions : Subordinating conjunctions, the largest class of conjunctions, **connect subordinate clauses to a main clause**. A **Subordinating conjunction** *comes at the beginning of a* **Subordinate clause** *and establishes a relationship between the dependent clause and the rest of the sentence.* It also turns the clause into something that depends on the rest of the sentence for its meaning. Some most commonly used Subordinating conjunctions are;***after,although,as,as if,as long as,as though,because,before,even if,even though, if, if only,in order that,now that ,after,although,once, rather than ,since ,so that ,than,that , though, till, unless ,until ,when ,whenever ,where ,whereas ,wherever, while.***

NOTE *that some of the subordinating conjunctions in the above examples such as ;after, before, since — are also prepositions, but as subordinate conjunctions they are being used to introduce a clause and to subordinate the following clause to the independent element in the sentence.*

Examples

After : (a) We are going out to eat after we finish our work. (Conjunction)

(b) After the rain stopped, the dog ran into the mud to play. (Preposition)

Since : (a) Since we have lived in Mexico,we have gone to every exhibit at the Royal Hall. (Conjunction)
(b) I have been here since the end of January. (Preposition)
While : (a)While I was waiting in line for my turn , I ate my lunch. (Conjunction)
(b) Shalini steamed the corn while Jack fried the steaks. (Conjunction)
Although : Although the shooting has stopped now, the destruction left behind is enormous. (Conjunction)
Even if : Even if you have already bought your ticket, you will still need to wait in queue.
Because : (a) I love her works because she uses colour so brilliantly. (Conjunction)
(b) The snowman melted because the sun came out. (Conjunction)
Even though : Even though Jack fell asleep, the mobile salesman kept talking. (Conjunction)

(C) Correlative Conjunctions : Correlative conjunctions also connect sentence elements of the same kind : however, unlike coordinating conjunctions, **correlative conjunctions are always used in pairs**. Such Conjunctions are ; ***Either.......or, Neither...............nor, Both..........and, Whether ... or, Not only........but also.***

NOTE *When joining singular and plural subjects, the subject closest to the verb determines whether the verb is singular or plural.*

Coordinating conjunctions are the simplest kind, and they denote *equality of relationship between the ideas* they join. Their relatives, correlative conjunctions, not only denote equality, but they also make the joining tighter and more emphatic.

Coordinating and Correlative conjunctions are greatly used *when two ideas are of the same importance*, but many times one idea is more important than another. Subordinating conjunctions are used *to show which idea is more and which is less important*. The idea in the main clause is the more important, while the idea in the subordinate clause (made subordinate by the subordinating conjunction) is less important. The *subordinate clause supplies a time, reason, condition, and so on for the main clause.*

Conjunction/Relative Pronoun/Relative Adverb/Preposition

Conjunctions merely join two words or two sentences and do nothing more. *Relative pronouns* not only join but also *refer to the noun* (antecedent). *Relative adverbs* also join two parts of the sentence and *modify the verbs* also. *Prepositions* join two words and also *govern the noun.*

(a) This is the pen that she gifted me.	Relative Pronoun
(b) This the place where I was born.	Relative Adverb
(c) He sat beside Shyam	Preposition
(d) He came and he worked.	Conjunction

In sentence (a) 'that', relative pronoun is not only joining two sentences but also referring noun; 'pen'. In sentences (b) and (c) the underlined words (where, beside) are not only functioning as adverb and preposition but also joining two sentences. In sentence (d) conjunction–'and' is just joining two sentences.

USE OF COORDINATING CONJUNCTION

'AND'

(i) 'And' is used to suggest that one work is sequential to another :
Kamini sent in her application and waited by the phone for a response.

(ii) To suggest that one work is the result of another :

Ramesh heard the weather report and promptly went to his house.

(iii) 'And' is used to suggest that one idea is in contrast to another (' and' is frequently replaced by '*but*' in this usage.):
Naresh is brilliant and Shalini has a pleasant smile .

(iv) To reflect an element of surprise (sometimes replaced by '*yet*' in this usage) :

Mumbai is a rich city and suffers from many elements of urban blight .

(v) To reflect that one clause is conditionally dependent upon another [usually the first clause (given in italics below) is an imperative.] :

(a) *Use your credit cards without care* and you'll soon find yourself deep in debt.

(b) *Waste your time carelessly* and you will soon find yourself out of time to prepare for the examinations.

(vi) To suggest a kind of 'comment' on the first clause 'and', is used :

Rajesh became addicted to gambling and that surprised no one who knew him.

'BUT'

(i) **To reflect a contrast that is unexpected in light of the first clause,** *'but' is used* :

(a) Jony lost a fortune in the stock market, but he still seems able to live quite comfortably.

(ii) **To reflect** *in an affirmative sense* **what the first part of the sentence implied** *in a negative way* (sometimes replaced by on the contrary) :

(b) The club never invested foolishly, but used the services of some intelligent counsellors.

(iii) **'But' is used to connect two ideas with the meaning of 'with the exception of'** (and then the second word takes over as subject) :

(c) Everybody but (with the exception of) Jai Kishan is trying out for the team.

'OR'

(i) **'Or' is used to suggest that only one possibility can be realized, excluding one or the other :**

(a) You study hard for this exam or you will not get good marks. .

(ii) **To suggest the inclusive combination of alternatives :**

(b) We can cook dinner tonight, or we can just eat leftovers.

(iii)To suggest a refinement of the first clause 'or' is used :

(c) Saraswati College is the premier all-girls' college in the State, or so it seems to most Saraswati College alumnae.

(iv) **To suggest a restatement or 'correction' of the first part of the sentence :**

(d) There are no tigers in this sanctuary, or so our guide tells us.

(v) To suggest a negative condition **'Or' is used** :

(e) The sayings of one of the freedom fighters was very important 'Do or die'.

(vi) To suggest a negative alternative without the use of an imperative (see use of 'and' above, rule v, (a), (b)) :

(f) They must approve his political style or they wouldn't keep electing him Chairman.

'NOR'

The conjunction 'nor' is *not used as often as the other conjunctions*. **It is commonly used in the correlative pair, *'neither-nor'*** (see below) :

(a) He is neither sane nor intelligent.

(b) That is neither what I said nor what I wanted to say.

'Nor' can also be used with other negative expressions :

(c) That is not what I wanted to say, nor should you interpret my statement as an admission of guilt.

'YET'

The word 'yet' functions sometimes as an adverb . **It can be used reflecting several meanings : (i) in addition** ('yet another cause of trouble' or 'a simple yet noble woman'), **(ii) even** ('yet more expensive'), **(iii) still** ('he is yet a novice'), **(v) eventually** ('they may yet win'), **(vi) and so soon as now** ('he's not here yet').

'Yet' also functions as a coordinating conjunction *meaning something like* **'nevertheless'** or **'but.'** :

(a) Jack plays basketball well, yet his favorite sport is cricket.

(b) The visitors complained a lot about the heat, yet they continued to play golf here every day.

'FOR'

The word 'for' is most often used as a preposition. It is also used, **as a coordinating conjunction**. Beginning a sentence with the conjunction 'for' should be avoided . Its function is **to introduce the reason for the preceding clause**.

See the following examples :

(a) Ramesh thought he had a good chance to get the job, for his uncle was on the company's board of directors.

(b) Most of the visitors were happy just relaxing under the shade, for it had been a long, dusty journey on the cart .

'SO'

'So', sometimes connects two independent clauses along with a comma, *but sometimes it doesn't*. For instance, in this sentence :

(a) He is not the only Olympic athlete in his family, so are his brother, sister, and his niece Chetna.

Here the word **'so' means–'as well' or 'in addition,'**.

In the following sentence, 'so' means–'therefore,'; the conjunction and the comma are adequate to the task :

(b) She has always been nervous in large gatherings, so (therefore) it is no surprise that she avoids crowd of her fans.

When 'so' is used at the beginning of a sentence, **it acts as a kind of summing up word,** in that case **comma is used after it** 'so' as following :

(c) So, the Judge peremptorily removed the child from the custody of the claimants.

SUBORDINATING CONJUNCTION

A **Subordinating Conjunction comes at the beginning of a Subordinate Clause** and establishes the relationship between the dependent clause and the rest of the sentence.Some of the subordinating conjunctions like; after, before, since etc. are also prepositions, but as subordinators they are being used to introduce a clause and to subordinate the following clause to the main clause .

Remember : Always put a comma at the end of the adverbial phrase when it precedes the main clause.

Classification of subordinating conjuctions :

Subordinating conjunctions can also be classified as per their meanings and their functions :

1. **Time :** Such conjunctions are ; ***when, whenever, till, until, before, after, as soon as, as, since, while*** etc.They denote *time of action* :
   (a) *When* I went to office, the peon was going to his house.
   (b) I have been searching her *since* I met her.
   (c) Ramesh went to his home, *after* he completed his work.
   (d) You should complete the work, *before* you go to market.
   (e) Make hay *while* the sun shines.
   (f) I will start the business, *as soon as* I get the licence.
   (g) He will stay in office *until* you reach there.
2. **Cause or Reason :** Such subordinating conjunctions are ; ***'As, because, since',*** etc. These denote *cause or reason of an action* :
   (a) I telephoned to her father *as* she was not available in office.
   (b) He is allowed to enter *as* he is invited by us.
   (c) I can't buy this car, *since* it is very costly.
   (d) She is crying *because* someone has stolen her purse.
3. **Purpose :** Such conjunctions are ; ***'that, so that, in order that, lest'*** etc.These denote *purpose of an action* :
   (a) We eat that we may live.
   (b) He came here, so that he can discuss the plan.
   (c) Run fast lest you should miss the train.
   (d) He is working hard in order that he can succeed.
4. **Result or Consequences :** Such conjunctions are ; ***'so that, such that, that'*** etc.These denote *result or consequence of an action :*

   Read the following sentences :

   (a) The coffee is so hot that I can't drink it.
   (b) He spoke in such a loud voice that everyone could hear him well.
   (c) She is such a nasty girl that you can't rely on her .

5. **Condition** : Such subordinating conjunctions are ; ***if, unless, provided, that, supposing*** etc.These denote a *condition for happening of an action* :
(a) You cannot succeed unless you work hard.
(b) He will help you if you ask him.
(c) I will pay your dues provided you allow proper discount.
(d) He will be penalised provided that the charges are proved.
(e) Supposing you won a lottery, what would you do?

6. **Place** :Such conjunctions are subordinating ; ***'where, wherever, whither*** (to what place), ***whence'*** (from what place) etc.These *denote place of an action* :
(a) I found my purse where I left it.
(b) Let her go wherever she likes to go.
(c) Can you inform me whither she has gone?
(d) He went back whence he came.

7. **Comparison** : Such conjunctions are; ***'as...as', 'so.....as', 'than'*** etc.These are used for comparison :
(a) He is as strong as your brother.
(b) She is as intelligent as her brother.
(c) He is not so intelligent as her brother.
(d) He is not so strong as your brother.
'As.....as' is *used for likeliness* and 'so ... as' is *used for unlikeliness.*

8. **Concession** : Such conjunctions are ; ***'though, although, yet, notwithstanding, however'***, etc.These conjunctions *refer concession* :
(a) She is poor yet she is trustworthy.
(b) I shall not meet her though she comes.
(c) Although he is intelligent, he is simple.
(d) I didn't support him, however I didn't oppose him.
(e) He passed the examination notwithstanding he was not fully prepared.

9. **Manner** : Such subordinating conjunctions are ; ***'As, as though, so far as'*** etc. These are used to denote the *manner in which an action takes place.*
(a) He spoke as if he were drunk.
(b) She was speaking the truth so far I could judge.
(c) He acted upon as he was instructed.
(d) He protested as though he were in opposition.

Look at the following *subordinate conjunctions* and their use with different meanings :

As = because, when :

1. **Because : As** he is my friend, I will cooperate him. (as = because)
2. **When : We watched as the train departed. (as = when)**
3. **After =later in time** :
later in time : After the train left, I went to my office directly .
4. **Although** or **though = in spite of the fact that :**
Although he is poor, he is honest.
5. **Before : 'Before' means–'earlier than' :**
(a) I arrived **before** the shops were open.

6. Because : It means :

(a) **for the reason that** : We had to wait, **because** the chief guest arrived late.

7. For : 'For' is used as 'because' :

(a) **because** : He is happy, **for (because)** he has good job.

8. If : It means :

(a) **on condition that** : **If** he is here, we will meet him.

9. Lest : 'lest' means :

(a) **for fear that** : We ran **lest** we should miss the train.

10. Providing or **provided :** It means

(a) **on condition that** : All will be well, **providing** you take interest in the function.

11. Since = from a past time , as , because :

(a) **from a past time** : I have been here **since** he came.

(b) **as, because :** Since you are here, we can discuss the matter .

12. So or **so that = consequently, in order that :**

(a) **consequently :** It was raining, **so** we did not go shopping.

(b) **in order that :** I am saving money **so** I can buy a car.

13. Supposing : 'Supposing' means :

(a) **if : Supposing** a monkey comes here, what will you do?

14. Than : It is :

(a) **used in comparisons** : He is taller **than** you.

15. Unless : It means :

(a) **except when, if not : Unless** he works hard , he will not succeed .

16. Until or **till :** It means :

(a) **up to the time when** : I will wait **until** he comes.

17. Whereas = because , on the other hand :

(a) **because : Whereas** this is the temple, it is open to everyone.

(b) **on the other hand :** He is short, **whereas** you are tall.

18. Whether : 'Whether' means—'if' :

(a) I do not know **whether** I was invited.

19. While = at the time when, on the other hand, although :

(a) **at the time when : While** it was raining, we were watching a movie.

(b) **on the other hand :** He is poor, **while** his friend is rich.

(c) **although : While** I am not an expert, I will do my best.

In addition, the following phrases are often used at the beginning of subordinate clauses :

20. As if : It means :

(a) **in a similar way** : She behaves **as if** she is my sister.

21. As long as = if , while :

(a) **if : As long as** we work fast, we can finish the work today.

(b) **while** : She has lived there **as long as** I have known her.

22. As soon as : It means :

(a) **immediately when :** Inform me **as soon as** you reach there.

23. As though : It means :

(a) **in a similar way :** It looks **as though** it will rain today.

24. Even if : It means :

(a) **in spite of a possibility :** I am going out **even if** it rains.

25. In case : It means :

(a) **because of a possibility** : Take a sweater **in case** it gets cold.

26. Or else : 'Or else' means—'otherwise'

(a) Please be careful, **or else** you may have an accident.

27. So as to : It means—

(a) **in order to :** I hurried **so as to** be on time.

NOTE *Some words, such as **after**, **before**, **since** and **until** may function as prepositions and as well as subordinate conjunctions. However it should be noted that in some cases different words must be used as prepositions and subordinate conjunctions, in order to express similar meanings.*

PREPOSITIONS AND CONJUNCTIONS

Look at the following examples to understand the difference between preposition and conjunction :

The girls were upset **because of** the delay.	Preposition
The girls were upset **because** they were delayed.	Conjunction
Despite the rain, we enjoyed ourselves.	Preposition
Although it rained, we enjoyed ourselves.	Conjunction
We stayed indoors **during** the storm.	Preposition
We stayed indors **while** the storm raged.	Conjunction
It looks **like** rain.	Preposition
It looks **as if** it wilol rain.	Conjunction

NOTE *The prepositions have noun objects, while the conjunctions introduce subordinate clauses.*

The Case of 'Like' and 'As' :

Strictly speaking, the word '*like*' is a preposition, not a conjunction. It can, therefore, be used to introduce a prepositional phrase ('My brother is tall like my father'), but it should not be used to introduce a clause ('My brother can't play the piano ~~like~~ as he did before the accident' or 'It looks ~~like~~ as if basketball is quickly overtaking baseball as America's national sport.'). To introduce a clause, it's a good idea to use *as*, *as though*, or *as if*, instead.

(a) ~~Like~~ As I told you earlier, the lecture has been postponed.

(b) It looks ~~like~~ as if it's going to snow this afternoon.

(c) Johnson kept looking out the window ~~like~~ as though he had someone waiting for him.

In formal, academic text, it's a good idea to reserve the use of *'like'* for situations in which similarities are being pointed out :

(d) This community college is like a two-year liberal arts college.

However, when you are listing things that have similarities, *'such as'* is probably more suitable :

(e) The college has several highly regarded neighbours, ~~like~~ such as the Mark Twain House, St. Francis Hospital, the Connecticut Historical Society, and the UConn Law School.

CORRELATIVE CONJUNCTIONS

Correlative conjunctions are used in pairs, in order to show the relationship between the ideas expressed in different parts of a sentence. Correlative conjunctions join various sentence elements that must be grammatically equal.
The most commonly used correlative conjunctions are **both ... and, either ... or** and **neither ... nor, hardly ... when, not only ... but also,** etc. Note that in the construction **if ... then**, the word **'then'** can usually be omitted.

Correlative Conjunctions are illustrated as follows :

(a) **both ... and :** She is **both** intelligent **and** liberal.
(b) **either ... or** I will **either** go for a picnic **or** take rest.
(c) **neither ... nor :** She is **neither** rich **nor** good natured.
(d) **hardly ... when :** He had **hardly** begun to work, **when** it started raining
(e) **if ... then : If** that is true, **then** what happened can't be imagined.
(f) **no sooner ... than : No sooner** had I reached the station, **than** the train arrived.
(g) **not only ... but also :** She is **not only** clever, **but also** intelligent.
(h) **rather ... than :** I would **rather** go swimming **than** go to the hospital.
(i) **scarcely ... when : Scarcely** had we left college, **when** it started to rain.
(j) **whether ... or :** Have you decided **whether** you will go there **or** not?

Important : Parallel construction

Correlative conjunctions *(both... and; not... but; not only... but also; either... or; first... second... third*; and the like) **should be followed by the same grammatical construction**. Thus, whenever possible, parallel construction should be employed when correlative conjunctions are used. Many violations of this rule can be corrected by rearranging the sentence. *The repetition of a particular grammatical construction is often referred to as* ***parallel construction***. This is illustrated in the following examples.

(a) I am **neither** happy **nor** excited.
(b) The resort contains open bars, swimming pools and a library.

In the first example, the two phrases **neither happy** and **nor excited** show parallel construction. In the second example, the three phrases open bars, swimming pools and a library also show parallel construction.

Correlative conjunctions and Parellel constructions :

Parallel construction should always be employed when correlative conjunctions are used. In the following example, the correlative conjunctions are printed in bold type.
Look at the following examples :

She has **both** a good education, **and** she has good work habits. *Incorrect*
She has **both** a good education **and** good work habits. *Correct*

In first sentence, '**both**' and **'and'** are followed by different grammatical constructions, so it is an incorrect sentence. **Both** is followed by the phrase **a good education**; whereas **and** is followed by the clause **he has good work habits**. The second sentence has been corrected by changing the clause **he has good work habits** into the phrase **good work habits**.

See more such examples :

(a) She turned neither right nor to the left. *Incorrect*

She turned neither right nor left. *Correct*

Or

She turned neither to the right nor to the left. *Correct*

(b) It was both a long ceremony and very tedious. *Incorrect*

The ceremony was both long and tedious. *Correct*

(c) A time not for words, but action. *Incorrect*

A time not for words, but for action. *Correct*

(d) Either you must grant his request or incur his ill will. *Incorrect*

You must either grant his request or incur his ill will. *Correct*

(e) Ram is watching not only T.V but also playing football. *Incorrect*

Ram is not only watching T.V. but also playing football. *Correct*

(f) Not only Ram gave me five coins but also thanked me. *Incorrect*

Ram not only gave me five coins but also thanked me. *Correct*

CONJUNCTIVE ADVERBS

The **conjunctive adverbs** *are used to create complex relationships between ideas. They show* **logical relationships between two independent sentences or between sections of paragraphs.**

Such most commonly used Conjunctive Adverbs are : ***also ,hence ,however ,still ,likewise , otherwise, therefore ,conversely,rather , consequently, furthermore, nevertheless , instead, as a result, moreover, then ,thus ,meanwhile ,accordingly.***

Examples of conjunctive adverbs

The following are examples of words which may be used as connecting (cojunctive) adverbs. Each connecting adverb is followed by its meaning and an example of its use :

accordingly = so : He was very persuasive; **accordingly**, I did what he asked.

also = in addition : She is my neighbor; she is **also** my best friend.

besides = in addition : I like the job, **besides**, I need the money.

consequently = so : She had fever, **consequently**, she stayed at home.

furthermore : in addition : You should stop smoking, **furthermore**, you should do it at once.

hence = for that reason He is a good friend; **hence**, I was not embarrassed to ask him for help.

however = but We wanted to arrive on time; **however**, we were delayed by traffic.

likewise = in addition :

The region is beautiful; **likewise**, the climate is excellent.

moreover = in addition : She is very intelligent; **moreover**, she is very ambitious.

nevertheless : but : They are proud, **nevertheless**, I like them.

nonetheless = but : The ascent was dangerous, **nonetheless**, he decided to attempt it.

otherwise = if not, or else : We should consult them; **otherwise**, they may be upset.

still = but : It is a long way to the beach, **still**, it is a fine day to go swimming,

then = 1. next afterwords : We went shopping, **then** we had lunch.

= 2. **So** : If you are sure, **then** I must believe you.

Therefore = for that reason : I was nervous; **therefore,** I could not do my best.

Thus = so, in this way : He travelled as quickly as possible ; **thus**, he reached Boston the next day.

EXPLETIVES

Expletives are closely related to conjunctive adverbs. Expletives convey no meaning of their own but instead **serve only to emphasize the statement to which they are attached**. As such, then, they technically do not show a logical relationship like time or cause between ideas, and that fact prevents them from being treated as conjunctive adverbs.Such expletives are :***of course, indeed, naturally, after all, in short, I hope, at least, remarkably, in fact, on the whole, I suppose, it seems, in brief , I think, clearly, assuredly, definitely, to be sure, without doubt, for all that, in any event, importantly, certainly .***

Examples :

1. The flashlight hit the floor and broke into a hundred pieces. *At least* there was a candle in the room.
2. They all began to use appropriate expletives in their writing. They were convinced, *I suppose*, by the excellent examples.
3. The conjunction list has left the building. *On the whole*, I hope you enjoyed it.
4. I was hungry and more *importantly,* my children were hungry.
5. *Clearly* the police cannot break the law in order to enforce it.

SOME SPECIFIC CONJUNCTIONS

1. "Neither.......nor.........nor........nor" and "Either........or........or........or"

Some grammarians feel that only one 'nor' can be used with 'neither' and only one 'or' can be used with 'either'.Please note the views of Mr Vallins in this matter :

"The correct correlatives are 'either.....or'and 'neither.....nor'. Strictly speaking, we should not add another 'or'or 'nor'since either and neither imply two and two only."

But Mr **T.S. Eliot** and **H. Walker** have opined differently.

Look at the following sentences :

(a) Either from the moralist's point of view, or from the theologian's point of view or from the psychologist's point of view, or from that of the political philosopher, or judging by the ordinary standards of likeableness in human beings, Milton is unsatisfactory. **(T.S. Eliot)**

(b) Neither the brilliancy of Haglitt, nor the harmony of De Quincey, nor the vigour of Macaulay, nor the eloquence of Ruskin, nor the purity of Goldsmith could for a moment H. Walker be thought capable of expressing the meaning of lamb. **(H. Walker)**

2. No/Not/Never........or

Use 'or' (but not 'nor') with Not/Never/No **in a sentence if an alternative conjunction is needed :**

(a) I have no chair or stool. (b) I have never read about her or heard of her.

(c) She does not speak or weep. (d) He did not say or write anything.

3. That

(A) 'That' is not used in 'direct narration'.It is usually used in 'indirect narration' :

(a) He said to me, "That I will go there". *Incorrect*
He told me that he would go there. *Correct*

(B) ***After some verbs such as*; agree, assert, avert, assume, hold, calculate, conceive, learn, maintain, state, reckon, suggest, understand** etc, *it is incorect to omit* **'that' :**

(a) I agree your proposal is very good *Incorrect*
I agree **that** your proposal is very good. *Correct*

(b) He asserted he could do **that**. *Incorrect*
He asserted that he could do **that**. *Correct*

(c) He suggested we should go there. *Incorrect*
He suggested **that** we should go there. *Correct*

(D) *After some verbs such as*; **believe, hope, suppose, think, presume, afraid of etc, it is appropriate to omit 'that' :**

(a) I hope, he is right. (b) We presume you are innocent.
(c) I suppose you have a good dictionary. (d) I think he will come.

OMITTING CONJUNCTION : 'THAT'

The word **THAT** is used as a conjunction to connect a subordinate clause to a preceding verb. In this construction 'that' is sometimes called the **'expletive that.'** Indeed, the word is often omitted to good effect, but the very fact of easy omission causes some editors to take out the red pen and strike out the conjunction 'that' wherever it appears. **In the following sentences, we can happily *omit* the *'that'*** (or keep it, depending on how the sentence sounds to us) :

(a) Isabel knew [that] she was about to be fired.
(b) She definitely felt [that] her fellow employees hadn't supported her.
(c) I hope [that] she doesn't blame me.

Sometimes omitting the **THAT** creates a break in the flow of a sentence, a break that can be adequately bridged with the use of a comma :

(i) The problem is, (that) production in her department has dropped.
(ii) Remember, (that) we didn't have these problems before she started working here.

As a general rule, if the sentence feels just as good without the **THAT**, if no ambiguity results from its omission, if the sentence is more efficient or elegant without it, then we can safely omit the that.

Theodore Bernstein lists three conditions in which we should maintain the conjunction 'that' ***:***

(a) When a time element intervenes between the verb and the clause, conjunction 'that' is used :
'The boss said yesterday **that** production in this department was down fifty percent.' (Notice the position of 'yesterday.')

(b) When the verb of the clause is long delayed :
'Our annual report revealed **that** some losses sustained by this department in the third quarter of last year were worse than previously thought.' (Notice the distance between the subject 'losses' and its verb, 'were.')

(c) When a second that can clear up who said or did what :

'The CEO said that Isabel's department was slacking off and **that** production dropped precipitously in the fourth quarter.' (Did the CEO say that production dropped or was the drop a result of what he said about Isabel's department? The second that makes the sentence clear.)

.... **'Do's, Don'ts and Maybes of English Usage' by Theodore Bernstein.**

4. However But:

'However' and 'but' should never be used together in a sentence .

(a) But his behaviour, however has not changed. *Incorrect*
His behaviour however has not changed. *Correct*

(b) But that, however is not repairable. *Incorrect*
But that is not repairable. *Correct*

5. Though, although and even though

'Though', 'although' and 'even though' are *used to show a contrast between two clauses. 'Yet'* (not but) **is used with *'though/although'*.**

(a) Our new neighbours are quite nice (this is good) though their two dogs bark all day long. (this isn't good)

We can use 'though or although' with no difference in meaning. But, **some differences are :**

(i) ***'Though' is more common than 'although'*** in conversation or writing.

(ii) **'Though' (but not although)** *can come at the end of a sentence :*
My new bike is really fast. I don't like the colour, though.

(iii) **'Though' (but not although)** *can also be used as an adverb :*
I'm not good at reasoning but I can help you with your geography, though, if you want.

(iv) *The meaning* of '**though**' *is similar* to *'however'*, but 'though' *is much more common than 'however'* in conversation.

'Even though' can be used *to make the contrast between two clauses stronger* :

(a) My father got back from work really late, even though he had promised to take mum to the cinema.

(b) Although he is poor, yet he is honest. (c) Though he is poor, he is honest.

6. Until-Unless

'Until' is used in reference of time while *'unless' refers a condition.*

(a) I will stay here until you return.
(b) He will wait until the train arrives.
(c) He can't succeed unless he works hard.
(d) You cannot achieve your goal unless you try for that.

7. AS, When and While

We can use; *'as, when or while'* in ***situations or actions that take place simultaneously.*** Note the following points.

1. We can use any of the these words *to introduce a longer background action or situation*, which is / was going on when something else also happens/ happened :
(a) As I was walking down the street I saw Jack driving a jeep.
(b) The telephone always rings when you are having a bath.
(c) While they were playing cards somebody broke into the house.

As, 'when and while' clauses can be used at the beginning or end of sentences, but **'as'** *clauses usually come at the beginning.*

A continuous tense is usually used for the longer background action or situation (*was walking, are having, were playing*). But 'as and while' can be used with a simple tense especially with a verb like sit, lie or grow which refers to a continuous action or state :

(a) As I sat reading the paper the door burst open.

2. We use **while** to say that *two longer actions or situation go / went on at the same time.* We can use continuous or simple tenses :

   (a) While you were reading the paper, I was watching T. V.

   (b) John cleaned the house while I watched T. V.

   'As' is used (with simple tenses) to talk about *two situations which grow or change together* :

   (a) As he gets older he gets more liberal.

   'When' is used , **to refer to ages and periods of life :**

   (a) When I was a child we wore half pants. (NOT As / while I was a child ....)

   (b) His father died when he was fourteen. (NOT .... while he was fourteen.)

3. 'As' is used to denote *two short actions* or **events that happen/ happened at the same time :**

   (a) As I opened my eyes I heard a loud noise.

   (b) She always arrives **just as** I start work.

8. As if/As though

1. **'As if'** and **'as though' mean the same**. We use them to say what a situation seems like :

   (a) It looks as if / though it's going to rain.

   (b) I felt as if / though I was dying.

   (c) She was acting as if / though she was the owner.

2. We can use a past tense with a present meaning after 'as if / as though'. This shows that a comparison is unreal :

   (a) She looks as if she's rich. (Perhaps she is rich.)

   (b) He behaves as if he owned the palace.(But he doesn't own it.)

   (c) He talks as if he was rich.(But he is not.)

   (d) He orders me as if I were his servant. (But I am not.)

3. We use past perfect after, 'as if / as though' , when referring to a real or imaginary action in the past :

   She talks about Newyork as if she had been there itself.

   He seems/seemed as though he hadn't had a nice meal for many days.

9. Because, as and since

'Because', 'As' and 'Since' are used to answer the question : *'Why?'*.

(i) They join two clauses in the same sentence :

(a) I lost my job because I was often late.

(b) Ram resigned because he wanted to spend more time with his family.

(ii) 'Because', 'As' and 'Since' *show the relationship between the two clauses :*

(a) Why did you resign from such a well-paid job, Ram ?

Because I wanted to spend more time with my family.

Because is more common than 'As' and 'Since' when the *'reason' is the most important* thing. The **because-clause is usually placed after the main clause :**

I went to Chennai for a holiday last October **because** I knew it would be warm and sunny every day I was there.

As and **Since** are used when the *reason is already well-known and / or less important*. The **'As' or 'Since'-clause** *often comes at the beginning of the sentence* and **is separated from the main clause by a comma :**

(a) As my family had finished dinner when I got home, I went to this really good beer bar. (I'm telling you about the beer bar. It's not so important 'why' I went there.)

(b) Since it's your birthday, I'll make you breakfast in bed. (I'm going to make you breakfast.(I know, and you know, it's your birthday.)

(c) Since I have no money, I can't go to the movie.

CORRECT YOURSELF EXERCISE : CONJUNCTION

CYE : 01 Join the following pairs of sentences using the connectors given in brackets :

1.My father is ill. My wife is ill.(both.............and)
2. The teacher was not in the class. The monitor was not in the class. (neither.............nor)
3. He is poor. He is honest. (though............yet)
4. The book may be in the bag.It may be in the cupboard. (either .... or)
5. There was a violent storm. Many trees were uprooted. (such........... that)
6. The doctor reached .The patient died. (hardly .... when)
7. He is strong. He is brave.(not only .... but also)
8. Do not be a borrower. Do not be a lender. (neither.............nor)
9. It was very dark. We could see nothing. (so............. that)
10. The thief saw the policeman .He ran away at once. (no sooner............ than)

CYE : 02 Combine each pair of sentences below into one sentence, choosing the right conjunctions from the following :

since, besides, lest, nevertheless, before, after, otherwise.

1. Walk carefully.You may fall.
2. It's raining.We won't play the match today.
3. Don't write.The bell has gone.
4. He was busy. He attended to me.
5. He is a rich man. He is an M.P.

CYE : 03 Fill in the blanks by choosing the correct connector given in bracket :

1. A student will fail .... he does not work hard.(because, if, until, though, unless)
2. He was late................. it was raining heavily. (while, after, so, that, when, because)
3. .... you have any doubt,please ask me. (in case, because,unless, until, though)
4. She is more intelligent .... her sister. (as ,than,before,because, that)
5. She has changed a lot .... I saw her last. (when ,before, while,as, since)
6. She could not get the prize,................ she tried hard for it.(yet, though, but, when, and)
7. We must leave now .... it is getting dark. (as long as, as soon as,when, since)

8. I was taking a bath .... somebody rang the bell.
(as, while ,when, as soon as, than)

9. He failed in the examination;................ , he didn't lose heart.
(moreover, then, while, nevertheless, until)

10. She tried her best; ...., she couldn't succeed.
(besides, in case, however, instead, as long as)

CYE : 04 Fill in the blanks with suitable connectors chosen from the ones given in brackets:

1. We want others to respect our feelings................ , we should respect the feelings of others. (nevertheless, similarly, on the other hand)
2. We lost the key.We had .... to break the lock open. (still, for, therefore)
3. His parents were transferred to Agra ....he was five years old. (when, since,while)
4. A mechanic was sent for .... our car broke down. (since, as soon as, because)
5. The rent being very high he will not take that house; ....it is very far away from his office. (because, moreover, still)
6. The police asked the suspect question after question, ...he did not open his mouth. (yet, still, however)
7. I have been to the hanging garden four times,.......I won't mind going there again. (but, nevertheless, however)
8. .... much I tried, I could not help him. (though,however, as)
9. My uncle left for Mexico...................... I was six years old. (when, since, while)

CYE : 05 Correct the following sentences :

1. I could neither contact Lila nor Sarla.
2. Neither he plays nor reads.
3. She both accused me and my friend Shyam.
4. Ram not only built a temple but also a mosque.
5. He has visited both to Newyork and Mexico.
6. English is not only difficult to speak but also to write.
7. She is as much noted for her beauty as for her wisdom.
8. I have both visited America and Russia.
9. He neither knows me nor my wife.
10. Ramesh neither went to Jaipur nor Delhi.

CYE : 06

1. No sooner had he reached the station when the train arrived.
2. Though he is poor but he is trustworthly.
3. Hardly had she left the hospital, than it began to rain.
4. He had neither a car or a scooter.
5. There was much disturbance both in Jammu as well as in Pahalgaon.
6. One cannot be both present at New Delhi as well as at Jaipur.
7. He cannot either read nor write English.
8. She cannot run nor walk.
9. He has not any book nor any copy.
10. I have never seen her nor heard of her.

CYE : 07

1. I do not know that when she will go.
2. I cannot say that where he is working now a days.
3. I understand she will attend the function.
4. I hope that you are well now.
5. I can assert it is right.
6. I cannot explain that why I like her so much.
7. I asked my assistant that bring a chair and my mobile.
8. I agree it is a good oportunity to invest the money.
9. As she started late, she will miss the train.
10. Since Ram is a poor fellow, he couldn't buy a new dress.
11. The reason is because he is not well.

CYE : 08

1. It was generally doubted that India would permit the use of her soil.
2. It is not doubtful whether she will attend the party.
3. Is there any doubt whether she will come ?
4. Keep your body fit like I do.
5. You are as dear to me as her.
6. Until he works hard, he can't pass.
7. Take an umbrella in case it may rain.
8. You wait here unless the train arrives.
9. You will succeed, if you will work hard.
10. If I had wings, I will fly to london.
11. If I won a lottery, I will buy a big house.
12. If he had worked hard, he would pass.

CYE : 09

1. It is a year since I have met her.
2. It is a month since she has left for U.S.A.
3. He speaks as if he was the master.
4. Ram orders as though he would be a millionaire.
5. Five years have passed since I had seen her.
6. A year passed since his wife died.
7. I was playing when he was watching T.V.
8. I will go when he will come.
9. I went there while he awoke.
10. I will meet you before I shall leave for home.

SOLUTIONS CORRECT YOURSELF EXERCISE

Solutions CYE : 01

1. Both my father and my wife are ill.
2. Neither the teacher nor the monitor was in the class.
3. Though he is poor,yet he is honest.
4. The book may be either in the bag or in the cupboard.

5. There was such a violent storm that many trees were uprooted.
6. The doctor had hardly reached when the patient died.
7. He is not only strong but also brave.
8. Neither be a borrower nor be a lender.
9. It was so dark that we could see nothing.
10. No sooner did the policeman see the thief than he ran away.

Solutions CYE : 02

1. Walk carefully lest you should fall.
2. Since it's raining,we won't play the match today.
3. Don't write after the bell has gone.
4. He was busy, nevertheless, he attended to me.
5. He is a rich man, besides,he is an M.P.

Solutions CYE : 03

1. if, 2. because, 3. In case, 4. than, 5. since,
6. though, 7. since, 8. when, 9. nevertheless, 10. however.

Solutions CYE : 04

1. similarly, 2. therefore, 3. when, 4. because, 5. moreover,
6. still, 7. but, 8. however, 9. when.

Solutions CYE : 05

1. I could contact neither Lila nor Sarla.
2. He neither plays nor reads.
3. She accused both me and my friend Shyam.
4. Ram built not only a temple but also a mosque.
5. He has visited both to Newyork and to Mexico.

   Or

   He has visited to both Newyork and Mexico.
6. English is difficult not only to speak but also to write.
7. She is noted as much for her beauty as for her wisdom.
8. I have visited both America and Russia.
9. He knows neither me nor my wife.
10. Ramesh went neither to Jaipur nor to Delhi.

Solutions CYE : 06

1. No sooner had he reached the station than the train arrived.
2. Though he is poor yet he is trustworthly.
3. Hardly had she left the hospital, when it began to rain.
4. He had neither a car nor a scooter.
5. There was much disturbance both in Jammu and in Pahalgaon.
6. One cannot be present both at New Delhi and at Jaipur.
7. He cannot either read or write English.
8. She cannot run or walk.
9. He has not any book or copy.
10. I have never seen her or heard of her.

Solutions CYE : 07

1. I do not know when she will go.
2. I cannot say where he is working now a days.
3. I understand that she will attend the function.
4. I hope you are well now.
5. I can assert that it is right.
6. I cannot explain why I like her so much.
7. I asked my assistant to bring a chair and my mobile.
8. I agree that it is a good oportunity to invest the money.
9. As she started late, she missed the train.
10. Since Ram is a poor fellow he can't buy a new dress.
11. The reason is that he is not well.

Solutions CYE : 08

1. It was generally doubted whether India would permit the use of her soil.
2. It is not doubtful that she will attend the party.
3. Is there any doubt that she will come ?
4. Keep your body fit like me. or Keep your body fit as I do.
5. You are as dear to me as she.
6. Unless he works hard, he can't pass.
7. Take an umbrella in case it rains.
8. You wait here until the train arrives.
9. You will succeed, if you work hard.
10. If I had wings, I would fly to london.
11. If I won a lottery, I would buy a big house.
12. If he had worked hard, he would have passed.

Solutions CYE : 09

1. It is a year since I met her.
2. It is a month since she left for U.S.A.
3. He speaks as if he were the master.
4. Ram orders as though he were a millionaire.
5. Five years have passed since I saw her.
6. A year has passed since his wife died.
7. I was playing while he was watching T.V.
8. I will go when he comes.
9. I went there when he awoke.
10. I will meet you before I leave for home.

16

The Interjection (!)

Definition : The interjection is always a spoken word that *expresses an emotion.*
or an **Interjection is a word, used to *express some sudden feeling of mind.*** Always use sign of exclamation (!) after the Interjection.
The word 'interjection' literally means 'something thrown in between' from the Latin words; *'inter'* ('between') and *'jacer'* ('throw').
An *interjection*, sometimes called a **filled pause**, *is a part of speech* that usually **has no grammatical connection to the rest of the sentence** and simply expresses emotion on the part of the speaker, although most interjections have clear definitions.
Interjections can be **'phrases'** or even **'sentences'** as well as 'words' :
As I entered the room —*Oh, my God! What I saw*! — he was still standing there.
Read the following sentences :

(i) *Hurrah* ! Our team has won.
(ii) *Alas* ! He lost his son.
(iii) *Bravo* ! Well played my boys.
(iv) *Ah* ! She has gone.
(v) *Fie* ! She did such thing.
(vi) *Oh* ! You are here.
(vii) *What* ! She failed ?
(viii) *Shh* ! Don't make a noise.
(ix) *Hush* ! Don't talk here.
(x) *Hello* ! How do you do ?

'Hello' and 'Goodbye' are also interjections, as are exclamations like 'Cheer's! and 'Hurray!'. In fact, very often they are characterized by exclamation marks depending on the stress of the attitude or the force of the emotion they are expressing. 'Well' can also be used as an interjection, for example when put at the beginning of a sentence.
Note the following interjections used to express different feelings :

1. **Joy** Hurrah! Ha ! Ha !
2. **Sorrow** Alas !, Ah !, Ha !
3. **Surprise** Oh !, What !,
4. **Contempt** Fie !, Bosh !, Shame ! Shame !
5. **Greetings** Bravo ! Welldone !
6. **Calling** Hello ! Hey !
7. **Attention** Listen !, Lo ! Hush ! Shh !, Behold !

Interjections are uninflected function words that express the attitude or emotion of the speaker. They are used when the speaker encounters events that cause these emotions — unexpectedly, painfully, surprisingly or in many other sudden ways.

17

Pronoun

Pronouns are words which are used in the place of nouns. Normally (but not always) pronouns stand for '*pro* + noun' or refer to a noun, an individual or individuals or thing or things (the pronoun's antecedent) whose identity is made clear earlier in the text.
In the following examples, pronouns are used in the place of nouns :

1. I saw a boy on the roof. He seemed to recognize me.
2. My friend and her brother like to play chess. They play whenever they can.

In the first example, the pronoun **'he'** is used instead of repeating the noun **'boy'**. In the second example, the pronoun **'they'** is used instead of repeating the nouns **'friend'** and **'brother'**

KINDS OF PRONOUN

Pronouns are classified as per following :

1. Personal Pronoun
2. Reflexive Pronoun
3. Emphatic Pronoun
4. Reciprocal Pronoun
5. Demonstrative Pronoun
6. Indefinite Pronoun
7. Interrogative Pronoun
8. Relative Pronoun
9. Distributive Pronoun
10. Exclamatory Pronoun

PERSONAL PRONOUNS

Personal pronouns refer persons or things. **Personal Pronouns change form**, according to their different uses in a sentence. Thus ***'I'*** is used as the subject of a sentence (I am satisfied.), ***'me'*** is used as an object (He taught me. He gave me a pen.), and '*my*' is used as the possessive form (This's my book.) . These forms are called **Cases**.

Personal pronouns in the subjective and objective cases :

Subjective Case	Objective Case
I	me
you	you
he	him
she	her
it	its
we	us
they	them

Personal pronouns can also be characterized or distinguished by **person**. First person denotes the speaker(s); 'I' for singular, 'we' for plural. Second person denotes the person or people being spoken; 'you' for both singular and plural. Third person refers to the person or people being spoken about; 'he,' 'she,' and 'it' for singular, 'they' for plural. Each person can change form, reflecting its use in a sentence. Thus, 'I' becomes 'me' when used as an object and 'my' when used in its possessive role ; 'they' becomes 'them' in object form and 'their' in possessive .

SINGULAR AND PLURAL PRONOUNS

Person	Singular	Plural
First Person	I	we
Second Person	you	you
Third Person	he, she, it	they

POSSESSIVE FORMS OF PERSONAL PRONOUNS

The forms of personal pronouns which indicate possession are called *possessive forms of personal pronouns*. In the following sentences, the italicized words are the possessive forms of personal pronouns :

1. This is *your* pen. This pen is *yours*.
2. *His* house is large, but *mine* is small.
3. *Their* rooms are bigger than *ours*.

The subjective, objective and possessive forms of the personal pronouns are shown in the following table :

Subjective	Objective	Possessive form case	Possessive form case (Adjective)
I	me	my	mine
you	you	your	yours
he	him	his	his
she	her	her	hers
it	it	its	[its]
we	us	our	ours
they	them	their	theirs

NOTE *It can be seen that only* **his** *and* **its** *have the same form when used as pronouns as when used as adjectives. The possessive pronoun* **its** *is rarely used.*

POSSESSIVE ADJECTIVES

The personal pronouns have two possessive forms. One form *shows possession by preceding a noun.* A personal pronoun in this form may be referred to as a **possessive adjective**, since, *like an adjective, it modifies the noun*.

PERSONAL PRONOUN : USE AND RULES

1. **If a pronoun refers a noun which has already been mentioned, the noun is called as the *antecedent of the pronoun*.**

(a) The mangoes are cheap, but they are not ripe yet : In this example, the noun '**mangoes**' is the antecedent of the pronoun '**they**'. An antecedent (noun) usually precedes the pronoun. A noun can also follow the pronoun provided that it is obvious, to what the pronoun is referring.

(b) Because they are sour, the mangoes will be used for making pickle : In this example, the pronoun '**they**' stands for the noun '**mangoes**', which occurs later in the sentence.

2. The third person singular pronoun '**he**' is used to refer to male antecedents and **she** is used to refer to female antecedents.These are the only pronouns in the subjective case which are differentiated with respect to gender.

(a) A girl was standing on the balcony. She was waiting for her parents.
(b) A boy was reading newspaper. He seemed to be very busy.

In the above sentences, the pronoun '**she**' agrees with the female antecedent '**girl**', and the pronoun '**he**' agrees with the male antecedent '**boy**'.

3. Singular and plural antecedents : If the antecedent of a pronoun is singular, a singular pronoun must be used. If the antecedent of a pronoun is plural, a plural pronoun must be used.

(a) I have a pen. It is quite smooth.
(b) I have two pens. They are quite smooth.
(c) This is my brother. He is younger than I am.
(d) These are my brothers. They are younger than I am.
(e) This is my friend Rani. She is older than I am.
(f) These are my friends. They are older than I am.

In the above examples (a), (c), and (e), the singular pronouns '**it**', '**he**' and '**she**' agree with the singular antecedents '**pen**, **brother** and **friend**'. The plural pronoun '**they**' agrees with the plural antecedents **pens**, **brothers** and **friends** [examples; (b), (d), (f)].

NOTE *The third person plural pronoun '**they**' can be used to stand for either male or female antecedents.*

4. Human and non-human antecedents : The pronouns '**he**' and '**she**' usually refer to human beings. However, **he** or **she** may also be used to refer to an animal, *if the gender of the animal is known to the speaker :*

(a) My sister is very clever. She has a degree in maths.
(b) His uncle was there, because he had to wait for us.
(c) Her dog is well trained. He is a good ball catcher.
(d) The tiger saw a girl sitting on a tree. He tried to attack her.

NOTE *The pronoun '**it**' is usually used to refer the animals or things.Sometimes 'ships' and 'countries' are referred to as '**she**'.*

1. This is a good book. It is interesting and well-written.
2. The *Vikrant* is a warship. She plays very crucial role during the war.

'**it**' is used to refer to things which are not human. In the second example, '**she**' is used to refer to a thing (ship) which is not human.

NOTE *The pronoun '**they**' can stand for either human or non-human antecedents :*

1. The children bought bread, because they felt hungry.
2. The mobiles are popular, but they are expensive.

In the first example, '**they**' stands for the human antecedent '**children**'. In the second example, '**they**' stands for the non-human antecedent '**mobiles**'.

5. *A pronoun should clearly refer the noun it stands for.* In the following examples, it is not clear to which nouns the underlined pronouns refer :

1. My friend was there with her aunt. She was wearing a red saree. *Incorrect*
2. The children stared at the dogs. They were ready to jump. *Incorrect*

In the first example, the pronoun '**she**' could stand either for the noun **friend** or for the noun **aunt**. Similarly, in the second example, the pronoun '**they**' could stand for either '**children**' or '**dogs**'.

NOTE *When it is not obvious to which antecedent a pronoun refers, the sentence should be corrected. This can be done either by repeating the noun, or by rewriting the sentence to make the meaning clear. For instance, the preceding examples could be corrected as follows. It will be assumed that* '**she**' *refers to* '**friend**', *and that* '**they**' *refers to* '**dogs**'.

1. My friend was there with her aunt. My friend was wearing a red saree. *Correct*
   or, My friend, wearing a red saree, was there with her aunt. *Correct*
2. The children stared at the dogs. The dogs were ready to jump. *Correct*
   or, The children stared at the dogs, which were ready to jump. *Correct*

6. When the verb '**to be**' is immediately followed by a personal pronoun, the pronoun must be in the subjective case.

(a) It is I. (b) That was he. (c) This is she. (d) Those are they.

NOTE *Nowadays this rule is usually ignored. The verb* '**to be**', *is also being followed by the objective form of the pronoun.. Thus, in informal English the sentence* '**It is I**' *would usually be expressed* '**It is me**', *and the sentence* '**That was he**' *would usually be expressed* '**That was him**'. *Both are acceptable these days.* ***Strictly speaking the use of subjective form of pronoun is grammatically correct.***

7. When a personal pronoun is the object of a verb, the pronoun must be in the objective case.

(a) They like me. (b) We respect you.
(c) They understand her. (d) I wanted him to assist them.

8. A noun or pronoun which forms part of a prepositional phrase is said to be the object of the preposition. *Personal pronouns in the objective case are used as objects of prepositions :*

(a) Please give the copy to him. (b) They went with her.
(c) I purchased a pen for him. (d) She walked across it.

NOTE *The underlined pronouns are the objects of the prepositions* ***to, with, for,*** *and* ***across.***

9. Possessive adjectives : The personal pronouns have two possessive forms. One form shows possession by preceding a noun, it is referred as a possessive adjective, since, like an adjective, it describes the thing to which the noun refers. The possessive adjectives must agree with their antecedents. Look at the following sentences :

(a) The boy obeys **his** father.
(b) The girl likes **her** mother.
(c) The bird sat on **its** nest.
(d) The cows have lost **their** way.

10. **Possessive adjectives used with gerunds :** When a gerund is preceded by a personal pronoun, the pronoun must be in the form of a possessive adjective :

(a) The girl said that **her** writing had improved.
(b) The boy entertained the guests with **his** singing.
(c) They think **their** lobbying for proper water supply will be effective.

In the above examples, the gerunds are underlined, and the possessive adjectives are printed in bold type.

11. **Possessive pronouns :** The possessive form of a personal pronoun, can be used in the place of a noun :

1. He did not bring his briefcase, but I brought mine.
2. Because I forgot my pen, she lent me hers.
3. Their teacher is stricter than ours.
4. Our teacher is nice, but theirs is short-tempered.

In the above sentences, the possessive pronouns are underlined.

NOTE *Except for the pronoun '**mine**', all of the possessive pronouns end in '**s**'. However, it should be noted that, unlike possessive nouns, the possessive personal pronouns are not spelled with an apostrophe. Care should be taken not to confuse the possessive form '**its**' with the contraction '**it's**', which stands for '**it is**' or '**it has**'.*

12. **Pronoun follows 'Let' :** When a pronoun follows 'let', we use the objective form of the pronoun.

We say -- Let **us** go to hospital.
We should not use subjective form after 'let'.

(a) Let you and I decide the matter once for all. *Incorrect*
Let you and me decide the matter once for all. *Correct*
(b) Let he who is without guilt throw the first stone. *Incorrect*
Let him who is without guilt throw the first stone. *Correct*

13. **Different person pronouns with the same verb :**

If pronouns of different persons are used with the same verb in a sentence, **they should be placed in following sequence :**

(a) **If all the pronouns are in singular form** then the ***good manners demand*** that second person pronoun should come first and then the third person.The first person should take the last position.i.e. **2 → 3 →1.**

(a) You, he and I are partners.
(b) He and I are good friends.
(c) You and he are working in the same office.
(d) You and I can do this work.

(b) **If pronouns are in plural forms** then the sequence should be **1→2→3;** it means the first person plural pronoun is followed by second and third person plural pronouns :

(a) We and you cannot live together.
(b) We, you and they can purchase that complex.

(c) Sometimes the sentence has some **apologetic sence or negative sense or sense of some error committed** etc , in such sentence the ***good manners demand ; to accept the guilt first*** by the speaker, that means by the first person .In such case the sequence should be **1→2→3.**

(a) I and you are responsible for the loss.
(b) You and he spoiled the party.
(c) I and he will beg sorry for the misconduct.

14. If a pronoun ['our, your, our' in the examples (a) to (d) given bellow] refers to more than one noun or pronoun of different persons (I, you, he), it must be of the first person plural, in case nouns or pronouns are first and second person (see example (a) below) and if nouns or pronouns referred by the pronoun are second and third person (see example (b) below) it must be second person plural.In case of nouns or pronouns are of first and third person (see example (c) below) the pronoun must be first person plural :

II + I--------------- I Person plural
II + III ------------- II Person plural
III + I ----------------I Person plural

Example

(a) You and I have done our job.
(b) You and he have completed your job.
(c) He and I have done our duty.
(d) You he and I have completed our duty.

15. ***If a collective noun is used as a unit*** denoting a unitary action as a whole, **the pronoun used is singular and in neutral gender :**

(a) The crew revolted and murdered its captain. ('crew' is a collective noun.)
(b) After three days, the jury gave its verdict. ('jury' is a collective noun)
(c) The fleet will reach its destination in a month. ('fleet' is a collective noun)

If the collective noun denotes separation or division, the pronoun used is plural :

(a) The jury were divided in their opinions.
(b) The Government decided to revise their plan outlays.

16. When two or more nouns are joined by 'and' the pronoun used would be plural :

1. Ram and Mohan went to *their* school.
2. Suresh and his family members have completed *their* work.

NOTE *If both the nouns joined by 'and' denote the same person, the pronoun used would be sigular :*

The collector and magistrate is negligent in his duty. (Collector and magistrate are same person.)

17. When two singular nouns are joined by *'and'* and preceded by *'each or every'*, the pronoun used would be **singular** :

(a) Every teacher and every boy was in his room.
(b) Each officer and each clerk has joined his duty.

18. Singular pronoun and singular verb is used with; *Each, Either* and *Neither* :

(a) Each of the students is ready to do his duty.
(b) Either of the two students gets his gift.
(c) Neither of them gets his turn.

19. Singular pronoun is used when two or more singular nouns are joined by 'or', *'Either.....*or', *'Neither.....nor'* :

(a) Ram or Shyam should deposit his dues.
(b) Either Ramesh or Ganesh lost his purse.
(c) Neither Ram nor Shyam has completed his work.

NOTE *But if one noun is plural, then the pronoun should be plural and plural noun should be placed near the verb :*

(a) Either the principal or the *teachers failed* in **<u>their</u>** duty.
(b) Neither the teacher nor the *students have done* **<u>their</u>** work.

PRONOUN - 'IT' :

'It' is used :

1. **For things without life :**
   (a) Here is your pen. Please take *it*. (Pen is 'without life'.)
2. **For animals :**
   (a) He has a cat. It is very beautiful. (b) I have a dog. It is very faithful.
3. **For young child** (if sex differentiation is not referred) :
   (a) When he saw the child, it was playing. (b) The baby has spoiled its dress.
4. 'It' is used **to emphasise a noun/pronoun in following type of sentences :**
   (a) It is you, who can solve this problem.
   (b) It was I, who called you.
   (c) It was at Shimla, where the agreement was signed.
   (d) It is the place where he was murdered.
5. **'It' is also used as indefinite nominative :**
   (a) It rains. (b) It snows.
   (c) It thunders. (d) It blows.
6. 'It'is also **used for time , weather etc :**
   (a) It is 7 O'clock. (b) It is fine.
   (c) It is winter. (d) It is summer.
7. 'It' is also **used in exclamatory expressions :**
   (a) What a beautiful bird it is ! (b) What a large building it is !
8. 'It' is also used **in following type of expressions :**
   (a) It is easy to find faults with others.
   (b) It is confirm that he is wrong.
   (c) It is doubtful whether she will join here.
   (d) It is uncertain that she will come.
   (e) He is telling what is not true : as he knows it.
   (f) He deserved the award : as we knew it.
   (g) I think it is wrong to travel without proper ticket.
   (h) I consider that it is pity to waste time.

'It' is also called an *Impersonal pronoun*.

'It' and 'This' :

'This'is used for introducing a person or for things. 'This' also refers to things that are nearby either in space or in time.We also use 'this' for informing telephone numbers to the caller and introducing the broadcasting channels. 'This' shows intimacy :

(a) This is my friend. (b) This is a cat.
(c) This is All India Radio. (d) This is my brother.

(e) This is 2345714.
(f) This is BBC / Voice of America.

We can't use 'this' for time, weather etc, 'it'is used for the purpose.

(a) It is 7 O'clock.
(b) It is very cold today.
(c) It is morning.
(d) It is winter.
(e) It is raining.
(f) It is 7 :30 by my watch.

REFLEXIVE PRONOUNS :

The *reflexive pronouns*, **ending in -*self*,** are used when the action denoted by the verb is directed toward the thing referred to by the subject.The reflexive pronoun shows that the subject also receives the action of the verb. This use of reflexive pronouns is illustrated in the following examples.

(a) She washed **herself** thoroughly before putting on new dress.
(b) Did you hurt **yourself**?
(c) We ruined **ourselves.**
(d) You ruined **yourself**.
(e) Students who cheat in this test are only harming **themselves.**

This means that whenever there is a reflexive pronoun in a sentence there must be a person to whom that pronoun can 'refer.'

NOTE ***Avoid the use of reflexive pronouns (ending in -self) where they are neither appropriate nor necessary*** *:*

(a) Ram and ~~(myself~~)I are responsible for this decision.
(b) This matter will be decided by ~~(myself)~~ me.
(c) If you have any questions, please contact ~~(myself)~~ me or Ramesh.

Rule 1. When pronouns are combined, the reflexive will take either the first person or, when there is no first person in the combination, the second person :

(a) Ram , and I have deceived ourselves about purchasing a house.
(b) You and Ram have ruined yourselves.

2. Transitive verbs take object with them. **If a trnsitive verb has no object , the reflexive pronoun fills the place of object.** Such commonly used verbs are **:** ***avail, absent, enjoy, resign, apply, revenge, exert etc*** **:**

(a) I absented myself from the office.
(b) I revenged myself upon her.
(c) He availed himself the opportunity.
(d) They enjoyed themselves the pleasure of weather.

3. Verbs when used intransitively don't need an object.In such case **we should not use any reflexive pronoun as object**. Such commonly used verbs are : ***keep, break, set, bathe, make, stop, steal, qualify, move, open, draw, rest, roll, burst, hide, feed, gather*** etc. These verbs are commonly used intransitively.

(a) He kept away from the function. *Correct*
He kept himself away from the function. *Incorrect*
(b) Let us rest at the bed. *Correct*
Let us ourselves rest at the bed. *Incorrect*
(c) She hid in the room. *Correct*
She hid herself in the room. *Incorrect*

4. The indefinite **pronoun '*one*' has its own reflexive form** ('One must have faith in oneself.'), but the *other indefinite pronouns use either* ***himself*** or ***themselves*** as reflexives.

'One' as pronoun :

Sometimes the **pronoun '*one*' functions as a numerical expression :**

(a) Those are goodlooking shirts. I think I'll buy one.

(b) One is red, the other green.

(c) The four brothers get along quite well; in fact they respect one another.

(d) One of the students will lead the group to the parliament.

(e) The white jeep is fast, but I think the green one will win.

As a pronoun, **'*one*' can also function** in an impersonal, objective manner, **standing** for all **people in general** who belong to a class :

(a) The young actoress was awful; one felt embarrased for her.

(b) If one fails, then one must try again .

When the pronoun '*one*' is used in the numerical sense, a different pronoun can be used in a subsequent reference :

(a) We watched as one [of the birds] dried its feathers in the sun.

(b) One [person] pulled her car over to the side.

NOTE *We should not match the impersonal 'one' with another pronoun, especially in the same sentence :*

(a) If one fails, then he/you must try again. *Incorrect*

If one fails then one must try again. *Correct*

One's Reflexive and Possessive Forms :

In the United States, the possessive and reflexive forms of '*one*'— one's and oneself — are often replaced by other pronoun forms. **In British English**, they are commonplace : One must be conscientious about one's dental hygiene.

In the U.S. that '*one's*' is apt to be replaced by a third-person 'his' or (more informally) a second-person 'your' :

(a) One must learn from one's [or his] mistakes.

(b) One must be conscientious about one's [or his] dental hygiene.

(c) One must be conscientious about your dental hygiene.

In formal writing, the use of *'your'* in sentence (c) above, in either American or British English—would be regarded as too casual or even sub-standard. On the other hand, the problem with using 'his' is obvious : it runs counter to the *tendency to remove gender bias from one's language* as much as possible. Thus, even in American English, this mixture of 'one' with 'he/his/him' is slowly disappearing.

'*Oneself*' is used in formal writing and speech as the proper reflexive form of '*one*' :

(a) If one slipped on this icy walk, one could hurt oneself badly.

Note that there is usually no apostrophe used in the spelling of *'oneself'*.

The Plural of 'One' :

As a singular numerical pronoun, we don't have trouble with '*one*' : It is possible, sometimes, to pluralize '*one*' :

(a) I really like the chocolate ones.

(b) Are these the ones you want?

(c) Do you want these ones?

When the word '*ones*' is preceded by a plural determiner (like '*these*'), we usually drop the '*ones*' and the determiner turns into a demonstrative pronoun : 'Do you want these?'

NOTE *The phrases 'one in [plural number]' and 'more than one' always take a singular verb :*

(a) One in four doctors recommends this medicine.
(b) One out of every six instructors gets this question wrong.
(c) There is more than one reason for this.
(d) More than one lad has lost his heart to this lass.

Formation of Reflexive Pronoun

It should be noted that the *first and second person reflexive pronouns* are formed from the *corresponding possessive adjectives*, whereas the *third person reflexive pronouns* are formed from the *corresponding pronouns* in the objective case. This is illustrated in the following table :

Subjective	Objective	Possessive Adjective	Reflexive Pronoun
I	me	my	myself
you	you	your	yourself, yourselves (plural)
he	him	his	himself
she	her	hers	herself
it	it	its	itself
we	us	our	ourselves
they	them	their	themselves

EMPHATIC PRONOUNS

The Emphatic pronouns (such as myself, yourself, herself, ourselves, themselves) **consist of a personal pronoun plus *self* or *selves*.** *The Emphatic pronoun is used* ***to emphasize a noun***. It is possible (but rather unusual) for an emphatic pronoun to precede the noun it refers to; eg– Myself, I don't believe a word she says.). *Usually Emphatic pronoun is* ***placed after the noun it refers*** **:**

(a) I myself solved this question.
(b) She herself found the solution.
(c) He himself came to see the patient.
(d) You yourself admitted your fault.

Reciprocal Pronouns

Reciprocal pronouns refer to persons or things which are acting on each other. '*Each other*' and **'*one another*'** are only two reciprocal pronouns. These are always used objectively.Both phrases may be used to refer to either persons or things :

(a) You and I saw each other last week.
(b) The houses faced each other.
(c) The two friends helped one another with their work.
(d) The wires were touching one another.

They are used for combining ideas. If Ram gave Sita a book, and Sita gave Ram a book , we can say that they gave each other books (or that they gave books to each other). **'Each other' usually refers idea of 'two'** :

(a) My mother and I give each other a hard time.

If more than two people are involved (let's say a large book club), we would say that they gave one another books :

(a) The two friends quarrelled with each other.
(b) They all gave gifts to one another.

(c) These two students love each other.
(d) They saved themselves by helping one another.

NOTE *As per traditional theory 'each other' is used for two and 'one another' for more than two, but now the rule is not strictly adhered to :*

(a) For you and I are foreigners to one another. - *Aldous Huxley*
(b) The artistic result of Volpone is not due to any effect that Volpone, Mosca, Corvino, Corbaccio, and Voltore have upon each other. - *T.S. Eliot.*

Reciprocal pronouns can also take possessive forms :

(a) They borrowed each other's ideas.
(b) The students in this lab often use one another's equipments.

DEMONSTRATIVE PRONOUNS

The family of demonstratives *(this/that/these/those/such)* functions either as pronouns or as **determiners.**

As pronouns, **they identify or refer to nouns :**
(a) *That* is incredible! (referring to something you just saw)
(b) I will never forget *this*. (referring to a recent incident)
(c) *Such* is my belief. (referring to a statement just made)

The words '**this, that, these** and **those**' **are Demonstrative pronouns**. **These are used to denote specific persons or things**. In the following examples, the words '**this, that, these** and **those**' are used as **demonstrative pronouns** :

(a) This is an umbrella. (b) That is a good idea.
(c) These are my friends. (d) Those are our shops.

NOTE *When these words* ***(this, that, these and those)*** *are used immediately* ***preceding a noun****, they function as* ***demonstrative adjectives(determiners)****.*

(a) This umbrella is made of Swiss cotton. (b) That idea seems workable.
(c) These people are my friends. (d) Those shops are ours.

In the preceding examples, '**this, that, these** and **those**' act as adjectives, modifying the nouns.

This and These :

'**This**' and '**these**' are used to *indicate persons or things that are near* to the speaker :
'**This**' takes a singular verb, and is used when referring to a *single person or thing* :
(a) This is my sister. (b) This book belongs to Shyam.
'**These**' takes a plural verb, and is used when referring to *more than one person or thing* :
(a) These are my friends. (b) These books belong to him.

That and Those :

'**That**' and '**those**' are used to *indicate persons or things that are at a distance* from the speaker.
'**That**' takes a singular verb, and is used when referring to a single person or thing :
(a) That is a table. (b) That man is our principal.
'**Those**' takes a plural verb, and is used when referring to more than one person or thing :
(a) Those are tables. (b) Those men are our teachers.

INDEFINITE PRONOUNS

A pronoun that refers to person or thing in a general way (not in a definite way) is called Indefinite Pronoun. The indefinite pronouns ***(everybody / anybody / somebody /all/ each/every / some/none/one)*** do not act for specific nouns but function themselves as nouns.

Indefinite pronouns may be used without antecedents. Look at the following sentences :

(a) One cannot get everything one desires.

(b) I will try to think of somebody who can help you.

(c) Nobody will believe it!

(d) Is there anyone here by the name of Sujak?

Following are the examples of Indefinite pronouns :

one, anyone, anybody, anything, everyone, everybody, everything, no one, nobody, nothing, someone, somebody, something.

All of the pronouns listed above take verbs in the **third person singular**. The phrase **'no one'** is used like the other indefinite pronouns, but is spelled as two separate words.

The pronoun **'one'** can refer to persons or things :

(a) One of the boys will help you. (b) Please hand me one of the boxes.

NOTE *When used in a general sense, the pronoun '**one**' is usually understood as referring to persons :*

(a) One should always look both ways before crossing the street.

As shown in the following table, the **indefinite pronouns which refer to persons, form possessive adjectives by adding'*s*.**

Indefinite Pronoun	**Possessive Adjective**
one	one's
anyone	anyone's
everyone	everyone's
no one	no one's
someone	someone's
anybody	anybody's
everybody	everybody's
nobody	nobody's
somebody	somebody's

The indefinite pronouns which refer to things usually do not form possessive adjectives.There are other **indefinite pronouns, words that are used as Determiners** also. **These are** : **'enough, few, fewer, less, little, many, much, several, more, most, all, both, every, each, any, either, neither, none, some etc.'**

NOTE *In formal English, it is considered grammatically correct to use the adjective '**his**' to agree with indefinite pronouns such as **anyone** and **everyone**.*

(a) Everyone took his seat.

INTERROGATIVE PRONOUNS

The Interrogative pronouns **are used for making** ***querries or asking questions***. The pronouns *'**who**, **what** and **which**'* are used as interrogative pronouns.

(a) Who telephoned?

(b) What did you say?

(c) Which is your brother?

The interrogative pronouns are 'who,' 'whom,' 'which,' 'what' and their **compounds formed with** the suffix *'ever'* ***('whoever,' 'whomever,' 'whichever,' and 'whatever').*** 'Who' and 'Whom' usually refer to people and 'Which' too can refer to people occasionally . **'Which' and 'What' usually refer to things and animals**. 'Who' acts as the subject of a verb, while 'whom' acts as the object of a verb or preposition. **'Which' is generally used with more specific reference than *'what*'**. If we're taking a test and I ask 'Which questions do you find the most difficult?', I am referring to specific questions on that test. If I ask 'What questions do you find most difficult'? I could be asking what kind of questions on that test (or what kind of question, in general) you find difficult.

NOTE *'which' or 'what' can also be used as an interrogative adjective, and that 'who', 'whom', or 'which' can also be used as a relative pronoun .*

Look at the following sentences :

The **highlighted** word in each of the following sentences is an interrogative pronoun :

(a) **Which** wants to see the dentist first? ('Which' is the subject of the sentence.)

(b) **Who** wrote the Mahabharat? ('who' is the subject of the sentence.)

(c) **Whom** do you think I should send there?('whom' is the object of the verb 'send')

(d) To **whom** do you wish to speak? ('whom' is the object of the preposition 'to')

(e) **Who** will meet the students at the college ground? ('who' is the subject of the compound verb 'will meet'.)

(f) To **whom** did you give the purse? ('whom' is the object of the preposition 'to')

(g) **What** did he say? ('what' is the direct object of the verb 'say')

DIRECT AND INDIRECT QUESTIONS

Direct questions :

When interrogative pronouns are placed at the beginning of a sentence in order to ask a question, such questions can be referred to as *direct questions*.

In a direct question, when the interrogative pronoun is the subject of a verb, the verb follows the subject.

(a) **What** has happened? (b) **Who** has been invited?

In these examples, '**what**' is the subject of the verb '**has happened**', and '**who**' is the subject of the verb '**has been invited**'. When the interrogative pronoun is the object of the verb or the object of a preposition, *inverted word order* must be used, with the first auxiliary preceding the subject of the verb. In the case of verbs in the simple present or simple past, the auxiliary **do** or **did** is used.

(a) What do **you** say? (b) Which did **he** choose?

(c) What is **she** playing? (d) To what can **one** attribute their success?

In the preceding examples, the subjects **you, he, she** and **one** are preceded by the auxiliaries **do, did, is** and **can**. In the first three examples, **what** and **which** are the objects of the verbs. In the fourth example, '**what**' is the object of the preposition '**to**'.

Indirect questions :

A direct question forms a complete sentence in itself, *an* ***indirect question is part of a longer sentence***. As well as being used at the beginning of direct questions, interrogative pronouns and adjectives can also be used at the beginning of **indirect** questions.The following examples show the difference between a direct question and an indirect question.

(a) Who is there ?—Direct question

(b) She wants to know who is there —Indirect question

(c) Will you tell me who is there?—Indirect question

In the first example '**Who is there?**' is a direct question. In the second example, '**who is there**' is an indirect question which is part of a longer statement. In the third example, '**who is there**' is again an indirect question which is part of a longer question.

RELATIVE PRONOUNS

A ***relative pronoun*** is a word such as ***'who'***, ***'whom' 'that'***, or ***'which'*** that **is used to introduce a relative clause**. These words are called **relative pronouns.** The compounds ***'whoever,' 'whomever,'*** and ***'whichever'*** are also relative pronouns.

In other words **'A pronoun which is used to begin a subordinate clause can be referred to as a *relative pronoun***, since it indicates the relationship of the subordinate clause to the rest of the sentence.' A *subordinate clause which is introduced by a relative pronoun is often referred to as* a **relative clause**.

Look at the following sentences :

(a) The woman **who** is wearing red saree is a doctor.

(b) The door, **which** is dark blue, is very tight.

(c) Have you found the magazine **that** was missing?

In above sentences the words in bold type are relative pronouns.

We can use a **relative pronoun** to **link one phrase or clause to another phrase or clause**. You can use the relative pronouns 'who' and 'whoever' to refer to the subject of a clause or sentence, and 'whom' and 'whomever' to refer to the objects of a verb or a preposition.

DEFINING AND NON-DEFINING RELATIVE CLAUSES

Relative clauses can be divided into two types : those which merely give a description *of the object to which they refer*, and **those which define the object (noun)** *to which they refer*.

(i) ***Defining Relative Clause***

The clause which describes the preceding noun is called 'defining relative clause'. A relative clause has the function of defining the object being referred to.

For instance, in the following example :

(a) The woman **who is wearing red saree** is a doctor.

NOTE *There is no coma (,)between the noun and the defining relative clause.* ***The absence of commas indicates*** *that the clause '****who is wearing red saree****' is a defining relative clause. In other words, the clause has the function of identifying; to which woman the speaker is referring.*

(ii) ***Non-defining Relative Clauses :***

When a **relative clause merely describes an object to** which the speaker or writer is referring , the ***clause must be placed between commas****. Such a clause can be called* a **non-defining relative clause.**

For instance, in the following example :

(a) The door, which is dark blue, is very tight.

The commas indicate that the clause '**which is dark blue**' is a non-defining relative clause. In other words, presence of commas in this sentence implies that it has already been made clear to which door the speaker is referring, and the clause '**which is dark blue**' simply gives descriptive information about the door.

Relative Pronouns—*'Who, Whom and Whose Who'* :

'**Who**' *is used as the subject of a verb*, '**whom**' is used as the *object of a verb or the object of a preposition*, and '**whose**' is used as an *adjective denoting possession.* The relative pronouns '**who, whom** and **whose**' **generally refer only to persons**, and are used either in defining or non-defining relative clauses. '**Who**' *refers to the subject of the sentence*, '**whom**' referes to the *object of a verb* or a *preposition* , while '**whose**' refers the *possession* and it is *used as adjective.*

In the following examples, '**who**' introduces the defining relative clause '**who secures the highest marks**' and the non-defining relative clause '**who is learning Russian**'.

(a) The child who secures the highest marks will receive a trophy.

(b) My brother, who is learning Russian, wants to travel to Kazhakistan.

In these examples, '**who**' has the antecedents '**child**' and '**brother**', and acts as the subject of the verbs **secures** and **is learning**.

Relative Pronouns—*'Whom, Whose, that, which, what, whatever-whoever, whomever' discussed separately :*

1. Whom :

In the following examples, '**whom**' introduces the *defining relative clause* '**whom we visited**' and the *non-defining relative clause* '**whom we will meet tomorrow**'.

(a) The girl whom we visited is her sister. (Mark the absence of commas.)

(b) Mr.Francis, whom we will meet tomorrow, will be our guide.

In these examples, '**whom**' has the antecedents '**girl'** and '**Mr. Francis**', and acts as the object of the verbs '**visited**' and '**will meet**'.

In the following examples, '**to whom**' introduces the defining relative clause **to whom you gave your umbrella** and the non-defining relative clause, **'to whom we send a birthday card every year**'.

(a) The girl to whom you gave your umbrella lives near my house.

(b) His aunt , to whom we send a birthday card every year, is ninety-eight years old now. In these examples, '**whom**' has the antecedents '**girl'** and '**aunt**', and is the object of the preposition '**to**'.

2. Whose :

In the following examples, '**whose**' introduces the *defining relative clause* '**whose house was sold**' and the *non-defining relative clause* '**whose family lives in America**'.

(a) The man whose house was sold will leave this town.

(b) My brother, whose family lives in America, will visit us for a few days.

In these examples, '**whose**' has the antecedents '**man**' and '**brother**', and modifies the nouns '**house**' and '**family**'. *In the case of 'whose', it should be noted that it is the antecedent which must be a person; the noun being modified may be a person or a thing.*

We may find use of '**whose**' at the beginning of a clause occasionally. '**Whose**' can also be used to referring to things , in order to make a simpler sentence.

For example :

(a) The tree, the branches of which overhung the street, was laid with fruits. *Correct*

The tree, whose branches overhung the street, was laid with fruits. *Incorrect*

However, this use of '**whose**' is considered to be grammatically incorrect in formal English.

3. That :

As a relative pronoun, '**that**' can **refer to either persons or things**. The relative pronoun '**that**' is generally **used only in defining relative clauses :**

(a) The girls that were here yesterday will return in a week.

(b) The bag that was on the steps belongs to our tenant.

In these examples, '**that**' has the antecedents '**girls**' and '**bag**', and introduces the defining relative clauses '**that were here yesterday**' and '**that was on the steps**'. Here, '**that**' acts as the subject of the verbs '**were**' and '**was**'. When '**that**' acts as the object of a verb or preposition, it is usually omitted :

(a) The magazines that we bought are very useful.

(b) The city that this road leads to is twenty kilometres away.

In the first sentence, '**that**' acts as the object of the verb '**bought**'. In the second sentence, '**that**' acts as the object of the preposition '**to**'. Therefore, these sentences *can also be written* as following :

(a) The magazines we bought are very useful.

(b) The city this road leads to is twenty kilometres away. Here '**that**' **has been omitted.**

NOTE

(A) ***'That'* can be used for *living and non living* nouns, for *singular* as well as *plurals* :**

(a) I have lost the *book* that you gave me. (non-living noun)

(b) I haven't read the *magazine* that the teacher suggested to me.

(c) *He* that is content is happy. (living noun)

(d) Uneasy lies the *head* that wears a crown.

(B) ***No preposition is used before 'that'*, if any preposition is required to be used , it is used in ending position :**

(a) We know the hotel that she lives *in*. ('in'—preposition)

(b) This is the lady that I told you *about*.

(c) I understand the point that you are hinting *at*.
(d) This is the house that I told you *about*.

(C) In a sentence after the following words 'that' is generally used : *All, any, anybody, anything, much, nothing, little, somebody, no one, none, 'the same + noun + that', 'the only + noun +that'* etc :

(a) *All* that glitters is not gold.
(b) There was *none that* didn't support the cause.
(c) It is for *nothing that* I have been trying to find.
(d) There is *much that* he needs.
(e) There was not *any that* could be followed.
(f) There was *somebody* that raised the matter.
(g) This is the *same girl that* we met yesterday. ('the same + noun + that')
(h) This is *the only girl that* secured more than 90% marks. ('the only + noun + that')

(D) After interrogative pronoun - *'who'* and *'what'*, *'that'* is used :

(a) What is it that you can't solve.
(b) What is there that I can't see.
(c) Who am I that you should care for.
(d) Who was there that you were talking with.

4. Which :

It is important to note that when used as a relative pronoun, **'which'** refers only to things, when used as an adjective or interrogative pronoun, **'which'** can refer to either persons or things.

The relative pronoun **'which'** can be used in either defining or non-defining relative clauses.

(a) The book which I purchased last week is very useful.
(b) The bag, which was full of coins, was very heavy .

In the first example, **'which'** has the antecedent **book**, and introduces the defining relative clause **'which I purchased last week'**. In the second example, **'which'** has the antecedent **'bag'**, and introduces the non-defining relative clause **'which was full of coins'**.

'That, Which and Who' :

*The use of the relative pronouns **'that,'** **'which'** and **'who'** is summarized in the following table.*

Relative Clause	Type of Clause	Type of Antecedent
that	defining clause only	persons or things
which	defining or non-defining	things only
who/whom/whose	defining or non-defining	persons only

NOTE *As shown in above table in case of defining relative clauses, **'that'** may be used to replace **'who, whom or which'**.*

Look at the following sentences :

(a) The girl whom we saw is his sister.
(b) The coat which you are wearing is rather large.

We can well write these sentences as following :

(c) The girl that we saw is his sister.
(d) The coat that you are wearing is rather large.

As in case of 'that', **'whom' and 'which' can also be omitted** when they act as the object of the verb in a relative clause; the above sentences could also be rewritten as :

(e) The girl we saw is his sister.

(f) The coat you are wearing is rather large.

NOTE *When '**whom**' or '**which**' is the object of a preposition, the preposition should immediately precede the relative pronoun :*

(a) The boy to whom we sent the parcel was very glad.

(b) The house to which you will be conducted has large rooms.

In these examples, '**whom**' and '**which**' are immediately preceded by the preposition '**to**'. *Note also: When the relative pronoun '**that**' is the object of a preposition, the preposition is normally placed at the end of the relative clause. For instance, if '**that**' is used, the above example (f) must be rewritten as follows :*

(a) The house that you will be conducted to has large rooms.

Preferring 'that' to 'who' or 'which' :

(A) **'That' is preferably used after superlative degree** *instead of 'who' or 'which'* :

(a) He is the *most* (superlative degree) eloquent speaker that I have ever heard.

(b) Patel was the *greatest* (superlative degree) man that India produced.

(B) **After two antecedents** one referring a person and the other referring an animal or a thing , use 'that', instead of 'who' or 'which'.

(a) The boy and his dog that entered the temple were caught by the people.

(b) The lady and her cat that created the nuisance were arrested by the police.

(C) **After *'same'* or *'such'* use *'as'* or *'that'* not *'who'* or *'which'* :**

(a) This is the same fellow that came yesterday also.

(b) My books are same as yours.

(c) His reply was such as we never expected from him.

5. What :

Relative pronoun ***'what'* is used without antecedents**. When used as a relative pronoun, ***'what'* has the meaning - *the thing or things that*** :

(a) What you say is not true.

(b) What he did was not wrong.

In above examples, '**what**' introduces the clauses '**what you say**' and ''**what he did**'. Such clauses are called as **noun clauses**, since they serve functions of a noun. For instance, in the preceding sentences, the clause '**what you say**' acts as the subject of the verb '**is**', and the clause '**what he did**' acts as the subject of the verb '**was**'.

6. Whatever and whoever :

'Whatever'* and *'whoever'* are also normally used without antecedents**. ***'Whatever'* means *no matter what, or ***anything which***. '**Whoever' means *no matter who***, or ***anyone who***.

(a) You can tell me whatever you think fit. (b) Let in whoever comes to our house.

In these examples, the noun clauses '**whatever you think fit**' and '**whoever comes to our house**' act as the objects of the verbs in the main clauses.

7. Whomever :

***'Whomever'* refers to the objects of a verb or a preposition.**

Look at the following sentences :

(a) You may invite **whomever** you like to the function.

The relative pronoun 'whomever' is the direct object of the compound verb 'may invite'.

(a) The coach will select **whomever** he pleases.

Here the relative pronoun 'whomever' is the direct object of the compound verb 'will select'.

NOTE *The **expanded form of** the relative pronouns — **whoever, whomever, whatever — are known as indefinite relative pronouns.***

Antecedent of a relative pronoun :

(A) The antecedent of a relative pronoun should not be in possessive case :

(a) These are chairman's instructions that must be followed. *Incorrect*

(b) I went to Sarla's house, who is my class fellow. *Incorrect*

It is an incorrect structure.These sentences should have been written as following :

(a) These are the instructions of the chairman that must be followed.

(b) I went to the house of Sarla who is my class fellow.

(B) The relative pronoun should be of same number and person as its antecedent. It means the verb should agree with the number and person of the antecedent :

(a) The girl who was late was fined.

(b) The girls who were late were fined.

(c) I, who am responsible for the loss , shall pay .

(d) They who live in glass houses should not throw stones .

(e) This is the only one of his books that is worth reading.

(f) We, who seek your help, are new to this place.

NOTE : ***In the end of the** chapter, 'who/whom' and whose/who's (relative pronouns) are **studied comparatively.***

DISTRIBUTIVE PRONOUNS

Each, either and neither are classified as *distributive pronouns.* They denote person or thing one at a time. *These pronouns* **are always treated as singular and take singular verbs.**

Look at the following sentences :

(a) Each of the students gets a prize.

(b) Each got his turn.

(c) Either of the two will win the race.

(d) Neither of those two students can secure first position.

(e) Every one of the students was happy.

(f) Each of the two students received a medal.

NOTE 'Each' (adjective and pronoun)and 'Every' (adjective) :

'Each' means–a ***number of persons or things considered individually.***

'Every' can have this meaning but *with 'every' there is less emphasis on the individual :*

(a) Every student got a prize.
(b) Each student got a prize .

'Every' is an adjective only :

(a) Every man knows about the incident.

'Each' can be used of *two or more persons or things* and *is normally used of small number. Every* is not normally used of *very small numbers*. 'Each' can be used for more than two when the number is usually definite.Both take a singular verb.

For example :

(i) Each of these six houses has a guard tower.
(ii) Each of the five reports starts with a question.

Neither and Either : Either is the negative of Neither.

1. ***'Neither'** means **'not one and not the other'***. It takes an affirmative singular verb.

   It can be used by itself or followed by a noun or by **of + the/ these/ those/ possessives or personal pronouns :**

   (a) I tried both keys but neither (of them) worked.
   (b) Neither of them knew the way/ Neither boy knew ....
   (c) I've read neither of these (books).

2. ***'Either'** means—**'any one of two'***. It takes a singular verb and like 'neither' can be used by itself or followed by a **noun/ pronoun or by of + the/ these/ those** etc.

3. Either + negative verb can replace neither + affirmative, except as in example (b) above, but could replace in (c) :

   (a) I haven't read either of these (books).

   Though 'either' cannot be the subject of a negative verb, it can be subject or object of an affirmative or interrogative verb :

   (a) Either (of these) would do.
   (b) Would you like either of these?

   'Either' and 'Neither' is used for speaking of two persons or things. For more than two, 'any, no one or none' is usually used.

NOTE (A) With 'distributive pronouns' the third person, singular pronoun, masculine gender **(he, his, him)is used :**

(a) Everyone should obey his parents.
(b) Neither of there two students has received his prize.

(B) If feminine gender noun follows the distributive pronoun use personal pronoun 'her':

(a) Neither of these two girls has deposited her fees.
(b) Either of the two girls has received her gift.
(c) Each of the girls has donated her pocket money.
(d) Everyone of the women has a choice of her own.

(C) If a plural pronoun(*us / them / you*) follows the distributive pronoun use singular masculine gender pronoun.

(a) Neither of them has done his duty. (b) Each of them has forgotten his purse.

Position of Pronoun 'Each'

Where to put 'each' in a sentence is an important point. 'Each' can have three positions.

Look at the following sentences :

(a) I bought each of these books for rupees fifty. *Incorrect*
I bought these books each for rupees fifty. *Incorrect*
I bought these books for rupees fifty each. *Correct*
'Each' is used after a numeral :

(b) These tables cost each two hundred rupees. *Incorrect*
These tables cost two hundred rupees each. *Correct*
When there is no numeral :

(c) These men received each a prize. *Incorrect*
These men received a prize each. *Incorrect*
Each of the men received a prize. *Correct*
In such cases begin the sentence with 'each'.

EXCLAMATORY PRONOUN

A pronoun used as an exclamation is called an exclamatory pronoun :

(a) What ! You don't know Sonia Gandhi ? (b) What ! You lost the chain ?

In above sentences ***'What'*** is *functioning as an* **exclamatory pronoun.**

WHO/ WHOM

1. **Who and whom (for persons) :** 'Who' and 'whom' are normally reserved for persons, but they **may be used for animals** when they are thought of in a semi-personal way; My dog, who is getting old now; and of countries, when the people rather than the territory are referred to : India, *who* feels very strongly on this matter....).
2. **'Who' and 'whom' as relative pronouns**. As relative pronouns, **'who and whom'** are preceded by a comma when they introduce a non defining clause, but the comma must not be used when the clause is a defining one.
3. ***'Who'* as subject, *'whom'* as object :**

   '**Who**' is used for the subject and the complement of a verb :

   (a) My father, who works in a bank, is retiring soon.

   (b) My father, who is sixty next year, works in a bank.

   '**Whom**' is used for the object and when governed by a perposition :

   (a) The man whom you rescued from the sea has recovered.

   (b) The newspaper editor, to whom we all owe so much, is leaving the company.

   But in questions introduced by an interrogative pronoun which is governed by a preposition which comes at the end of the sentence it is more usual to use '*who*' :

   (a) Who is that letter from? (b) Who was this poem written by ?

   In spoken English or colloquial written style, '**who**' is now almost universally used. But even here, '**whom**' must always be used *after a preposition* at the beginning of a sentence :

   (a) To whom do I send it?
4. **Who/whom in relative clauses :** A frequent source of trouble is sentences of this type :

   (a) The person **who (or whom?)** we thought was guilty proved to be innocent.

(b) The man **who (or whom?)** we feared we had injured proved to be unharmed.
In above sentences the temptation is always to use '**whom**', presumably because it is felt that the word **('whom')** is the object of **'thought'** and **'feared'** (or whatever verb tkes their place in other sentences); but it is not .In the first sentence, it is the subject of '**was guilty**', hence '**who**' is correct, and in the second **'who/whom'** is , the object of **'had injured'** hence '**whom**' is required. **'We thought'** and **'we feared'** *have the force of parentheses*, and could be moved to another part of the sentence :

(c) The person who was guilty we thought.... ;

(d) **The man whom we had injured we feared...** Even the **Times Literary Supplement** had this sentence : *Incorrect*

(e) The German people, whom Hitler had determined should not survive defeat, did in fact survive. *Incorrect*

Obviously 'who' should have been used, since it is the 'subject of should not survive'.
And The Sunday Times made the same mistake in this headline, that follows :

(f) The entire Magazine, except Lifespan, is devoted this week to 100 men and women **whom** Sunday Times, writers and expert consultants believe will be making headlines in the Britain of the 1980s .

Again, **'who' should have been used** as it is the subject of 'will be making' when it goes with an infinitive, however, 'whom' is always required as follows :

(g) The person **whom** we thought to be guilty.

If there is any doubt, a useful test is to substitute the personal pronoun he or him; if he would be used, the correct relative is 'who' ; if 'him', it is 'whom' :

(a) We thought *he* was guilty (therefore who),
(b) We feared we had injured *him* (therefore whom),
(c) We thought *him* to be guilty (therefore whom).

5. A similar difficulty may arise with questions :

(a) Who (not whom) do you think we saw?
because it is the object of saw.

6. **'Whom' is never indirect object :** 'Whom' is not used as an indirect object. We do not say 'the boy whom I gave the book', or ask 'whom did you give the book ?' It must be 'to whom' (or the preposition may be placed at the end) :

(a) The boy *to whom* I gave the book .... or,
(b) The boy whom I gave the book to ....
(c) To whom did you give the book?

7. **The verb after 'who' :** 'Who' is the same number and person as its antecedent, and takes its verb accordingly :

(a) It is *I* who *am* to blame.

The rules regarding the use of the co-ordinating conjunctions '**and**' and '**but**' before '**who**' are the same as those for 'which' : .... ***Current English Usage by F.T.Wood .***

WHOSE AND WHO'S

Care chould be taken not to confuse 'whose' with 'who's' (meaning 'who is ,or ,'who has'), a mistake that is easily made as, like 'its and it's', they are also pronounced the same. Even the journalists of *The Times Educational Supplement* are not always so careful as they should be, as this headline shows :

(a) *Whose* Afraid of the Big Bad Comprehensive? *Incorrect*

And here is the mistake the other way round from ***The Observer*** :

(a) I relished the anticipation of clever people, cleverly swapping anecdotes, cleverly punning, cleverly imitating others, indiscreetly prognosticating who'd get *who's* job.

....***Current English Usage by F.T.Wood.*** *Incorrect*

POINTS TO REMEMBER

(A) REFER CLEARLY to a specific noun : Don't be vague or ambiguous.

- (a) Although the motorcycle hit the tree, it was not damaged. (Is 'it' the motorcycle or the tree?)
- (b) I don't think they should show violence on T.V. (Who are 'they'?)
- (c) Vacation is coming soon, which is nice. (What is nice; the vacation or the fact that it is coming soon?)
- (d) Jack worked in a national forest last summer. This may be his life's work. (What word does 'this' refer to?)
- (e) If you put this sheet in your notebook, you can refer to it. (What does 'it' refer to; the sheet or your notebook?)

Such type of ambiguity must be avoided.

(B) The indefinite pronouns 'anyone, anybody, everyone, everybody, someone, somebody, no one, and nobody' are always singular. This is sometimes perplexing to learners who feel that everyone and everybody (especially) are referring to more than one person. The same is true of 'either' and 'neither', which are always singular even though they seem to be referring to two things.

CORRECT YOURSELF EXERCISE : PRONOUN

CYE : 01 Correct the following sentences :

1. Let you and I go to play.
2. There is close relation between he and I.
3. You, he and I have done their job.
4. You and he could not complete his work.
5. He and I have fastened his belts.
6. I, you and he were present in the function.
7. I and you are strangers.
8. You and I are responsible for this loss.
9. He and I were the main accused.
10. You, he and I must beg sorry for the misconduct.

CYE : 02 Correct the following sentences :

1. Neither of these four vehicles will do.
2. Anyone of the two girls can solve this puzzle.
3. Either of the three students is responsible for the loss.
4. None of the two girls could complete the job.

5. One should obey his elders.
6. One should respect not only his own parents but also others'.
7. One should take care not to make himself obnoxious to others.
8. Each girl and every madam tried their best to finish the work before 7P.M.
9. Every man and every woman have their own fascinations.
10. Every leader and every citizen have a duty towards their country.

CYE : 03 Correct the following sentences :

1. Each of the employees have to arrange their own vehicle.
2. Every one of them were given their table and chair.
3. Either Ramesh or Sita have left their tiffin box.
4. Either the teacher or the students have left his classroom unlocked .
5. Please take the buffaloe to her shed.
6. The cow has hurt her legs.
7. This is easy to get her agree.
8. This was he who arrived first in the meeting.
9. It is to certify that Mr. A is our employee.
10. This is 8 O'clock by my watch.

CYE : 04 Correct the following sentences :

1. All which she said was incorrect.
2. Who was the girl which came to meet you?
3. What is his opinion about the work which you have completed?
4. I always purchase the item which is best in the market.
5. This is the same shirt which I saw in the shop.
6. Who is she who can abuse me like this?
7. Only those employees should be promoted whom are sincere.
8. The leaders which do not love their country are not respected.
9. Those whose live in glass houses should not throw stones at others.
10. What was the reply, which she submitted?

CYE : 05 Correct the following sentences :

1. It was me who telephoned you yesterday.
2. The girl whom you spoke to in the office is my friend.
3. My brother and myself are glad to get your greetings.
4. I am not one of those who cannot keep his promise.
5. It is not us who are responsible for the delay.
6. They admired his wife and he.
7. What place are you going?
8. Which house do you live?
9. She has absented from duty today again.
10. I could not avail of the opportunity I got last year.
11. The treatment received by me was such, which I never expected.
12. His expectation is the same which is hers.
13. One cannot bear his insult like this.
14. My house is bigger than their.
15. This is a secret between you and I.

CYE : 06 Fill in the blanks with interrogative pronouns :

1. We went to Ranjana's party .... we enjoyed very much.
2. Anajali went to the doctor .... told her to rest for seven days atleast.
3. .... does your sister live?
4. .... book do you like?
5. .... did you finish the game?
6. The woman .... I met yesterday lent me her umbrella.
7. The horse .... I selected won the race yesterday .
8. He did not know .... to say then .
9. Shakespeare, ... is the world's greatest dramatist, was born in a cottage .
10. The Superintendent of Police, ... work is very precarious, takes care of public safety and law and order .

CYE : 07 Fill in the blanks with interrogative pronouns :

1. What is the name of the man .... car you borrowed?
2. I don't know the name of the woman to .... I spoke on the phone.
3. .... teaches you Sanskrit?
4. .... is your problem?
5. I gave him all the money .... I had.
6. Ashish is the man .... son won the scholarship.
7. Our flight was delayed .... meant we had to wait for hours at the airport.
8. Jitu is one of my friends .... I have known for a very long time.
9. The book .... you gave me is very useful for the pregnant ladies.
10. Swimming , ... is a good sport also , makes people healthy and bold.

CYE : 08 Add the relative pronouns to the following sentences :

1. Gypsum is a mineral .... is extracted from the earth.
2. There is nothing .... I can do for you.
3. This is the house .... I was born.
4. My parents had left for college .... I reached home.
5. He is a famous scientist about ....many books have been written.
6. Madam Curie, ... discovered radium, was one of the greatest women of her age.
7. The book ,............ you gave me is not so useful for learning English speaking..
8. Where is the man .... sold me the detergent powder ?
9. That is the lady .... golden chain was snatched yesterday?
10. The girl .... you see at the desk is the receptionist.

CYE : 09 Correct the following :

1. Everyone should obey their parents.
2. Sita must do their duties.
3. Each girl and every student was busy in her their work.
4. Either Pramod or Narendra has learnt their lesson.
5. Nisha or Sushma was teaching their son.
6. Either Rohan or his friends forgot his books.
7. You, he and I am friends .
8. He I and you went to Nehru garden yesterday.
9. Manish and I should learn my lesson.
10. You and Sushma should read her book.
11. He, you and I must do my work.

12. Ram and Shyam help one another.
13. Three children love each other.
14. Two friends love one another.
15. It is I who is your friend.

CYE : 10 Correct the following :

1. That is one of the girls who has stolen eggs.
2. It is me, who am speaking on this topic.
3. That is one of the interesting books that has appeared this year.
4. This is the only one of his stories that are worth reading.
5. It is I, who is answering the question.
6. The boy which is sitting in the corner reads in my class.
7. She who walk in the evening gets energy.
8. The sun whom rays give life to earth is a source of energy.
9. This is the same toy which I gave you.
10. Uneasy lies the head which wears the crown.
11. All which glitters is not silver.
12. Man is the only animal which can use his intelligence.
13. That is the best which you can do.
14. The girl and her cat who had entered my house were locked.
15. I have read Milton's poems who was a romantic poet.

CYE : 11 Correct the following :

1. You self did this work.
2. Who do you want?
3. Neither Sushma nor Indu were wanted.
4. The girls absented from the class.
5. One should do his duty.
6. I was not so rich as him.
7. This is the boy whose all admire.
8. This is the girl whom marks are highest.
9. Either of these roads lead to the hospital.
10. Yourself admitted the guilt.
11. You, he and I are in the wrong.
12. You are stronger than me.
13. It is me.
14. Only you and him can do that work.
15. If I were him, I should help you.

CYE : 12 Correct the following :

1. This is mine pen.
2. Between tyou and I, Mohan is a thief.
3. Let me take your leave .
4. He cannot bearing separation from me.
5. Good girls like you and she should not abuse others.
6. This pen is superior to your.
7. Every men and every women should obey their elders.
8. He availed of he chance.
9. He will not object to me going there.
10. He is a good player is not it ?

SOLUTIONS : CORRECT YOURSELF EXERCISE

Solutions CYE : 01

1. Let you and me go to play.
2. There is close relation between him and me.
3. You, he and I have done our job.
4. You and he could not complete your work.
5. He and I have fastened our belts.
6. You, he and I were present in the function.
7. You and I are strangers.
8. I and you are responsible for this loss.
9. I and he were the main accused.
10. I, you and he must beg sorry for the misconduct.

Solutions CYE : 02

1. None of these four vehicles will do.
2. Either of the two girls can solve this puzzle.
3. Anyone of the three students is responsible for the loss.
4. Neither of the two girls could complete the job.
5. One should obey one's elders.
6. One should respect not only one's own parents but also others'.
7. One should take care not to make oneself obnoxious to others.
8. Each girl and every madam tried her best to finish the work before 7 P.M.
9. Every man and every woman has his own fascinations.
10. Every leader and every citizen has a duty towards his country.

Solutions CYE : 03

1. Each of the employees has to agrrange his own vehicle.
2. Every one of them was given his table and chair.
3. Either Ramesh or Sita has left his/her or this tiffin box.
4. Either the teacher or the students have left their class room unlocked.
5. Please take the buffaloe to its shed.
6. The cow has hurt its legs.
7. It is easy to get her agree.
8. It was he who arrived first in the meeting.
9. This is to certify that Mr.A is our employee.
10. It is 8 O'clock by my watch.

Solutions CYE : 04

1. All that she said was incorrect.
2. Who was the girl that came to meet you?
3. What is his opinion about the work that you have completed?
4. I always purchase the item that is the best in the market.
5. This is the same shirt that I saw in the shop.
6. Who is she that can abuse me like this?
7. Only those employees should be promoted who are sincere.
8. The leaders who do not love their country are not respected.
9. Those who live in glass houses should not throw stones at others.
10. What was the reply that she submitted?

Solutions CYE : 05

1. It was I who telephoned you yesterday.
2. The girl who you spoke to in the office, is my friend.
3. My brother and I are glad to get your greetings.
4. I am not one of those who cannot keep their promise.
5. It is not we who are responsible for the delay.
6. They admired his wife and him.
7. What place are you going to?
8. Which house do you live in?
9. She has absented herself from duty today again.
10. I could not avail myself of the opportunity I got last year.
11. The treatment received by me was such as I never expected.
12. His expectation is the same as is hers.
13. One cannot bear one's insult like this.
14. My house is bigger than theirs.
15. This is a secret between you and me.

Solutions CYE : 06

1. which,	2. who,	3. Where,	4. Which,	5. When,
6. whom ,	7. which,	8. what,	9. who,	10. whose.

Solutions CYE : 07

1. whose,	2. whom,	3. Who,	4. What,	5. that,
6. whose,	7. that,	8. whom,	9. which,	10. which.

Solutions CYE : 08

1. which,	2. that,	3. where,	4. when,	5. whom,
6. who,	7. which,	8. who,	9. whose,	10. whom.

Solutions CYE : 09

1. Eveyone should obey his parents.
2. Sita must do her duties.
3. Each girl and every student was busy in work.
4. Either Pramod or Narendra has learnt his lesson.
5. Nisha or Sushma was teaching her son.
6. Either Rohan or his friends forgot their books.
7. You, he and I are friends.
8. You, he and I went to Nehru garden yesterday.
9. Manish and I should learn our lessons.
10. You and Sushma should read your books.
11. You, he and I must do our work.
12. Ram and Shyam help each other.
13. Three children love one another.
14. Two friends love each other.
15. It is I who am your friend.

Solutions CYE : 10

1. That is one of the girls who have stolen eggs.
2. It is I, who am speaking on this topic.
3. That is one of the interesting books that have appeared this year.
4. This is the only one of his stories that is worth reading.
5. It is I, who am answering the question.
6. The boy who is sitting in the corner reads in my class.
7. She who walks in the evening gets energy.
8. The sun whose rays give life to earth is a source of energy.
9. This is the same toy that I gave you.
10. Uneasy lies the head that wears the crown.
11. All that glitters is not silver.
12. Man is the only animal that can use his intelligence.
13. That is the best that you can do.
14. The girl and her cat that had entered my house were locked.
15. I have read poems of Milton who was a romantic poet.

Solutions CYE : 11

1. You yourself did this work.
2. Whom do you want?
3. Neither Sushma nor Indu was wanted.
4. The girls absented themselves from the class.
5. One should do one's duty.
6. I was not so rich as he.
7. This is the boy whom all admire.
8. This is the girl whose marks are highest.
9. Either of these roads leads to the hospital.
10. You yourself admitted the guilt.
11. I he and you are in the wrong.
12. You are stronger than I.
13. It is I.
14. Only you and he can do that work.
15. If I were he, I should help you.

Solutions CYE :12

1. This is my pen.
2. Between you and me, Mohan is a thief.
3. Let me take leave of you.
4. He cannot bear separation from me.
5. Good girls like you and her should not abuse others.
6. This pen is superior to yours.
7. Every men and every women should obey their elders.
8. He availed himself of the chance.
9. He will not object to my going there.
10. He is a good player, isn't it?

18

Conditional Sentences

Conditional sentences have two parts :

1. 'If' clause, 2. Main clause.

There are three kinds of conditional sentences :

1. 'If' clause in present tense
2. 'If' clause in past tense
3. 'If' clause in past perfect tense

CONDITIONAL SENTENCE 'IF' CLAUSE

(A) Conditional sentence- 'If' clause in present tense :

1. If + simple present + future

(The verb in the **'if 'clause is in the present tense** and the verb in the main clause is in the future simple.) :

(a) If it rains , he will not come in time. (b)If he runs fast, he will reach in time.

2. Instead of 'if + present + future' we may have **if + present + may/ might (possibility) :**

(c) If the fog gets thicker, the plane may be late.

3. If + present + may (permission) or *can* (permission or ability) :

(d) If it stops raining ,we can go to the top. (permission or ability)

(e) If your ticket is confirmed you may/ can board the plane. (permission)

4. If + present + must / should /could, etc. :

(f) If you want to lose weight eat less potatoes.

(g) If you meet Sita in the party, could you tell her to ring me?

(h) If you want to lose weight, you should eat less potatoes.

NOTE *The 'if clause' may come after future clause also :*

(i) He will reach in time if he runs fast..

(j) The plane may be late if the fog gets thicker.This type of sentences denotes that the action in the if clause is quite probable.

The meaning here is present or future but the verb in the if clause is in present.

5. If + present + another present tense

(such construction shows automatic or habitual results)

(k) If you heat ice, it turns to water.(the use of **'will turn'** is also possible)

(l) If you boil water, it turns to vapours.

(m) If there is shortage of a commodity, its price goes up.

6. Instead of 'if + present tense' we can also have :

if + present continuous +...

(Such construction shows a present action or a future arrangement)

(n) If you are waiting for a taxi(present action), you should better go there.

(o) If you are looking for Raju (present action), you may find him in the park.

(p) If you are staying for another day(future arrangement), I'll ask the manager to charge you at concessional rate.

(q) If you are going to purchase a car(future arrangement), I will ask my assistant to show you the dealer's shop.

7. If + present perfect conditional sentence :

(r) If you have finished dinner, I will ask the waiter for ice cream.

(s) If she has written the thesis ,I will send it to the professor.

(t) If you haven't seen the Victoria Palace we would better go there today.

(B) Conditional sentence -'If' clause is in past tense :

1. if + simple past, + would + V-I

(a) If I had an umbrella I would lend it to you.
[But I haven't an umbrella.]

(b) If I had a brief case, I would give it to her.
[But I haven't a brief case.]

This construction refers to the present or future and *the past tense in the 'if clause' is not a true past* but a subjunctive which indicates unreality.

2. When we don't expect the action in the 'if clause' to take place :

(a) If he tried to threaten me I would inform his father.
(But I don't expect that he will try to threaten me).

(b) If a thief came into my room I would call you.
[But I don't expect a thief to come into my room.]

(c) If she dyed her hair green every one would laugh at her.
(But I don't expect that she will dye her hair green.)

The above construction refers improbability.

NOTE *'Might' or 'could' may be used instead of would :*

(a) If he tried again he would pass. (certain result)

(b) If he tried again he could pass. (ability)

(c) If he tried again he might pass. (possibility)

The use of 'would' refers certainty, 'might' refers possibility, and 'could' refers ability.

3. If + past tense can also be followed by another past tense when we wish to express automatic or habitual reactions in the past :

(a) If anyone abused him he became angry.

(b) If she interrupted him he got angry.

(c) If there was a scarcity of milk, its prices went up.

(d) If there was a short supply of any commodity, prices of that commodity increased.

(C) Conditional sentences -If clause is in 'past perfect tense' :

1. if + past perfect, would + have + past participle

In this type of conditional sentences ,the verb in the if clause is in the past perfect tense; the verb in the main clause is in the perfect conditional. The condition cannot be fulfilled because the action in the 'if clause' didn't happen :

(a) If he had come to me I would have helped him.
(But he didn't come to me.)

(b) If she had invited me I would have attended the function.
(But she did not invite me.)

(c) If he had tried to cheat me I would have dismissed him.
(But he didn't try to cheat me.)

NOTE : (i) 'Could' or 'might' may also be used instead of 'would' in the same constructions:

(a) If we had found her earlier we could have saved her life. (ability)

(b) If we had found her earlier we might have saved her life. (possibilities)

(c) If you had got valid visa you could have left for USA .(ability or permission)

(ii) 'Had' can be placed first and the 'if' omitted :

(a) If he had come to me I would have helped him.

(b) Had he come to me I would have helped him. ('of' omitted.)

2. We can also use, past perfect continuous in the 'if' clause :

I was wearing helmet. If I hadn't been wearing the helmet I would have been seriously injured.

OTHER TYPES OF CONDITIONAL SENTENCES

(A) Normally *will/would /should is not used after* 'if' in conditional sentences, *but there are certain exceptions* :

1. For making request : if you will/ would +....

is often used in ***polite requests***. ***'Would'* is the *more polite* form :**

(a) If you will / would wait a moment I'll see your work is done (Please wait.)

(b) I would be very grateful if you would accept the cash after 3 p.m. (More polite)
('Would' is the more polite form for making request.)

if you would + infinitive

is used for the **requests which would normally be complied as a matter of course :**

(a) If you would fill up this form.(at a bank)

(b) If you would just sign the register.(in a hotel)

(c) If you'd put your address on the back of the cheque.(in a departmental store)

2. If you would like / care + ... *is more polite than* **if you + want/ wish,** and *is more common in use :*

(a) If you would like to come I will arrange a party for you.

(b) If you would care to see the photos I will bring them for you.

(c) If he would like to leave his scooter here he can do so.

3. *If + should* +..... denote that the action though possible is not very likely.

It is combined with an imperative and is mainly used in written instructions :

(a) If you should have any difficulty in getting newspaper, ring at this number.

(b) If these packets should arrive in a damaged condition please inform the company at once.

NOTE : *'Should' can also be placed first and the 'if' omitted :*

(c) Should these packets arrive in a damaged condition, please inform the company at once.

(B) *If + were / was* +...construction is used for advice :

(a) If I were you ,I would forgive him. (I advise you to forgive him)
(b) If I were you , I would punish him. (I advise you to punish him.)

(C) The use of *'Otherwise'*

Otherwise – if this doesn't happen / didn't happen / hadn't happened :
(a) We must reach there before10 O' clock; otherwise we'll be debarred.
(= If we do not reach there before10 O' clock; we'll be debarred)
(b) His father paid his dues; otherwise he wouldn't be in college.
(= If his father didn't pay his dues he wouldn't be in college.)
(c) I used my computer ; otherwise I'd have taken many more hours.
(= If I hadn't used my computer I'd have taken many more hours.)

(D) Unless+ affirmative =If + negative :

(a) You cannot pass *unless you attend* the college. (unless + affirmative)
(=You cannot pass *if you do not attend* the college.) (if + negative)
(b) She cannot go to America *unless she has* a valid visa.
(= She cannot go to America *if she does not have* a valid visa.)

(E) Use of *'In case'* in conditional sentences :

(a) Inform me in case you need more money.
(b) Turn on the light in case you need my help.
(c) Ring my doorbell in case he comes here.

NOTE *'In case' appears similar to 'if' and is often confused with it. But the two are completely different. An 'in case' clause causes an action in the main clause.*

(F) Use of *'So long'* in conditional sentences :

'So long' imposes restriction / limitation .
(a) I shall support him so long he is here.
(b) You can stay here so long the owner is out of station.
(c) So long I am here I will assist in your work.

(G) Use of *'provided'* in conditional sentences :

'Provided' imposes a restriction / limitation :
(a) I shall attend the meeting provided he also attends.
(b) We shall support you provided you favour us .
(c) I can pay you rent provided you get the roof repaired .

(H) Use of *'suppose'* in conditional sentences :

suppose/ supposing ....? = what if .... ?
(a) Suppose a monkey comes here what will you do?
(=What if a monkey comes here what will you do?)
(b) Suppose the train is late?
What if if the train is late?

(I) Use of *'But for'* in conditional sentences :

but for = if it were not for/ if it hadn't been for

(a) But for his help Ramesh would have ruined.
(b) But for the flood, I would have arrived here yesterday.
(c)But for your company I would have bored.

CORRECT YOURSELF EXERCISE : CONDITIONAL SENTENCES

CYE : 01 Correct the following Sentences :

1. If he came to me, I would have given him a pen.
2. Had he invited me, I would attend the function.
3. If he had telephoned me, I would have gave him the address.
4. If a monkey came here, what you will do?
5. If I had an umbrella, I would have given it to her.

CYE : 02 Correct the following Sentences :

1. If he will work hard, he will get promotion.
2. Unless he will ask me, I shall not help him.
3. If I had a brief case, I will have lend it to her.
4. If you will heat ice, it may turn to water.
5. If you are looking for Sita, you would find her with Ram.

CYE : 03 Correct the following Sentences :

1. If I was you, I would dismiss him.
2. Unless he comes back, wait for him.
3. Until you work hard, you can't beat him.
4. Suppose she does not agree, what could you do?
5. If he tried again, he can pass.

CYE : 04 Fill in the blanks :

1. I will stay here ...... you come. (until/unless)
2. .... you work hard, you can't secure first position. (until/unless)
3. If I .... you, I would forgive him. (was/were)
4. If I were him, I .... dismiss you. (will/would)
5. If it rains, he .... not come. (will/would)
6. If you boil water it .... to vapours. (turns/ will turn)
7. If you are waiting for a taxi, you .... better go there. (should/would have)
8. If he had come here I .... given him a room to stay. (would/would have)
9. If she .... me, I would have attended the function. (had invited/invited)
10. If he tried again he .... pass. (will/would)

CYE : 05 Complete the conditional sentences (type I). Remember to use the auxiliary verbs.

1. If it doesn't rain, we (can / go) swimming tomorrow.
2. If you train hard, you (might / win) first prize.
3. If we go to Canada next year, we (can / improve) our English.
4. I (may / go) to the disco in the evening if I do the washing-up now.
5. If we go on holiday next week, I (not / can / play) tennis with you.
6. If you see Ganesh tomorrow, you (should / tell) him that you love him.
7. If my parents go shopping in the afternoon, I (must / look) after my little sister.

8. He (must / be) a good drummer if he plays in a band.
9. If you are listening to the radio after 10 pm, you (should / turn) the volume down.
10. If you like that shirt, you (can / have) it.

SOLUTIONS : CORRECT YOURSELF EXERCISE

Solutions CYE : 01

1. If he came to me I would give him a pen. or If he had come to me, I would have given him a pen.
2. Had he invited me, I would have attended the function.
3. If he had telephoned me, I would have given him the address.
4. If a monkey came here what would you do?
5. If I had an umbrella I would give it to her.

Solutions CYE : 02

1. If he works hard, he will get promotion.
2. Unless he asks me I shall not help him.
3. If I had a briefcase, I would lend it to her.
4. If you heat ice, it turns to water.
5. If you are looking for Sita, you will find her with Ram.

Solutions CYE : 03

1. If I were you, I would dismiss him.
2. Until he comes back, wait for him.
3. Unless you work hard, you can't beat him.
4. Suppose she does not agree, what can you do?
5. If he tried again he could pass.

Solutions CYE : 04

1.until, 2. unless, 3. were, 4. would, 5. will,
6. turns, 7. should, 8. would have, 9. had invited, 10. would.

Solutions CYE : 05

1. If it doesn't rain, we can go swimming tomorrow.
2. If you train hard, you might win first prize.
3. If we go to Canada next year, we can improve our English.
4. I may go to the disco in the evening if I do the washing-up now.
5. If we go on holiday next week, I cannot play tennis with you.
6. If you see Ganesh tomorrow, you should tell him that you love him.
7. If my parents go shopping in the afternoon, I must look after my little sister.
8. He must be a good drummer if he plays in a band.
9. If you are listening to the radio after 10 pm, you should turn the volume down.
10. If you like that shirt, you can have it.

19

Question Tag

Question Tag is a special construction in English. It is a statement followed by a mini-question. **The whole sentence is a '*tag question*', and the mini-question at the end is called a '*question tag*'.** They are like short questions added to sentences, asking for aggreement or confirmation.

FRAMING QUESTION TAG-RULES

Rule : 1

1. **We use questions tag at the end of statements** to ask for confirmation. They mean something like : 'Am I right?' or 'Do you agree?' They are very common in English.

   Structure of Question Tag :

   For positive statement,-negative question tag?

   Helping Verb + n't + Subject?-Negative

   For negative statement, positive question tag?

   Helping Verb + Subject ?-Positive

2. **We always use the auxiliaries to make question tags.** ***Negative verbs in the tags are usually contracted. (didn't you? did you not?)***

CONTRACTED FORM OF AUXILIARIES WITH 'NOT'

do + not= don't	will + not= won't
does + not= doesn't	can + not= can't
did + not= didn't	should + not= shouldn't
am I not...= aren't	I would + not= wouldn't
is + not= isn't	could + not= couldn't
are + not = aren't	may + not= mayn't
has + not= hasn't	might + not= mightn't
have + not= haven't	ought + not= oughtn't
had + not= hadn't	must + not= mustn't
was + not= wasn't	used + not = usedn't
were + not = weren't	need + not= needn't
shall + not = shan't	dare + not= daren't

3. **The subject of the tag is always a pronoun :**

   (a) Ram is going to Jaipur, isn't *he* ? (b) Sita is not cooking, is *she*?

4. **If there is no auxiliary in the sentence, we add *'do, does*, or *did'*, depending on the tense :**

(a) He goes to office, doesn't he ?
(b) They played football, didn't they?

5. **If the subject of the statement is a personal pronoun , use the *same pronoun in question tag. If*** the statement contains a name , the pronoun should agree with the gender and number of the subject.If the subject is singular number third person use 'he'(pronoun) in question tag :

(a) It is not correct, is it?
(b) It is true, isn't it?
(c) They play, don't they?
(d) He is watching TV, isn't he?
(e) You know it, don't you?
(f) Ram and Sita are swimming, aren't they?
(g) She is very beautiful, isn't she?
(h) We played a match, didn't we?

6. **If the subject of the statement is; *there, this, that, those, these,one*, we use the following pronouns as subject of the question tag :**

Subject of statement	Subject in Question Tag
There	There
One	One
This	It
That	It
These	They
Those	They

(a) There is a cow, isn't there?
(b) One can hold it, can't one?
(c) This is his pen, isn't it?
(d) That is his house, isn't it?
(e) These are animals, aren't they?
(f) Those are birds, are't they?

7. **If ; *one , this , that , those* etc. are used in the statement as *adjective*,** it means these are modifying a noun, the subject of the question tag is governed by the gender and person of the noun .

(a) One man can pull it, can't he?
(b) This girl was present there, wasn't she?
(c) This book is very useful, isn't it?
(d) That boy has no manners, has he?
(e) This boy won the race,didn't he?
(f) Those books are mine, aren't they?

8. **When the subject of the sentence is :**

'anyone, no one, anybody, nobody, none, neither everyone, everybody, someone, somebody',

We use the pronoun *'They'* as *subject of the tag* :

(a) None can say so, can they?
(b) No one voted against the bill, did they?
(c) Someone invited me, didn't they?
(d) Somebody will be there, won't they?
(e) Anyone can attend the function, can't they?
(f) Nobody has praised the move, have they?

9. **If the subject of the statement is ; *'nothing, anything, something or everything'* we use *'it'* as subject of the question tag :**

(a) Everything is arranged, isn't it?
(b) Something is missing, isn't it?
(c) Anything can be arranged, can't it?
(d) Nothing can be seen, can it?

10. **If the subject of the statement is ; *All of us, Some of us, Any of us, None of us, Most of us, Everyone of us, Either of us, Neither of us* etc., *we use 'we'* as subject of the question tag.**

If 'us' is substituted by 'you' or ' them' , the subject of the question tag will be 'you' or 'they' respectively :

(a) All of us are invited, aren't we?
(b) All of you are invited, aren't you?
(c) All of them are invited, aren't they?
(d) Either of you can join, can't you?
(e) Neither of you can do it, can you?
(f) None of us was present there, were we?

11. When the statement contains '*I am*' as subject , the construction of the question tag in negative, will be *'aren't I' (not amn't I)* :

(a) I am going to meet her, aren't I ?
(b) I am not going there, am I ?
(c) I am your friend, aren't I ?
(d) I am not your friend, am I ?

12. When **'*dare/need*' are used in the statement as *modal auxiliaries*, the question tag will use *dare / need* as following**. If these verbs are used as main verbs, we use ***'do /does/did'*** in the question tag as usual .

(a) He dare not speak so, dare he?
(b) She need not come here, need she?
(c) He dares to speak like this, doesn't he?
(d) They dare to meet the chairman, don't they?
(e) He needs your help, doesn't he?
(f) They need my assistance, don't they?

13. If the statement contains *'used to'*, we can use *'usedn't'or 'didn't'* in negative question tag (used or did in positive) as following :

(a) She used to go to temple, usedn't she? or didn't she?
(b) He used to smoke, usedn't he ? or didn't he ?
(c) He usedn't smoke, used he ? or did he?
(d) They usedn't go to temple, used they ? or did they?

14. Statements containing words such as :

neither, no, none, no one, nobody, nothing ,scarcely, barely, hardly, hardly ever, rarely, and seldom are treated as negative statements and followed by an ordinary interrogative (positive question) tag :

(a) None was present there, were they?
(b) No one can solve this question, can they?
(c) Nobody believes it, do they?
(d) They said nothing about it, did they?
(e) I know little about U.S.A, do I ?
(f) She rarely comes here, does she?
(g) Neither of them was available there, were they?
(h) Few people can live in such circumstances, can they?
(i) Nothing was said, was it ?
(j) No salt is allowed, is it ?
(k) Neither of them complained, did they?
(l) Prakash hardly ever studies, does he ?
(m) I don't think anyone will come, will they?

15. With imperatives :

Sometimes we use question tags with imperatives (invitations, orders), but the sentence remains an imperative and does not require a direct answer. We use *'won't* in the question tag' for invitations. We use *can, can't, will, would* for orders.

notion imperative + question tag *notes* :

invitation : Take a seat, won't you? (polite)
request : Help me, can you? (quite friendly)
order : Help me, can't you?quite friendly (some irritation?)
order : Close the door, would you? (quite polite)
order : Do it now, will you? (less polite)
order : Don't forget, will you? (with negative imperatives only '*will*' is possible)
order : Use your own vehicle, can't you ? (some irritation)
order : Keep shut, can't you? (some irritation)
order : Mind your own business,can't you? (some irritation)

16. Statement with *'Let's' (Let us)* have question tag *'shall we'* and statement with *'let him , let them , let you'* will have question tag 'will you' :

(a) Let's play, shall we ?
(b) Let us sing, shall we?
(c) Let's go , shall we ?
(d) Let them play, will you?
(e) Let him work, will you?
(f) Let her cook, will you?

17. *Same-way question tags* :

Although the basic structure of tag questions is positive-negative or negative-positive, it is sometime possible to use a *positive-positive* or *negative-negative structure.* **We use same-way question tags *to express interest, surprise, anger* etc, and not to make real questions :**

(a) So you're having a baby, are you? That's wonderful!
(b) She wants to marry him, does she? Some chance!
(c) So you think that's amusing, do you? Think again.
Negative-negative tag questions usually sound *rather hostile* :
(d) So you don't like my looks, don't you?

CORRECT YOURSELF EXERCISE : QUESTION TAG

CYE : 01 Complete the following by using the correct question tags :

1. Everybody was watching the cricket match on TV,......?
2. He is a very wise man, ...?
3. Mrs. Meena is a good teacher,......?
4. We saw a rainbow in the sky yesterday , ...?
5. Sita is a beautiful girl,......?
6. You should not smoke, ...?
7. Miss Neha does not play tennis, ...?
8. I am older than you, ...?
9. You always have your lunch at 1 o'clock,......?
10. I can do it for you, ...?
11. She doesn't want to go to college today, ...?
12. Let's pray to Almighty, ...?
13. He had met you before, ...?
14. We couldn't enjoy the picnic,......?

CYE : 02 Write the letter a, b, c, or d of the correct answer in the brackets :

1. Do as I say, ...?
   (a) didn't you (b) won't you
   (c) needn't you (d) shan't you ( )
2. Now you can make question tags, ...?
   (a) can you (b) won't you
   (c) can't you (d) will you ( )
3. You fell on your back, ...?
   (a) didn't you (b) weren't you
   (c) have you (d) did you ( )
4. Few people know that you are an artist, ...?
   (a) do they (b) don't they
   (c) aren't they (d) haven't they ( )
5. Tomorrow we will attend our college, ...?
   (a) shall we (b) will we
   (c) won't we (d) shouldn't you ( )
6. The Bishnois of Rajasthan protect trees and animals, ...?
   (a) have they (b) weren't they
   (c) do they (d) don't they ( )
7. Everyone wanted a ticket, ...?
   (a) didn't they (b) didn't he
   (c) didn't she (d) haven't they ( )
8. Let's take a little rest before we start again, ...?
   (a) will we (b) should we
   (c) shall we (d) needn't we ( )
9. Anjali dances very well, ...?
   (a) does she (b) doesn't she
   (c) aren't she (d) isn't she ( )
10. Both Ram and Shyam are engineers, ...?
    (a) isn'the (b) isn't she
    (c) are they (d) aren't they ( )
11. He knows nobody in the colony, ...?
    (a) does he (b) did he
    (c) doesn't he (d) didn't he ( )
12. Jahangir was a great judge, ...?
    (a) doesn't he (b) didn't he
    (c) wasn't he (d) weren't he ( )
13. I am looking after the garden, ...?
    (a) amn't I (b) aren't I
    (c) isn't I (d) don't I ( )

14. It is quite hot outside today, ...?
(a) is it (b) isn't it
(c) doesn't it (d) aren't it ( )

CYE : 03

1. Nisha dances very well, ...?
(a) doesn't she (b) does she
(c) aren't she (d) isn't she ( )
2. We have not met before, ...?
(a) did we (b) didn't we
(c) haven't she (d) have we ( )
3. I am senior to you, ...?
(a) do I (b) don't I
(c) aren't I (d) amn't I ( )
4. You are a bit late today, ...?
(a) aren't you (b) don't you
(c) are you (d) do you ( )
5. I do not now live in this colony , ...?
(a) did I (b) aren't I
(c) don't I (d) do I ( )
6. We are learning English Grammar , ...?
(a) are we (b) shall we
(c) aren't we (d) shan't we ( )
7. She is too old , ...?
(a) doesn't she (b) isn't she
(c) aren't she (d) is she ( )
8. You will come tomorrow , ...?
(a) will you (b) shouldn't you
(c) won't you (d) needn't you ( )
9. The house needs immediate repairing , ...?
(a) does it (b) isn't it
(c) is it (d) doesn't it ( )
10. You don't like sugar in your coffee, ...?
(a) didn't you (b) do you
(c) will you (d) don't you ( )
11. Open the window, ...?
(a) don't you (b) aren't you
(c) will you (d) should you ( )
12. I have already taken tea, ...?
(a) didn't I (b) haven't I
(c) did I (d) have I ( )

13. I am working hard on this book, ...?

(a) don't I (b) won't I

(c) aren't I (d) can't I ( )

14. He was asleep, ...?

(a) was he (b) wasn't he

(c) didn't he (d) did he ( )

15. Let us start now, ...?

(a) shall we (b) should we

(c) could we (d) would we ( )

CYE : 04 Complete the following by using the correct tags :

1. Delhi is not very far from Meerut, ...?
2. Shalini is very young ....?
3. You are always punctual, ...?
4. Students are learning swimming, ...?
5. They don't like to bathe in winter, ...?
6. You should not drink wine , ...?
7. Miss Minu does not play chess, ...?
8. I am elder to you, ...?
9. You always have your lunch at 12 O'clock, ...?
10. I can do it for you, ...?

CYE : 05 Complete the following by using the correct tags :

1. He doesn't want to go to college today,................................?
2. Let's pray to God, ...?
3. You had met me before, ...?
4. We couldn't enjoy the picnic, ...?
5. He is a rude man, ...?
6. Everybody was watching the TV, ...?
7. Mrs.Saxena is a good lady ....?
8. Something must be done for us, ...?
9. Someone might come, ...?
10. He needs money, ...?
11. I needn't write, ...?
12. Nisha need not go there, ...?

SOLUTIONS : CORRECT YOURSELF EXERCISE

Solutions CYE : 01

1. weren't they 2. isn't he 3. isn't she 4. didn't we 5. isn't she
6. should you 7. does she 8. aren't I 9. don't you 10. can't I
11. does she 12. shall we 13. hadn't he 14. could we.

Solutions CYE : 02

1. (b) 2. (c) 3. (a) 4. (a) 5. (c) 6. (d) 7. (a)
8. (c) 9. (b) 10. (d). 11. (a) 12. (c) 13. (b) 14. (b)

Solutions CYE : 03

1. (a) 2. (d) 3. (c) 4. (a) 5. (d) 6. (c) 7. (b)
8. (c) 9. (d) 10. (b) 11. (c) 12. (b) 13.(c) 14. (b) 15. (a)

Solutions CYE : 04

1. is it 2. isn't she 3. aren't you 4. aren't they 5. do they
6. should you 7. does she 8. aren't I 9. haven't you 10. can't I

Solutions CYE : 05

1. does he 2. shall we, 3. hadn't you 4. could we 5. isn't he
6. weren't they, 7. isn't she 8. mustn't it 9. mightn't they 10. doesn't he
11. need I 12. need she

20

Question Framing with 'Wh' Words

Questions beginning with *'Wh words'(what, when, who, why, whom ,whose, which* etc .) **are called** *'Wh questions'*.

We can **classify** these questions in ***Direct*** and ***Indirect*** questions.

DIRECT QUESTIONS

(A) When interrogative pronouns are placed at the beginning of a sentence *in order to ask a question*, **such questions can be referred to as *direct questions*.**

In a direct question, when the interrogative pronoun is the subject of a verb, the verb follows the subject.

(a) **What** has happened? (b) **Who** has been invited?

In these examples, '**what**' is the subject of the verb '**has happened**', and '**who**' is the subject of the verb '**has been invited**'.

(B) When the interrogative pronoun is the object of the verb or the object of a preposition, *inverted word order* must be used, with the first auxiliary preceding the subject of the verb. In the case of verbs in the simple present or simple past, the auxiliary '**do**' or '**did**' is used.

(a) What do **you** say? (b) Which did **he** choose?
(c) What is **she** playing? (d) To what can **one** attribute their success?

In the preceding examples, the subjects '**you, he, she** and **one**' are preceded by the auxiliaries '**do, did**', **is** and '**can**'. In the first three examples, '**what**' and '**which**' are the objects of the verbs. In the fourth example, '**what**' is the object of the preposition '**to**'.

(C) Questions with pronoun 'Who' :

The pronoun '**who**' usually refers to persons. **The pronoun 'who' has following three forms :**

(i) Who :

When '**who**' is the subject of a verb, we should use the subjective case :

(a) Who opened the window?

(b) Who will assist me?

It should be noted that when '**who**' is used with the verb '**to be**', or with verbs in the passive voice, the subjective case is usually used, as such verbs do not take an object :

(a) **Who** was it? 'verb to be'
(b) **Who** is the fastest runner? 'verb to be'
(c) **Who** will be there? 'verb to be'
(d) **Who** has been nominated? 'verb in passive'

(ii) Whom : It is the objective form of 'who'.

When the pronoun '**who**' is the object of a verb or the object of a preposition, the objective form '**whom**' must be used :

Whom did you see in the club ?
To whom did you send the invitations?

In the first example, '**whom**' is the object of the verb '**see**'. In the second example, **whom** is the object of the preposition '**to**'.

In informal English, the form **'who'** is often used for the objective as well as for the subjective case. For instance, in informal English, the preceding examples might be expressed : '**Who did you see in the club?**' and '**Who did you send the invitations to?**' Grammatically this use is considered **incorrect** in formal English.

(iii) Whose : Possesive form of 'who'.

'**Whose**' can be used either as a possessive adjective followed by a noun, or as a possessive pronoun :

(a) **Whose** sarees are these? possessive adjective
(b) **Whose** are these? possessive pronoun

The possessive form '**whose**' expresses the idea of '**belonging to**'. For instance, the idea expressed in the sentence: **Whose sarees are these?** could also be expressed by the sentence: **To whom do these sarees belong?**

(D) What and Which :

'**What**' and '**which**' are **used either as interrogative pronouns, or as interrogative adjectives.**

(a) What is this? used as interrogative pronoun
(b) Which is his brother? used as interrogative pronoun
(c) What time is it? used as interrogative adjective
(d) Which man is his brother? used as interrogative adjective

'What' and '**which**' can **refer to either persons or things**. e.g

(a) What man would not like to own a horse?
(b) What colour are the oranges?
(c) Which boy is the best horseback rider?
(d) Which road leads to New Delhi?

NOTE *It should be noted that when used as a relative pronoun, '**which**' can refer only to things.*

'**Which**' as an adjective or interrogative pronoun usually **implies a choice of one or more things from a limited number of alternatives :**

(a) Which magazine would you like?
(b) Which girls were ready on time?

The first example (a) implies a **choice of one magazine from two or more magazines**. The second example (b) implies that an answer is expected which will *indicate certain girls from a limited group of girls.*

In contrast, '**what**' as an adjective or interrogative pronoun *is usually used in order to ask for* **general information.**

(a) What time is it?

(b) What does she want?

'**What**' *is also used in* **exclamations**. For instance, the exclamation '**What!**' can be used to express surprise or disbelief.

(a) What nonsense!

(b) What a shame!

(c) What a beautiful day!

In written English, an exclamation must be followed by an exclamation mark: **!**

Indirect questions :

A direct question forms a complete sentence in itself, ***an indirect question is part of a longer sentence***.As well as being used at the beginning of direct questions, interrogative pronouns and adjectives can also be used at the beginning of **indirect** questions.

The following examples show the difference between a direct question and an indirect question :

Who is there?	*Direct Question*
She wants to know who is there.	*Indirect Question*
Will you tell me who is there?	*Indirect Question*

The first example '**Who is there?**' is a direct question. In the second example, **'who is there'** is an indirect question which is part of a longer statement. In the third example, '**who is there**' is also an indirect question which is part of a longer question.

As well as being used at the beginning of direct questions, ***interrogative pronouns and adjectives can also be used at the beginning of indirect questions :***

(a) Interrogative word as the subject :

When the '**Wh' word** is the subject of a verb, or modifies the subject of a verb, the word order of an indirect question is usually the same as that of a direct question.

Look at the following examples;

(a) **What** hashappened?	*Direct Question*
We shall ask **what** has happened.	*Indirect Question*
(b) Which **student** won the match?	*Direct Question*
They will ask which **student** won the match.	*Indirect Question*

In the first pair of examples, the interrogative pronoun **'what'** is the subject of the verb '**has happened**'. In the second pair of examples, the interrogative adjective '**which**' modifies '**student**', the subject of the verb '**won**'. In both pairs of examples, the word order of the indirect questions is the same as that of the direct questions.

(b) Interrogative word as the object of a verb or preposition :

When the '**Wh' word** is the object of a verb or preposition, or modifies the object of a verb or preposition , the word order of an indirect question differs from that of a direct question. In a direct question, the first auxiliary precedes the subject, and the auxiliary '**to do**' must be used for verbs in the simple present and simple past. In an indirect question, the subject precedes the verb, and the auxiliary **to do** is not used. Thus, in an indirect question, the word order used is the same as that used for an affirmative statement.

Look at the difference in word order:

(a) What is **she** doing? — *Direct Question*
I will ask what **she** is doing. — *Indirect Question*

(b) What story did **Ram** tell you? — *Direct Question*
I wonder what story **Ram** told you. — *Indirect Question*

(c) Which does **he** prefer? — *Direct Question*
We asked which **he** prefers. — *Indirect Question*

(d) Whom did **she** meet? — *Direct Question*
Tell me whom **she** met. — *Indirect Question*

(e) To whom has **he** sent the invitations? — *Direct Question*
They will ask to whom **he** has sent the invitations. — *Indirect Question*

(f) For which guest did **they** make the arrangements? — *Direct Question*
Do you know for which guest **they** made the arrangements? — *Indirect Question*

As shown in the above examples, when the interrogative word is the object of a verb or preposition, or modifies the object of a verb or preposition, the first auxiliary precedes the subject in a direct question, but the subject precedes the verb in an indirect question.

(c) The verb 'To Be' with a noun or pronoun complement :

When '**what**' or '**who**' is followed by both; the verb '**to be**' and a noun or pronoun complement of the verb, the word order of an indirect question usually differs from that of a direct question. As illustrated in the following examples, *in a direct question, the verb '**to be**' is followed by its complement; whereas in an indirect question, the verb '**to be**' is usually preceded by its complement.*

In each of the following examples, the verb **to be** is underlined, and its noun or pronoun complement is printed in bold type.

What is **this**? — *Direct Question*
Can you tell me what **this** is? — *Indirect Question*
What was **that noise**? — *Direct Question*
I wonder what **that noise** was. — *Indirect Question*
What time is **it**? — *Direct Question*
Ask him what time **it** is. — *Indirect Question*
Who is **he**? — *Direct Question*
Do you know who **he** is? — *Indirect Question*
Who was **that girl**? — *Direct Question*
I will ask who **that girl** was. — *Indirect Question*
Whose books are **these**? — *Direct Question*
I wonder whose books **these** are. — *Indirect Question*

Similarly, when **which** is followed by the *verb '**to be**', followed by a pronoun*, the pronoun complement generally precedes the verb in an indirect question.

Which was **it**? — *Direct Question*
I want to know which **it** was. — *Indirect Question*
Which organization is **that**? — *Direct Question:*
Please ask which organization **that** is. — Indirect question

However, when '**which**' is followed by *the verb '**to be**' followed by a noun or noun phrase*, the noun complement often follows the verb in an indirect question.

Which <u>is</u> **the Qutab road**?________________ *Direct Question*
Please tell me which <u>is</u> **the Qutab road**.________________ *Indirect Question*
Which animals <u>are</u> **predators**?________________ *Direct Question*
He wants to know which animals <u>are</u> **predators**.________________ *Indirect Question*

It should be noted that in sentences with the verb **'to be'**, the word order of indirect questions differs from that of direct questions only when the verb is accompanied by a <u>noun</u> or <u>pronoun</u> complement.

If the *verb **to be** is accompanied by an <u>adjective</u>*, the word order of direct and indirect questions is the same. In each of the following examples, the verb **to be** is underlined, and the accompanying adjective is printed in bold type :

Who <u>is</u> **here**?________________ *Direct Question*
I will ask who <u>is</u> **here**.________________ *Indirect Question*
Who <u>was</u> **sad**?________________ *Direct Question*
Tell me who <u>was</u> **sad**.________________ *Indirect Question*
Which answer <u>is</u> **correct**?________________ *Direct Question*
Please tell us which answer <u>is</u> **correct**.________________ *Indirect Question*

CORRECT YOURSELF EXERCISE : QUESTION FRAMING

CYE : 01 Frame a question to get the following answers :

Q. 1. When ....?
Ans. I play football in the evening.
Q. 2 When ....?
Ans. He will go to Delhi next week.
Q. 3. How many ....?
Ans. She has two sons and a daughter..
Q. 4. Where ....?
Ans. He keeps his money in a nationalised bank.
Q. 5. How many ....?
Ans. There are 366 days in the leap year.
Q. 6. How much ....?
Ans. Our cow gives twenty kilo milk in a day.
Q. 7. Whose ....?
Ans. It (car) is mine.
Q. 8. How old ....?
Ans. My son is ten years old.
Q. 9. Have..?
Ans. Yes, I have paid my tuition fees.
Q. 10. Who ....?
Ans. Mr. Sharma teaches us Physics.

CYE : 02 Frame a question to get the following answer :

Q. 1. Why ....?
Ans. He has gone to the railway station to see off his cousin.
Q. 2. Who ....?
Ans. It is my friend Rajendra (at the gate).

Q. 3. How many ....?
Ans. I got three prizes.
Q. 4. How far ....?
Ans. It (my village) is forty kilometers from here.
Q. 5. How much ....?
Ans. We buy two kilo milk of cow daily.
Q. 6. What ....?
Ans. My hobbies are reading novels and making friends.
Q. 7. Which ....?
Ans. I play football and cricket.
Q. 8. Could..?
Ans. No, she could not catch the train.
Q. 9. What ....?
Ans. He (my brother) is an engineer.
Q. 10. Do ....?
Ans. Yes, we have tea in the morning.

CYE : 03 Frame a question to get the following answers :

Q. 1. How far .... ?
Ans. It (Delhi) is 160 kilometers from here.
Q. 2. What ....?
Ans. I am writing a letter.
Q. 3. How ....?
Ans. She was welcomed warmly by her friends.
Q. 4. Where ....?
Ans. You can find it on the table.
Q. 5. Why ....?
Ans. We eat to live.
Q. 6. Are ....?
Ans. Yes , I'm afraid of ghosts.
Q. 7. How many ....?
Ans. I made 58 runs yesterday.
Q. 8. Who ....?
Ans. My friend has invited me.
Q. 9. How long ....?
Ans. We have been living in this country for three years only.
Q. 10. When ....?
Ans. I go to school at seven 'o clock in the morning.
Q. 11. Is there..?
Ans. Yes, there are three cinema halls in our town.
Q. 12. How often ....?
Ans. I go to the cinema every Sunday.
Q. 13. How ....?
Ans. He (my father) is 55.

Q. 14. Who ....?

Ans. Mr. S.K. Jain is my class teacher.

Q. 15. When ....?

Ans. I reached home at 9 p.m.

SOLUTIONS : CORRECT YOURSELF EXERCISE

Solutions CYE : 01

1. When do you play football ?
2. When will he go to Delhi. ?
3. Howmany children has she ?
4. Where does he keep his money ?
5. Howmany days are there in the leap year ?
6. Howmuch milk does your cow give in a day?
7. Whose car is it ?
8. How old is your son ?
9. Have you paid your tuition fees ?
10. Who teaches you Physics ?

Solutions CYE : 02

1. Why has he gone to the railway station ?
2. Who is at the gate ?
3. How many prizes did you get ?
4. How far is your village from here ?
5. How much milk of cow do you buy daily ?
6. What are your hobbies ?
7. Which games do you play ?
8. Could she catch the train ?
9. What is your brother ?
10. Do you have tea in the morning ?

Solutions CYE : 03

1. How far is Delhi from here ?
2. What are you doing/writing ?
3. How was she welcomed by her friends ?
4. Where can I find it ?
5. Why do we eat ?
6. Are you afraid of ghosts ?
7. How many runs did you make yesterday?
8. Who has invited you on this occasion ?
9. How long have you been living in this country ?
10. When do you go to school ?
11. Is there any cinema hall in your town ?
12. How often do you go to the cinema ?
13. How old is your father ?
14. Who is your class teacher ?
15. When did you reach home ?

21

Transformation of Sentences

The transformation of a sentence means **to change it from one grammatical form to another, without changing its meaning**. A sentence can be transformed to another grammatical form in various ways.

WAYS OF TRANSFORMATION

A. Interchanging degree of Adjective :

We can transform sentences by changing degree of adjective in the following ways:

There are three degrees of adjectives:

1. Positive, 2. Comparative, 3. Superlative.

1. Changing positive to comparative

Positive degree is used in *three structures* :

I. As..........as, II. So...........as, III. No other.......as...as..

I. As.......as :

	Positive	Comparative
(a)	Hira is as tall as Ram.	Ram is not taller than Hira.
(b)	Shalu is as intelligent as Ram.	Ram is not more intelligent than Shalu.
(c)	She is as beautiful as her sister.	Her sister is not more beautiful than she.
(d)	Ramesh is as wise as his father.	His father is not wiser than Ramesh.

II. So..........as :

(a)	Ram is not so strong as Shyam.	Shyam is stronger than Ram.
(b)	Sita is not so beautiful as Rani.	Rani is more beautiful than Sita.
(c)	She is not so intelligent as her brother.	Her brother is more intelligent than she.
(d)	Raju is not so wise as Rahim.	Rahim is wiser than Raju.

III. No other.......as.........as:

(a) No other city in Rajasthan is as beautiful as Jaipur. *Positive*
Jaipur is more beautiful than any other city in Rajasthan. *Comparative*

(b) No other student in college is as strong as Rahim. *Positive*
Rahim is stronger than any other student in college. *Comparative*

(c) No other book in the market is as good as this. *Positive*
This is better than any other book in the market. *Comparative*

(d) No other girl in the college is as beautiful as Sita. *Positive*
Sita is more beautiful than any other girl in the college. *Comparative*

2. Interchange of positive, comparative and superlative :

(a) This is most beautiful building in our town. *Superlative*
This is the more beautiful than any other building in our town. *Comparative*
No other building in our town is so beautiful as this. *Positive*

(b) Ramesh is the strongest man in the village. *Superlative*
Ramesh is stronger than any other man in the village. *Comparative*
No other man in the village is so strong as Ramash. *Positive*

(c) Kolkata is the largest city in India. *Superlative*
Kolkata is larger than any other city in India. *Comparative*
No other city in India is as large as kolkata. *Positive*

(d) Mohan is the best student in our college. *Superlative*
Mohan is better than any other student in our college. *Comparative*
No other student of our college is as good as mohan . *Positive*

NOTE (i) *Structure :* **One of the + superlative**

(a) Kalidas was one of the greatest poets. *Superlative*
Kalidas was greater than most other poets. *Comparative*
Very few other poets were as great as Kalidas. Positive

(b) Mumbai is one of the most beautiful cities in India. *Superlative*
Mumbai is more beautiful than most other cities in India. *Comparative*
Very few other cities in India are as beautiful as Mumbai. Positive

(ii) **Removal of adverb 'Too'**
'Too' means *excess*. The structure *too....to*, shows a negativity.

(a) He is too weak to run.
He is so weak that he cannot run.

(b) She is too old to climb up the tree.
She is so old that she cannot climb up the tree.

(c) He was too tired to do anything.
He was so tired that he could not do anything.

(d) The mountain is too high to climb it up.
The mountain is so high that one cannot climb it up.

(e) The wall is too hot to touch.
The wall is so hot that one cannot touch it.

(f) The scene was too pathetic to see.
The scene was so pathetic that one couldn't see that.

B. Interchange of Affirmative and Negative Sentences :

1. Using Antonyms:

Affirmative	Negative
(a) He is a rich man.	He is not a poor man.
(b) I am innocent.	I am not guilty.
(c) The boss is always night.	The boos is never wrong.
(d) Man is mortal.	Man is not immortal.

(e) This knife is sharp.	This knife is not blunt.
(f) Ram dislikes you.	Ram does not like you.

Negative	**Affirmative**
(a) He is not an honest person.	He is a dishonest person.
(b) You do not trust him.	You distrust him.
(c) He is not a wise fellow.	He is a foolish fellow.
(d) His habits are not good.	His habits are bad.
(e) She is not a dull girl.	She is an intelligent girl.
(f) You should not deny it.	You should accept it.

2. Using double negatives :

Affirmative	**Negative**
(a) I love her.	I am not without love for her.
(b) I have a car.	I am not without a car.
(c) Every rose has thorns	There is no rose without thorns.
(d) She is wise .	She is not without wisdom.

Negative	**Affirmative**
(a) There is no smoke without fire.	Where there is fire there is smoke.
(b) I am not without money.	I have money.
(c) He left no plan untried.	He tried every plan.
(d) No gains without pains.	For gains one has to take pains.

3. Using 'To fail':

Affirmative	**Negative**
(a) He played the match.	He did not fail to play the match.
(b) He delivered his speech.	He didn't fail to deliver his speech.
(c) I saw the Taj Mahal.	I did not fail to see the Taj Mahal.
(d) Consult the doctor.	Do not fail to consult the doctor.

Negative	**Affirmative**
(a) He couldn't catch the train.	He failed to catch the train.
(b) She didn't fail to help the needy.	She helped the needy.
(c) He couldn't see me.	He failed to see me.
(d) He couldn't meet the chairman.	He failed to meet the chairman.

4. Miscellaneous sentences :

Affirmative	**Negative**
(a) Only the poor can beg like this.	None but the poor can beg like this.
(b) Only a fool can say like this.	None but a fool can say like this.
(c) The brave alone deserves the award.	None but the brave deserves the award.
(d) Only Ram was present there.	None but Ram was present there.
(e) As soon as I reached there, it started raining.	No sooner did I reach there than it started raining.
(f) As soon as he saw the police, he ran away.	No sooner did he see the police than he ran
(g) It always pours when it rains.	It never rains but pours.

Negative	**Affirmative**
(a) None but a girl can talk like this.	Only a girl can talk like this.
(b) None but Nisha can solve it.	Only Nisha can solve it.

(c) No sooner did the thief see the police than he ram away.	As soon as the thief saw the police, he ran away. than he ran away.
(d) No sooner did I hear the noise, than I came out.	As soon as I heard the noise I came out.
(e) I never rains but pours, .	It always pours, when it rains.
(f) There is nobody but like mangoes.	Everybody likes mangoes.
(g) It is a unique item.	There is no item like this.
(h) All the people wept.	There was none but wept.
(i) She seldom comes here.	She does not come here very often.
(j) He goes to office daily.	He never absents himself from office.
(k) We won all the matches.	We didn't lose any match.
(l) His position became worse gradually.	His position didn't improve.
(m) Smoking is prohibited here.	Don't smoke here.
(n) Have patience please.	Don't be impatient.
(o) Keep silence.	Don't make a noise.
(p) A few persons were present there.	Not many persons were present there.
(q) Work hard lest you should fail.	Work hard so that you may not fail.
(r) Run fast lest you should miss the train.	Run fast so that you may not miss the train.

C. Interchange of Assertive and Interrogative Sentences:

1. Interrogative sentences beginning with *Helping Verbs* (Auxiliaries) :

Interrogative	Assertive
(a) Am I not your friend?	I am your friend.
(b) Isn't she beautiful?	She is beautiful.
(c) Didn't I study?	I did study.
(d) Can a blind see?	A blind can't see.
(e) Don't I love her?	I love her.
(f) Shall we ever forget you?	We shall never forget you.
(g) Haven't I a car?	I have a car.
(h) Did I tell a lie?	I did not tell a lie.
(i) Don't I know you?	I know you
(j) Does not the earth revolve round the sun?	The earth revolves round the sun.
(k) Won't you have a cup of tea?	Have a cup of tea.

2. Interrogative sentence beginning with 'Wh' words :

Interrogative	Assertive
(a) Who does not know Amitabh?	Everyone knows Amitabh.
(b) Who does not love his mother?	Everyone loves his mother.
(c) Who will tolerate such an insult?	No one will tolerate such an insult.
(d) Who can live more than 100 years?	No one can live more than 100 years.
(e) Who is more powerful than God?	No one is more powerful than God.
(f) Who does not love his country?	Everyone loves his country.
(g) Who can surpass him in intelligence?	No one can surpass him in intelligence.
(h) What more can I do?	I can't do any more.
(i) Why waste money here?	It is useless wasting money here.
(j) When will you have sense?	You will never have sense.
(k) Why cry over spilt milk?	It is no use crying over spilt milk.

(l) What if you are more intelligent than I?	It does not matter much, even though you are more intelligent than I.
(m) Where will I have peace of mind?	I will nowhere have peace of mind.
(n) How can I forget you?	I can't forget you.
(o) How can I repay you?	I can't repay you.
(p) How does it matter, if you lose?	It does not matter much even if you lose.

D. Interchange of Exclamatory and Assertive Sentences :

1. Exclamatory sentences beginning with What/How :

Exclamatory	Assertive
(a) What a bird it was !	It was a beautiful bird.
(b) How fast she moves!	She moves very fast.
(c) How hot it is !	It is very hot.
(d) What a nice weather it was!	It was a very nice weather.
(e) How odd it looks!	It looks very odd.
(f) What a busy life she leads!	She leads a very busy life.
(g) What a scene!	It is a beautiful scene.
(h) What an art!	It is a great work of art.
(i) What a hotel!	It is a grand hotel.
(j) What a fall!	It is a great fall.

2. Exclamatory sentences beginning with 'Oh that/ O that/ would that/ Alas ?

Exclamatory	Assertive
(a) Would that I had not wasted my money!	I wish I had not wasted my money.
(b) O that she were young again!	I wish that she were young again.
(c) Alas! She died so young.	It is sad that she died so young.
(d) O that I were a king!	I wish that I were a king.

3. Exclamatory sentences beginning with 'Hurrah/ Bravo/ Well-done ?

Exclamatory	Assertive
(a) Bravo! You secured highest marks.	It is a matter of praise that you secured highest marks.
(b) Hurrah! we have won the match!	It is a matter of joy that we have won the match.
(c) Well done! you got selected!	It is matter of praise that you got selected.
(d) Hurrah! he scored a goal!	It is matter of joy that he scored a goal.
(e) Fie, fie! he is a thief .	it is a matter of contempt that he is a thief.
(f) Fie, fie! she is a prostitute.	It is a matter of contempt that she is a prostitute.

4. Exclamatory sentences beginning with if only :

(a) If only I could meet her once.	I wish to meet her once.
(b) If only I could once get selected.	I wish to get once selected .

5. Miscellaneous Sentences

(a) How kind of you to help me! *Exclamatory*
You were kind enough to help me. *Assertive*
It was kind of you to help me. *Assertive*

(b) How foolish of him to abuse the chairman! *Exclamatory*
He was foolish enough to abuse the chairman. *Assertive*
It was foolish of him to abuse the chairman. *Assertive*

(c) A navyman afraid of water ! *Exclamatory*
It is strange that a navyman should be afraid of water. *Assertive*
(d) An army man and such a coward! *Exclamatory*
It is shocking that an army man should be such a coward. *Assertive*
(e) To think of our getting married ! *Exclamatory*
It is strange that we should get married. *Assertive*
(f) To think of my seeing you in this foreign land! *Exclamatory*
It is strange that I should see you in this foreign land. Assertive

E. Interchange parts of speech

1. Changing into verb :

(a) Smoking is injurious to health. *Adjective*
Smoking injures health. *verb*
(b) You should give assistance to him. *Noun*
You should assist him. *Verb*
(c) Grahmbell made the invention of telephone. *Noun*
Grahmbell invented the telephone *Verb*
(d) Her action caused disgrace to the country. *Noun*
Her action disgraced the country. *Verb*
(e) You must render help to her. *Noun*
You must help her. *Verb*

2. Changing into noun :

(a) Who discovered India? *Verb*
Who made the discovery of India? *Noun*
(b) Who invented computer? *Verb*
Who made the invention of computer? *Noun*
(c) Listen to him attentively. *Adverb*
Listen to him with attention. *Noun*
(d) She is healthy . *Adjective*
She enjoys good health. *Noun*
(e) Walk carefully. *Adverb*
Walk with care. *Noun*
(f) He fought courageously. *Adverb*
He fought with courage. *Noun*

3. Changing into adjective :

(a) He confessed his guilt. *Noun*
He confessed that he was guilty. *Adjective*
(b) Wine injures liver. *Verb*
Wine is injurious to liver. *Adjective*
(c) Fortunately she escaped unhurt. *Adverb*
She was fortunate to escape unhurt. *Adjective*
(d) He solved the puzzle easily. *Adverb*
It was easy for him to solve the puzzle. *Adjective*

4. **Changing into Adverb :**

(a) His success is sure. *Adjective*
He will surely succeed. *Adverb*
(b) He does not intend to speak. *Verb*
He does not speak intentionally. *Adverb*
(c) Sita sang a sweet song. *Adjective*
Sita sang a song sweetly. *Adverb*
(d) He fought with courage . *Noun*
He fought courageously. *Adverb*

F. Transformation of conditional sentences:

(a) If you work hard, you will pass.
Unless you work hard you will not pass.
Work hard and you will pass.
Work hard in case you want to pass.
Should you work hard you would pass.
(b) Had he come to me, I would have helped him.
If he had come to me, I would have helped him.
(c) In case you support me, I will make a protest
If you support me,I will make a protest.
Provided you support me, I will make a protest.
(d) One more try and you will achieve it.
If you make one more try, you will achieve it.
(e) If she does not turn up, you will get the job.
In case she doesn't turn up you will get the job.
Supposing she does not turn up, you will get the job.

G. Conversion of simple / compound / complex Sentences:

1. **Conversion of simple sentence into compound :** A simple sentence has one principal clause and a compound sentence has two principal clauses which are joined together by a coordinating conjunction. A simple sentence can be converted into a compound sentence by enlarging a word or a phrase into a coordinate clause as in sentences (b), (c), (d), (e), (f) etc. below :

(a) In spite of his poverty he is trustworthy. *simple*
He is poor yet he is trustworthy . *compound*
(b) The sun having risen the fog disappeared. *simple*
The sun rose and the fog disappeared. *compound*
(c) Besides being beautiful she is intelligent. *simple*
She is beautiful as well as she is intelligent. *compound*
(d) The chief rewarded the officer for his excellent work. *simple*
The clerk did excellent work and so the chief rewarded him. *compound*
(e) Seeing a lion he fled away. *simple*
He saw a lion and he fled away. *compound*
(f) Notwithstanding his problems he is trying again. *simple*
He has problems yet he is trying again. *compound*
(g) You should work hard to achieve your goal. *simple*
You should work hard or you can't achieve your goal. *compound*
(h) The officer punished the boy for his misbehaviour. *simple*
The boy misbehaved so the officer punished him. *compound*

2. Conversion of compound (double) sentences to simple sentences :

To change a compound sentence into simple ,ensure that after conversion we have only one finite verb :

(a) He finished his work and put away the tools. *compound*
Having finished his work he put away the tools. *simple*

(b) Not only did her mother give her gift but her sister too. *compound*
Besides her mother giving her gift her sister also did the same. *simple*

(c) She must not be late or she will be fined. *compound*
In the event of her being late she will be fined. *simple*

(d) You must either pay the rent at once or vacate the godown. *compound*
Failing prompt payment the godown must be vacated by you. *simple*

(e) You must eat or you cannot live. *compound*
You must eat to live. *simple*

3. Conversion of compound sentence into complex sentence :

A compound sentence is composed of two simple sentences joined together by a coordinating conjunction. To convert a compound sentence into a complex one , we need to make one clause principal and another subordinate :

(a) Run fast or you will miss the train. *compound*
Unless you run fast you will miss the train. *complex*

(b) I am not well so I shall not come to the office. *compound*
I shall not come to the office as I am not well. *complex*

(c) She was ill so I helped her. *compound*
I helped her because she was ill. *complex*

(d) Check his room and you will find the money. *compound*
If you check his room you will find the money. *complex*

(e) He is innocent and I know it. *compound*
I know that he is innocent. *complex*

(f) She lost her child and she found it. *compound*
She found her child that she lost. *complex*

4. Conversion of complex sentences into compound sentences :

To convert a complex sentence into a compound one , we need to use coordinating conjunction; and the subordinate clause should be changed to independent clause :

(a) I am certain you have stolen my purse. *complex*
You have stolen my purse and of this I am certain. *compound*

(b) I am glad that she has recovered from cholera. *complex*
She has recovered from cholera and I am glad of it. *compound*

(c) We can prove that the sun rises in the east. *complex*
The the sun rises in the east and we can prove it. *compound*

(d) I have found the bag that I had lost. *complex*
I had lost a bag but I have found it. *compound*

(e) As soon as she got the message she left in a car. *complex*
She got the message and immediately she left in a car. *compound*

(f) We sow so that we may reap. *complex*
We wish to reap so we sow. *compound*

5. Conversion of simple sentence into complex sentence :

A simple sentence can be converted to a complex sentence by expanding a word or phrase into a subordinate clause. This clause may be a Noun, Adjective or Adverb clause :

(a) I know his address. *simple*
I know what his address is. *complex*

(b) She accepted her guilt. *simple*
She accepted that she was guilty. *complex*

(c) You should work hard to achieve your goal. *simple*
You should work hard so that you can achieve your goal. *complex*

(d) I drink to enjoy. *simple*
I drink so that I can enjoy. *complex*

(e) He is too poor to pay his fees. *simple*
He is so poor that he can't pay his fees. *complex*

(f) This is my office. *simple*
This is the office where I work. *complex*

6. Conversion of complex sentences into simple sentences :

While converting a complex sentence into simple sentence, ensure that after conversion you have only one finite verb.Look at the followng examples:

Noun Clause

(a) Tell me where you live. *complex*
Tell me your address. *simple*

(b) It is informed that all students found with papers will be rusticated. *complex*
According to the information all students found with papers will be rusticated. *simple*

(c) He commented how beautiful the girl was. *complex*
He commented on the girls's beauty. *simple*

(d) How long he will stay is uncertain. *complex*
The duration of his stay is doubtful. *simple*

Adjective Clause

(a) I have no advice that I can offer her. *complex*
I have no advice to offer her. *simple*

(b) We came upon the quarter where she lived. *complex*
We came upon hers quarter. *simple*

(c) She died in the village where her parents were born. *complex*
She died in her parental village. *simple*

(d) The time which is lost is lost for ever. *complex*
A lost time is lost for ever. *simple*

Adverb Clause

(a) The colonel was annoyed that I had not obeyed his orders. *complex*
The colonel was annoyed at my not having obeyed his orders. *simple*

(b) You can eat as much as you like. *complex*
You can eat to your heart's content. *simple*

(c) She will not pay unless she is forced. *complex*
She will pay only by force. *simple*

(d) She has succeeded better than she hoped. *complex*
She has succeeded beyond her hopes. *simple*
(e) He was so tired that he could not walk. *complex*
He was too tired to walk. *simple*

CORRECT YOURSELF EXERCISE : TRANSFORMATION

CYE : 01 Convert the following simple sentences into compound sentences :

1. The teacher punished the boy for disobedience.
2. Running at top speed, he got out of breath.
3. By his pleasant manners he gained many friends.
4. Raleigh, taking off his cloak politely, placed it in the muddy street.
5. In this tower sat the poet gazing on the sea.

Transform the following sentences according of the diirections given in brakets :

6. If you do not take exercise, you will be ill. (Convert this into a compound sentence.)
7. The moment which is lost, is lost for ever. (Convert this into a simple sentence.)
8. Self-made men are always respected. (Turn this into a complex sentence.)
9. He will not pay unless he is compelled. (Turn this into a simple sentence.)
10. In the absence of the cat the mice will play. (Turn this into a complex sentence.)
11. To everyone's surprise, the enterprise completely failed. (Convert.) this into a compound sentence.)
12. You must work hard to win the first prize. (Convert this into a compound sentence.)
13. He was very tired but he kept on working. (Turn this into a simple sentence.)
14. His silence proves his guilt. (Turn this into a complex sentence.)
15. Consult the dictionary and you will find the meaning of this word. (Convert this into a complex sentence.)

CYE : 02 Join the following pairs into single sentences :

1. Storms may come. They may destroy the dam.
2. The girl has gone away. I wanted to marry her.
3. The king talked to a woman. The woman's four sons had been killed in the war.
4. He is very clever. He cannot be deceived.
5. Hiroshima was once a prosperous town. It is now a heap of ruins.
6. The moon rose. Their journey was not ended.

CYE : 03 Rewrite the sentences using 'than' (superlative to comparative degree) :

1. Switzerland is the most beautiful country in the world (use 'more beautiful').
2. Delhi is the biggest city of Inda (use 'bigger').
3. Mahima is the most beautiful girl in the class. (use 'more')
4. Morning walk is the best exercise for us. (use 'better').
5. Anil Ambani is the richest man in India (use 'richer').

CYE : 04 Rewrite the sentences using 'as .... as' (comparative to positive degree) :

1. Nikita is taller than Babita (use'tall').
2. Reeta is more intelligent than Nita (use 'intelligent').
3. America is richer than India (use 'rich').
4. Kavita's hair is more beautiful than Vimla's hair (use 'beautiful').

5. Alwar is bigger than Tonk (use 'big').
6. She is taller than any other girl in the school (use 'tall').
7. Mohan is poorer than any other man in the village (use 'poor').
8. My mother is more beautiful than any other lady in our colony (use 'beautiful').
9. Ganga is more famous river than any other river in India. (use 'famous')
10. Jodhpur is hotter than Simla (use 'hot').

CYE : 05 Change comparative to superlative:

1. Subhash Chandra Bose was greater than any other leader of India. (use 'the greatest ')
2. Kolkata is bigger than any other city of India. (use 'the biggest')
3. Iron is heavier than any other metal. (use 'the heaviest')
4. Everest is higher mountain in the world. (use 'the highest')
5. Sonu is fatter than any other boy in the house. (the fattest)
6. Rani is better than any other girl (use "the best").

CYE : 06 Interchange of exclamatory sentences to assertive sentences:

1. How cute she is !
2. What a beautiful sight it is!
3. What a stupid she is!
4. What a big building it is!
5. Oh that, I were the queen of Britain !
6. O that, I were a bird !
7. Alas! She died in an accident.
8. Bravo! You have done well.
9. Hurrah ! I won the game.
10. What an attractive person he is !
11. What a good book it is!
12. How fast she reads !
13. What a fine weather it is!
14. What a sight it is!
15. How funny!
16. What a hut!
17. What a style!
18. Oh that, I had the wings of bird!
19. Oh, for a beautiful car to drive !
20. If I were Miss -India !

CYE : 07 Interchange of exclamatory sentences to assertive sentences:

1. Such a woman and my wife!
2. How kind of her to help me!
3. Fie!fie! you are a murderer.
4. How sweetly she sings!
5. How sad was the sight of that deserted place!
6. What a girl she is!
7. What a lovely flower!
8. How strange!
9. Would that I had never left my village!
10. Would that my son were alive!
11. O for a cup of tea!
12. If only I could find my lost love!
13. A child and so brave!
14. How clever of him to cheat her!
15. How cool the moonlit night is!
16. Would that I were an I.P.S. officer!
17. If I could only see her!

CYE : 08 Transform the following sentences into assertive :

1. Is this the kind of dress to wear in marriage party?
2. Won't you come in?
3. Can the dumb speak?
4. Didn't I tell her to stay here?
5. Is it not a wise step?
6. Why wait for him?
7. Do you like to lose money?
8. Haven't I warned you against the danger?
9. Why to accuse him?
10. How can one change one's nature?

CYE : 09 Use the following words as noun and as verb:

1. Close, 2. Court, 3. Back, 4. Head, 5. Light.

CYE : 10 Use the following words as noun and as adjective:

1. Fast, 2. Less, 3. Like, 4. Down, 5. Master.

CYE :11 Use the following words, as adverb and as adjective:

1. Round, 2. Next, 3. Near, 4. Well, 5. Slow.

CYE : 12 Transform the following simple sentences into compound sentences.

1. He should work hard to pass the examination.
2. Besides making a promise, she keeps it.
3. For all the problems, he is happy.
4. The principal rusticated the boy for misbehaviour.
5. The sun having risen, the fog dispersed.
6. He died a brilliant death, leaving an example to the world.
7. Having finished his work, he went to market.
8. Owing to ill health, she could not prepare the breakfast.

CYE : 13 Transform the following simple sentences into complex :

1. She owed hr success to my support.
2. Wise persons do not talk nonsense.
3. His silence proves his guilt.
4. Non-vegetarians are not allowed to enter into the temple.
5. Listen to the elders.
6. We are sure to win the match.
7. Intelligent students always succeed.
8. His ambition is to become an engineer.
9. Tell me your address.
10. I have no moneey to spend.

CYE : 14 Transform the following compound sentences into complex sentences :

1. He is a poor man, but he is honest man.
2. My brother gave me a watch and I have lost it.
3. She was very tired and so she didn't cook food.
4. She is still in teens, but she has the wisdom of a matured woman.
5. I had lost the purse but I have found it now.
6. She is very affable and so I love her.
7. He is doing his best and I am sure of it.
8. Be sincere and you will be respected by every one.
9. Send the money in advance or you will not get the magazine.
10. You are a teetotaller and I know it.

CYE : 15 Transform the following affirmative sentences into negative:

1. My sister is wise.
2. That is impossible.
3. I shall always remember your kindness.
4. He is always careful.

5. A true man is always right.
6. Sita's voice is harsh.
7. We like him.
8. This student is dull.
9. We are innocent.
10. She is always present .
11. They won the game.
12. I always treat her fairly.
13. This knife is blunt.
14. Everyone was hopeful.

CYE : 16 Transform the following affirmative sentences into negative:

1. She is a bad teacher.
2. They were doubtful whether it was her.
3. Ram is a dishonest man.
4. He is sometimes foolish.
5. My uncle is a poor man.
6. Always speak the truth.
7. I am always happy.
8. Everyone hates you.
9. Everyone hides his sorrow.
10. Everyone praised her dance.
11. I love him.
12. She had clothes.
13. Every rose has thorn.

CYE : 17 Transform the following affirmative sentences into negative:

1. Only the rich can buy that house.
2. Only Ram can solve this problem.
3. Only Manish came to see you.
4. As soon as the thief saw the police,he ran away.
5. As soon as he saw the monkey, he fled.
6. As soon as I went inside, it began to rain.
7. Only seniors need apply.
8. He disbelieves me.
9. He failed to catch the thief .
10. It is wrong to do this work.
11. Nisha is always sure.
12. Ram will stay here.
13. She dislikes you.

CYE : 18 Rewrite the following sentences :

1. Sachin is the best cricket player in India. (use 'better')
2. Mr. Ganguli is the richest man of our city. (use 'richer')
3. Neetu is the cleverest girl of our college. (use 'cleverer')
4. Hockey is the most popular game in India. (use 'more populer')
5. Akbar was the greatest Muslim ruler in India. (use 'greater')

6. Morning walk is the best exercise for young people (use 'better')
7. Pt. Nehru was one of the greatest leader of India. (use 'greater')
8. Rahul Dravid is one of the best batsman of our country. (use 'better')
9. Atal Bihari Vajpayee was the most impressive Prime Minister of India. (use 'more impressive')
10. Nisha is the most intelligent student in the school. (use "more intelligent")

CYE : 19 Rewrite the following sentences using positive degree :

1. Mumbai is the best part of our country (use 'good').
2. My brother is the wisest man in the office. (use 'wise')
3. Naresh is the poorest man in our village.
4. Mr. Rohan is the most popular member in our office (use 'popular').
5. Iron is the most useful metal (use 'useful').
6. Bikaner is the hottest city in Rajasthan (use 'hot').
7. Shatabdi Express is the fastest train (use 'fast')
8. Nisha is the tallest girl of our school. (use 'tall').
9. Rajasthan is the most desert state of India. (use 'desert')
10. America is the richest country in the world. (use 'rich')
11. A lion is the strongest animal in the forest. (use 'strong')

SOLUTIONS : CORRECT YOURSELF EXERCISE

Solutions CYE : 01

1. The boy was disobedient, and so the teacher punished him.
2. He ran at top speed so he got out of breath.
3. He has pleasant manners and therefore he gained many friends.
4. Raleigh took off his cloak politely and placed it in the muddy street.
5. The poet sat in this tower and gazed on the sea.
6. Take exercise otherwise you will be ill.
7. The moment once lost is lost for ever.
8. The men who are self-made are always respected.
9. He will pay only under compulsion.
10. The mice will play when the cat is absent.
11. The enterprise completely failed and it surprised everyone.
12. You must work hard so that you many win the first prize.
13. In spite of being very tired he kept on working.
14. The fact that he is silent proves his guilt.Or
    His silence proves that he is guilty.
15. If you consult the dictionary you will find the meaning of this word.

Solutions CYE : 02

1. Storms may come and destroy the dam.
2. I wanted to marry the girl who had gone away.
3. The king talked to the woman whose four sons had been killed in the war.
4. He is too clever to be deceived. *Or*
   He is so clever that he cannot be deceived.
5. Hiroshima, which was once a prosperous town, is now a heap of ruins.
6. The moon rose before the end of their journey.

Solutions CYE : 03

1. Switzerland is more beautiful than any other country in the world.
2. Delhi is bigger than any other city in the world.
3. Mahima is more beautiful than any other girl in the class.
4. Morning walk is better than any other exercise for us.
5. Anil Ambani is richer than any other man in India.

Solutions CYE : 04

1. Babita is not as tall as Nikita.
2. Nita is not as intelligent as Reeta.
3. India is not so rich as America.
4. Vimla's hair is not as beautiful as Kavita's hair.
5. Tonk is not as big as Alwar.
6. No other girl in the school is as tall as she.
7. No other man in the village is as poor as Mohan.
8. No other lady in our colony is as beautiful as my mother.
9. No other river in India is as famous as Ganga.
10. Simla is not as hot as Jodhpur.

Solutions CYE : 05

1. Subhash Chandra Bose was the greatest leader of India.
2. Kolkata is the biggest city of India.
3. Iron is the heaviest metal.
4. Everest is the highest mountain in the world.
5. Sonu is the fattest boy in the house.
6. Rani is the best girl.

Solutions CYE : 06

1. She is very cute.
2. It is a very beautiful sight.
3. She is a great stupid.
4. It is a very big building.
5. I wish that I were the queen of Britain.
6. I wish I were a bird.
7. It is sad that she died in an accident.
8. It is a matter of praise that you have done well.
9. It is joyful that I won the game.
10. He is a very attractive person.
11. It is a very good book.
12. She reads very fast.
13. It is very fine weather.
14. It is a lovely sight.
15. It is very funny.
16. It is a beautiful hut.
17. It is a good style.
18. I wish that I had the wings of bird.
19. I wish that I had a beautiful car to drive.
20. I wish that I were Miss-India.

Solutions CYE : 07

1. It is shocking that such a woman should be my wife.
2. She was kind enough to help me.
3. It is a matter of contempt that you are a murderer.
4. She sings very sweetly.
5. That deserted place presented very sad sight.
6. She is a peculiar girl.
7. This is a very lovely flower.
8. It is very strange.
9. I wish I had never left my village.
10. I wish my son were alive.
11. I wish I had a cup of tea.
12. I wish I could find my lost love.
13. It is strange that a child should be so brave.
14. He was clever enough to cheat her.
15. The moonlit night is very cool.
16. I wish I were an I.P.S.officer.
17. I earnestly desire to see her.

Solutions CYE : 08

1. This is not the kind of dress to wear in marriage party.
2. You come in please .
3. The dumb can't speak.
4. I told her to stay here.
5. It is a wise step.
6. It is useless to wait for him.
7. You do not like to lose money.
8. I have warned you against the danger.
9. It is wrong to accuse him.
10. One can't change one's nature.

Solutions CYE : 09

1. **Close :**

   The metting came to a close at 6 p.m. (Noun)
   Please close the shop now. (Verb)

2. **Court :**

   I am going to attend the court of law tomorrow. (Noun)
   She is regularly courting her boss. (Verb)

3. **Back :**

   He carried the load on his back. (Noun)
   I am not going to back your arguments. (Verb)

4. **Head :**

   He has a big head full of white hair. (Noun)
   She headed the list of investors. (Verb)

5. **Light :**
There is no light in the corridor. (Noun)
Light the candle in the room. (Verb)

Solutions CYE : 10

1. **Fast :**
She keeps fast on every Tuesday. (Noun)
He is a fast runner. (Adjective)

2. **Less :**
I won't be contended with less. (Noun)
She paid less attention to sports. (Adjective)

3. **Like :**
You cannot see her like again. (Noun)
They are man of like physique and stature. (Adjective)

4. **Down :**
I have seen the ups and downs of business. (Noun)
The down train was very late yesterday. (Adjective)

5. **Master :**
She is my master. (Noun)
He conceived a master strategy. (Adjective)

Solutions CYE : 11

1. **Round :**
He brought her round to my point of view. (Adverb)
It is a round floor. (Adjective)

2. **Next :**
What next are you planning? (Adverb)
I shall meet you at the next crossing. (Adjective)

3. **Near :**
Come near and sit here. (Adverb)
She is my near relative. (Adjective)

4. **Well :**
Well begun is half done. (Adverb)
You are well now. (Adjective)

5. **Slow :**
She is workin in a slow manner. (Adverb)
She is a slowg worker. (Adjective)

Solutions CYE : 12

1. He should work hard or he will not pass the examination.
2. She not only makes a promise but also keeps it.
3. Though he is in great problems, yet he is happy.
4. The boy misbehaved so the principal rusticated him.

5. The sun rose and the fog dispersed.
6. He died a brilliant death and left an example to the world.
7. He finished his work and he went to market.
8. She was in ill health and so she could not prepare the breakfast.

Solutions CYE : 13

1. It was due to my support that she succeeded.
2. The persons who are wise do not talk nonsense.
3. The fact that he is silent proves his quilt.
4. If you are a non-vegetarian, you can't be allowed to enter into the temple.
5. Listen to what the elders say.
6. We are sure that we shall win the match.
7. The students who are intelligent always succeed.
8. His ambition is that he wants to become an engineer.
9. Tell me where you live.
10. I have no money that I can spend.

Solutions CYE : 14

1. He is a honest man although he is poor.
2. I have lost the watch which my brother gave me.
3. As she was very tired, she didn't cook food.
4. She has the wisdom of a matured woman, although she is still in teens.
5. I have found the purse that I had lost.
6. I love her because she is very affable.
7. I am sure that he is doing his best.
8. If you are sincere, you will be respected by every one.
9. You will not get the magazine unless you send the money in advance.
10. I know that you are a teetotaller.

Solutions CYE : 15

1. My sister is not a fool.
2. That is not possible.
3. I shall not forget your kindness.
4. He is your never careless.
5. A true man is never wrong.
6. Sita's voice is not sweet.
7. We do not dislike him.
8. This student is not intelligent.
9. We are not guilty.
10. She is never absent.
11. They did not lose the game.
12. I never treat her badly.
13. This knife is not sharp.
14. No one was without hope.

Solutions CYE : 16

1. She is not a good teacher.
2. They were not sure whether it was her.
3. Ram is not an honest man.
4. He is not always foolish.
5. My uncle is not a rich man.
6. Never tell a lie.
7. I am never unhappy.
8. There is no one who does not hate you.

9. There is no one who does not hide his sorrow.
10. There was none who did not praise her dance.
11. I am not without love for him.
12. She is not without clothes.
13. There is no rose without thorn.

Solutions CYE : 17

1. None but the rich can buy that house.
2. None but Ram can solve this problem.
3. None but Manish came to see you.
4. No sooner did the thief see the police than he ran away.
5. No sooner did he see the monkey than he fled.
6. No sooner did I go inside than it began to rain.
7. None but seniors need apply.
8. He did not believe me.
9. He could not catch the thief.
10. It is not right to do this work.
11. Nisha is never in doubt.
12. Ram will not go any where.
13. She does not like you.

Solutions CYE : 18

1. Sachin is better than any other cricket player in India.
2. Mr. Ganguli is richer than any other man of our city.
3. Neetu is cleverer than any other girl of our college.
4. Hockey is more popular than any other game in India.
5. Akbar was greater than any other Muslim ruler in India.
6. Morning walk is better than any other exercise for young people.
7. Pt. Nehru was greater than most other leaders of India
8. Rahul Dravid is better than most other batsman of our country.
9. Atal Bihari Vajpayee was more impressive than any other Prime Minister of India.
10. Nisha is more intelligent than any other student in the school.

Solutions CYE : 19

1. No other part of our country is so good as Mumbai.
2. No other man in the office is as wise as my brother.
3. No other man in our village is as poor as Naresh.
4. No other member in our office is so popular as Mr. Rohan.
5. No other metal is so useful as Iron.
6. No other city in Rajasthan is so hot as Bikaner.
7. No other train is so fast as Shatabdi Express.
8. No other girl is as tall as Nisha.
9. No other state of India is so desert as Rajasthan.
10. No other country in the world is so rich as America.
11. No other animal in the forest is as strong as lion.

22

Words Used as Different Parts of Speech

Traditional Grammar classifies words based on ***eight parts of speech* : the verb, the noun, the pronoun, the adjective, the adverb, the preposition, the conjunction, and the interjection.**

Each *part of speech* **explains not what the word *is*, but how the word *is used*. In fact, the same word can be a noun in one sentence and a verb or adjective in the next.**

It is difficult to say whether a particular word is a **noun** or a **verb .Only by studying the use and position of the *word in a sentence*, we can say that it *is used as noun or pronoun or as verb or as an adjective or an adverb*.** *We are giving below some of the important words which are used as different parts of speech in the sentences*. A careful study of the use of these words will help the students increasing their grammatical knowledge of words and their uses :

All :

Noun	All is well that ends well.
Adjective	All men are mortal.
Adverb	They are now all right.
Pronoun	All were in favour of the motion.

Any :

Pronoun	Do any of you know anything about her temperament?
Adjective	Take any magazine that you like.
Adverb	We must take lunch before doing any other work.

As :

Pronoun	He is not such a good man as looks.
Adverb	She wrote as fast as she could.
Conjunction	As he was poor so I helped him.

About :

Adverb	She wandered about in inner garments.
Preposition	There is nothing pleasing about her gait .

Above :

Noun	The blessings came from above.
Adverb	The Gods live above in heaven.
Prepostion	The sun was above our head at that time.

After :

Adverb	She arrived soon after .
Conjunction	She went away after her husband had left.
Preposition	He looks after his mother.

Age :

Noun	Age is more important than the physical fitness.
Verb	He is aging, my dear.

Arm :

Noun	He received a serious wound in his right arm.
Verb	Border people were asked to arm themselves with weapons.

Before :

Adverb	I have not met you before.
Conjunction	She went away before he came.

Better :

Noun	Give place to your betters.
Adjective	I think yours is a better pen.
Verb	Let us first better our financial position.
Adverb	You are working better today.

Both :

Pronoun	Both of them have gone.
Adjective	You cannot make it both ways.
Conjunction	Both the cashier and the clerk are on tour.

But :

Pronoun	There is no one but praise her
Adverb	It is but a natural consequence.
Conjunction	He tried hard, but failed.

Back :

Noun	She carried the load on his back.
Verb	Do not back false friends.

Book :

Noun	He is writing a book.
Verb	Please book a cycle for Kota through this train.

Bare :

Adjective	He has bare feet.
Adverb	He walked bare feet.
Verb	Bare your arm.

By :

Adverb	Time passes by.
Preposition	He was much loved by his wife.

Close :

Noun	The meeting came to a close at 5 p.m.
Adjective	They are very close friends.
Verb	The school will close tomorrow.
Adverb	Both walked close to each other.

Calm :

Noun	The calm of mind ,is in fact required.
Adjective	Today the weather is very calm and quiet.
Verb	First calm yourself and then write your report.

Cold :

Noun	Wear the woolen clothes lest you should catch cold.
Adjective	It is very cold today.

Court :

Noun	Ramesh was summoned to the court of law.
Verb	He courted her all the week.

Cane :

Noun	This is a beautiful cane.
Verb	He was caned publicly by the teacher.

Cut :

Noun	I do not like the cut of your hair.
Verb	Cut the paper in desired sizes.

Cover :

Noun	Put a cover on your copy.
Verb	Cover your head lest you should catch cold.

Down :

Noun	He has seen the ups and downs of life.
Adjective	The man was thrown from the down train.
Verb	Down with dowry.
Preposition	The engine came rushing down the hill very fast.

Deep :

Noun	She fell down into the deep.
Adjective	It is a very deep river.
Adverb	My pen fell deep into the tank.

Drive :

Noun	My brother has gone out for a drive.
Verb	You are driving very fast.

Date :

Noun	His date of birth is 26th April.
Verb	The Vikram era dates from 57 B.C.

Either :

Pronoun	Ask either of them to bring a pen.
Adjective	Either pen is good enough.
Conjunction	He must either work or take rest.

Enough :

Adjective	There is enough time to go there.
Adverb	He knows well enough what she means to say.

Even :

Adjective	The chances of winning the game are even.
Verb	Let them even the field first.
Adverb	He cannot even see me.

Else :

Adjective	He brought something else for her.
Adverb	We should look anywhere else.
Conjunction	Walk fast, else you should miss the bus.

Eye :

Noun	He has one eye only.
Verb	The policeman eyed him with suspicion.

Elder :

Noun	We must show respect to our elders.
Adjective	He is my elder brother.

For :

Conjunction	We should help him for he is very poor.
Preposition	I was looking for her.

Fast :

Noun	He keeps fast on Tuesday.
Adjective	He is a very fast today.
Verb	He fasted for a week.
Adverb	He ran so fast to win the race.

Free :

Adjective	We are citizen of a free country.
Verb	Let us free ourselves from social bondage .

Fix :

Noun	He was in a terrible fix .
Verb	Fix some other date for our marriage.

Face :

Noun	There are red pimples on her face.
Verb	He faced the situation with courage.

Fool :

Noun	He is a fool to behave like that.
Verb	He cannot fool me now.

Fish :

Noun	Whale is a kind of large fish.
Verb	Do not try to fish in troubled water.

Half :

Noun	One half of this task is completed.
Adjective	Half hearted man do not succeed.
Adverb	She was half dead with fear.

Help :

Noun	His timely help saved him.
Verb	God help those who help themselves.

Hand :

Noun	A bird in hand is better than two in the bush.
Verb	The postman handed him two parcels.

Head :

Noun	His head was bald.
Verb	He headed the list of successful students.

Less :

Noun	She won't be happy with less.
Adjective	He paid less attention to sports and more to studies.
Adverb	The soil of her garden is less fertile than that of yours.

Like :

Noun	You cannot see her like again.
Adjective	They are man of like physique and stature.
Verb	I like to take some fruit after dinner.

Light :

Noun	There is no light in the room.
Adjective	It is not a light matter.
Verb	Light the candle, please.

Love :

Noun	I have great love for her.
Adjective	She does not like love stories.
Verb	I love you.

Laugh :

Noun	She raised many a laugh at his cost.
Verb	Do not laugh at the poor .

Much :

Adjective	He has wasted much time.
Adverb	I am much annoyed with you.

More :

Adjective	He wants more workers like you.
Adverb	You must talk less and work more.

Meek :

Noun	God helps the meek and gentle.
Adjective	She is quite meek.

Master :

Noun	She was my master in all matters.
Adjective	He conceived a master plan.
Verb	She has mastered this book.

Move :

Noun	The army is on the move.
Verb	Let us move to some other hotel.

Make :

Noun	What is the make of you T.V. ?
Verb	Do not make a noise.

Near :

Adjective	He is my near relative.
Verb	We are nearing the end of the project.
Adverb	Come near and listen to me.
Preposition	His house is near the temple.

Needs :

Noun	My needs are few.
Verb	It needs great care.

Neither :

Pronoun`	Neither of them can be relied.
Adjective	Neither charge is true.
Conjunction	Neither he nor his brother was present there.

No :

Noun	His answer was a perfect no.
Adjective	It is no joke.
Verb	She is no more with me.

Next :

Adjective	I shall see you next Monday.
Adverb	What next ?
Preposition	He was sitting next to her.

Number :

Noun	Put it on the tenth number.
Verb	His days are now numbered.

Once :

Noun	Let me see her for once.
Adverb	I was young once.
Conjunction	Once you hesitate, you are dead.

One :

Noun	The little one cried for joy.
Pronoun	One would think he was mad.
Adjective	One day I met her in a function.

Only :

Adjective	It was his only chance.
Adverb	He was only foolish.

Over :

Noun	In first over he took three wickets.
Adverb	Read it over carefully.
Preposition	Last year, a chance came over to him again.

Off :

Adjective	Ramesh picked the horse's off nail.
Adverb	He is falling off.
Preposition	The rider fell off the bike.

Open :

Adjective	This is an open letter.
Verb	Please open the door.

Poor :

Noun	The rich should help the poor.
Adjective	He is a poor man.

Pocket :

Noun	I have two rupees in my pocket .
Verb	He pocketed the insult patiently.

Right :

Noun	I asked him favour as a right.
Adjective	He is the right man for the job.
Verb	This is a fault that will right itself.
Adverb	She stood right in my gate.

Round :

Noun	That night was a round of pleasures.
Adjective	It is a round hole.
Verb	You can not round it by pen.
Adverb	He brought her round to my point of view.
Preposition	The earth revolves round the sun.

Reach :

Noun	The bunch of grapes was not within his reach.
Verb	I shall reach there in time.

Refuse :

Noun	The refuse of the hospital is put into public drains.
Verb	She refused to help her.

Since :

Adverb	I have not seen him since.
Conjunction	Since there is no way , let us kiss and part.
Preposition	Since Monday I have not seen her.

Some :

Pronoun	Some say one thing and other say another.
Adjective	We must find some way out of this problem.
Adverb	Some thirty people were present in the party.

Still :

Noun	I could hear her cry in the still of night.
Adjective	Still waters run deep.
Verb	With his name the mothers still their babes.
Adverb	They are still sleeping.

Such :

Pronoun	Such was not his meaning .
Adjective	Don't move in such a hurry.

So :

Adverb	I am so tired that I cannot go.
Conjunction	He was poor, so they helped him.

Slow :

Adjective	He is a very slow writer.
Verb	The car slowed down as it reached the hotel.
Adverb	How slow she works ?

Sound :

Noun	Hearing the sound of the trumpets, the people woke up.
Adjective	His arguments were not sound and acceptable.
Verb	Sound the horn, please.

Spring :

Noun	It was a spring of fresh water.; Spring has set off.
Adjective	We use spring water for bathing.
Verb	See how the dog springs upon the cat.

Stone :

Noun	The house is made of stone.
Adjective	That house has stone walls.
Verb	He was stoned to death.

Stand :

Noun	Everybody praised him for his stand against the injustice.
Verb	Stand in a queue.

Stay :

Noun	He has to cut short the period of his stay at Alwar.
Verb	She will stay with me for a few days.

Second :

Adjective	He is second to none.
Verb	No one seconded her candidature.

School :

Noun	There is no school in our colony.
Verb	He was not schooled properly .

Silence :

Noun	There was perfect silence in the hall.
Verb	He soon silenced her with his arguments and the evidence.

That :

Pronoun	That is what I want.
Adjective	What is that noise ?
Adverb	You have done that much only.
Conjunction	He says that he wants to leave.

Till :

Conjunction	Do not start till I say.
Preposition	He put off this work till tomorrow .

Than :

Conjunction	He likes this more than that.
Preposition	He was fond of any drink other than milk.

Time :

Noun	What is the time by your watch ?
Verb	The train is timed to come at 10.p.m.

Touch :

Noun	Midas loved the Golden touch.
Verb	She will not touch this point.

Turn :

Noun	There is a turn after five kilometers
Verb	He turned to be a thief.

Up :

Adjective	She will come by the next up train.
Adverb	These days prices are up.
Preposition	Can you climb up this tree.

Well :

Noun	There are only two wells in the village.
Adjective	I hope you are now well.
Adverb	Well begun is half done.

While :

Noun	Sit down and rest a while.
Verb	They while away their days with books and watching T.V.
Conjunction	He was reading while his friends were playing.

Why :

Noun	You should not be worried about why and wherefore of it ?
Adverb	I know why she did it.

Wrong :

Noun	The Minister did no wrong.
Adjective	It is a wrong policy.
Verb	He was wronged by the leader of his party.
Adverb	I think that my son is going wrong.

Watch :

Noun	I have lost my watch.
Adjective	I require a watch-man.
Verb	Let us watch her movements.

Water :

Noun	Bring me some cold water.
Adjective	There are water snakes and land snakes.
Verb	He is watering in the garden.

Walk :

Noun	They go for a walk in the evening.
Verb	She was so weak that she could not walk.

Which :

Pronoun	Which of these two pens you like more ?
Adjective	Which coaching you have joined ?

Want :

Noun	Owing to the want of rains, there occurred a drought.
Verb	I want to purchase a good new T.V. set .

Whose :

Pronoun	He is the man whose brother met me yesterday.
Adjective	Whose book is this ?

Yet :

Adverb	There is more evidence yet to be given.
Conjunction	Though he worked hard, yet he failed.

23

Formation of Words

The basic part of any word is the **root. Word formation is the process of forming new words usually by adding prefix or suffix to the root** .

VARIOUS WAYS OF FORMATION OF WORDS

1. **By prefix:** Prefix is a syllable added before the root :

Un + lucky	unlucky ,
In + dependent	independent,
Im + polite	impolite.

2. **By suffix:** Suffix is also a syllable , added at the end of the root :

Great + ness	Greatness,
Social + ism	Socialism,
Leak + age	Leakage.

3. **Compounding of two words :**

Drawing + room	Drawing room
Tax + paid	Taxpaid
Pre + paid	Prepaid

4. **Merging of two words :**

Break fast and lunch	Brunch
Hotel for motorist	Motel

5. **Cutting or clipping :**

Telephone	Phone
Teenagers	Teens
Picture with movement	Movie.

1. **Prefix** ; im,is, ir, il, re, em, en, de, un, dis, mis, pre, non, mini, semi, vice,etc are used in the formation of words :

impolite,	impotent,	impure,
indiscipline,	incompetent,	immaterial,
irregular,	irrelevant,	immoral,
illogical,	illegal,	illiterate,
recast,	refund,	reclaim,
empower,	embody,	embark,

encourage, enrich, enlist,
deform, defame, demoralise,
unfortunate, untie, unexpected
disappear, dislike, discourage,
miscarriage mistrust, mismanage,
premature prepaid, prefix,
non cooperation, non refundable, non sense,
mini computer, mini-car, mini-skirt,
semi modal, semi-circle,. semi colon,
vice captain, vice chairman, vice president.

2. **Suffix** ; age, ed, ist, ing, em, ish, ful, en, ly, ship, ness, ment,etc are used in formation of words:

artless, cheerful, graceful,
gifted, ruined, talented,
socialist, artist, rightist,
painting, gardening, watering,
bolden, hidden, maiden,
selfish, boyish, womanish,
joyful, truthful, fearful,
godly, manly, suddenly,
friendship, membership, hardship,
kindness, fastness, goodness,
tasteless colourful, powerful,

Conversion of Words-One Form Into Another

CHANGING NOUN INTO ADJECTIVE

Noun	Adjectives	Noun	Adjectives
Angle	angular	Brass	brazen
Adam	adamic	Body	physical
Ancestor	ancestral	Beast	bestial
Authority	authoritative	Contempt	contemptuous
Advice	advisable	Coward	cowardly
Brother	fraternal	Cat	feline
Blue	bluish	City	urban
Beginning	initial	Calamity	calamitous
Bounty	bounteous	Circle	circular
Brute	brutal	College	collegiate
Conscience	conscientious	Nose	nasal
Circumstance	circumstantial	Ocean	oceanic
Dog	canine	Offence	offensive
Emperor	imperial	Omen	ominous
Expectation	expectant	People	popular
Example	exemplary	Population	populous
Enemy	inimical	Professor	professorial
Earth	earthen	Patriot	patriotic

Essence	essential	Pathos	pathetic
Elephant	elephantine	Picture	picturesque
Explanation	explanatory	Prejudice	prejudicial
Egg	oval	Problem	problematic
Eye	optical	Punishment	penal
Famine	famished	Sentence	sententious
Fraud	fraudulent	Place	local
Foot	pedal	Palace	palatial
Flower	floral	Ruin	ruinous
Fear	timorous	Sedition	seditious
Fable	fabulous	Service	serviceable
Fever	feverish	Secretary	secretarial
Fate	fatal	Study	studious
Flesh	carnal	Paradise	paradisiacal
Grief	grievous	Series	series
Grass	grassy	Salt,	saline
Hand	manual	Serpent	serpentine
Hypocrite	hypocritical	Superstition	superstitious
Island	insular	Ship	naval
Industry	industrious	Sky	etherial
Spring	vernal	Joy	joyous
Sun	solar	Joke	jocular
Star	starry	Judge	judicial (judicious)
Tooth	dental	Tribe	tribal
Licence	licentious	Town	urban
Lustre	lustrous	Talk	talkative
Love	amorous	Table	tabular
Money	monetary	Youth	juvenile
Moon	lunar	Vice	vicious
Merchant	mercantile	Voice	vocal
Metal	metallic	Village	rural
Medicine	medicinal	War	martial
Myth	mythical	Title	titular
Minister	ministerial	Worth	worthy
Muscle	muscular	Watch	vigilant
Merit	meritorious	Wood	sylvan
Night	nocturnal	Year	annual
Neighbour	neighbourly	Zodiac	zodiacal
Nihil	nihilistic	Zenith	zenithal

CHANGING NOUN INTO VERB

Noun	**Verb**	**Noun**	**Verb**
Authority	authorise	Hard	harden
Assertion	assert	Harmony	harmonise
Apology	apologise	Haste	hasten
Allusion	allude	Height	heighten

Blood	bleed	Idol	idolise
Beauty	beautify	Justice	justify
Black	blacken	Knee	kneel
Brass	braze	Loss	lose
Bed	embed	List	enlist
Body	embody	Monopoly	monopolise
Circle	encircle	Magnet	magnetise
Centre	centralise	Memory	memorise
Cipher	decipher a	Nature	naturalise
Class	classify	Notice	notify
Certainty	ascertain	Necessity	necessitate
Colony	colonise	Night	be night
Collision	collide	Origin	originate
Company	accompany	Office	officiate
Conception	conceive	Perception	perceive
Custom	accustom	Patron	patronise
Character	characterise	Peace	pacify
Danger	endanger	Person	personify
Drop	drip	Prison	imprison
Enthusiasm	enthuse	Power	empower
Excellence	excel	Relief	relieve
Economy	economise	Robe	enrobe
Electricity	electrify	Society	associate
Furniture	furnish	Sermon	sermonise
Frost	freeze	Spark	sparkle
Food	feed	Shrine	enshrine
Force	enforce	Slave	enslave
Friend	befriend	Title	entitle
Fraud	defraud	Tomb	entomb
Grass	graze	Utility	utilise
Glory	glorify	Vapour	evaporate
Gold	gild	Verse	versify
Habit	habituate	Vacancy	vacate
Hand	handle	Vice	vitiate

CHANGING NOUN INTO ABSTRACT NOUN

Noun	Abs.Noun	Noun	Abs.Noun
Beggar	beggary	Machine	mechanism
Coin	coinage	Priest	priesthood
Coward	cowardice	Person	personage
Cunning	cunningness	Royal	royalty
Creature	creation	Regent	regency
Elector	electorate	Servant	service
Hero	heroism	Witch	witchery

CHANGING ADJECTIVE INTO VERB

Adjective	Verb	Adjective	Verb
Abundant	abound	Large	enlarge
Able	enable	Lamp	lamp
Abusive	abuse	Little	belittle
Bitter	embitter	Long	prolong
Brief	abbreviate	Liquid	liquidise
Brutal	brutalise	Mad	madden
Base	debase	Moist	moisten
Clear	clarify	Noble	ennoble
Civil	civilise	Public	publish
Clean	cleanse	Popular	popularise
Dense	condense	Poor	impoverish
Different	differentiate	Perpetual	perpetuate
Double	duplicate	Pure	purify
Dramatic	dramatise	Real	realize
Equal	equalise	Rich	enrich
Fat	fatten	Safe	save
Fertile	fertilise	Stupid	stupidity
Firm	confirm	Sweet	sweeten
Fresh	refresh	Solid	solidity
Feeble	enfeeble		

CHANGING ADJECTIVE INTO NOUN

Adjetive	Noun	Adjective	Noun
Adequate	adequacy	Intense	intensity
Acid	acidity	Just	justice
Bankrupt	bankruptcy	Merry	merriment
Brief	brevity	Magnificent	magnificence
Busy	business	Notorious	notoriety
Chaste	chastity	Obedient	obedience
Civil	civility	Pious	piety
Compulsory	compulsion	Public	publicity
Dense	density	Rival	rivalry
Gay	gaiety	Solitary	solitude
Double	duplicate	Perpetual	perpetuate
Grand	grandeur	Splendid	splendor
Hot	heat	Vain	vanity
Humble	humility	Wide	width
Local	locality	Worthy	worthc

CHANGING VERB INTO NOUN

Verb	Noun	Verb	Noun
Acquit	acquittal	Conceive	conception
Bathe	bath	Commit	committal
Betray	betrayal	Compare	comparison

Deceive	deception	Precise	precision
Defy	defiance	Predict	prediction
Deny	denial	Precede	precedence
Do	deed	Pursue	pursuit
Prohibit	prohibition	Yean	yeanling
Heal	health	Recede	recess
Know	knowledge	Rely	reliance
Lend	loan	Respond	response
Give	gift	Redeem	redemption
Narrate	narration	Steal	stealth
Oblige	obligation	Urge	urgency
Move	motion	Seize	seizure
Please	pleasure	Weave	web
Persuade	persuasion	Vary	variety

CORRECT YOURSELF EXERCISE : FORMATION OF WORDS

CYE : 01 Write the adjective form of the following nouns :

1. Calamity, 2. Coward, 3. City, 4. Blue, 5. Emperor,
6. Brute, 7. Cet, 8. Beast, 9. Body, 10. Brass.

CYE : 02 Write the 'noun' form of the following words :

1. Floral, 2. Fatal, 3. Populous, 4. Inimical, 5. Penal,
6. Saline, 7. Naval, 8. Solar, 9. Dental, 10. Jocular.

CYE : 03 Change the following nouns into verbs:

1. Hard, 2. Loss, 3. Magnet, 4. Centre, 5. Bed,
6. Circle, 7. Food, 8. Grass, 9. Collision, 10. Nature,
11. Origin, 12. Office.

CYE : 04 Change the following verbs into noun:

1. Bathe, 2. Predict, 3. Defy, 4. Please, 5. Lend,
6. Move, 7. Pursue, 8. Steal, 9. Oblige, 10. Respond,
11. Yean, 12. Do.

CYE : 05 Form the words as directed, from the following words :

(i) a noun from *err*, (verb)
(ii) a noun from *flow*, (verb)
(iii) a noun from *precise*, (adjective)
(iv) an abstract noun from *witch*, (noun)
(v) a verb from *office*, (noun).
(vi) adjectives from *coast, home*
(vii) Abstract noun from *fool, poor, laugh*.

CYE : 06 Use each of the following words as a noun and as a verb in your own sentences :

1. quarrel, 2. book, 3. hand, 4. lock., 5. water.
6. stand, 7. field, 8. chair, 9. notes, 10. sacrifice,
11. train, 12. work, 13. present, 14. record.

CYE : 07 Fill in the blanks with the appropriate word in the second sentence in the following pairs of sentences :

1. The corrupt politician is about to be exposed.
   The corrupt politician faces ....
2. Most of the cups broke in transit.
   Most of the cups suffered............ in transit.
3. The passengers were annoyed at the delay.
   The passengers expressed their .... at the delay.
4. The Court ordered the building to be demolished.
   The Court ordered .... of the building.
5. The strange word is repeated in all his poems.
   All his poems show.............. of the strange word.
6. He told me not to be in such haste.
   He told me not to ....so much.
7. My grandfather fell down.
   My grandfather had a ....
8. The visitor frightened the child.
   The visitor gave the child a ....look.

SOLUTIONS : CORRECT YOURSELF EXERCISE

Solutions CYE : 01

1. Calamitous, 2. Cowardly, 3. Urban, 4. Bluish, 5. Imperial,
6. Brutal, 7. Feline, 8. Bestial, 9. Physical, 10. Brazen.

Solutions CYE : 02

1. Flower, 2. Fate, 3. Population, 4. Enemy, 5. Punishment,
6. Salt, 7. Ship, 8. Sun, 9. Tooth, 10. Joke.

Solutions CYE : 03

1. Harden, 2. Lose, 3. Magnetise, 4. Centralise, 5. Embed,
6. Encircle, 7. Feed, 8. Graze, 9. Collide, 10. Naturalise,
11. Originate, 12. Officiate.

Solutions CYE : 04

1. Bath, 2. Prediction, 3. Defiance, 4. Pleasure, 5. Loan,
6. Motion, 7. Pursuit, 8. Stealth, 9. Obligation, 10. Response,
11. Yeanling, 12. Deed.

Solutions CYE : 05

(i) error, (ii) flow, (iii) precision, (iv) witchery, (v) officiating,
(vi) coastal, homely, (vii) folly, poverty, laughter.

Solutions CYE : 06

Use as noun

1. *Quarrels* take place over the property.
2. The *books* written by Mr.S.C. Gupta are very useful.

3. The *hands* of Mafia are many.
4. The *locks* of Aligarh are durable .
5. *Water* is necessary for life.
6. You should have taken a tough *stand.*
7. The *field* of Red Corner, China is plane.
8. This is a comfortable *chair* .
9. She has taken my *notes*.
10. The *sacrifice* made by Subhash Bose is indeed great.
11. The *train* is a good mode of travel.
12. Complete your *work* today positively.
13. This is a good *present* for her.
14. Sachin has made several *records*.

Use as a verb

1.You should not *quarrel* with your brother.
2. The scooter was *booked* for Alwar.
3. A representation was *handed* over to the Chairman.
4. *Lock* the house properly while going out.
5. He is *watering* the plants..
6. The inflation rate now *stands* at 4% only.
7. Sachin *fields* the ball very quickly.
8. The Home Minister *chaired* the meeting of M.P.s.
9. Please *note* down my telephone number.
10. Subhash Bose *sacrificed* his service and fought for independence.
11. Pakistan is *training* militants.
12. He *works* in this office.
13. She *presented* a wrong information.
14. Please *record* my dissent in this matter.

Solutions CYE : 07

1. Exposure, 2. Breakage, 3. Annoyance, 4. Demolition, 5. Repetition,
6. Hurry, 7. Fall, 8. Frightening.

24

Spelling Rules

Here are a few rules. Keep the principle in mind—but don't bog down in the rules. (You'll do better simply memorizing the words you misspell.) Actually, English spelling does follow specific rules.Knowing some basic rules of English spelling can eliminate many common errors even though there are usually exceptions.

BASIC SPELLING RULES

1. **Whether *'ie'* or *'ei'*** ? : Remember the following poem to decide if a word should be spelled ***'ie'*** or ***'ei'***.

   "Put i before **e** , except after **c**
   Or when it sounds like **a**
   As in **neighbour** or **neigh.**"

   Examples

mischief	believe	field	('i' before 'e')
receiver	conceit		(except after 'c')
eight	weigh	freight	(sounds like 'a')

   Exceptions

   friend, neither , leisure, foreign

2. **Doubling a consonant** : Follow these steps to decide **if a final consonant needs to be doubled** *when a suffix or verb ending is added* :

   If the word is one syllable or is stressed on the last syllable,
   And has a single final consonant,
   And that single final consonant is preceded by a single vowel,
   And the suffix begins with a vowel,
   Then double the final consonant.

Example : Control + able

The stress is on the last syllable - **trol,**
There is a single final consonant - **l,**
The final consonant has a vowel before it - **o,**
The suffix, **able**, begins with a vowel,
Therefore, you double the **'l'** before adding the suffix—**'able'**.
Write **'controllable'**.

Other examples : 'occur- occurring', 'swim - swimming', 'ship - shipping'.

Now see : **enter + ing,**

The stress is on the first syllable - **en** - not the last,

Therefore, you do not double the final consonant 'r'.

Write '**entering**'.

Other examples: visit-visiting, develop-developing, dread-dreading,appeal-appealing.

3. ***Handling final* 'e' when adding a suffix or verb ending:**

   If the suffix or verb ending begins with a vowel, drop the final **'e'.**

   Example : amuse + ing = amusing.

   Other examples : create-creating, type-typing, bake-baking

   If the suffix or verb ending begins with a consonant, keep the final **'e'.**

   Examples : measure + ment = measurement

   definite + ly = definitely

4. ***Adding a suffix* or verb ending, with words** ending in 'y' :

   If the word has a consonant before the **y**, change the **y** to **i.**

   Example : mercy + less = merciless.

   If the word has a vowel before the **y**, keep the **y**.

   Example : employ + ed = employed.

5. **Words ending in two vowels** (a vowel + final 'e') : Retain the final vowel (e) before adding a suffix. (see/seeable; shoe/shoeing; canoe/canoeing)

6. **For words ending in 'c',** insert k before adding -ing or -y. (picnic/picnicking; traffic/trafficking; panic/panicky, etc.)

7. **To retain the soft sound of the** 'c' ('s' sound) **and of the** 'g' ('j' sound) in words ending in 'ce' and 'ge', we keep the final 'e' (peace/peaceable; replace/replaceable; arrange/arrangement; advantage/advantageous; notice/noticeable; change/changeable).

8. **Pluralizing noun :** Most of the nouns in English spell their plural by simply adding a final *-s*. Nouns that are noncountable or abstract (***e.g., cheese, sugar, honesty, intelligence***) generally take a singular verb, but in some instances can be plural, in which case they follow the rules for plural based on their spelling. Also, there are some categories of words which are only plural, even though their spelling does not reflect this

   (a) Words that end in **'ss, sh, ch'** or **'x'-add es.**

   Example : pass -passes, buzz-buzzes, coax-coaxes, wash-washes, watch-watches.

   (b) Words that have a consonant before a final **'y'**- change the **'y'** to **'i'** before adding **es.**

   Example : summary– summaries, cry – cries, try–tries.

   (c) Most nouns ending in **'f'** or **'fe'** –add **'s'**. However, some nouns change the **'f'** to **'v'** and add **'s'** or **'es'** in plural.

   There is no rule to follow here.

   Examples : belief = beliefs

   half = halves , calf = calves.

   Most nouns ending in 'o' add 's'. However, some add 'es'.

   There is no rule to follow here.

   Examples : studio = studios, cargo = cargoes.

9. The spelling of a word does not change when you add a prefix to it even *when the first letter of the word and the last letter of the prefix are the same :*

Examples : **mis + step = misstep,**
pre + eminent = preeminent,
un + necessary = unnecessary.

10. No rule for **irregular plurals** .These just need to be memorized :

child	children	foot	feet
goose	geese	louse	lice
man	men	mouse	mice
ox	oxen	tooth	teeth
woman	women		

11. Sometimes **words have silent letters**. These words follow patterns that can be memorized.

Examples : gn, pn, kn= n,
gnome, pneumonia, knife.

Examples : rh, wr = r,
rhyme, wrestle —.

Examples : pt, ght = t,
ptomaine, height —.

Examples : ps, sc = s,
psalm, science —.

Example : wh = h,
whole. —.

LIST OF COMMONLY MIS-SPELT WORDS

Autumn	Conscience	Irresistible	Phenomenon
Accommodate	Cigarette	Irrelevant	Physique
Accustom	Colloquial	Irreparable	Psychology
Agility	Commemorate	Indefatigable	Potato
Athlete	Competition	Indigenous	Pharmaceutical
Accommodate	Convenient	Incorrigible	Pursue
Acquaintance	Conceive	Juggler	Quarrel
Assailant	Condemn	Jealousy	Queue
Aggregate	Curriculum	Jubilee	Quinine
Acquiesce	Deceive	Juvenile	Rogue
Abbreviate	Discernible	Knave	Routine
Ascetic	Deficiency	Kitchen	Regrettable
Annihilate	Dialogue	Knee	Restaurant
Appropriate	Descendant	Knight	Repetition
Aerodrum	Division	Kneeled	Referee
Architecture	Dilemma	Knives	Rehearsal
Acquiesce	Deteriorate	Leniency	Rupee
Alcohol	Dysentery	Leisure	Sceptre
Adherent	Ecclesiastical	Laurel	Scissors
Abhorrence	Etiquette	Luxurious	Schedule
Accessible	Erroneous	Lieutenant	Strategy
Acknowledgment	Exaggeration	Manageable	Simultaneous
Acquittal	Ecstasy	Magnificent	Symmetrical

Apparatus
Amateur
Appetite
Acclamation
Affectionate
Aesthetic
Alienate
Ambassador
Ambition
Assassin
Bankruptcy
Beneficent
Behaviour
Bequeath
Besiege
Bureaucracy
Budget
Buffoon
Circumstance
Commitment
Committee
Condescend
Connoisseur
Correspondence
Counterfeit
Catalogue
Convalesce

Equilibrium
Exchequer
Extravagance
Efficiency
Efficacious
Embarrass
Fallacious
Fascinate
Facilitate
Felicitate
Freight
Favourable
Fourth
Genuine
Guarantee
Gorgeous
Grievance
Grotesque
Geometry
Grammar
Gazette
Harassment
Heinous
Heterogenous
Hygiene
Inflammable
Incarcerate

Martyr
Manoeuvre
Misdemeanor
Meagre
Moustache
Mosquito
Missionary
Millionaire
Massacre
Museum
Mischievous
Musician
Noticeable
Nuisance
Neighbour
Necessary
Necessitate
Occurrence
Omitted
Oscillate
Ominous
Parallel
Pneumonia
Proletariat
Perceive
Proprietor
Perspicuous

Soliloquy
Sovereign
Stomach
Technique
Transience
Tenacious
Transgressor
Utterance
Vacation
Vaccination
Vicissitude
Vocabulary
Vicious
Villainous
Wednesday
Weigh
Woolen
Written
Writing
Xenomania
Xylography
Yawning
Yeoman
Zodiac
Zealous
Zootomy
Zythepsary

SPELLING : AMERICAN AND BRITISH

Here are some general differences between British and American spellings:

1. Words ending in –'or' (American) –'our' (British) :
   American English Labor, Color, Rumor,Humor,Neighbor etc.
   British English Labour, Colour , Rumour, Humour, Neighbour.
2. Words ending in –'ize' (American) – 'ise' (British) :
   American English recognize, patronize.
   British English recognise,, patronise.
3. Words ending in–'og' (American), 'ogue' (British English) :
   American English catalog,dialog.
   British English catalogue, dialogue.
4. Words ending in–'l' (single or double):
   American English Traveler, leveling.
   British English Traveller, levelling
5. Words ending in–'ter' (American English) and 'tre' (British English) :
   American English Theater, Meter, center
   British English Theatre, Metre, centre

6. Spelling difference in some more words:

American	British
tire	tyre (on a vehicle)
program	programme
jail	gaol, jail
aluminum	aluminium
defense	defence
jewelry	jewellery

We use British English in India : The best way to make sure that you are being consistent in your spelling is to use the spell check on your word processor (if you are using the computer of course) and choose which variety of English you would like. As you can see, there are really very few differences between standard British English and standard American English. However, the largest difference is probably that of the choice of vocabulary and pronunciation.

CORRECT YOURSELF EXERCISE : SPELLING RULES

CYE : 01 Insert 'ance' or 'ence' into the following :

(a) exist, (b) attend, (c) correspond, (d) magnific, (e) occurr,
(f) persist, (g) entr, (h) emin, (i) prud, (j) vigil,
(k) compli, (l) hindr, (m) acquaint, (n) assure, (o) repent,
(p) differ, (q) refer.

CYE : 02 Insert 'ant' or 'ent' into the following :

Attend–	cog–	immigr–	complim–	disinfect–
immin–	serp–	inhabit–	serv–	brilli–
monum–	pertin–	fragr–	promin–	perman–
vali–	adjac–	restaur–	resist–	suffici–
excell–	benefic–			

CYE : 03 Add 'tion', or 'sion' to complete the spellings of the following :

Applica–,	discus–,	deci–,	colli–,	posses–,
profes–,	combina–,	explo–,	confu–,	permis–,
sugges–,	atten–,	ambi–,	ammuni–,	associa–,
determina–,	divi–,	exclu–,	compul–,	conclu–,
commis–,	direc–,	administra–,	resolu–,	reputa–,
ses–,	founda–,	man–,	excur–,	popula–,

CYE : 04 Insert 'ary', 'ery,' 'ory' or 'ry' into the following :

Brav–,	bound–,	contra–,	sal–,	slav–,
jewell–,	gallant– ,	second–,	prim–,	secret–,
cook–,	coroll–,	dai–,	geomet–,	laborat–,
liter–,	mercen–,	milit–,	mission– ,	monast–,
myst–,	necess–,	satisfact–,	machin–,	fact–,
begg–,	carpent–,	surg–.		

CYE : 05 Insert 'cial' or 'tial' in the following words :

pala–,	residen–,	superfi–,	ra–,	par–,
spe–,	influen–,	pruden–,	provin–,	sacrifi–,
finan–,	judi–,	cru–,	nup–,	prejudi–,
presiden–,	preferen–,	essen–.		

CYE : 06 Insert 'eous' or 'ious' into the spellings of the following :

nutrit–,	courag–,	court–,	notor–,	erron–,
meritor–,	supersitit–,	bount–,	industr–,	licent–,
prec–	prodig–,	cur–,	feroc–,	grac–,
conscient–,	luxur–.			

CYE : 07 Add the suffix 'able' or 'ible' with the following words :

agree,	love,	resist,	blame,	move,
access,	value,	eat,	change,	reduce,
contempt,	force,	pay,	profit,	discern.

CYE : 08 Fill in 'age', 'dge' or 'ege' in the following :

pill–,	coll–,	carri–,	mess–,	man–,
line–,	ple–,	dam–,	bu–,	bri–,
he–,	pres–,	pack–,	mortg–,	post–,
vill–,	suffr–,	lo–,	pass–,	cartri–.

CYE : 09 Insert 'cious' or 'tious' into the following words :

Mali–,	fero–,	supersti–,	conscien–,	ostenta–,
ambi–,	vi–,	ficti–,	deli–,	perni–,
atro–,	vora–,	sedi–,	infec–,	saga–,
avari– .				

CYE : 10 Insert 'ei' or 'ie' into the following :

Perc–ve,	hyg–ne,	bel–f,	ach–ve,	ch–f,
dec–ve,	rel–f,	conc–t,	th–f,	v–l,
n–gh,	y–ld,	br–f,	n–ce,	forf–t,
I–ge,	surf–t,	f–gn,	retr–ve,	rec–pt,
gr–ve,	pr–st.			

CYE : 11 Tick mark the words with correct spellings :

1. (a) temperature,	(b) temprature,	(c) tempareter,
2. (a) definate,	(b) definite,	(c) difinite,
3. (a) expirience,	(b) exparience,	(c) experience,
4. (a) incident,	(b) insident,	(c) insidant,
5. (a) extasy,	(b) ecstacy,	(c) acstasy.

CYE : 12 Find out the wrongly spelt words :

1.(a) pompous,	(b) populous,	(c) prejudiced,	(d) pretentous,
2.(a) exempleary,	(b) embarrass,	(c) envious,	(d) excellence,
3.(a) dispose,	(b) dipose,	(c) demote,	(d) denote,

4.(a) casual, (b) candid, (c) convercant, (d) catastrophe,
5.(a) procession, (b) passion, (c) posession, (d) profession,

CYE : 13 Find out the wrongly spelt words :

1. (a) rein, (b) neigh, (c) neither, (d) neice,
2. (a) efficient, (b) reticent, (c) magnificient, (d) deficient,
3. (a) vocal, (b) focal, (c) mystical, (d) vehical,
4. (a) altogether, (b) alrigt, (c) almighty, (d) allottee,
5. (a) pretence, (b) offence, (c) dence, (d) deference.

SOLUTIONS : CORRECT YOURSELF EXERCISE

Solutions CYE : 01

(a) existence, (b) attendance, (c) correspondence, (d) magnificence,
(e) occurrence, (f) persistance, (g) entrance, (h) eminence,
(i) prudence, (j) vigilance, (k) compliance, (l) hindrance,
(m) acquaintance, (n) assurance, (o) repentance, (p) difference,
(q) reference.

Solutions CYE : 02

attendant, cogent, immigrant, compliment, disinfectant,
imminent, serpent, inhabitant, servant, brilliant,
monument, pertinent, fragrant, prominent, permanent,
valiant, adjacent, restaurant, resistant, sufficient,
excellent, beneficent,

Solutions CYE : 03

application, discussion, decision, collision, possession,
profession, combination, explosion, confusion, permission,
suggestion, attention, ambition, ammunition, association,
determination, division, exclusion, compulsion, conclusion,
commission, direction, administration, resolution, reputation,
session, foundation, mansion, excursion, population.

Solutions CYE : 04

bravery, boundary, contrary, salary, slavery,
jewellery, gallantry, secondary, primary, secretary,
cookery, corollary, dairy, geometry , laboratory,
literary, mercenary, military, missionary, monastery,
mystery, necessary, satisfactory, machinery, factory,
beggary, carpentry, surgery,

Solutions CYE : 05

palatial, residential, superficial, racial, partial,
special, influential, prudential, provincial, sacrificial,
financial, judicial, crucial, nuptial, prejudicial,
presidential, preferential. essential.

Solutions CYE : 06

nutritious, courageous, courteous, notorious, erroneous,
meritorious, superstitious, bounteous, industrious, licentious,
precious, prodigious, curious, ferocious, gracious,
conscientious, luxurious.

Solutions CYE : 07

agreeable, lovable, resistible, blamable, movable,
accessible, valuable, eatable, changeable, reducible,
contemptible, forcible, payable, profitable, discernible .

Solutions CYE : 08

pillage, college, carriage, message, manage,
lineage, pledge, damage, budge, bridge,
hedge, presage, package, mortgage, postage,
village, suffrage, lodge, passage, cartridge.

Solutions CYE : 09

malicious, ferocious, superstitious, conscientious, ostentatious,
ambitious, vicious, fictitious, delicious, pernicious,
atrocious, voracious, seditious, infectious, sagacious,
avaricious.

Solutions CYE : 10

perceive, hygiene, belief, achieve, chief,
deceive, relief, conceit, thief, veil,
neigh, yield, brief, niece forfeit
surfeit,liege, feign, retrieve, receipt, grieve,
priest,

Solutions CYE : 11

1. (a), 2. (b), 3. (c), 4. (a), 5. (b).

Solutions CYE : 12

1. (d), 2. (a), 3. (b), 4. (c), 5. (c).

Solutions CYE : 13

1. (d), 2. (c), 3. (d), 4. (b), 5. (c).

25

Punctuation Marks

Punctuation : The right use of *putting in marks or stops in writing* is called Punctuation. Knowledge of proper use of punctuation marks is necessary for writing and reading english correctly. These are signals to the readers. In speaking, we can pause, stop, or change our tone of voice. In writing, we use these marks of punctuation to emphasize and clarify what we mean.

Following is the list of the punctuation marks used in writings :

Apostrophe	'	Colon	:
Semicolon	;	Comma	,
Dash	—	Ellipse	...
Exclamation Mark	!	Hyphen	-
Parentheses	( )	Period	.
Question Mark	?	Quotation Marks	" " and ' '

1. Apostrophe' is used,

(a) **to take the place of missing letters in *contractions* :**
I *won't* go there.

(b) **to form *possessive nouns* :**
This is Ram's house.

(c) **to refer to the *plural of letters and words* :**
I wrote three *r's* in terrific.
You have written too many *and's* in this paragraph alone.

2. Colon : is used,

(a) after the greeting in a ***business letter* :**
Dear Chairman: , Dear Sir: , Dear Dr. Suneel : etc.

(b) between ***hours and minutes*** in the time of day :
It is already 6:30 P.M.

(c) before ***lists in sentences :***
I will bring the following items to class tomorrow: a board, a torch, a bucket, and a string.

(d) to introduce a ***long direct quotation :***
At the school assembly, the headmaster said :
Please read the new instruction booklet being handed out right now. In it there are many new rules that apply to everyone in the school. The first states that there are no mobile phones allowed within school premises. Also, no drinks are allowed on the lawns.Further...

(e) **When definition or description of a noun is given :**
Noun : Name of any person or a thing.
Peacock : A large beautiful bird with blue neck and colourful feathers.

(f) **To denote *proportion or ratio* :**
15 : 3 :: 5 : 1
4 : 3 : 7

(g) **In writing plays :**
Ram : I shall forgive Ravana for his misdeeds.
Laxman : I shall kill Ravana.

3. Semicolon; is used,

(a) **to *join between independent clauses*** in compound sentences that do not have a coordinating conjunction :
The hotel burnt down ; it was the biggest hotel in the city.
The efforts must continue; war can be fruitless.

(b) in front of adverbial conjunctions *that join two simple sentences* :
He was not well ; so, he could not attend the meeting.
Registrations exceed all expectations; however, there is shortage of good teachers.

(c) *to separate items in a series* when the items already contain commas :
The nominated members are S.Krishnan, Chairman ; K.Krishnan, Vice Chairman; L.Krishnan, Secretary; and M.Krishnan,Joint Secretary .

4. Comma (,) is used,

(a) **between *words, phrases,* or *clauses* in a series** (three or more items) :
She purchased an eraser, a pen, and some copies.
She is a dedicated, sincere and honest lady..

(b) **between the *day* and *year* in a date; eg**– *December 29, 2006.*

(c) ***between* names of a *road /colony , a city*, and a *state* :**
I live at129 South West Block ,Alwar , Rajasthan.

(d) **to set off a *dialogue* :**
He said to me, "I will come on Monday".

(e) ***to end a dialogue***, the comma comes at the end of a sentence (and is not an exclamation or question :
"My favorite pet is my cat," asserted Smith.

(f) **to set of interruptions :**
Come, come ; don't delay.
Try, try, and try again.

(g) **with mild *interjections* :**
Oh dear, where did I leave my purse?

(h) **in direct addresses :**
Now remember, Nitu, to never leave the gas on.

(i) **after introductory words :**
Next, I woke up for a glass of milk.

(j) **to enclos a *title*, a *name*, or *initials* :**
Akbar , the great king , was a great religious scholar also.
Ramesh, the son of a millionaire, was sent to jail.
Mr. Hillman, M.D., said that she still had trouble with the computer.

(k) **In compound sentences** to show the coordinate clauses separately :
He sold hies house, sold his furniture, rented his computer, and left the city.
We went to hill station, made some purchasing, visited the temple,and returned home at 12 P.M.

(l) **after a dependent *clause* or *phrase*** that is followed by an independent clause :
How he passed, is a point of controversy.
If he does not go there, he will loose.

(m) ***to separate adjectives*** that equally modify the same noun :
Technically, the scheme is quite feasible.
Pleased with the result, she called a press conference.

(n) **to set off appositives :**
Akbar , the great king , was a great religious scholar also.
Ramesh, the son of a millionaire, was sent to jail.

(o) **after the greeting and closing in *letters :***
My dear father, My dear friend, Yours faithfully, Yours sincerely, etc.

(p) **to set off the *omission* as following :**
Rakhi is seventeen; Sarita, ten. (is-omitted).
Rahul is twenty; Suraj, eighteen. (is-omitted).

5. Dash – is used,

(a) **to show a *break of thought* in a sentence :**
He lost the game – but I am to go to hospital.
He was passed in interview – but his father is ill..

(b) **to introduce a *list of items* :**
The bus driver said that three things were not allowed on the bus - food, beverage, and gum.

(c) **to show *interruption* or a *little stop*** :
Rahul, don't go now – you are too late.''

(d) **to show hesitation :**
"Well", he said, "You – you can't speak like this."

(e) **to clarify the point , we use dash instead of a bracket :**
The other man – Mukul – didn't know me.

(f) **to set of the omitted figures / numbers** etc. :

6. Ellipse (...) is used,

(a) **to show that words have been left out :**
... a beautiful girl she ... with her sister.

(b) **to show that words have been left out to the end of the sentence** (use four dots) :
Rahul went to Jaipur with ....
Ramseh is the man who ....

7. Exclamation mark (!) is used,

(a) **after an exclamatory sentence :**
What a beautiful bird it is!
What! he expired.

(b) **after an *interjection* :**
Hurrah! we have won the match.
Alas! I am ruined!

(c) **after a strong *command*** (imperative sentence)
Go do your homework!

8. Hyphen (-) is used,

(a) **to separate *compound numbers*** (from twenty-one to ninety-nine); eg—
Thirty-nine feet, Thirty-seven miles.

(b) **to separate *some compound* words :**

Anti-government,	Ex-President,
Ex-wife,	Pre-planned,
A 10-days journey,	Self-respect,
H-Bomb,	Door-to-door campaign,
House-to-house service,	Co-operation,
Co-ordination,	Bell-like,

(c) **to break a word at the end of a line :**
(i) Ram was not pre-
sent yesterday.
(ii) Sita was indeed an int-
elligent girl.

(d) **to denote stammering or hesitation**
P-p-p-please madam, R-r-r-Rahul don' t beat me.

9. Period (.) is used,

(a) **at the end of a sentence :**
He is a good boy. (Statement)

(b) **after a mild command** in imperative sentence :
Do not open the gate. (Command)

(c) **after an *indirect question :***
He asked me where I was. (Indirect question)

(d) **after *initials* :**
R.K. Sharma, P.K.Jain.

(e) **after most *abbreviations***
F.I.R., M.Sc., M.A., A.M., U.S.A.

10. Question mark (?) is used,

(a) **at the end of a question** (interrogative sentence) :
Who invited you to dinner?
Where does she live?
"Is everything ok?", Ram asked.
Open the window, will you?
Whom shall we elect? Rahul? Meenakshi?

(b) **to ask question** (in uncertainty mood) **in affirmative understood sense :**
Gandhiji died in 1948?

11. Parentheses [( )] are used,

(a) **to enclose an *explanation*** that is extra information :
Go to Module 6 (pages 14-21) for more information on computers.

(b) **around the *abbreviation* or acronym** that follows its full name :
The Department of Telecommunications (DOT) is having an official meeting today.

(c) **around an added sentence** that is included in another sentence :

June (Is she also your friend?) invited me to her party .

My brother (The one that is really fat.) came to visit me yesterday.

12. Quotation marks (“ ”) are used,

(a) ***in direct speech****, around the speaker’s exact words :*
He said, “Where do you live?”
She said to me, “I am going to market.”

(b) **around *titles* of short stories :**
I haven’t read ‘Hamlet’ so far.
“An arrogant Hare” is a good story.

(c) **around *titles* of poems :**
“Leap year” is a famous poem.

(d) **around *titles* of songs :**
My favorite song is “Kabhi kabhi mere ….”

(e) **around *titles* of articles :**
The Word ‘Nature’ is also used to mean the aptitude of a person.
Many persons were jailed under ‘POTA’ in Tamilnadu.

(f) **around *titles* of chapters :**
The chapter “The Encounter with God” was quite interesting.

(g) use ***single quotation marks*** (only *one quotation mark*) **around a quote that is in another quote.**
She said to me, “Have you read ‘Godan’ of Prem Chand?”
Ram said to me. “Haven’t you seen ‘The Spider man’ so far?”

ENGLISH ALPHABETS AND USE OF CAPITAL LETTERS

English is a *West Germanic* language related to *Dutch, Frisian and German* (languages) with a significant amount of vocabulary from *French, Latin, Greek* and many other languages.

Approximately 341 million people speak English as a native language and a further 267 million speak it as a second language in other 104 countries including the UK, Ireland, USA, Canada, Australia, New Zealand, South Africa, American Samoa, Andorra, Anguilla, Antigua and Barbuda, Aruba, Bahamas, Barbados, Belize, Bermuda, Botswana, British Indian Ocean Territory, British Virgin Islands, Brunei, Cameroon, Cayman Islands, Cook Islands and Denmark.

Each letter of the English alphabet can be written as a ‘small letter’ and as a ‘large letter’. Large letters are also called ‘capital letters’ or ‘capitals’ :

A B C D E F G H I J K L M N O P Q R S T U V W X Y Z —Capitat letters
a b c d e f g h i j k l m n o p q r s t u v w x y z —Small letters

Small letters are sometimes called ‘lower case’ and large letters ‘upper case’.

Use of Capital Letters

1. Use a capital letter for the *personal pronoun* ‘I’:

(a) What can I say? (b) I am a boy.

2. Use a capital letter *to begin a sentence* or to begin *speech*:

(a) The woman arrived. (b) She sat down.
(c) Fortunately she came on time.

3. Use capital letters **for many *abbreviations* and *acronyms* :**

G.M.T. or GMT (Greenwich Mean Time),
N.A.T.O. or NATO or Nato (North Atlantic Treaty Organization).

4. Use a capital letter **for names of *days* of the *week, months of the year, holidays* :**
   Monday, Tuesday, Wednesday, etc.;
   January, February , March ,etc. ;
   Christmas , Deepawali, etc. ;
   Armistice Day , Father's day.
5. Use a capital letter **for the names of *countries, languages & nationalities, religions*:**
   China, France, India ;
   Japanese, English , French ;
   Christianity, Buddhism , Sikhism.
6. Use a capital letter **for persons' *names* and *titles*:**
   Anita, Ram, William Shakespeare;
   Professor Jhons, Dr Smith;
   Captain Kailash, King Henry V.
7. Use a capital letter **for *trade-marks* and names of *companies* and other *organizations*:**
   Coca Cola, Waterman;
   Microsoft Corporation, Maruti;
   the United Nations, the Red Cross.
8. Use a capital letter **for names of *places* and *monuments* :**
   London, Tokyo, the Latin Quarter ;
   the Eiffel Tower, St. Paul's Cathedral;
   Jaisingh Palace, the White House;
   Oxford Street, Fourth Avenue;
   Jupiter, Mars, Syrius, Neptune;
   Asia, the Middle East, the South Pole.
9. Use a capital letter **for *names of vehicles*; like—ships, trains and spacecraft:**
   the Titanic . the Vikrant;
   the Orient Express, the Flying Scotsman;
   Challenger 2, the Enterprise
10. Use a capital letter **for *titles of books*, poems, songs, plays, films etc:**
    War And Peace;
    If, Futility;
    Like a Virgin,
    The Taming of the Shrew,
    The Lion King, Gone With The Wind.
11. Use capitals letters (**sometimes!**) **for headings, titles of articles, books etc, and newspaper headlines:**
    (a) HOW TO WRITE CORRECT ENGLISH (a heading)
    (b) Chapter VI : CLINTON'S EARLY LIFE (Title of an Article)
    (c) LIFE ON MARS (Title of a book.)

PARAGRAPH WRITING

What is a paragraph?

A paragraph is a collection of related sentences dealing with a single topic or we can say that a ***Paragraph is a unit of thoughts with one idea developed adequately.*** A paragraph should contain each of the following : *Unity, Coherence, A Topic Sentence*, and *Adequate Development*. All of these traits overlap, so using and adapting them to our specific purpose will help us to construct effective paragraphs.

1. Unity : The entire paragraph should concern itself with a single focus. If it begins with *one focus or major point of discussion,* it should not end with another or wander within different ideas.

2. Coherence : Coherence is the trait that makes the paragraph easily understandable to a reader. Coherence can be created or maintained in your paragraphs by ***carrying over the same idea from sentence to sentence.*** These sentences are related to the main idea and give more information about the main idea. These sentences include; facts, details, explanations, reasons, examples, illustrations.

3. A Topic sentence(Main idea sentence) : ***A topic sentence is a sentence that indicates in a*** *general way what* ***idea or thesis the paragraph is going to deal with.*** Although not all paragraphs have clear-cut topic or main idea sentences, and despite the fact that topic sentences can occur anywhere in the paragraph (as the first sentence, the last sentence, or somewhere in the middle), an easy way to make sure your reader understands the topic of the paragraph is to *put your topic sentence near the beginning of the paragraph.*

***A main idea sentence* (topic sentence) answers the following questions:**

- What is the paragraph about?
- What is the main point I want to make?
- What do I want to say?

4. Adequate development : The topic (which is introduced by the topic sentence) *should be discussed fully and adequately.* Again, this varies from paragraph to paragraph, but it solely depends on the purpose of writing and demand of the examination.

Some points to make sure your *paragraph is well developed* :

(a) Use examples and illustrations,

(b) Cite *data* in your paragraph (*i.e.*, facts, statistics, evidence, details, and others),

(c) Examine *testimony* (what other people say; such as-quotes and paraphrases),

(d) Use an *anecdote* or story to illustrate or prove your arguement in the paragraph,

(e) *Define* terms in the paragraph,

(f) Compare and contrast,

(g) Evaluate causes and reasons,

(h) Examine effects and consequences,

(i) Analyse the topic of the paragraph, you want to write,

(j) Describe the topic,

(k) Offer a chronology of an event (time segments) if need be.

Solved Examples :

THE VALUE OF TIME

Time is very precious. We should not waste our time. Time, once lost is lost for ever. If you waste your time,time will waste you. Money spent can be earned again . It is not so with time. Time once spent, is spent and gone. It can never be got back. Almost everything in the world can be purchased, but time lost cannot be purchased.As each second ticks away, that second moves from the present to the past. If you have not properly used that single second when it was in the present, it is a second wasted and it is already lost and becomes the past. No amount of crying or trying can bring you back the past. If you want success in life , make proper use of time. Mind the present and make full use of it.

I WON A LOTTERY

I am from a middle-class family. My life was going on easily. One day, I was coming back from school. A lottery ticket seller came to me. He requested me to purchase a ticket. He told me the possibility of winning the first prize. He drew a very promising picture before me. I purchased a ticket in the name of God. On due date, the draw was opened. Next day, I saw the newspaper. I brought my ticket. I was surprised to see that I had won the first prize of Rs.fifty lakh. At first, I did not believe it. I was mad with joy. When luck favours, it knows no limits. I cried with happiness. My parents, brother and sisters came to me. They also checked the ticket number. They were extremely happy. My relatives and friends came to congratulate me. My father brought sweets from the market. We gave sweets to everyone who came to our house. Everyone was telling us that we were very lucky. I have no words to express my joy and feelings. That day really brought happiness to all of us.

GOOD MANNERS

Good manners are not born with us. They are learnt. Good manners help to make a man popular. They are the ornaments of a gentleman. They make a person a useful member of the society. They are a ladder to success. They are more important than the laws of the government. If a man has good manners, he is liked by all. People praise him and respect him.

Good manners cost nothing, but their effects are very valuable. Good manners give colour and grace to life. We should demonstrate good manners at home, at school and everywhere. We should respect our parents, neighbours, teachers and elders. We should have affection (love) for those, who are younger to us. We should respect the feelings of others. We should look to the comforts of each member of our family. Politeness is a very necessary element of good manners. We should not unnecessarily argue with others. We should not lose our temper. We should not hurt the feelings of others. We must remember, that our rights are limited by the rights of others. Good manners bring us honour.

MY AMBITION IN LIFE

Life without an ambition is like a ship without rudder.Man is the maker of his life. Those who aim at nothing get nothing. In fact, without aim, a man wanders about in dark. Life without aim is no life at all. Aim gives direction to the life. Ambitions differ from man to man. Some people aim at wealth, some at power and some at eminence.

The service to man is the service to God. I also want to serve human beings. My ambition is to become an ideal teacher. Teachers are the builders of nation . Teaching is a peaceful job. A teacher is always young among the students. A teacher feels pleasure in teaching.A mother simply gives birth to a child , a teacher makes him capable. He wishes that his students should bring a good name to him and to his country. A true teacher does not run after money. A true teacher has a respectable position in the society. People respect a true teacher.

Students are the true wealth of a teacher. A teacher follows the principle-'simple living and high thinking'. A teacher has morals and teaches morals to his students.

So, my ambition is to become a true teacher.

A MORNING WALK

Walking is the best exercise. It is a natural tonic. It is good for the old and the young alike. It keeps the body healthy and strong. There is a saying "A healthy mind lives in a healthy body." A morning walk keeps our mind fresh and makes us active. Early rising is a good habit.

Nature is full of peace and beauty. Through morning walk, we come into close contact with nature. We enjoy the beauties of nature. The air is cool and pleasant. We see that birds are singing. Flowers are laughing and leaves are dancing. We feel pleasure. We notice green trees and green fields. They look very beautiful. The air is fresh and full of natural fragrance. Peace prevails everywhere. A walks in the morning gives us pleasure and peace. We forget our worries. Noble ideas come to our mind. We are not in a hurry and walk slowly. We feel that God is really a big artist. We get free fresh air (oxygen). It makes our lungs and heart strong and keeps illness away.

After some time, the sky begins to become red in the eastern horizon. It shows that the sun is about to rise. Slowly, the sun peeps out at the horizon. It looks like a big red ball! The scene of rising sun has its own charm. In short, we can say that morning walk is a boon.

GOING TO A DOCTOR

I detest the idea of being sick. However, sickness does not care for one's likes and dislikes. One day, I got up feeling quite uneasy. I thought it was the outcome of lack of sleep. When it persisted, my parents and I knew some sickness was in the offing. My father took me to Dr. Joshi , a well known physician of the town. There was a great rush at his clinic. The doctor was examining the patients one by one. We had to wait for over forty five minutes. The doctor asked me to open my mouth and show him the tongue saying, 'ah'. An assistant of the doctor took my temperature. The doctor told my father that I had a bad cold. He asked me to stay in bed for a week. I was asked to take light food only. The doctor prescribed me some capsules, some tablets and a cough syrup. The behaviour of the doctor impressed my father and me a lot.

A ROAD ACCIDENT

It was 21st December. I was going to my school. The road between Ashoka Circle and Bhagat Singh Circle was very busy. Everybody seemed in a hurry. A young man on a motorcycle came . He was driving the bike at a great speed. A girl was going on a bicycle. The motorcyclist tried to control his speed but it was too late. There was a severe collision. He knocked down the girl. The girl started screaming with pain. Some people ran to help the girl. The motorcyclist and I took her to the general hospital. We took the girl to 'Emergency Ward'. The doctor on duty quickly examined the girl and gave her some tablets. I telephoned the parents of the girl. They immediately arrived and thanked me. The motorcyclist was very ashamed for the accident.

There has been a great rise in traffic recently. The number of road accidents is fast increasing. Rash driving and lack of effective traffic control are mainly responsible for it.

A RAINY DAY

It was a cloudy day. Before I set off to office, my mother insisted on taking an umbrella. So I took an umbrella along with my briefcase. Hardly had I started, when it started drizzling. Within minutes the drizzle turned to heavy showers. The road was completely wet with water gushing into the drains near the road. I took shelter in the varandah of a shop near the bus stop.

As I looked around, I saw boys and girls splashing water on one another. Little children were dancing and jumping with joy. One small boy was trying to float a little paper boat. Some people were fully drenched but did not care and went on walking. Buses, cars, rickshaws and scooters flashed past splashing water.

After about half an hour, the rain stopped and I set off to office.

MY HOBBY

Every person has some hobby. Hobbies differ from man to man. My hobby is gardening. It gives me pleasure and satisfaction. It also helps me to keep fit as physical labour is involved in it. Mostly, I am free in the morning. So I devote an hour every day for the sake of my hobby. I have grown a beautiful lawn in front of my house. This lawn is surrounded by flowering plants. I have a good variety of 'English roses' besides the seasonal flowers that I grow. I have collected a good number of fine species of cacti and crotons. In the evenings, I sit in the lawn, see the blooming flowers and feel as if I am living in a garden of happiness. My parents like the hobby I pursue and my neighbours praise me.

A VILLAGE FAIR

I live in a village. Last Monday I went to see the fair of Baba Ramdeoji. I went there with my friends. Hundreds of men, women and children were there. They were in fine clothes. The ground looked like a sea of people. People were going and coming here and there in groups. Some women were singing songs. There were many beggars also. They were begging. There were some scouts and policemen to help the people.

There were many stalls. They were decorated with toys, bangles, rings, ear-rings, combs, clothes, balloons and many other things. There was rush on every stall. Stall-keepers were doing good business. There were some stalls selling sweets, namkins and tea. We were also enjoying the fair. We saw a small boy weeping. He had lost his parents. We took him to the police-chowki. His parents were waiting there. They were very sad. When they saw the boy with us, they were very happy. They thanked us.

We went to the temple. There was a long queue of people. We also stood in the queue. After some time we had 'darshan' of Baba. We took one more round of the fair. We were tired. We went to a tea stall. We took a some 'chat' and tea. There were some merry-go-rounds. They were attracting many people. We went there. We also enjoyed them.

It was evening. I purchased some toys and balloons for my younger brother. We came back to our houses. I was very happy. I cannot forget this fair in my life.

IMPORTANCE OF TREES

Trees are called 'GREEN GOLD'. It means trees are as valuable as gold. We get wood from trees. Wood is used in making furniture, houses and other useful things. Trees give us fruits, spices, timber and many useful medicines. They give fodder to animals. Trees breath out oxygen. We breathe in oxygen and so are alive. Every country is suffering from air-pollution. Trees help in reducing air-pollution. Many industries depend on trees.

Trees attract clouds, and clouds bring rain. Trees check soil-erosion. Wild animals and birds live in forests. They are useful in many ways.

Trees are our helpful and useful friends.In reality, trees are the valuable gifts of nature to man. We should honour and preserve trees.

THE IMPORTANCE OF NEWSPAPERS

Newspaper is a mirror which reflects the political, economical and the social conditions of the country . Newspapers try to give us the latest news about the country and the world. Newspapers are the windows through which we see the happenings of the world and the country.

They enhance our general knowledge. They have educational value. They serve the society in many ways. We should inculcate the habit of reading newspapers.

The government programmes and policies are made public through newspapers. If a particular policy is good, people appreciate it; and if it is harmful, a cry against it can be raised in newspapers. They are an eye-opener for the government. In this way, newspapers are very important for democracy. A good newspaper is a watchdog of democracy.

AN INDIAN WEDDING

Marriage is a social necessity. It is said that marriages are settled in heaven and celebrated on the earth. Indian weddings are colourful.

Last month I attended the marriage ceremony of my friend Ramesh. The house was decorated with colourful lights and paper-flags. In the evening, his friends and relatives gathered at his house. All were in fine dresses. Ladies were singing songs. My friend put on a special dress. He sat on a decorated mare. There was a music-band-party with the 'barat'. We went to the bride's house in a procession. On the way, groom's friends danced at many places .

The house of the bride was also decorated. The relatives of the bride welcomed us. There was a tent and there were chairs. We took our seats. The groom went at the gate. The bride came in a fine bridal-dress. She was looking very beautiful. They garlanded each other.

They served us tasty dinner. We enjoyed it. The groom also took food. Then he was taken into the house. There was a 'Pandit'. The bridegroom and the bride sat side by side. The 'Pandit' chanted out some promises. The bride and bridegroom repeated them. The pair took seven rounds of the holy fire. The ceremony took about two hours. Now they were husband and wife. Next morning, the 'barat' came back to the bridegroom's house with the bride . They were welcomed there.

FAMILIARITY BREEDS CONTEMPT

Familiarity means-closeness; means- lack of formalities; means-knowing all the ins and outs of the others. 'Familiarity' also means lot of expectations , which result in giving rise to cause of dispute and also breed reasons for quarrel or contempt, as expectations can't be calculated and are very difficult to be fulfilled in this world, where everyone is busy in his own affairs. On the other hand, in formal acquaintances we know little about others and take more formal care and pay more formal respect, so there is little cause of quarrel or contempt.A reasonable distance in relations so, is necessary to avoid quarrel and contempt.Rightly said, "A hedge between, keeps the friendship green'' and also, ''familiarity breeds contempt".

ROMANCE IS THE MAGIC OF DISTANCE

One likes to acquire what is not within one's ambit.Any rare thing once possessed , lost charm of having it, but a thing of whatever quality till not acquired is a rare thing and so has its importance.There is a saying : 'Distant bells are charming'. The future is always more charming because that is far from the present.A man generally pines for distant objects and moments in the hope of getting imaginative pleasure. We often discover an element of magic in the distant obects.Romance vanishes as soon as the object of romance is achieved or acquired by us. The fact is that 'the element of distance' casts some magical spell on us. All human faces and objects look romantic till they are at a distance. Keats has so rightly said, "Heard melodies are sweet, but those unheard are sweeter".

GOD HELPS THOSE WHO HELP THEMSELVES

God has gifted the man with such wonderful and tremendous powers that he can achieve anything. A person, who is sincere and dedicated to his task, gets success. In time of distress , when one aspires some divinely help to get one free from the period of distress, the divine help comes only to those who help themselves . God only helps those who do not loose heart and fight tooth and nails to get success.One, who is hard working , sincere and devoted honestly to one's work, is certain to achieve his goal and get success and to such fellows, God is there to come to aid and rescue. So, one must not keep oneself idle and waste one's time in the hope of any divine help as God helps those who help themselves. 'Every one pushes the moving cart, but none lifts the bogged down one'.

THE FRUITS OF LABOUR ARE SWEETER THAN THE GIFTS OF FORTUNE

What is received in gift or what is inherited from the parents is never as charming or important as the things achieved by us by our own efforts, by our own labour.The 'sweet' acquired through 'sweat' will be much sweeter than the sweet given to us by someone. Nothing tastes so sweet as that is earned by hard labour. 'By the sweat of thy brow thou shalt earn thy bread'-was the divine wish.The things achieved by hard work shall be more permanent, more delicious, more lovable, more enjoying and rendering us real happiness.

Anything acquired by the grace of God or by luck will not give you the real enjoyment and real respect, because this fortune does not have anything your own.The history remembers those who change the path of adversity by their hard labour.The world adores those who make their own fortune and create examples for others.Abraham Lincon, Dhiru Bhai Ambani etc. are several examples of persons who achieved the success by their sheer hard work and so they are adored today.'Honest labour bears a beautiful face.'

SPARE THE ROD AND SPOIL THE CHILD

What is good and what is bad can't be understood by a child.He tries to do what he feels good and enjoyful. Sometimes he puts unreasonable demands and presses upon it to get it fulfilled by all the means he knows. If we fulfill such demands it means we are not sincere to our child in real terms and spoiling his habits, making him peevish and obstinate. To make a child disciplined and hardworking, we have to put a check on the wrong demands , wrong actions of the child .Even if we are to use some force, we must not hesitate , because if we spare the rod we spoil the child. Unjustified and wrong demands must be nipped in the bud.

TIME AND TIDE WAIT FOR NONE

Time and tide have their own course , their own routine as per nature's rule.They do not wait for anyone. They come and go their own ways. A wise man makes the best use of his tims .The time once gone never comes back. Those who do not make a proper use of opportunity, often repent later on.One should siege the opportunity, whenever it is within one's reach.If you loose, other fellow will grab it and then you will be blaming your luck or anything else for your loosing such a good opportunity. Time and tide wait for none and they will not wait for us also.

ONLY THE WEARER KNOWS WHERE THE SHOE PINCHES

It is very difficult to calculate the sufferings or problems of others without putting oneself entirely in others' place. Looking from the outside, a man of power, like a king or a minister, seems enoying all the luxuries of life ,but his problems and pains can't be understood by ordinary people.The pains, the difficulties and responsibilities of enjoying position of authority are so immense that can't be realised until we are in the same position.Crown carries with it not only the power but the liabilities and the responsibilities also. So it is rightly said that only the wearer knows where the shoes pinches.

STORY WRITING

Story-telling is not a difficult task .You also know how to tell a story. You do it every day! Every time you tell someone about something that happened to you or something you saw or you did, you tell a story. For example, if something new happens at your school, you tell a friend about it, you've created a story. The point is how to write it ?

You can write a story about anything you want. All you need to know are the basics — the ingredients of your story. You can't bake a cake without ingredients, right? So, before you begin to write, sit and think for a little while about the beginning, middle and end of your story. You must have the whole plot clear in your mind.

In this exercise, you are not asked to make up a story. The plot of each story is given to you more or less fully in the outlines provided. *You are to complete the story* with a well connected narrative and make it fully interesting .

Points to Remember:

1. Set your mind free. Set a clear idea of the plot of the story in your mind before you begin to write.
2. Keep in mind the outline given ; i.e. do not leave any point and keep to the track of the outline.
3. Connect the points given in the outline properly , so that the whole story looks well connected, compact and interesting.
4. If need be, you can introduce *dialogue or conversation;* but be careful that these should be relevant.
5. The *conclusion* should be written in such a manner that the whole story leads up to it naturally and it should not come to the end abruptly.
6. While writing *a heading or title to the story,* choose the main character object or incident of the story (e.g., "The Barber of Baghdad," or "The Pot of Olives," or "An Accident") or a proverb or well known quotation that suits the theme of the story (e.g. "Something is better than nothing" "Failures are the pillar of success", etc.)
7. Your composition should be grammatically correct .
8. Do spell check and revise the work until it is as per your choice.

Examples:

ROBERT BRUCE AND THE SPIDER

(Robert Bruce .... King of Scotland .... loses repeatedly on battle field .... notices a spider .... climbing up to the roof .... at last it reaches the roof .... learns a lesson .... fights against the English .... wins back the liberty of Scotland.)

Once there lived a King in Scotland. His name was Robert Bruce (his kingdom was over-powered by the English). He fought very hard to free his country from the English. But he lost repeatedly on the battle field. He was badly defeated. He had to run for his life into the forest. There he hid himself in a cave.

One day he was feeling much depressed, he noticed a spider, trying to climb up the wall to reach the roof. Bruce for the time being forgot his own troubles and watched the efforts of the insect with interest. It climbed and fell again and again but the spider did not lose heart.The spider began to climb up again. It went up steadily inch by inch and at last reached the roof.

The king at once rose up crying, "I must try again and again like the spider and the success will surely be mine." He learnt a lesson. He once again raised a strong army. He fought against the English. He won back the liberty of his country.

Moral : **Try again and again, till you succeed.**

A WISE TRAVELLER

(A thirsty traveller .... through a forest .... in search of water .... coconut tree .... high for the traveller .... monkeys .... plan .... stones at monkeys .... coconuts at the traveller .... breaks coconuts .... drinks water .... quenches his thirst.)

Once upon a time there was a traveller. He was passing through a forest. He was very thirsty. He searched for water everywhere but all in vain. At last he came under a coconut tree. Coconuts were hanging down from it. He could not climb up the tree because coconuts were very high on it.

There were many monkeys on the tree. The wise traveller thought of a plan. He threw some stones at the monkeys. The monkeys got very angry. They too, plucked coconuts and threw at the traveller. The traveller collected the coconuts and broke them and drank their water. In this way, he quenched his thirst.

Moral : **Wisdom always pays.**

THE HIDDEN TREASURE

(A farmer .... four sons .... very lazy .... father advises them to work hard .... never listen to him .... falls ill .... calls for his sons .... tells them of treasure in the field .... farmer dies .... sons dig up .... no treasure .... sow seed .... good crop .... earn a lot of money .... thank father .... they become rich.)

Once there lived an old farmer in a village . He had four sons. All were very lazy. He often advised his sons to work hard. But the lazy sons never listened to his advice. The old man was much worried.

One day the farmer fell ill. His condition was serious. He wanted to teach his sons the value of hard work. So he called his sons and said to them, "There is a big treasure in my field. I am on deathbed. If you dig up the field, you will surely find it. Dig it out only after my death. But I do not know the exact place where I have buried it." Soon after this the old farmer died.

After some days, the sons dug up all the field to search the treasure. But they found nothing. They were disappointed.

In the meantime, an old man passed that way. He knew what their father meant. He advised them to sow seeds. They did so. There was a good crop . They became rich. Thus they learnt the value of hard work.

Moral : **No pains, no gains.**

BLESSINGS IN DISGUISE

(A merchant .... returning home on his horse .... money under the saddle .... passing through a thick forest .... begins to rain heavily .... sad .... curses God .... starts journey again .... meets a robber .... the robber says, "Your money or your life." .... does not agree .... the robber fires .... the gun does not go off .... the merchant saved .... thanks God.)

Once there was a merchant. One day he went to a fair. He sold all his wares and made huge profits. He started back for his village in the evening. On his way was a thick forest. There were some robbers in the forest. So he hid his money under the saddle of his horse. It began to rain heavily. The merchant was drenched to the skin. He cursed God for such a nasty weather.

A robber came out of the bushes. He aimed a gun at the merchant. He asked the merchant to hand over the money. The merchant was frightened. He spurred his horse to run fast. The robber pressed the trigger of his gun. But it did not go off because it was wet due to rain.So the merchant escaped unhurt. He thanked God for saving his life from the robbers.

***Moral :* One can't judge the acts of God.**

THE WISE KING

(Two women .... claim the same child .... no witness .... difficult to decide .... go to the King .... child to be cut into two parts .... the first woman .... quiet .... the second woman falls at king's feet .... "do not divide" .... agrees to give up the child .... the second woman .... the real mother .... the first woman sent to jail.)

There were two women. Once there was a quarrel between them over a child. Both of them claimed the same child. Each said that she was the child's real mother. There was no eye witness or fullproof evidence to know the reality. So it was very difficult to settle the case.

Both of them went to the king for justice. The king was very wise. He heard their statements. The King said, "There is only one solution to your problem. The child should be cut into two halves. Each of you will get half the child."

The first woman kept quiet but the other one fell at the king's feet and prayed to the king not to kill the child. She said, "My Lord, give this child to her (the other woman) but do not cut it." This affection was a clear proof that she was the real mother. The king gave her the child. The first woman was sent to jail for her wickedness.

A TIGER AND A BRAHMIN

(Tiger .... encaged .... requests Brahmin to set free .... he frees him .... he wants to eat the Brahmin .... a fox comes .... it asks the tiger to show how it was encaged .... tiger enters the cage .... Brahmin asked to shut the cage tightly .... the fox asks the Brahmin to go .... thus he is saved by fox.)

Once a tiger was encaged. He requested a Brahmin to set him free. The Brahmin set the tiger free. Now the tiger wanted to kill the Brahmin and eat him up. A fox was passing that way. The Brahmin requested the fox to arbitrate in that case.The fox understood the wickedness of the tiger. The fox asked the tiger to show how it was encaged. The tiger entered the cage. The fox asked the Brahmin to shut the door tightly.Brahmin did so. Then the fox asked the Brahmin to go home. Thus the cunning fox saved the life of the Brahmin.

***Moral :* Never believe the 'wicked'.**

THE WISE JUDGE

(A merchant .... riding .... city .... a sick man ....wants .... a lift .... puts him on horse back .... refuses to get down .... wants the horse .... both go to the judge .... wise judge .... go to the stables one by one .... horse turns head towards his master .... looks at him with affection .... does not look at the sick man .... judgement.)

Once a merchant was going to the city riding on his horse. He met a sick man on the way. The sick man requested the merchant to give him a lift on his horse. The merchant put the sick man behind himself on the horse-back.

Both of them reached the city. The merchant asked the sick man to get down. But he refused to get down the horse. He said that the horse belonged to him. They took the dispute to a judge. The judge was very wise. He sent the horse to the stable. He asked both the men to come to him next morning.

Next morning, the judge asked the sick man to wait for some time. The wise judge took the merchant to the stable. The horse turned his head towards his master and looked at him with great affection. Then the judge returned with the merchant.

Now the judge took the sick man to the stable. The horse did not look at him. Thus the judge knew, who was the real master of the horse. The sick man was sent to jail for his dishonesty. The merchant got his horse.

***Moral :* Lie has no legs.**

HALF THE PROFIT

(A fisherman .... catches a golden fish .... to the king .... the gate-keeper wants half the reward .... allowed .... the king happy .... offers reward .... demands fifty lashes on his back .... surprised .... dishonesty of the gate-keeper discovered .... punished.)

Once there was a fisherman who used to catch fish daily. One day he caught a golden fish. He wanted to present it to the king. So he reached the king's palace. But the gate-keeper did not allow him to enter the palace and demanded half of what the fisherman would get. The wise fisherman agreed.

The fisherman gave the golden fish to the king. The king was very happy to see such a beautiful fish. The king offered rewards to fisherman; asked him what he wanted .

The fisherman said, "Sir, I want fifty lashes on my back." The king thought that the fisherman was a mad fellow. He ordered his servant to give him fifty mild lashes.

The fisherman asked the king that he wanted to call his partner in the reward. The fisherman called the gate-keeper. Then he told the king how the gate-keeper demanded half the reward. The king understood the whole case and was very angry. The gate-keeper was punished severely and was dismissed from his service. The king rewarded the fisherman handsomely, and praised his wisdom and honesty.

***Moral :* Corruption under the nose must be checked.**

REPRODUCTION OF A STORY POEM

In this exercise, students are required to write the *story of a poem in their own words.* The students should read the poem well, understand the story and then tell the story in their own words in their own way.

Tips to Remember :

(a) Read the whole poem thoroughly and try to understand the theme of the story of the poem. If the story is not quite clear after first reading, *read the poem again and again,* until the theme is quite clear in your mind.

(b) *Note down briefly the main points of the story,* so that these could be helpful to you in writing your narration. Do not leave out any important point.

(c) Now try to write out the story in your own words in simple English. Write straightforwardly and in natural manner.

(d) *Avoid using the language of the poem.* Don't use literary adjectives etc.,use simple and plain words.

(e) The sentences used should be well connected. *Check again if any important point is left.* Also *check* the *spelling* and *punctuation*. The whole composition should be well construed and compact.

Example 1. ***Read the following poem thoroughly and reproduce the story of the poem, concisely in your own words.***

KING BRUCE AND THE SPIDER

King Bruce of Scotland threw himself down
In a lonely mood to think;
It's true he was king and wore a crown,
But his heart was beginning to sink.
For he had been trying to do a great deed
To make his people glad;
He had tried, and tried, but couldn't succeed;
And so he became quite sad.
He threw himself down in low despair,
As grieved as a man could be;
And after a while as he pondered there,
"I'll give it all up," said he.
Now just at that moment a spider dropped
With its silken cobweb clue;
And the king in the midst of his thinking stopped
To see what the spider would do.

It was a long way up to the ceiling dome
And it hung by a rope so fine,
That how it would get to its cobweb home
King Bruce could not divine.
It soon began to cling and crawl
Straight up with strong endeavour;
But down it came with a slippery sprawl,
As near the ground as ever.
Up, up it ran, not a second did stay,
To make the least complaint,
Till it fell still lower, and there it lay,
A little dizzy and faint.
Its head grew steady- again it went,
And travelled a half-yard higher;
It was a very thin thread it had to tread,
A road where its feet would tire.
Again it fell and swung below,
But again it quickly mounted;
Till up and down, now fast, now slow,
Nine brave attempts were counted.
'Sure' cried the king, 'that foolish thing
will strive no more to climb;
When it toils so hard to reach and cling,
And tumbles every time.
But up the insect went once more,
'Ah' me!' it's an anxious minute;
He's only a foot from his cobweb door;
Steadily, steadily, inch by inch,
Higher and higher he got;
And bold little run at the very last pinch
Put him into his own small cot.
'Bravo, bravo!' the king cried out,
'All honour to those who try;
The spider up there showed no despair;

He conquered, and why shouldn't I?

And so king Bruce felt stronger in mind,

And people tell the tale

This he tried once more as he tried before,

And that time did not fail.

Reproduction:

KING BRUCE AND THE SPIDER

King Bruce of Scotland wanted to make his people glad. He was not successful. He was very sad. He went away to a lonely place.He thought of the situation. He was lying down. He saw that a spider was trying to climb up the ceiling. But it fell down again and again. It tried nine times. It did not lose heart. It tried tenth time, It was successful. The king was watching the spider. The spider inspired the king. He also decided to try again. Bruce learnt two lessons; (1) we should not lose heart at failures, (2) we should try and try again. So king Bruce tried again and got success.

Example 2. ***Read the following poem thoroughly and reproduce the story of the poem, in four paragraphs in your own words:***

PEACE

I'd like to build the world a home

And furnish it with love.

Grow apple trees and honeybees

And snow-white turtle doves.

I'd like to teach the world to sing

In perfect harmony.

I'd like to hold it in my arms

And keep it company.

I'd like to see the world for once

All standing hand in hand;

And hear its echo through the streets

For peace throughout the land.

Last night I had the strangest dream

I ever had before

I dreamt the world had all agreed

To put an end to war.
I dreamt I saw a room somewhere
And the room was full of men;
And the paper they were singing said
We'd never fight again.
And when the paper was signed and sealed
And million copies made
There was cheering in the streets
And grateful prayers were said.
I dreamt I saw the world for once
All marching hand in hand
And swords and guns and uniforms
Were banned throughout the land.
Last night I had the strangest dream
I ever had before
I dreamt the world had all agreed
To put an end to war.

Reproduction:

PEACE

The poet has a noble desire. He wishes to change the whole world into a dream home and equip it with all comfortable things. There he wishes to grow apple trees and keep beehives for honey. He would like to rear white doves. White doves are a symbol of peace. He would also like to teach the world to sing in complete harmony. He would like to keep this peace and harmony with him. Thus he would be happy to hear the echo of the music of peace all over the world.According to him, what the world needs today is only peace.

The poet says that he had a strange dream last night. He had never had such a dream before. He dreamt that all the world had agreed to put an end to war. He also saw a big hall. It was full of men. They were from all parts of the world. They were signing of an agreement, never to fight in future.

And when they had signed the agreement and sealed it, they made millions of copies of this agreement, perhaps to distribute them all over the world. They, perhaps, wanted to tell the people about this agreement of peace. People also cheered this agreement and said prayers in a gesture of thanks.

The poet dreamt that the people were marching hand in hand with one another. All the weapons of war and military uniforms were banned forever. People would not fight anymore in future. Then last night he had one more dream. It was the strangest of all. And he had never had such a dream before. He dreamt that all the people had agreed to put an end to war. There would be no war in future.

LETTER WRITING

Letter writing is an art. A well written letter not only conveys your message to the receiver in clear terms but also reflects on him about your overall personality. Everyone has to write letters of some sort in his life, so one must learn the art of letter writing.

Letter can be classified broadly in *two categories.*

(1) *Personal* or *friendly* letters, including invitational letters,

(2) *Business* letters, including letters to government or semi-government officials, letters to newspapers , letters of application etc.

All letters in general consist of *following parts:*

1.The Heading,

2. The Greeting,

3. The Body,

4. The Complimentary close (The subscription), and

5. The Signature line.

PERSONAL LETTERS

Personal letters, also known as **friendly letters,** normally **have *five parts*:**

1. The Heading : This includes the ***address, line by line, with the last line being the date***. Skip a line after the heading. The heading is indented to the middle of the page.If using pre-addressed stationery, just add the date.

The heading of a friendly letter contains the *return address,* followed by the date.

In a friendly letter, the **heading is always indented to the middle of the page.**

If the correspondents are familiar enough and the recipient knows the writer's address, or if the stationery is imprinted with the return address, then the return address may be omitted. (Although another reason for mentioning the return address is a backup, in case the envelope gets damaged....) But don't forget to include the date. For example:

129, South West Block,
Alwar (Rajasthan).
August 24, 2006.

(Most writers skip a line between the address and the date.)

2. The Greeting (Salutation): The greeting always *ends with a comma.* The greeting may be *formal,* beginning with the word ***"dear"*** and using the person's given ***name or relationship,*** or it may be *informal*, if appropriate:

Formal greeting : Dear Uncle Jimmy, Dear Mr. Walker,

Informal greeting : Hi Joe, Greetings,

The greeting in a friendly letter *capitalizes the first word and any noun*. It normally ends with a comma, though it might be all right *to end with an exclamation mark* when writing to someone with whom we are very familiar and the emphasis is appropriate.(Occasionally very personal greetings may end with an exclamation mark *for emphasis.*)

3. The body: ***The body*** **of the letter contains the** ***main text*** **.** This includes *the message you want to write.* Normally in a friendly letter, the beginning of paragraphs is indented. If not indented, be sure to *skip a space between paragraphs. The block style* (no indented paragraphs) is considered too formal for a friendly letter, so each new paragraph should be indented.Skip a line after the greeting and before the close. Skipping a line between paragraphs, especially in typed or printed copy, helps the reader.

4. The complimentary close (The subscription) : This short expression is always–a few words on a single (eg. **Sincerely yours, Truely yours**). The complimentary close begins with a capital letter and ends with a comma. It should be indented to the same column as the heading. Skip one to three spaces for the signature line.

5. The signature line : Type or print your name. The *handwritten signature goes above this line* and *below the close.* The signature line and the handwritten signature are indented to the same column as the close. If the writer and reader are very friendly, or if the letter is handwritten in the same script as the signature, the signature line or the last name in the signature line may be omitted.

Unless there is great familiarity between the correspondents, *the signature should be in blue or black ink.* For example:

Truly yours,
(Signature goes here)
Suresh Gupta.

Postscript : If your letter contains a postscript, *begin it with* ***P.S.*** and *end it with your initials.* Skip a line after the signature line to begin the postscript.

ENVELOPE FORMAT

The following picture shows what an addressed envelope should look like. The horizontal lines represent lines of type.

Follow this format regardless of letter style you used:

Stamped Addressed Envelope

Postage

The postage (stamp or prepaid imprint) goes in *the upper right hand corner* of the envelope.

Do not cover a stamp with adhesive tape.

Make sure the stamp is positioned so that its cancellation will not affect the addresses.

Be sure that the *postage is sufficient as per norms.* Always check letters containing more than three pages, letters with inserts, or letters to foreign countries for correct postage. There are few things that will annoy a correspondent more than having to pick up and pay for penal postage due to letter.

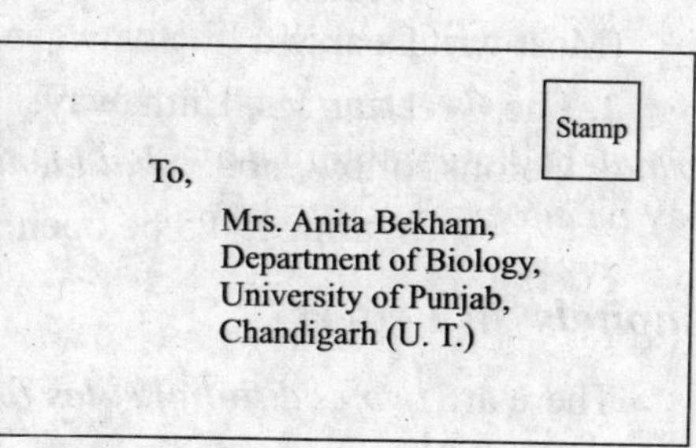

Address

The name and address of the recipient should be *centered on the envelope.* Make sure the address begins far *enough down on the face of the envelope*, so that it will not be covered by the cancellation of stamps.

If you are using envelopes with windows, make sure the address is visible clearly through the window.

Addresses on envelopes are normally single-spaced.For example:

Mrs Anita Bekham,
Department of Biology,
University of Punjab,
Chandigarh(U.T.).

PUNCTUATING THE LETTERS

Commas

(a) Use commas *after the salutation* (also called the *greeting*) in a personal letter and *after the complimentary closing* in all letters:

(i) Salutation:

Dear Ram,
My dearest Hina,

(ii) Closing:

Sincerely,
Truly yours,

Colons (:) used in Special Cases

1. Numerical expressions of time,

   Example : 5:31 p.m.

   The colon (:) goes *between the hour and minute.* If seconds are noted, a colon goes *between the minute and second* also.

2. We can also use 'colon' with *salutations* in business letters, as per following:

   Dear Sir:

   Dear Ms. Hathaway:

3. Colons follow *labels that identify important ideas meant to get attention*:

   Warning: To be opened by authorized personnel only.

Capitals in Letters

There are ***two additional rules for capitalizing a word'* when writing letters**:

1. Capitalize the *first word and all nouns in the salutation* (greeting):

   Dear Sir:
   My dearest Aunt,
   Greetings!

2. Capitalize the *first word in the complimentary closing:*

Sincerely,
Truly yours,

With best wishes,

Examples of Personal Letters

Q. 1. Letter from a father, giving advice to his son, who has taken admission in a college.

1/42,Aravali Vihar,
Rajgarh(Alwar).
July 14, 200.

My very dear Son,

This is the first letter I am writing to you, after you left home for higher studies at the college. You have been a very sincere and hard working student so far. You are at the threshold of making and shaping your future career . If you would be sincere to your studies , you could get what you desire .These four years of sincerity and devotion to the studies are very important in shaping the career of a student.You are venturing into a new life where you find everything to decide yourself. There is none to tell to study or play or watch T.V. You are to manage all your time.

I know that you will not disappoint me with respect to your studies, but you are in your youth , and know little of the temptations and allurement with which youth is beset nowadays. The bad habits and evils caught during this period can spoil not only your own career but also destroy the aspirations of the parents .

Companions influence one's character greatly; good companions make one's character and bad companions mar one's career. Choose the friends who are sincere, honest and industrious. Education plays very important role in the formation of character. Morals are of greater importance in life than the subjective knowledge.

Indolence is the worst habit a student can form. Remember that doing nothing may do you even more harm. You may find plenty of books in your college library. Read history and biographies, both for instruction and amusement and also if you feel inclined for something lighter.

I don't want to say anything more.You are yourself wise boy. Remember :

"Heights by the great men reached and kept , were not attained by sudden flight, but while their companions were sleeping, they were toiling upwards in the night".

Write to me regularly and unreservedly. Always look upon me as your best friend, hiding nothing, not even your mistakes or faults.

Your mother conveys you her fondest love.

Your affectionate father,
S.C. Gupta

Q. 2. *Write a letter to your friend, congratulating him on his success in the RAS examination.*

32/31,West Patel Nagar,
Jaisalmer.
July 23, 200.

My dear Pramod,

I am glad to see your result in the Rajasthan Patrika of today; that you have been successful in the RAS examination and secured good rank. I conveyed this happy news to my father who was sitting beside me. He too was overjoyed.

I thank God for His Kindness and wish you a bright future. I know well that you have been intelligent and diligent in your school and college days. Certainly your success is due to God's grace as well as your hard work and also timely guidance of your respected parents.

Please convey my respectful compliments to your parents.Again congratulations to you.

Yours sincerely,
Raj Kumar

Q. 3. *Write a letter to your friend, who has recently lost his mother.*

10,Barkat Nagar,
Jaipur.
May 4, 200.

My dear Mahesh,

It is really a very sad news that you have lost your mother. I knew your mother was ill, but the illness was not so serious. The news of your mother's death came to me as a shock. I know you will feel it deeply, for you always thought so much of your mother and loved her very much. I also feel it as a personal loss to myself. She was always very kind and loving to me. I can't forget her love and affection for me and her motherly care and worries for me. She was such a good and noble lady.

In such sorrow, we are always alone. Words, I know, can't soothe the wounds. May God give you strength to bear this loss!

Yours sincerely,
Kailash Jaiman

Q. 4. Write a letter of apology to a friend for not keeping an appointment.

29,Janta Colony,
Jaipur. N.P. June 19, 200.

My dear Pradeep,

I am sorry, I could not join you at dinner last night. You must have waited for me and cursed me as well for not keeping the appointment. But this lapse on my part was due to the fact that I met with an accident while coming over to your place.

Near Ghat Gate, a motorcycle came from the opposite direction. It was without lights. It hit my scooter. I fell off the scooter and lay on the road. My left arm was badly injured. Some people took me to hospital. I was allowed to leave the hospital only after midnight. My arm was plastered. I hope you will excuse my absence.

Yours Sincerely,
Ashok

Q. 5. Write a letter to your younger brother, advising him to take part in evening games.

12, South West Block,
Alwar.
February15, 200.

My dear Tapan,

I met your class teacher yesterday. He told me that you stood first in the class. I was glad to hear it. But he also told me that you have become a bookworm. You do not take part in any kind of games. It is not good. It will affect your health.

I suggest you to take part in evening games. Do not study at the cost of your health. Play hockey or football . Play the game for an hour. It will refresh your mind and keep you physically fit. This will also help you in your studies. Do study hard, but do play a while. Work, while you work and play, while you play; that is the way to be happy and healthy.

With love,

Yours affectionately,
Prakash Gupta

Q. 6. Letter to your elder brother from the town in which you have just joined a new appointment, describing the important features of the town, and of the people with whom you are associated.

13,Mayur Colony,
Bhilwara.
April 25, 200.

My dear Brother,

I am glad to receive your loving letter and happy to learn that everyone is fine at home. You have asked me to give you a brief description of this town. I like this town and the people here. I am sure that the description as follows will make you like the place and fill you with a longing to see it.

It is a big trade centre. There are two cloth mills here, which supply cloth to the whole of the country. There is a large cloth market where you can buy cloth of all qualities and printing designs . There are four boys' colleges and eight senior secondary schools.There are two girls' college also. There are three government hospitals , one for male, other for female and child and several private nursing homes .Besides these, there is a charitable Eye hospital also.It has a Railway junction . Three beautiful Picture Halls are also situated in the town. There is one Engineering and one Dental College too, located in the Industrial Area about 8 kilometers from the town. The most interesting feature of the town is its magnificent temples where hymns are sung and cymbals are clashed daily in the morning and evening.

People here, are nice, honest, straighforward, hardworking and trustworthy. They are by and large not addicted to any vices; as-drinking and gambling. My colleagues are also very cooperative and of helping nature. The General Manager of my company is a thorough gentleman and takes keen interest in the welfare of the staff. He is very kind and sympathetic to all the employees.

I am fine here. Everything is going on here nicely as per schedule routine.

Regards to Daddy and Mom.

Yours affectionately,
Maneesh

Q. 7. Personal letter from a student to his friend, telling him about the first impression of the college :

215, Aravali Vihar,
Near Jain Temple,
Alwar (Raj.) 301001.

Dear Shankar,

As you know, I got admission in Rajasthali Commerce College, New Delhi this year. You have asked me to tell you about my new college.

The atmosphere and the environment of the college is entirely different from that of our school.The discipline in the college is not as strict as in our school. No bindings of wearing any uniform. The professors treat us in very friendly way. No terror of the teachers as in school . Professors just come in the class, deliver the lectures and generally do not bother to ask any question from the students. They are not worried whether any student follows them or not.All kinds of facilities; like-library, sports, games, canteen are available in this college.

Students enjoy the freedom of college life. Everyone is at liberty to go wherever he likes, do whatever he likes, and speak what he has in his mind within some limits. There is none to check the students . They can spoil or make their lives.

I can't afford to waste my time in useless things and have started making notes, consulting the library books for the last one week.

I have to do a lot of hard work to achieve good marks.Tell me about you.

Convey my regards to your parents.

Yours sincerely,
Dinesh

Q. 8. Letter to your elder brother, writing him the reasons of your failure in Public Service Commission Examination.

304, Shastri Nagar,
Jodhpur (Raj.),
Jan.16, 200.

My dear Brother,

I am in receipt of your letter. You have asked me the reasons of my failure in Public Service Commission Examination. I do not like to take any excuses but believe in narrating the facts of my failure as per my imaginations. As you also know, this was not an easy competition. I made full preparations for all the four papers, but the time table of my exams was very cumbersome. I had to take three papers continuously. The Economics paper was on 12th Jan. from 3 PM. to 6 PM. and the paper of Statistics -I was scheduled on 13th Jan. from 10 Am. to 1 PM. and after that I had to take the paper of Statistics -II from 3 PM. on the 13th Jan, itself. This all caused a lot of tension to my mind. I couldn't sleep even for a minute on the night of 12th Jan. and so when I went to the examination hall on 13th Jan., I could take the paper of Statistics -I satisfactorily but I could not take the paper of Statistics -II properly and so in this paper I got only 31 marks out of 100 marks. That spoiled my percentage. I did make very good preparations for all the papers, but to whom can I blame, it is my hard luck or say, I was unfortunate as the time table was so uneasy and tedious.

This is the first time, when all the students who opted Economics and Statistics have suffered a lot, because of such time scheduling. I am myself not happy with the result but nothing can be done now. I am determined to take this examination again with more hard work. I remember your words, "A man who wins, is the man who thinks, he can".

Convey my regards to Papa and Mummy.

Yours loving brother,
Prakash

Q. 9. Write a letter to your uncle, thanking him for the birthday gift you have received from him.

105, Mangal Vihar,
Alwar.
February 28, 200.

My very dear Uncle,

Yesterday was my birthday. I received many gifts, but your gift was the best. You have sent me a beautiful wrist watch. Everybody liked it. I thank you very much for such a lovely gift.

Your gift is very precious to me. I was often late for school. Now I shall be punctual. This wrist watch will help me during my examination days also.The watch is a token of your love for me. I shall always keep it with me. Once again, I thank you.

With best regards,

Yours lovingly,
Harsh

Q. 10. Write a letter to your father, asking for some money.

415, Lajpat Nagar,
Alwar(Rajasthan),
February 23, 200.
My dear Father,

I hope this letter will find everybody at home in the best of health and happiness. I am well here; you might have received my progress report from the school. You will be glad to know that I secured first position in my terminal examination. I assure you that I will maintain this position in the annual examination also. As you know, my fees for the next quarter are due, kindly send me Rs. 11000/- by draft at the earliest.

Please pay my respects to dear mother and convey my love and affection to Puppy and Raju.

Yours loving son ,
Harish

Q. 11. You are Putin, your sister Ragini has just completed X standard and has sought your advice in the matter of opting Science or Commerce group. Write a letter to her, advising her therein to select the group in XI standard.

KH-3, South West Block
Near Eid Gah,
Alwar (Raj.).
18th June, 200.
Dear Ragini,

I am in receipt of your letter dated 15th June . You have sought my advice in the matter of opting Science or Commerce group in your XI standard.

First of all I like to tell you very frankly, that whatever stream you opt, you are to put hard to achieve success. In the present competitive world ,poor show in any stream is of no use. In Science group , you can opt either Engineering or Medical.If we compare Engineering and Medical profession , the medical profession is more suitable, particularly for female candidates . On the other hand, through Commerce stream, you can become a Chartered Accountant, ICWA, Company Secretary and can also go for MBA. Along with Commerce stream, you are required to take computer training also, because nowadays all business is being carried through the computer. As such commerce also opens new vistas of career opportunities to you.

So, if you are interested in becoming an Engineer or a Doctor, you should opt for the Science stream and if you are interested in the work of accounting nature, the Commerce stream is more suitable to you. Anyway, choice is yours.

Whatever may be your decision, please convey me positively.I also like to tell you that you should also improve your English alongwith your academic achievements.English is very important for achieving higher qualifications.

Everything is normal at my end. Do write for any work.

Convey my regards to Mummy and Papa.

Yours loving brother,
Putin

Q. 12. You are Sweta , living in the hostel of PQR School, New Delhi. Write a letter to your sister Rashmi, describing your hostel life.

Indira Hostel,
PQR School,
New Delhi.
25th May, 200.
My dear Rashmi,

I received your loving letter three days ago, but because of my preoccupation in making preparations for the annual function of our hostel , I could not spare time to reply you.

I feel pleasure in informing you that I stood first in the quiz competition and our team stood second in folk dance competition held during the annual function programmes. As I am staying in the hostel, I am devoting more than two hours daily in improving my General Knowledge and General Awareness, in addition to course studies. Ours is a very good hostel. Most of the students are well disciplined and sincere. Our hostel warden Mrs. Savita Vermani is a very strict lady. She keeps close watch on every student. All the students are required to attend the morning and evening prayers daily and both the time attendance is marked.

The quality of food, served here is very good, consisting of two vegetables, curd and salad, with Tawa chapatis and a sweet dish. Breakfast is served at 8 AM , after that I go to school and take lunch at 12 PM and dinner is served from 7 PM to 9 PM .In the evening we play games like badminton, hockey, cricket in the hostel playground from 4 PM to 7 PM. As such, I find this hostel a well maintained one, with everything of good quality and caring.

What about you ? How are your studies going on ? Do write to me for any help or work.

Convey my regards to Mummy and love to Sunni.

Yours loving sister,
Sweta

Q. 13. You are Sarwesh, living at 1215, Qutab Enclave, New Delhi. Write a letter to your father telling him of your plan to go to a village with a group of students to teach illiterate villagers.

1215,Qutab Enclave,
New Delhi,
22nd April, 200.
Respected Daddy,

I received your affectionate letter three- four days ago, but I was busy in my examinations, so I could not reply earlier.I am very happy to note that Sonu has been selected in IIT with very good rank. Please congratulate him on my behalf . He deserves the kudos.

As I informed you earlier that my annual examination will be over on 29th April. On 30th April I, along with a team of ten students, are planning to go to a nearby village Hatina , to educate the illiterate villagers. The team will be headed by our professor Dr.Pannikaran. We will teach them how to read and write our mother tongue, Hindi. We will also train them to write their signatures.

Illiteracy is a curse in our society .Many problems and hardships faced by the poor villagers are because of the illiteracy .Our tour will not only help the villagers but it will also be beneficial for us to get the first hand knowledge of rural problems. I will write you about our detailed programme later on. Every other thing is fine at my end. I am preparing well for my annual examinations.

Convey my deep regards to Mom and heartily congratulations to Sonu.

Yours loving son,
Sarvesh

Q. 14. You are Girish, living in a hostel of BTR School, New Delhi. Write a letter to your friend Mohan, telling him, about an interesting weekend that you spent at your friend's house recently.

Subhash Hostel,
BTR School,
New Delhi.
30th March, 200.

Dear friend Mohan,

I have been thinking to write to you for the last several days about my short but enjoyful stay at my friends.As you are aware that I am well settled in the hostel now. I have got some very good friends here . I wrote you earlier about my friend Pankaj , who belongs to Kolkata. The school was closed for winter vacations. Pankaj took me with him to Kolkata. His father is Executive Engineer in PHED. He owns a big house and a small farm house . Kolkata is a large metropolitan city. We visited National library, Victoria Palace, New A.C. market. We also travelled in tram, a small train with two coaches. It was really thrilling to visit zoo and Birla Planetarium there. I also visited Bara Bazar, a commercial market. I purchased two shirts and a wrist watch from the Maidaan Market at very economical prices.

I really enjoyed my short stay with Pankaj. His parents are very generous and amiable. Every family member gave me love and affection. Their love and affection will always be fresh in my mind.

What about you ? When are you going to London ? Please write me your exact programme, so that I may plan to visit you accordingly.

Yours truly,
Girish

Q. 15. You are Anubhuti , write your friend, Rina, about the futility of exploding crackers on Deepawali.

1876, Mount Villa,
Mount Abu.
24th May 200.

Dear friend Rina,

Hope this letter finds you happy and enjoying the leisure time after examinations. You know that the festival of Diwali is approaching fast. I like to inform you that in our town, I, along with my four friends have decided to make the people aware of futility of using crackers on Diwali.

I do not find any reason for wasting so much money on firing and exploding crackers, which not only pollutes the atmosphere but also causes out break of fire on many occasions.. Many times the fire caused by the crackers endangers human lives and destroys huge properties. On the one side, people are wasting money in exploding crackers and on the other side people are not having sufficient food to eat and clothes to cover their bodies. We have decided to collect rupees fifty from every house and to distribute sweets and clothes to the poor. I think by this way, we will be celebrating this festival in real sense. Tell me, what you think about our unique plan of celebrating Diwali as above.

Convey my regards to your parents.

Yours friend,
Anubhuti

Q. 16. Your are Prakash. Write a letter to your friend Ramesh, asking him about his studies for competitive examinations.

103, Narpat Colony,
Near Ahinsa Circle,
Jaipur (Raj.) 302015.
15/03/200.

Dearest Ramesh,

I haven't heard from you since long. It seems that you are very busy in preparing for the State Service Commission Examinations or something else ? Anyway, tell me about your preparations. I think you should have completed all the optional papers so far. I like to tell you only one thing that whenever you start revising your papers, try to prepare short notes, so that you can revise the same again during examination period. This will help you in making several revisions and you will be able to secure good marks. A good percentage in theory papers means, your selections is almost confirm.

I know, you must be putting all your strength and wisdom, as you are a very hard working and devoted guy. I wish to see you among the first fifty candidates.

I am doing my job well. My good wishes for the exams.

Do write for any deserving service.

Yours truly,
Prakash

Q. 17. Write a letter to your father, explaining him the reasons of your not securing good marks in English paper.

24, Subhas Hostel,
WXT College,
Jaipur.
March 26, 200.

Respected Papa,

I received your letter today in the morning. You have asked me the reasons of my securing poor marks in English paper.

First of all, I like to tell you that I put very hard labour in English. As you are aware, that I am not good at Grammar, so I couldn't attend the Grammar portion so well. I need tuition for English Grammar. I have talked with our Grammar teacher, who consented to give me tuitions for two months only. Without good command over English Grammar, it is not possible to secure good marks in English. Please allow me to take the tuition. so that the problem of English is solved for ever.

You can see, that in other subjects I have secured more than 85 % marks, but in English I could not manage to secure more than 40% .

Convey my regards to Mom, and Grand mom.

Yours loving son,
Jaipal

Q. 18. Write a letter to your elder brother, telling him about the discomforts of a railway journey without reservation.

214,Nehru Nagar,
Ambala.
3rd March, 200.
Dear brother.

As I informed you telephonically also, I reached here safe and sound yesterday.

I like to tell you about the discomfort I suffered because I had no reservation .As you Know, I could not get the reservation, so I had to travel in second class general compartment. The Journey was very tiring and cumbersome. First of all, the train was late by two hours. As soon as the train arrived, I somehow managed to push myself into the general compartment. It was overcrowded, but after one hour , I got half a seat; just managed to sit on the corner of a seat. Six persons were sitting on a seat for three, still it was comparatively comfortable. It was not possible to take rest or sleep the whole night, but I had no option .

However, the night passed and the train reached Ambala at 5 A.M. . I found myself safe and sound but extremely tired. I took a lesson to plan any future journey in such a way that either I get a reservation or if not, better travel by bus.

How the things are going at your end .Convey my regards to Mom and love to Tini.

Yours younger brother,
Pulkit

SOCIAL LETTERS

(INVITATIONS)

Invitations are *of two kinds*. *Formal* and *Informal* Invitations.

A *formal invitation* is generally written *in third person*, and *contains no heading*, *no salutation*, and *no complimentary*.The writer's name should appear in the body of the invitation. The address of the writer and the date should be written to the left, below the communication.

Formal Invitation:

Smt and Shri Chawla
Request the pleasure of Shri S.K. Mathew's company
At dinner on Monday , the 24th of July at 8 P.M.
At Jai palace, Jaipur.20th July2002.

Informal invitations are like *ordinary letters*, though *using more formal language*. They are addressed to the recipient by name, and the *formal close is generally any of the follwing*:-

Sincerely yours, Yours sincerely, Yours affectionately, etc.

Informal Invitation:

My dear Shri Verma,

Will You please give me the pleasure of your company at dinner on Monday, the 18th July, 2002 at 8.30 P.M., at my residence.

Yours very sincerely,
Prakash Jha
12, Alka Puri, Alwar.

15th July

Examples of Invitations

Q. 19. As Mrs. and Mr. Ramesh Dutt, invite Mrs. and Mr. C. R. Pathak on the occasion of their daughter Anu's marriage with Uttam at 8 P.M., on Monday, 4th Oct. 200.

Mrs. and Mr. Ramesh Dutt
request the pleasure of the company of Mrs. and Mr. C. R. Pathak
on the occasion of the marriage of their daughter.
ANU
with
UTTAM
S/o Mrs. and Mr. Vivek Dutt
at 8 P.M., on Monday, 4th Oct. 200.
AT THEIR RESIDENCE

R.S.V.P.
49 Manu Marg,
Alwar.

Q. 20. As the Principal of Bal Bharati School, which is holding its Annual Day Function at 6.00 P.M. on 12th November ..... in the school auditorium, design an invitation card to be sent to the parents and other invitees. The Chief Minsiter of Delhi has agreed to be the chief guest on this occasion. Do not exceed 50 words.

BAL BHARATI SCHOOL, ALWAR
Celebrates its
ANNUAL DAY FUNCTION
on
12th Novemeber, ...
at
6.00 P.M., in the
SCHOOL AUDITORIUM
CHIEF GUEST : The Hon'ble Chief Minister of Delhi

The Honourable Chief Minister will give away the prizes to all the meritorious students. You are cordially invited to grace the occasion with your benign presence.

PRINCIPAL

Q. 21. *Write a formal letter of invitation to a friend of your son, inviting him to your son's birthday party.*

MRS. AND MR. GAURAV NAGPAL
request the pleasure of the company of
MR. HITESH SHARMA
on the occasion of the 20th birthday of their son.
RAHUL
at 7.00 P.M., on 12th August
at their residence

R.S.V.P.
6-C Model Town
Delhi-110007
Phones : 2334329

With Compliments
Friends & Relatives

Q. 22. *Write a formal letter of invitation to your friend, inviting him to your son's birthday party.*

Mrs. and Mr. P. K. Sharma
request the pleasure of the company of Mrs. and Mr. S. C. Gupta
on the auspicious occassion of the 18th birthday of their son
GAURAV
at 6.00 P.M., on 5th January
at-132/13 Panchsheel Colony, Udaipur

Phone No. : 4312342
4769790

R.S.V.P.
X.Y.Z.

Q. 23. *Draft an invitation card for a formal dinner at Home.*

Mrs. and Mr. S. C. Gupta
invite
Mrs. and Mr. P. K. Sharma
to
THE BIRTHDAY PARTY
of their son
HEMANT
On Tuesday, the 1st Oct., 200., at 6.00 P.M.
at their residence, M-3 Satyawadi Colony, Purjan Vihar, Jaipur.
Please grace the occasion with your benign presence.

Q. 24. Write a formal reply to your neighbour, accepting the invitation to his brother's birthday party. Invent names, date, time and place etc.

Mrs. and Mr. G.K. Kapoor
of Kota City
Thank
Mrs. and Mr. K. L. Arora
for their invitation
on
the auspicious occasion
of
the birthday of
Mr. S. L. Arora
(younger brother of Mr K.L.Arora)
and
accept the same and promise to be there
on Tuesday, 5th October, ... at 6.30 P.M.
at their residence at
M-43, Purjan Vihar....Udaipur.

Q. 25. You are R. Kumar S/oShri K. Kumar of 31, Janta Colony,Jaipur. Prepare a draft for an invitation card to be sent on behalf of your parents on the occasion of the wedding of your sister.

Smt. and Shri K. Kumar
request the pleasure of your company
on the auspicious occasion of the marriage
of their daughter
REENA
with
MAYANK
(Son of Smt. and Shri K.L. Gupta of Rohtak)
on Friday, 4th December, 200. at 8.00 P.M.
at their residence 31,Janta Colony, Jaipur
as per the following programme:
Reception of Barat 7.00 P.M.
Dinner : 9.30 P.M.
Doli: (5th December, 200.) at 500 A.M.
With Best Compliments from

R.S.V.P.
M/s R. K. Garments,
20 Park Square, Bangalore.
Phone : 653434

All Relatives
&
Friends.

Q. 26. You are Miss Komal Mittal of 134/32, Panchsheel Colony, Udaipur. You are celebrating your 20th birthday next week. Draft a formal invitation to a tea party. (Do not mention the invitee's name).

MISS KOMAL MITTAL
requests the pleasure of your company
at a
TEA PARTY
on the occasion of her 20th birthday
at 5.30 P.M, on Sunday, August 12th
at her residence-134/32, Panchsheel Colony, Udaipur.

R.S.V.P.
Mittal Refractories,
Udaipur(Rajasthan).
0294 2512103

Q. 27. You have set up a cooperative store in your colony, Nayabans, Alwar. You have decided to invite one member from each family settled their, to its inaugural ceremony. Prepare a draft of the invitation letter for the purpose.

M/S G. N. Nagpal and Sons
announce the opening of their new establishment
NAGPAL COOPERATVE STORE
Nayabas, Alwar
INAUGURATION
On Sunday, the 2nd October, at 9.00 P.M.
by Dr. Gaurav Mittal
One member from each family settled in Nayabans, Alwar
is cordially invited .
Visit for all kinds of domestic items : Readymade Garments
Cosmetics, Medicines and Electrical items.
AVAIL INAUGURAL DISCOUNT OF 10% ON ALL GOODS

R.S.V.P.
Nagpal Cooperative Store.
Phone : 2334329.

BUSINESS LETTERS

Business Letters

A business letter is *more formal than a personal letter.* It should have *sufficient margin* (at least one inch) on all four edges. It is usually written on 8½" × 11", unlined stationery (plain paper). **There are six parts to a business letter:**

1. The Heading : The heading of a business letter contains the ***return address* with the *date* on the last line**. If the stationery is imprinted with the return address, then the return address may be omitted.

Sometimes it may be necessary to include a line after the address and before the date for a phone number, fax number, E-mail address, or something similar.

Often a line is skipped between the address and date. If you are using stationery with the return address already imprinted, you need not write return address above the date:

Lacme Stores,
140-B, Ganesh Apartment,
Mansarovar, Jaipur.
(0141) 2760795
July 18, 2006

2. The Inside Address : This is the address, you are sending your letter to.It should be complete .Include titles and names if you know them.

This is always on the left margin. If an 8½" × 11" paper is folded in thirds to fit in a standard 9" business envelope, the inside address can appear through the window in the envelope.

An inside address also helps the recipient route the letter properly and is of much help , should the envelope be damaged and the address become unreadable.

Skip a line after the heading before the inside address. Skip another line after the inside address before the greeting :

Dr. Govind Raghvan
Cross Country Coach,
Dept. of Athletics,
University of Jodhpur,
Jodhpur (Rajasthan).

3. The Greeting (Salutation) : The greeting in a business letter is always formal. It normally begins with the word 'Dear' and always includes the person's last name.

It normally has a title; such as-**Mr., Mrs., Dr.,** or a political title. Use a first name only, if the title is unclear. The greeting in a business letter may end in a colon (:) or comma (,), *eg.*

Dear Mr. Sharma:
or
Dear Mr. Sharma,

Names and Titles of People in Greetings:

Use the full name in standard writing unless the person uses an initial as part of his or her name. For example:

George Smith ,
Robert E. Lee

[The initial is fine here, because that is the name he (Robert) went by.]

Social titles before a proper name are capitalized. **All but *Miss'* and *'Master'* are abbreviated** and *end with a period.*

Social titles: Mr., Master, Mrs., Miss, Ms.

4. The Body : *The body* is the *main letter.* It is written as text. A business letter is usually typed . Depending on the letter style you choose, *paragraphs may be indented.* Regardless of format, skip a line between paragraphs. The first line of a new paragraph is indented in the semiblock style. The block and modified block style have all lines of the body to the left margin.

Skip a line between the greeting and the body. Skip a line between the body and the close.

5. The Complimentary Close(Subscription) : This *short, polite closing* ends with a comma. It is either at the left margin or its left edge is in the center, depending on the style that you use. It begins at the same column as the heading does. The *complimentary close begins* with a *capital letter and ends with a comma;* eg. —***Yours faithfully***, etc.

6. The Signature Line: Skip two lines and type out the *name to be signed.* This customarily includes a *middle initial,* but does not have to. Women may indicate how they wish to be addressed by placing *Miss, Mrs., Ms. or similar title in parentheses* before their name.

The signature line may include *a second line for a title*, if appropriate. The term 'By direction', in the second line means that a superior is authorizing the signer. Sign the name in the space between the close and the signature line, starting at the left edge of the signature line.For example:

Sincerely Yours,

(Signature goes here)

Prakash Jha

By direction: General Manager (Finance)

See another example :

Sincerely,
(Signature goes here)
(Mrs.) Ben Jackson
Director of Acquisitions (This is the second line for the title.)

The signature should start directly above the first letter of the signature line in the space between the close and the signature line. *Use blue or black ink.*

Business letters should not contain postscripts.

SOME IMPORTANT BASICS OF GOOD BUSINESS LETTERS

Following phrases* are usually found in any *standard business letter. By using these standard phrases, you can give a professional touch to your business letters. These phrases are used as a kind of *frame* and *introduction* to the content of business letters:

1. The Beginning :

(a) Dear Personnel Manager,

(b) Dear Sir or Madam (use, if you don't know who you are writing to.)

(c) Dear Mr, Mrs, Miss or Ms (use, if you know who you are writing to, and have a formal relationship with)

VERY IMPORTANT: ***use 'Ms' for women unless asked to use 'Mrs' or 'Miss'.***

(d) Dear Frank (use, if the person is a close business contact or friend)

2. The Reference: 'The Reference' line in business letters *may include following phrases*:–

With reference to your advertisement in the Times of India ,

Your letter of 3rd May,

Your phone call today,

Thank you for your letter of March 25th.

The Reason for Writing;

I am writing to....

(a) enquire about, or

(b) apologise for, or

(c) confirm ....

Requesting;

(a) Could you possibly ....?

I would be grateful if you could ....

Agreeing to Requests:

(a) I would be delighted to....

Giving Bad News:

(a) Unfortunately ....

I am afraid that ....

Enclosing Documents:

(a) I am enclosing herewith....

(b) Please find enclosed here with ....

(c) Enclosed, you will find....

Closing Remarks:

(a) Thank you for your help.

(b) Please contact us again.

(c) If we can help in any way....
(d) If there are any problems....
(e) If you have any questions....

Reference to Future Contact:

(a) I look forward to ....
(b) hearing from you soon.
(c) meeting you next Tuesday.
(d) seeing you next Thursday.

The Finish:

(a) *Yours faithfully*, (If you *don't know the name* of the person you're writing to),
(b) *Yours sincerely*, (If you *know the name* of the person you're writing to),
(c) Best wishes,
(d) Best regards, etc. (If the person is a close business contact or friend.).

EXAMPLES OF BUSINESS LETTERS

Q. 28. Write a letter from M/s V.K.Gupta & Sons, Jaipur to M/s Arihant Prakashans, Karol Bagh, New Delhi, requesting them to supply certain books.

M/s V.K.Gupta & Sons
UniversityRoad, Jaipur.

Ref.:Un/

Date 08/3/200.

M/s Arihant Prakashans,
106, Karol Bagh,
New Delhi 110013.

Subject: Supply of books.

Dear Sir,

We are sending herewith draft no. 1478952, dated 25/01/05, drawn on Punjab National Bank, favouring yourselves, payable at New Delhi, for Rs 15000/-in advance, against the supply of following books:

1. 60 days Grammar	By S.C. Gupta	200 copies
2. Objective Physics	By Sharma & Gupta	150 copies

Please send the above books through Jaipur Golden Transport company, duly packed with polythene.Please send the bill after allowing discount as usual.

Thanking You,

Yours faithfully,
V.K.Gupta
Partner,

V. K.Gupta & Sons

Q. 29. ***Write a letter to the retailer from whom you purchased a TV, but its picture tube seems not functioning well. Write him to get it changed.***

15, Ganesh Colony,
Alwar (Raj),
Aug. 25, 200.

M/s Preeti Electronics,
Jayanti Market,
Jaipur.

Subject : Replacement of TV.

Dear Sir,

I have purchased a TV, make BPL-21FSTW, from you vide-bill no. 2581, dated 1/7/2004, for Rs 11300/-.

The picture tube of the TV is not functioning properly. You have sent the mechanic twice to check the same, but of no avail.

As the TV is under one year guarantee period, you are requested to get the TV changed immediately.

Taking into account your good will and market reputation, I am sure that the TV will be replaced without any delay,

Thanking you,

Yours faithfully,
Vikas Sharma

Q. 30. ***Write a letter to the Publisher, returning the books, wrongly supplied by him and asking him to supply the proper books.***

R.K. Book Depot
155, Nangali Circle, Alwar.

Ref. : Po/ Dated 16/3/200.

M/s Jaipur Publications
Chaura Rasta,
Jaipur.

Subject : Supply of Books.

Dear Sir,

Today, we have received the parcel of books sent by you. We are surprised to find that you have sent all the twenty books of English Grammar written by some Mr. Sarraf, while we have ordered for the English Grammar books, written by Mr. Gupta & Gupta.

We are returning the books. You are requested to dispatch the books of English Grammar written by Mr. Gupta & Gupta.

Please be kind enough to supply the proper books immediately. The parcel be packed properly with polythene.

Thanking you,

Yours faithfully,
R.K. Jain
Partner

Q. 31. As Principal of a college, place an order for supplying some sports items to M/s Sports & Sports, Ludhiana.

Subhash Gandhi College.
Lucknow (U.P.)

Ref. :Ord/sport

Dated 18/4/200.

M/s Sports & Sports
Lal Bazar, Ludhiana.

Subject : Supply of Sports Goods.

Dear Sir,

You are requested to supply the following sports goods, at the rates mentioned by you in your quotation dated 10/3/200.

Name of items	*Quantity*
1. Cricket Bats	12 Pieces
2. Volley Balls	12 Pieces
3. Badminton Rackets	12 Pieces

Please dispatch the above items duly packed, to avoid any damage in transit.

Thanking you,

Yours faithfully,
R.P. Ojha

Q. 32. You are Anil Shah, General Manager of M/s Cement Associates, Karol Nagar Nimbahera. Mr. R.K & Sons have placed with you an order for two thousand bags of cement . Please write a letter, asking them to send 50% amount in advance by draft and also to submit you two reference, as this is the first dealing.

M/s Cement Associates,
Karol Nagar, Nimbahera.

Ref. : Adv/ Dated 27/8/200.

Mr R.K & Sons,
Akbar Nagar,
Shri Ganganagar(Rajasthan).

Subject : Supply of 2000 bags of cement.

Dear Sir,

We thankfully acknowledge your order no. 1841, dated 21/8/200., for supplying of two thousand bags of cement.

Please be informed that this is our first dealing, and as per our business policy, yours being a new firm, you need to send 50 % advance payment by draft and also two references for all future dealings.

For your ready reference, we are attaching herewith a list of firms in Rajasthan who are registered with us.

We hope, you will get these formalities fulfilled at the earliest.

Thanking you,

Yours faithfully,
Anil Shah
General Manager.

Q. 33. You are the dealer of Pakija Biscuits for the state. Due to strike of Transporters operators, your supply of biscuits has been disrupted. One of your distributors has asked you to arrange the supply of biscuits at whatever cost. Draft a letter to your distributer telling him regarding increase in the supply rates.

BENGAL Bakeries Ltd.
Registered Office:181, Nanitalla Lane,
Kolkata 700023

Ref.: Supply/ad/ Dated 17/4/200.

M/s Priya Distributers,

Asansol (W.B.)

Sub : Supply of Pakija Biscuits

Dear Sir,

We are in receipt of your urgent call for supplying the biscuits at whatever cost.

As you are aware, due to strike of transport operators, it has become impossible to supply the biscuits by trucks.

We are sending you biscuits with our sales executive, Mr P.V. Vardhan, by passenger train as per your requirements.

You are requested to pay him Rs 350 /- extra, as excess charges borne by us in supplying the biscuits through train.

Thanking you,

Yours faithfully,
Kamal Bose
Marketing Executive.

Official letters, Applications and Complaints

Q. 34. Write a letter to the Post Master, complaining that your sister at Ambala has not received the parcel sent by you last month.

129, South Block
Alwar (Raj.)
26/4/200.

The Post Master,
Head Post Office,
Alwar.

Subject: Non receipt of parcel, sent on 25/03/200.

Dear Sir,

I had sent a Registered Parcel to my sister Jaya at: 16, Sector 5, Ambala, on date 25/3/200., vide- receipt no.1479. The parcel has not so far been received by her. More than one months have since passed. It appears, either the parcel is delivered to somebody else or it has been lost in transit.

You are requested to enquire into the matter and apprise us the factual position without any further delay.Your early action will be highly appreciated.

Thanking you,

Yours faithfully,
S.K. Gupta

Q. 35. Draft a First Information Report regarding theft of your Scooter.

15, Kalindi Market,
Near University,
Jaipur.
28/5/200.

The S.H.O.
University Road Thana,
Jaipur.

Subject: FIR regarding theft of Scooter.

Dear Sir,

I have to lodge an FIR for the theft of my scooter from the University Road . It was about 1 P. M. in the noon, I went to the market to make some purchasing . I locked my scooter as usual and parked it outside the shop; M/s K.K. & sons, UniversityRoad, Kalindi Market . After about half an hour, I came out of the shop and was shocked to find that my scooter was missing. I made enquiries from the nearby shopkeepers, but of no avail. The Scooter was of 2006 model, Hero Honda, blue coloured, 100 cc, self start, bearing registration no. RJ 02, C 2879.

I request you to lodge the FIR and arrange to trace the scooter at the earliest. Your immediate action in the matter is solicited.

Yours faithfully,
Pramod Jhalani.

Letters to and from Bank

Q. 36. ***You are Rajesh, you have deposited a cheque for collection in your current account. Even after passing of more than one month, the amount of cheque has not been credited in your account so far. Write a letter to the manager of the bank, to get the amount of cheque deposited in your account and also make a demand for payment of interest for the delayed period.***

The Manager,
Quick Bank,
New Delhi.

Subject : Non crediting the proceeds of cheque.

Dear Sir,

I had deposited a cheque no. 175896, dated 25/03/200., for Rs 56200 /-, drawn on State Bank of India, Alwar for collecting the proceeds in my current account no. 7816 with your branch.

I regret to note that even after passing of more than a month, the amount of cheque has not been credited in my account so far.

You are requested to look into the matter and arrange to get the amount of cheque credited in my current account immediately, along with the interest for the delay, as per norms.

Thanking you,

Date
27.4.200.

Yours faithfully,
Rajesh
Current A/c No. 7816
12/ 7, Vikas Nagar,
New Delhi.

Q. 37. As manager of a bank, write a letter to a customer that his cheque has been dishonoured.

Quick Bank Ltd.
Ram Nagar, Jaipur.

Ref.: Com/05/ Dated : 29th April, 200.

Mr. Rajesh Sharma,
12/ 7, Vikas Nagar,
New Delhi.

Subject : Your cheque No. 175896, dated 25/03/200., for Rs 56200/-, drawn on SBI, Alwar.

Dear Sir,

In reference to your letter dated 29.4.200., we beg to inform you that your above cheque was received back by us for the following reason:

1. Funds insufficient.

The cheque has since been sent to you by Registered Post, on 25.04.200. at your residential address. We are taking up the matter with the Post Master to ascertain the reason of non delivery.

You are also requested to consult the postman of your area in the matter.

We are always at the service of our clients.

Thanking you,

Yours faithfully,
T.K.Bose
Sr.Manager

Q. 38. There is an advertisement in the local newspaper for the post of Office Assistant. Make an application and write your biodata.

The General Manager,
Tilak Associates,
Faluja road,
New Delhi.

Subject: Application for the post of Office Assistant.

Dear Sir,

With reference to your advertisement in the Indian Express, dated ...., for the post of 'Office Assistant', I am sending my biodata with this application.My biodata contains all the details regarding my qualifications and experience.

I like to assure you that if I am given a chance to serve in your esteemed organisation, you will positively feel satisfied with my attitude and working.

Yours faithfully,
R.K. Sharma

BIO-DATA

1. Name : R.K. Sharma
2. Father's Name : Mr. P.K. Sharma
3. Address : 4/47, Shah Nagar, near Nai Mandi, New Delhi. 110007.
4. Telephone No. : 011-22094521 (R)
5. E-mail : rksharma_147@yahoo.com.
6. Date of Birth : 25th April, 1984.
7. Qualifications :

Degree	University	% Marks	Year of passing
B.A.(Maths)	University of Delhi	78 %	2001
M.A. (Economics)	University of Delhi	75 %	2003

8. Experience : One year at Sandeep Associates, as cashier cum-accountant (Experience certificate enclosed).
9. Hobbies : Playing cricket, Reading Newspapers, Watching T.V. serials.
10. Extra Activities :
    1. English Typing speed on computers 60 w pm.
    2. Hindi Typing speed on computers 40 w pm.
    3. Well versed in Tally 5.4 and 6.3 versions
    4. Have good knowledge of MS Word, MS Excel .

I hope, you will find my bio-data as per your requirements.

R.K. Sharma
Signature.

Q. 39. *Write an application to the Principal of your college/school, requesting him to grant you concession in fees.*

The Principal
____
____

Subject : Concession in Fees.

Sir,

Most humbly, I beg to state that I am a student of class 11th in your school. My father is a retired clerk. He is getting a pension of Rs 1800 /- P.M. I have two younger brothers. They are also studying in this school. There is no other source of income. My father is unable to pay my fees. Last year too, your goodness granted me 100 % concession in my school fees. This year too, I request you to grant me 100 % concession in my school fees, so that I shall be able to continue my studies. I like to apprise you that I secured 96 % marks in 10th standard and secured 12th position in state merit list.

Please be kind enough to grant me full fees concession.

Thanking you,
Dated
24/3/200.

Yours obediently,
Saurabh

Q. 40. Send a reply to the following advertisement, published in a newspaper. Indicate to which post you are applying. Include your Bio Data. Suppose you are Satish Pradhan from New Delhi.

ADVERTISEMENT

Wanted male/female Marketing Executives, Accountants, well qualified, experienced.
Salary no constraint for the right candidate.
Apply to General Manager, XYZ Company, New Delhi, within seven days.

The General Manager ,
XYZ Company,
New Delhi.

Sir,

With reference to your advertisement in the Hindustan Times, dated January 28, 200., for various posts. I offer myself as a candidate for the post of Accountant. As far as my academic and other qualifications are concerned, these are indicated in the bio-data attached herewith:

1. Name	:	Satish Pradhan
2. Father's Name	:	Shiv Kumar Pradhan
3. Date of Birth	:	11.7.82
4. Educational Qualifications	:	M.Com.
5. Nationality	:	Indian
6. Marital Status	:	Bachelor
7. Experience	:	One year experience of working in a private company
8. Reference	:	(a) Mr. P.K. Mishra (Bank Manager), 142, Nehru Nagar, New Delhi-18 Tel. : 011- 25761081 (b) Sh. S .R. Sharma, MBBS (Councillor), 145, Patel Nagar, New Delhi-11
9. Extra curricular activities		Apart from the above mentioned Bio Data , I have additional record of extra–curricular activities; I participated in debates, dramas and sports and won many prizes from time to time. In light of the above-mentioned facts, I request you to consider my application favourably.

I like to assure you, that you will never feel disappointed with my work and attitude. I believe in working with full dedication and positive attitude.

Date 30/01/200.

Yours faithfully,
Satish Pradhan

Q. 41. Write a letter to the District Education Officer, Jaipur, applying for the post of a temporary teacher.

231, Arya Nagar,
Alwar,
February 14, 200.

The District Education Officer,
Jaipur District,
Jaipur.

Sir,

I have been given to understand that a post for a teacher of English is lying vacant in one of the schools under your control. I beg to apply for the same. As regards my qualifications and experience, I submit as follows :

I passed the Matriculation examination from the D.S. High School, Jaipur, in the year 1974, securing 87% marks and stood first in the school. I passed the B.A. examination from D.S. College, Jaipur in 1978, with 76%. I took my M.A. degree in English from University of Rajasthan,Jaipur with first division, securing 61% marks in 1980, and stood first in the University in the B.Ed. Examination in 1982.

I have seven months' experience of teaching English in a Higher Secondary School. The experience certificate is enclosed herewith, for your kind persual.

I like to assure you that if I am selected, I shall do my best for the students and everybody concerned shall feel satisfied with my conduct and devotion.

Yours faithfully,
Vijay Kumar

Q. 42. *Write an application to the Director of Education, Rajasthan, Jaipur, asking for a job as a teacher in an educational institution.*

The Director of Education,
Rajasthan,
Jaipur.

Sir,

With reference to your advertisement in 'The Hindustan Times' dated-15th January, for the post of teachers , I beg to offer my services as a candidate for one of them.

Relevant particulars of my career are given below :

Name : Bahadur Khan

Age : 25 years (Date of Birth 1.1. 1978)

Examinations Passed	Division	Year
High School	2nd	1990
Intermediate	2nd	1992
B.A.	2nd	1995
B.Ed.	2nd	1996

Experience : Working as a temporary teacher of English teacher in a private college, since July, 200.

I am enclosing photocopies of my qualifications and the experience certificates for your kind persual.A favourable decision will oblige me.

My address :

Bahadur Khan,
S/o Mr. Rashid Khan,
20, Nai Basti,
Jaipur (Rajasthan)

April 25, 200.

Yours faithfully,
Bahadur Khan

Complaints and Letters to the Editor

Q. 43. Write a letter to the editor of a newspaper, complaining against the increasing nuisance of beggars in the city.

S.K. Joshi,
17, Mahabir Colony,
Asansol (W.B.)
Jan. 23, 200.

The Editor,
'The Times of India',
New Delhi.

Dear Sir,

Through the columns of your esteemed newspaper, I like to draw the attention of local authorities towards the increasing nuisance of beggars in our city.

Nowadays, the population of beggars has abruptly increased in the city. Everywhere in the city, whether market, park or outside, at restaurant or even in every street and on Red Light stoppage, you will find such obstinate beggars, who can't be easily put off. The pity is that most of them are physically fit. Begging is their well thought of profession.

Some of them must be involved in other crimes also. Some of the beggars also suffer from highly contagious diseases such as-leprosy, TB etc., and while begging, they come in contact with general public. It is necessary that such cases be taken care of and be treated in General Hospital and other able bodied beggars be taken to the task. Either they be given jobs or they must not be allowed to make the begging their profession.

I am sure, the authorities will positively take care of this increasing nuisance of beggars, at the earliest.

Thanking you,

yours faithfully,
S. K. Joshi

Q. 44. Write a letter to the editor of a newspaper about very irregular and scanty water supply in your locality.

The Editor,
The Times of India,
New Delhi.

Subject : Irregular and scanty water supply.

Dear Sir,

I crave the hospitality of the 'HELP LINE' columns of your esteemed newspaper to draw the attention of local authorities, particularly the authorities of 'Water Works Department'.

For the last many days the water supply in our colony has become very irregular and scanty. Out of last seven days, the supply was given on three days only and that too for an hour or 90 minutes.

On yesterday and day before yesterday , the water was supplied only for 35 minutes. When we contacted, the Assistant Engineer concerned, he replied that due to electricity problem, the water supply has become irregular.His reply was very evasive.I was not satisfied with the reply. It appears that the concerned A.En. is not taking the problem seriously.

In summer season, water is of utmost necessity. I hope you will be kind enough to publish this letter in your daily, so that the higher authorities take notice and solve this acute problem immediately and warn those who are responsible for it.

Dated 28/4/200.

Yours faithfully,
Ram Chand
21/ 7, Janakpuri Road,
New Delhi 1100031

Q. 45. Write a letter to the District Collector, drawing his attention to the nuisance caused by loudspeakers in the city during examinations days.

The District Collector,
Hoshiyarpur (Punjab).

Subject : Nuisance caused by the loudspeakers during examination days.

Dear Sir,

I beg to draw your kind attention to the problem of nuisance being caused by the loudspeakers in the city.

Nowadays, students are preparing for their examination. The loud noise of loudspeakers is causing a lot of problems to the students . Every year, a prohibitive order is issued by your office, banning the use of loudspeakers during the days of examination, but this year no such action has been taken so far.

I request you to ban the use of loudspeakers totally for the period of two months, so that the students can prepare well for the ensuing examinations and not suffer due to this unwarranted noise of loudspeakers.

Hope to get your immediate attention.

Thanking you ,
Date: 15th March, 200.

Yours faithfully,
P.K. Mehra
Student of B.E. (Computers) III year
17, Janta colony,
Hoshiyarpur (Punjab)

Q. 46. *Write a letter in not more than 200 words, to a national daily, about the neglect of priceless historical monuments in and around your city. Suggest ways and means to preserve them.*

The Editor,
The Hindustan Times,
New Delhi.

Sir,

Through the esteemed columns of your prestigious newspaper,I like to draw the attention of the general public, on the neglectful and miserable conditions of the historical monuments which are the evidential witnesses of our past glory and grandeur. They are the proven records of our past history, but have fallen victims to the criminal neglect of the officials. I had earlier brought it to the notice of the Department of Archaeological Survey of India , but there was no response. This callous indifference on the part of concerned authorities has compelled me to approach you through this letter.

Sir, if you personally visit some of the monuments, like– the Humayun Tomb, Tughlak Qila , Qutab Minar etc, you will realise that they are gradually losing their shape and are getting dilapidated day by day, in the flames of times. Their walls are mouldering, their roofs are getting cracked, their bricks and stone pieces are losing plaster and the top corner of walls have already crumbled. All this is due to the lack of proper maintenance and criminal neglect by the government servants. These monuments are the heritage of the glorious period of our past history. We must realise that even the present will be past one day. I was shocked to witness the sight of these worn and torn monuments. I request you to publish this letter in your esteemed paper, so that the concerned authorities are awakened in time, and the priceless historical monuments are saved and preserved.

Thanking you,

Yours truly,
XYZ.

Q. 47. ***Write a letter in about 200 words, to the Municipal Corporation of your city, describing therein the miserable condition of roads in your locality,also suggest some remedies for improvement.***

The Commissioner,
Municipal Corporation ,
New Delhi.

Sir,

I would like to attract your kind attention to the miserable condition of roads in my locality, Nehru Nagar, near Subzi Mandi, Delhi. The roads are broken at many places.One can't drive the vehicle even for ten minutes regularly, without making adjustments with the broken roads. The buses, trucks, cars, three-wheelers and two- wheelers all have to halt at every five to seven minutes, just to adjust with the road breaks and pits. It has been repeatedly brought to the notice of M.C.D., but all in vain. There is always a traffic problem on the roads. The first showers of monsoon will put the things in its worst shape. The residents are in deep distress on this account and they have repeatedly expressed their resentment through Press, as well as through written complaints, but nothing has so far been done. People have also staged demonstrations last month and the authorities have assured to take necessary action in the matter, but so far, all the assurances are proved only the assurances for the sake of assurances.

I request you to get the roads constructed without any further delay, lest the anger of the public should explode.I hope to get your immediate attention.

25th Aug., 200.

Yours sincerely,
Secretary,
Nehru Nagar Residents Society,
near Sabji Mandi,
Delhi.

Q. 48. You are a resident of Indira Nagar, a posh colony of DDA . There are no street lights on the main road leading to this colony. The road gets so dark after seven in the evenings that the possibility of some major accident cannot be ruled out. Write a letter to the Editor of a Daily, drawing attention of the authorities to this serious problem . (Word limit = 200 words)

The Editor,
The Hindustan Times,
New Delhi.

Subject : Provision for street lights on the main road.

Sir,

Through the columns of your esteemed newspaper, I want to draw the attention of the authorities concerned towards the provision of street lights on the main road leading to Indira Nagar. I like to apprise that Indira Nagar is a posh colony of DDA and is inhabited by more than 3500 flats on both the sides of the road. The electricity board has installed poles on either side of the road to supply electricity to the residents , but they are just poles without the electricity. The civic authority is lacking in providing basic amenities to the residents.During these days of winter, after seven, there is pitch dark. There is every possibility of occurance of some major accident, because heavy traffic passes over this road round the clock .The necessity for electrification requires no emphasis.In addition to accidents, cases of thefts and robbery can also not be denied. Darkness may lead to any kind of mishappening . It may also be stated that many residents go on pouring into their flats even after late hours in the night.The residents pay house tax to the Municipality regularly but facility of street lights is denied to them.The matter has been taken up with the authorities time and again, every time mere assurances were given but problem still persists in the same way.

I hope, if the letter is published in your esteemed newspaper , the authorities shall be awakened from the slumber and the problem will be finally solved.

Thanking you,

Yours faithfully,
XYZ
(A Resident of Indira Nagar)
152, Indira Nagar,
New Delhi

27th Oct., 200.

Q. 49. You are a resident of the 'Aparna Apartments', Mayur Vihar, New Delhi. There is no bus-stop within the radius of 2 km. from the apartments, causing a lot of inconvenience to the residents. Write a letter to the Editor of The Hindustan Times, drawing attention of the concerned authorities to this problem .

271, Aparna Apartments
Mayur Vihar, New Delhi
23rd Jan, 200.

The Editor,
The Hindustan Times,
New Delhi.

Subject : Providing nearby Bus-stops

Sir,

Through the columns of your esteemed newspaper, I like to attract the attention of the concerned Government officials and the leaders representing the public, towards the problem of nonavailability of bus stops in the surrounding area, near Mayur Vihar, Aparna Apartments. These apartments are spread within the radius of at least 4 km and are situated on the main road to Mayur Vihar.One can notice the running of buses on the main road to all the destinations, of Delhi, after every five minutes. But it is very strange to note that the Government has not provided enough bus stops to cover all the apartments and colonies, on the road. The residents have to run for more than two km. to catch a local bus. Hiring of a rickshaw or three wheeler is very costly for all of us in order to reach the bus stand. The chilly or the hot rough weather often puts the passengers in a great dolldrum. This also wastes time, energy, stamina and strength of a traveller.

For lady passengers, it is all the mone awesome from the safety point of view.No investment or no financial burden will be passed on to the government in making more bus stops, keeping in view the necessities and the convenience of the residents. It being fully residential area, it is need of the hour to provide bus stops at the nearest points in this area, instead of having a bus stop at a distance of even more that 2 kms.

I hope the government would definitely consider our difficulty and provide enough bus stops for the convenience of the passengers. It will provide relief to all of us, as moving to a long distance of 2 km. in winter and hot summer is very troublesome and tiresome.

I request you to publish this letter in your esteemed newspaper, so that the concerned authorities could take notice and relieve the residents from this problem. Thanking you,

Yours faithfully,
XYZ
A resident of Aparna Apartments,
Mayur Vihar,
New Delhi

Q. 50. ***You are resident of Mangal Vihar Colony, Alwar. Write a letter to the Editor, Rajasthan Patrika ,about the misuse and poor maintenance of the public park in your area.***

118-A, Mangal Vihar Colony,
Alwar.
December 15, 200.

The Editor,
Rajasthan Patrika
Alwar.

Subject : Poor Maintenance of Public Park

Sir,

Through the columns of your esteemed daily, I want to draw the attention of the authorities concerned towards the poor maintenance of the public park in our area.

Public parks are the lungs of the locality, where residents come and refresh their tired and fatigue minds. But in our colony, the park is not well maintained or say not at all maintained. The park suffers from the utter neglect of the authorities. The residents of a nearby basti are using the area as a public convenience. Some rowdies create disturbance and obstruct in proper upkeeping of the park.The park has become the favourite halting place of stray cattle and dogs and pigs. Miscreants sit and gamble here in the broad daylight. They create disturbance and affect the normal health and hygiene of the common man. In reality, the park has become a safety heaven for all types of evil characters.

If no immediate action is taken, the park will turn into a devil's den and a cause of nuisance for the colony.

I hope the authorities concerned will take immediate steps in the matter.

Yours faithfully,
XYZ

Q. 51. You are a resident of South-West Block, Alwar .Write a letter to the Superintendent of Police about the unauthorised construction of a block of three shops adjacent to the public park.

329-South West Block,
Alwar.
15th Dec, 200.

The Superintendent of Police,
Alwar (Rajasthan).

Subject : Unauthorised construction adjacent to the public park.

Sir,

May I lodge a complaint against Sh. Ram Nath, who has constructed a block of three shops adjacent to the Nehru Park in our colony. The construction was completed in the late hours of night when there was none to oppose. In morning, a block of shops was found disfiguring the park area. This has created a good example for others to occupy the government land ,in any way they like. There is complete "Goonda Raj" in this area. Powerful men are usurping the property of the Government for their own benefits. It is not out of place to mention that the saying "Might is Right" stands true here. In the morning, some residents opposed the construction but instead of listening to their voice, he threatened them to shoot. There is complete chaos and an atmosphere of fear prevails in the area.

It looks, he has got good relations with high ups. If this remains the state of affair, a day will come when others will also occupy the available land. This is the only main park where children can play and rest in the morning and evening.

Please take action and protect the park from the miscreant, spoiling its use and beauty.

Yours faithfully
XYZ

Q. 52. You are Pralay Kumar of 125, Jahangir Road, New Delhi. Write a letter to the Police Commissioner (Traffic) about inadequate parking facility in the Connaught Place area of New Delhi.

125, Jahangir Road,
New Delhi.
20th Aug., 200.

The Police Commissioner (Traffic),
Connaught Place,
New Delhi.

Subject : Inadequate parking facility at Connaught Place

Sir,

Connaught Place is the heart and soul of our capital . It is the busiest and cleanest site of the capital.It attracts a large number of businessmen, foreigners and tourists daily. Being the center of trade, there is great hustle and bustle in the market. During the peak hours one cannot park his car at a safe place here, because the parking facilities are very much inadequate. If one has to park his vehicle, he has to look here and there for safety of vehicle and availability of a parking place. If a suitable site is available by chance, it becomes difficult to get one's vehicle back because of the shortage of sufficient space. Under these circumstance, it is imperative on the part of the authorities to make sufficient spots available for parking the vehicles.

I hope, you will definitely realise the inconvenience caused to all, as above . Please take suitable steps to solve this genuine problem.

Thanking you,

Yours faithfully,
Pralay Kumar

Q. 53. You are Tek Chand of 115, Subhash Nagar, Jaipur. Write a letter to The Post Master, complaining about the irregular delivery of letters and parcels etc.

115, Subhash Nagar,
Jaipur.
25th August, 200.

The Post Master,
General Post Office,
Jaipur(Rajasthan).

Subject : Irregular Delivery of Letters.

Sir,

I want to draw your kind attention towards the negligent working style of Mr. P.K.Verma, the postman of this area. He is very irregular and negligent in his work. He does not deliver the letters and parcels on daily basis. He never comes in time. He often throws the letters either in the 'Ganda Nala' or delivers them to the small children playing in the streets. Many times, the letters are lost. The business is also hampered due to irregular and late delivery of letters. This is a matter of great concern and can cause a great loss. On many occasions he has been warned to mend his ways, but he paid a deaf ear to the requests of the residents.

Kindly take necessary action in this matter and immediately transfer Mr Verma to some other area , lest he should take revengeful action against some of the residents.

Thanking you,

Yours faithfully,
Tek Chand

Q. 54. You have visited the general hospital by chance . You find the condition of cleanliness in the hospital very pathetic. Write a complaint to the CMHO,Jaipur Hospital, in the matter.

12, Gurunanakpura,
Adarsh Nagar,
Jaipur.
24th September, 200.

The CMHO,
General Hospital ,
Jaipur (Rajasthan).

Subject : Uncleanliness and negligence of the staff in the General Hospital.

Sir,

May I lodge a simple but very important complaint to draw your attention towards the poor facilities available in the general hospital and the neglectful attitude of the medical staff. The nurses hardly attend to their duties and generally found busy in gossiping . Even the low priced medicines remain out of stock in the hospital. The toilets are never found clean; always emit a very foul smell. Yesterday, an attendant of a patient took her father to toilet , the nauseating smell made her nervous and she fainted. A complaint was also lodged with the staff nurse on duty, but she took no care of the complaint.

The electric wiring is lying uncovered and tubes don't emit proper lights. Even the sweepers leave rubbish in the corners.Every where a foul smell , uncleanliness ,dust and negligence prevail. I don't know how the hospital staff is so indifferent and working in such unhygienic conditions.

I hope you will take steps to improve the conditions and make proper arrangements, to keep the hospital clean immediately.

Thanking you,

Yours faithfully,
XYZ

Q. 55. You are Dipti Sharma of 110, Raja Park, Jaipur. Write a letter to the General Manager, Rajasthan Roadways, Jaipur, complaining about rude and irresponsible behaviour of the drivers and conductors of the roadways buses.

110, Raja Park,
Jaipur
25th June, 200.

The General Manager,
Rajasthan Roadways,
Jaipur (Rajasthan).

Subject : Complaining about rude and irresponsible behaviour of the drivers and conductors of the roadways buses.

Sir,

I want to draw your kind attention towards the rude and irresponsible behaviour of both the drivers and bus conductors with the commuters. They look towards the passengers with indifference and behave with them in a very strange and absurd way. They lack etiquettes and use filthy language.

Generally, the bus drivers do not stop the bus at the fixed stops, they rather disdain the travellers and stop before or after the stop, so the passengers have to run after the bus. The passenger hardly approaches the bus when it starts. In this way many commuters fall and feel lot of irritation and humiliation.

No less irresponsible is the behaviour of conductors. They never bother whether the passengers have got into the bus or not but are bent on blowing the whistle. The bus moves while passengers have only one foot on the foot board. This leads to the falling of the poor passengers and sustaining injuries by them several times.

They forget the elementary duties of a good conductor and behave indecently. They show no courtesy and sympathy towards the senior citizens and the ladies.

It is my humble suggestion that at the time of their recruitment, and during the initial training, they must be taught how to deal with the passengers. Regular training in this matter may help them understand the problems of the commuters. Presently, they must be instructed and advised suitably to mend their ways and a surprise checking in this respect be also done.

Your faithfully,
Dipti Sharma

Q. 56. Write a suitable letter in reply to the following advertisement , signing yourself as 'Some body':

ADVERTISEMENT :
FOUND A SUITCASE

A suitcase is found in Jammu Mail on 28/02/200..., the owner should contact the Station Master, Delhi Cantt, with proof of belongings.

B-423, Man Singh Park,
New Delhi.
April 27, 200...

The Station Master,
Delhi Cantt.

Subject : Missing suitcase

Dear Sir,

Please refer to your advertisement in the 'Times of India' on dated 23.3.200..., regarding the suitcase found in the Jammu Mail on 28.2.200..., I want to bring to your kind notice that the said suitcase belongs to me.

It is a VIP suitcase-22 inches, of gray colour. My name 'Some body' is pasted on it. It contains three white shirts, two trousers, one blue-coloured pant, one towel, a comb, one ball pen and some coins also. It also contains my original certificates (Matric and MA Economics) with attested copies, one issue of 'Akhand Jyoti ' monthly, as well as a newspaper of that day. I had returned on that day from Kanpur after attending an interview.

I shall feel obliged if the same is returned to me. Please let me know the date and the time, convenient to you, when I may collect my suitcase.

Yours faithfully,
Somebody

COMPREHENSION

"Comprehensions judge your capability and ability of *understanding the passage,* your power of *analysing* the problem in proper perspective and your ability of *presenting your answers* systematically".

Verbal comprehension measures your ability to read and understand the written passage. Through the comprehension exercise, you are asked to answer questions about the passage.

In answering the questions based on the reading passage, it is important that you answer the questions only according to the information given in the passage. If you have information from your own experience and knowledge, you should not use it to answer a question of this type. Even if you think that there is a mistake in the reading selection (paragraph), you must still answer the question on the basis of the information given in the reading passage.

There are certain techniques that will help you do well on reading comprehension questions. **Here is a summary of the most important techniques:**

(a) **Use your pencil:** To begin with, use your pencil as a *pointer.* Using the pencil *to guide your eye* along a line of text, helps you to focus on the details in the reading; it holds *your attention to the precise words in the passage.* In a long test, attention may weaken. Fatigue may blunt your attention to details. But using your pencil as a pointer will help to preserve your attention to details.

(b) Another ***benefit of using the pencil as a pointer*** is that it will probably *speed up your reading.* The steady flow of the pencil across the page with each line of text draws the eye along at a *steady pace.* Do not go faster than you can grasp the text, but do try to keep your reading going at a steady pace set by the pencil.

(c) **Circle key words and phrases:** Remember, you are not reading for just a vague general understanding of the passage. You usually have to read for detailed understanding. There will be individual *words which are important for grasping a point exactly.* Circling key words or phrases which *will enable you to zero in on precise points* needed to answer a question.

(d) **Keep forging ahead :** Do not get bogged down if there is a word or sentence you do not understand. *You may get the main idea without knowing the individual word or sentence.* Sometimes you can sense the meaning of the word from the context. Sometimes the word or sentence may not be the basis of any question. If there is some idea, regarding which you need to answer a question but do not understand, read it one more time. If *you still do not understand it, move on.* You can come back to this question later if you have more time at the end of the test.

(e) Another good reading comprehension strategy is to **read the questions before starting the passage**. This does not mean reading the answer choices at this time. By reading the questions, *you will have an idea of what information you will need* after reading the passage. This may *alert you to certain details,* ideas and specific areas in the paragraph, where the questions are being drawn from.

RIGHT APPROACH TO ANSWER THE QUESTIONS :

1. Questions are to be answered on the basis of the information provided in the passage, and you **are not expected to rely on outside knowledge** of a particular topic. Your own views or opinions may sometimes conflict with the views expressed or the information provided in the passage. Be sure that you *work within the context of the passage*. You should not expect to agree with everything you encounter in reading passages.
2. You should analyse each passage carefully before answering the accompanying questions. As with any kind of close and thoughtful reading, *look for clues* that will help you understand less explicit aspects of the passage. Try to *separate main ideas from supporting ideas or evidence*.
3. Note *transitions from one idea to the next,* and examine the relationships among the different ideas or parts of the passage. For example, are they contrasting? Are they complementary? Consider the points the author makes, the conclusions drawn, and how and why those points are made or conclusions are drawn.
4. *Read each question carefully* and be certain that you understand exactly what is being asked.
5. Always read all the answer choices before selecting the best answer.
6. **The *best answer* is the one that *most accurately* and *most completely* answers the questions** being posed. Be careful not to pick an answer choice simply because it is a true statement. Be careful also not to be misled by answer choices that are only *partially true* or only partially satisfy the problem posed in the question.

COMPREHENSIONS : SOLVED EXAMPLES

Direction : ***Read the following passage carefully and answer the questions given below it:***

PASSAGE 1

Many people believe that science and religion are contrary to each other. But this notion is wrong. As a matter of fact, both are complementary to each other. The aim of both these institutions is to explain different aspects of life, universe and human existence. There is no doubt that the methods of science and religion are different. The method of science is observation, experimentation and experience. Science takes its recourse to progressive march towards perfection; the rules of religion are faith, intuition and spoken word of the enlightened; in general, while science is inclined towards reason and rationality, spiritualism is the essence of religion.

In earlier times when man appeared on earth, he was over-awed at the sight of violent and powerful aspects of nature. In certain cases, the usefulness of different natural objects of nature overwhelmed man. Thus began the worship of forces of nature-fire, the sun, the rivers, the rocks, the trees, the snakes, etc. The holy scriptures were written by those who had developed harmony between external nature and their inner self. Their object was to ennoble, elevate and liberate the human spirit and mind. But the priestly class took upon itself the monopoly of scriptural knowledge and interpretation to its own advantage. Thus the entire human race was in chains. Truth was flouted and progressive, liberal and truthful ideas or ideas expressing doubt and skepticism were suppressed and their holders punished. It was in these trying circumstances, the science emerged as a saviour of mankind But its path was not smooth and safe. The scientists and free thinkers were tortured. This was the fate of Copernicus, Galileo, Bruno and others. But, by and by science gained ground.

Q. 1. Why does man worship the force of nature?
(a) The holy scriptures advocate the worship of forces of nature,
(b) The worship elevates and liberates the human spirit and mind,
(c) The worship makes man believe in faith and intuition,
(d) Forces of nature reach us spiritualism,
(e) None of these.

Q. 2. Which of the following statements is true in the context of the passage?
(a) Science and religion are antagonistic to each other,
(b) Science encourages worshipping of nature,
(c) Religion is essential for external peace and harmony,
(d) Regimental religion was replaced by scientific principles,
(e) Science is essential for inner peace of mind.

Q. 3. According to the passage, science and religion both :
(a) rely on the spoken word of the enlightened,
(b) emerged out of the fear of man,
(c) emerged from the desire of man to worship the forces of nature,
(d) employ different methods of enquiry,
(e) work at the cross-purpose of each other.

Q. 4. Why is it said in the passage that, 'science emerged as a saviour of mankind'?
(a) Many great thinkers contributed to the progress of science,
(b) Science takes recourse to progressive march towards perfection,
(c) Science is inclined towards reason and rationality,
(d) Man was bound in chains by religious orthodoxy,
(e) The free thinkers and enlightened men were tortured.

Q. 5. Which of the following statements is not true in the context of the passage?
(a) Man worships the forces of nature,
(b) Methods of science and religion are different,
(c) Regimental religion got degenerated into orthodoxy,
(d) Galileo and Bruno were disciples of Copernicus.
(e) The holy scriptures were written by people who had tremendous inner strength.

Q. 6. Choose the word which is most nearly the same in meaning as the word 'flouted', as used in the passage.
(a) Mocked, (b) Nourished, (c) Expressed, (d) Deflated,
(e) Concealed.

Q. 7. According to the passage, science and religion :
(a) are contrary to each other,
(b) have the same origin,
(c) are supportive to each other,
(d) have the same aim of controlling universe,
(e) do not allow any deviation from their rules.

Q. 8. According to the passage, at the present juncture, there is a need to :
(a) encourage spiritualism as much as possible,
(b) teach people to worship the forces of nature,
(c) free man from all sorts of bondages,
(d) explain to the people different aspects of life and universe,
(e) judiciously mix the principles of science and true spirit of religion.

Q. 9. What was the object of the authors of the holy scriptures?
(a) To teach man the methods of worshipping nature,
(b) To advocate the progressive and liberal ideas,
(c) To educate and raise the human spirit and mind,
(d) To develop harmony between external nature and their inner self,
(e) None of these.

Q. 10. Choose the word which is most opposite in meaning to the word ' enlightened' as used in the passage :
(a) Uninformed, (b) Derogatory, (c) Downtrodden, (d) Educated,
(e) Authority.

Answers :

1. (b), **2.** (d), **3.** (d), **4.** (d), **5.** (d), **6.** (a), **7.** (c), **8.** (e),
9. (c), **10.** (a).

PASSAGE 2

Direction : ***Read the following passage carefully and answer the questions given below it:***

Mountaineering is now looked upon as the king of sports. But men have lived amongst the mountains since prehistoric times and in some parts of the world, as in the Andes and Himalayas, difficult mountain journeys have inevitably been part of their everyday life. However, some of the peaks there, were easily accessible from most of the cities of Europe. It is quite interesting that while modern mountaineers prefer difficult routes for the greater enjoyment of sport, the early climbers looked for the easiest ones, for the summit was the prize they all set their eyes on. Popular interest in mountaineering increased considerably after the ascent of the Alpine peak of Matterhorn in 1865 and Edward Whymper's dramatic account of the climb and fatal accident which occurred during the descent.

In the risky sport of mountaineering, the element of competition between either individuals or teams is totally absent. Rather, one can say that the competition is between the team and the peaks themselves. The individuals making up a party must climb together as a team, for they depend upon one another for their safety. Mountaineering can be dangerous, unless reasonable precautions are taken. However, the majority of fatal accidents happen to parties which are inexperienced or not properly equipped. Since many accidents are caused due to bad weather, the safe climber is the man who knows, when it is time to turn back, however, tempting it may be to press on and try to reach the summit.

Q. 1. Mountaineering is different from other sports because :
(a) it is risky and dangerous,
(b) it can be fatal,
(c) it is most thrilling and exciting, there is no competition between individuals.

Q. 2. People living in the Andes and the Himalayas made mountain journeys because :
(a) it was a kind of sport,
(b) they had to undertake them in their day-to-day life,
(c) they lived in pre-historic time,
(d) of the challenge offered by the difficult journey.

Q. 3. Mountaineers climb as a team because :
(a) the height is too much for one individual,
(b) the competition is between the team and the peak,
(c) they have to rely on each other for safety,
(d) there is no competition among them.

Q. 4. "..........the summit was the prize they all set their eyes on." In the context of the passage, this means :
(a) reaching the top was their exclusive concern.
(b) they kept their eyes steadily on reaching the summit.
(c) they cared for nothing but the prize of reaching the summit.
(d) they chose a route from which they could see the summit clearly.

Q. 5. "to press," in the last sentence of the passage, means :
(a) to struggle in a forceful manner,
(b) to force upon others,
(c) to work fearlessly,
(d) to continue in a determined manner.

Answers :

1. (c), **2.** (b), **3.** (c), **4.** (a), **5.** (d).

PASSAGE 3

Direction : ***Read the following passage carefully and answer the questions given below it :***

On the morning of August 31, 1573, 3000 horsemen of the imperial Mughal army paused at the banks of the Sabarmati. The rebels, they were after, lay just beyond the swollen river, but the soldiers were exhausted; they had traversed 960 kilometers of difficult terrain in nine days, riding almost continuously. Suddenly a warrior on a chestnut charger plunged into the raging torrent. As man and horse struggled on to the opposite bank, a thrill ran through the army. It was the emperor, Jalal-uddin Akbar ! With a roar, the soldiers followed him across and within two days, they had put down the rebellion so thoroughly that Gujrat remained in Mughal hands for the next 185 years.

Q. 1. The rebels were camped :
(a) across the Sabarmati river,
(b) on the banks of Sabarmati river,
(c) in Gujrat,
(d) in imperial Mughal courts.

Q. 2. The expression "swollen river" means :

(a) a river in flood, (b) a calm and serene river,
(c) a deep river, (d) a shallow river.

Q. 3. The Mughal soldiers didn't cross the river because :

(a) they were cowards,
(b) they had joined hands with the rebels,
(c) they were waiting for the king to arrive,
(d) they were tired after a difficult journey.

Q. 4. The sudden arrival of King Akbar :

(a) surprised the soldiers, (b) angered the soldiers,
(c) dismayed the soldiers, (d) enthused the soldiers.

Q. 5. The attack on the rebels turned out to be :

(a) a dismal failure, (b) a grand success,
(c) of no particular significance, (d) an ordinary affair.

Answers :

1. (b), **2.** (a), **3.** (d), **4.** (d), **5.** (b).

PASSAGE 4

Direction : ***Read the following passage carefully and answer the questions given below it :***

He saw nothing, he had no knife or sharp instrument, the grating of the window was of iron and he had too often assured himself of its solidity. His furniture consisted of a bed, a chair, a table, a pail and a jug. The bed had iron clamps, but they were screwed to the wall and it would have required a screwdriver to take them off.

Dantes had but one resource, which was to break the jug and with one of the sharp fragments attack the wall. He let the jug fall on the floor and it broke in pieces. He concealed two or three of the sharpest fragments in his bed, leaving the rest on the floor. The breaking of the jug was too natural an accident to excite suspicion, and next morning the gaoler went grumblingly to fetch another, without giving himself the trouble to remove the fragments. Dantes heard joyfully the key grate in the lock as the guard departed.

Q. 1. Dantes was in :

(a) a hostel, (b) a dining room,
(c) an army barracks, (d) a prison.

Q. 2. Dantes was planning to :

(a) carve his name, (b) make his escape,
(c) tease the guard, (d) call for breakfast.

Q. 3. The guard left the fragments because he:

(a) didn't notice them, (b) wished to punish Dantes,
(c) was too lazy to bother, (d) wanted Dantes to clear up.

Q. 4. Dantes probably broke the jug:

(a) in the morning, (b) during the night,
(c) after breakfast, (d) at exactly 3 p.m.

Q. 5. Dantes heard the key grate in the lock, when the:

(a) cell door was shut, (b) cell door was opened,

(c) storeroom was opened , (d) storeroom was shut.

Answers :

1. (d), **2.**(b), **3.** (c), **4.** (b), **5.** (a).

PASSAGE 5

Direction : ***Read the passage given below carefully and then answer these questions based on what is stated or implied in the passage :***

One simple concept lies behind the formation of the stars : gravitational instability. The concept is not new. Newton first perceived it late in the 17th Century. Imagine a uniform, static cloud of gas in space. Imagine then that the gas is somehow disturbed, so that one small spherical region becomes a little denser than the gas around it so that the small region's gravitational field becomes slightly stronger. It now attracts more matter to it and its gravity increases further, causing it to begin to contract. As it contracts its density increases, which increases its gravity even more, so that it picks up even more matter and contracts even further. The process continues until the small region of gas finally forms a gravitationally bound object.

Q. 1. The primary purpose of the passage is to :

(a) describe a static condition,

(b) support a theory considered outmoded,

(c) depict the successive stages of a phenomenon,

(d) demonstrate the evolution of the meaning of a term.

Q. 2. It can be inferred from this passage that the author views the information contained within it as:

(a) lacking in elaboration, (b) original but obscure,

(c) speculative and unprofitable, (d) uncomplicated and traditional.

Q. 3. With which of the following words can you replace the word uniform as given in this passage ?

(a) Uniting, (b) Varying, (c) Gaseous, (d) Unvarying.

Q. 4. What does the underlined word 'it' stands for in he passage ?

(a) Gravitational instability, (b) Cloud of gas,

(c) Small spherical denser region, (d) Matter.

Q. 5. The author provides information that answers which of following questions ?

(A) What causes the disturbances that changes the cloud from its original static condition?

(B) How does this small region's increasing density affect its gravitational field ?

(C) What is the end result of the gradually increasing concentration of the small regionof gas?

(a) A only, (b) B only,

(c) B and C only, (d) A,B and C.

Answers :

1. (c), **2.** (d), **3.** (d), **4.** (c), **5.** (c).

PASSAGE 6

Direction : ***Read the following passage carefully and answer the questions given below it :***

A great deal of the world's work is neither producing material things nor altering the things that Nature produces, but doing services of one sort or another.

Thoughtless people are apt to think a brickmaker more of a producer than a clergyman. When a village carpenter makes a gate to keep cattle out of a field of wheat, he has something solid in his hand which he can claim for his own until the farmer pays him for it. But when a village boy makes a noise to keep the birds off, he has nothings to show, though the noise is just as necessary as the gate. The postman does not make anything ..... The policeman does not make anything ..... The doctor makes pills sometimes; but that is not his real business, which is to tell you when you ought to take pills, and what pills to take, unless indeed he has the good sense to tell you not take them at all, and you have the good sense to believe him, when he is giving you good advice instead of bad. The lawyer does not make anything substantial ..... They are all in service.

Q. 1. Thoughtless people think a brickmaker more of a producer than a clergyman because :
(a) a clergyman is an idler,
(b) a brickmaker produces something solid which he can keep with him till he gets its price,
(c) a brickmaker, being physically stronger than a clergyman, can naturally produce more,
(d) he cannot understand the philosophical lectures of the clergyman.

Q. 2. According to the author of the passage, a large number of persons :
(a) are producing material things,
(b) are altering the things that Nature produces,
(c) are doing nothing in particular,
(d) offer services.

Q. 3. The writer thinks that :
(a) both the doctor and the patient are sensible when one makes pills and the other buys them,
(b) the doctor is sensible and the patient is insensible,
(c) the doctor is insensible and the patient is insensible,
(d) both the doctor and the patient make sense when the doctor tells not to take the pills and the patient believes him.

Q. 4. The writer's description of the doctor's business :
(a) strengthens the main argument of the passage because the doctor's business is to make pills,
(b) is irrelevant to the main argument of the passage,
(c) weakens the main argument of the passage,
(d) illustrates the difference between producing something and offering a service.

Answers :

1. (b), **2.** (d), **3.** (d), **4.** (d).

PASSAGE 7

Direction : ***Read the passage carefully, then answer the questions which are based on what is stated or implied in the passage :***

Since the world has become industrialised, there has been an increase in the number of animal species that have either become extinct or have neared extinction. Bengal tiger, for instance, which once roamed the jungle in vast numbers, now number only 2300 and by the year 2025 their population is estimated to be down to zero. What is alarming about the case of Bengal tiger is that this extinction will have been caused almost entirely by poachers who according to some sources, are not interested in material gain but in personal gratification. This is an example of the callousness that is part of what is causing the problem of extinction. Animals like the Bengal tiger, as well as, those belonging to other endangered species, are a valuable part of the world's ecosystem. International laws protecting these animals must be enacted to ensure their survival, and the survival of our planet. Countries around the world have begun to deal with the problem in various ways. Some countries, in order to circumvent the problem, have allocated large amount of land to animal reserves. They then charge admission fees to help defray the costs of maintaining the parks, and they often must also depend on world organisations for support. With the money get, they can invest in equipment and patrols to protect the animals. Another solution that is an attempt to stem the tide of animal extinction is an international boycott of products made from endangered species. This seems fairly effective, but it will not, by itself, prevent animals from being hunted and killed.

Q. 1. What is the author's main concern in this passage ?
(a) Problems of industrialisation, (b) The Bengal tiger,
(c) Endangered species, (d) Callousness of man.

Q. 2. According to the passage, poachers kill for :
(a) material gain, (b) personal satisfaction,
(c) both, (d) None of the above.

Q. 3. Which of the following words is closest in meaning to the underlined word 'alarming' ?
(a) Serious, (b) Dangerous,
(c) Distressing, (d) Frightening.

Q. 4. Certain species are becoming extinct because of :
(a) industrialisation, (b) poaching,
(c) love of products made from them, (d) all the above.

Q. 5. The Phrase 'Stem the tide' means :
(a) save, (b) stop,
(c) touch, (d) spare.

Q. 6. Which of the following, best describes the author's attitude ?
(a) Concerned, (b) Vindictive,
(c) Surprised, (d) Generous.

Answers :

1. (c), **2.** (b), **3.** (d), **4.** (d), **5.** (b), **6.** (a).

PASSAGE 8

Direction : *Read the passage carefully and then choose the one best answer for each question given below :*

The conservative is not an extreme individualist. He may be willing to concede numerous arguments of the unqualified individualists, for his own respect, for the dignity of the individual is not surpassed by that of any man. Yet, he cannot agree to the full implications of individualism, which is based so he thinks, on an incorrect appraisal of man, society, history, and government. In his own way, the individualist is as much a perfectionist as the Socialist, and with perfectionism the conservative can have no <u>truck.</u>

In particular, the conservative refuses to go all the way with economic individualism. His distrust of unfettered man, his recognition to groups, his sense of the complexity of the social process, his recognition of the real services that government can perform - all these sentiments make it impossible for him to subscribe to the dogmas and shibboleths of economic individualism : laissez-faire, the negative state, enlightened self-interest, the law of supply and demand, the profit motive. The conservative may occasionally have kind word for each of these notions, but he is careful to qualify his support by stating other, more important social truths. For example, he does not for a moment deny the prominence of the profit motive, but he insists that it be recognised for the selfish thing it is and be kept within reasonable, socially imposed limits.

Q. 1. The conservative is :
(a) a perfectionist,
(b) an economist,
(c) a socialist,
(d) none of above.

Q. 2. The conservative is against Econo+mic Individualism for all the following reasons except:
(a) he does not trust free men,
(b) he believes in the authority of the government,
(c) he believes in groups,
(d) he feels that social processes are important.

Q. 3. The author mentions all the following catchwords of economic individualism except:
(a) free trade,
(b) the profit motive,
(c) balance of trade,
(d) the negative state.

Q. 4. Which of the following words can replace the underlined word 'truck' ?
(a) Dealing,
(b) Bargain,
(c) Debate,
(d) Transport.

Q. 5. Which of the following statements is true ?
(a) The socialist and the individualist tend to be broadly similar in their views,
(b) The conservative believes that profit motive originates in selfishness,
(c) The conservative is also an extreme individualist,
(d) None of the above.

Q. 6. Which of the following could be an appropriate title for the passage ?
(a) Anarchy and freedom,
(b) Progress and The conservative,
(c) A conservative apology
(d) The conservative stand.

Answers :

1. (d), **2.** (d), **3.** (a), **4.** (a), **5.** (b), **6.** (d).

PASSAGE 9

Direction : ***Read the following passage carefully and answer the questions given below :***

An old gentleman was walking slowly along a street. One day he saw a little boy who was trying to reach a door-bell which was too high for him. He was a kind-hearted old man, so he stopped and said, "I will ring the bell for you," and then he pulled the bell so hard that it could be heard all over the house.

The little boy looked up at him and said, "Now we will run away, come on," and before the old gentleman knew what was happening the naughty boy had run round the corner of the street leaving the man to explain to the angry owner of the house why he had rung the bell.

Q. 1. Write the letter a, b, c, or d of the correct answer in the answer book :
The old man rang the bell because :
(a) he wanted to help the little boy,
(b) he wanted to have some fun,
(c) the boy asked him to do so,
(d) he wished to see the owner of the house.

Q. 2. Who did the owner of the house see at the door ?

Q. 3. Who did the little boy want to make fun of ?

Q. 4. ".......... so he stopped and said ...."
Who does the word 'he' here refer to ?

Q.5. "............ I will ring the bell for you."
Who does the word 'you' here refer to ?

Q. 6. Why did the boy ask the old man to run away with him ?

Answers :

1. (a).

2. The owner of the house saw the old man at the door.

3. The little boy wanted to make fun of the owner of the house.

4. The 'old man'.

5. The word 'you', here refers to the 'little boy'.

6. The boy asked the old man to run away , because he knew that the owner of the house would be angry.

PASSAGE 10

Direction : ***Read the following passage carefully and answer the questions given below :***

Once a smart looking young man visited the office of a business firm to look for a job. The manager though pleased with his behaviour said, "There is no vacancy for a clerk." The young man was very unhappy and turned to go. As he was passing out of the door way, he found a pin lying near it. He at once picked it up. The manager saw this and was greatly impressed. He thought that the applicant was good enough to be employed in the office. So he called him back and appointed him a clerk in his office. The young man in due course became the head of the firm. It was his love of order and economy, that brought him success in life.

Q. 1. Write the letter a, b, c, or d of the correct answer in the answer book :
The young man was very :

(a) happy, (b) unhappy,
(c) sorry, (d) pleased.

Q. 2. What was the young man in need of ?

Q. 3. What made the young man very sad ?

Q. 4. What did the young man see when he was leaving the room ?

Q. 5. What did the manager see the young man doing ?

Q. 6. "............ and appointed him a clerk ...." Who does the word 'him' here refer to ?

Answers :

1. (b)

2. The young man was in need of a job.

3. On hearing the words of the manager that there was no vacancy for a clerk, the youngman became very sad.

4. The young man, while passing out of the door way, saw a pin lying near it.

5. The manager saw the young man picking up the pin .

6. The word 'him' here refers to the young man.

PRECIS WRITING

What is a Precis?

It is a **short summary of the essential ideas of a longer composition;** the basic thought of a passage is reproduced in miniature, *retaining the mood and tone of the original.* It must possess clear, emphatic diction and effective sentence construction. Its unity and coherence should be emphasised through smooth, unobtrusive transitions.

Precis denotes a brief, concise and clear, well connected abstract, summary or gist of a given passage.

As per the *Oxford dictionary,* Precis means-a *concise or abridged statement*, a summary. **To make precis of a given passage,**we should **extract its main points, and then express them clearly in as few words as possible.** Precis is a summary or a condensed composition of bare facts.

Essentials of a Good Precis :

[1] *Completeness :* Precis must have complete idea of the passage.
[2] *Compactness* or *Well connected :* The sentences must be well connected and the whole precis should reflect a necessary compactness.
[3] *Brevity* : Brevity is the soul of a good precis .
[4] Precis is usually written in *Indirect narration* in past tense in third person.
[5] Precis *must not contain our own opinion or biased vieus.*
[6] Precis must be *grammatically correct.*
[7] *The heading* of the precis should *reflect theme or idea of the passage.*

How to Write a Good Precis?

First, *write an outline of the main ideas* – those you see as most important. Think of it this way – you are summarising the lecture for a friend who missed the class and the material will be on an upcoming test. Also, you may want to include a brief statement about the *tone, audience, or purpose* of the article.

Second, *put your outline into sentence/paragraph form.*

Third, count the *number of words* and make necessary changes.

Note : 1. A summary or a precis is NOT a personal interpretation of a passage or an expression of your opinion of the idea; it is, rather, an exact replica in miniature of the passage, ***often reduced to one-quarter to one-fifth of its size***, in which you express the complete argument.

2. ***Do not copy a single sentence from the article***! You may use key words and phrases only when you are expressing ideas which are technically precise or when you feel comfortable using the writer's own words, i.e., you understand exactly what he or she means, and there is really no better way to express the concept.

Do's and Don'ts of Precis Writing

(a) Start your precis by stating the main idea of the passage.
(b) Do not use the words *"in this article."* Use the style *"Jackob argues that* the most significant contribution of the Iraqies was . ."

(c) When writing about history, use the past tense.
(d) Do not use *abbreviations* or *contractions*.
(e) Avoid words, like-*big, good, bad, little*, and *a lot*. Also, do not use the phrase ''*throughout history*.'' This is cliché.
(f) *Count your 'ands.' Avoid use of 'ands'* unnecessarily.
(g) *Title of text* should be put in *italics* or *underlined.*

PRECIS WRITING

Examples

Q. 1. Make a precis of following passage . The precis should be, as far as possible, in your own words. Suggest a suitable title for your precis :

When our childhood has fallen behind us and taken on some of the glamour of distance, we often ransack our memories in order to call up to our mind's eye the picture of the children we were. Then we are surprised to discover how little we remember of our earliest days; they have gone for ever and seemingly have left nothing behind them . All is lost in haze, and no definite image rewards our efforts, made to recapture the incidents of infancy.

Some, however, can recall more than others; one may remember something that happened when he was only a child of two, while another may find his memory blank- a clean sheet of paper, as far as anything is concerned, which befell him before he was five. Yet, perhaps as regards things generally, the memory of the latter may be stronger than that of the former, it is only in regard to the early childhood that the first man's memory is stronger.

To account for these variations is not easy; there are so many factors to be taken into account. Nature and circumstances have to be considered. One may be markedly introspective, unconsciously looking into himself from his earliest days; another may have had an accident which could not fail to impress itself on his memory. Again, one man may remember earlier events because his memory is a visual one, while another looks not so far back because his memory is more of the mind and ''a child's mind is of slower development than his sight."

Some Tips

Heading : "*Memory of Childhood*."

Main points of the passage are to *be noted down* as follows :

(1) We remember little of our earlier days.
(2) The memory of some extends farther back than that of others.
(3) Variations in the memory of childhood are due to a person's nature and early circumstances.

Use these points to write a precis , leaving aside unimportant and superfluous items:

PRECIS

Title : "Memory of Childhood."

After some years , if we look back to our earliest days of childhood, we would find that we remember very little. The memories of some 'however' can go back farther than that of others. It is not necessarily the stronger memory that does it. It is the nature of a man and his circumstances, that determine the extent of his memory.A man with visual memory may have better memory than others.

Q. 2. *Make a precis of following passage. The precis should be, as far as possible, in your own words. Suggest a suitable title for your precis :*

"It is possible to score goals and lose the game. It is possible to win battles and lose the campaign. It is possible to make money and miss a fortune. The short-sighted man suffers, no matter where he is found ; he may see some things with excessive clarity, but he fails to get the true perspective, which will enable him to arrive at wise conclusions. He gains one thing, but he loses something better.

This is a very common error. The student makes it when he forgets the life-goal in thinking of the medal or the scholarship. The saint forgets it when he thinks of to-day and forgets the greater tomorrow. The business man misses his way when he choses a present gain and forfeits ten times as much in the future. The youth makes such a mistake when he marries good looks, and forgets the character which will be necessary to command his respect for forty years to come.

Man was made to think and unless he uses his brain he will stumble into no end of unseen morasses.There is a future, and it cannot be evaded ; and when it is reached, it cannot be changed, for we are just deciding what it shall be.We are our own destiny-makers . It is well to face the future with care and caution ."

How to make the precis ? Learn through the following example :

Heading : *Disadvantages of Short-Sightedness.*

Main points of the passage are to be noted down:

(1) Winning and losing game and money are possible in life of everybody. A man who suffers from short-sightedness, sees only the immediate gain with clarity, but loses something better and greater in the future.

(2) The student who cares more for the medal than for the goal of life, the saint who thinks of the present and not of the glorious future, the business man who for an immediate gain forgoes greater future gain, and the youth who marries a woman of good looks rather than of character, all are the victims of this grave error.

(3) Our future lies in our own hands. We are our own destiny-makers. We should face the future with care and caution.

Now, use these points to write a precis, leaving aside unimportant and superfluous items:

PRECIS

Title : 'Disadvantages of Short-Sightedness'

Wining and losing, game or money are part of life. A short-sighted person loses the greater future gain for an immediate small gain. The student misses his life-goal for the medal or scholarship, the saint ignoring future bliss for the present achievement, the business man forgoing a larger future fortune for the present trifle gain and the youth marrying a good-looking girl rather than one of character, all reflect short-sightedness of the respective fellows. We are the architect of our future and, therefore, of our destiny; we should face it warily and carefully.

Q. 3. *Make a precis of following passage. The precis should be, as far as possible, in your own words. Suggest a suitable title for your precis :*

" How many apparent defeats, enthusiasm has transformed into victories ? It is one of the most vital elements in all successes, but in the sphere of religious activity, its value cannot be over-estimated. Nevertheless, it must be admitted, that enthusiasm is not something that can always be had merely for the asking.

In the first place, to be effective, enthusiasm must be genuine. Simulated enthusiasm is a weak, vapid, dull thing that soon dies. People do not become enthusiastic merely by wanting to be. It is not something that can be thrust upon others at will. Nothing could be more ridiculous than for some one to rise before a large gathering and say, " I moved them all and they became enthusiastic ! " Enthusiasm is not necessarily a noise or shouting or even feverish activity. These may be, and sometimes are, manifestations of its presence, but not necessarily so. Often, indeed, such symptoms are merely spurious imitations, and as far from the genuine articles as the counterfeit money from the real money.

All genuine, lasting enthusiasm must be built upon knowledge. This is the true fountain from which it bubbles up, and nothing will take its place. People cannot be lastingly enthusiastic about that of which they know nothing."

Learn to make Precis through the following example:

Heading: '*The Power of Enthusiasm*'

Main points of the passage are to be noted down:

(1) Enthusiasm has transformed many apparent defeats into victories.

(2) It is the most vital element in all successes. But enthusiasm cannot be had for the asking.

(3) Genuine enthusiasm is effective. Simulated enthusiasm is a dull and temporary thing. Enthusiasm cannot be forced upon others.

(4) Genuine enthusiasm can be built upon knowledge alone. One cannot be enthusiastic about a thing for long unless one has complete knowledge of it.

Use the above points to write a precis , leaving aside unimportant and superfluous items:

PRECIS

Title : 'The Power of Enthusiasm'

Enthusiasm is one of the most important elements to achieve successes and has turned many sure tumblings into victories. But in order to be effective and lasting, it must be genuine. Simulated enthusiasm dies soon. We should distinguish real from false enthusiasm which consists in noise, shouting or feverish activity. Genuine enthusiasm can be built upon knowledge alone. To be lastingly enthusiastic about a thing,the people should have complete knowledge of it.

Q. 4. *Make a precis of following passage. The precis should be, as far as possible, in your own words. Suggest a suitable title for your precis :*

When in the course of human events it becomes necessary for one people to dissolve the political bonds which have connected one-another and to assume among the powers of the earth, a separate and equal station, a decent respect for the opinions of mankind requires that they should declare the causes which impel them to separation .

We hold truth to be self evident: that all men are created equal; that they are endowed by their creator with certain inalienable rights; that among these are life, liberty and the pursuit of happiness; that to secure these rights, governments are instituted, deriving their just powers from the consent of the governed; that whenever any form of government becomes destructive of these ends, it is the right of the people to abolish it and to institute a new government, laying its foundation on such principles and organising its power in such form, as to them shall seem most likely to effect their safety and happiness.

Prudence will dictate that governments long established should not be changed for light and transient causes and accordingly, all experience hath shown that mankind are more disposed to suffer while evils are sufferable than to right themselves by abolishing the forms to which they are accustomed. But when a long train of abuses and usurpations, pursuing invariably the same object, evinces a design to reduce them under absolute despotism, it is their duty to throw off such government, and to provide new guards for their future security.

PRECIS

Title : 'The People and the Government'

Whenever one people forces to break the political bonds with another and assumes an independent status as a separate nation, they should declare the causes of such a separation.

All men are created equal and they possess certain inalienable rights-life, liberty and pursuit of happiness. Governments are created by the people to protect these rights. If a government fails to secure these, the people have a right to change that government. Prudence requires that long-established governments should not be changed for trivial causes. Only when constant abuses and usurpations threaten to bring them under despotism, then such a govrnment should be thrown off to secure the future well beings.

Q. 5. Make a precis of following passage in about 100 words. The precis should be, as far as possible, in your own words. Suggest a suitable title for your precis :

Trading is a social activity. Whoever undertakes to sell any kinds of goods to the public, does what affects the interest of other persons and of society in general. Thus his conduct, in principle, comes within the jurisdiction of society. Accordingly, it was once held to be the duty of governments, in all cases which were considered of importance, to fix prices, and regulate the process of manufacture. But it is now recognized, though not till after a long struggle, that both the cheapness and the good quality of commodities are most effectively provided for by leaving the producers and sellers perfectly free,under the sole check of equal freedom to the buyers for supplying themselves from elsewhere. This is the so-called doctrine of Free Trade, which rests on grounds different from, though equally solid with, the principle of individual liberty. Restrictions on trade or on production for purposes of trade are indeed restraints; and all restraints, as restraint, is evil. But the restraints in question affect only that part of conduct, which society is competent to restrain and those are wrong solely because they do not really produce the results which are desired to be produced by them. As the principle of individual liberty is not involved in the doctrine of Free Trade, so neither is in most of the questions which arise respecting the limits of the doctrine : as, for example, what amount of public control is admissible for the prevention of fraud by adulteration; how far sanitary precautions, or arrangements to protect working-people employed in dangerous occupations, should be enforced on players. Such question involves considerations of liberty, only in so far as leaving people to themselves is always better than controlling them.

PRECIS

Title : 'Control over Trade'

Trade affects the society . Governments in the past, as a duty , fixed the prices and regulated the manufacturing processes. Things of cheap and good quality can be available only when the buyers and sellers are free to deal with each other. This is called a Free Trade which may or may not have personal freedom. Restraints for the sake of restraints on trade are unjustified. Restraints imposed by the society itself, are improper because the result is not as desired. Enforcement of control to prevent adulteration and to protect people from health hazards, again, involves the point of liberty . So it is always better to leave the people free and let them control themselves.

Q. 6. Make a precis in your own words, of the following passage, in about one- third its length. Give a suitable title.

Although our age far surpasses all previous ages in knowledge, yet there has been no correlative increase in wisdom. The agreement between the two ceases as soon as we attempt to define 'wisdom' and consider means of promoting it. I want to ask first what wisdom is, and then what can be done to teach it.

There are, I think, several factors that contribute to wisdom. Of these, I should put first a sense of proportion ; the capacity to take account of all the important factors in a problem and attach to each, its due weight. This has become more difficult than it used to be, owing to the extent and complexity of the specialized knowledge required of various kinds of techniques. Suppose, for example that you are engaged in research in scientific medicine. The work is difficult and is likely to absorb the whole of your intellectual energy. You have not time to consider the effect which your discoveries or inventions may have outside the field of medicine. You succeed (let us say) as modern medicine has succeeded, in enormously lowering the infant death-rate, not only in Europe and America but also in Asia and Africa. This has the entirely unintended result of making the food supply inadequate and lowering the standard of life in the most populous parts of the world. To take an even more spectacular example, which is in everybody's mind at the present time : You study the composition of the atom from a disinterested desire for knowledge and incidentally place in the hands of powerful lunatics the means of destroying the human race. In such ways, the pursuit of knowledge may become harmful unless it is combined with wisdom; and wisdom, in the sense of comprehensive vision, is not necessarily present in specialist in the pursuit of knowledge.

Comprehensiveness alone, however, is not enough to constitute wisdom. There must be also, a certain awareness of the ends of human life. This may be illustrated by the study of history. Many eminent historians have done more harm than good, because they viewed facts through the distorting medium of their own passions. Hegel had a philosophy of history which did not suffer from and lack of comprehensiveness, since it started from the earliest time and continued into an indefinite future. But the chief lesson of history which he sought to inculcate was, that from the A.D.400 down to his own time, Germany had been the most important nation and the standard-bearer of progress in the world. Perhaps, one could stretch the comprehensiveness that constitutes wisdom to include not only intellect but also feeling. It is by no means uncommon to find men, whose knowledge is wide, but whose feelings are narrow. Such men lack what I am calling wisdom.

PRECIS

Title : 'Knowledge v/s Wisdom'

Our age is far ahead of previous ages in the matter of knowledge, but not so in case of wisdom. Wisdom means a sense of proportion. It further means to analyse a problem in the light of all the related factors .Comprehensiveness itself does not mean the 'wisdom'. Technical knowledge about medicines and atomic energy does not bother about the far-reaching consequences of its use. So, there should be wisdom to control and guide the use of knowledge. Besides comprehensiveness, wisdom includes the awareness about the ends of our lives. The study of history well throw light on this point. Some historians distorted the facts of history because of their personal passion and interest. Indifferently pursuing for acquiring the knowledge may result in its misuse , if used by a man having no wisdom. A man with wide knowledge but no feelings is a man without wisdom.

Q. 7. Make a precis of the following passage in about 200 words. As far as possible, the precis should be in your own words.Suggest a suitable title far the precis :

What is a perfectly free person ? Evidently, a person who can do what he likes, when he likes and where he likes, or do nothing at all if he prefers it. Well, there is no such person; and there never can be any such person. Whether we like it or not, we must all sleep for one-third of our lifetime; wash and dress and undress; we must spend a couple of hours eating and drinking; we must spend nearly as much time in getting about from place to place. For half the day, we are slaves to necessities which we cannot shirk, whether we are monarchs, with a thousand servants or humble labourers , with no servants. And the wives must undertake the additional heavy slavery of child-bearing if the world is still to be full of people.

These natural jobs cannot be shirked. But they involve other jobs which can. As we must eat, we must first provide food; as we must sleep, we must have beds and beddings in houses with fireplaces and cool; as we must walk through the streets, we must have clothes to cover ourselves. Now, food, houses and clothes can be produced by human labour. But when they are produced they can be stolen. If you like honey you can let bees produce it by their labour, and then steal it from them. What you can do to a bee, you can also do to a man or a woman or a child if you can get the upper hand of them by force or fraud or trickery of any sort, or even by teaching them that it is their religious duty to sacrifice their freedom for yours.

So beware, if you allow any person, or class of persons, to get the upper hand of you, they will shift all that part of their slavery to Nature that can be shifted on to your shoulders; and you will find yourself working form eight to fourteen hours a day when, if you had only yourself and your family to provid for, you could do it quite comfortably in half the time or less. The object of all honest governments should be to prevent your being imposed on in this way. But the object of most governments is exactly the opposite. They enforce your slavery and call it freedom. But they also regulate your slavery, keeping the greed of your master within certain bounds. They promise that in future you shall govern the country for yourself. They redeem this promise by giving you a vote, and having a general election every five years or so. At the election, two of their rich friends ask for your vote : and you are free to choose which of them you will vote for to spite the other–a choice which leaves you no freer than you were before, as it does not reduce your hours of labour by a single minute. But the newspapers assure you that your vote has decided the election, and that this constitutes you as a free citizen in a democratic country. The amazing thing about it is, that you are foolish enough to believe them.

PRECIS

Title : 'Perfect Freedom'

Perfect Freedom is an illusory thing. None can be perfectly free.Neither the Kings nor the labourers are perfectly free. They also have to obey the natural calls of sleeping, eating, clothing, drinking, etc. For fulfilling these calls, we need food, beddings, which is produced by human labour but which can be stolen also, just as man steals honey from bee hives. In the same way, man exploits other weak people through force or fraud.Strong are the slaves of nature.They in turn, enslave the weak by forcing them to work from eight to fourteen hours a day.This exploitation should have been stopped by the governments, but instead of stopping this ,they perpetuate slavery in the name of freedom. By extending a right to vote, they hoodwink the people with the idea of self governance ,i.e, choosing their rulers themselves. But the choice is limited because the poor have to choose one rich man every time, who does not bother to give any relief to the poor.The newspapers also make the people feel that they have chosen their leaders and they are befooled to believe that they are the free citizens of a democratic country.

Q. 8. Make a precis of the following passage . As far as possible, the precis should be in your own words. Suggest a suitable title for the precis :

Disarmament assumes a very special importance for us, overriding all other issues. For many years past, there have been talks on disarmament and some progress has undoubtedly been made in, so far as the plans and proposals are concerned. Still, we find that the race for armaments continues, as also the efforts to invent ever more powerful engines of destruction. If even a small part of these efforts was directed to the search for peace, probably the problem of disarmament would have been solved by this time. Apart from the moral imperative of peace, every practical consideration leads us to that conclusion. The choice today in this nuclear age, is one of utter annihilation and destruction of civilization or of some way to have peaceful co-existence between nations. There is no middle way. If war is an abomination and an ultimate crime which has to be avoided, we must fashion our minds and policies accordingly. In order to achieve peace, we have to develop a climate of peace and tolerance and to avoid speech and action which tend to increase fear and hatred. It may not be possible to reach full disarmament in one step, though every step should be conditioned to that end. Much ground has already been covered in the discussion on disarmament. But the sands of time run out, and we dare not play about with this issue or delay its consideration. This, indeed, is the main duty of the United Nations today and if it fails in this, the United Nations fails in its main purpose.

PRECIS

Title : Importance of 'Disarmament'

Disarmament has acquired a special significance today. Inspite of talks, plans and proposals to stop it , mad race for armaments and search for more destructive weapons still continue. In this Nuclear Age we are to choose, either total destruction or an atmosphere of peaceful coexistence. To create a peaceful environment, we must avoid speeches and talks mounting tensions, fear and hatred. Total disarmament is not possible in one step , but gradual move towards this goal can be fruitful. In order to prove its utility, the U.N.O.must endeavour to achieve this goal.

Q. 9. Make a precis of the following passage . As far as possible, the precis should be in your own words.Suggest a suitable title for the precis :

If the rule of reason in the region of thought is the aim of science, the rule of equality in the region of behaviour is the aim of democracy. Democracy is not a political arrangement or a form of government. It is a pattern of life, an active conviction, which informs and inspires every thought, word and deed. Our present constitution of society induces in its more fortunate members, far too great readiness to accept privileges as though it were inherent in the social order; as though it were normal and even proper and just.

If we are sincere in our professing of democracy, we should not shut our eyes to the most obvious defects of the present social order. A system which does not offer security and decent employment to multitudes of trained young men, suffers from fundamental vice. Society is in danger of splitting to pieces if the few who have the benefits of civilization, are not willing to share them with the rest. No state is stable, unless it procures for all its members the essentials of a good life. We acknowledge that health is better than disease, sufficiently better than poverty; shelter better than cold and exposure, ease of mind better than racking anxiety. It is our duty to obtain these essentials of civilized life or the mass of the population to work for basic economic justice for all, if necessary, by the imposition of higher taxes on incomes, land , property and inheritance. Riches were created by the maker for being spent on social purposes. It was Blackstone, not Lenin, who wrote ; " The law not only regards life and protects every man in enjoyment of it, but also furnishes him with everything necessary for its support. For, there is no man so indecent or wretched but that he may demand a supply sufficient for all the necessities of life, from the more opulent part of the community."

PRECIS

Title : 'Essentials of Democracy'

Precis: The aim of democracy is to establish the rule of equality in the behavioural conduct of society. Democracy is not simply a form of government, but a way of life, an important mode of conduct. In the prevailing order of our society a few classes flourish but masses suffer.

Unless the inequality is removed, and the States provide security, employment, health, shelter, peace of mind,basic economic justice and other essentials of civilized life to all the citizens, it cannot be said to be truly democratic.A few affluent can't be safe if the masses are wretched. For its own existence, it is the first duty of the State to protect the basic rights of the poor and to provide economic justice to all .

Q. 10. Make a precis of the following passage. As far as possible, the precis should be in your own words.Suggest a suitable title for the precis :

We talk so much about democracy, without going into ancient records. Parliamentary democracy, roughly speaking, is something of the growth of the last 150 or 200 years. We might remember that, say in England and in other countries too, this parliamentary democracy and the system of giving the franchise to the people was very strictly limited. Till quite recently, some 20 to 30 years ago, relatively small number of people had the vote. Even now in quite advanced countries, half the population consisting of women do not have the vote. Therefore, democracy in those countries is presumably thought of in terms of 'male democracy', not female.

When we talk about democracy in the nineteenth century', it was a democracy which was limited very strictly to certain classes and gradually, after great struggles, it widened out ; the franchise went wider and wider. Then again after a good deal of trouble, the actual representatives, who were chosen, also spread out from certain limited classes to other. It is a relatively slow process, therefore, it is only in the last, I believe, thirty years or so, that adult franchise has come into being in a number of countries. That clearly is long enough, I suppose, and yet it is not long enough really to tell us what ultimate effects of this are likely to be in solving problems. etc., because the ultimate test, of course, is how far a system of governance solves the problems which the country and the people have to face. Any broadly theoretical approach to this question, good as it may be, does not take you very far if the best of these fails to solve the problems that the country has to face. Of course, the problems are solved not merely by good machines, or the structure of government, but by many other things ; by the quality of human beings, by their training, by their education, by their character and any number of other things. All that the machine can do is to make it easier for these qualities to develop and remove any element of suppression and actually encourage them to grow.

Now, we talk about democracy again. Democracy has been spoken of chiefly, in the past, as political democracy, roughly represented by every person having a vote. This is a substantial idea but it becomes obvious that a vote by itself does not represent very much to a person who is down and out ; to a person, let us say, who is starving or hungry or has no other resources. He is much more interested in getting food to eat than a vote apart from some few individuals who might be. Therefore, political democracy, by itself, is not enough except that it may be used to obtain a gradually increasing measure of economic democracy, equality and the spread of the good things of life to other and removal of gross inequalities. That process has,no doubt, continued for some time in countries where there is political democracy and brought about a lessening of these differences, and because of the growth in other ways it has lessened internal tensions,though not completely.

PRECIS

'Parliamentary Democracy'

Precis: Parliamentary democracy is a product of gradual growth of 150 to 200 years. In the past, franchise was limited in many countries to a few people. Even now, there are countries where women do not have any franchise. It was after a long drawn struggle, that the right of voting was extended to others. But the ultimate effect of this change has to be seen not simply in the kind of government that it promises to introduce, but in the way it helps the people in solving their economic and other problems. A vote by itself has no value for a starving person.For true political democracy, it is necessary that it leads to economic equality, equal distribution of wealth among the people, and to the lessening of their social and economic differences and for all round gradual growth with little internal tensions.

EXPANSION-WRITING

What is an Expansion ?

Expansion means an ***enlargement of the topic/*** **theme or the statement given.** It is therefore, precisely *opposite in nature to precis writing,* where we have to compress and concise the given passage.In Expansion, a sentence or a short passage has to be enlarged into paragraphs by elaborating in detail, adding therewith illustrations, examples or proofs etc.The exercise of expansion practically amounts to *writing a miniature essay on the subject* or topic given. No strict rule can be laid down as to the length of the expansion , it should be neither so short nor so large as to become an essay.

Normally, *a proverb, maxim* or a *statement packed with meaning is given for expansion*, e.g., *A stitch in time saves nine* ; *Rome was not built in a day* ; *Honesty is the best policy* etc.

How to Write an Expansion?

Some Important Tips:

(1) First of all, try to understand the *precise meaning*, *signigicance* and *implications of the statement* or the topic, given for expansion. Devote a few minutes.

(2) Having grasped the subject and meaning of the passage, proceed to *expand it by adding illustrations*, *examples*, and other relevant details etc., until it becomes **a mini essay**.

(3) *Arrange your ideas* and *note down the important points* in the order to be mentioned. Mention only those points that are relevant to the subject.

(4) If you are given a *metaphor*, describe its full meaning in plain langauge, and give reasons to support it.

(6) Do not use or begin your expansion with such *stereotyped* or *uninteresting phrases*, as; 'The meaning of the saying is', or 'This proverb means', or 'These lines teach us', or 'Instances are not wanting to prove the truth of this statement', or 'It is a common saying and does not require any explanation'. Such openings are "dull, flat and unproductive,"and indicate lack of originality.Begin your expansion in some striking way.

(7) Write simply and *to the point.*Use grammatically correct language , taking care, if a *limit* has been set, not to exceed it.

(8) Finally, *examine your composition*. Your expansion should read as a complete piece of composition couched in good English.

Avoid :

(1) *Misunderstanding the subject*, or not understanding it fully.

(2) Lack of arrangement, and consequent *confusion in the expresion of ideas*.

(3) *Repetition of ideas*/ arguments.

(4) Inclusion of *irrelevant matter*

(5) Writing *too little* or *too much*.

(6) Inaccurate *illustrations*.

(7) Grammatical and *spelling errors*.

Solved Examples:

EXPAND : KNOWLEDGE IS POWER

Doing right things, at right time, in the right way, produces the right results, we aspire. In other words; knowing, what to do, at what time, in what direction and how, are the various parameters that lead to sure success. Knowing the timings well, knowing our goals well, knowing our strengths and weaknesses well, and shaping them in right direction, we can achieve what we aspire to achieve. Knowledge gives one power to mobilise the things in right direction and so it is said that knowledge is power.

If one ventures to establish any business, wishes to achieve any goal, he must acquire full knowledge of all the things concerned, including his own limitations and weaknesses. Knowledge gives one, capacity and capabilities to know the result of his actions, probability ratio of success and failure, propriety of his venture and so knowledge is said to be the power.

For a country, knowledge about its friends and foes, knowledge about the capabilities of its, enemies, is very important. In the present world scenario many satellites and spy aircrafts are deployed for the purpose of gaining maximum knowledge of activities going on in other countries. A country having the maximum and accurate knowledge of other countries, can use them for its advantage; it is the 'Knowledge' that rules the world.

Knowledge can be acquired, enhanced through reading. Reading is the key to knowledge. *Napolean* once remarked, " Show me a family of readers and I will show you the people who move the world." All learned men, all successful and powerful men have been great readers. Again through our readings, we can get to know about the lives of great and successful men, the problems they faced, and the means they employed to over come them. Often their biographies give us a clue to solving our problems.

In times of adversity, danger, misfortune, a man of knowledge proves to be a man of resources. He can overcome the problems with his knowledge. No knowledge is better than the knowledge of self. Knowing oneself means, mastering one's passions and controlling one's traits and faculties. Thus, knowledge gives one immense power, so rightly said, 'Knowledge is Power.'

MONEY IS A GOOD SERVANT, BUT A BAD MASTER

No doubt, money is an essential, almost indispensable article in the present day world. It is the 'money' through which we can purchase all the necessary comforts and amenities of life.If you have money, you can obtain what seems impossible to others. It is the money which gives man, *c*onfidence, *c*redit worthiness, *c*redentials, *c*apacity, *c*apabilities and *c*ourage. In present day materialistic world, money, has become very powerful. All the present day corruption, cut throat competition, callous degradation of moral and ethical values, are for the sake of grabbing and accumulating more and more money.The prestige, respect, social status commanded by a person is calculated as per his monetary status.

Time has gone, when we valued a person in terms of his moral and ethical values.People were earlier known for keeping their words, for donating every thing to a donee. Now people are known in terms of their ranking, in the list of rich of the world. Money has become the centre of all activities. Money power and muscle power have become essential ingredients of a successful political leader.

Can you purchase everything with the power of money?

No, you cannot. You cannot purchase inner satisfaction through money, you cannot purchase the lost youthfulness through money, you cannot purchase time to live more from the death, at any cost.

Those who earn money simply to a have more money, more balance in their accounts, are no better than the proverbial miser king Midas. Excessive love for money, makes a man slave to money. Money is important in our life, but it is not the most important thing for a human being.Those who use money for fulfilling their necessities, acquiring reasonable comforts, and for the sake of a common good, are the masters of money. But those who earn money just for the sake of increasing its volume and number, are slave to the money. They are the most unfortunate creatures who know well that whatever money they are earning, an cota of that can't be carried along when they die, still they are minting more and more money.What a paradox ! Money has become their master and they are just slaves, having no peace of mind, no moral and ethical values, no inner satisfaction.

So it is rightly said that 'money is a good servant but a bad master'. Let us earn the money for our comfort, not for the sake of money, minting more and more money.

THE CHILD IS THE FATHER OF MAN

This line which has since taken the shape of a proverb, really occurs in the the famous poem 'My heart leaps When I behold' of Wordsworth, the great poet. It implies that the qualities and characteristics shown by a child often indicate, what the child is going to be as a grown up man. The childhood is the reflection of future personality. The habits, traits and qualities of a man are usually the development of the habits, traits and qualities he had as a child. A careful study of the characteristics and qualities of a child can help us to foretell his future prospects :

"The childhood shows the man,
As morning shows the day."

The child is father of man, is proved true in many cases. See the example of Shivaji who during his childhood, loved so much to hear the stories of famous heroes of Ramayana and Mahabharat, became later a great warrior himself. Michael, the famous sculptor and painter, during his childhood used to make drawings on the pots, easels, stools and other things belonging to an old painter. The old painter once said, " One day this boy will beat me." A Young Italian lad, Titian, was very fond of painting pictures, but had no paints to colour with. He was so genius, he made his own paints. Nelson, the daring Naval Commander of British Navy, shown his traits of courage and fearlessness during his childhood.

Many more examples; like that of-Florence Nightingale, Macaulay, can be quoted to prove the veracity of the proverb that 'The child is the father of man', but we can find hundreds and thousands other examples, where childhood of a man did not reflect anything about the grown up personality of the man.George Bernard Shaw was known as a hopeless dullard. Mahatma Gandhi was inclined to become a rich Barrister. Shelley, the great poet and writer, never shown such traits during his childhood. Amitabh Bachhan, the great Super Star of today, didn't show such traits and qualities in his childhood.

Inspite of apparent exceptions, it is generally observed that the characteristics and qualities reflected during childhood are developed in the grown up personaliity of a man. An old proverb, "As the twig is bent, so the tree will grow," endorses the saying, "The child is the father of the man."

PREPAREDNESS FOR WAR FOR PRESERVING PEACE

Very strange and paradoxical, it seems, that preparedness for war is essential for preserving peace. But the saying, appears to be true for, if a country is well equipped with all the modern war gadgets and weapons, other nations will have to think twice before entering into any conflict with it.On the other hand, a weak nation becomes prey to the whims and aggressions of powerful neighbours.

Peace means-freedom from war, but how can one preserve it; unless or until you are well equipped, you can't preserve your peace. A peace loving nation may not have the intention to enlarge its empire, but who can guarantee the dictates of other neighbour countries.

What happened with our country, when China attacked in 1962 ? We, being fully peace loving country, never felt necessity till then to equip ourself with modern war gadgets and weapons. China, saw the opportunity and attacked us, made encroachment on our land. What did UNO do? What other Super Power could have done ? None came to our rescue. Think of today, when we are equipped with all kinds of nuclear and other weapons, can China dare to attack us now? No, because China knows well of our preparedness for war. Our 'No First Attack' stand with Pakistan,since 1971, is because of our full capacity to destroy that country, in all eventualities. In the present world, your power, decides your relation with neighbours.

The attack of USA on Iraq, the removal of Osama-bin Laden from Afghanistan, all show the same thing, that best guarantee for peace is your best preparedness for war.

But 'Peace,' if taken in a broader sense, reflects something different. Actually peace can't be preserved only with the preparedness for war. Preparedness for war could be a deterrent for an attacking country, but the real thing is the removal of cause of war, removal of cause of discontent, removal of disparities. Think of a situation, when none has any war weapons, will the mankind not survive then peacefully? The actual requirement for preserving peace is of, faith in principles of co-existence, faith in principles of integrity and sovereignty of all nations, faith in the inherent values of humanity and mankind. Total disarmament, destruction of nuclear and other weapons, making the UNO the real effective body, must be done in order to keep the whole world in peace. The terrorism, imperialistic intensions, racial and religious hatredness must be eliminated at all cost, only then, we can think of preserving the peace in this world.

ALL THAT GLITTER IS NOT GOLD

Guided by the appearance can be disastrous. In this world of deception and deceit, what is seen outwardly, is not the reality. Often the glittering appearance, hides the foulness of wickedness. When advertisements, display, showiness, have all become the day of life, the judgement of the reality has become very difficult. The good looking innocent people are the perfect cheat of the day. The only way to save ourselves from such hypocrites, is to be very attentive and careful in life with good observance.

What is exhibited and displayed outwardly, should not be taken as creditworthy. Visual appearances are commonly deceptive. The quality of a thing can only be judged by its use. In many cases, a thing that appears, to be very durable and cheap, may turn out a duplicate. Duplicates or imitations commonly radiate more shine and glitter than the genuine one.

A person can be judged by his deeds, attitude and aptitude. A coarse man may be more helpful and cooperative than a person of pleasant countenance. A well dressed, gentlemanly looking person is apt to deceive you by his outwards looks. What he intends to show, may not be his actual intentions. His appearance may be delusory and misleading.Try to ascertain his motives, and analyse his actions. Keep a close vigil.What appears to be gold, may turn out a yellow metal, a polish of Gold on iron, a fake colour of gold on brass. So beware of the appearance, judge the things from its original contents, "All that glitter is not gold".

EXPAND : POVERTY IS THE MOTHER OF ALL CRIMES

A hungry man can commit any sin or crime. He knows no morality no ethics. How can we expect from a hungry man to think of good or bad, reasonable or unreasonable action, when his own existence is at stake. Right to life is the paramount right.Rightly said that 'poverty is the mother of all crimes'. A poor person can commit any crime to save his family from the clutches of illness, hunger etc. When a person finds that his wife and children are starving to death, he can resort to any measure to save his wife and his children. Crimes, like-theft, robbery, dacoity, pick-pocketing are generally committed by those, whose means of living are very meagre.

The poor parents cannot afford to educate their children. They fail to teach them what is right and what is wrong. A poor man, in fact, has no idea of ethics.It also does not mean that all the crimes are committed by the poor. Nowadays, the abductions, murders, kidnapping, rapes , high-jackings and all other heinous crimes are being committed by the rich, who have never seen the face of poverty. They commit such crime not for the sake of hunger of stomach but hunger of power, hunger of more and more money. In the present world, the above saying should be amended to mean that ''the poverty is *not alone* a cause of crimes''.

THE FRUITS OF LABOUR ARE SWEETER THAN THE GIFTS OF FORTUNE

What is received in gift or what is inherited from the parents is never as charming or important as the things achieved by us by our own efforts, by our own labour. The sweet acquired through 'sweat' will be much sweeter than the sweet given to us by someone. Nothing tastes so sweet as that is earned by hard labour. 'By the sweat of thy brow thou shalt earn thy bread'- was the divine wish. The things achieved by hard work shall be more permanent, more delicious, more lovable, more enjoying and rendering us real happiness.

Anything acquired by the grace of God or by luck will not give us the real enjoyment and real respect, because this fortune does not have anything our own. The history remembers those who change the path of adversity by their hard labour. The world adores those who make their own fortune and create examples for others. Abraham Lincoln, Dhiru Bhai Ambani etc. are several examples, who achieved, the success by their sheer hard work and so they are adored today; 'Honest labour bears a beautiful face.'

AS YOU SOW SO SHALL YOU REAP

In other words, you shall harvest what you plant, spiritual or natural, as God said, if you sow the flesh, you shall reap corruption, but if you sow the spirit of love for all, you shall reap life everlasting.God is the great paymaster, we are His workmanship, we are the clay and He is the Potter, so do something for the God, who made you and He will not forget the things that you do instead you shall receive your pay, good or bad.

The theory of Karma is spoken about in many of the sacred texts of all the religions in the world and is implied in the Golden Rule: 'Do unto others as you would have them do unto you'. The implication: as you treat others, so will you be treated.

Every tragedy we live through is the result of some terrible wrongs we did in our past life. A child who dies of an illness at an early age, for example, might simply have chosen to experience the birth, young, and adult stages of life before deciding what he wanted to do with his life as an adult in his next incarnation.

Karma is inescapable. Your actions do return to you. It may not be in this lifetime, but it certainly will return in some way. "As you sow, so shall you reap" has relevance in today's competitive market place, as well as, in the timeless arena of human relationships. At every juncture, in all times, this theory of karma (As you sow so shall you reap) is well respected and well observed.

EXPAND : DELAYED JUSTICE NO JUSTICE

Many Chief Justices, Judges of the Supreme Court, the High Courts, The Law Ministers, members of the Law Commission, the media, the great writers and thinkers have all lamented over the delay in the dispensation of justice. The inordinate delay in the provision of relief amounts to the virtual denial of any relief found in number of cases.

The litany of woes caused by delay in the administration of justice is disastrous. A layman does not want to understand anything or any reason for the delay in administration of justice, he just wants and understands that he has the right to get the justice and that too within reasonable time. An aggrieved, if doesn't get the justice within reasonable time, then all his sufferings and hardships because of such delay, are like a punishment inflicted on him for no fault of his own.

Delayed justice is the biggest cause of prevalent corruption in the country. Many political leaders are enjoying the chairs of Ministers while a number of cases are pending against them. Are our courts not their accomplice ? It is unimaginable, how much loss our nation may be suffering from ethical and moral point of view at least, because of the delay in disposing of the cases. Innocent person is the worst effected unfortunate, who has to take shelter of the courts for getting justice, which he can never calculate as to when that so called justice will finally arrive. None can compute his worries and the frustrations. Such sufferings and hardships make him to conclude that, "Delayed justice is no justice".

One Paragraph Expansions:

THEY ALSO SERVE WHO ONLY STAND AND WAIT

This is one of the crucial lines from Milton's sonnet- 'On His Blindness'. This concluding and proverbial sentence of the poem means that God does not require any active service from his creatures. What He requires from man, is obedience to His commandments. Those who only stand and wait at His service, also serve him as do His trusted angels. It means, those who surrender themselves to His will and act as per the wishes of the Almighty, are also doing a service. The persons who are, though, not putting any active service but always at the call of Him, are not lesser devotees.

EXPAND : MAN IS A SOCIAL ANIMAL

The functions of Man and other animals are to a great extent similar. Man has a developed brain while other animals do not have such a developed brain. But man is also an animal. The natural impulses, like-hunger, thirst, sex and pugnacity are found in all animals alike. Because of the gift of brain possessed by the man, he is superior and created a world of its own; developed families, societies, towns , cities , countries .Man acts and lives for the welfare of his family , society . All the actions of the man are oriented for the good causes and for the welfare of the human beings, while other animals live only for themselves. Therefore, 'man is called a social animal.'

FAME IS THE LAST INFIRMITY OF A NOBLE MIND

Fame does not make a man noble; nobility makes a man famous.If a noble mind becomes sensitive to the fame, he is no more noble. 'Noble' means doing everything without any ambition.Nobility does not require or aspire any reward.A noble mind works with selfless, detached spirit and considers work to be its own reward. *Milton*, the author of this quotation, has well said that a noble soul may conquer all weaknesses, but he cannot override the desire to acquire fame. But whatever said or done by anybody, it is undoubtedly true that the day the noble mind gets influenced by the lust of fame , his nobility diminishes upto the degree the lust is there. It is right that desire of getting famous is a powerful desire, which an ordinary man cannot over ride, but for a noble man nothing is more important than the nobility in real terms.

EXPAND : CHARACTER IS DESTINY

A fatalist believes in destiny. According to him fate is a pre written thing, can't be changed or made by the human being.Such people believe that a man's fate is preordained by God, and man has no power over his fate. To such people, destiny is character. While many persons believe that man is the maker of his own destiny and fate. A man who wins, is the man, who thinks he can. That man can change his fate, create his fortune, who believes in himself, has positive attitude, strong will, firm determination and zeal to achieve the goals.Character is nothing but these qualities, which shapes the conduct of a person. So character is the real destiny and it is wrong to think that destiny is somewhat a pre-written thing. God also helps those who help themselves.

ATTACK IS THE BEST FORM OF DEFENCE

Defence is necessary for the happy living. The imperialistic persons try to grab the neighbours territory and so attack them.Under such circumstances, it is better to make first attack instead of waiting for an attack and then defend. All the planning should be made in advance, considering the imminent attack first by the enemy. It also does not mean that one should not resort to the peaceful means to avoid war, but after exhausting all the solutions of maintaining peace, if the war seems definite, then it is always better to attack first, than to wait for an attack to take place and then defend. Attack is the best defence in such circumstances.

'ESSAY WRITING'

How to Write an Excellent Essay?

'Essay writing is an art.One may have thorough knowledge of a topic or a subject, but *to put* this *knowledge in a logical and coherent way* is a task, requires skill, practice and subtle technique'.

1. What is an essay?

The word ***essay means an 'attempt'.*** For an attempt to be crowned with success, certain techniques , methods and perseverance are necessary. ***An essay is an organised collection of ideas, facts and figures* about the topic , nicely written and elegantly presented.**

In other words, the essay must be well structured,organised, well planned and presented in a way that the reader finds clear and easy to follow. It must look *tidy* and not present any obstacle to the reader. It must have a clear *readable interesting style*. But, above all, it must consist of ideas, facts and figures relevant to the subject .

An essay can have many purposes, but the basic structure is the same, no matter what the subject or the topic is. You may be writing an essay to argue for a particular point of view or to explain the steps necessary to complete a task. Either way, your essay will have the *same basic format.* If you follow a few simple steps, you will find that the essay is almost written itself. You are to supply ideas, facts and figures, which are the important parts of the essay anyway.

2. Classification of Essays.

Essays are divided roughtly into four classes :

(1) Narrative Essays: : Narrative Essays consist of the *narration of some events* about *historical facts* or *eminent personalities.* Such events may be :

(a) Historical or legendary events,

(b) True or imaginary stories,

(c) Biographical sketches.

(2) Descriptive Essays : Descriptive Essays consist of the *description of some place or thing.* These may be about:

(a) Countries, islands, mountains, seas, rivers.

(b) Aspects and phenomena of nature.

(c) Towns and buildings.

(3) Reflective Essays : Reflective Essays consist of *reflections upon some topic*, which are generally of an *abstract nature*. These may be in respect to:

(a) Habits, qualities, etc.

(b) Social, political, economical or domestic affairs.

(4) Expository or Argumentative Essays : These consist of the exposition or *explanation of a saying, or a thesis* :

"Truth always triumphs".

"I am the maker of my destiny"

"Get started"!

These *simple steps* will guide you through the *essay writing process*:

1. *Select* the topic.
2. Prepare an *outline* of your ideas.
3. Write the *introduction*.
4. Write the *body*.
5. Write the *main points*.
6. Write the *subpoints*.
7. *Elaborate* on the *subpoints*.
8. Write the *conclusion*.

Select a Topic for Your Essay :

Selection of topic out of the given topics is an important task.Evaluate each topic .You must simply consider each one individually. *Select the topic about which you have detailed facts and figures*. You must be sure it is a subject about which you are particularly well-informed. You must be sure it is a subject about which you are at least moderately passionate. Of course, the most important factor in choosing a topic is the number of ideas you have about that topic.Even if none of the topic you find particularly appealing, in that case *select a topic which may not be selected by other candidates* or select a topic which is selected by only a few candidates, that will minimise the chances of immediate comparison of the essay written by you with others'.

Before you are ready to move on in the essay-writing process, *look one more time at the topic* you have selected.Once you have determined that your topic will be suitable, you can move on.

Organise Your Ideas:

The purpose of an outline or diagram is to put your ideas about the topic on paper, in a moderately organised format. A well thought-out structure is the *heart* of every good essay.

Outline:

1. Begin your outline by *writing your topic at the top* of the page.
2. Next, write the *Roman numerals* I, II, and III, spread apart down the left side of the page.
3. Next to each Roman numeral, write the main ideas that you have about your topic, or *the main points that you want to make*. If you are trying to persuade, you write your best arguments.If you are trying to explain a process, you write the steps that should be followed.You will probably need to group these into categories.If you have trouble grouping the steps into categories, try using *Beginning, Middle, and End*. If you are trying to inform, you write the major categories into which your information can be divided.
4. Under each Roman numeral, write A, B, and C down the left side of the page.
5. Next to each letter, write the *facts or information that support the main idea.*

Now you have finished, *you have the basic structure* for your essay and are ready to continue.

Introduction :

The introduction should be designed *to attract the reader's attention* and give him *an idea of the essay's focus* :

1. Begin with an attention grabber : Which attention grabber you use, is up to you, but *here are some ideas* :

(a) Startling information : This *information must be true and verifiable*. It could simply be a pertinent fact that explicitly illustrates the point you wish to make.If you use a piece of startling information, follow it with *a sentence or two of elaboration*.

(b) Anecdote : ***An anecdote is a story that illustrates a point***. Be sure, your anecdote is *short, to the point*, and *relevant* to your topic. This can be a very effective opener for your essay, but use it carefully.

(c) Dialogue or Quotation : An appropriate dialogue or quotation does not have to identify the reader, but the reader must understand the point you are trying to convey.

Write the Body Paragraphs :

In the body of the essay, all the preparation up to this point comes to fruition. The topic you have chosen must now be explained, described, or argued. ***Each main idea,*** *that you wrote down in your outline, will become one of the body paragraphs*. If you had three or four main ideas, you will have three or four body Paragraphs.

Each ***body paragraph*** will have the same ***basic structure***.

1. Start by writing down one of your *main ideas*, in sentence form.
2. Next, write down each of your *supporting points* for that main idea.
3. In the space under each point, write down *some elaboration* for that point.Elaboration can be further description or explanation or discussion.

Write the Conclusion :

Now, you need a tight, powerful conclusion which is the logical consequence of everything that has gone before.The conclusion brings closure of the essay to the reader, summing up your points or providing a final perspective on your topic.All that the conclusion needs, is three or four strong sentences which do not need to follow any set formula. Simply *review the main points* (being careful not to restate them exactly) *or briefly describe your feelings about the topic*. Even an *anecdote can end your essay* in a useful way. The conclusion completes the paragraphs of your essay.

Remember:

If your essay is badly-written, you will be losing marks. And, in the outside world, you would be a failure. It is very important to write in a crisp, *clear style*, with *good sentence construction* and proper *punctuation*. Needless to say, *spelling* mistakes also fail to impress.

Some 'Tips' on writing an excellent Essay

1. Use simple words rather than complex words : Keep your writing style simple. Follow the standard rule in all editing: prefer the simpler word to the complex word. **This means writing**

'*extra*' or '*more*' rather than '*additional*' '*help*' rather than '*assistance*'; use rather than '*utilise*'. Although you might need specialist or technical words, depending on your subject, you should choose the simpler word instead of the more difficult word, whenever you can.

"*When something can be read without effort, great effort has gone into its writing.*"..

Enrique Jardiel Poncela

Your essay should be interesting but also easy to read. As well as the advice to use the simpler word to the complex word, you can also make your essay read much better if you cut down on heavy words.

2. Structure your essay to help your reader : All documents need a start, a middle and an end. Traditionally, we think of the *Introduction, Body and Conclusion* as the key parts of an essay. Logically, this helps us set the context for the essay (introduction), present the facts and develop the arguments (body) and summarize the main points or the answer to the question set (conclusion).

3.Writing Introduction : This introduces the main idea of your essay and draws the reader into the subject. *A good introduction gets to the heart of the subject* and *captures the interest* of the reader. Most students write poor introductions, that needlessly repeat information and turn off the reader, with too much background information. If you want to gain a top grade for your essay, you have to start strongly and gain your reader's attention immediately.

4. Writing the Body of Essay : This consists of *supporting paragraphs*, logically arranged to develop your main ideas. *List the points* you wish to develop, place each point in its own paragraph, and expand on each point with *supporting facts, details and examples*. Each paragraph should clearly present the relevant information, discuss and evaluate information and opinions, and develop an argument based on the information and a review of opinions.*This is 80-90 percent of the essay* and must satisfy the reader's appetite. To do this, the body of the essay must reflect solid research, show a clear understanding of the subject, and develop your points logically.

5.Writing Conclusion : The conclusion is vital. It is the last impression, the reader has of the essay. Use it well, making sure your essay doesn't fizzle out. Make it *a strong statement*, confidently answering the question, summarizing the position, and *reviewing the topic*. If you are in doubt what to put in the conclusion, think about the key information or argument the essay has presented and repeat it in a short, direct form.

"*Do not write so that you can be understood, write so that you cannot be misunderstood.*"

Epictetus

A VISIT TO A MUSEUM

It was Sunday. The college was closed for the day. Weather was cloudy and the breeze was blowing. My friend Ramesh came from my native village to meet me .We made a programme for visiting the museum . We spent about two hour there, and saw many wonderful things. There were works of art-paintings, sculpture, pottery, embroidery; clay models of various scenes from the village life, of social and religious caremonies, were very interesting. Among the most interesting articles we saw , were the antiquities of the stone and bronze periods, consisting of daggers, swords, shields and early pottery and sculptural urns, and weapons and personal ornaments of that period. In one room we noticed several old coins of India and fine brass articles .

The dresses worn by the people of that time; the dresses of the ancient Rajput and Sikh warriors of this country were amazing to be seen. Old swords, shields and armours of the old inhabitants of this country were nicely arranged and attracted the sight of the visitors. The models of the Kohinoor, the Taj Mahal, the Golden Temple and the Bhakra Dam pleased us greatly.

Passing into another room, we saw thousands of years old, big statues of Gautam Buddha and some other Buddhist saints. We saw the history of India written on stone and paper by hand. We also saw the pillars on which were recorded the edicts of Asoka. All these carried us into the past.

The most intersting thing that caught our eyes, was an Egyptian mummy- a man in a glass case, wrapped in a hundred yards of cloth. The Egyptians did not bury their dead, but preserved them from decay with salts and spices and other chemicals.

The Museum contained many things of interest and instruction. One could learn much from an inspection of its treasures and also derive amusement from the various curiosities stored therein.It was a fine , memorable and educative visit.

A WALK BY THE RIVER-SIDE

It was a little before sunset on a hot evening that I, with two of my friends, went out for a walk by the river side. The sight was charming and eye catching. The trees spreading out their branches to catch the breezy air, the flowers 'tossing their heads in sprightly dance' in the cool and mild breeze, the birds with their variegated plumes singing on the trees; the buterflies flitting from one flower to another , the children also enjoying in their own way , the acquatic birds swimming and diving, the boys rowing and larking, and the fish coming up here and there in the river water–all presented a fascinating and mesmerizing sight. The blue vault of the sky, reflected in the trasparent water, was beautiful to behold. The whole landscape was captivating; scenery all round was charming. Wonderful was the whole ramp show of the Nature. It filled our hearts and minds with peace and exhilarating excitement.

The dusk fell, the stars started showing their twinkling lights and the smiling moon rose in the sky. The twinkling stars were reflected beautifully in the calm water of the river; the moon sailing through the clouds in the sky, now smiling upon us, now blushing, and bathing trees, flowers, buildings and gardens, in her light blue silvery beams, presented a beautiful scene. Every thing seemed asleep in the soothing beams of the moon.The sight was too mesmerizing to forget.

CAUGHT IN A SHOWER OF RAIN

The clouds which have been gathering on the horizon for a long time, have become dark and the rain started pouring down heavily . Those who were caught in, ran in all directions, some laughing and some yelling.

I always find particular amusement in such sudden helter-skelter. It seems as if each person, taken by surprise, loses the personality which he poses to the world and now appearing in his true colours.For example, that big man with deliberate steps, who suddenly forgot his indifference made to order, and ran like a schoolboy. He is a thrifty gentleman, who, with all his fashionable airs, is afraid of spoiling his hat.

That pretty lady, on the contrary, whose looks are so modest, and whose dress is so elaborate, slackens her pace with the increasing storm. She seems to find pleasure in braving it, and does not think of her valvet cloak spotted by the hail. She is evidently a lioness in sheep's clothing.

Here, a young man who was passing, stops to catch some of the hailstones in his hand, and examines them. By his quick and businesslike walk just now, you would have taken him for a commercial traveller on his rounds . And those schoolboys, who left their ranks to run after the sudden gusts of whirlwind ; those girls, just now so demure,who flew with bursts of laughter ; those guardsmen, who quit the martial attitude of their days of duty, and took refuge under a porch ! The sudden rain storm has caused all these transformations.

THE POSTMAN

The postman is a very humble member of our society. His work looks very simple but it's indeed very important and valuable work.His work facilitates us to know about our near and dears.

He symbolises what duty is. He performs his duty even in odd weather.It may be raining in torrents, thunder and lightning , the day may be blazing hot or stormy, he is ever punctual in delivering letters. He is a very sincere and dedicated worker and is strictly devoted to his duties. He is a fountain-head of good humour, contentment and happiness, and ever comes with a smiling face. He is an embodiment of the virtues of obedience, courtesy and civility.

And when we think of what he carries in his bag from door to door along the streets of the city, or through the jungles and along mountain paths to distant villages, he seems to be the messenger of good luck. People wait for him anxiously ,with mixed feelings, some with hope, some in dread, for he carries messsages. In his bag may be the long-expected letter from a soldier in a far-off country to his anxious parents; the letter that will tell a newly married girl about the date of arrival of her husband ; the letter that will tell a poor widow of the death of her only son; the letter informing an anxious candidate of his success or failure in an examination; letters of joy and sorrow, complaint and request, success and failure, upbrading and praise, death and life, fortune and ruin. And the humble postman, all unknowing, passes on indifferently, scattering all sorts of news.

With the advent of other sources of communication , now a lot of role of the postman is taken over by courier-man, telephones, mobiles etc, yet the imporatnce of post man in rural area is still high.

DILIGENCE IS THE MOTHER OF SUCCESS

The heights by great men reached and kept
Were not attained by sudden flight,
But they, while their companions slept,
Were toiling upward in the the night.
Longfellow.

If we glance at the biographies of great men, we find that the most of the successful persons, whether inventors, artists, scientists, thinkers, leaders, and workers of any kind, owe their success to their indefatigable hardwork and dedication. They were the men, who achieved their sucess with dedication, devotion and true hard work. Disraeli hold that the secret of success consisted in being master of our subject. Such mastery is attainable through continuous application and study. Walter Scott, the famous novelist of Scotland, who started his life as an ordinary clerk, attained the great heights of eminence, by dint of his sheer diligence. He used to rise at 5 O'Clock, and by the time his family assembled for breakfast, he had done enough, to use his own words, to break the neck of the day's work.

Those who work diligently, not only achieve their goals and get success, but also remain happy, cheerful and active, which is it self a great reward even if the work does not bring success. Idleness or laziness is worse as it brings jealousy, gloom, frustration, depression, which are more degrading than the failure itself.

Those who consider themselves born to ill luck, very aptly assume that all their failures and misfortunes are because of their hard luck. They don't analyse their weaknesses, shortcomings and lack of efforts but lament for their ill fate. Fate is nothing, but a creation of an idle fancy, an invention of superstitious brains. Dr.Johnson, has rightly said, "All the complaints which are made of the world are unjust, I have never known a man of merit and diligence neglected ; it was by his own fault that he failed of success.'' Several proverbs signifiy the importance of diligence; No pains, no gains; no sweat no Sweet; Heaven help those, who help themselves; The World is His, who has Patience and Industry. These proverbs have stood test of time and experience of everyday and still bear force of truth and accuracy.

But one should not forget, the importance of intelligence, along with the diligence. Labour and hardwork, pay, when applied intelligently. Just as diligence alone can't help in achieving success, in the same way, intelligence alone can't help in making one successful. It is the result of both diligence and intelligence, which makes a man successful, fortunate .

FAILURES ARE THE PILLARS OF SUCCESS

Failure is not fatal, it can be the stepping stone to success, if you can make 'the failure' to work for you.

Every successful man fails at some time. Failure tells you about your weaknesses, shortcomings, lack of preparations,lack of efforts, so if you can manage to learn from failures, you will definitely go where you started out to go. Making a mistake is not a crime, the ability to learn from it contributes to lasting success. Extract the lesson to be learnt from failure and try again with redoubled vigour. Facing failure makes the strong, more wise and more resolute, spurs them on to greater efforts. There is no failure in truth, save from within; unless we are beaten there, we are bound to succeed.

Nothing that comes too easily is worth having? When you want to succeed, be ready to pay the price for it, which includes braving failures and setbacks and keeps persisting with your efforts, till the goal is achieved. The reasons of failure may seem staggering if viewed collectively, but looked at individually, they will no longer be formidable. You can either be defeated or discouraged by failure, or you can learn from it and analyse the causes of failure, remove them and endeavour again with all your strength and energy, then you are sure to get success.

Our greatest glory is not in never falling, but in rising every time we fall. Little minds are tamed and subdued by failures, misfortunes, but great minds rise above it. We must face every adverse circumstance as its master and not let it master us. Many men owe the grandeur of their lives to their failures in the beginning.

Mere idle talk, day dreaming or aimless drifting, will not take you to goal, but only divert your attention and dissipate your energy and strength. Hardships, obstacles, failures are the various points in the path of success. They are not to be evaded, but to be faced bravely, courageously and with double vigour.

A child can seldom learn to walk, without making sustained and sincere efforts; in the process tumbling and falling down any number of times. His failure never deters him to stop standing again. The doggedness in the child's resolve lies in making any number of attempts to stand up and walk whatever be the pain or fear of fall.

The failures are the real path-indicators of success. The failures give us clues of our mistakes and tell us, how to club our efforts in a right manner, so that we get success one day positively.

CRIMINALISATION OF POLITICS

Politics has become such a lucrative and beneficial business, that whoever can invest or bid both money power and muscle power, can earn through, for a few future generations and enjoy unfettered power and respect among the society.

Criminals enter politics to become politicians and then patronise other criminals. The dire consequences of this unholy alliance between criminals and politicians is, that at every level from bottom; Panch at Panchayat level to Chief Minister or Ministers at State and Central level, criminals are being elected and appointed to the positions of power.

Politics has now become a shortcut way of earning. Once elected, a person can accumulate money, sufficient for his few generations. Neither Gandhiji nor the other freedom fighters, who sacrificed their all luxuries and comfort, for the cause of nation would have ever dreamt that a day would come, when India's governance would pass into the hands of criminals and corrupt anti-social elements.

An indomitable Chief Election Commissioner, Mr. T.N.Sheshan tried his best to cleanse the system, but failed. Mr. Sheshan's successor, Mr. Gill faced the same problem. Mr. Lingdoh also found himself in such a pitiable position, that he had no concrete remedy to cleanse the system, but to appeal the voters: Not to vote for the criminals.

Most of the dreaded dacoits of Chambal or Murena ravines were driven to crime as a result of victimisation or because of some social, economic or personal causes. But for the modern criminals turned politicians, crime has become a way of life and most of them thrive with the blessings of the senior Politicians, Ministers and even the Chief Ministers and Union Ministers. Pity the parties that have given tickets to such candidates. During last elections, many candidates in Bihar collected illegal guns and explosives to be used by them to ensure electoral victory. A big number of candidates contested elections from inside the Jail. Thousands of unauthorised arms manufacturing units worked overtime to meet the increasing demand for fire arms. Tickets were given to the candidates with criminal records even by National Parties. U.P. is not behind Bihar in fielding candidates with criminal background. The case of Amar Mani Tripathi, Minister in the Mayawati and Mulayam singh Yadav Governments, being charged for the murder of Madhumita, a poetess, is a flagrant example of nexus between crime and politics.

A virtual impression seems to have gained ground that you could commit crime and get away with it, if you have political patronage at the proper level. The police dare not proceed against you or if having initiated an action, shall drag away their feet to defeat the ends of justice. With politics and crime intertwined, bureaucracy and the police have also become part of nexus. This unholy affinity is having a malignant effect over the public life and poses a threat to the democratic structure of the country.

The enormous problem of the nexus between criminals and politicians cannot be ignored any longer . The supreme court has recently pronounced its judgement on the issues, raised in a public interest litigation on this subject and asked the government to establish a powerful, independent body to look into such cases of corruption and crime. The recent decision of Supreme Court and the directions of Chief Election Commission that every candidate filing his nomination for State Legislature or Lok Sabha has to submit an affidavit, mentioning therein, all kinds of cases filed , decided or pending against him in any court as well as the details of the wealth and the property owned by the candidate.It may have some deterrent effect , but seems as it will also result in a futile exercise as in India votes are being cast on the basis of caste, creed and religion. Moral values and ethics have long been vanished from the political arena of our country, but we cannot have such an indifferent attitude. We shall have to find a solution to eradicate the menace for which we are also responsible to a great extent.

In a democratic country, all the power lies in the hands of the voters, that is, the general public. An awakening among the general mass can only show the right place to such criminal politicians.

TERRORISM

Millions of innocent people and thousands of cops have lost their lives fighting terrorism, but the thirst for human blood of the creators and fumigators of terrorism has not been quenched so far .

Terrorism has now become a world wide phenomena. Terrorism can be defined as an organised way of intimidation and violence especially for political purpose. Political frustration, political necessities, religious and racial fanaticism and personal political interests are some of the main causes of terrorism. Terrorists are encouraged by the interested countries, external powers, to create instability in certain country or region. Terrorists indulge in looting, kidnapping, murdering, shooting, arson and other unlawful activities to serve their very purpose of creating instabilities or deter the innocents, so that either they support them or don't support the legal government machinery.

As far as India is concerned, terrorism has become endemic here since early 1980s. India has been fighting the cross border terrorism on its own for the last 20-30 years. India has been the worst sufferer of global terrorism, having lost more than 65000 people during the last 20 years. The terrorism in India is mainly nurtured by external agencies, especially Pakistan, in the bordering states of Kashmir and Punjab. In North- Eastern states, ULFA and NSCN like organisations have also indulged in terroristic activities.

The much talked about 'Global war against Terrorism' is one of the most cruel jokes of present time. It is ironical that Pakistan, the epicenter of Global Terrorism, is the greatest ally of USA, fighting Global Terrorism.India has regularly been drawing the attention of the US and other countries to the atrocities committed by the terrorists, trained and funded by Pakistan but of no avail.Rightly said by someone 'Only the wearer knows where the shoe pinches'.USA realised the danger of terrorism only when terrorists struck at its heart, on 11th Sept, 2001, when twin towers of 'World Trade Centre', New York, were reduced to debris by suicide squads of terrorists. USA, that boasted of its Super Power status, military might and intelligence, suddenly was forced to realise its vulnerability. USA feared that its fortress was also not impregnable and therefore wanted to eliminate the kingpin, the notorious dreaded Osama-bin Laden and its Al-Queda. But President Bush couldn't identify the God-Father of all the mischief in the terrorist world, Gen. Pervez Mushrraf, instead joined hand with Mr. Musharraf to fight the terrorism globally. The removal of Osama-bin Laden from Afganistan, has not eliminated the threat of terrorists' attack on USA. The American people even today are living under the long shadow of fear. The military might and word's most powerful intelligence agency CIA could no longer eliminate the fear from the general American's mind. The taps of Osama-bin Laden released by Al-Zazira, time and again threaten the USA Government of his (Laden's) determination to teach a lesson to the US Government.

Every person entering USA, is being frisked by the authorities thoroughly. There have been thousands of instances when passengers are out loaded on strength of suspicion. Once bitten, twice shy, they don't want to leave anything to chance. But in spite of all that, insecurity prevails among the minds of Americans. The US ambassador to India has time and again asserted that global terrorism will not end until the problem of trans-border terrorism across India's borders is tackled. The crux of the story is, that the USA is having double standard in dealing with terrorism and formulating its foreign policy to suit its interest. In the name of destruction of WMD(Weapons of Mass Destructions) , US destroyed the Iraq, ousted the Saddam and till date, not even a trace of Biological, Chemical or Nuclear weapons has been found there. Indian government time and again drew the attention of US' appeasement policy towards Pakistan. Appeasement of devilish elements can result in more unforeseen catastrophe.

India has to fight on its own with the terrorism, being funded and encouraged by the neighboring countries.How can we expect that USA or Britain will feel the pinch of terroristic attack in India? To look for support from either of them would be a folly. Just like any other country, we have to empower ourselves, we have to tackle our problems in our own way. Terrorism has to be dealt firmly with determined efforts and indomitable political will, with the full and all out support of all political parties and every citizen.

CASTE POLITICS IN ELECTIONS

Caste has polarised the national politics and caste politics breeds caste parties. Not a single party, however avowedly opposed to casteism, is free from the dominant influence of caste factor.

During election time, when the question of number game becomes most important, candidates seek to mobilise the support of not only their own caste members but also those belonging to other castes.

Caste has played very important role in the success of Indian Democracy by mobilising India's mass electorate to participate in the election process effectively and meaningfully. Use of caste for political purpose has begun long before the introduction of adult franchise. Organisations based on castes for social, economic and political system came into existence even before the constitution came into force. The illiterate people, who didn't understand politics were mobilised to organise themselves by appealing to their caste sentiments by the self interested politicians.

The casteism has penetrated in Indian politics so deeply, as to shape and reshape not only the political parties, but also, their manifestos for the elections. The various caste groups, like the Nair, the Christian and Ezhava in Kerala, the Brahmin and non-Brahmin in Tamil Nadu,The Khamma and Reddy in Andhra, the Vokkaliga and Lingayats in Karnataka, the Maratha and Mahar in Maharashtra, the Patidar and the Rajput in Gujrat, the Jat, Rajput, Meena, Brahmin and Vaisya in Rajasthan, organised likewise in all states and determine the political scenario in the states to a great extent.

In Bihar there is a communal triangle formed by the Bhumihar, the Rajput and the Kayastha. Caste politics in U.P. varies from region to region. The Thakurs from the majority community nurture strong anti Brahmin feelings. Not only the groups among the castes, a strong lobby of Dalits and Non-Dalits further exists nowadays with the active support of their so-called Dalit leaders, making propaganda, against so called Manuwadis or other Castes.

Caste has polarised the national politics and caste politics breed caste parties. Not a single party, however avowedly opposed to casteism, is free from the dominant influence of caste. Even in the National parties, whether Congress or BJP, while allocating tickets to the candidates, allocating portfolios to the Ministers, a proper analysis of caste factor is done. Caste tends to determine electoral nominations, voting behaviour nowadays . Numerous castes have started making numerous demands, whether for reservation, or to categorise them in OBCs etc, vitiating the representative principles envisaged and emphasised under the democratic pattern of our country.

See the flagrant example of demands for reservation put forth by Gurjars,Rajputs, Brahmin and Vaisya community in Rajasthan, at the eve of elections. Congress and BJP, both parties are assuring to fulfill their demands as per their capabilities. Several regional parties are advocating the justification of the demands made by these castes and communities before the elections, knowing well, that it is not possible to get any demand fulfilled but they do so just to fish in troubled water of elections.

Every government orients its policies on caste on caste lines, as it is found most convenient and politically expedient keeping the caste factor in view, not only while forming ministeries, but also while deciding the placement of individual members in government organizations and institutions.

Caste which has a past history of three thousand years in our country, can't be abolished altogether. The future of democracy and the system of parties in this country depends upon the willingness of the society to change according to the demands of democracy. Illiteracy among the backward castes, poverty among the downtrodden, lack of awakening among the rural folk, are some of the factors responsible for the prevalence of casteism in elections. The socalled Dalit leaders or caste Headmen are encashing the votes of their fellow caste members as per their vested interests.

Political parties have an enormous role to play in the social awakening of India on democratic pattern. Instead of being influenced by caste and their current interests, they must endeavour to educate the people as per the ethics and demands of democracy and organise public opinion to regularise the progressive changes and withdrawal of privileges based on castes. For the real success of democracy, casteism is a big obstacle.

REPORT WRITING

HOW TO WRITE A GOOD REPORT ?

What is a Report ?

A report is a *factual description of some incident*, or a consolidated statement of some *plan* or *scheme* either existing or being implemented, based upon some logics collected verbally or in writing.

Reports can be classified in *four categories* :

1. *Official* report.
2. Report to a *newspaper* by a reporter.
3. Report for a *specific purpose*.
4. *Technical*/Research report.

1.Official Report : An official report is prepared usually on a matter of public importance or official interest.It is submitted by an official to a higher authority or to a committee. An official report is quite formal . While submit the report, it begins like this .. "The report is submitted by.... to ......". In an official, report only the immediate and practical aspects of the subject matter need discussed. In an official report, its subject and scope is limited upto the official terms of reference. When a report is submitted by a junior officer in respect to any happening , the immediate and practical aspects of the subject matter are discussed in it and suitable suggestions and his recommendations are also given.

2. Report to a Newspaper by a reporter : *A correspondent* or a *reporter* prepares such reports for the publication in a newspaper. He is either deputed for the purpose or the incident about which he is submitting his report, pertains to his area of operation.Usually, he is well acquainted with the situation or event. This report should reflect the detailed study made by the reporter.

A reporter who reports on an event, say, an accident, a riot, a strike, a rally etc., collects facts and figures from a number of persons involved in that particular event. From their accounts he prepares his report, but he must make sure that the facts and figures submitted in the report are correct.

This reporter should be *objective* , *impersonal* and unbiased in his report.

3. Report for a Specific Purpose : Sometimes, a reporter is deputed for preparing a report on a specific subject or he himself suo motto prepares a detailed report .Such report is not in respect to any incident, like-accident , fire or terrorist attack etc. but it usually covers the after effects of an official policy or is in respect to a long prevailing problem being faced by the society, country etc. The data and information collected are not only on verbal basis but also from official records.While analysing the figures in preparing the report, the personal bias must be avoided.

4. Technical Report : These reports are prepared by *economists / engineers/scientists* and other *technical persons* as a part of their duty. Such reports help the policy makers to take major decisions.While preparing such reports the reporter is required to base his reports on the basis of all the relevant data and the conclusions must be drawn very sincerely , meticulously, as the conclusions may have far reaching effects.

A good report must have the *following characteristics* :

1.Factual Description : Report must be factual and free from personal prejudices.All the data and informaton collected should be *relevant* and *unbiased*.

2.Clear, Compact and Concise : The *object* of the report should be clear ,the *suggestions* and *recommendations* submitted should also be very clear ,The report should not be unneccesarily detailed and should not cover irrelevant points . In short, it should be clear , compact and concise.

3. Purpose : The purpose of the report is very important.A good report must contain *relevant points as per the purpose of the report.*

4. Free from personal prejudices : The *report* prepared, *data* collected, should be free from the personal prejudices of the reporter.The *recommendations* given in the report should also be free from any personal interest.The conclusion drawn must be based on the well accepted principles .

4. Simple and logical : The *language* used should be simple and not be couched in typical or unnecessary technical words. No round-about statement should be used while making recommendations or giving suggestions.All the report and the final conclusion must be logical and to the point.

Solved Examples :

(1) As a staff reporter of the Hindustan Times , who witnessed a multiple collision of a Maruti car, a scooter and a tourist bus in a road accident, write a report in not more than 100 words.

TWO DEAD, SIX INJURED IN ROAD ACCIDENT

New Delhi : 10th May, 200. From our staff reporter

It was perhaps the most unfortunate and saddest day of many people who witnessed a multiple collision of a Maruti car, a scooter and a tourist bus, near I. T.O., New Delhi. A tourist bus of U.P. Roadways, full of passengers was on a picnic tour to India Gate. When it reached near I.T.O, it hit a Maruti car from the left side and a scooter from the back . The two young boys in their teens on the scooter were thrown on the road and died at the spot. The dead bodies were lying on the road in a pool of blood.The scooterists were not wearing helmets, so they sucumbed to the head injuries caused in the accident. Even the driver of the Maruti car lost his sense, hit a wall, but didn't get hurt. Passengers in the bus, got a sudden jerk. Six passengers got seriously injured. All were crying for help. There was a loud hue and cry. The injured were taken to the hospital for immediate medical aid. The whole traffic came to a stand still. The police arrived in no time and registered a case for negligent driving and homicide against the bus-driver.

(2) You are Mohan, a staff reporter at Times of India. You have witnessed a severe road accident involving a Truck and a Maruti car. Write a report including details about number of people injured and extent of damage caused to the colliding vehicles, in not more than 100 words.

TRUCK HITS MARUTI, ONE DEAD

New Delhi : 16th September, 200.

A serious accident took place near Naraina in which a truck bearing Regd. Number DLI 023, D 4573 jumped the red light and suddenly turned to right. It was about to collide with a Maruti car Regd. No. DLJ 012, J 1572,but the driver was very smart and careful. He saw the impending danger and took a turn to the left but could not escape fully . The truck hit the Maruti on the side and lost its balance and hit a wall in the right. The truck was overturned causing a serious injuries to the passengers, sitting in the cabin . The driver was thrown out and his head struck against the wall and he died on the spot . The three passengers sitting in the cabin of the truck, were badly injured, two other suffered minor injuries.The Maruti driver got minor injuries. The traffic came to a standstill. The injured were removed to the hospital. Police rushed to the sight and a case of rash and negligent driving was lodged against the truck driver.

(3) You are Nisha, working as a newspaper reporter for the 'The Hindustan Times'. Yesterday, you were invited to attend a press conference convened by the Union Minister for Parliamentary Affairs on the proposed changes in the constitution of India . Write a report for publication in the newspaper in not more than 150 words.

CONSTITUTIONAL AMENDMENTS NECESSARY FOR STABILITY: MINISTER

New Delhi : 24th March, 200... By Miss Nisha, staff reporter, H.T., New Delhi.

The Union Minister for Parliamentary Affairs Mr...convened a press conference at his residence on the proposed changes in the Constitution of India in order to provide a stable government to the country. India being a democratic country , the representatives are elected to run the government. In case any political party fail to get a clear majority to form a government, it has to get the support of other political parties to form the government. Thus a coalition government takes place. At present we are having a coalition government but its success is neither certain nor admirable, as the allied parties in general force its motives and decisions on the government.This poses great hurdles in the smooth functioning of the Government.Sometimes the coalition partners start working against the Government. In order to put a check over such practice, certain changes in the Constitution are under process; The majority party shall be allowed to form a government. In the first instance, no candidate should be allowed to change a party after winning the election. On the issues of national interest all parties have to give their consensus. There should be only four political parties, which have secured at least 20% votes in the last three elections.Once accepted as coalition partner, that party shall not be allowed to withdraw the support.Once a government is formed , it can not be thrown out, unless a majority of two third of the total membership put a demand in writing to the President, and a no-confidence motion is passed by the same majority .When asked about the feasibility of such a move, the Minister replied that it is well in the interest of the nation and for the peace and progress, stability is must.

(4) ***Paresh Tak, a correspondent from Statesman, was asked to submit a report on Environmental Pollution. Write a report on "Environmental Pollution" in 100-120 words .***

ENVIRONMENTAL POLLUTION

New Delhi, 25th Oct, 200. From our special correspondent Mr. Paresh Tak.

Environmental Pollution has assumed alarming proportions, resulting in a serious health hazard nowadays. Not only air but also water has become dangerously polluted. Smoke pollutes the air, sewage pollutes the water and solid wastes (garbage and junk etc.) pollute the land. Population explosion, urbanisation and industrialization are the biggest causes of the present pollution . Industrial units throw their waste and chemicalised water in the rivers. Sewage of big cities is being dumped into rivers. This has resulted into spreading of harmful chemicals in the environment which are harmful for the living creatures. Plants,animals and human beings are suffering from many known and unknown diseases because of this pollution.The polluted water causes cancerous diseases like cholera, jaundice and diarrhoea etc. The smoke coming out of the chimneys of the factories and vehicles causes serious health problems. We regularly breathe the polluted air and as a result headache, nausea and many diseases of lung and heart take place. This is a serious health hazard to all of us. The public be made aware to the harms and the problems caused due to environmental pollution.Public be advised to use anti- pollutant instruments in their vehicles and regular tuning and pollution check be made compulsory. Industrial Units be forced to take anti pollution measures. A proper arrangement for dumping of Industrial and sewage wastes be made. Use of polythene bags be banned.A mass awareness programme be launched by the Governmental and Non Governmental agencies. To save the younger generation from the effects of the environmental pollution, it is but necessary that immediate and proper action be initiated effectively.

(5) ***You are Mr. Ashok Jain. You have seen a students' demonstration near Moti Nagar, New Delhi. Write your report in about 80–100 words for the newspaper.***

STUDENTS DEMONSTRATED AGAINST FEES HIKE

New Delhi, 29th August From our special correspondent Mr. Ashok Jain.

The students of senior classes of Government School, Moti Nagar walked out of their classes and held massive demonstration against the hike in board fees.They were raising slogans against the government decision for increasing Board fees and abolishing the compartment examinations altogether. They were having hand bills and many posters. They were shouting slogans for restoring the compartment examination and maintaining the status quo in the matter of Board fees. This peaceful procession proceeded towards the office of Education Minister. Approximately 20,000 students gathered at the office of the Education Minister from all corners of Delhi. The police tried to disperse the students but they did not budge even a single inch. There was complete chaos and the traffic was jammed. The Minister arrived on the spot and had discussion with the student leaders, assured the student for prompt and positive action. The situation was thus controlled and then the students left the place winningly and peacefully.

(6) *You are Sarala. You visited the Industrial Exhibition at Pragati Maidan. Your teacher has asked you to write a report for the school magazine. Write your report in about 100 words.*

A REPORT ON EXHIBITION

Delhi, 25th Dec, 200... Report by Miss Sarala: a staff correspondent.

An all-States Exhibition started at Pragati Madan today , inaugurated by the Home Minister. On the inauguration the Home Minister said, "Exhibitions are the reflections of a country's progress in toto and this exhibition is unique in which all the states and the union territories are participating". Every year, many exhibitions and trade fairs are organised by the Governmental and Non Governmental Agencies. This year a specific industrial exhibition was held in Pragati Maidan.All the States participated in this exhibition. It attracted a throng of visitors from all over the country. It reflects that India has made exemplary progress in the field of Industry. People could be seen in long queues before the different pavilions. At the machinery section, one could not find a place to keep foot on. Agricultural implements of Punjab were in great demand.Hand made Galichas and dresses of Kashmir also attracted a lot of visitors.The pavilion of Rajasthan was also very interesting as it had very cheap and beautiful items of clay and mud. Some of the stall -keepers distributed hand-bills to the visitors. People were walking here and there in an enthusiastic mood. Small children were enjoying the merry-go-rounds, horse and camel rides. The refreshment corner was also full of hustle and bustle .

(7) *Imagine you are posted as SDM in a district, prepare a report on the Pulse Polio Programme carried out in the district.*

From:

Sub Divisional Magistrate,

District ....

To,

The Chief Secretary,

Govt of ....

....

Subject : Pulse Polio Programme

Sir,

Under National Programme of Polio Eradication, we have carried out the Pulse Polio Campaign on 14th August in the district. A good advance publicity campaign was launched to make the general public aware of the Programme and about the date, 14th August, the day of vaccination. A wide publicity was made not only in the city area but in remote rural areas also.

Forty teams of doctors and nurses,fifteen for the city and twenty five for the rural areas were deployed on the vaccination day to provide polio drops to every child.Male and Female nurses were deployed to visit door to door and give the drops to the children wherever possible. More than twenty thousand children were given the polio drops on that day.

We are planning to repeat this campaign in the month of October again .This time we shall be covering only the rural areas of the district. Our target for the district is 90000 children, we have already covered twenty thousands plus forty thousands (in earlier camps), total sixty thousands so far. We hope not only to achieve our target but also to exceed the same. Every child will be given the drops positively.We are determined to make the Polio Eradication programme a grand success positively.

23rd August, 200.

R.K.Purohit

S.D.M.

(8) You are posted as District Family Planning Officer in the district. Submit a report to the Director, Medical and Health Department of the State,in respect to the Family Planning Campaign launched in your district.

From:
District Family Planning Officer,
District....................
To
Director,
Medical and Health Department,
....
....

Subjict : Family Planning Campaign in this district of...

Sir,

As per the instructions received from your office, vide-letter no. RJ/FP/103/2004, dated 25th Dec, we launched the Family Planning Campaign on 20th January, 200.

All the staff of our department was deployed for the purpose. Various voluntary organisations, Panch, Sarpanch and the respected persons of each village were motivated to make the campaign a grand success. In city area, the public is well aware to the advantages of adopting family planning measures, but in rural area, more awareness is required to be created.

During this campaign, 315 operations were done and three thousand packets of condoms were distributed.

To make this programme a regular feature, I like to suggest that at least two Mobile Operation Vans be made available for the district to cover the rural areas.We want to fix a day for every village, on which the pending cases and the interested cases may be operated on a regular basis.

However we will be achieving our targets positively.

22nd Jan., 200.

P.K.Sharma
D F P O

(9) You are posted as Assistant Collector in a district. Flood has caused a lot of damage in the district, submit a factual report to Chief Secretary of the State, stating therein the measures taken by you to control the situation and your recommendations to assist the flood hit people.

From:
Assistant Collector,
District ....
To
The Chief Secretary,
....
....

Subject : Flood in the district of....

Sir,

I have personally visited the area affected by the recent flood. The villages lying in the path of river 'Sone' are the worst affected. As there had been little rain during the last three four years, so the people started settling nearby the river. The sudden rains have over flooded the river and all the huts and houses within approximately one km range of the river were completely washed away and destroyed. Flood water entered the houses. People have taken shelter in hills. A huge damage to properties have been done.Two persons died in Takupaka village.An acute shortage of eatables, drinking water and dry fire wood, is being faced. We have taken all measures to help the flood victims. Packets of food,bottles of drinking water, wheat flour ,kerosene etc.are being supplied to the people, with the assistance of the generous people, the NGOs, other voluntary organisations and selfless clubs. To check the spread of any epidemic, CMHO was called to take necessary measures. A team of doctors was dispatched to every affected village to take care of spreading of any water borne or any other kind of diseases.

We are taking all possible measures to assist the flood hit people. But looking at the heavy damage caused by the flood, more funds are required immediately.

You are requested to arrange at least five crore rupees urgently, so that the relief work can be carried out effectively.

Sept, 19,200.

J.C. Bhagat
Assistant Collector.

(10) Suppose, you are Collector of a district. Submit a report to the Chief Secretary of the State in respect to the drought situation in the district. Inform the remedial measures taken by you and further measures required, to control the situation.

From:
Collector,
District............
To :
The Chief Secretary,
Govt of................
....

Subject : Havoc caused by the drought in the district of...

Sir,

Our district has been suffering from the shortage of rains regularly for the last four years. Due to scanty rainfall, the water level in whole of the district has gone down tremendously. Without water in the wells, and no rainfall, all the crops have dried up, thus causing huge loss to every farmer. Our agriculture depends mainly on rainfalls. The dams and ponds are also fully dried up. An acute shortage of water is being faced. Cattle are either sold by the farmers or left to die for the shortage of water and fodder. The cost of fodder has increased tremendously. This drought has so far claimed 120 lives of cattle and affected more than 600 villages of the district with a population of 78 lacs.

'No rains' and 'shortage of water' have created famine like conditions. The drought has rendered lacs of villagers jobless. The dead bodies of animals are stinking in the fields and creating a health hazard. The danger of an epidemic spreading is immense.

I have visited almost all the affected villages.I found the situation very alarming.We are arranging fodder from the nearby State, water is being supplied in tanks from the city area. Loans are being arranged for the farmers for deepening and electrification of wells. The CMHO is instructed to check the out-break of any disease. Free dry wood is made available for the cremation of dead animals.

We have also taken assistance of voluntary organisations, NGOs and other generous people to help the affected people.

The situation is under control, yet, lot of fund is needed to help the affected people. We need at least 150 crores rupees to start relief work in a proper manner.

Please arrange the necessary funds, so that the situation caused due to the drought may be checked effectively.

28th Aug., 200.

Piyush Dixit
District Collector

(11) *As a newspaper correspondent of a national daily, write a report for your paper on the destruction caused by flood and the relief measures that have been taken by the administration.*

The Editor,
Indian Express,
Bahadur Shah Zafar Marg,
New Delhi - 110002

Sir,

I hereby submit to you a report on the flood situation in district Ropar of Haryana.Floods have become a common feature in our country during rainy season. This time, it has affected many areas of Haryana but the situation in district Ropar is the worst. Thousands of people have been rendered homeless. At least twenty-two persons are reported to have been drowned.Thousands of huts/houses have been marooned owing to heavy rainfall. One railway track is badly damaged and many roads are under knee-deep water. Property worth crores of rupees has been washed away.

The people of the area are facing the calamity bravely. The Haryana Government is handling the situation on a war footing. The rescue and relief operations are going on in full swing. The medicines, clothes and other necessary articles are being supplied to the flood-stricken people by the Government and voluntary organisations. Many boats have been pressed into service to rescue the marooned people. The Chief Minister of Haryana is personally supervising the relief operations and he has announced an outlay of Rs.250crores to rehabilitate the affected people. Many voluntary organisations from neighbouring states; Punjab , Rajasthan and Delhi have sent men and materials to assist the relief work. The Government has exempted the farmers from payment of land revenue and postponed the repayment of loans. The situation now appears to be quite under control though most of the areas in the district are still submerged in water. An active team of policemen and two battalion of military soldiers have been keeping round the clock vigil on strategic points. Due to active role played by the political leaders and vigilance of the Government machinery, a lot of sufferings of the affected people have since mitigated.It is hoped that, in a week or so, there will be a remarkable improvement in the situation.

XYZ
Correspondent

(12) ***'Imagine that you have conducted a survey in your city on teenagers and the television programmes they watch.' Write a report for a newspaper about the survey, your findings and your critical remarks.***

The Editor,
The Indian Express,
New Delhi.

Sir,

I have conducted a survey of TV- watching teenagers about their preferances. A peculiar similarity was observed in the likings of the present teens. A few important points which are universally applicable to all the children, who fall between the age of thirteen and nineteen, are being discussed hereunder.

A few special traits and tendencies govern their minds. The teenagers generally select those T.V. programmes which are action oriented or have love triangle. They prefer adventurous stories, serials involving love, romance and separation, detective episodes, comedy serials and some other programmes like cartoon films etc. They do not relish things of lofty and sublime nature. They enjoy funny, imaginative, romantic and tragedy items , which can make them jump and find in themselves, one of the heros of the serials. Some serials, which show conflict with the society in the matter of love and marriage are also liked by the teenagers very much. They do not need things of intellectual nature.

I think, such type of tendencies are not good for their real development. They are living in the realm of imaginations and dreams. They are being carried away by the imaginations involved in the serials and unable to understand the reality of the life,of the world.They should be inspired to watch different programmes based on political, social, religious and economic subjects. It is must for the healthy development of the teenagers.The parents should check the children and try to discuss with them and quench their querries.Something radical should be done to raise the level of teenagers' thinking. In fact the parents can play a vital role in this matter.

I request you to publish this survey report in one of the columns of your leading daily and oblige.

Yours faithfully,
Rajesh Prasanna
A free lancer.

(13) *You participated in an inter-college debate competition as a contestant, organised by the Lions Club of your area, in which you spoke in favour of the motion and stood first. The topic for the debate was. "In the opinion of the house, free education upto secondary level should be the fundamental right of every Indian child". Write a report in not more than 120 words, for publication in your college magazine.*

Jaipur: 15th August, 200. From RajdeepTDC, IInd Yr Sc.

Yesterday, an inter college debate competition was organised by Lions Club in our college. Total twelve participants spoke in favour of the topic, 'free education upto the secondary level should be the fundamental right of every Indian child. Simultaneously, twelve contestants spoke against the motion. Many college lecturers,students and parents were there to listen to the different ideas. I was also one of the contestants. I pleaded that without education a man is just like a devil who can disrupt the life of a nation. It is the education that ennobles our souls and removes darkness from our minds. Education is a window that opens channels to achieve the highest learning. It joins us with the master minds of other nations, whose achievements can be made use of, in the best possible way. Getting education upto secondary level should be a Fundamental Right of every child of India. The government should see that every child of school going age must attend the school. It is the education that provides wisdom, wealth, prosperity and what not.The audience clapped time and again when I cited many examples supporting my contentions.When the result was declared, I was adjudged as the best contestant. The function was a grand success. Chief Guest, the District Collector, exhorted the president of the 'Lions Club' to organise such competitions on regular basis, as such debate opens the minds of the students and make them a good citizen.

(14) *You are a reporter from The Times of India News service. Being an eye-witness to AN. 52 aircraft crashing near the New Delhi airport, draft a report of the crash in about 150 words.*

New Delhi : 21st Sept, 200.. By a Staff Reporter

An Indian Air Force transport aircraft crashed near the upcoming Dwarka township in South-West Delhi on 21st Sept, killing 22 persons including all the 17 IAF officials and the pilot on board and injuring seven. The U. K. built AN-52 first hit electric wires strung across two poles, with one of its wheels breaking off after hitting a concrete structure.It burst into flames after hitting a ten-feet high boundary wall and finally crashed into an under construction DDA water tank. As per one eyewitness, the pilot saved the residential area by slightly changing the direction of the plane, otherwise a huge loss to the lives and the property could have taken place. The accident took place at about 7:20 A.M. Besides the IAF Men, a 60 Year old mason, two children of another mason and two other passerby were also killed due to the burning fuselage of the aircraft. The aircraft's fuselage lay embedded in the water-tank with parts of its engine, wings, scattered on top the structure. Broken wings of metal and the debris of the aircraft were spread over an area of around 500 meters, around large stretches of vacant land. IAF sources said, a court of inquiry has been constituted.The Government of Delhi has also ordered a judicial enquiry into the cause of accident.

AUTOBIOGRAPHIES

Autobiography : An autobiography is the ***history of the life of a person written by himself*** e.g. *Benjamin Franklin's* "Autobiography." Mahatma Gandhi's "My Experiments with Truth".

The autobiography of Benjamin Franklin, the first secular biography published in the United States, served as a model for subsequent American autobiographies.

Biography : Biography is the history of the life of a person ***written by some one else*** e.g., *Southey's* **'Life of Nelson'**, *Bosell's* **'Life of Johnson.'** etc.

Writing an Autobiography : Some Important Hints

In this exercise the students are generally asked to write the autobiography of an animal or an inanimate object. **Learn the following points well** :

(1) In writing the autobiography of an animal or an inanimate object you must *imagine yourself to be that animal or object* and write as that animal or object might be supposed to tell its story.

(2) You must write in the *First Person*.

(3) You must be careful **not to fall into such *errors* as the following** :

(a) "I was very useful to my master till *I died.*"

(b) "*I died* in harness."

(c) "Till at last one day *I died.*"

(d) "My master wrote a fine *epitaph on my tomb.*"

How can any one *write after his death*?

(4) Do not write anything that is *affected* or *unnatural*. Try to describe only those things that are natural and possible. *Beware of writing such* **absurdities as the following** in *'The Autobiography of a Horse'* :

(a) "After six years, I got married."

(b) "Every night I retire to my bed of soft cotton."

Can you imagine a *horse getting married* or *sleeping on a bed* of soft cotton?

(5) Lastly, you must make the story as interesting as possible and tell it in *simple language* such as is used in *ordinary everyday talk*.

Examples of Autobiographies :

1. The Autobiography of a Horse

I am an old horse,feel my joints stiff now a days. I recall , while grazing in the pasture about the period of my very young age i.e. my foal days. In my opinion that was the happiest period of my life. I was not required to do any work. I could run about after my mother who was a fine grey Arabic mare. I spent most of my time in the pastures and meadows where I loved basking in the sun, rolling on the grass, frisking about and nibbling the tender green grass while my mother went on steadily grazing.

When I was old enough the trainer came and to my great indignation, fastened a long rope round my neck and then I was driven round and round in circles with his long whip. What a hard time it was for me! I felt great pain and anger. But I was helpless before the whip of the cruel trainer. He believed only in whipping, and beat me constantly and left me only when I was too tired to stand up. My mother told me that it was no use resisting and that I should go through the training bravely and sincerely . In this way I was thoroughly trained as a riding horse.

Soon I was bought by a rich zamindar. He was a kind master. Everyday he washed my sides, allowed me to graze the green grass in the fields and gave me plenty of fodder. I carried my master, the farmer,' to cities situated at a distance. Sometimes I brought my master's hay home. Sometimes I gave the children joy rides. I liked doing this task most. I loved to hear the children laugh, to feel them on my back and to hear their merry voices thanking me and saying ''Run up Pegasus!" Very often the dear children would come to see me in the evening when I remained in the stable. They would pat my back and sides and feed me with delicious hay or handfuls of juicy green grass. Sometimes, as a treat they would thrust a loaf of bread into my mouth or a lump of sugar or a couple of biscuits or even an apple. All this was a happy time for me. But after some time the zamindar got into debt and had to sell me to a rich merchant, who kept a buggy and I was trained to run in shafts. I hated this work; and I am afraid I gave him a lot of trouble by going as slowly as I could. The driver often gave me a sound whipping, but this would not make me go any faster; I would stand still for some minutes then I would start shying at every object on the road. Whenever I was harnessed in the buggy and whipped strongly, I simply reared or backed. My owner got disgusted at last and sold me to an official who used to visit villages on horseback.

I was very happy to get back to saddle-work and thoroughly enjoyed my daily gallop over the plains. I was proud of my new master who was respected in all the neighbouring villages. The syce looked after me carefully and I was always kept neat and tidy. My glossy skin and mane soon began to shine again. But an accident put an end to this jolly life; for one day my master forced me to take a long jump over a tunnel which I knew I could not take. I tried my best but unfortunately I was a bit short. My master was thrown off and broke his arm.My front legs were badly sprained.

I was in hospital for some weeks and then was sold to a gentleman who wanted a quiet mount. He is a kind master and feeds and uses me well. I am in his service for a number of years. His daughter is a fashionable collegian.She regularly rode me along the Mall every evening.She is very kind girl. She takes full care of me. Now that I am quite old, I am given a little work. I spend most of my time grazing in the field and leading a peaceful life.

2. *The Autobiography of a Butterfly*

"Agile as a butterfly" - I have often heard that said of a cheerful and lively person. Yes, I am agile. I do lead a very active and happy life. Life to me is all pleasure, a continual feast and a sunny holiday.My life is all play and merry making. You might envy my life which is so happy so glorious and so shining. Just have a look at my wings! How glorious they are to behold! Azure and jet yellow and red, in fact all the rainbow colours are present therein. What need have I to adorn myself with gold or silver ornaments and to put on gorgeous garments? My wings are already fringed with silver and sprangled with gold. I am decked all over with the flimsiest and most sparkling silken garments that glisten in the rays of the sun. I proudly perch on a rose or idly flutter on some fragrant flower. Off I fly to hill or dale wood, or bower to bower, intoxicated with the joy of life and take pleasure in visiting the golden daffodils, growing by the margin of a lake, the herbs growing in the vale, the tall and majestic trees spreading their budding twigs in the breezy air. I love to hear the larks and nightingales and other singing birds pouring forth a flood of rapturous music. I cannot but be gay in such jolly surroundings. Sometimes, I bask in the sun and ruminate over my joyful existence. Sometimes, I flit from flower to flower, tasting and sipping honey and little caring to settle upon any one. In this way, I pass from one beautiful object to another. My silken wings and delicate feet never do any damage. On the other hand, my presence beautifies a garden and makes it a lovely and charming spot.

But I have bad times also. Many a time, I have been chased by wicked, naughty children with caps in their hands. Every beautiful thing attracts them and they are charmed by my gorgeous wings. I have heard with horrors that some of them delight in making collection of butterflies of every kind. I hate this act.

3. *The Autobiography of an Ant*

We ants are very tiny creatures. People often trample us to death without any regard or concern for us. Many persons despise us because we are found everywhere. Place sweetmeats safely locked in a tin cupboard and you will find swarms of us there; place sugar in a vessel and we are sure to reach there as if by magic. We go after sweet, fragrant, savoury, and tasteful things. We like their taste; we love their smell. Our smelling power is so strong that we can at once detect a thing, even though at a distance. People dislike us because they think that we spoil their foodstuffs, liquid drinks, beverages and other eatables.

We are also good friends of human beings. We remove dead and poisonous insects which would be harmful to men. We do scavenger work by removing matter which would otherwise decay and be gravely injurious to their health.

We are as wise as men. You can learn many lessons of wisdom from us. We do not believe in wasting time in sleeping or playing. We always work , we collect corn and food articles for the rainy days. Don't you appreciate our intelligence, strength and skill ? You can't find any other creature which possess such a great power of organisation as we? We build nests and store them with food and divide ourselves up into classes such as workers, soldiers, carriers and so on. It may be news to you that some of us even keep slaves and get work from them and others keep inseets, from which they get a sort of milk just as you keep cows.

Our industry is proverbial, nobody doubts it, I am sure. There is a saying "Go to the ant, thou sluggard, consider her ways and be wise", which tells the lazy person to take a lesson in industry and thrift from our kind. We are ever toiling and moiling and we preach you a sermon daily nay hourly; ''Work , work and work to keep youself happy."

4. *The Autobiography of a Rupee*

I am now an old coin. I have been in circulation for many years. Now I have become much dull and all my shining has worn out. My face is now very faint and the lettering on my back is almost rubbed out with the years of hard work I have done. But I can still remember my early youth. If you had seen me when I was in the Government Treasury in the company of my bright companions soon after we were issued fresh from the Mint, you would hardly have recognized me them. I was then shining like silver, looking very beautiful and distinct. I was indeed proud then of my bright and smart appearance.

I have a very long history of mixed events in my life. My active life began when I was paid over the counter of a bank along with other new rupees to a college student who cashed a cheque. We went on merrily jingling in his pocket; but I was not there for long, as he soon passed me on to a Panwalla. The Panwalla looked pleased with my smart appearance; he picked me up and threw me into a drawer where there were already many other dull coins.

I soon found myself in a mixed company. I took no notice of the other small coins as I knew, they were of very base extraction. I knew that I was twice valuable as the best of the 50 paisa coins and four time better than the small 25 paisa coin . I also realised that I was much more liked than the old rupees, dull and worn. Some of them were jealous of my smart appearance and made nasty remarks, but an old rupee that was somewhat of bigger size, advised me not to despise the company of old rupees as "A rupee is always a rupee, however old and worn."

Then I passed into the hands of the daughter of that Panwalla, a pretty girl who put me in her purse. But the purse had a hole in it and as she walked along the street, I fell out and rolled into a gutter where I was lost for a long time. Eventually a dirty and ragged person picked me up, took me home and clapped me into an iron chest where I found thousands of my own kind being under the same confinement. After a year of imprisonment, we heard somebody knocking it open with a hammer. This we found was the old man's heir. We thanked him for our release. He separated me from my fellow prisoners that very day. What was the fate of my companions, I know not; as for myself, I was paid to a merchant in return for a piece of cloth. The merchant handed me over to a woman, the woman to a butcher, the butcher to a brewer, the brewer to his wife who made a present of me to a priest. In this way, I made my way merrily through the world and rambled from pocket to pocket.

I can't narrate you to even, the hundredth part of my adventures.However, I am lucky that every person likes my company.

5. *The Autobiography of a Euro*

It took three long years for my comming to existence, after I was conceived as money form. Actually I was conceived and given name on Ist Jan., 1999,when eleven European countries decided to have a new money form i.e. me (Euro.) My value was determined as per the conversion rate fixed by these countries in terms of their own currencies. On 1st Jan., 2002 I came into being in the shape of a currency note when tweleve countries put me into circulation. Some countries opposed my being and refused to accept me as currency initially. But now almost all the civilized countries have started accepting me as a valid currency. My cousin, Dollar, brother Lira, sister Sterling ,were quite jealous of me but sooner they started accepting my existence and started respecting me.

I now enjoy a place of pride among all the currencies in the world and almost everyone is accepting me freely with confidence.

6. *Autobiography of a Parrot*

I am a bird. I am called by the people 'Parrot'. No doubt, I am loved by the people. But their love has altogether taken away my freedom. I am imprisoned in a cage. I am being given good food, my favourite dal and green chilly, but I am not happy with all this.

I remember the days when I was free and could fly in the limitless sky up to any distance with my brothers and sisters. One day, as we were flying in a group of ten, we saw some fresh food lying at a roadside. We were allured to grab this food but we were deceived; it was a net of a fowler and I along with six more friends were trapped in the net. Second day, I was sold to my present master. My master is a kind and gentle person.His wife is also a kind hearted lady. They have a son who is very naughty. He sometimes tries to pinch me with a sharp stick. My master has taught me to speak a few words—

Good morning,
Good evening,
Thank you etc.

He insists me to utter these words again and again and as I speak these, he becomes very happy. I don't have any other problem here. I am getting proper food and care, but my freedom is altogether curtailed. I pray to God to get me free again.

DIALOGUE WRITING

Dialogue is a *conversation between two persons*. Writing dialogue is an important form of composition, especially for those who want to have command on spoken English. It enables a student to learn the colloquial way of talking in English and trains him to express his thoughts in easy and natural language. **Dialogue writing is just putting our spoken sentences and words in writing**. The spoken English of the students is often bookish and hampered with hesitation because the students don't get proper environment to speak English.

The dialogue written should be composed in such a way that it appears to be *spontaneous* and natural. The reader should find it as free flow of conversation, unbookish and unstilted The writer of the dialogue has to put himself in *two imaginary persons* so as to make them express their opinions as two different persons in a natural way.As regards the matter of conversation try to develop it logically, observe the principles of unity, consistency and coherence.

Note the following points :

(1) Be natural. *Don't be formal, affected, or bookish*. Remember that colloquialism, slang etc. are permissible to only a limited extent.

(2) *Think out your characters and make them variant*. For doing this, you should have in your mind a clear idea of the way in which each character is to express his views.

(3) Give your *characters consistency*, life and movement.

(4) Carefully think over the topic given and note down briefly the *arguments or opinions* about it which might reasonably be expressed by the imaginary characters. *Arrange* your ideas in a logical order, so that one may directly follow from the other in the course of the conversation.

(5) Avoid *clumsy repetitions* like; *he said, I said* etc.

"In the writing of imaginary dialogues on given subjects the student should in the first place *set the scene as vividly as possible in a few words*. In doing so, he should take care to select appropriate occasions or likely spots for his conversations as this makes for reality. The more real and convincing his work seems, the nearer it approaches true art. The important thing is to make the dialogue *spirited* and *natural* and as true to life as possible.

A. Conversation about hazards of smoking :

Ram : Hello Shyam, where are you going?

Shyam : I am going to fetch cigarettes.

Ram : Dear, you must not smoke so many cigarettes. Smoking is injurious to health and it is well mentioned on all packets.

Shyam : Brother, I know it. I have thought to give it up many times but this habit can't be given up.

Ram : Look dear, smoking spoils not only your health but also of your friends' and members' of the family. It can cause cancer also. Smokers don't have sound sleep and it is the root of many other problems.

Shyam : I know Ram, whatever you are telling, but inspite of that it is very difficult to give up this habit.

Ram : Well, you do one thing .You make a promise that now onwards you will not smoke at your home. If you are to somke, you will go out of the home.

Shyam : That's O.K. It is my promise. I am also joining a Naturopathy course from the next week to give up smoking.

Ram : Very nice. The day you will give up the smoking, I will organise a party for you.

Shyam : O.K ,then I will certainly give up smoking this time . It's my promise.

Ram : If you make a promise, then keep it.

Shyam : Surely, I shall try from today itself. I shall give up this habit within 15 days.

Ram : May God grant you success!

B. Conversation about superstitions :

Mr. Sharma : What're you doing? Don't you go for a walk?

Wife : Coming, wait a bit please.

Mr. Sharma : You have delayed a lot, let's move now.

Wife : Well, let's go now. Er....., a cat has crossed the path .Now we'll not go. It's a bad omen.

Mr. Sharma : What do you mean? What happened , if a cat crossed the path? It is merely a superstition .Several such superstitions are well prevailing in the society.

Wife : You may treat it a superstition. If any thing untoward will take place what will we do?

Mr. Sharma : Happening good or evil doesn't depend upon cat . Sneezing is also treated, a bad omen by many people. Some fear number 13. You should know that crossing path by a cat is treated a bad omen here, but at many places, cat is treated lucky. A single sneeze is supposed to be a bad omen at ours but in many other countries, single sneezing is lucky while sneezing twice is bad . Owl is considered a signal of death and misfortune at ours, while in Persia the owl is looked upon as a bird of luck. Do you understand my point ?

Wife : I haven't much knowledge, but we have been observing the same since long.

Mr. Sharma : Really , superstitions have been in existence in society since time immemorial. The man who truely believes in God, does not believe in such superstitions. Believing in superstitions means lacking faith in God.

Wife	:	You are right. Now onwards, I shall also not believe in them. Let's move.
Mr. Sharma	:	Very good you are really my good wife.

C. *Conversation between two students regarding preparation for the examinations :*

Ram	:	Hello! Rahim, how are you? I have seen you after a long period. What are you busy in?
Rahim	:	Hello, Ram, I am fine. I haven't seen you too since long. I am actually preparing for State Administrative Services competitive examinations.
Ram	:	Oh, that's the reason . But so far my knowledge goes, the State Service examinations are generally held in the month of June or July. This is October, the vacancies are also not declared so far.
Rahim	:	You are right Ram, but you must know that after declaration of vacancies, one gets only two to three months to prepare for the examination.This is not an academic examination Here one is to secure marks better than others. Last year too, I filled up the form but I couldn't prepare well due to lack of time, so I didn't take the examination.
Ram	:	You look very serious this time. I certainly endorse your views. If one wants to prepare for Administrative Services one should be serious and dedicated to the task. Which optional papers are you going to opt?
Rahim	:	I have chosen History and Economics. As you know, I have done my M.A. with Economics and I have to prepare History additionally.
Ram	:	What about General Knowledge, English and Hindi?
Rahim	:	General knowledge is a very lengthy subject. I am regularly preparing it. So far Hindi and English are concerned, I don't have any problem.
Ram	:	Could you guide me which optional should I opt ? I may also start preparing for the Administrative Services.
Rahim	:	I think you should opt Statistics and History. As you are M.A. with Statistics, only History you are to prepare additionally. Opting History as optional helps us in preparing General Knowledge also.
Ram	:	Thank you Rahim, for your kind advice and guidance. I shall meet you after finalising my papers. Bye!
Rahim	:	Good bye!

D. Conversation between Police Inspector and a girl whom someone tried to kidnap.

Police Inspector : Hello, Tina, I am Inspector P.K Jha. I am handling your case. The kidnapping attempt must have been a terrible experience for you.

Tina : Oof, indeed a nightmare ! Such criminals must be put behind bars.

Police Inspector : For that purpose, I am here. If you help, we shall be able to catch them. I heard that there were two men. Is'nt that right?

Tina : Yes, but I saw only one man who tried to grab me, the other one was in the car.

Police Inspector : If you are O.K., then we may draw a description of the person who tried to grab you. Let's start with his size. How tall was he approximately? What was his age as per you?

Tina : About as tall as you, no a little bit shorter than you . His age should be around forty.

Police Inspector : What sort of build was he? I mean, what was the general shape of his body?

Tina : He wasn't thin. He might be considered stocky and also had a fat stomach.

Police Inspector : That's very good. Tina do you remember anything about his clothes?

Tina : Yes, I remember well. He was wearing a blue coloured white striped shirt and a black coloured trousers?

Police Inspector : His face Tina?

Tina : His face was round. He had dark staring eyes. His eyebrows were bushy. His face was short and bumpy. His hair was black and straight.

Police Inspector : Did he wear spectacles? Anything specific about his nose or any scar etc on the face? Do you remember anything about his teeth, lips?

Tina : Yes, he was wearing a plastic frame glasses and they kept slipping down his nose. He had a sharp pointed nose. Regarding teeth, I remember that he had one of his upper teeth on his right, yes.... on the right side missing. Oh yes, one more thing I do remember that he had a scar on his upper lip, where the tooth was missing.

Police Inspector : Was he clean shaved? I mean whether he had a beard or moustache?

Tina : Oh. I see , he didn't have a beard, but he did have moustache.

Police Inspector : Very nice. Can you remember any other thing that may help us to catch them?

Tina : No, I don't think so... Oh, one more thing, the man, who tried to grab me, had a mark of tatoo of a snake on his right arm. It was a beautiful and multicoloured tatoo .That's all, I can remember sir.

Police Inspector : Thank you very much Tina. You have been very helpful. With such a detailed description, I am sure to catch them very early.

E. *Conversation about democracy:*

Leena : Papa, Papa, Tell me something about democracy. I am to deliver a speech on this topic. First of all tell me, what is democracy?

Papa : Dear daughter Leena, it is a big question. Let me think over it. Democracy, yes, democracy means People's rule.

Leena : It means, democracy means Jantantra.

Papa : Yes, it is so.

Leena : Papa, you and I are people, but we don't rule? What's actually the meaning of democracy?

Papa : (Laughing).... If everyone rules, then who will do all other works. Democracy here means, rule by the representatives of the people. We may call it Representative Democracy.

Leena : How do we elect the representative?

Papa : Every citizen of India, who is 18 years of age, can cast his vote to elect the representatives. We elect the representatives through our votes.

Leena : I shall be of 18 years of age this year, then I shall also be able to cast my vote.

Papa : Yes dear, you would be able to cast your vote in the next elections.

Leena : Papa, whom should we vote?

Papa : We must vote to such a candidate, who is honest and hard working; who has desire and feelings to serve the people. We must not cast our votes on the basis of caste or religion.

Leena : Papa, do you know the definition of democracy given by Abraham Lincoln?

Papa : Yes, of course. Lincoln's definition is being followed in our country also. "Government of the people, by the people and for the people" This is the definition of democracy, by Lincoln.

Leena : Now I understand what is democracy. Thank you Papa.

Papa : My child, it's my pleasure.

F. *Conversation between a mother and the class teacher :*

Mother : Good morning Mrs Khanna. I am Rajani Sharma, mother of Shilpa. You want to tell me something about Shilpa.

Mrs Khanna : Mrs Sharma, please come in. Have a seat please. Shilpa is an intelligent girl. She secures good marks in all the subjects, but she is very weak in English. She has been securing very poor marks in English regularly.

Mother : Yes, I have seen her progress report. I have discussed this matter with her too. Actually, before taking admission in this school, she has studied in a Hindi medium school. I am also worried in this matter. Please tell me about any good teacher who can give her tuitions.

Mrs Khanna : Well. I will send you a teacher of English tomorrow. Her name is Mrs Sangeeta Jhalani .You talk to her. She can help you out.

Mother : Thanks a lot. You have solved my problem. Any other problem about Shilpa?

Mrs Khanna : No, nothing. She is otherwise a good and well behaving girl.

Mother : Please inform me definitely , if there is any problem about Shilpa in future also. Thank you again.

Mrs Khanna : Sure, sure. You are welcome.

G. *Conversation between a boy and an uncle:*

Dimple : Hello uncle, good evening.

Uncle : Hello, what's your name?

Dimple : I am Dimple.

Uncle : In which class do you read?

Dimple : I read in 9th class.

Uncle : In which school do you read?

Dimple : I read in Saint Anslems' school.

Uncle : How do you go to your school?

Dimple : I go by school bus.

Uncle : How is your school?

Dimple : My school is one of the best schools of Jaipur.

Uncle : Who is your class teacher?

Dimple : Miss. Renu is our class teacher.

Uncle : How many students are there in your class?

Dimple : There are total thirty five students in my class.

Uncle : Who is your best friend?

Dimple : My best friend is Rahim.

Uncle : What is you hobby?

Dimple : Playing cricket is my hobby.

Uncle : What do you want to become in your life?

Dimple : I want to become a doctor.

Uncle : Dimple, if you work hard,you can become whatever you want.

Dimple : Yes uncle, I shall positively do hard work.

Uncle : May God grant you success!

Dimple : Thank you uncle.

H. Conversation between two brothers, going to see a Magician's Show :

Raju : Bade Bhaiya (Elder brother), Good morning.

Ramesh : Good morning Raju.

Raju : Brother, have you brought the tickets for the Magician's Show, as you promised ?

Ramesh : Yes, dear, I have five tickets of noon show.

Raju : Oh! brother, you are great. At what time are we to go?

Ramesh : We shall move at 1 P.M.

Raju : Who else, except Bhabhiji, will accompany us?

Ramesh : My friend Mukesh and his wife will also accompany us.

Raju : Woh ! that will be excellent.

Ramesh : Now you get ready. Bring vegetables from the market, so that lunch could be cooked timely.

Raju : O.K. brother. Don't worry. I am just getting ready.

Raju : Brother, May I take your scooter.

Ramesh : Yes, you can,but park it at a proper place.

Raju : Thank you, that's right.

I. Conversation between Father and Son, while going to school :

Father : Sonu, get up. It is ten past seven. You may be late for school.

Sonu : Good morning Daddy. I am just getting up within ten minutes.

Father : Just get up and get fresh quickly.

Sonu : O.K. Daddy. Where is Mummy?

Father : Mummy has gone to temple.

Sonu : Daddy, I am ready. Where is my breakfast and my lunch box?

Father : Your breakfast is on table and lunch box is in the kitchen.

Father : You haven't polished your shoes today.

Sonu : No I just brushed them.

Father : Good, take your breakfast and put your lunch box in your school bag.

Sonu : Daddy, I have had my breakfast. I am ready now.

Father : Very good. I will just drop you at the bus stop.

Sonu : Thank you Daddy.

Father : Bye Sonu!

J. Conversation between two friends :

Ram : Hi ! Shyam, how are you?

Shyam : Hello ! What about you, Ram ?

Ram : I am fine, thank you. I have seen you after many days.Where have you been so long?

Shyam	:	I am at Bangalore nowadays. There I have joined a company as computer engineer.
Ram	:	Very good. I am very glad to know it. How are you feeling there?
Shyam	:	I am feeling well. Ours is one of the reputed companies of India. I am getting good salary and free accommodation also.
Ram	:	That's great .You must work hard there. In private sector, lot of importance is given to a hard worker.
Shyam	:	I am putting very hard there and with dedication. What about your transport business?
Ram	:	It's good. We have lately purchased two new trucks. One has to be very careful in transport business.
Shyam	:	Yes, in transport business, a lot depends upon the honesty of the drivers.
Ram	:	Our all drivers are very laborious and honest. We also take care of them as members of our family.
Shyam	:	So you are successful in this business.
Ram	:	Now, I am to go. See you tomorrow.
Shyam	:	Bye Ram!

K. *Conversation between two college girls :*

Rani	:	Hi! Anu, how are you?
Anu	:	I am fine, what about you?
Rani	:	I am quite well. Thanks.
Anu	:	What new are you doing nowadays?
Rani	:	I am doing 'O' level computer course nowadays.
Anu	:	What's the duration of this course? How many papers are there in this course?
Rani	:	This is only one year course. There are four theoretical and one practical papers only.
Anu	:	That's good. Where's your elder brother nowadays.
Rani	:	He is a financial adviser in a company at Delhi and has also joined some professional course there.
Anu	:	What professional course is he doing?
Rani	:	I don't know exactly, but it is some course relating to finance or commerce.
Anu	:	When does he come here? I am to seek his advice.
Anu	:	He comes here on Sunday.Now let's go to canteen and have coffee.
Rani	:	Yes, let us go.

L. Conversation between two strangers :

Traveller : Excuse me, sir. I am trying to find my way to Lyod church. Please tell me as to how can I reach there.

Native A : You must be new to this city. Are you having your own vehicle or taking public bus.

Traveller : You're right. I came here yesterday only. I will like to go there by bus.

Native A : That's good. It's slower, but you'll get more of the city, riding the bus. First you take bus no. 54 from here and get down at the next crossing. Therefrom, you take bus no.361 and ask the conductor to get you down at the church. The bus will take only 20 minutes up to Lyod church.

Traveller : Thank you. I appreciate your help.

Native A : It's O.K.

Native B : Hello stranger! I have overheard your conversation with that gentleman, who just told you the way for the church. I think he must be confused, because the route he told you is not correct.

Traveller : What should I do then?

Native B : Walk with me. I am going in the direction where you will be catching the bus. By the way where are you from?

Traveller : I am from Rajasthan. This is my first visit to Delhi.

Native B : I am Shyam. I am from Bhopal, Madhya Pradesh.

Traveller : Very glad to meet you.

Native B : Well! here we are. Here is your bus stop. Take bus no. 363 from here and it will drop you in front of the church itself. The bus will take only 20 minutes up to church.

Traveller : Thank you very much. You have given me the right way.

Native B : If you have a good map, then it is not difficult to find your way around. I advise you to buy one.

Traveller : Oh ! bus no. 363 is coming. Thanks a lot for you help. Good bye!

M. Conversation between a Doctor and a Patient :

Doctor : You told me on telephone that you were feeling listless. What's wrong!

Patient : I do not feel good. I feel that I have no energy.

Doctor : Any other thing specific?

Patient : No. Nothing specific, but I feel mostly rundown and tired. I don't have proper sleep.

Doctor : Do you eat well? What about your appetite?

Patient	:	I generally don't eat well. I eat a lot of fried and junk food. I don't even eat vegetables.
Doctor	:	You have also gained some weight since I last checked you. Do you take exercises?
Patient	:	I am not so active physically. I have my own business and I work very hard at it.
Doctor	:	Doesn't matter, please take off your coat and roll up your shirt's sleeve. I am to check your blood pressure. What's you age, probably fifty?
Patient	:	I am 53.
Doctor	:	Your blood pressure is high, but nothing to be much worried so far. But you have to restrict your salt intake and take more exercises. Are you short of breath some times?
Patient	:	Yes, I sometimes get dizzy. I can't walk long enough and can't lift heavy items. I start panting immediately.
Doctor	:	You're still smoking.
Patient	:	I tried to give up smoking, but did not get success. I smoke up to two packets a day.
Doctor	:	You smoke two packets in a day. You don't take exercise. Your diet is also not proper, even then you complain why you are not fit and healthy. I wonder, why you are not dead so far!
Patient	:	What should I do then, doctor?
Doctor	:	You are to take care of your health more seriously. You are to take care of your diet also.
Patient	:	Taking care of diet is very difficult because of my very busy schedule.
Doctor	:	Your health is more important than your business. Taking exercise is also very necessary. If you can't exercise, start walking in the morning. Start swimming also. Swimming is a good exercise.
Patient	:	I joined a health club lately, but I never had time to go there.
Doctor	:	Spare time. It is very necessary and for God's sake, stop smoking!
Patient	:	Well, I shall try again. It's very difficult to give up this habit. What about my dizziness and feeling weak?
Doctor	:	I am prescribing you this medicine, so that you will get proper sleep. Without proper diet and exercises, you will not be fit. Giving up smoking is must. Do you hear me?
Patient	:	Yes, doctor. I appreciate your sayings. I shall positively give up smoking, thank you very, very much.

N. Conversation on a Birthday Party:

Misha	:	Many-many congratulations on your birthday. This is your gift please.
Anu	:	Thank you very much.
Anu	:	Misha, meet my brother, This is Rajesh and Rajesh, this is my dear friend Misha. She is a very good dancer also.
Rajesh	:	Very pleased to meet you, Misha.
Misha	:	Me too. What do you do?
Rajesh	:	I am a computer Engineer.
Anu	:	Misha, come here please.
Misha	:	Excuse me, Rajesh.
Misha	:	O.K. Anu, what's the matter?
Anu	:	Meet my parents. These are my very lovely parents.
Misha	:	Hello uncle, Hello aunty. Anu in always speaking very high of you people.
Anu's Mother	:	Hello, Misha. How are you?
Misha	:	I am quite well aunty.
Anu's father	:	Misha, feel at home here. If you need anything, please tell me. You are the fast friend of Anu, so as our daughter.
Misha	:	Thank you, uncle.
Anu	:	Misha please take some cold.
Anu's father	:	Anu, all the guest, have arrived, please cut the cake now. All are requested to come here please.

(Anu cuts the cake. Everybody conveys 'happy birthday, and good wishes' to Anu.)

Anu	:	Many-many thanks to all of you. Please have cake.
Misha	:	What's the programme now?
Anu	:	Now we will dance and then take dinner.
Misha	:	O.K. let us dance. (Every body dances)
Anu's father	:	The dinner is ready. All are requested to have the dinner please.
Misha	:	Today every thing was very fine here.
Rajesh	:	Misha, you really dance beautifully.
Misha	:	Thank's for the compliments.
Rajesh	:	No, I am indeed speaking the truth.
Misha	:	It's all right. Thank you.
Misha	:	O.K. Anu, Bye!
Anu	:	Thanks for coming here. Good bye!

O. *Conversation with the librarian:*

Student : Good morning, sir.

Librarian : Good morning .

Student : I have taken admission in B.Sc, Ist year in this college. I want to take some books from the library.

Librarian : Books can be issued to the members only. First of all you become the member of this library.

Student : What's to be done to get the membership

Librarian : Take this form and fill it up. Get it signed by Mr. P.K. Srivastava, lecturer and submit here.

Student : Thank you sir.

(After some time.)

Student : Sir, take this form. It is filled up completely and also signed by Srivastavaji.

Librarian : Alright. You will be issued two cards. You can collect these cards after a short period from here.

Student : O.K. I should read some magazines etc. for such period in the library itself.

Librarian : That's O.K.

(Again, after some time)

Student : Are my library cards ready?

Librarian : Yes, take these cards and sign here on this register. First of all, read all the library rules carefully. The main points are, that you can get issued, two books at a time. These books are to be returned within seven days. If not deposited within 7 days, a fine of Rs. 5/- per day, per book is to be deposited.

Student : What is the working-time of library?And on what day, is the library off?

Librarian : The library opens from 9 A.m. to 6 P.M. daily and whenever the college is off, the library also remains off.

Student : Could I also see the old newspapers here?

Librarian : Yes, you can also see the old newspapers, but these can't be issued to you.

Student : Thank you very much for your kind cooperation.

Librarian : You're welcome.

P. Conversation at the Railway station:

Passenger	:	Coolie, Collie !
Coolie	:	Yes sir.
Passenger	:	Take this luggage. I am to go by Toofan Express.
Coolie	:	Toofan Express will arrive at platform no. 16. You are to pay rupees twenty for this luggage.
Passenger	:	It's O.K. Take the luggage carefully.
Coolie	:	This is platform no16. In which coach, you got the reservation?
Passenger	:	It's S-3 and berth number 45.
Coolie	:	S-3 coach will stop there.
Passenger	:	See, perhaps Toofan Express is arriving.
Coolie	:	Yes, it is Toofan. Please don't make a hurry. I shall put your luggage well at your birth.
Passenger	:	That's O.K.
Coolie	:	Sir, check your luggage. Is every thing OK?
Passenger	:	It's all right .Please take your charges, rupees twenty.
Coolie	:	Thank you sir.

Q. Conversation regarding importance of Computer education:

Rina	:	Hi Seema. Where from are you coming?
Seema	:	I am coming from the computer centre.
Rina	:	Computer centre! Are you doing any course there?
Seema	:	I am doing DOEACC 'O' level course.
Rina	:	Please don't mind. There is no use of doing computer course. It does not guarantee you any job. Moreover, we are to study for one year.
Seema	:	Rina, listen! It's correct that there is no guarantee of getting any job, after 'O' level. But you can do 'A' level after that and then 'B' level and then you will positively get a good employment.
Rina	:	It means, you will have to do computer courses for 5-6 years.
Seema	:	Oh no! one year for 'A' level and for 'B' level, just two years .As such total three years in computers will make you equivalent to MCA. Though I haven't thought so much in advance, yet I understand that in the present world, computer education is must.
Rina	:	I too agree with you that one must have knowledge of computers. Nowadays, computers have entered in all fields.
Seema	:	You also do at least 6 months' Basic computer course.
Rina	:	It's right, I shall accompany you to the computer centre tomorrow.
Seema	:	That's very good. Now I leave. See you tomorrow. Bye.
Rina	:	Good bye.

FIGURES OF SPEECH

A figure of speech is also termed as *rhetorical figure* or *elocution*. It is a word or phrase that departs from ordinary, literal language. Figures of speech are often *used for greater emphasis, freshness of expression, or clarity*. However, sometimes clarity may also suffer from their use.

Classification

Figures of speech have been classified by scholars of classical Western rhetoric into **two main categories**: ***Schemes*** and ***Tropes***. Schemes (from the Greek *schema = form or shape*) are figures of speech in which there is a *deviation from the ordinary or expected pattern of words*. For example, the phrase, "Ram, my best friend" uses the scheme known as apposition. Tropes (from the Greek *tropein = to turn*) involves *changing* or *modifying the general meaning of a term*. An example of a trope is the *use of 'irony'*, which is the use of word in a way that conveys a meaning opposite to its usual meaning ("For Brutus is an honourable man; / So, are they all, honourable men").

Schemes :

Accumulatio	:	Summarization of previous arguments in a forceful manner
Alliteration	:	Repetition of consonants in nearby words
Anacoluthon	:	A change in the syntax within a sentence
Anadiplosis	:	Repetition of a word or words at the end of a clause, at the beginning of the next.
Anaphora	:	The repetition of the same word or group of words at the beginning of successive clauses
Anastrophe	:	Inversion of the usual word order
Antimetabole	:	Repetition of words in successive clauses, in reverse order
Antistrophe	:	The repetition of the same word or phrase at the end of successive clauses
Antithesis	:	The juxtaposition of opposing or contrasting ideas
Aposiopesis	:	Breaking off or pausing speech for dramatic or emotional effect
Apposition	:	The placing of two elements side by side, in which the second defines the first
Assonance	:	The repetition of vowel sounds, most commonly within a short passage of verse.
Asyndeton	:	Omission of conjunctions between related clauses
Cacophony	:	The juxtaposition of words producing a harsh sound
Chiasmus	:	Reversal of grammatical structures in successive clauses
Climax	:	The arrangement of words in order of increasing importance
Dystmesis	:	A synonym for tmesis
Ellipsis	:	Omission of words

Enallage	:	The substitition of forms that are grammatically different, but have the same meaning
Enthymeme	:	Informal method of presenting a syllogism
Epanalepsis	:	Repetition of a word or clause following intervening matter.
Epistrophe	:	Repetition of a word at the beginning and end of a clause
Hendiadys	:	Use of two nouns to express an idea when the normal structure would be a noun and a modifier
Hendiatris	:	Use of three nouns to express one idea
Hypallage	:	Changing the order of words, so that they are associated with words normally associated with others
Hyperbaton	:	Schemes, featuring unusual or inverted word order
Isocolon	:	Use of parallel structures of the same length in successive clauses
Parallelism	:	The use of similar structures in two or more clauses
Paraprosdokian	:	Unexpected ending or truncation of a clause
Parenthesis	:	Insertion of a clause or sentence in a place, where it interrupts the natural flow of the sentence
Perissologia	:	The fault of wordiness
Pleonasm	:	The use of superfluous or redundant words
Polyptoton	:	Repetition of words derived from the same root
Polysyndeton	:	Repetition of conjunctions
Synchysis	:	Interlocked word order
Synesis	:	An agreement of words according to the sense, and not the grammatical form
Synonymia	:	The use of two or more synonyms in the same clause or sentence
Tautology	:	Redundancy due to superfluous qualification; saying the same thing twice
Tmesis	:	Insertion of one word between the syllables of a word or between the elements of a compound word
Tropes	:	Allegory; An extended version in which a story is told to illustrate an important attribute of the subject
Anacoenosis	:	Posing a question to an audience, often with the implication that it shares a common interest with the speaker
Antanaclasis	:	A form of pun, in which a word is repeated in two different senses
Anthimeria	:	The substitution of one part of speech for another, often turning a noun into a verb
Antiphrasis	:	A word or words, used contradictory to their usual meaning; often with irony
Antonomasia	:	The substitution of a phrase for a proper name or vice versa

Aphorism	:	Calling into question the meaning of a term
Aporia	:	Deliberating with oneself, often with the use of rhetorical questions
Apostrophe	:	Addressing a thing, an abstraction or a person not present
Archaism	:	Use of an obsolete, archaic word
Auxesis	:	A form of hyperbole, in which a more important sounding word is used in place of a more descriptive term
Catachresis	:	A mixed metaphor (sometimes used by design and sometimes a rhetorical fault)
Circumlocution	:	'Talking around' a topic by substituting or adding words, as in euphemism or periphrasis
Denominatio	:	Another word for metonymy
Erotema	:	Synonym for rhetorical question
Euphemism	:	Substitution of a less offensive or more agreeable term for another
Hysteron proteron	:	Reversal of anticipated order of events
Hyperbole	:	Use of exaggerated terms for emphasis
Irony	:	Use of word in a way, that conveys a meaning-opposite to its usual meaning
Litotes	:	Emphasizing the magnitude of a statement by denying its opposite
Malapropism	:	Using a word through confusion. with a word that sounds similar
Meiosis :		Use of understatement, usually to diminish the importance of something
Metalepsis	:	Referring to something through reference to another thing, to which it is remotely related
Metaphor	:	An implied comparison of two things
Metonymy	:	Substitution of a word to suggest what is really meant
Oxymoron	:	Using two terms together, that normally contradict each other
Parable	:	An extended metaphor told as an anecdote to illustrate or teach a moral lesson
Paradox	:	Use of apparently contradictory ideas to point out some underlying truth
Paralipsis	:	Drawing attention to something while pretending to pass it over
Paronomasia	:	A form of pun, in which words similar in sound but with different meanings are used
Pathetic fallacy	:	Using a word, that refers to a human action on something non-human
Periphrasis	:	Substitution of a word or phrase for a proper name

Personification/ prosopopoeia/ anthropo-morphism	:	Attributing a personality to some impersonal object
Praeteritio	:	Another word for paralipsis
Procatalepsis	:	Refuting anticipated objections as part of the main argument
Prolepsis	:	Another word for procatalepsis
Proslepsis	:	An extreme form of paralipsis, in which the speaker provides great detail while feigning to pass over a topic
Rhetorical question	:	Asking a question, as a way of asserting something
Simile	:	An explicit comparison between two things
Syllepsis	:	A form of pun, in which a single word is used to modify two other words, with which it normally would have differing meanings
Synecdoche	:	A form of metonymy, in which a part stands for the whole
Transferred epithet	:	The placing of an adjective with what appears to be the incorrect noun.
Zeugma	:	A figure of speech related to syllepsis, but different in that the word used as a modifier is not compatible with one of the two words it modifies.

DESCRIPTION OF SOME IMPORTANT FIGURES OF SPEECH

Simile :

A simile is a figure of speech in which the ***subject is compared to another subject***. Frequently, similes are marked by use of the words '*like*' or *'as'*, "The snow was like a blanket". However, "The snow *blanketed* the earth" is also a simile and not a metaphor because the verb blanketed is a shortened form of the phrase covered like a blanket.

The phrase "The snow was a blanket over the earth" is the metaphor in this case. **Metaphors differ from similes in that the two objects are not compared, but *treated as identical***, "We are but a moment's sunlight, fading in the grass." *Note*: Some would argue that a simile is actually a specific type of metaphor

Examples :

1. As good as gold —*Charles Dickens*
2. Yellow butterflies flickered along the shade like flecks of sun —*William Faulkner*
3. Woo the moon like the tide —*Vladimir Mayakovsky*

Metaphor :

A metaphor is defined as a figure of speech, or something that we use to *replace 'normal' words* in order to help others understand or enjoy our message. For example, we use the phrase "a blanket of snow" to describe a snowfall that covers the ground evenly, as if the snow were a fabric. The popular software '*Windows*' is named for the rectangular units that show information in much the same way as the windows on our houses allow us to look outside in different directions and see different things. When you see ***a word that substitutes the real word*** one would use, it's probably a metaphor.

Apostrophe :

Apostrophe (turning away) is an *exclamatory rhetorical figure* of speech, when a speaker or writer breaks off and directs speech in an abstract direction, *to a person not present, or to a thing*. In dramatic works and poetry, it is *often introduced by the word* 'O' (not the exclamation 'oh').

Examples :

1."O eloquent, just, and mighty Death!"—*Sir Walter Raleigh*, 'History of the World'.

2."Roll on thou dark and deep blue ocean."—*Lord Byron.*

Personification :

A type of metaphor in which distinctive *human characteristics*, e.g., honesty, emotion, volition, etc., *are attributed to an animal, object or idea*, as "The haughty lion surveyed his realm" or "*My car was happy to be washed*" or "*Fate frowned* on his endeavors." Personification is commonly used in allegory.

Symbol :

An image transferred by something that stands for or represents something else, like-flag for country, or *autumn for maturity*. Symbols can transfer the ideas embodied in the image without stating them, as in Robert Frost's 'Acquainted With the Night', in which *night is symbolic of death or depression*, or Sara Teasdale's 'The Long 'Hill', in which 'the climb up the hill' symbolizes life and 'the brambles' are symbolic of life's adversities.

Hyperbole :

A bold, deliberate ***overstatement***, e.g., "I'd give my right arm for a piece of pizza." *Not intended to be taken literally*, it is used as a means of emphasizing the truth of a statement.

Sidelight : A type of hyperbole in which the exaggeration magnified so greatly that it *refers to an impossibility* is called ***an adynaton***.

Litotes :

A type of meiosis *(understatement)* in which an *affirmative is expressed by the negative of the contrary*, as in "not unhappy" or "a poet of no small stature."

Imagery, Image:

The elements in a literary work used to *evoke mental images*, not only of the visual sense, but of sensation and emotion as well. While most commonly used in reference to figurative language, imagery is a variable term which can apply to any and all components of a poem that *evoke sensory experience*, whether figurative or literal, and also applies to the concrete things so imaged.

Figure of Sound :

Sometimes called **sound devices**, these include *onomatopoeia*, *alliteration*, *assonance*, *consonance*, *euphony*, *resonance*, and others. Not all of these are considered figures of speech, exactly, but they're included here because they're part of what you'll find if you look closely at the language and word choice of many poems. They work hand-in-hand with rhythm and all types of rhyme.

Alliteration :

Also called ***head rhyme*** or ***initial rhyme***, the repetition of the initial sounds (usually consonants) of stressed syllables in neighbouring words or at short intervals within a line or passage, usually at word beginnings, as in "wild and woolly" or the line from Shelley's 'The Cloud :' "I bear *light shade* for the leaves when Iaid

Sidelight: Alliteration has a gratifying effect on the sound, gives a reinforcement to stresses, and can also serve as a subtle connection or emphasis of key words in the line, but alliterated words should not 'call attention' to themselves by strained usage.

Assonance :

Assonance is the relatively close juxtaposition of the *same or similar vowel sounds*, but with *different end consonants* in a line or passage; thus a vowel rhyme, as in the words, '*date*' and '*fade*'.

Onomatopoeia :

Strictly speaking, **Onomatopoeia is the formation or *use of words which imitate sounds***, like *whispering*, *clang* and *sizzle*, but the term is generally expanded to refer to any word whose sound is suggestive of its meaning.

Sidelight :

Because sound is an important part of poetry, the use of onomatopoeia is another subtle weapon in the poet's arsenal for the *transfer of sense impressions through imagery*, as in *Keats*'-"*The murmurous haunt of flies on summer eves*," in '*Ode to a Nightingale*'.

Sidelight :

Though impossible to prove, some philologists (linguistic scientists) believe that all languages originated through the onomatopoeic formation of words.

Cacophony :

Discordant sounds in the jarring juxtaposition of *harsh letters or syllables*, sometimes inadvertent, but often deliberately used in poetry *for effect*, as in the lines from *Whitman's 'The Dalliance of Eagles*':

The clinching interlocking claws, A living, fierce, gyrating wheel,
Four beating wings, two beaks, A swirling mass tight grappling,
In tumbling turning clustering loops,
straight downward falling,

Sidelight : Sound devices are important to poetic effects; to create sounds appropriate to the content, the poet may sometimes prefer to achieve a cacophonous effect instead of the more commonly sought for-*euphony*. The use of words with the consonants *b, k* and *p*, for example, produce harsher sounds than the soft *f* and *v* or the liquid *l, m* and *n*.

Caesura :

A rhythmic break or *pause in the flow* of sound which is commonly introduced in about the middle of a line of verse, but may be varied for different effects. Usually placed between syllables rhythmically connected in order to aid the recital as well as to convey the meaning more clearly, it is a pause dictated by the sense of the content or by natural speech patterns, rather than by metrics. It may coincide with conventional punctuation marks, but not necessarily. A caesura within a line is *indicated in scanning by the* **symbol (||)**, as in the first line of *Emily Dickinson's*, '*I'm Nobody*!' Who Are You?' :

'I'm no | body! || Who are | you?'

Sidelight : As a grammatical, rhythmic, and dramatic device, as well as an effective means of avoiding monotony, the caesura is a powerful weapon in the skilled poet's arsenal.

Sidelight : Since caesura and pause are often used interchangeably, it is better to use metrical pause for the 'type' of 'rest' which compensates for the omission of a syllable.

APPRECIATION OF POETRY

What is Poetry ?

Poetry can be defined briefly as a *short piece of imaginative writing*, of a personal nature and laid out in lines *with usual rhythm and rhyme*.

Defining Poetry is a difficult task, as it is aesthetics in nature. It can also be said that poetry is a *responsible attempt to understand the world* in human terms through literary composition.

Poetry is now a days regarded as *an amalgamation of three distinct viewpoints*. ***Traditionalist*** argue that a poem is an *expression of a vision* that is rendered in a form intelligible and pleasurable to others and so likely to arouse kindred emotions. For ***Modernists***, a poem is an *autonomous object* that may or may not represent the real world but is created in language made distinctive by its complex web of references. ***Post modernists*** look on poems as *collages of current idioms* that are intriguing but self-contained—they employ, challenge and/or mock preconceptions, but refer to nothing beyond themselves.

Poetry is an art form in which human language is used for its *aesthetic qualities* in addition to, or instead of, its notional and semantic content. It consists largely of oral or literary works in which language is used in a manner that is felt by its user and audience to differ from ordinary prose.

Nature of Poetry

Poetry can be differentiated most of the time from prose, which is language meant to convey meaning in a more expansive and less condensed way, frequently using more complete logical or narrative structures than poetry does. This does not necessarily imply that poetry is illogical, but rather that poetry is often created from the *need to escape the logical,* as well as expressing feelings and other expressions.

Sound in Poetry :

The most vital element of sound in poetry is *rhythm.* Usually the rhythm of each line is arranged *in a particular meter*. Poetry in English and other modern European languages often uses *rhyme. Rhyme at the end of lines* is the basis of a number of common poetic forms, such as *ballads, sonnets* and *rhyming couplets*. However, the use of rhyme is not universal. Much modern poetry, for example, avoids traditional rhyme schemes.

Verse and Poetry :

Relation between verse and poetry is very typical .Poetry is usually *written in verse form.* Verse is generally *written in a particular pattern*. If we read the verse form we find regular rhythm of sound like regular beat of pleasing trumpet. A regular swing of sound is heard .The poet arranges the words in such a peculiar way in the verse that the *accented syllables* on which we naturally stress upon , while speaking *comes at almost equal intervals*. **The regular ups and downs; increase and decrease of tone of sounds; loud and low sounds recurring at regular intervals is called Rhythm**. Rhythm is the essential ingredient of verse or we should say *Rhythm is the chief characteristic of Verse.*

Rhyme :

When *words have the same vowel sound* and *end with the same consonant sound* they are said to rhyme. Verse is generally rhymed though rhyme is not necessary to verse. **Rhyme gives musical tone to the verse.**

Stanzas :

You might have noticed that many poems are divided into *units of equal lines and length.* Such units or divisions in a poem are called stanzas. Most of the poems are written in stanzas of equal and same patterns.

Rhythm, Rhyme and stanzas are usually characterized with the verse.

Rhythm is an essential characteristic of the verse. We can't have verse or poetry without rhythm. We can find *Rhyme and Stanza* in most of the poems but these *are not essential characteristics of poetry.*

Essential Characteristics of True Poetry

These are as follows :

(1) Verbal Music, (2) Vision,

(3) Imagery, (4) Emotions,

(5) Refinement, (6) Harmony.

(1) Verbal Music : The foremost essential of poetry is Verbal Music. To produce effective and pleasing music the poet selects and arranges the distinctive words of beautiful sounds in a special way. A skilled poet varies the *music to suit his subject* in order to make the sound of line more clear and pleasing. The verbal music doesn't depend solely on the musical sound of words but it depends upon the rhythm also. It is the proper combination of rhythm and melodious words that produces the pleasant music of poetry.

Let us analyse in detail, how poet creates the musical effects in poetry :

(a) Rhyme : You might have noticed that in many poems the *words at the end of the lines have the same sound* like; '*star , are;*' '*keep, peep;*' '*September, November*' etc.**When words have the *same vowel sound and end with the same consonant sound*, they are said to *rhyme*.** Verse is generally rhymed though rhyme is not necessary to verse.Rhyme gives musical tone to the verse.Words *rhyming together give a musical sound* and so rhyme is extensively used in poetry :

"O rudder than the cherry!
O sweeter than the berry!
O nymph more bright!
O than moonshine right!"

Internal rhyme (means-*rhyme within the line*) also produces a pleasing music :

"The ice was here the ice was there, the ice was all around.
It cracked and growled and roared and howled,
Like noises in a swound."

(b) Consonance : Consonance is a pleasing combination of sounds; *sounds in agreement with tone*. Also, the close repetition of the same end consonants of stressed syllables with differing vowel sounds.

Consonance is often used in poetry. It is the repetition of consonant sounds in a short sequence of words, *for example, the 't' sound in "Is it blunt and flat*?" ***Alliteration differs from consonance*** insofar as alliteration requires the repeated consonant sound to be at the beginning of each word. In *half rhyme*, the terminal consonant sound is repeated. A special species of consonance is using a series of *sibilant sounds* (/s/ and /sh/, for example); this is sometimes *known simply* as **sibilance**.

(c) Dissonance : In poetry, dissonance is the *deliberate avoidance of patterns of repeated vowel sounds*. The most strict definition of dissonance includes all sounds which are considered "unpleasant", while the most general definition includes only those which are restricted in their use.Dissonance has been defined differently by different people in different places, at different times. Western musical history can be seen as progressing towards a wider definition of consonance, culminating in the '*emancipation of the dissonance*', such as in the view of *Arnold Schoenberg. Henry Cowell* viewed *tone clusters* as the use of higher and higher overtones. While the perception and definition of dissonance is obviously culturally influenced, dissonance may also have some objective basis. In general *the closer the frequencies of two pitches the more dissonant they are*. Consonance between two notes may also be defined as greater coincidence of their harmonics or partials, which collectively are overtones. Dissonance is then defined by the *amount of beating between non-common harmonics*. By this definition dissonance is dependent not only on the quality of the interval between two notes, but the harmonics and thus sound quality of those notes themselves.

(d) Assonance : Assonance is the *repetition of vowel sounds* within a short passage of verse or prose. If the *repeated sounds are consonants, the figure of speech is* **consonance** when the repeated consonants are in the middle of the word, or ***alliteration*** *when the repeated consonants are the first letters of the word.* A combination of terminal assonance and consonance (the final vowel/consonant combination being repeated) results in *rhyme*. Assonance is more a feature of verse than prose. It is used in (mainly modern) English-language poetry, and is particularly important in Old French, Spanish and Celtic languages.

(e) Onomatopoeia: In linguistics and poetry, onomatopoeia is the device of a word, or occasionally, a grouping of words, with a sound imitating the sound it is describing, such as '*bang*', '*click*', '*fizz*', '*hush*'. **For animal sounds, the following words are typically used in English**:

Bee	—	'Buzz'
Cat	—	'Meow'
Chickadee	—	'Chickadee'
Chicken	—	'Cluck', 'Cockadoodledoo'
Cow	—	'Moo'
Crow orraven	—	'Caw'
Dog	—	'Woof'

A number of animals, especially *birds, get their names also from the onomatopoeic link* with the calls they make, such as the *Cuckoo* and the *Chiffchaff*.

(f) Alliteration : Alliteration is the repetition of the same sounds or of the *same kinds of sounds at the beginning of words* or in stressed syllables, as in "*on scrolls* of *silver snowy sentences*" (*Hart Crane*). Modern alliteration is predominantly *consonantal*; certain literary traditions, such as Old English verse, also alliterate using vowel sounds.

Alliteration is the repetition of the same starting sound in several words of a sentence. *Shakespeare* parodies alliteration in *Peter Quince's* Prologue in '*A Midsummer Night's Dream:*'

> ''Whereat, with *blade*, with *bloody blameful blade*,
> He *bravely breach*'d his boiling bloody breast.''

Modern poets have continually renewed the possibilities of alliteration, e.g., Gerard Manley Hopkins's "*Pied Beauty*":

> ''Glory be to God for dappled things...
> Landscapes plotted and pieced—fold, fallow and plough;
> And áll trádes, their gear and tackle and trim.''

(g) Repetition : Repetition of words often produces *a musical and pleasing effect* of the poem.

For example :

Word : "Alone, alone, all, all alone,
Alone on a wide, wide sea"

Phrases : "A weary time! A weary time!
How gazed each weary time!''

Sentence : "The ice was here,the ice was there;
The ice was all around."

(h) Burden or Refrain : A refrain is also a form of repetition. In some poems, a particular line or a part of it is repeated *at the end* of each verse. Such *a repeated line or phrase is called a burden or refrain.*

Such repetition gives a peculiar *pleasing musical regularity* to the poem :

"The Seraph band, each waved his hand!
It was a heavenly sight!
They stood as signals to the land,
Each one a lovely light!
The Seraph band, each waved his hand ,
No voice did they impart
No voice but O, the silence sank,
Like music on my heart."

(2) Vision : A great poet has the capability *to see truth that others can't*. A poet is endowed with some *spiritual insight*. He feels and visualises the things around him in a different way. A poet has a distinct power to communicate and prevails upon others to share his feelings and emotions A poet by his imaginative power sees into the life of things. He has a great vision, a distinct power to visualise and feel the things differently, lively and curiously. *The poet idealizes the real*. He helps us to see natural objects.There is nearly always suggestiveness in great poetry. It has a depth of meaning which can't be visualised by us on one reading.

(3) Imagery : Imagery is the content of thought *where attention is directed to sensory qualities: mental images*, figures of speech and embodiments of non-discursive truth.It is often written off as *decoration* or illustration,but imagery actually lies at the heart of a poem.

There are seven kinds of mental images — those of *sight, sound, taste, smell, touch, bodily awareness and muscular tension*. All are used by poets, though rarely to the same extent. The key point is the purposes to which imagery is put. *Metaphor, simile, allegory, personification, metonymy* (attribute for whole) and *synecdoche* (part for whole) *all involve imagery*. Often the things compared are both images, but one of them may also be a feeling or concept.

A poet uses art of imagery in following ways :

(a) By description : The poet *paints a scene*, real or ideal in words. Note the following wonderful description of the rain in summer by *Long Fellow* :

"How it clatters along the roofs
Like the tramp of hoofs!
How it gushes and struggles out
From the throat of the everflowing spout!
Across the window pane
It pours and pours;

And swift and wide,
With a muddy tide,
Like a river down the gutter roars
The rain the welcome rain!''

(b) By Figures of speech : Another way of suggesting mental pictures is by *comparison.* A poet compares one thing with another and thereby suggests some important point about it by an image. He does this by either simile or metaphor or personification. *Christina Georgina Rossetti* describes in the following words, the wonderful love that existed between the two sisters, Laura and Lizzie:

"Golden head by golden head,
Like two pigeons in one nest
Folded in each other's wings
They lay down in their curtained bed!
Like two blossoms on one stem.
Like two flakes of new fall'n snow,
Like two wands of ivory
Tipped with gold for awful kings."

To Blake, feeling himself and wishing to make us feel the insatiate fierceness cruelty, energy, and splendour which are the essence of the tiger's nature, comes the revelation that all these are the essential attributes of fire also; he can, if he chooses compress them all into a single simile; but he does more, he compresses them in one marvellous metaphor :

'Tiger, tiger burning bright.'

probably the finest single word metaphor in all literature.

(c) By Picturesque Epithets : A poet can also call *up a picture with a single illuminating word* or phrase. Mark, how the epithets or adjectives in the following lines call up a picture of colour:

"All in a hot and copper sky,
The bloody sun of noon." —*Coleridge.*

A poet stands on high cliff and looks down on the sea below; it moves, it murmurs, it heaves, it ebbs and flows, it shimmers, it flatters, it has waves and troughs made to look tiny by the immense height, what among all this are its typical traits by which we may know it and in what words the perfect expression of them? *Tennyson* answers with two words each as common as life and death:

''The wrinkled sea beneath him crawls.''

That is final. So long as language lasts and men have eyes, that picture of the sea from above remains for men to approve.

(4) Emotions : The fourth essential of poetry is emotion. In poetry, we usually find expression of *deep feeling;* that of love or hate; of joy or pain; of contempt or respect .The feelings are expressed in such a way *that arouse a sympathetic feeling in the heart of the reader.* Robert Herrick sees the daffodils .They rouse in him a strong emotion, and that emotion the poet marvellously communicats in his poem :

"Fair Daffodils we weep to see
You haste away so soon :
As yet the early rising Sun
Has not attain'd his noon,
Stay, stay,
Until the hasting day
Has run
But to the even song:
And, having pray'd together, we
Will go with you along."

(5) Refinement : It is essential that poetry should be *refined in thought and language*; also, that it should have a refining influence upon the mind of the reader. Hence we find that the great poets idealize not only the character of men and women but also the scenes of Nature. Hence too, the spirit of their work is *optimistic rather than pessimistic* even in the face of great calamities as may be seen by reference to the great tragedies.

(6) Harmony : Just as a painter must secure harmony of form and colours, so must the poet secure *harmony of thought and expression* in a poem. Or just as in a Persian carpet, various devices and colours are all interwoven into a complete whole of beauty and delight, so should the various *ideas of a poem be interwoven by the choicest form.*

APPRECIATING A POEM : (SOLVED EXAMPLES)

You have learnt a lot about the poetry and appreciation of poetry. With the following exercises, you will be able to understand well about the method or procedure of appreciations of a poem.

Example 1

Daffodils

I wandered lonely as a cloud,
That floats on high o'er vales and hills,
When all at once I saw a crowd,
A host, of golden daffodils;
Beside the lake, beneath the trees,
Fluttering and dancing in the breeze.

Continuous as the stars that shine,
And twinkle on the milky way,
They stretched in never-ending line,
Along the margin of a bay :
Ten thousand saw I at a glance,
Tossing their heads in sprightly dance.

The aves beside them danced; but they
Out-did the sparkling waves in glee:
A poet could not but be gay,
In such a jocund company:
I gazed—and gazed—but little thought,
What wealth the show to me had brought:

For oft, when on my couch I lie,
In vacant or in pensive mood,
They flash upon that inward eye,
Which is the bliss of solitude;
And then my heart with pleasure fills,
And dances with the daffodils.w

— *William Wordsworth*

Appreciation :

(1) Subject and Substance : First of all, you should try to learn the theme of the poem well. Read the poem thoroughly and carefully. Learn and grasp the subject and substance of the poem.

The poem is essentially a comment on the pleasure, Wordsworth obtained from solitary contemplation.Here the poet tells us that as he was *walking alone beside a lake on a fine breezy morning in Spring*, he suddenly came to view a sight that filled him with immense pleasure.He wondered at the beauty of the daffodils .He was amazed to watch uncountable(thousands of) yellow daffodils beside the sparkling waters of the lake.The fluttering daffodils appeared, as if they were dancing in the breeze, filled him with so unforgettable pleasure that the scene came to his memory again and again and filled his heart with gladness even afterwards.The beauty made him spell bound and the poet remembered the scene in his lonely hours even afterwards.

(2) Language : The beauty of the poem lies in the *simplicity of the language*. Every word used, is easy to understand. *Daffodil is a plant of the lily family*, which has yellow flowers of trumpet shape. These flowers bloom fully in the spring season.

(3) Imagery :

(i) The ordinary people see flowers, the poet saw in them-stars, dancers, happy celebrations of nature's miracles and it gave him immense pleasure.The poet has narrated about the daffodils, the yellow coloured floweres in the first three verses.

(ii) **Similes :** Wordsworth had utilized the metaphors and similes elegantly. ''I wandered lonely as a cloud'', comparing the loneliness of a man to a cloud, drifting through the sky. The another's comparison, between the *endless line of daffodils and countless stars in the milky way* is also a beautiful lively comparison.

(iii) The poem contains notable *personification* in second and third stanzas. The poet described the *daffodils as 'dancing in glee* and *tossing their heads like human beings'* (second stanza) and as '*enjoying themselves in such a jocund company*' (third stanza).

The line, ''ten thousand saw I at a glance is an example of *'hyperbola'* (figure of speech). It is poet's imaginative exaggeration, not to be taken in literal meaning.

(4) Sound :

(a) Note, that the use of word '*Dance*' in every stanza gives rythm to the poem.

(b) There is also a little use of *alliteration in line six of the fourth stanza*- "and dance with the daffodils". The repetition "I gazed and gazed" in line five of the third stanza is also noteworthy. It points out the regular and long duration for which the poet stood, looking spell bound, at the amazing beauty of the daffodils.

(5) Important lines : The most important lines are; lines-third and fourth of the last stanza. "They flash upon that inward eye, which is the bliss of the loneliness'': show dreaming the beauty of such memorable scenes afterwards. This shows imaginative and visualising faculty of the poet, that when he is alone he enjoys that wonderful sight at leisure.

EXERCISES

Exercise 1

Read the following poem and answer the questions given below :

Whose woods these are, I think I know,
His house is in the village though;
He will not see me stopping here,
To watch his woods fill up with snow.
My little horse must think it queer,
To stop without a farmhouse near;
Between the woods and frozen lake,
The darkest evening of the year.
He gives his harness bells a shake,
To ask if there is some mistake.
The only other sound's the sweep,
Of easy wind and downy flake.
The woods are lovely, dark and deep,
But I have promises to keep;
And miles to go before I sleep,
And miles to go before I sleep.

Questions :

Q. 1. What is the central idea of the poem?

Ans. The poem tells us about the relation between the call of beauty and the call of duty. Duty is first in life. One has to complete many important assignments before he departs finally from this world.

Q. 2. On the surface, the poem seems to be a simple descriptive piece of poetry. But there is a deeper meaning to it. What, do you think, is the message of the poem?

Ans. Apparently, the poet gives a description of nature's beauty in the poem. The woods appear to be so beautiful that the poet feels an attraction to stay there.He stays there to enjoy them . The horse warns him by shaking his harness bells that duty is more important and that duty must be done first; he should not have stopped there to enjoy the beauty of the woods. The poem gives out a message that duties should be done first; promises should be fulfilled first.

Q. 3. Explain the following line:

"But I have promises to keep."

Ans. The poet reminds of the duties he has to perform . He is to fulfil his promises before he takes rest or stops to enjoy something else.

Q. 4. Explain "And miles to go before I sleep."

Ans. This line has been repeated. It means, that poet wants to stress upon the idea that he should complete his journey or complete his important work or achieve his goal, before he sleeps or before he finally departs from this world.

Q. 5. Explain the deep meaning of the line:

"The woods are lonely, dark and deep."

Ans. Many charms of the beauty, like lonely, dark and deep wood, come in the way of achieving the goal. They distract people from the right path,but man should not be attracted by these charms, until he attains his goal.

Exercise 2

Read the following poem and answer the questions given below :

A an's destination is his own village,
His own fire, and his wife's cooking;
To sit in front of his own door at sunset,
And see his grandson, and his neighbour's grandson;
Playing in the dust together.
Scarred but secure, he has many memories,
Which return at the hour of conversation;
The warm or the cool hour, according to the climate
Of foreign men, who fought in foreign places,
Foreign to each other.
A man's destination is not his destiny,
Every country is home to one man
And exile to another.
Where a man dies bravely,
At one with his destiny, that soil is his.
Let his village remember.

Questions :

Q. 1. What is the central idea of the poem?

Ans. The destination of a man is his own village The land where a person dies fighting bravely becomes his destination because he is buried there.

Q. 2. Explain ' scarred but secure'.

Ans. The soldier was wounded while fighting in the war and the wound marks are on his body. But he was saved, so was secure.

Q. 3. What is the poet's idea of a war hero? Why should the village remember this?

Ans. A war hero means a soldier who fought bravely in the war. It does not matter whether he is dead or alive. If he is alive, he has all memories of war. He describes the brave deeds to the villagers. If he is dead, people will tell others about his heroic deeds.

The villagers should remember this. All the villagers are proud of the brave hero, and his deeds. He has brought fame to the village.

Q. 4. What is the poet's concern about the righteousness or wrongness of war or the individuals who fought it?

Ans. The poet is not concerned about the righteousness or wrongness of war. The soldiers are ordered to fight the war. It is not their duty to see the rightness or the wrongness of war. The poet is definitely concerned about the soldiers who fought it.

Q.5. Explain why 'a man's destination is not his destiny?'

Ans. Destination means a goal which a man wants to get; or destination means the final place where a person is to go. Therefore, a man's destination is the grave or the cremation ground. Destiny is decided by God. An Indian is born in India. It was his destiny. He dies in India and is cremated in India. It was his destiny. But an Indian soldier goes to England to fight a war, and if dies there fighting bravely, he will be cremated in England and not in India. In this way, a man's destination is not his destiny.

Exercise 3

Read the following poem and answer the questions given below:

Leave this chanting and singing and telling of beads!
Whom dost thou worship in this lonely dark corner
of a temple with doors all shut?
Open thine eyes and see
thy God is not before thee.
He is there where the tiller is tilling the hard
ground and where the pathmaker
is breaking stones.
He is with them in sun and in shower,
And his garment is covered with dust.
Put off thy holy mantle and even like him
Come down on the dusty soil
Deliverance?
Where is the deliverance
to be found?
Our master himself has joyfully
Taken upto him the bonds of creation;
He is bound with us all for ever.

Questions :

Q. 1. What's the central idea of the poem?

Ans. The central idea of this the poem is very deep. The poem tells us that we cannot find God through ceremonial rites. God actually lives with the tillers, the labourers, and the hard working people.

Q. 2. What message does the poet want to give us when he says :

'Meet him and stand by him in toil and in sweat of thy brow'?

Ans. The poet wants to give us the message that we should go where workers are doing hard work. And we should support them with toil or otherwise.

Q. 3. "........... and his garment is covered with dust."

Whose garment is the poet referring to?

Ans. The poet is referring to the garment of the tiller and the pathmaker.

Q. 4. What according to the poet, will be the gains of hard work and labour?

Ans. According to the poet, deliverance will be the gains of hard work and labour.

Q. 5. "He is with them in sun and shower."

(i) Who does 'them'refer to?

(ii) What is the meaning of 'in sun and in shower'?

Ans. (i) 'them'refers to the tiller and the pathmaker.

(ii) 'in sun and in shower'means-in all circumstances.

Exercise 4

Read the following poem and answer the questions given below :

How beautiful is the rain!
After the dust and heat,
In the broad and fiery street.
In the narrow lane,
How beautiful is the rain!
How it clatters along the roofs,
Like the tramp of hoofs!
How it gushes and struggles out,
From the throat of the overflowing spout!
Across the window pane
It pours and pours;
And swift and wide,
With a muddy tide,
Like a river down the gutter roars

The rain, the welcome rain!
The sick man from his chamber
Looks at the twisted brooks;
He can feel the cool
Breath of each little pool;
His fevered brain
Grows calm again,
And he breathes a blessing on the rain.
From the neighbouring school
Come the boys,
With more than their wonted noise
And commotion;
And down the wet street sail their mimic fleets,
Till the treacherous pool
Engulfs them in its whirling
And turbulent ocean.
In the country, on every side,
Where far and wide,
Like a leopard's tawny and spotted hide,
Stretches the plain,
To the dry grass and the drier grain,
How welcome is the rain!
In the furrowed land
The toilsome and patient oxen stand;
Lifting the yoke-encumbered head,
With their dilated nostrils spread,
They silently inhale
The clover-scented gale,
And the vapours that arise
From the well-watered and smoking soil.
For this rest in the furrow after toil,
Their large and lustrous eyes
Seem to thank the Lord,
More than man's spoken word.
Near at hand
From under the sheltering trees,

The farmer sees
His pastures, and his fields of grain,
As they bend their tops
To the numberless beating drops,
Of the incessant rain.
He counts it as no sin,
That he sees there in
Only his own thrift and gain.

H. W. Longfellow

Q. 1. What's the central idea of the poem?

The poet wants to tell us the beauty and importance of rain to the sick man, boys of school, and the farmers etc.

Q. 2. The poet has compared the rain to various objects. Mention two of them and explain the similarity.

Ans. Two examples of the above asked similarities from the poem:

(i) How it clatters along the roofs
Like the tramp of hoofs.

(ii) In the country, on every side,
Where far and wide,
Like a leopards' tawny and spotted hide.

Q. 3. How do the boys, the sick man and the farmer enjoy the rain?

Ans. Everyone enjoys the rains. Boys from the schools come and make much noise. They float paper ships on the rainy water in the streets. A sick man feels the cool. His fevered brain grows calm. The farmer also feels happy. He sees his own thrift and gain due to rain.

Q. 4. How do boys enjoy the rain?

Ans. Boys make more noise than they usually do. They make paper ships in large number and float it on in the rainy water.

EXERCISE 5

Read the following poem and answer the questions given below :

I'd like to build the world a home
And furnish it with love.
Grow apple trees and honeybees
And snow white turtle doves.
I'd like to teach the world to sing
In perfect harmony.
I'd like to hold it in my arms

And keep it company.
I'd like to see the world for once
All standing hand in hand;
And hear its echo through the streets
For peace throughout the land.
Last night I had the strangest dream
I ever had before
I dreamt the world had all agreed
To put an end to war.
I dreamt I saw a room somewhere
And the room was full of men;
And the paper they were signing said
We'd never fight again.
And when the paper was signed and sealed
And million copies made;
There was cheering in the streets
And grateful prayers were said.
I dreamt I saw the world for once
All marching hand in hand
And swords and guns and uniforms
Were banned throughout the land.
Last night I had the strangest dream
I ever had before
I dreamt the world had all agreed
To put an end to war.

Q. 1. What's the central idea of the poem?

Ans. The poet desires, that there should be no war in the world. The world today, needs only the PEACE.

Q. 2. What is the dream of the poet?

Ans. He dreamt, many men were in a big room. They signed a paper declaring that they would not fight again. People lived peacefully. They were happy.

Q. 3. "Grow apple trees .... doves."

Why does the poet use verb 'grow' with bees and doves which are clearly not grown the way apple trees are grown?

Ans. 'Grow apple trees', does not mean to grow them actually. It means to 'make apples available'. In the same way, the poet means that honey-bees and 'doves'should be made available.

Q. 4. What picture of the world does the poet have?

Ans. The poet thinks that there should be peace in the world. There should not be any kind of wars.

Q. 5. How did people in the street react?

Ans. They were very happy that there would be no wars. They said grateful prayers to God.

PARAPHRASING

Paraphrasing is the **process of changing another person's words into your own words.** A paraphrase is a reproduction of another writer's text, argument,explanation or narrative in our own words. It is **approximately of the same length as the original,** but is substantially different in wording and sentence structure. Paraphrasing is *used* as *a study technique* or as a *writing technique.*

Why Paraphrase?

The purpose of paraphrase is usually one of the following :

(a) to discuss someone's argument or text directly;

(b) to use as *expert evidence* for a point you are making in your own argumentative text;

(c) to make sure that you fully understand what the text (for example, a poem or a Bible verse or a speech from a play by Shakespeare) says;

(d) to present an opposing point of view that you wish to refute, and

(e) to restate a difficult passage the reader may not understand.

Paraphrasing is Better than Quotation.

A paraphrase is an indirect quotation. Paraphrases are more *flexible* than quotations. It must be documented because it relates in your own words and style the thoughts you have borrowed from another person. They fit more smoothly into your text, and you can express your own interpretations as your paraphrase. It is better than quoting information from an undistinguished passage.It is a good *way of using another person's ideas to prove your own thesis.*

There are two ways to paraphrase :

Verbatim Paraphrasing :

In this method, you **substitute the original words of each sentence with *synonyms*.** You can use the method as a first step towards learning the drafting of paraphrases.But this method has two shortcomings; 1. Since you paraphrase sentence by sentence, your overall *structure may be awkward*; and 2. You also run a greater risk of *plagiarism*.

Free Paraphrasing:

Under this method, you can borrow the original ideas *without necessarily keeping the same organization and structure*. You can use synonyms and rearrange the sentence structure. This form of paraphrasing sounds more natural and is recommended.

Effective and Legitimate Paraphrasing :

(a) *Reread* the sentence or section several times until you completely understand it.

(b) Set the original aside,and '*translate*' it into your own words .

(c) Break *long sentences into shorter ones*, and combine short sentences for variety.

(d) Use a *thesaurus for synonyms*, but be careful of subtle changes in the meaning of words.

(e) Make sure, your paraphrase considers the *complete meaning* of the original quotation. Check your drafted paraphrase with the original to make sure that your version accurately expresses all the essential information in a new form.

(f) Use *quotation marks* to identify any unique term or phraseology you have borrowed exactly from the source.

(g) When including a paraphrase in your text, introduce the topic in your own words, but make it clear that you are presenting someone else's ideas with wording like "*H. H. Smith argues* that . . ." or "According to medical researcher Donald Smith, . . ." or "*Smith also claims that* . . .".

SOLVED EXAMPLES TO COMPARE

1. The original passage : Students frequently overuse direct quotation in taking notes, and as a result they overuse quotations in the final [research] paper. Probably only about 10% of your final manuscript should appear as directly quoted matter. Therefore, you should strive to limit the amount of exact transcribing of source materials while taking notes.

A legitimate paraphrase : In research papers, students often quote excessively, failing to keep quoted material down to a desirable level. Since the problem usually originates during note taking, it is essential to *minimize the material recorded verbatim.*

2. The Original Quotation : "Four score and seven years ago, our fathers brought forth on this continent a new nation, conceived in liberty and dedicated to the proposition that all men are created equal . . . ."

A Verbatim Paraphrase : Eighty-seven years before, our ancestors founded in North America a new country, thought of in freedom and based on the principle that all people are born with the same rights.

A Free Paraphrase : Our ancestors thought of freedom when they founded a new country in North America eighty-seven years ago. They based their thinking on the principle that all people are born with the same rights.

3. The original Paragraph : "I had to explain to him that I was deaf. I said, 'Wait; I can't hear; please talk slowly.' He looked at me and said, 'What?' I told him again I was deaf, and he said, 'Oh.' He pointed to a door and told me to go through that door. I followed his instructions. I opened the door and walked through it, closing the door behind me. I found that I was in the hallway near the elevator where I had just come up. I was shocked! He had rejected me without any explanation. I got into the elevator, and as it descended, I felt very letdown. I couldn't understand why he didn't give me a chance to explain that I could do the job well. It didn't require hearing!"

— *Bernard Bragg, My First Summer Job, A Handful of Stories, 19.*

A Legitimate Paraphrase : In 'A Handful of Stories', Bernard Bragg tells a story of trying to get a job. One time, he told a potential employer he was deaf, and the man just pointed to the door. Mr. Bragg, not realizing the man was telling him to leave, opened the door and stepped out. Not until he went out of the door, did he realise, he had been rejected because he was deaf.

4. Original Text : "If you're coping with an illness or want to exchange views about a medical topic, you'll want to find your way to a newsgroup. Despite the name, these are not collections of news items. They are, in effect, virtual bulletin boards open to anyone who cares to participate. The messages generally consist of plain text" (*Schwartz 28*).

Legitimate and Effective Paraphrase : In a recent Consumer Reports article, the author suggests finding a relevant newsgroup if you have a particular medical problem or if you want to talk with others about a medical subject. Newsgroups are online bulletin boards that are available to anyone; in spite of their name, they are not news reports. Anyone who wishes to, may join in a newsgroup discussion(*Schwartz 28*).

5. Original Text : "In some respects, the increasing frequency of mountain lion encounters in California has as much to do with a growing human population as it does with rising mountain lion numbers. The scenic solitude of the western ranges is prime cougar habitat, and it is falling swiftly to the developer's spade. Meanwhile, with their ideal habitat already at its carrying capacity, mountain lions are forcing younger cats into less suitable terrain, including residential areas. And that, cougars have generally grown bolder under a lengthy ban on their being hunted, and an unsettling scenario begins to emerge" (*Rychnovsky*, "*Clawing into Controversy*," *p.* 40)

Legitimate and Effective Paraphrase : Californians are encountering mountain lions more frequently because increasing numbers of humans and a rising population of lions are competing for the same territory. Humans have moved into mountainous regions once dominated by the lions, and the wild habitat that is left cannot sustain the current lion population. Therefore, the older lions are forcing younger lions out of the wilderness and into residential areas. And because of a ban on hunting, these younger lions have become bolder—less fearful of encounters with humans.

6. Original Text : "Because the intracellular concentration of potassium ions is relatively high, potassium ions tend to diffuse out of the cell. This movement is driven by the concentration gradient for potassium ions. Similarly, the concentration gradient for sodium ions tends to promote their movement into the cell. However, the cell membrane is significantly more permeable to potassium ions than to sodium ions. As a result, potassium ions diffuse out of the cell faster than sodium ions enter the cytoplasm. The cell, therefore, experiences a net loss of positive charge, and as a result the interior of the cell membrane contains an excess of negative charge, primarily from negatively charged proteins." (p. 204).

An Appropriate Paraphrase : A textbook of anatomy and physiology reports, that the concentration of potassium ions inside of the cell is relatively high and, consequently, some potassium tends to escape out of the cell. Just the opposite occurs with sodium ions. Their concentration outside of the cell causes sodium ions to cross the membrane into the cell, but they do so at a slower rate. According to the authors, this is because the permeability of the cell membrane is such that it favors the movement of potassium relative to sodium ions. Because the rate of crossing for potassium ions, that exist in the cell, is higher than that for sodium ions that enter the cell, the inside portion of the cell is left with an overload of negatively charged particles, namely, proteins that contain a negative charge.

SOLVED EXERCISE

Directions : *Write a paraphrase of each of the following passages :*

1. "The Antarctic is the vast source of cold on our planet, just as the sun is the source of our heat, and it exerts tremendous control on our climate," Cousteau told the camera. "The cold ocean water around Antarctica flows north to mix with warmer water from the tropics, and its upwellings help to cool both the surface water and our atmosphere. Yet the fragility of this regulating system is now threatened by human activity." From "*Captain Cousteau*," *Audubon* (May 1990):17.

2. The twenties were the years when drinking was against the law, and the law was a bad joke because everyone knew of a local bar where liquor could be had. They were the years when organized crime ruled the cities, and the police seemed powerless to do anything against it. Classical music was forgotten while jazz spread throughout the land, and men like Bix Beiderbecke, Louis Armstrong, and Count Basie became the heroes of the young. The flapper was born in the twenties, and with her bobbed hair and short skirts, she symbolised, perhaps more than anyone or anything else, America's break with the past. From *Kathleen Yancey, English 102 Supplemental Guide* (1989): 25.
3. Of the more than 1000 bicycling deaths each year, three-fourths are caused by head injuries. Half of those killed are school-age children. One study concluded that wearing a bike helmet can reduce the risk of head injury by 85 percent. In an accident, a bike helmet absorbs the shock and cushions the head. From "*Bike Helmets: Unused Lifesavers,*" Consumer Reports (May 1990): 348.
4. Matisse is the best painter ever at putting the viewer at the scene. He's the most realistic of all modern artists, if you admit the feel of the breeze as necessary to a landscape and the smell of oranges as essential to a still life. "The Casbah Gate" depicts the well-known gateway Bab el Aassa, which pierces the southern wall of the city near the sultan's palace. With scrubby coats of ivory, aqua blue, and rose delicately fenced by the liveliest gray outline in art history, Matisse gets the essence of a Tangier afternoon, including the subtle presence of the bowaab, the sentry, who sits and surveys those who pass through the gate. From *Peter Plagens*, "*Bright Lights.*" Newsweek (26 March 1990):
5. While the Sears Tower is arguably the greatest achievement in skyscraper engineering so far, it's unlikely that architects and engineers have abandoned the quest for the world's tallest building. The question is: Just how high can a building go? Structural engineer, William LeMessurier has designed a skyscraper nearly one-half mile high, twice as tall as the Sears Tower. And architect Robert Sobel claims that existing technology could produce a 500-story building. From *Ron Bachman*, "*Reaching for the Sky.*" Dial (May 1990):

Answers :

1. According to *Cousteau*, the activity of people in Antarctica is jeopardizing a delicate natural mechanism that controls the earth's climate. He fears that human activity could interfere with the balance between the sun, the source of the earth's heat, and the important source of cold, the Antarctic waters, that flow north and cool the oceans and atmosphere ("*Captain Cousteau*" 17).
2. During the twenties, lawlessness and social nonconformity prevailed. In cities organized crime flourished without police interference, and in spite of nationwide prohibition on liquor sales, anyone who wished to buy a drink knew where to get one. Musicians, like-Louis Armstrong became favourites, particularly among young people, as many turned away from highly respectable classical music to jazz. One of the best examples of the anti-traditional trend was the proliferation of young 'flappers,' women who rebelled against custom by cutting off their hair and shortening their skirts.
3. The use of a helmet is the key to reducing bicycling fatalities, which are due to head injuries 85% of the time. By cushioning the head upon impact, a helmet can reduce accidental injury by as much as 85%, saving the lives of hundreds of victims annually, half of whom are school going children.

4. Matisse paintings are remarkable in giving the viewer the distinct sensory impressions of one experiencing the scene first hand. For instance, "The Casbah Gate" takes one to the walled city of Tangier and the Bab el Aassa gateway near the Sultan's palace, where one can imagine standing on an afternoon, absorbing the splash of colours and the fine outlines. Even the sentry, the bowaab, vaguely eyeing those who come and go through the gate, blends into the scene as though real.
5. How much higher skyscrapers of the future will rise than the present world marvel, the Sears Tower, is unknown. However, the design of one, twice as tall, is already on the boards, and an architect, Robert Sobel, thinks we currently have sufficient know-how to build a skyscraper with over 500 stories.

PARAPHRASING OF POETRY

Paraphrasing of poetry requires some additional knowledge of words specifically used in the poetry. **We are giving below a number of such words, quite common in poetry** *but rare in ordinary prose.*

Nouns :

Words specifically used in poetry	Meaning
swain	for peasant or husbandman
billow	for wave
swine	for pigs
maid or damsel	for girl
main	for sea or ocean
steed or charger	or yeoman for peasant or husbandman
tilth or tillage	for agriculture
thrall	for distress
might	for strength
bliss	for happiness
bane	for poison or mischief
marge	for margin
spouse	for wife
numbers	for verse or meter
quest	for search

bower	for summerhouse
scribe	for writer
victor	for conqueror
morn	for morning
foe or foeman	for enemy
mead	for meadows
meed	for reward
goblet	for cup
troth	for veracity or faithfulness
ought	for anything
naught	for nothing
eve	for evening
ken	for perception
guile	for deceit
chanticleer	for cock
combat	for battle
realm	for kingdom
brand	for sword
carol	for song
cot	for cottage
argosy	for merchant ship
dame	for lady
sire	for father
steed	for horse
sprite	for fairy
wirydome	for bird-cage; etc.

Adjectives :

fond	for foolish
wrathful	for angry
dire	for dreadful
darksome	for dark
hapless	for unlucky
artless	for innocent
lone or *lonesome*	for lonely
drear	for dreary
dread	for dreadful
lovesome	for lovely
rapt	for delighted
hallowed	for holy
baleful	for pernicious
doleful	for sorrowful
yon	for yonder
dauntless	for brave
lowly	for low or humble
forlorn	for distressed
sequestered	for retired
bootless	for unprofitable
aweary	for weary
ingrate	for ungrateful
recreant	for unfaithful
mute	for silent
quenchless	for inextinguishable
stilly	for still

jocund	for merry
reckless	for careless
sylvan	for woody
joyless	for unhappy
plenteous	for plentiful
sheen	for brightness
azure	for blue

Verbs :

smite	for hit or strike
quit	for leave
wax	for grow
quoth	for said
list	for listen
sojourn	for lodge or dwell
trow	for believe
lorry	for remain or stay
hearken	for hear or attend
vanquish	for conquer quaff for drink deep
hie or speed	for hasten
wrought	for worked
clad	for clothed
clomb	for climbed
clove	for cleft
bade	for bid
begat	for begot
crew	for crowed

drave	for drove methinks for I think
chid	for scold
I ween	for I think
doff	for abandon or discard
don	for put on (garment)
avaunt	for begone

Conjunctions :

Albeit	for although
ere or *'are*	for before
natheless	for nevertheless
an	if for if

PECULIAR GRAMMATICAL CONSTRUCTIONS OF VERSES

Verses have some peculiar grammatical construction, *different from prose* :

1. In verse, a *verb is often used alone*, so when you paraphrase the verse into prose, you should have an auxiliary verb attached to it. Examples :
   - (i) Tell me not in mournful numbers.
     (Do not tell me in mournful numbers)
   - (ii) Gives not the hawthorn bush as sweet a shade?
     (Does not the hawthorn bush give as sweet a shade?)
   - (iii) Long die thy happy days before thy death!
     (May thy happy days die before thy death.)
   - (iv) This day be bread and peace my lot!
     (May peace and bread be my lot this day.)
2. Sometimes an adjective is used to qualify a verb. While paraphrasing verse into prose, *substitute an adverb for the adjective*. Example :-
   - (i) 'First they praised him *soft* and *low*'. —*Tennyson.*
     (First they praised him *softly* and *lowly*.)
   - (ii) 'The green trees whispered *low* and *mild*'. —*Longfellow.*
     (The green trees whispered *lowly* and *mildly*.)
3. Sometimes an adjective is used for the noun. In paraphrasing, *substitute a noun for an adjective*. Examples :

(i) 'Below the chestnut, when their bunds.
Where glistening to the breezy blue' (=sky)–*Tennyson*.

(ii) The dread vas (=expanse) of night–*Milton*.

(iii) The palable obscure (= darkness)–*Milton*.

(iv) The kinding azure (=sky).–*Thomson*.

4. In verse, there is free use of *impersonal* verbs for *personal*. In a paraphrase, all such impersonal verbs should be changed into personal ones. Examples :

(i) 'Methinks' should be changed into 'I think'.

(ii) 'Melists' should be changed into 'it seems to me'.

5. Substitute an adjective for a *possessive noun* :

(i) Pity women's (*womanly*) compassion.— *Longfellow*.

(ii) The *mother's* (*motherly*) nature of Althre.—*Lowell*.

6. While paraphrasing verse into prose, place the *adjective before the noun it qualifies* :

Or, where the gorgeous East with richest hand.
Showers on her kings barbaric pearl and gold.—*Milton*.

Here 'barbaric' is intended to qualify 'kings' and not 'pearl.'

7. While paraphrasing verse into prose, place the verb after the subject.

(i) '*Roar the mountains*, thunders all the ground.'
(The *mountains roar*, all the ground thunders.)

(ii) '*Again returned* the scenes of youth.'
(The scenes of youth *returned again*.)

8. Place the *object after its verb* and the subject before it :

(i) 'A transient calm the happy scenes bestow.'
(The happy scenes bestow a transient calm.)

9. Place a *qualifying phrase after*, instead of before, *the noun* it qualifies :

(i) 'Thou sun, of this great world both eye and soul'.—*Milton*
(Thou sun, both eye and soul of this great world.)

10. While paraphrasing verse into prose, use-*either* ... *or* for *or*... *or,* and neither ...nor for *nor*... *nor.* Examples :

(i) 'Nor grief nor pain shall break my rest'.
(*Neither* grief *nor* pain shall break my rest.)

(ii) 'Remote, unfriended, solitary, slow.
or by the lazy scheldt or wandering Po.'- *Goldsmith*.
(*Either* by the lazy scheldt *or* wandering Po.)

11. While paraphrasing verse into prose, change *adjectives or participles into clauses*. Examples:-

(i) 'See that your polished arms be primed with care'.
(See that your weapons are well polished and primed with care.)

(ii) 'Forth goes the woodman, leaving unconcerned.
The cheerful haunts of men'.

(The woodman goes forth, leaving unconcerned the haunts of men, however cheerful they may be.)

(iii) 'From loveless youth to unrespected age.
No passion gratified except her rage.'

("Her youth was devoid of love, the peculiar grace of youth; and her old age was devoid of respect, the peculiar privilege of age; she gratified no passion except her evil temper.")

Inversion : Inversion is very commonly found in verses. While paraphrasing we should avoid the inversion and *restore the usual order*.

Original. "Mine be a cot beside a hill."

Paraphrase. "May a cot beside a hill be mine."

Original. "Now through the gloom appears,
Far to left and far to right,
In broken gleams of dark blue light.
The long array of hamlets bright,
The long array of spear."

Paraphrase : "Now the long line of gleaming helmets and of spears in order appears through the gloom etc.

Original : "Our remedies oft in ourselves do lie.
Which we ascribe to heaven."

Paraphrase : "Although we look to heaven for help in our troubles, the remedy often lies with ourselves."

Original : "There is some soul of goodness in things evil.
Would men observingly distil it out."

Paraphrase : "It is possible to find some good even in evil things if men will only take the trouble to look for it."

Flowery and Ornamental Language :

We very often come across flowery and ornamental language.Such language *should be simplified* in paraphrasing :

Original : "Do not as some ungracious pastors do.
Show me the steep and thorny way to heaven,
Whilst, like a puffed and reckless libertine,
Himself the primrose path of dalliance treads,
And recks not his own rede."

Paraphrase : Do not act like unworthy preachers who show others the difficult virtues which lead to heaven and never practise them themselves. They lead lives of luxury and debauchery and do not care at all for the future.

Metaphors in Paraphrasing Verse into Prose:

Most of the poetry are abound in metaphors. In paraphrase, the metaphors should *be expanded into similes*. For example :

"Silently one by one, in the infinite meadows of heaven.
Blossomed the lovely stars. The forget me nots of the angels."

This might be *paraphrased* thus :

"The stars came out one by one silently in the vast sky like forget me nots'flowering in the fields."

In some cases the *metaphor may be dropped altogether*, and the literal meaning given instead. For instance :

"Then the few whose spirits float above the wreck of happiness.
Are driven ov'r the shoals of guilt, or ocean of a cess;
The magnet of their course is gone or only points in vain.
The shore to which their shiver'd sail shall never stretch again."

May be paraphrased as follows :-

"Then the few whose hearts (but not their spirits) are wrecked, plunge into a career of wickedness or reckless dissipation. Men who lose the genial guidance of a youthful heart are driven towards careers of guilt or excess."

Simile in Paraphrase :

In paraphrasing elaborate similes, we may make the chief points of comparison clear by *expansion*.

Original. "Our hearts, though stout and brave,
Still, like muffled drums, are beating.
Funeral marches to the grave."

Paraphrasing. "However brave our hearts may be, they are like drums covered up to deaden the sound, and beat in a funeral procession, for every heart beat brings us nearer to our grave."

Original. "All down his cold white side
The crimson torrent ran, dim now and soiled,
Like the soil'd tissue of white violets
Left, freshly gathered, on their native bank,
By children whom their nurses call with haste
Indoors from the sun's eye."

Paraphrasing : All his cold white body covered with dark streaks of blood, looked like stained and withered white violets, plucked and left on the bank where they grew, by children, called indoors from the hot sun by their nurses.

Rhetorical Questions in Paraphrase :

Rhetorical questions be changed into *direct affirmations or negations* while paraphrasing verse into prose :

Original. Are we not better armed than our foes?

Paraphrase : We are better armed than our foes.

Metonymy :

When abstract is used for concrete, in paraphrase we should *restore concrete*.

Original : Let not ambition mock their useful toil.

Paraphrasing : Ambitious men should not despise the useful labour of poor peasants.

Original : The hawthorn bush with seats beneath the shade.
For talking age an whispering lovers made.

Paraphrasing : The hawthorn with shady seats provided for talkative old men and whispering lovers.

Concrete for Abstract :

When conerete is used for abstract, in paraphrase we have the concrete :

Original. ''I see a lily on thy brow
With anguish moist and fever dew,
And on thy checks a fading rose
Fast withereth too.''

Paraphrasing : Your forehead, pale as a lily is wet as though with the agony of a fever. The colour on your cheeks is disappearing like the glow of a withering rose.

Exclamations :

Exclamations should also be *changed into simple statements* :

Original. "O for a lodge in some vast wilderness!"

Paraphrase : I wish I had a secluded refuge far from the society of men.

Symbol for the thing signified :

When in the verse, a symbol is used for the thing signified, in paraphrasing it into prose, we should *mention the actual things* :

Original : "She was bred to the purple."

Paraphrasing : She was brought up in imperial surroundings.

Apostrophe:

Apostrophe in a paraphrase should be changed from the *second to the third person* :
Original : "Others abide our question. - Thou art free!"
Paraphrase : "We can freely criticize other authors, but you are beyond criticism."

Rhythm and Rhyme :

Rhythm and Rhyme are characteristic of verses in general.These have no place in prose and *should be avoided in paraphrasing.*

METHOD OF PROCEDURE : PARAPHRASING

(1) Read carefully through the original passage and try to understand its meaning .You can *read carefully twice or thrice* to make sure that you have grasped its exact meaning.

(2) Now read the passage again and *note down all the uncommon or difficult words*, all *idioms*, inversons and other unusual grammatical constructions, metaphors.Now concentrate your mind and express them by their *appropriate equivalents*.It must be well remembered that a good paraphrase contains all the essential details of the original.

(3) Your paraphrase should not be a literal translation ; a word for word paraphrase will invariably make nonsense. Render phrase by phrase or sentence by sentence; that is, ***render the thought rather than the words***.

(4) Do whatever is necessary, either to bring out the *full meaning of the passage* or to avoid redundancy. Thus, sometimes you will have to amplify and sometimes to condense a phrase or sentence from the original.

(5) If the original word or phrase is in all respects suitable, retain it. There is no need to find a substitute for every word.

(6) *Long and involved sentences* should be broken up into shorter ones. You may rearrange the *order of sentences*, even of the whole passage, if this will make the meaning clear.

(7) Explanatory notes should be avoided altogether. All explanations of difficulties must be in the body of the paraphrase itself. If you add *explanatory notes* at the end, it clearly shows that you have bungled in paraphrasing.

(8) Lastly, your finished paraphrase should be *compact* and *well connected*, look like a piece of good prose.

EXERCISES (SOLVED)

Exercise 1.

"Our life is not the life
Of roses and of leaves;
Else wherefore this deep strife,
This pain our soul conceives?
The fall of ev'n such short-lived things.
To us some sorrow brings."

Paraphrase 1.

The life of man is different from the life of roses and leaves .No doubt man too, like them is mortal, but the difference is that man's soul experiences a deep struggle against earthly limitation and always longs for eternal bliss and for life everlasting. Other earthly things know not of the soul. Man alone experiences this spiritual struggle. He alone yearns for immortal life. He alone feels the shortness of human life. Only he is pained to see the decay of such short lived things, as; the roses and leaves and struggles for an eternally better and happier life.

Exercise 2.

Ah love, let us be true
To one another! for the world, which seems
To lie before us like a land of dreams,
So various, so beautiful, so new
Hath really neither joy nor love not light,
Nor certitude, nor peace, nor help for pain;
And we are here as on a darkling plain
Swept with the confused alarms of struggle and flight,
Where ignorant armies clash by night.

—Matthew Arnold

Paraphrase 2.

Let us be true to the spirit of love, for the world which seems to lie before us, is like a dream land fascinating but delusive, unreal and unrealisable. There is in the world, though it appears to be full of variety and beauty and freshness neither everlasting joy nor unchangeable love. We find no thing of this world certain, our restless souls know neither peace nor help in case suffering and agonies befall. In this world, which is full of moral darkness, we are like the two armies that struggle and fight against each other, knowing not friend from foe and filling the plain with their confused din.

Exercise 3.

Let not Ambition mock their useful toil
Their homely joys, and destiny obscure:
Nor Grandeur hear, with a disdainful smile,
The short and simple annals of the poor
The boast of heraldry the pomp of pow'r
And all that beauty all that wealth e'er gave,
Awaits alike the inevitable hour:
The paths of glory lead but to the grave.

—Gary.

Paraphrase 3.

Ambitious men should not despise the useful labour of poor peasants. They should not laugh at their simple enjoyments or at the insignificant lives they lead. Nor should the people who think grand, noble and aristocratic, look with a smile of contempt at the short and eventless lives of the poor. Everything awaits death. The pride of power, the pride of beauty or wealth, all must meet the hour of death. All human fame and glory must end in the grave.

Exercise 4.

The glories of our blood and state
Are shadows, not substantial things;
There is no armour against Fate;
Death lays his icy hands on kings.
Sceptre and crown
Must tumble down.
And in the dust be equal made
With the poor crooked scythe and spade.

Paraphrase 4.

Nobility of birth and exalted rank, of which men so proudly boast. are mere illusions and quickly pass away. There is no protection against the common fate of all mankind-death. It does not spare even kings. Death is a great leveller, it destroys all artificial distinctions of birth and rank by making the proud kings lie side by side with the humblest and poorest of their subjects in the grave.

Exercise 5.

How happy is he born or taught,
That serveth not another's will;
Whose armour is his honest thought,
And simple truth his highest skill?
Whose passions not his masters are,
Whose soul is still prepared for death,
Untied unto the world with care
Of princes' grace or vulgar breath.

—Henry Wotton

Paraphrase 5.

He is happy , who because of inborn disposition or careful upbringing, does not serve to the will of others. He who cherishes honest and sincere thoughts in his mind, is really happy because his sincere thoughts protect his mind from harbouring any evil ideas and thus act as a defensive armour against all evil thoughts entering his mind. Such a man takes pains to speak the plain and unvarnished truth and this is greatest skill he possesses.

He is happy ,who is not a slave to his passions, but exercises a perfect control over them .He is happy, who is always prepared to welcome death and for whom death has lost all its terrors. He is happy, who is not devoted too much to the world, its worries and anxieties. He is truly happy, who does not hanker after favours from princes and who does not pine for winning public fame or popular applause.

Exercise 6.

What is this life, if full of care,
We have no time to stand and stare?
No time to stand beneath the boughs,
And stare as long as sheep or cows,
No time to see, when woods we pass,
Where squirrels hide their nuts in grass,
No time to see, in broad daylight,
Streams full of stars, like skies at night,
No time to turn at beauty's glance,
And watch her feet, how they can dance.

Walter de la Mare

Paraphrase 6.

It is but a dull and monotonous life if we are so engrossed in worldly cares and material pursuits, that we can find no time to stand and look idly about us. Life is not worth much if we get no leisure to stand beneath a tree and enjoy the sight of the sheep and cows grazing in the pastures. Life is not worth it, if we are so preoccupied as to not notice squirrels hiding their nuts in grass, and be charmed by the sight of the ripples playing upon a stream like the stars of night twinkling in the sky. If we are not overpowered by the looks of a beautiful woman and do not feel overjoyed at the rhythmic dance of her movements, we have missed the glory of life.

Exercise 7.

It is not growing like a tree,
In bulk, doth makes Man better be:
Or standing long an oak, three hundred year
To fall a log at last, dry bald, and sere;
A lily of a day
Is fairer far in May,
Although it fall and die that night;
It was the plant and flower of light,
In small proportions we just beauties see;
And in short measures life may perfect be.

—Ben Johnson

Paraphrase 7.

A man is not like a tree. An oak tree grows to a huge size, and lives for hundreds of years, only to fall at last to the ground, like a withered, dry and leafless log. Even so, a man may live for a long term of years without becoming noble in character; he has acquired bodily strength, but not good nature.

On the contrary, nature shows us that the smallest of her creatures, though they are short lived ; yet may be perfect and beautiful in every way; a lily that blossoms in summer, though it lives only for a few hours, is far more beautiful than the great oak and during its brief life, its radiant whiteness sheds joy and cheerfulness all around. So men, though they may live for a short period, can also make their lives beautiful and perfect by doing truly noble deeds.

FREQUENTLY USED SYNONYMS

Word	Synonyms
Abstain	Refuse, Renounce, Avoid, Shun,
Abandon	Desert, Forsake, Leave, Relinquish
Absurd	Ridiculous, Silly, Foolish, Preposterous
Abhor	Hate, Detest, Loathe, Abominate
Abase	Degrade, Disgrace, Humiliate, Demean, Dishonour, Stigmatize
Aberration	Deviation, Wandering, Errant, Irregular, Weird, Abnormal
Abbreviate	Curtail, Abridge, Compress, Shorten, Truncate
Abut	Adjoin, Border, Verge on, Join
Abet	Aid, Assist, Condone, Favour, Support, Promote
Abstruse	Recondite, Hidden, Difficult, Complex, Profound.
Assiduous	Painstaking, Diligent, Industrious, Laborious, Meticulous
Abundant	Ample, Copious, Plentiful, Bountiful
Adequate	Enough, Sufficient, Proportionate
Accommodate	Adapt, Adjust, Reconcile
Acme	Summit, Apex, Zenith, Peak
Acclaim	Applaud, Cheer, Celebrate, Extol
Acquiesce(in)	Assent, Rest, Accede, Comply, Concur, Consent, Submit
Admiration	Esteem, Praise, Respect, Approval, Approbation, Awe, Regard
Adherent	Sticking to, Follower, Partisan, Devotee
Affliction	Distress, Ordeal, Suffering, Sorrow
Adversity	Misfortune, Calamity, Catastrophe, Hostility
Ameliorate	Make better, Improve, Amend
Ally	Colleague, Helper, Partner, Accomplice
Audacious	Bold, Brazen, Impudent, Daring
Astonish	Amaze, Surprise, Astound, Flabbergast
Assistance	Help, Aid, Succor, Collaboration, Sustenance
Aphorism	Maxim, Apothegm, Axiom, Proverb, Motto, Adage
Apprehend	Seize, Know, Fear, Arrest, Understand
Appraise	Evaluate, Estimate, Assess, Assay
Antithesis	Contrasting, Reverse, Converse, Contrariety
Alms	Dole, Gratuity, Charity, Donation
Beg	Implore, Solicit, Supplicate, Beseech, Request, Plead
Behaviour	Conduct, Demeanour, Deportment, Manner
Base	Ignoble, Mean, Low, Foundation
Bad	Evil, Wicked, Devilish, Naughty, Worthless

Blame	Censure, Reprove, Condemn, Reproach
Blessing	Benediction, Benison, Benedicite
Banish	Exile, Ostracize, Deport
Barbaric	Savage, Uncivilized, Primitive.
Bait	Snare, Trap, Decoy
Brittle	Frail, Fragile, Crisp, Breakable.
Bizarre	Unusual, Grotesque, Fantastic
Bewilder	Confound, Perplex, Befuddle, Befog, Baffle, Daze, Stun
Belligerent	Warlike, Pugnacious, Hostile
Bedlam	Pandemonium, Chaos, Mayhem, Clamor, Confusion
Bravo	Fearless, Intrepid, Dauntless, Valiant, Bold
Burlesque	Mock, Imitate, Tease, Satirize, Ridicule, Jeer, Deride
Browbeat	Intimidate, Bully, Frighten, Threaten
Backlash	Repercussion, Reaction, Recoil
Banal	Dull, Trite, Hackneyed, Prosaic
Bigoted	Biased, Prejudiced, Dogmatic, Opinionated
Calm	Quiet, Tranquil, Peaceful, Sedate, Composed, Placid,
Cajole	Persuade, Flatter, Wheedle, Coax
Captious	Censorious, Hypercritical, Faultfinding
Care	Solicitude, Anxiety, Misgiving, Foreboding
Charlatan	Impostor, Mountebank, Quack, Chicane, Trickster
Choleric	Irascible, Petulant, Peevish, Irritable, Irascible.
Conceit	Pride, Vanity, Ego, Arrogance
Colossal	Gigantic, Huge, Enormous, Mammoth, Vast
Cynical	Surely, Misanthropic, Moody, Eccentric, Sardonic, Sarcastic
Conversant(with)	Familiar, Well versed, Acquainted
Condign	Due, Merited, Well deserved, Due, Suitable
Condone	Pardon, Forgive, Excuse, Overlook
Confess	Admit, Apologise, Own, Acknowledge
Contingent(on)	Liable, Possible, Uncertain
Constant	Eternal, Perpetual, Incessant, Continuous
Cross	Crusty, Fretful, Ill-humoured
Cursory	Hasty, Superficial, Careless
Concise	Short, Brief, Abridged, Compact
Crafty	Cunning, Artful, Sly, Calculating
Cruelty	Tyranny, Persecution, Brutality, Oppression, Ferocity

Damage	Loss, Harm, Injury, Detriment
Decay	Wither, Fade, Corrode, Decline
Destitute	Needy, Forsaken, Orphan
Didactic	Teaching, Instructive, Perfecting
Denounce	Accuse, Condemn, Arraign, Decry, Censure
Divine	Heavenly, Celestial, Graceful, Godlike
Dangerous	Perilous, Risky, Hazardous, Precarious
Dear	Expensive, Costly, Loved, Endeared.
Definitive	Limiting, Final, Positive
Desultory	Discontinuous, Irregular, Rambling
Diffident	Modest, Bashful, Shy
Discourse	Lecture, Sermon, Exhortation, Dissertation
Dissipate	Scatter, Waste, Disperse, Diffuse.
Economy	Management, Frugality, Thrifty, Judicious expenditure
Effete	Exhausted, Old, Worn out, Tired
Elicit	Draw out, Discover, Evoke, Extort
Elude	Baffle, Avoid, Cheat, Fool
Emancipate	Free, Liberate, Release, Deliver, Uplift
Emulate	Imitate, Rival, Copy, Follow
Entice	Lure, Persuade, Allure, Entrap
Extravagant	Prodigal, Wasteful, Spendthrift, Squander
Exquisite	Elegant, Fine, Matchless, Exclusive
Exceptional	Anomalous, Unique, Extraordinary
Extricate	Disentangle, Untangle, Disengage
Ephemeral	Transient, Short-lived, Evanescent, Fleeting
Exterminate	Uproot, Eradicate, Eliminate, Destroy, Annihilate
Exacerbate	Magnify, Heighten, Enlarge, Overstate, Amplify
Exculpate	Absolve, Vindicate, Exonerate, Forgive.
Exigency	Emergency, Distress, Contingency
Fascinate	Charm, Enchant, Mesmerize, Bewitch
Fastidious	Dainty, Squeamish, Hard to please
Fate	Lot, Destiny, End, Fortune, Luck
Fatuous	Silly, Purposeless, Inane, Foolish, Idiotic
Fight	Battle, Contention, Combat, Struggle, Conflict, Strife
Fury	Anger, Rage, Wrath, Ire (eg. Fury of Nature)
Fecund	Prolific, Fertile, Fruitful, Luxuriant, Productive

Ferocious	Savage, Barbaric, Fierce, Wild, Uncivilized
Fictitious	False, Imaginative, Illusionary, Fabricated, Fanciful
Flagrant	Notorious, Outrageous, Disgraceful
Fortuitous	Chance, Accidental, Serendipitous
Forerunner	Precursor, Herald, Harbinger
Forbid	Prohibit, Preclude, Inhibit, Debar
Flippant	Pert, Frivolous, Impudent, Saucy
Flamboyant	Bombastic, Ostentatious, Ornate
Fatal	Deadly, Mortal, Lethal, Virulent
Fallacy	Imperfection, Ambiguity, Quirk, Error
Fallible	Imperfect, Erring, Wrong
Furbish	Polish, Spruce, Renovate
Fortitude	Strength, Firmness, Valor, Determination
Guile	Fraud, Trickery, Cunning
Gratification	Satisfaction, Enjoyment, Pleasure, Delight
Garrulous	Talkative, Loquacious
Humane	Kind, Generous, Benevolent, Compassionate
Haughty	Arrogant, Proud, Egoist, Obstinate
Humility	Politeness, Meekness, Modesty
Hamper	Hinder, Block, Impede, Prevent
Illiterate	Unlearned, Ignorant, Uneducated
Impotent	Powerless, Disabled, Inadequate, Incapable (to reproduce etc.)
Immaterial	Unimportant, Insignificant, Useless, Irrelevant
Imminent	Threatening, Impending, Approaching
Irresolute	Undecided, Wavering, Vacillating, Unsettled
Indignant	Angry, Furious, Irate, Exasperated, Outraged
Inanimate	Lifeless, Dead, Dormant, Stagnant, Extinct
Ingenuous	Artless, Sincere, Naive, Innocent
Insidious	Cunning, Clever, Inventive, Deceitful, Sly
Intimate	Close, Confidant, Inform, Cherished
Inexorable	Relentless, Merciless, Apathetic, Harsh
Impertinent	Irrelevant, Impudent, Insolent, Saucy
Jolly	Jovial, Merry, Cheerful, Affable
Jubilant	Elated, Triumphant, Exultant, Rejoicing
Joy	Delight, Pleasure, Ecstasy, Elation
Knave	Fraud, Cheat, Scoundrel, Rogue

Lament	Sorrow,. Mourn, Grieve
Liberal	Generous, Kind, Tolerant, Permissive
Lenient	Forbearing, Forgiving, Compassionate, Mild
Lethargy	Laziness, Stupor, Sluggishness, Idleness
Likeness	Similarity, Resemblance, Affinity
Lively	Active, Enthusiastic, Agile, Brisk
Loyal	Devoted, Faithful, Trustworthy, Honest
Meagre	Small, Tiny, Inadequate, Scanty
Mean	Low, Petty, Abject, Selfish
Misery	Sorrow, Distress, Affliction, Grief
Morbid	Unhealthy, Diseased, Ghastly, Horrid, Sickly
Mournful	Sad, Sorrowful, Gloomy, Dejected
Mighty	Powerful, Massive, Strong, Almighty
Malice	Bitterness, Spite, Ill-will, Rancour, Malevolence
Melancholy	Sadness, Sorrow, Dejected, Dispirited, Unhappy
Magnificent	Splendid, Grand, Good, Glorious
Notorious	Infamous, Dishonourable, Flagrant, Blatant
Notable	Memorable, Remarkable, Renowned, Eminent
Obscene	Filthy, Indecent, Awful, Bawdy, Vulgar, Gross, Crude
Obsolete	Antiquated, Old-fashioned, Extinct, Outworn
Obtrude	Thrust, Pressure, Importunate, Interfere
Obliterate	Destroy, Efface, Demolish, Erase
Opportune	Timely, Convenient, Appropriate, Well-chosen
Pensive	Thoughtful, Rational, Contemplative, Reflective
Pathetic	Moving, Touching, Distressing, Lamentable
Pious	Religious, Holy, Devout, God-fearing
Perennial	Perpetual, Permanent, Long lasting, Constant
Portray	Delineate, Depict, Draw, Sketch
Possess	Have, Own, Acquire, Occupy, Seize
Prate	Chatter, Babble, Tattle, Talkative
Prodigal	Extravagant, Wasteful, Spendthrift, Squander
Precocious	Premature, Forward, Advanced, Developed
Philanthropist	Altruist, Charitable, Benevolent, Kind
Patronize	To act as a patron, To be kind or helpful
Penalize	Castigate, Chastise, Punish
Picturesque	Charming, Pictorial, Scenic, Sylvan

Prerogative	Privilege, Advantage, Exemption, Right
Prohibit	Forbid, Interdict, Prevent, Ban
Pillage	Plunder, Loot, Rob, Destroy, Steal
Poignant	Touching, Moving, Heart-rending
Quaint	Queer, Odd, Singular, Whimsical
Quirk	Whim, Caprice, Fancy, Vagary, Idiosyncrasy.
Quip	Retort, Repartee, Remark, Jest
Quarantined	Separated, Isolated, Restrained
Qualm	Scruple, Doubt, Uncertainty, Suspicion
Queer	Strange, Odd, Indifferent, Weird
Questionable	Doubtful, Disputable, Accountable, Objectionable
Quest	Search, Pursuit, Inquisitive, Crusade
Quick	Alive, Swift, Keen, Fast
Radiant	Brilliant, Bright, Intelligent, Beaming
Refined	Elegant, Polished, Cultured, Sophisticated
Rebellion	Mutiny, Revolt, Struggle, Fight
Reiterate	Repeat, Do it again, Rewrite, Emphasis
Remorse	Repentance, Regret, Anguish, Grief
Renown	Reputation, Fame, Famous, Distinguished
Rejoice	Exult, Delight, Happy, Glad
Relevant	Execute, Applicable, Pertinent, Implement
Resistance	Opposition, Hindrance, Combat, Struggle
Ruin	Destruction, Downfall, Wreckage, Devastation
Rigid	Stiff, Unyielding, Stern
Rash	Impetuous, Hasty, Foolhardy, Impulsive, Heedless, Brash
Refute	Disprove, Answer, Deny
Ricochet	Rebound, Reflect, Bounce, Carom
Rut	Groove, Hollow, Furrow, Habit, Course, Routine, Practice
Rural	Suburban, Rustic, Agrarian, Country
Radical	Fundamental, Native, Original, Extreme, Progressive, Rebellious
Rimy	Frosty, Hazy, Blurred
Remote	Far, Distant, Interior place, Aloof
Ridiculous	Absurd, Silly, Comical, Ludicrous
Sane	Wise, Sensible, Sound, Balanced
Satiate	Satisfy, Surfeit, Glut, Happy
Sacred	Holy, Consecrated, Blessed, Divine

Scanty	Meagre, Slender, Insufficient, Limited
Scold	Chide, Rebuke, Rail, Complain
Scrutinize	Examine, View, Study, Analyse, Inspect
Scorching	Sweltering, Searing, Burning, Fiery
Spry	Nimble, Agile, Animated, Brisk, Lively, Quick
Statute	Law, Decree, Ordinance, Edict, Rule, Act, Bill
Stipulation	Prerequisite, Condition, Qualification, Requirement, Clause
Subterfuge	Ploy, Scheme, Stratagem, Deceit, Deception
Substantiate	Authenticate, Validate, Confirm, Verify, Corroborate, Attest
Succinct	Brief, Concise, Terse, Abbreviated
Sensual	Carnal, Fleshy, Voluptuous, Attractive
Servile	Slavish, Docile, Timid, Menial, Obsequious
Shrewd	Astute, Perspicacious, Canny, Calculative
Shy	Bashful, Coy, Diffident, Hesitant
Solitary	Single, Hermetic, Isolated, Desolate
Sordid	Ugly, Dirty, Squalid, Debauched
Specimen	Prototype, Model, Sample, Dummy
Static	Firm, Adamant, Fixed
Spurious	Fake, Counterfeit, Artificial, False
Sterile	Unproductive, Barren, Impotent, Disinfected
Sublime	Exalted, Elevated, Improved, Magnified
Superficial	Shallow, Illusion, Dream, Outward
Synonymous	Identical, Equivalent, Alike, Similar
Taboo	Forbidden, Banned, Prohibited
Tenacious	Resolute, Persistent, Obstinate
Tenet	Belief, Conviction, Dogma, Doctrine, Creed, Theology
Therapeutics	Curative, Restorative, Recuperative, Remedial
Temperate	Moderate, Balanced, Controlled, Sensible
Thrive	Flourish, Succeed, Grow
Temporal	Worldly, Materialistic, Impermanent, Ephemeral
Tirade	Outburst, Denunciation, Harangue, Speech, Diatribe
Thankful	Grateful, Obliged, Indebted, Appreciative
Tentative	Temporary, Transitory, Brief
Tyrant	Autocrat, Despot, Dictator, Oppressor
Tyro	Amateur, Novice, Apprentice, Neophyte
Ulterior	Concealed, Shrouded, Obscured

Urchin	Waif, Stray, Foundling, Orphan
Urbane	Sophisticated, Suave, Polite, Refined, Polished
Unique	Unparalleled, Single, Peerless, Unusual, Exceptional, Matchless
Urge	Incite, Press, Implore, Instigate, Drive, Impel, Goad, Stimulate
Utopian	Idealistic, Perfect, Visionary, Quixotic
Vigilance	Watchfulness, Alertness, Attentiveness, Caution
Vindictive	Revengeful, Malicious, Resentful, Spiteful
Vehemence	Force, Passion, Emphasis, Obsession
Veracity	Truth, Honesty, Accuracy, Exactness, Correctness
Veto	Reject, Discard, Void, Nullify, Invalidate, Dismiss
Vilify	Malign, Slur, Defame, Slander
Vivacious	Sprightly, Spirited, Energetic
Weary	Exhausted, Tired, Devitalised, Drained
Wreck	Destroy, Devastate, Ruin, Demolish
Wistful	Melancholic, Sentimental, Plaintive, Nostalgic
Wile	Trickery, Artifice, Ruse, Chicanery, Hoax
Winsome	Beautiful, Captivating, Comely, Delightful, Charming
Waive	Forgo, Relinquish, Defer, Renounce
Yield	Surrender, Submit, Admit, Agree
Yearn	Crave, Desire, Aspire, Urge
Zeal	Zest, Passion, Enthusiasm, Fervour, Tempo
Zenith	Peak, Apex, Summit, Acme

ANTONYMS

Word	Opposite	Word	Opposite
Accustomed	Unusual	Active	Inert
Alert	Careless	Ample	Scanty, or meagre
Acquittal	Conviction	Economical	Extravagant
Arrogant	Humble	Ancient	Modern
Aches	Ecstasy	Elevation	Depression
Activity	Passivity	Ease	Difficulty
Barbarism	Civilization	Enthrone	Dethrone
Blunt	Sharp	Enrich	Impoverish
Bravery	Cowardice	Expedite	Impede
Belief	Disbelief	Entrance	Exit
Beauty	Ugliness	Ebb	Flow

Beneficial	Injurious, Harmful	Earning	Spending
Barren	Fertile	Enjoy	Suffer
Bride	Bridegroom	Fame	Infamy
Bless	Curse	Faith	Doubt
Blustering	Gentle	Genuine	Spurious
Boon	Bane	Faithful	Treacherous
Care	Neglect	Fail	Succeed
Cheerfulness	Gravity	Frankness	Reserve
Comparison	Contrast	Fresh	Stale
Classicism	Romanticism	Friendly	Hostile
Confidence	Diffidence	Full	Empty
Consent	Dissent	Firm	Infirm
Concord	Discord	Fortune	Misfortune
Confession	Denial	Fatigue	Refresh
Credit	Cash, Discredit	Flexible	Rigid
Continuity	Discontinuity	Front	Rear
Conceited	Modest	Fine	Coarse
Courage	Timidity	Favour	Frown
Complication	Simplification	Foreign	Native
Converge	Diverge	Gain	Lose
Civilized	Savage	General	Particular
Creation	Destruction	Genuine	Spurious
Cause	Effect	Guest	Host
Christian	Pagan	Gaiety	Gravity
Celebrated	Obscure	Giant	Dwarf
Optimist	Pessimist	Tragedy	Comedy
Principal	Subordinate	Town	Country
Prodigality	Parsimony	Top	Bottom
Philanthropist	Misanthropist	Uniform	Varied
Patriot	Traitor	Uncle	Nephew
Peace	War	Virtue	Vice
Plenty	Scarce	Violent	Gentle
Persuade	Dissuade	Vivacious	Languid
Plaintiff	Defendant	Voluntary	Compulsory
Pride	Humanity	Victor	Vanquished
Prohibition	Permission	Venturesome	Timid

Pure	Adulterated	Vague	Definite
Polite	Impolite	Written	Verbal
Pursuit	Avoidance	Poverty	Affluence
Wild	Domestic	Paradise	Purgatory
Worry	Comfort	Obscure	Clear
Salubrious	Unhealthy	Ruthless	Humane

PARONYMS

In English, we find several words, which are ***derived from the same root word***.These **words differ slightly in form but their meanings differ a lot**. Such words are called ***Paronyms*** :

1. **Alternate (by turn) :** He comes here on *alternate* days.
   Alternative (choice between two things) : There were *alternative* methods of travel available.
2. **Acceptance (accepting a thing, consent) :** I am happy to learn that she has given her *acceptance* for the attending the court.
   Acceptation (interpretation) : There are several *acceptations* of the word 'Nature'.
3. **Access (approach) :** I was not allowed *access* to a lawyer.
   Accession (becoming sovereign) : Today is the 50th anniversary of the queen's *accession* to the throne.
4. **Act (to do) :** I shall *act* as per the wishes of my parents.
   Action (doing things) : His timely *action* saved him from the loss.
5. **Admission (being admitted) :** He has taken *admission* in evening college.
   Admittance (to let in) : He was denied *admittance* in the hall.
6. **Artist (performer of fine art) :** A poet is no less an *artist* than a sculpture.
   Artiste (performer in singing, dancing etc.) : The group consists of several *artistes*.
7. **Artistic (having aesthetic values) :** This painting is indeed very *artistic*.
   Artful (cunning, clever) : He wants to achieve success by *artful* means.
   Artificial (Antonym of natural) : City life is becoming more *artificial* day by day.
   Artisan (well versed in handicrafts); The *artisans* of Nepal are very hardworking and efficient.
8. **Appropriation (to take possession of) :** He was charged for *appropriation* of Bank's fund.
   Appropriateness (suitability) : The work of Harivansh Rai Bachchan is renowned for its *appropriateness* in style.
9. **Affecting (touching, pathetic) :** The movie has many *affecting* scenes and situations.
   Affectation (false pretense) : Political leaders speak with *affectation* and artfulness.
10. **Besides (in addition) :** *Besides* paying my debt, he also gave me money for the medicines.
    Beside (by the side) : In Republic day function, none was sitting *beside* the President.

11. **Barbaric ('smple'-used in good sense) :** I like her *barbaric* simplicity.

Barbarian (primitive) 'Johar'and 'Sati' are the *barbarian* customs.

Barbarous (cruel-used in bad sense) : War is indeed a *barbarous* act.

12. **Barbarism (uncivilised condition) :** In some part of Bihar, absolute *barbarism* prevails even nowadays.

Barbarity (cruelty) : Aurangzeb was notorious for his *barbarity*.

13. **Confident (certain) :** I am *confident* that she will come.

Confidant (reliable) : He is a cheat, don't make him your *confidant*.

14. **Completion (end)** After *completion* of this work you are to go to Kolkata.

Completeness (perfection) : None can claim *completeness* of knowledge in any field.

15. **Ceremonious (overdone formalities) :** His greetings and salutations are too *ceremonious*.

Ceremonial (pertaining to ceremony) : Diwali is a *ceremonial* occasion for Hindus.

16. **Comprehensive (involves all aspects) :** This book gives us *comprehensive* knowledge of English.

Comprehensible (understandable) : His views on this subject are not only clear but *comprehensible* also.

17. **Considerable (much) :** I have spent a *considerable* time to solve this problem.

Considerate (thoughtful) : He being a *considerate* man, can't refuse to sign this proposal.

18. **Continuous (uninterrupted) :** He has been *continuously* working on computer for the last three hours.

Continual (occasional breaks) : There has been *continual* raining since yesterday.

19. **Child-like (in good sense-act like a child) :** Her *child-like* face attracts everybody.

Childish (in bad sense -silly act) : His childish habits annoyed everybody.

20. **Complacent (pleasing look, self satisfied) :** Indian farmer are *complacent* in their look.

Complaisant (polite) : She is a *complaisant* and intelligent girl.

21. **Dependent (adjective-to rely on) :** I am not *dependent* on anybody for my livelihood.

Dependant (*noun*-depend on others) : My younger brother is *dependant* on me (for home. food etc).

22. **Disinterested (without self interest) :** Mother Teresa rendered *disinterested* service to downtrodden.

Uninterested (indifferent) : Amitabh is *uninterested in* politics.

23. **Divers (several)** : *Divers* men are trying to reach the top.

Diverse (dissimilar-different) : *Diverse* opinions were given by the members on this proposal .

24. **Decided (past of decide) :** He *decided* to go to Europe the next week.

Decisive (that which decides some thing important) : The battle of Plassey was a *decisive* one.

25. **Destination (the place to reach) :** The last *destination* of this train is Puri.

Destiny (fate) : One can make his *destiny* with hard labour.

26. **Envious (feeling envy) :** You should not be *envious* of your friend's progress.

Enviable (arousing envy) : His *enviable* posting made many jealous of him.

27. **Effectual (creating desired effects) :** He adopted the *effectual* means and so got the contract.

Efficacious (sufficient to have desired result) : Quinine nowadays is not *efficacious* in malaria.

28. **Egotist (self conceited) :** I can not discuss anything with an *egotist* like you; Egotist-always talks of himself; a self admirer.

Egoist (selfish, self interested) : He is an *egoist*, he believes that self interest is the base of all actions; Egoist-always thinks of himself.

29. **Especially (pertaining to exceptional degree) :** Her mother was *especially* invited on the occasion.

Special (for the purpose) : I came *specially* to attend the function.

30. **Exceptional (unusual) :** J.L.Nehru was a man of *exceptional* qualities.

Exceptionable (objectionable) : His speech was full of *exceptionable* remarks.

31. **Exposition (description) :** Tennin's *exposition* of Ramayan is incomparable.

Exposure (open air, to cold etc.) : Protect yourself from *exposure*, otherwise you may catch cold.

32. **Economic (relating to economy) :** The *economic* condition of our country is not so good.

Economical (thrifty) : He is very *economical* in spending the money .

33. **Funeral (ceremony after death) :** More than ten thousand persons attended the *funeral* of his father.

Funereal (gloomy) : He came to the office with a *funereal* countenance.

34. **Fatal (deadly) :** He received a *fatal* wound in his chest.

Fatalist (believer in fate) : I am not a *fatalist*.

Fateful (lucky, important) : Fifteen August is a *fateful* day in Indian History.

35. **Forceful (commanding force) :** He enjoys a *forceful* personality.

Forcible (under compulsion) : Police made a *forcible* entry in his house.

36. **Godly (pious) :** Mahatma Gandhi led a *godly* life.

God-like (like God) : Mahatma Gandhi was a *God-like* man.

37. **Graceful (handsome-smart) :** She has a *graceful* appearance.

Gracious (kind) : God is *gracious*.

38. **Honorary (without any remuneration) :** He was nominated '*Honorary*' Chairman of the society.

Honourable (deserve honour, respected) : I request the *honourable* Principal to come on the dais.

39. **Imaginary (not real) :** Equator is an *imaginary* line.

Imaginative (pertaining to imagination) : A good writer must have *imaginative* ideas.

40. **Industrious (laborious) :** Nothing is impossible for an *industrious* and sincere student.

Industrial (relating to industry) : Bhiwadi is an *industrial* town.

41. **Intelligent (wise)** : He is an *intelligent* guy.

Intelligible (understandable) : He delivered an *intelligible* speech on educational necessities of rural area.

42. **Judicial (pertaining to legal system or Judge)** : Government has ordered a *judicial* enquiry in the matter.

Judicious (prudent , wise) : Going for a war is not a *judicious* decision.

43. **Loudly (high volume)** : Please do not speak so *loudly* in library room.

Aloud (audible voice) : He spoke *aloud* so that all could hear him.

44. **Luxuriant (refer more growth)** : There is a *luxuriant* growth of vegetables in our kitchen garden.

Luxurious (luxury) : He is leading a *luxurious* life after the death of his father.

45. **Lovable (worthy of love)** : He is a *lovable* person.

Lovely (charming) : What a *lovely* girl she is !

46. **Limit (boundary)** : Keep yourself within the *limits*, otherwise you have to face the music.

Limitation (restrictions) : Being a girl, I have many *limitations*.

47. **Memorial (statue or building to commemorate)** : You can find many *memorials* at Rajpath, New Delhi.

Memorable (rememberable) : 26th January is a *memorable* day in Indian History.

48. **Momentary (for a moment)** : His anger is *momentary*, soon things will be okay.

Momentous (important) : The battle of Plassey was a *momentous* event in the history of India.

49. **Negligible (unimportant)** : There is a *negligible* difference between this shirt and the shirt we saw in that shop.

Negligent (careless) : She is generally *negligent* about her health.

Neglectful (careless about a thing) : She is so *neglectful* that she does not care even for her career.

50. **Officious (over kind)** : His *officious* attitude towards her, creates doubts.

Official (relating to office) : As a responsible *official* of a company you must behave properly.

51. **Practical (antonym of theoritical)** : He failed in *practical* examination;

He is a practical business man

Practicable (capable of being carried out) : This is not a *practicable* plan.

52. **Political (relating to politics)** : We should not trust the *political* statements of leaders.

Politic (sagacious, prudent) : It is not *politic* to argue with an intoxicated person.

53. **Pitiable (relating to pity)** : His condition is indeed *pitiable*.

Pitiful (feeling pity) : Seeing her pitiable condition, every one became *pitiful*.

54. **Prophecy (*noun*-forecast)** : He made a *prophecy* that whole of the world would be destroyed in 2202.

Prophesy (to forecast) : I can *prophesy* that within five years India will be a very powerful country.

55. **Respective (particular thing or person)** : After prayer, students should join their *respective* teams.

Respectful (respected) : One should be *respectful* to one's teachers, elders.

56. **Righteous (just)** : Her anger was *righteous* as no girl can tolerate such insult.

Rightful (just claim) : I am the *rightful* owner of this car.

57. **Regrettable (causing regret)** : It is quite *regrettable* that you are not taking care of your father.

Regretful (full of regret) : I am not at all *regretful* for my actions.

58. **Servility (flattery)** : I can't adopt an attitude of *servility* to get promotion.

Servitude (slavery) : Try to come out of this state of *servitude*.

59. **Sociable (fond of getting social)** : She has a *sociable* nature.

Social (relates to society) : She is not only *social* but also very cooperative.

60. **Sensuous (used in good sense for appreciation of beauty)** : Keats was a *sensuous* poet.

Sensual (used in bad sense, means-voluptuous) : He was jailed for his *sensual* advancement towards his college friend.

61. **Sensitive (touchy)** : Cow slaughter is a *sensitive* issue for Hindus.

Sensational (exciting) : There are many *sensational* stories of murder in this magazine.

62. **Spirituous(alcoholic)** : Gujarat has banned the use of *spirituous* drinks in restaurants.

Spiritual (pertaining to soul) : She is a *spiritual* lady.

63. **Tolerant (refer to a person, who respects different opinions also)** : Akbar was regarded as a *tolerant* king.

Tolerable (bearable) : Because of his *tolerable* nature, he didn't lodge FIR against you.

64. **Temperament (disposition)** : Because of his violent *temperament*, he gets into trouble.

Temperance (sobriety) : He should observe *temperance* in drinking and dancing.

65. **Temporal (antonym to spiritual)** : Nowadays, people are ready to do anything for *temporal* gains.

Temporary (a short time) : I offered her a *temporary* job.

66. **Transitory (short lived)** : The life is not eternal but *transitory*.

Transient (of short duration) : The world is *transient*.

67. **Union (to be united)** : *Union* is strength .

Unity (one ness) : There is no *unity* among different classes of the society.

Unison (harmony) : There was a good *unison* of Tabla and Violin in the cultural programme.

68. **Virtual (in effect)** : Sanjay Gandhi was the *virtual* head of Congress Party.

Virtuous (of good moral values) : Sita was a *virtuous* lady.

69. **Wilful (knowingly)** : He was charged for *wilful* negligence.

Willing (ready) : I am *willing* to help her.

70. **Womanly (used in good sense-affectionately)** : My wife possesses all *womanly* qualities.

Womanish (used in bad sense, means-cowardly and weak like woman) : Everyone likes to dominate a man of *womanish* temperament.

71. **Wait (generally used intransitively)** : Please *wait* for me .

Await (used intransitively) : A surprise *awaited* them at their home.

72. **Weary(tired)** : You look pale and *weary*.

Wearisome(tiring) : The journey was *wearisome*.

73. **Yield (return)** : What is the annual *yield* from the fields?

Yielding (submissive) : He is a man of *yielding* nature.

ONE WORD SUBSTITUTIONS

1. Abdication	:	Voluntarily renouncing throne.
2. Aborigines	:	Original inhabitants of a country.
3. Accessible	:	Which can be approached.
4. Acclimatize	:	To accustom oneself in new climate.
5. Aggressor	:	One, who attacks first.
6. Alimony	:	Allowance paid to wife on legal separation.
7. Altruist	:	One, who loves others.
8. Amateur	:	One, who does things for pleasure and not for money.
9. Ambassador	:	Person representing a state in a foreign country.
10. Ambidextrous	:	One, who can use either hand without any problem.
11. Ambiguous	:	That can be interpreted in any way.
12. Amnesia	:	Loss of memory
13. Amphibia	:	Animals, that live both on land and in water; eg., frog.
14. Anarchy	:	Absence of rule or law and order.
15. Annual	:	Which happens once a year.
16. Anomaly	:	Deviation from common rule.
17. Anonymous	:	Which does not bear the name of writer.
18. Antiseptic	:	Medicine used to save plants and animals from being rotten or decayed.
19. Antonym	:	Words which are opposite in meaning.
20. Aphasia	:	Loss of speech

21. Aquarium : Vessel in which fish and water plants are kept.
22. Aquatic : Animals, that live in water.
23. Archaeology : Study of antiquities
24. Aristocracy : Government by the rich/aristocrats.
25. Ascetic : One, who tortures himself for the realisation of soul.
26. Atheist : One, who does not believe in existence of God.
27. Audible : Sound, which can be heard.
28. Auditor : One, who audits the accounts.
29. Aurist : A specialist with regard to the ear.
30. Autobiography : Life history written by self.
31. Autocracy : Government by one man.
32. Autograph : Signature of some important person in his handwriting
33. Bachelorhood : State of being unmarried.
34. Bankrupt : One, who can't pay the debts.
35. Bellicose : One, who is fond of fighting .
36. Belligerents : Nations or persons engaged in war.
37. Bibliophile : One, who loves and collects books.
38. Biennial : Happening every second year.
39. Bigamy : Having two husbands or two wives at a time.
40. Biography : Life history of a person.
41. Biped : Animal having two feet.
42. Blasphemy : Speaking disrespectfully about sacred or religious things.
43. Bookworm : One, who devotes full time in studying course books.
44. Botany : Study of Plants.
45. Brigand : A bandit or robber, esp. one of a band living by pillage and ransom.
46. Brittle : Which can be easily broken.
47. Bullion : Gold or silver before using for manufacturing ornaments.
48. Bureaucracy : Government run by officials.
49. Caducity : The infirmity of old age, senility.
50. Calligraphy : The art of beautiful handwriting; elegant penmanship.
51. Cannibal : One, who eats human flesh.
52. Centrifugal : Anything, tending to move away from centre.
53. Centripetal : Anything, tending to move towards the centre
54. Century : One hundred year.
55. Colleagues : Persons, working in the same office.

56. Compatriot : Belonging to same country.
57. Congenital : Belongs to a person by birth.
58. Contemporaries : Persons, living at the same time; Ram and Valmiki were *contemporaries*.
59. Convalescence : Period of gradual recovery after illness.
60. Cosmopolitan : A citizen of the world; Many plants are *cosmopolitan* in distribution.
61. Credulous : One, who easily believes others.
62. Cryptography : Study of secret writing and coded words.
63. Curable : Which can be cured.
64. Cytology : Study of cell.
65. Dead letter : An unclaimed letter.
66. Deaf : One, who can not hear.
67. Democracy : Government of the people, for the people, by the people.
68. Dermatology : Study of skin.
69. Digestible : That which can be digested.
70. Dipsomania : A strong desire to take liquor
71. Divisible : That which can be divided.
72. Dotage : Extreme old age, when one behaves like a child.
73. Drawn : A game in which no party wins, III form of the verb-'draw'.
74. Dumb : One, who can't speak.
75. Edible : A thing fit to eat.
76. Effeminate : Womanish in habits.
77. Eligible : One, who is fit for the post.
78. Emigrant : One, who goes to live in a foreign country.
79. Employee : One, who is employed.
80. Employer : One, who employes.
81. Endemic : A disease prevailing in a locality.
82. Entomology : Study of insects.
83. Epic : A long narrative poem.
84. Epicure : One, who is fond of sensuous enjoyment.
85. Epilogue : A speech given after conclusion of drama.
86. Epitaph : Words, inscribed on the tomb of the dead.
87. Etymology : Science, dealing with formation of words.
88. Etymology : Study of word.
89. Examinee : One, who is taking examination.

90. Examiner	:	One, who examines the copies of examinees.
91. Expatriate	:	To send out of native country.
92. Expurgate	:	To remove all objectionable matter;eg., from records.
93. Extempore	:	A speech without previous preparations.
94. Extradite	:	To send back the criminal to the country of his origin.
95. Fanatic (Bigot)	:	Unreasonably enthusiastic about religion.
96. Fastidious	:	Having very selective taste, Hard to please.
97. Fatalist	:	One, who believes in fate.
98. Feminist	:	One, devoted to the welfare of women.
99. Foster child	:	Child brought by persons, who are not his parents.
100. Franchise	:	Constitutional right to cast vote.
101. Fratricide	:	Murder of brother.
102. Garage	:	A shed for motor car.
103. Geology	:	Study of Earth.
104. Germicide	:	Which destroy germs.
105. Glutton	:	Fond of eating too much.
106. Gratis	:	Without any payment, Free.
107. Gregarious	:	Animals, that live in flocks, persons who like being in company.
108. Harangue	:	A noisy and loud speech before a large gathering.
109. Hearse	:	Vehicle to carry dead bodies.
110. Herbivorous	:	Animals, that live on herbs.
111. Heterogeneous	:	Things of different nature.
112. Histology	:	Study of tissue.
113. Homicide	:	Murder of a human being.
114. Homogeneous	:	Things of same nature.
115. Honeymoon	:	The first night of newly married couple.
116. Honorary	:	A post without any remuneration.
117. Hydra	:	A mythological serpent with many heads.
118. Hydrophobia	:	A fear from water.
119. Hygienist	:	Who cares fully for his health.
120. Hypothesis	:	A tentative assumption, made to drive a logical conclusion
121. Iconoclast	:	Breaker of art, literature and icons.
122. Idiosyncrasy	:	Peculiar temper of an individual.
123. Idolatry	:	Worshiping of idols.
124. Ignorant	:	Person, who has no knowledge of any happening.
125. Illegal	:	Unlawful.

126. Illegible	:	Which cannot be read.
127. Illiterate	:	One, who can neither read nor write.
128. Imitable	:	Which can be imitated, copied
129. Immigrant	:	A person from another country, who comes to our country to settle.
130. Immovable	:	Which can't be moved, Fixed.
131. Imposter	:	One, who assumes name or title of someone else for deceiving others.
132. Impregnable	:	A fort which can't be entered into.
133. Incorrigible	:	That cannot be corrected.
134. Incredible	:	Which can't be believed.
135. Inevitable	:	That cannot be avoided.
136. Infallible	:	One, who cannot make a mistake or do wrong, Never failing.
137. Infanticide	:	Murder of an infant.
138. Infections	:	A disease spread by contact, through air or carriers, like-mosquito etc.
139. Inimitable	:	That cannot be imitated.
140. Insomnia	:	Loss of sleep.
141. Interpolate	:	Inserting new matter in a book.
142. Intervenes	:	Anything pushed inside veins
143. Invisible	:	That which cannot be seen.
144. Invulnerable	:	Cannot be wounded.
145. Irreparable	:	That can't be repaired.
146. Irrevocable	:	A decision that can't be revoked.
147. Itinerant	:	One, who travels from place to place (eg. band of musicians).
148. Kindergarten	:	A school for small children.
149. Kleptomania	:	An abnormal desire to steal.
150. Linguist	:	One, who knows many languages.
151. Loquacious	:	A continuous talker.
152. Lunar	:	Eclipse of moon, pertaining to moon.
153. Maiden speech	:	Speech delivered for the first time.
154. Mammals	:	Animals, which give milk.
155. Manuscript	:	Script of book , as first written out or typed .
156. Masochism	:	The condition or state of deriving (esp. sexual) gratification from one's own pain or humiliation.
157. Materialistic	:	One, for whom money is the most important thing.

158. Matins : Morning prayer in church.
159. Matricide : Murder of own mother.
160. Matrimony : State of being married.
161. Maxim : An established principle, aproverb, a saying.
162. Meadow : A low level tract of uncultivated grassland.
163. Meditation : The action or practice of profound spiritual or religious reflection or mental contemplation.
164. Melodrama : A sensational dramatic piece with crude appeals to the emotions and usually a happy ending.
165. Mercenary : One who fights for the sake of money.
166. Mesomorph : A person whose build is powerful, compact, and muscular.
167. Meteorology : Study of climate or weather.
168. Meticulous : Very particular, even about small details.
169. Migratory : That moves from one place to another; eg-migratory birds.
170. Misogamist : One, who hates the custom of marriage.
171. Misogynist : Hater of women.
172. Misologist : One, who hates learning.
173. Mobocracy : Rule by mob.
174. Monogamy : Marrying one at a time.
175. Morphology : Study of animal and plant structure
176. Narcotic : Medicine which induces sleep.
177. Neologism : New word coined by an author.
178. Neology : Study of formation of new words.
179. Notorious : A man with bad reputation, Infamous
180. Numismatics : Study of coins.
181. Obsolete : No longer in practice.
182. Oceanography : Study of ocean.
183. Odontology : Study of teeth.
184. Oligarchy : Government by a few.
185. Omnipotent : One, who is all powerful.
186. Omniscient : One, who knows everything.
187. Omnivorous : One, who eats every thing.
188. Opaque : That which can't be seen through.
189. Ophthalmology : Study of eye.
190. Optics : Study of light.
191. Optimist : One who sees bright side of things.

192. Ornithology : Study of birds.
193. Orography : Study of mountains.
194. Orphan : A child whose parents are dead.
195. Orthodox : One, who believes in traditional values.
196. Orthography : Study of correct spelling of words.
197. Ostracize : To expel from society.
198. Pacifist : One, who believes in total abolition of war.
199. Paleontology : Study of fossils.
200. Panacea : A remedy for all ills.
201. Pantisocracy : Government by all.
202. Pantomime : A dumb show.
203. Parasite : One, who depends on others.
204. Parasol : A lady's umbrella.
205. Pathology : Study of Disease.
206. Patricide : Murder of one's own father.
207. Patrimony : Properties inherited from one's father.
208. Patriot : One, who loves own country.
209. Pedagogy : Study of Art of teaching.
210. Pedantic : A style in which author displays his knowledge.
211. Pedestrian : One, who travels on foot.
212. Pessimist : One, who sees dark side of things.
213. Philanderer : One, who enjoys by love making.
214. Philanthropist : A lover of mankind.
215. Philately : Study of Stamp collection.
216. Philistine : One, who does not care for art or literature.
217. Philogynist : Lover of womankind.
218. Philology : Study of words and their roots.
219. Phonetics : Acoustics, Study of sound
220. Phrenology : Study of shape of skull with regard to human character.
221. Physiology : Study of normal functions of human (animal) body.
222. Pioneer : One, who leads others.
223. Plagiarism : Literary theft; Using ideas and words of another person, presenting them as own.
224. Platitudes : Common place remarks.
225. Plutocracy : Government by rich.
226. Polyandry : Marrying more than one man at a time.

227. Polygamy : Marrying more than one woman at a time.
228. Post mortem : An examination of body after death.
229. Primogeniture : Right of succession, belonging to the first born.
230. Pseudonym : An imaginary name of author, assumed to disguise himself.
231. Pugnacity : Tendency to quarrel.
232. Purist : One, who is particular about the purity of one's language.
233. Quadruped : Animal having four foot.
234. Rebel : One, who takes up arms against government or resists authority.
235. Redtapism : Too much official formalities.
236. Regicide : Murder of a king.
237. Reticule : A lady's purse.
238. Retrospective : Which takes effect from some earlier date.
239. Sacrilege : Violating sanctity of some religious place.
240. Sadist : A person who derives pleasure (esp. sexual) from inflicting pain, suffering, humiliation.
241. Shrew : A woman with peevish nature.
242. Simultaneous : Happening at the same time.
243. Smuggle : Importing goods illegally without paying custom duties.
244. Solar : Eclipse of Sun, pertaining to sun.
245. Soliloquy : Speaking himself, when alone.
246. Somnambulism : Walking in sleep.
247. Somniloquism : Talking in sleep.
248. Spokesman : One, who speaks on behalf of other.
249. Stoic : One, who is indifferent to pleasure and pain; has a great self control.
250. Suicide : Killing of self.
251. Synchronize : Two or more events, happening at a time; eg-Synchronize all the clocks in a builaling.
252. Teetotaller : One, who does not take alcoholic drinks.
253. Telltale : One, who enjoys talking about others' private affairs.
254. Thearchy : Government by the God.
255. Theist : One who believes in the existence of God.
256. Theomania : A belief that one is God.
257. Transmigration : Passing of soul (subtle body), from one body to another after death.
258. Transparent : That which can be seen through.

259. Truant : A student, leaving school or class without permission.
260. Truism : An often repeated truth.
261. Twins : Two child born together.
262. Usurer : One who lends money at higher rate of interest.
263. Utopia : A state of highest perfection impracticable to achieve.
264. Uxoricide : Murder of wife.
265. Valetudinarian : One who always thinks that he is ill.
266. Venial : An excusable fault.
267. Verbatim : Repetition - word by word.
268. Verbose : Style, full of words.
269. Vesper : Evening prayer in a church.
270. Veteran : A well and long experienced person in a particular occupation.
271. Wardrobe : An almirah, where clothes are kept.
272. Widow : A woman, whose husband has died.
273. Widower : A man, whose wife has died.
274. Zoology : Study of animals.

HOMONYMS

***Words similar in sound , but different in meanings** are called Homonyms :*

1. **Affect (to act upon, to pretend)** : She *affects* too much innocence. The drought *affected* a large part of the district.
   Effect (result) : Internet produces a bad *effect* on the young generation.
2. **Adapt (accomodate)** : One should *adapt* oneself to the new circumstances.
   Adept (expert) : He is an *adept* in Folk dance.
   Adopt (take up) : One should not *adopt* unfair means to secure good marks.
3. **Addition (putting more)** : I am to buy two more copies in *addition* to this one.
   Edition (of printing books) : The first *edition* of this book has sold like hot cakes.
4. **Accede (agree) :** He will not *accede* to your request.
   Exceed (to be greater) : Write an essay, not *exceeding* three hundred words.
5. **Access (approach, reach)** : Now a days, every person has an easy *access* to the temples irrespective to his caste.
   Excess (more than enough) : *Excess* of everything is bad.
6. **Accept (to take/agree)** : He can not *accept* this gift.
   Except (leaving out) : *Except* Nisha, everyone was present in the party.
7. **Alter (change)** : You can not *alter* my opinion about her.
   Altar (place of offering) : S.C. Bose sacrificed everything at the *altar* of freedom. In India incense is burnt at the altar in temples.

8. **Antic (odd, strange)** : His behaviour, yesterday, was antic.

Antique (ancient) : I am fond of collecting *antique* items.

9. **Assay (attempt, testing the purity of metals)** :

1. He *assayed* hard to secure top position.
2. He *assayed* the gold ornaments.

Essay (a piece of composition) : Write a brief *essay* on 'Indian Films'.

10. **All ready (all are ready)** : They were *all ready* to welcome the groom.

Already (earlier) : I have *already* informed him.

11. **Allusions(indirect reference)** : The poem is full of *allusions*.

Illusion (a deceptive show) : Indian mythology regards the material world as an *illusion*.

12. **Apposite (proper)** : His arguments were not *apposite* to the subject.

Opposite (contrary-in front of) : His house is *opposite* to the college.

13. **Assent (agreement)** : He gave his *assent* to the new proposal.

Ascent (going up) : He pushed the button and the elevator began its *slow ascent*.

14. **Arc (part of circle)** : If a straight line is drawn in a circle it will divide it into two *arcs*.

Ark (covered floating vessel) : He crossed the Black Sea with his family in an *ark*.

15. **Aloud (high volume)** : I can't hear you well,please speak *aloud*.

Allowed (permitted) : He was *allowed* to enter .

16. **Angle (An angle of degree)** : This is a ninety degree *angle*.

Angels (a divine messenger) : *Angels* reside in heaven while men reside on earth.

17. **Advice (noun)** : I need your expert *advice* in this matter.

Advise (verb) : Please *advise* me in this matter.

18. **Amiable (lovable)** : She is not only a beautiful but also an *amiable* girl.

Amicable (friendly) : Finally they came to an *amicable* settlement.

19. **Ail (to be ill)** : What *ails* the Industry is to be sorted out.

Ale (a drink) : He has gone to the *ale-house*.

20. **All together (in a body)** : Let us move there *all together*.

Altogether (completely) : It seems *altogether* impossible to cross the river in the night.

21. **Bale (package)** : I received thirty *bales* of cotton last month.

Bail (security) : The magistrate didn't grant him *bail* in theft case.

22. **Berth (sleeping place in train)** : I have booked two *berths* in Shatabdi express.

Birth (coming to life) : This is not the *birth* place of Buddha.

23. **Bare (uncovered)** : He came here *bare* footed.

Bear (to tolerate) : I cannot *bear* your insulting remarks.

Bear (an animal) : There are three *bears* in that circus.

Beer (a kind of wine) : I prefer to take *beer*.

24. **Blow (to whistle)** : A cool wind is *blowing*; Don't blow the whistle.

Below (under neath) : Hitting *below* the belt is not allowed.

25. **Born (To take birth)** : My wife was *born* in 1960.

Borne (supported) : He is suffering from water *borne* disease.

26. **Bad (not good)** : He is a *bad* man.

Bed (sleeping place) : I go to *bed* at 11P.M.

27. **By (assistance)** : A snake was killed *by* Ram with a stick.

Buy (purchase) : I want to *buy* a car.

28. **Beet (A vegetable)** : I prefer mango to *beet.*

Beat (to thrash) : It is wrong to *beat* the students with a stick.

29. **Borrow (to take loan)** : I have *borrowed* some money from Bank.

Burrow (a hole in earth) : A mouse lives in this *burrow*.

30. **Cell (a small cottage)** : There are more than twenty *cells* in that prison.

Sell (to dispose off) : He *sells* fruits and vegetables.

Sale (*noun-act* of selling) : I have purchased this dress from that shop *on sale*.

31. **Beach (shore)** : Many people like to walk along the sea *beach*.

Beech (a kind of tree) : There are many *Beech* trees near the railway station.

32. **Brake (lever)** : I am going to get the *brake* wire changed .

Break (to make apart) : Can you *break* this stick with your hands ?

33. **Bow (bend)** : Let us *bow* to our motherland India.

Bough (a branch of tree) : Many birds are sitting on the *bough* of the tree.

34. **Bridal (pertaining to marriage)** : She is looking beautiful in her *bridal* dress.

Bridle (reins) : It is not easy to *bridle* a vicious horse.

35. **Baron (a landlord)** : There was a time when all powers rested in the hands of rich *barons*.

Barren (not fertile) : In *barren* land, you can't cultivate any thing.

36. **Blue (a colour)** : I like *blue* colour.

Blew (whistled) : The refree *blew* the whistle again and again.

37. **Check (to verify, to stop)** : He *checked* my passport; He checked me from leaving the function.

Cheque (Bank document) : I issued a *cheque* favouring P.N.B.

38. **Calendar (chart showing Dates etc.)** : I have only one *calendar* in my office.

Calender (to press paper, cloth etc.) : Please *calender* my dress.

39. **Cannon (big gun)** : A *cannon* of ancient time is placed near the railway station.

Canon (rule) : He believes in *canons* of justice.

40. **Canvas (a kind of rough cloth)** : My shoes are made of *canvas*.

Canvass (to solicit votes) : Nowadays students are busy in *canvassing* for their friends.

41. **Casual (accidental, occasional)** : I was granted only one day *casual* leave.

Causal (showing cause) : There is a *causal* link between balanced diet and sound mind.

42. **Corpse (dead body)** : The *corpse* was covered with a white sheet of cloth.

Corps (a body of troops) : I want to join National Cadet *Corps*.

43. **Coma (state of senselessness)** : The patient has been in *coma* since Monday.

Comma (mark of punctuation) : One should be careful about proper use of *comma*.

44. **Cession (to yield)** : India should not have made a *cession* of an inch of its land for the establishment of Pakistan.

Session (sitting of assemble or court) : The winter *session* of parliament will be over tomorrow.

45. **Censer (a pot in which incense is burnt)** : Place some incense into the *censer*.

Censor (an official examination) : The *censor* board has awarded 'U' certificate to this film.

Censure (criticize adversely) : His conduct was *censured* by the parliament.

46. **Chord (a string of musical instrument)** : He is playing with the *chords* of the violin.

Cord (a thin rope) : I need a fifteen feet long *cord* for packing the luggage .

47. **Cease (discontinue)** : He resigned and thus *ceased* to be the chairman of our society.

Seize (to catch) : Heroin worth two lacs rupees is *seized* from his office.

Siege (surrounded) : Akbar's army *sieged* the castle of Chittorgarh.

48. **Career (profession)** : For better *career* opportunities, join computer courses.

Carrier (one who carries) : Mosquitoes are the *carriers* of malaria.

49. **Coarse (rough)** : Do not use a *coarse* cloth to clean the glasses.

Course (line of action) : A disciplined *course* of action is required to achieve success.

50. **Collision (clash)** : In a *collision* between train and bus, three persons died on the spot.

Collusion (secret agreement for an evil plan) : He planned to execute a robbery in *collusion* with the clerk.

51. **Cloth (unstitched cloth)** : I want to purchase *cloth* for a shirt and a trousers.

Clothe (stitched cloth) : I have given my *clothes* to washerman for drycleaning.

52. **Capital (centre of administration)** : Delhi is the *capital* of India.

Capitol (Roman temple of Jupiter, US Congress House) :
A meeting of US congress will be held in *Capitol* tomorrow.

53. **Defy (challenge)** : One should not *defy* the orders of one's superiors.

Deify (worship like a God) : Mr. M.K.Gandhi is *deified* by all Indians.

54. **Complacent (self satisfied)** : He seems *complacent* with his job and earning.

Complaisant (polite) : He is a man of very *complaisant* nature.

55. **Complement (which completes)** : Husband and wife are *complementary* to each other.

Compliment (regards) : Please convey my best *compliments* to your parents.

56. **Cautious (aware)** : I am quite *cautious* of his activities.

Conscientious (careful, scrupulous) : My mother is very hard working , sincere and *conscientious* lady.

57. **Council (assembly)** : He was nominated to the *Council* of State .

Counsel (advice) : He *counsels* in a right way.

58. **Credible (believable)** : He is not a *credible* person.

Creditable (worthy of praise) : His achievements are indeed *creditable*.

59. **Cymbal (a musical instrument)** : I like the melodious sound of the *Cymbal.*

Symbol (sign) : What was the *symbol* for last Olympic Games.

60. **Current (present)** : What is the *current* news?

Currant (dried grapes) : I am fond of *currants*.

61. **Cite (speak)** : He *cited* the example of bravery of Maharana Pratap.

Site (location) : In my opinion, this *site* for the departmental store is commercially viable.

Sight (view) : It was a pitiable *sight*.

Sight (vision) : Get your eye *sight* checked at the earliest.

62. **Caste (community)** : He belongs to schedule *caste*.

Cast (to give) : Please *cast* your votes in favour of me.

63. **Cattle (animal)** : *Cattle* were grazing in the field.

Kettle (vessel) : Put the *kettle* on the gas-burner.

64. **Corporal (pertaining to body)** : *Corporal* punishment is banned nowadays in all schools and colleges.

Corporeal (bodily, material) : God has no *corporeal* existence.

65. **Desert (a waste track of land -noun; to forsake-verb)** : Churu is a *desert* area in Rajasthan; He has deserted his wife.

Dessert (fruit served after dinner) : The *dessert* course after dinner was liked by all.

66. **Decry (to cry down)** : The Iraq policy of US government was *decried* by Indian Govt.

Descry (to see dimly) : Across the river you can *descry* a hut near the palm tree.

67. **Dye (a verb-to colour)** : *Dye* my shirt in sky blue shade.

Die (expire) : He *died* from cholera.

68. **Dose (quantity of medicine)** : I have already taken four *doses* of this medicine by now.

Doze (sleep) : You were *dozing* in the class yesterday.

69. **Draught (a quantity of liquid)** : The patient was given a *draught* of medicine.

Drought (want of rain) : Due to scanty rain, whole of the district is in the grip of *drought*.

70. **Dam (surrounding the area to stop flow of water)** : A *dam* is being built up here for storage of the rainy water.

Damn (condemn) : His behaviour is *damned* by all the members of the society.

71. **Dear (loving)** : He is my very *dear* friend.

Deer (an animal) : I saw many deer in that forest.

72. **Deduce (draw conclusion)** : You can't *deduce* such a conclusion from the discussion.

Deduct (to take something) : *Deduct* cash discount 3 % and make the payment by tomorrow.

73. **Deference (respect)** : I treat my elders with due *deference*.

Difference (dissimilarity) : There was a *difference* of opinion on this point.

74. **Decent (good)** : Because of his *decent* behaviour, he was promoted to the post of General Manager.

Descent (coming down) : That hill has a steep *descent* to the south.

Dissent (to differ) : He recorded his *dissent* on this proposal.

75. **Device (*noun*-plan)** : He used all *devices* to popularise the game.

Devise (*verb*- to plan) : You are to *devise* a plan to increase the turn over.

76. **Duel (a fight between two)** :There was a *duel* between Dara Singh and King Kong.

Dual (double) : *Dual* system of governance is a bad governance.

77. **Disease (illness)** : Malaria is a curable *disease*.

Decease (death) :The sudden *decease* of his father forced him to abandon his studies .

78. **Eruption (bursting out)** : There was an *eruption* of volcano near Gujrat border.

Irruption (Invasion) : The *irruption* of Mughals destroyed the glory of Rajput empire.

79. **Emerge (to come out)** : He *emerged* successfully out of the miserable circumstances.

Immerge (to plunge into) : He is *immerged* in mythological thoughts.

80. **Eminent (distinguished)** : Indira Gandhi was an *eminent* politician.

Imminent (impending) : Indian army is ready to face any *imminent* attack of Pakistan.

81. **Eligible (fit to be chosen)** : He is *eligible* for the post.

Illegible (that which cannot be read) : His writing is *illegible*.

82. **Facility (ease, opportunity)** : *Facility* of STD is also available in this hotel.

Felicity (happiness) : True *felicity* can't be enjoyed by a dishonest man.

83. **Foul (unfair)** : One can't achieve true success through *foul* means.

Fowl (a bird) : He is fond of *fowl's* meat.

84. **Find (to get)** : Go there, you will *find* a tree near the river.

Fined (to charge) : The court *fined* him Rs. 20000 for the offence.

85. **Floor (surface)** : Clean the *floor* with dettol and water.

Flour (wheat meal, pulp, powder) : He has a *flour* mill.

86. **Forth (onward)** : He alone came *forth* to assist that poor lady.

Fourth (third-fourth) : April is the *fourth* month of the year.

87. **Farther (more distant)** : Delhi is *farther* from Alwar in comparison to Jaipur.

Further (next) : Please settle the case without any *further* delay.

88. **Faint (to swoon)** : She *fainted* after taking wine yesterday.

Feint (pretension) : She made a *feint* of reading the books.

89. **Fain (gladly)** : She would *fain* on seeing me.

Feign (pretend) : When his boss scolded him, he *feigned* as a deaf.

90. **Fair (pure, a show)** : I believe in using *fair* means to achieve the target;

Let us go to the fair.

Fare (passage money) : A strike was called by the bus operators, demanding hike in minimum *fare.*

91. **Feat (an exploit)** : A racing car is an extra ordinary *feat* of engineering.

Feet (plural of foot) : Do not put your *feet* on the table.

92. **Forego (go before)** : We have already discussed this point in *foregoing* lessons.

Forgo (to let go) : I cannot *forgo* my rights .

93. **Gild (thin coating of metal)** : *Gilded* ornaments look more beautiful than the original.

Guild (group of persons from same profession) : Nowadays, all the workers have organised themselves into *guilds.*

94. **Gage (security)** : I do not lend with out sufficient *gage.*

Gaze (to look attentively) : She stood *gazing* at herself in the mirror.

95. **Gait (manner of walk)** : That model girl has a graceful and sexy *gait.*

Gate (large door) : You should not enter through the main *gate.*

96. **Goal (aim)** : To achieve this *goal* you are to work hard.

Gaol (jail) : He has been to *gaol* earlier also.

97. **Hail (frozen rain)** : It is *hailing*;.It hailed yesterday.

Hale (healthy) : May God keep you *hale* and healthy!

98. **Horde (a gang)** : A *horde* of mischievous students attacked the shopkeepers.

Hoard (to store) : *Hoarding* of sugar beyond the prescribed limit is an offence.

99. **Hair**-She has black ***hair.***

Heir (successor) : He is an *heir* apparent to the throne.

100. **Hurt (injury)** : Your comments can *hurt* her feelings.

Hart (a male deer) : I have a beautiful pair of *harts.*

Heart (an organ in the body) : He is suffering from *heart* disease.

101. **Humane (kind)** : UNO has advised the member countries to meet out *humane* treatment to the prisoners of war.

Human (pertaining to mankind) : You will find almost the same human nature everywhere.

102. **Heel (part of shoe)** : The *heels* of my shoe are pinching.

Heal (to cure) : This medicine will help you in quick *healing.*

103. **Hole (a burrow)** : A serpent lives in this *hole*.

whole (complete) : He ate *whole* of the breakfast.

104. **Idle (indolent)** : An *idle* man can't make any progress.

Ideal (visionary) : My teacher Mr. Shrivastava is an *ideal* for me.

Idol (an image of a deity) : A section of the Hindus believes in *idol* worship.

105. **Ingenious (clever)** : He is an *ingenious* engineer.

Ingenuous (Simple) : His *ingenuous* attitude is liked by all .

106. **Incite (to provoke)** : His arrogant behaviour *incited* me a lot.

Insight (a clear vision) : The circumstantial evidence gave an *insight* into the cause of murder.

107. **Indite (to compose)** : Though he *indited* the letter carefully, yet it was not liked by the chairman.

Indict (to accuse) : He was *indicted* for theft and murder.

108. **Jealous (envious)** : He is not liked by anybody because of his *jealous* nature.

Zealous (enthusiastic) : She is very *zealous* about her new book.

109. **Naughty (mischievous)** : She is a *naughty* girl.

Knotty (difficult) : This was indeed a *knotty* problem.

110. **Lightening (make lighter)** : We had appealed to the court for *lightening* the punishment, but of no avail.

Lightning (electric discharge in clouds) : There was occasional *lightning* in the sky last night.

111. **Loath (unwilling)** : Nothing *loath* he did, as he was saying.

Loathe (to dislike greatly) : I *loathe* her dressing pattern and arrogant way of talking.

112. **Latter (antonym of former)** : Between Ram and Shyam, the *latter* (Shyam) is a diligent student.

Later (comparative of late) : He came *later* than his friend.

113. **Lose (to part with)** : Where did you *lose* your briefcase?

Loose (to slack) : He was wearing a *loose* cotton shirt.

114. **Lesson (chapter)** : Learn your *lesson* well.

Lessen (to make less) : Even this medicine has not *lessen* my pain.

115. **Last (antonym to 'first')** : Bahadur Shah was the *last* emperor of India .

Latest (superlative of late) : She always prefers *latest* design clothes.

116. **Meat (flesh)** : I don't like eating *meat*.

Meet (to assemble) : She came here only to *meet* me.

117. **Mead (meadow)** : I met a beautiful girl in the *meads* yesterday.

Meed (reward) : Kalidas has got a universal *meed of* praise.

118. **Metal (iron, brass etc.)** : Silver is a white *metal.*

Mettle (spirit, courage) : Our leaders have no *mettle* to fight against corruption.

119. **Metre (poetic rhythm)** : Can you tell me,in what *metre* Shelley's 'Skylark' is written.

Meter (a measuring instrument =100 cm.,) : One *meter* is equal to hundred centimeters.

120. **Minor (underage)** : *Minors* are not allowed to open current account in Banks.

Miner (one who works in mine) : He is a *miner*, works in a coal mine.

121. **Moat (a ditch surrounding a castle)** : There is a bridge over the *moat* near main gate.

Mote (a particle of dust) : You can not see small *mote* by naked eyes.

122. **Monetary (pertaining to money)** : Have you any book on *monetary* theory?

Monitory (giving advice) : He acted against the *monitory* advise of his friends and so failed.

123. **Male(opp.to female)** : A *male* candidate can't be posted against the post reserved for a woman.

Mail (post) : Have you received my *mail* ?

124. **Mite (small thing)** : He contributed his *mite* for the service of mankind.

Might (strength) : Your *might* will be tested in battle against the foreign power.

Might (past of 'may') : He told me that he *might* come to attend the function.

125. **Marry (to get married)** : I want to *marry* your sister.

Merry (joyous) : Don't lose heart and be *merry.*

126. **Main (chief)** : Ramesh is the *main* culprit in the bank robbery case.

Mane (long hair of an animal's neck) : His horse had a fine *mane.*

127. **Marshal (A military officer)** : He is a *marshal* of the court.

Martial (war like) : He has a *martial* spirit and courage to fight in odd circumstances.

128. **Maize (corn)** : I like to eat *maize* cake.

Maze (labyrinth) : This castle has many hidden *mazes*.

129. **Nice (good)** : She is a *nice* and beautiful girl.

Niece (daughter of brother) : I am to attend the marriage of my *niece* positively.

130. **Our (plural of 'my')** : This is *our* house.

Hour (a period of time) : I have been waiting for you for half *an hour.*

131. **Oar (used for rowing a boat)** : Life without aim is like a boat without an *oar.*

Ore (mineral from which metal can be extracted) : Iron is extracted from its *ore* by melting.

132. **Ordinance (a rule)** : The President has promulgated an *ordinance* for administering the minority community.

Ordnance (gun) : There is an *ordnance* factory in Jamshedpur, w. Bihar.

133. **Pray (entreat)** : I *pray* to God every day.

Prey (hunt) : Do not *prey* upon the innocent animals.

134. **Principal (head of school or college)** : Sh. R.C. Jha is the new *Principal* of our college.

Principle (rule) : Do you understand anything about the *principles* of justice?

135. **Prophecy (*noun*-foretold)** : It is his *prophecy* that America will not attack Iran.

Prophesy (*verb*- to foretell) : He had *prophesied* that Iraq would attack Kuwait.

136. **Proffer (offer)** : Many lucrative proposals were *proffered* to him for acceptance.

Prefer (like) : I *prefer* coffee to tea.

137. **Practice (noun)** : *Practice* makes a man perfect.

Practise (*verb*-to practise) : Don't preach but *practise*.

138. **Plain (easy, simple)** : One should try to write his thoughts in *plain* language.

Plane (to smoothen, level) : I use cream to *plane* my hair.

139. **Peel (to remove the skin)** : You cannot eat a banana without *peeling* it.

Peal (sound of thunder or bells) : I am hearing *peals* of trumpets.

140. **Pare (to trim)** : *Pare* your nails and then polish them.

Pair (two) : I have only three *pairs* of shoes.

141. **Peace (tranquillity)** : *Peace* of mind is more precious than the materialistic richness.

Piece (fragment) : The dog found a *piece* of meat .

142. **Price (value)** : What is the *price* of this coat.

Prize (reward) : She could not win any *prize* this time.

143. **Persecute (to harass)** : Pakistani soldiers *persecuted* the Hindus in a cruel manner.

Prosecute (to bring before a court) : He was *prosecuted* for murdering his wife.

144. **Physic (medicine)** : No *physic* can cure him of cancer.

Physique (bodily fitness) : He possesses an attractive *physique*.

145. **Prescribe (to direct)** : The doctor has *prescribed* three doses of medicine after four hours daily.

Proscribe (to banish) : The minister was *proscribed* by the king.

146. **Patrol (going round)** : A chowkidar was *patrolling* at the main gate.

Petrol (oil) : *Petrol* is required to run vehicles.

147. **Popular (familiar)** : Mahatma Gandhi was a very *popular* leader.

Populous (thickly inhabited) : Delhi is a highly *populous* city.

Pail (bucket) : I have two *pails* full of water.

Pale (yellowish apperance, wanted) : On seeing a lion , his face turned *pale*.

148. **Quite (altogether)** : I am *quite* well now.

Quiet (silent) : Please keep *quiet*.

149. **Rein (bridle)** : Keep the *rein* tight, otherwise you may be thrown out by the horse.

Reign (rule) : The *reign* of Akbar is known for communal harmony.

150. **Rite (ceremony)** : Only a few *rites* were performed in his wedding.

Write (compose) : I am to *write* a letter immediately.

Right (antonym of left) : This is my *right* leg.

Right (antonym to wrong) : You have taken a *right* decision.

Wright (a worker) : He is a wonderful play *wright*.

151. **Raise (to lift)** : I will *raise* this issue in parliament.

Raze (to destroy) : The storm *razed* many buildings to the ground.

152. **Route (course)** : By which *route* you came here?

Rout (flight) : The Pakistan armies were put to *rout*.

153. **Rap (a sharp blow)** : He *rapped* her on the cheek.

Rape (to ravish) : He *raped* a college girl.

Wrap (to enclose) : The book was *wrapped* in a piece of white paper.

154. **Reclaim (to win back)** : He was *reclaimed* from his bad habits by his devoted wife.

Re-claim (to claim again) : He is thinking to *re-claim* the property on some other ground.

155. **Recover (regain)** : He has now *recovered* a lot from the weakness.

Re-cover (to cover again) : *Re-cover* the sweets with some clean cloth.

156. **Road (way)** : The *road* has recently been repaired.

Rode (Past of 'ride') : He *rode* on the horse yesterday.

157. **Ring (an ornament for fingers)** : This *ring* is made of gold.

Wring (to twist, to squeeze) : *Wring* the clothes well and put them on the ground.

158. **Rest (respite)** : I want some *rest* before starting the next assignment.

Wrest (snatch by force) : Ram *wrested* a bag from Shyam.

159. **Roll (turning over and over)** : What is your *roll* number ?

He *rolled* over the log to the right side of river.

Role (actor's part in a play) : I am playing the *role* of Ravana in this serial.

160. **Sooth (truth)** : *Sooth* to speak, he is not a good boy.

Soothe (to calm) : You can't *soothe* his anger with lame excuses.

161. **Spacious (enough space)** : His office is quite *spacious* and well decorated.

Specious (attractive) : With your *specious* look,you can't befool her.

162. **Stationary (fixed)** : Earth is not *stationary*, it moves round the sun.

Stationery (writing material) : I am going to market to purchase several *stationery* items for the office.

163. **Straight (opposed to curved)** : I believe in *straight* talks.

Strait (narrow) : The lane is too *strait* for an elephant to pass through.

164. **Sore (painful)** : I can't sing as my throat is *sore*.

Soar (to fly high) : Birds *soar* in sky.

Sour (not sweet) : The grapes were *sour*.

165. **Suit (an action in court)** : Bank has filed a civil *suit* against you for recovery.

Suite (a set of room) : I have reserved a *suite* for you in Alaska Hotel.

166. **Story (a tale)** : My grandmother told me a *story* of an old man.

Storey (floor of a building) : I have taken a room at first *storey*.

167. **Serge (a kind of cloth)** : This suit is made of *serge*.

Surge (move like waves) : The waves of ocean *surge* violently in night.

168. **Shear (to clip the wool)** : The sheep are being *shorn*.

Sheer (downright) : He achieved success by the *sheer* force of his hard labour.

169. **Sun (sun)** : The *sun* is a star.

Son (Boy) : He is my *son*.

170. **Sole (lower surface of shoe, one and only)** : The *sole* of the right shoe requires repairing; The *sole* aim of my life is to earn reputation in the society.

Soul (immaterial part) : You can't see *soul*; *Soul* is immortal.

171. **Stair (step)** : Let us go up *stairs*.

Stare (gaze) : It is wrong to *stare* at girls .

172. **Sing (melodious sound)** : She will *sing* a sweet song.

Swing (to oscillate) : She has gone to enjoy *swing* ride.

173. **Sale (to exchange for money)** : This is not for *sale*.

Sail (to travel in water) : Ships can *sail* in deep sea only.

174. **Team (a group of players)** : Our college *team* has won the trophy.

Teem (to be full of) : Rajasthan is a state *teeming* with natural resources.

175. **Toe (a part of foot)** : She hurt her left *toe* in an accident.

Tow (to draw by a rope) : The boat was *towed* with a tree near the shore.

176. **Tail (part of body)** : Cow has a long *tail*.

Tale (story) : My grandmother told me an interesting *tale*.

177. **Their (belong to they)** : They have learnt *their* lessons.

There (at that place) : I am to go *there* now.

178. **Throne (Royal seat)** : All the brothers are fighting for the *throne*.

Thrown (III form of 'throw') : She has *thrown* her certificates into the river.

Thorn (impediment; sharp, pointed growth on the stem of a plant) : You need a needle to get the *thorn* out.

179. **Tenor (purpose)** : The *tenor* of his speech was important from religious point of view.

Tenure (right of holding an estate) : The Zamindari Abolition Act has finished the big problem of land *tenure* system in our country.

180. **Umpire (a referee)** : You must not disobey the *umpire*.

Empire (dominion) : The king was unable to manage his *empire* properly.

181. **Vein (a blood vessel)** : *Veins* take the blood to all parts of body.

Vane (weather cock) : There is a *vane* at the top of the temple.

182. **Vale (valley)** : The beautiful *vale* of Manali is worthseeing.

Veil (a cover) : Muslim ladies generally put a *veil* on their face.

Wail (to lament) : Don't *wail* please, your husband is safe and sound.

183. **Wave (unevenness)** : The *waves* of ocean are rising higher and higher.

Wave (movement) : She *waved* her hand as the bus started.

Waive (relinquish) : I request the officer to *waive* the punishment.

184. **Waste (useless)** : Don't *waste* your precious time.

Waist (part of body) : The boy had a chain round his *waist*.

185. **Weather (atmosphere)** : It is cold *weather* today .

Whether (which of two) : I asked her *whether* she would come .

186. **Vain (useless)** : I made several request to our Principal but all in *vain* .

Wane (to decrease) : I see the moon *waning* these nights.

187. **Vary (to change)** : Your actions *vary* from the promise you made.

Very (more) : She is a *very* beautiful girl.

Wary (cautious) : Because of his *wary* nature, he was saved.

188. **Vacations (holidays)** : We are going to Delhi in summer *vacations*.

Vocation (occupation) : What *vocation* you intend to join after graduation?

189. **Weigh (to ascertain the weight)** : I am to purchase one *weighing* machine.

Way (passage) : This *way* leads to hospital.

190. **Weight (weight)** : He gained ten kilograms of *weight* within a month.

Wait (to attend) : Don't *wait* for me, I will go myself.

191. **Week (period of seven days)** : Monday is the first day of a *week*.

Weak (feeble) : Ramesh is too *weak* to walk.

192. **Ware (article)** : He has sold all his cook *wares*.

Wear (to put on) : I like to *wear* silk sarees.

Wear (to diminish) : My shirt has *worn* out .

193. **Wine (drink)** : Drinking *wine* is harmful for lever.

Vine (creeper plant) : The hut is covered with grape *vines*.

194. **Yearn (to long)** : I am anxiously *yearning* to meet my wife.

Yarn (thread) : I have purchased three bundles of *yarn*.

195. **Yoke (slavery)** : He is under the *yoke* of his master.

Yolk (yellow portion of an egg) : Some people eat only the *yolk* of an egg.

IDIOMS AND PHRASES

A gentleman at large (an unreliable person) : He is *a gentleman at large*, you must not trust him.

A wolf in sheep's clothing (a dangerous person pretending harmless) : Charles Shobhraj is *a wolf in sheep's clothing* for general public.

ABC (very common knowledge) : He doesn't know *ABC* of Physics.

Above board (fair and honest) : He is a straight forward man. His financial dealings are *above board*.

Again and again (repeatedly) : One who tries *again and again* gets success positively.

All and sundry (without making any distinction) : He invited *all and sundry* in the marriage party of his younger brother.

All in all (whole-sole, most important) : The Forest Minister is *all in all* of our department.

Alpha and omega (First and last letter of Greek alphabet, means-beginning and end) : The *alpha and omega* of British policy was to keep the Indians divided.

An eye wash (a pretence) : He does nothing without self interest, all his excuses are but *an eye wash*.

An iron hand (by force) : Indira Gandhi put down the opposition with *an iron hand*.

At sixes and seven (persons who are having different opinions) : Economists are *at sixes and seven* on the policy of rationing.

Back and call (at the service) : Don't worry, I am at your *back and call*.

Bag and baggage (with all goods) : He returned his village bag and baggage.

Between scylla and Charybdis : (choice between two unpleasant alternatives) : Don't make haste, take care so that in avoiding *scylla* you don't fall in *Charybdis*.

Between the cup and the lips : (On the point of achievement) : Until I got the appointment letter in hand, I was not sure of the posting, as there were many slips *between the cup and the lips*.

Black and white (in writing) : It is always better to get everything in *black and white,* before entering a partnership.

Blow hot and cold (having no stand, showing favour at one time and unfavour at another) : He can't be relied upon, as he *blows hot and cold* in this matter.

Body and soul (entirely) : She devoted *body and soul* to win the medal.

By fits and starts (irregularly) : Work done *by fits and starts* never completes in time.

By hook or by crook (by any means) : I want to get this licence *by hook or by crook*.

By leaps and bound (speedily) : The population is increasing *by leaps and bounds.*

Call a spade a spade (straight talk) : He believes in *calling a spade a spade.*

Cats and dogs (heavy rain) : It has been raining *cats and dogs* for the last three hours.

Cock and bull story (untrue story) : All his excuses seem *a cock and bull story.*

Confusion worse confounded (be in further worse position) : Such demonstrations and communal speeches in present situation make *confusion worse confounded.*

Cut and dried (readymade form) : There is no *cut and dried* method of English speaking.

Ever and anon (now and then) : She goes to temple *ever and anon.*

Fair and square (honest) : He is *fair and square* in his dealings.

Fair field and no favour (equal opportunity to all) : All the staff wants *fair field and no favour* in the matter of transfer.

Far and wide (every where) : Many tourists come to see the Taj from *far and wide.*

Fire and brimstone (fearful penalties) : The USA has threatened Iran with *fire and brimstone* if she refuses to follow the resolutions of UNO.

Fire and fury (extreme enthusiasm) : The speech of the leader was full of *fire and fury.*

First and foremost (highest priority) : To be sincere and devoted is the *first and foremost* requirement of a good employee.

Fishy (doubtful) : There seems to be something *fishy* going on.

Free and easy (natural and simple) : The principal found his arguments *free and easy.*

Gall and wormwood (source of irritation) : Her remarks about his father were *gall and wormwood* to him.

Gird up the loin (to be ready) : We should *gird up the loin* to fight the menace of poverty and dowery.

Goods and chattels (belongings of home) : On transfer, he brought all *goods and chattels* by road.

Hand and gloves (very intimate friends) : Ram and Rahim are *hand and gloves* to each other.

Hard and fast (certain) : There are no *hard and fast* rules to sanction the loan in the banks.

Haughty and naughty (arrogant and naughty) : The *haughty and naughty* attitude of the president is not liked by any memeber of the society.

Heart and soul (with full devotion) : He threw himself *heart and soul* to pass the examination.

Herculean task (a tedious job) : Getting selected in IAS is a *herculean task* for everybody.

Hit below the belt (contrary to principles of fairness) : By making his enemy's private secretes public, he hit *him below the belt.*

Hither and thither (here and there) : He is in the habit of putting his belongings *hither and thither.*

Hole and corner policy (a secret policy for an evil purpose) : The officer adopted *hole and corner policy* to get his P.A . trasferred.

Hue and cry (great noise) : A lot of *hue and cry* was raised in Parliament against this bill.

Ins and outs (full detail) : Before starting any new business you must know all *ins and outs* of it.

Intents and purposes (practically) : My wife is the incharge of the house for all *intents and purposes*.

Kith and kin (blood relatives) : All *kith and kin* were invited in the marriage function of his son.

Latin and Greek (unable to understand) : His speech in English was *Latin and Greek* to the rural folk.

Law and equity (legal and moral justice) : *Law and equity* demands that the reservations should be based on economic parameters.

Leave no stone unturned (make all possible efforts) : I shall leave no stone *unturned* to get the promotion.

Length and breadth (all over) : Anti-English agitation spread throughout the *length and breadth* of the country.

Life and soul (main support) : Soniya Gandhi is the *life and soul* of Congress (I).

Like a fish out of water (in every difficult and unsuitable situation) : Ram was given an unremunerative post. He is feeling like a *fish out of water.*

Loaves and fish (material interests) : Nowadays Government servants are concerned with the *loaves and fish* of the office than to solve the problems of common public.

Lock and key (in safe place) : He keeps the jewellery under *lock and key.*

Might and main (with all enthusiasm) : If you study with *might and main* you will positively secure the success.

Milk and water (weak) : The foreign policy of India is nothing more than a *milk and water* policy.

Neck and Crop (completely) : The Pak army ruined the border village *neck and crop.*

Need of the hour (necessity of time) : Providing full security for the residents of border area is the *need of hour.*

Nook and corner (everywhere) : I searched her in every *nook and corner.*

Not born yesterday (worldly wise) : You can't befool me as I was *not born yesterday.*

Now and then (Occasionally) : I visit church *now and then.*

Null and void (of no use, without force of application) : The law passed by legislature was declared *null and void* by the Supreme court.

Odds and ends (remaining goods) : Except *odds and ends*, all the items have since been arranged in order.

Often and often (frequently) : She visits her parents *often and often.*

Once and again (repeatedly) : I have told you *once and again* that I have no money to purchase the car at the moment.

Open and above board (very clear, transparent) : He believes in *open and above board* discussion on every point before arriving at a conclusion.

Out of gear (in disorder) : The strike of employees always puts the government machinery *out of gear*.

Over and above (besides) : I paid him rupees ten thousand *over and above* what he demanded.

Over head and ears (excessively) : He is *over head and ears* in debt.

Part and Parcel (being an important part of) : Each employee should feel himself *part and parcel* of the business enterprises.

Pell mell (putting one upon the other, in confusion) : He was in such a hurry that he put all the articles *pell mell* and closed the room .

Pick and choose (to choose selectively as per wish) : The management adopted *pick and choose* policy in the matter of promotions from clerical to assistant cadre.

Pins and needles (small items) : It is unwise to use swords and scissors where *pins and needles* can do.

Pros and Cons (merits and demerits) : Before signing this agreement you must understand all its *pros and cons* well.

Rain or shine (favourable or unfavourable circumstances.) : *Rain or shine*, I will speak to oppose the proposal.

Rank and file (everyone without discrimination) : For the actual prosperity of the nation, the economic conditions of *rank and file* should be improved.

Rank and ruin (complete destructions) : The present drought has put the farmers at the verge of *rank* and *ruin*.

Rhyme or reason (rational cause) : He resigned from the service without any *rhyme or reason*.

Right and left (in all ways) : The robbers looted the village *right and left* and fled away.

Root and branch (complete) : Poverty among the public is the *root and branch* of all the crimes.

Safe and sound (quite well) : She reached their *safe and sound*.

Speck and span (neat and smart) : Mr. J.L. Nehru was always *speck and span* in his dressing style.

Stuff and nonsense (worthless) : The judge found all his arguments *stuff and nonsense*.

Sum and substance (the actual theme) : The *sum and substance* of the paragraph must be reflected in a good precis.

The die is cast (decided finally) : *The die is cast*, there is not point of discussing over it now.

The last nail in the coffin (the last action which resulted in the complete end of something.) : The reservation policy of V.P. Singh was *the last nail in the coffin* of Janta Party.

Thick and thin (in all circumstances) : I shall support you through *thick and thin*.

Through fire and water (in all sort of difficulties) : He can go *through fire and water* to achieve his goal.

Time and tide (course of time) : *Time and tide* waits for none.

To and fro (going and coming, backward and forward) : What are the *to and fro* taxi charges for Alwar to Delhi?

To check by jowl (very near to each other) : As the space was short, so he kept all the articles *check by jowl.*

To move heaven and earth (to make all possible efforts) : I am ready *to move heaven and earth* to bring him to justice.

To play ducks and drakes (to waste money) : He is *playing ducks and drakes* with parental money.

Toil and moil (hard labour) : It requires too much of *toil and moil* to secure first position.

Tom Dick and Harry (everyone) : Every *Tom Dick and Harry* knows that Sachin is the greatest cricketer .

Tooth and nail (with all force) : Students of general caste opposed the reservation policy *tooth and nail* but of no avail.

Ups and downs (prosperity and adversity) : There are *ups and downs* in every business.

Warp and woof (essential parts of a thing) : Blood and bones are *warp and woof* of human body.

Watch and ward (careful guard) : At least three guards are required to have perfect *watch and ward* of the building.

Weal and woe (prosperity and adversity) : I will abide by you in all *weal and woe.*

Whips and spur (with greatest hurry) : He completed the project *whips and spur.*

Why and wherefore (the basic reason) : Please tell me the *why and wherefore* of your decision to take voluntary retirement .

Willy Nilly (wish or not wish) : *Willy nilly,* you are to obey the orders of your father.

ANIMALS : MALES, FEMALES, YOUNGS AND GROUP TERMS

Animal	Male	Female	Young	As a group
Antelope	Bull	Cow	Calf	Herd
Bear	Boar	Sow	Cub	Sloth
Cat	Tom	Queen	Kitten	Clowder
Cattle	Bull	Cow	Calf	Herd/Drove.
Chicken	Cock/Rooster	Hen	Chick	Flock
Deer	Buck/Hart/Stag	Doe/Hind	Fawn	Herd
Dog	Dog	Bitch	Pup	Kennel
Donkey	Jackass	Jeneet/Jenny	Foal/colt	Pace
Elephant	Bull	Cow	Calf	Herd
Fox	Dog	Vixen	Cub	Skulk
Giraffe	Bull	Cow	Calf	Herd

Goat	Billy/Buck	Nanny/Doe	Kid	Herd
Goose	Gander	Goose	Gosling	Flock/Gaggle
Horse	Stallion	Mare	Foalt/colt(male)	Herd/filly(female)
Kangaroo	Buck/Boomer	Doe/flier	Joey	Herd/troop/mob
Lion	Lion	Lioness	Cub	Pride
Ostrich	Cock	Hen	Chick	Flock/troop
Pig	Boar	Sow	Shoat/farrow/	Herd/drove/ piglet
Rabbit	Buck	Doe	Kindle/kitten	Warren
Rat	Buck	Doe	Mouse	Colony
Seal	Bull	Cow	Pup/whelp	Rookery/trip
Sheep	Ram	Ewe	Lamb	Flock
Swan	Cob	Pen	Cygnet	Flock
Turkey	Cock/gobbler/tom	Hen	Poult	Dule
Whale	Bull	Cow	Calf	School/pod
Zebra	Stallion	Mare	Foal	Herd

SOUNDS & CRIES OF SOME BIRDS, ANIMALS, INSECTS etc.

Names of Birds, Animals, Insects etc.	Cries
1. Dogs, foxes	Bark
2. Cows	Bellow
3. Sheep, goat, calf, lambs	Bleat
4. Donkey, ass	Bray
5. Bees, flies, wasps	Buzz
6. Sheep, lamb	Baa
7. Hunting dogs, hounds	Bay
8. Waves, guns	Boom
9. Geese, hen	Cackle
10. Crow, rook, raven	Caw
11. Monkey	Chatter
12. Sparrow/bird, grasshopper	Chirp
13. Hen	Cluck
14. Dove, pigeon	Coo
15. Frog	Croak
16. Cocks	Crow
17. Babies, mole, rook	Cry
18. Aircraft, bees	Drone

19. Of People talking inarticulately	Gabble
20. Monkeys, frightened persons	Gibber
21. Dogs,thunder, bears	Growl
22. Pigs, Camel	Grunt
23. Snake, fire, serpents	Hiss
24. Owl, horn, siren	Hoot
25. Dog, wolf, jackal, wind, tiger	Howl
26. Bees, flies,insects	Hum
27. Cattle, cows	Low
28. Cats, a sea bird	Mew
29. Horse	Neigh
30. Duck	Quack
31. Lion, tigers, traffic	Roar
32. Cats, babies, wind, hurricane, engine	Scream
33. Monkeys, old ladies, wheels, gate	Screech
34. Chorus	Sing
35. Dog, tiger	Snarl
36. Human beings Man	Talk/Laugh/Cry Grumble, Laugh, Smile,
37. Elephant, brass instruments	Trumpet
38. Birds, Sparrows	Twitter
39. Dogs	Yelp
40. Larks, nightingale, cuckoo	Warble

PHRASAL VERBS AND THEIR USE

act up : [***misbehave*** (for people); ***not work properly*** (for machines)] : "The babysitter had a difficult time. The children *acted up* all evening.;"I guess I'd better take my car to the garage. It's been acting up lately."

act on : [***produce effect***] : In general Acids *act on* metals.

act upon : [***in accordance with***] : The captain acting upon the secret information caught the militants.

act like : [***behave in a way that's like***] : "What's wrong with Bob? He's *acting* like an idiot."

add up : [***logically fit together***] : "His theory is hard to believe, but his research *adds up*.

" **Note: *This phrasal verb is often negative*** :

"His theory seems, at first, to be plausible, but the facts in his research don't *add up*."

add up : [*find the total*] : "What's the total of those bills? Could you *add* them *up* and see?"

add up to : [*to total*] : " The bills *add up to* Rs 8570/- only. That's more than I expected!"

ask out : [*ask for a date*] : "Shalu has a new boy friend. He *asked* her *out* last night."

back down : [*not follow a threat*] : "Tom was going to call the police when I told him I'd wrecked his car, but he *backed down* when I said I'd pay for the damages."

back off : [*not follow a threat*] : "Tom was ready to call the police when I told him I'd wrecked his car, but he *backed off* when I said I'd pay for the damages."

back up : [*move backward; move in reverse*] : "You missed the lines in the parking space. You'll have to *back up* and try again."

"The people waiting in line are too close to the door. We won't be able to open it unless they *back up*."

back up : [*drive a vehicle backwards (in reverse)]* : You're too close! *Back* your car *up,* so that I can open the garage door."

back up : [*confirm a story, fact*, **or** *information*.]

"If you don't believe me, talk to Dave. He'll *back me up*."

back up : [*make a 'protection' copy to use if there are problems with the original*].

"When my computer crashed, I lost many of my files. It's a good thing I, had *backed* them *up*."

beg off : [*decline an invitation; ask to be excused from doing something*]

"At first, Lily said she would be at the party. Later she *begged off*."

blow up : [*inflate*] : "We needs lots of balloons for the party. Will you *blow* them *up*?"

bear down : [*to crush by force*] : She was successful in *bearing down* the opposition group.

bear out : [*verify or confirm*] : Your arguments do not *bear out* the facts.

bear up : [*to face hardships bravely*] : He must try to *bear up* against this temporary phase of economic slump.

bear with : [*endure to have patience*] : A good wife *bears with* the habits of her husband.

beat down : [*to crush*] : He *beat down* the opposition with a single trick.

beat off : [*to repulse, to drive back*] : Indian army successfully *beat off* the enemy forces.

beat up : [*to beat*] : Ramesh was *beaten up* by Suresh for no reason.

blow up : [*explode*; *destroy by exploding*] :

A: "That old building really came down quickly!"

B: "That's because the construction company used dynamite to *blow it up*."

bone up on : [***review / study thoroughly for a short time***]
"If you're going to travel to the U.K, you'd better *bone up* on your English."

break down : [***stop working / functioning***] : "Shalini will be late for work today. Her car broke down on the way."

break in : [***enter by using force (and breaking a lock, window, etc.)***] : "John's apartment was burglarized last night. Someone *broke in* while John was at the movies.; "Somebody *broke into* John's apartment while he was at the movies.

break in : [***train; get someone / something accustomed to a new routine***] : "I hope, I can learn my new job quickly. The manager hasn't scheduled much time for *breaking* me *in*."

break up : [***disperse; scatter***] : "What time did the party *break up* last night?"

break up : [***end a personal relationship***] :"Tom and Jassi aren't going steady any more.They got really angry with each other and *broke up*.; "Have you heard the news? Jassi *broke up* with Tom! "I'm sorry to hear that their marriage *broke up*. I'm sure the divorce will be difficult for the children."

bring/take back : [***return something***] : "Yes, you can borrow my pen, don't forget to *bring* it *back to* me when you're finished."This book is due tomorrow. I guess I should *take* it *back* to the library."

bring off : [***accomplish something difficult; accomplish something people had considered impossible or unlikely***] : "No one thought Raju could get an 'A' in that course, but he *brought* it *off*.

bring up : [***raise; rear.***]" : Shalu's parents died when she was a baby. Her grandparents *brought* her *up*."

brush up on : [***review / study thoroughly for a short time***] : "If you're going to travel to the U.K., you'd better *brush up on* your English."

burn down : [***become destroyed / consumed by fire***] : **Note**: *For upright things--trees, buildings, etc.--only*; "Lightning struck Mr. Kalhan's barn last night. It *burned down* before the fire fighters arrived."

burn up : [***become destroyed / consumed by fire***] : *Note*: *For people and non-upright things only*; "All of Mr. Kalhan's hay *burned up* when his barn burned down."

butt in : [***impolitely interrupt (a conversation, an action)***] : "Hey, you! Don't *butt in*! Wait for your turn!"

butter up : [***praise someone excessively with the hope of getting some benefit.***] : "I guess Mohan really wants to be promoted. He's been *buttering* his boss *up* all week."

call off : [***cancel something that has been scheduled.***] "We don't have school today. The Collector *called* the classes *off* because of the snow."

call on : [***ask someone for an answer in class***.] "I don't know why the teacher never *calls on* you. You always know the answer."

calm down : [***become calm / less agitated or upset***; ***help someone become calm / less agitated or upset***.] : "Why are you so upset? Sheela didn't intend to spill orange juice on you. *Calm down*!/ "I know Raju is upset, but can you *calm* him *down*? He's making so much noise that he's irritating everyone in the office."

care for : [***like; want***.] ;
Note: *This phrasal verb is usually negative, though is may be used affirmatively in questions*. A: "Would you *care for* something to drink? We have coffee, tea, or orange juice." B: "Could I have water, please? I don't *care for* coffee, tea, or juice."

care for : [***take care of; supply care to; attend / watch***..] : "Ann's father got out of the hospital last week. The family is *caring for* him at home."

catch on : [***develop understanding or knowledge of something***.] : "Bholu had never used a computer until he took this class, but he *caught on* very quickly and is now one of the best students."

catch up (with) : [***stop being behind somebody or something***.] : "Toshu has stopped to rest for a few minutes. He'll *catch up*. / *Catch up* with us later."

check in (to) : [***register for / at a hotel, conference, etc***.] : "My plane will arrive around 5:00 P.M. I should be able to *check into* the hotel by 6:00 or 6:30."/ "When you arrive at the convention, be sure to check in at the registration desk."

check off : [***make a mark to indicate that something on a list has been completed***.] : "Here are the things you need to do. Please *check* each one *off* when you've finished it."

check out (of) : [***follow procedures for leaving*** (***a hotel***, etc.)] : "Don't forget to take your room key to the front desk when you *check out* (when you check out of the hotel)."

cheer up : [***help someone feel less worried/depressed/sad***.] : "Shalu's brother was depressed about not getting a promotion, so she sent him a funny card to *cheer* him *up*."

chew out : [***scold someone severely; berate***] : "Tom's father was really angry when Tom didn't come home until 3:00 A.M. He *chewed* Tom *out* and then said that Tom had to stay at home for three weeks."

chicken out : [***lose the courage or confidence to do something–often at the last minute***] : "Sahu said he was going to ask Tili for a date, but later on he *chickened out*."

chip in : [***contribute/donate*** (***often money***) ***towards something done by a group***.] : "We're going to buy a birthday cake for our boss and I'm collecting donations. Do you want to *chip* in?"

clam up : [***suddenly become quiet / refuse to talk about something***.] : "Lila wouldn't talk about the accident. When I asked her what happened, she *clammed* up."

come across : [*find* (*unexpectedly*)] : "I've lost my extra car keys. If you *come across* them while your're cleaning the room, please put them in a safe place."

come down with : [*become ill with........*]"George won't be at the office today. He *came down with* the flu over the weekend."

come to : [*total*] : "Your charges *come to* $124.38. Will you pay by check, in cash, or with a credit card?"

come to : [*regain consciousness*] : "When I told Gina that she'd won a million dollars, she fainted. When she *came to*, I told her it was a joke and she almost hit me!"

count on : [*depend on; trust that something will happen* **or** *that someone will do as expected*.] : "I'm *counting on* you to wake me up tomorrow. I know I won't hear the alarm."

cross out : [*show that something written is wrong or unnecessary by making an X across it*] : "We can't afford to buy everything on your shopping list, so I've *crossed all* the unnecessary things *out*."

cut back (on) : [*use less of something*.] : "You drink too much coffee. You should *cut back*."/ "You should *cut back* on the amount of coffee that you drink."

do in : [*cause to become very tired*] : "Those three games of tennis yesterday afternoon, really *did* me *in*. I slept for ten hours after I got home."

do over : [*do something again*] : "Oh, no! I forgot to save my report before I turned the computer off! Now I'll have to *do* it *over*!".

drag on : [*last much longer than expected or is necessary*] : "I thought the meeting would be a short one, but it *dragged* on for more than three hours."

draw up : [*create a formal document*] : "The Ajax and Tip-Top Banks have decided to merge. Their lawyers will *draw* all the official documents *up* sometime this month."

drop off : [*deliver something; deliver someone* (*by giving him/her a ride*)] : "Yes, I can take those letters to the post office. I'll *drop* them off as I go home from work./ "You don't have to take a taxi. You live fairly close to me, so I'll be happy to *drop* you *off*."

drop in (on) : [*visit informally* (*and usually without scheduling a specific time*)] : "If you're in town next month, we'd love to see you. Please try to *drop in*. /Please try to *drop in on* us."

drop by : [*visit informally* (*and usually without scheduling a specific time*)] : "If you're in town next month, we'd love to see you. Please try to *drop by* the house."

drop out (of) : [*stop attending/leave school or an organisation*] : "No, Paresh isn't at the university; He *dropped out*. / He *dropped out* of school."

draw out : [***prolong something (usually far beyond the normal limits)***] : "I thought that speech would never end. The speaker could have said everything important in about five minutes, but he *drew* the speech *out* for over an hour!"

eat out : [***have a meal in a restaurant***.] : "I'm too tired to cook . Why don't we *eat out*?"

egg on : [***urge/encourage greatly toward doing something (usually something negative)***.] : "At first Boby and Kaku were just having a mild argument, but Boby's friends *egged* them *on* until they started fighting."

end up : [***arrive somewhere as a result or consequence***.] : "You're working too hard. If you don't take it easy, you'll *end up* in the hospital!"

face up to : [***admit to; take responsibility for***.] : "You can't pretend that you're doing OK in this course, John. Sooner or later, you'll have to *face up to* the fact that you're failing it."

fall through : [***not happen***. (***Note***: *describes something that was planned but didn't happen*.)] : "We had originally intended to go to Morroco for our vacation, but our trip *fell through* when I got sick."

feel up to : [***feel strong enough or comfortable enough to do something***.] : "I know the accident was a terrible shock. Do you *feel up to* talking about it?"

figure out : [***logically find the answer to a problem; solve a problem by thinking about it carefully***.] : "For a long time I couldn't understand the last problem, but I finally *figured* it *out*."

fill in : [***add information to a form***.] : "The office needs to know your home address and phone number. Could you *fill* them *in* on this form?"

fill in (on) : [***supply information that someone doesn't know***.] : "I wasn't able to attend the meeting yesterday, but I understand that it was important. Could you *fill* me *in*? / Could you *fill* me *in* on what was discussed?"

fill in for : [***temporarily do someone else's work; temporarily substitute for another person***.] : 'Professor Neerja is in the hospital and won't be able to teach for the rest of the term. Do you know who's going to *fill in for* her?"

fill out : [***complete a form by adding required information***.] : "Of course, I completed my application form! I *filled* it *out* and mailed it over three weeks ago!"

fill out : [***become less thin; gain weight***.] : "Jerry used to be really skinny, but in the last year he's begun to *fill out*."

find out (about) : [***learn / get information*** (***about***)] : "I'm sorry that you didn't know the meeting had been cancelled. I didn't *find out* (find out about it) myself until just a few minutes ago."

get across : [***make something understood; communicate something understandably***] : "Alan is really intelligent but sometimes he has problems *getting* his ideas *across*."

get along (with) : [***have a friendly relationship*** (***with***); ***be friendly*** (***toward***)] : "Why can't you and your sister *get along*? Everyone else *gets along* with her just fine!"

get around : [***move from place to place***]"She doesn't have a car. She *gets around* by bicycle, bus, or taxi."

get around to : [***do something eventually***] : "I really should wash the dishes, but I don't feel like it. Maybe I'll *get around to* them tomorrow morning."

get by : [***survive***, ***financially***, ***in a difficult situation***] :"It's going to be hard to pay the rent now that you've lost your job, but somehow we'll *get by*."

get in : [***enter a small***, ***closed vehicle***] : "I don't know where Jasmine was going. She just *got in* her car and drove away."

get off : [***leave a large***, ***closed vehicle***] : "When you *get off* the bus, cross the street, turn right on Oak Street, and keep going until you're at the corner of Oak Hotel.

get off : [***make it possible for someone to avoid punishment***.] : "Everyone knew he was guilty, but his lawyer was clever and *got* him *off*."

get out of : [***escape having to do something***.] : "Liz said she had a terrible headache and *got out of* giving her speech today."

get over : [***finish***. (**Note**: *for individual activities*, *not the ones that happen again and again*.)] : "What time do your classes *get over*?"

get over : [***recover from an illness*** **or** ***painful experience***.] : "Kelly was really upset when she failed the test. She thought she would never *get over* feeling so stupid."

get rid of : [***dispose of***; ***give away or throw away***.] : "That shirt is really ugly. Why don't you *get rid of it*?"

get up : [***leave bed after sleeping and begin your daily activities***] : "You'll have to *get up* much earlier than usual tomorrow. We have to leave by no later than 6:00 A.M."/ "I know I won't hear the alarm tomorrow morning. Can you *get* me *up* at 6:00 A.M?"

give up : [***stop doing something*** (***usually a habit***)] : "He knows smoking isn't good for his health, but he can't *give* it *up*."

go out with : [***have a date with***.] : "You *went out with* Shalini last night, didn't you?"

go with : [***date regularly and steadily***] : "Is Hina *going with Joe*? I see them together all the time."

goof off : [***be lazy***; ***do nothing in particular***] : A: "Do you have any special plans for your vacation?" B: "No. I'm just going to stay home and *goof off*."

grow up : [***spend the years between being a child and being an adult***.] : "Did you know that Kallu *grew up* in Malaysia?"

hand in : [***submit homework***, ***an assignment***, ***etc***.] : "You'd better get started on your report. You know that you have to *hand* it *in* at 8:30 tomorrow morning!"

hand out : [***distribute***] : "Why don't you have a course description and list of assignments? The teacher *handed* them *out* on the first day of class."

hang up : [***end a phone conversation by replacing the receiver***] : "I'd like to talk longer, but I'd better *hang up*. My sister needs to make a call."

have to do with : [***be about***] : "This class *has to do with* the behaviour of people in groups."

hold up : [***raise***; ***lift to a higher-than-normal position***] : "The winner of the race proudly *held* his trophy *up* for all to see."

iron out : [***mutually reach an agreement***; ***mutually resolve difficulties***] : "Yes, I know we disagree on lots of things, Susan, but we can *iron* them *out*."

jack up : [***raise / lift by using a jack***] : "We'll have to *jack* the back of the car *up* before we can change the tire."

jump all over : [***severely scold someone***; ***berate someone***.] : "Amar is really upset. His boss *jumped all over* him because he's been late for work three times this week."

keep on : [***continue***] : "I'm not ready to stop yet. I think I'll *keep* on working for a while."

kick out : [***expel***; ***force someone to leave because of his/her poor performance or unacceptable behaviour***] : "Jim's club *kicked* him *out* because he didn't pay his dues or come to meetings."

knock out : [***make unconscious***] : "The boxing match ended when one boxer *knocked* the other one *out*."/"That medicine really knocked me out. I slept for 14 hours straight!"

knock oneself out : [***work much harder than normal or than what is expected***.] : "We completed the project on time because of Jack. He *knocked* himself *out* to be sure we didn't miss the deadline."

lay off : [***dismiss someone from a*** **job** ***because of lack of work or money*** (***not because of poor performance***)] : "I feel really sorry for Shalu's family. Her father was *laid off* yesterday."

leave out : [***forget***; ***omit***] : "Oh, no! When I made the list of those who attended the meeting, *I left* your name *out*!"

let down : [***disappoint***] : "I know, *I let* you *down* when I didn't do, what I promised. I'm really sorry."

let up : [***become less intense or slower***] : "It's been raining hard for a long time. Will it ever *let up*?"

look back on : [***remember***; ***reflect on / consider something from the past***] : "When they *looked back* on their many years together, they realised that their marriage had been a very happy one."

look down on : [***hold in contempt***; ***regard as inferior***.] : "It's not surprising that Ted has few friends. He seems to *look down on* anyone who doesn't like the same things that he does."

look forward to : [***anticipate pleasantly***; ***think about a pleasant thing before it* happens'**] : "I'm really *looking forward* to vacation. I can't wait for it to begin!"

look in on : [***visit in order to check something's / someone's condition***.] : "My father just came home from the hospital. I plan to *look in on* him today after I finish work."

look into : [***investigate / get more details about something***] : "Someone said there was a meeting at 9:30 but I haven't heard anything about it. Shall I *look into* it?"

look like : [***resemble*** (***in appearance***).] : "Does he *look like* his father or his mother?"

look over : [***check***; ***review***.] : "I think I may have some errors in this report. Could you *look* it *over*?"

look up : [***find something in a reference work***] : "I'm sorry, but I don't know what that word means. I'll have to *look* it *up*."

look up : [***find where someone lives or works and visit him/her***] : "Thanks for giving me your brother's address. When I'm in Chicago next month, I'll be sure to *look* him *up*."

look up to : [***respect***] : "Everyone *looks up to* Jane because she always makes time to help others."

luck out : [***be unexpectedly lucky***.] : "Gloria was worried because she wasn't prepared to give a report at the meeting, but she *lucked out* because the meeting was postponed."

make fun of : [***make jokes about*** (***usually unkindly***).] : "I agree that Bob looks ridiculous since he shaved his head, but don't *make fun of* him. You'll hurt his feelings."

make up : [***invent / create*** (***imaginary***) ***information***] : "Judy's story is hard to believe. I'm sure she *made* it *up*."

make up : [***compensate for something missed* or *not done*, *by doing extra or equivalent work***.] : "I'm sorry I missed the test. May I *make* it *up*?"

make up (with) : [***re-establish a friendly relationship by admitting guilt***] : "Jack and his girl friend were very angry with each other, but last night they finally *made up*."

make out : [***see / hear something well enough to understand what it means***. (**Note**: *often negative*.)] : "Kath's writing is very small. I almost need a magnifying glass to *make* it *out*."/ "What were the last two examples that he gave? I couldn't *make* them *out*."

make for : [***go to* or *toward***.] : "Her teen-aged children are always hungry. As soon as they arrive home from school, they *make for* the refrigerator."

make for : [***result in***; ***cause***] : "Many hands *make for* light work. (If many people work together, there's less work for everyone.)"

mark up : [***increase the price*** (***for resale***)] : "Mrs. Britt's import shop is profitable because she buys things inexpensively and then *marks* them *up*."

mark down : [***reduce the price (as an incentive to buy)]*** : "These shoes were really a bargain! The store *marked* them *down* by 40%!"

mix up : [***cause to become confused***] : "I didn't complete the assignment because I didn't know how. The directions *mixed* me *up*."

nod off : [***fall sleep*** (***usually unintentionally***)] : "The speech was so boring that several people in the audience *nodded off* before it was finished."

pan out : [***succeed***; ***happen as expected*** (***for plans***)] : (**Note**: *almost always negative when in statements*.) "I'll be here next week after all. My trip to Chicago didn't *pan out*."

pass away : [***die***] : "I was very sorry to hear that your grandfather *passed away*."

pass out : [***distribute***] : "Everyone in the room needs one of these information sheets. Who will help me *pass* them *out*?"

pick out : [***choose***; ***select***] : "Kelly's grandmother especially liked her birthday card because Kelly had *picked it out* himself."

pick up : [***arrange to meet someone and give her/him a ride***] : "Of course, we can go there together. What time should I *pick* you *up*?"

pick up : [***get***; ***buy***] : "The children just drank the last of the milk. Could you *pick* some more *up* on your way home this evening?"

pick on : [***bully***; ***intentionally try to make someone upset***] : "You should be ashamed of teasing your little brother, Tony! *Pick on* someone your own size!"

pitch in : [***help***; ***join together to accomplish something***] : "We'll be finished soon if everyone *pitches in*."

pull over : [***drive a vehicle to the side of the road***] : "When the policeman indicated that I should *pull over*, I knew he was going to give me a ticket."

put away : [***return something to the proper place***] : "I just took these clothes out of the dryer. Will you help me *put* them *away*?"

put off : [***postpone***; ***delay***; ***avoid***] : "I can't *put* this work *off* any longer. If I don't do it soon, it'll be impossible to finish it in time."/"When will Mr. Jack agree to a meeting? I keep asking for an appointment, but he keeps *putting* me *off*."

put on : [***begin to wear***; ***don***] : "It's a little bit chilly outside. You'd better *put* a sweater *on*."

put on : [***try to make someone believe something that is ridiculous or untrue***] : "Don't believe a word of what Jaru was saying. He was just *putting* us *on*."

put (someone) out : [***be inconvenient to someone***.] : "I hate to *put you out*, but I need a ride to the railway station and hope you can take me."

put up : [***return something to the proper place***] : "Your toys are all over the floor, Tinni. Please *put* them *up*."

put up : [***provide someone with a place to sleep***] : "There's no need for you to check into a hotel. I'll be happy to *put* you *up*."

put up with : [*tolerate*] : "It's really important to come to work on time. The boss won't *put up* with tardiness."

put back : [***return something to the proper place***] : "I've finished with these books. Do you want me to *put* them *back* on the shelves?"

rip off : [***cheat***; ***take advantage of***; ***charge too much***] : "Don't even think about buying a car there. They'll *rip* you *off*."

round off : [***change from a fraction to the nearest whole number***] : "*Round* all prices *off* to the closest whole rupee amounts. For example, round Rs. 83.71 off to Rs. 84.00."

run into : [***meet by chance***] : "Yesterday at the Supermarket, Jane *ran into* her former roommate. Before yesterday, they hadn't seen each other for nearly five years."

run out of : [***use the last of***] : "On the way home from work, my car *ran out of* gas."

set up : [***make arrangements for something***] : "You'll see Mr. Kamas tomorrow. I've *set* a meeting *up* for 9:30 A.M." tomorrow.

set back : [***cause a delay in scheduling***] : "We've had some problems with the project that have *set* us *back* at least two days. We'll give you a progress report tomorrow."

stand out : [***be noticeably better than other similar people or things***.]"Good job, Ann! Your work really *stands out*!"

stand up : [***rise to a standing position***] : "When the Chairperson entered the room, everyone *stood up*."

show up : [***arrive***; ***appear***] : "The boss was very upset when you didn't *show up* for the meeting. What happened?"

stand for : [***represent***] : "These letters seem to be an abbreviation. Do you know what they *stand for*?"

take after : [***resemble***; ***favour (in appearance)****]* : **Note***: used for people.* **"**Both my sister and I take after our father."

take / bring back : [***return***] : "This book is due tomorrow. I guess I should *take* it *back* to the library."/ "Yes, you can borrow my pen, but don't forget to *bring* it *back* to me when you're finished."

take care of : [***provide care for***; ***watch one's health***] : "Louis has been *taking care of* her father since he returned home from the hospital."/ "You've been working too hard lately. You'd better *take care of* yourself!"

take off : [***remove*** (***something you're wearing***)] : "Please *take* your hat *off* when you go inside the building."

take off : [***leave***; ***depart*** (***often suddenly or quickly***)] : "Was something wrong with Kelly?/ She *took off* without saying goodbye."/ "When does your plane take off?"

take up	:	[***begin*** (***a hobby or leisure time activity***)] : A: "Do you like to ski?" B: "I've never been skiing, but I think I'd like to *take it up*."
tell (someone) off	:	[***speak to someone bluntly and negatively, saying exactly what she/he did wrong***.] : "Julie was really angry at Bob; she *told* him *off* in front of all of us."
tick off	:	[***irritate someone***; ***make someone upset* or *angry***] : "It really *ticks* her *off* when someone is late for an appointment."
tick off	:	[***show that something has been completed by putting a tick (check) beside it***.] : "Here are the things you need to do. *Tick* each one *off* when you finish it."
throw away	:	[***discard***; ***put in the garbage***] : "You shouldn't *throw* those newspapers *away*; they're recyclable."
throw out	:	[***discard***; ***put in the garbage***] : "This food smells bad. You'd better *throw* it *out*."
throw up	:	[***vomit***] : "Rau was so nervous about his interview that he *threw up* just before he left for it."
try on	:	[***wear something briefly* to *check its fit*, *how it looks*, *etc***.] : "I'm not sure that jacket is large enough. May I *try* it *on*?"
try out	:	[***use a machine briefly to determine how well it works***.] : "I really like the way this car looks. May I *try* it *out*?"
turn around	:	[***make changes so that something that was unprofitable becomes profitable***] : "The company was doing poorly until it hired a new president. He *turned* it *around* in about six months and now it's doing quite well."
turn down	:	[***refuse***] : "I thought I could borrow some money from Joe, but when I asked, he *turned* me *down*."
turn in	:	[***report or deliver wrongdoers to the authorities***] : "Two days after the robbery, the thieves *turned* themselves *in*."
turn off	:	[***stop something by turning a handle or switch***] : "I'm feeling cold. Do you mind if I *turn* the air conditioner *off*?"
turn on	:	[***start by turning handle or switch***] : "It's cold in here. I'm going to *turn* the heater *on*"
turn up	:	[***appear unexpectedly***] : "We were all surprised when Rani *turned up* at the party. We didn't even know she was in town."
wait on	:	[***serve*** (***usually customers in a restaurant, shop, etc***.)] : "I want to make a complaint. The person who just *waited on* me was very impolite."
wait for	:	[***wait until someone / something arrives or is finished with something***] : "When will Jenny be finished with work? I've been waiting for her for almost an hour!"/"I'm tired of *waiting for* the bus. I guess I'll take a taxi instead."

wake up : [***rouse someone*; *cause someone to stop sleeping***] : "I have an important meeting tomorrow and I'm afraid I won't hear my alarm. Will you *wake* me *up* at 6:00 A.M.?"]

watch out for : [***be careful of*; *beware of***] : "There's a school at the end of this block. *Watch* out for children crossing the street."/"If you take that road, *watch out for* snow during the winter."

wear out : [***cause to become exhausted; cause to become very tired.***] : "I had four different meetings today. They *wore* me *out*."/

"I suppose I should get some new shoes. I've almost *worn* this pair *out*."

work out : [***solve a problem/resolve a difficult situation* (*usually by working together*)**] : "I know we disagree on many points, but I believe we can *work* things *out*."

wrap up : [***wear enough clothes to keep warm***] : "It's really cold today. Be sure you *wrap up* when you leave the house."

wrap up : [***finish something*; *bring something to a conclusion***] : "We've been talking about the problem for nearly three hours. I hope we'll be able to *wrap* the discussion *up* soon."

write down : [***record something in writing.***] : "Could you tell me your e-mail address again? I want to *write* it *down*."

write up : [***record; report in writing***]: "You'll need to make a report on your business meetings. Be sure you *write* them *up* as soon as possible after you return from your trip."

EXERCISES

1. Give the meaning of phrasal verbs, italicized in the following sentences, and then use them In your own sentences :

(a) Don't worry. I shall try to *bring him round*.

(b) You must *make up* your differences.

(c) He has promised to *go into the* matter.

(d) I shall *stand by* you through thick and thin.

(e) You will have to *make good* this loss.

2. Complete the phrasal verb in each of the following sentences :

(a) If the business continues to lose money, I'm afraid we'll have to close ....

(b) You'd better ring her...... and tell her you'll be late.

(c) I invited her to drop ..... any time she was passing, and have a cup of tea.

(d) He won't buy the car wihtout trying it .... on the road first.

(e) If you can't afford it, you'll have to do .... it.

3. **Complete the phrasal verbs in each of the following sentences :**

(a) They left the bomb in the street. Many people died when it blew ....

(b) The dacoits refused to give .... even though they were surrounded by the troops.

(c) The Prime Minister pulled .... his partymen for their rude behaviour.

(d) Each time a new problem cropped .... he rushed to his parents for advice.

(e) She broke ..... when she heard the news of her son's death.

(f) The chief guest gave .... the prizes.

Answers :

1. (a) persuade to accept something, (b) finish a quarrel, (c) investigate/go in detail, (d) support or help, (e) compensate.
2. (a) down, (b) up, (c) in , (d) out, (e) without.
3. (a) up, (b) in , (c) up , (d) up, (e) down, (f) away,

SPECIFIC USE OF WORDS (SIMILAR MEANING)

1. **Abstain (from a thing)** : One should *abstain* from sex without condom.

   Refrain (from doing) : One should *refrain* from making unwarranted comments.
2. **Revenge (to return injury for injury)** : She *revenged* herself upon Ramesh, her former lover.

   Avenged (to punish the evil doers) : He has devoted the past three years to *avenging* his daughter's death.
3. **Allow (giving permission for otherwise unreasonable thing)** : The girls were *allowed* to talk in the class by the principal.

   Permit (to give a positive assent) : 'I was *permitted* to appear in the M.A. examination.'
4. **Anger (a sudden feeling of unhappiness)** : The people showed great *anger* at the news.

   Resentment (more lasting feeling of unhappiness) : My words could not lessen her *resentment*.'
5. **Attain (to get by labour)** : *'We attained* a high degree of success through quality manage ment.

   Acquire (to have something permanently) : The students of this section have *acquired* a thorough knowledge of Naturopathy.
6. **Ancient (opposite to modern)** : 'We can learn a lot by the events of *ancient* history of India.'

   Old (opposed to new and to young) : 'The *old* dressing pattern is liked by the people even today. *'Old* people prefer simplicity to show.'

7. **Admit (to acknowledge as true)** : He didn't *admit* that he was present in the house.

Confess (to acknowledge responsibility or guilt) : He *confessed* that he had stolen the bike.

8. **Reply (to a letter)** : He always *replies* in time.

Answer (to a question) : *Answer* only five questions.

9. **Ability (intellectual quality)** : He is promoted on the basis of his *ability* to perform in a better way.

Capacity (capable to hold or achieve) : His *capacity* to work, regularly is praiseworthy.

10. **Surprise (when something unexpected happens)** : He was *surprised* to see the result.

Astonishment (extreme surprise) : I was *astonished* to see my ex-peon maintaining a car.

Wonder (surprise with admiration) : I *wondered* at his securing first position at all India level.

11. **Bravery (in the blood)** : The *bravery* of Rajputs is well known.

Courage (in mind) : He has the *courage* to speak the truth.

Valour (a quality more than bravery or courage) : The black commandoes are known for their deeds of *valour*.

Daring (rashness) : He is *daring* but not prudent.

Boldness (a short lived quality) : He showed his *boldness* in catching the robber single handed.

12. **Battle (a contest between two opposing armies)** : 'The third *battle* of Panipat was the last nail in the coffin of the Mughal Empire.'

War (a series of contests continued for a long time) : The World *War* I and II saw the pinnacle of inhumane face of the weapons made by the men.

13. **Begin (used on all occasions)** : 'The sooner you *begin* the better it is.

Commence (used only in official and formal language) : 'The examinations will *commence* on the 25th of May.'

14. **Beautiful (used for girls)** : She is a *beautiful* girl.

Handsome (used for man) : He is a *handsome* boy.

15. **Custom (relates to community or society)** : Wearing kumkum after marriage is a *custom* among the Hindus.

Habit (relates to individual) : Smoking is a bad *habit*.

16. **Crime (against law of the state)** : Theft is a *crime*.

Vice (offence against morals) : Drinking is a *vice*.

Sin (against law of religion or society) : Abusing elders is a *sin*.

17. **Ceiling (inner portion of roof)** : I want to purchase one *ceiling* fan.

Roof (upper covering of house) : They are playing at the *roof* of their house.

18. **Cite (is used for things or persons-give reference of)** : 'He *cited* the authority of the Supreme court Judgement.

Quote (is used for things only) : 'He *quoted* passage after passage from Geeta.'

19. **Compulsion (is physical, what is generally against our wishes)** : 'He was *compelled* by the court to be present on the next date of hearing.

Obligation (is moral; what is imposed on us as a duty) : 'We are *obliged* to maintain those who depend on us.'

20. **Confer (conferring is an act of authority)** : 'The government *confers* titles like Bharat Ratna, Padma Bhushan etc. on eminent persons.'

Bestow (an act of generosity / charity) : 'Many presents were *bestowed* on the refugees.'

21. **Character (mental or moral nature)** : 'A man of *character* overcomes all temptations.'

Conduct (one's actions) : 'None can blame you if your *conduct* is good.'

22. **Contentment (inner satisfaction, when nothing more is required)** : Actual happiness consists in *contentment.*

Satisfaction (fulfillment of one's desire) : She completed the preparations to my entire *satisfaction.*

23. **Contagious (disease spread by contact)** : Small pox is a *contagious* disease.

Infectious (disease spread through air or mosquitoes) : Malaria is an *infectious* disease.

24. **Cool (pleasant feeling)** : A *cool* wind is blowing.

Cold (unpleasant feeling) : Weather is very *cold* today.

25. **Defend (against an attack)** : Indian army is capable to *defend* the nation against any attack.

Protect (relates to an approaching injury) : Woollen clothes *protect* us from cold.

26. **Deny (relates to a past a action.)** : He *denied* his involvement in the murder.

Refuse (relates to a future action) : He *refused* to lend me any money.

27. **Doubt (a negative feeling)** : I *doubt* his loyalty (I think that he is not loyal).

Suspect (a positive feeling) : I *suspect* his involvement in the crime. (I am thinking that he was not involved).

28. **Discover (relates to thing already in existence)** : A new star was *discovered* by him.

Invent (a new thing is created) : Who *invented* telephone?

29. **Drown (relates to living beings)** : Many persons *drowned* in this river last year.

Sink (relates to things) : A ship dashed against this rock and *sank* last year.

30. **Wish (used in reference to a remote thing)** : I *wish*, I were a king.

Desire (used in reference to achievable things) : I *desire* to have a beautiful house and a name in the society.

31. **Want (relates to a thing, which is absent)** : I *want* to buy a car.

Need (relates to necessary things) : I *need* a pen to write with.

Require (to demand) : You are *required* to attend the meeting.

32. **Envy (bad feeling)** : He is *envious* of his friend's prosperity.

Jealousy (positive feeling of possessing something) : I am *jealous* of our ancestral heritage.

33. **Sufficient (necessary for)** : Two persons are *sufficient* for this job.

Enough (more than necessary) : I have *enough* money for the education of my children.

34. **Accident (an unexpected happening)** : Train *accidents* have become common now a days.

Incident (an ordinary occurrence) : Our newspapers are full of daily *incidents*.

Event (an important happening) : The third battle of Panipat was an important *event* in the History of India.

35. **Notorious (in bad sense)** : He is a *notorious* cheat.

Famous (in good sense) : Newyork is *famous* for multi-storeyed buildings.

Renowned (high reputation) : Shakespeare was a *renowned* dramatist.

36. **Excuse (courteously used for trifle matters)** : Please *excuse* me for troubling you at this time.

Forgive (used for comparatively big offences) : Please *forgive* me for my speaking ill about your friend.

Pardon = generally used for asking for repetition of something

I beg your pardon = Please repeat, I was unable to understand earlier

37. **Freedom (implies absence of restraint)** : We enjoy several kinds of *freedom* .

Liberty (implies previous restraint) : 'The prisoners were set at *liberty*.'

38. **Falsehood (something said or done with wrong intentions)** : 'He was guilty of *falsehood* when he spoke against the character of the Chairman.'

Lie (speak untrue words). Never tell a *lie*.

39. **House (refer to a dwelling unit)** : I am going to purchase a new *house*.

Home (Place to live with family association) : Men make houses, women make *homes*.

40. **Listen (to hear attentively)** : The teacher asked the students to *listen*.

Hear (to get through ears) : I am *hearing* your voice.

41. **Hope (is used when what we anticipate is welcome)** : I *hope* to get selected this time.

Expect (is used when what we anticipate is certain whether welcome or not) : 'Every student is *expected* to carry out the instructions given in the notes.

42. **Hardly (refers to degree)** : You can *hardly* imagine how much I suffered because of her allegation.'

Scarcely (refers to quantity) : Don't ask me for milk, I have *scarcely* enough for my own use.

43. **Idle (having nothing to do, due to circumstances)** : He has been sitting *idle* due to great slump in the market.

Lazy (habit of not doing things in active manner) : He is too *lazy* to reply letters.

44. **Sick (mental feeling)** : He is a *sick* man.

Ill (out of health) : She is *ill* nowadays.

45. **Libel (written)** : His statement in the press release amounts to *libel.*

Slander (spoken) : His public speech was taken note of and an action for *slander* is being initiated.

46. **Oral (spoken words)** : 'He was failed in *oral* examination.

Verbal (written words) : Teachers were abused *verbally* and assaulted physically.

47. **Presume (pre decision of a thing.)** : I *presume* he is responsible for the loss in business.

Assume (Assuming anything true) : I *assume* he will help you in case of need.

48. **Place (to put)** : *Place* the keys on the chair .

Keep (to put at some defined place) : *Keep* the books on the table.

49. **Possible (can be done)** : It is not *possible* to reach there by car .

Probable (likely to happen) : It is *probable* that she may agree with our proposal.

50. **Blunder (a gross mistake)** : Disclosing business secrets to the rivals is a *blunder* on your part.

Mistake (small act) : It is a *mistake* to go on leave without taking prior permission.

Error: (doing things against the recognised norms) : Your essay is full of grammatical *errors.*

51. **Praise (for actions)** : His actions are *praiseworthy.*

Admire (for qualities) : Everybody *admires* him for his benevolent nature.

52. **Prohibit (has force of law)** : The government has *prohibited* the cow slaughter.

Forbid (relating to personal life) : *Forbidden* fruits are more sweet.

53. **Recollect (remember after some efforts)** : Can you *recollect* what exact words did he use ?

Remember (having in memory) : I *remember* his words well.

54. **Regret (for a thing done or left undone.)** : I felt *regret* for not completing the job in time.

Sorrow (for big harm or evil) : Her husband's death caused her deep *sorrow.*

55. **Redress (to correct something wrong)** : A victim looks to the court for *redress.*

Relief (feeling happiness because something wrong did not happen) : I breathed a sigh of *relief.* When I saw my name in the list.

56. **Rob (to take away by force)** : 'He was *robbed* of his money and jewellery.

Steal (to take away secretly) : The thieves *stole* away all the goods of my house last Sunday.

57. **Talk (speaking with others)** : I want to *talk* to him in this matter.

Tell (to inform) : He *tells* me to wear neat dress.

Speak (to say in ordinary way) : He *speaks* loudly.

Say (to assert) How did you *say* so ?

58. **Seem (something assumed by our mind)** : The moon *seems* moving very fast.

Appear (impression of objects on us) : The statue *appears* to be of ancient time.

59. **See (in an ordinary way)** : I can *see* that house.

Look (see with some attention) : *Look* at that house.

Watch (to observe closely) : Keep a *watch* on that house.

60. **Scenery (a view of landscape)** : The *scenery* of Manali is indeed beautiful.

Scene (a place of any happening, a landscape) : He captured many beautiful *scenes* in his camera.

61. **Treaty (a written or formal arrangement)** : India and the U.S.A. have signed a *treaty* .

Truce (a temporary suspension of conflict) : On NewYear eve, there was a *truce* between the fighting militant groups.

62. **Trifling (no importance matter,)** : She never neglects even a *trifling* matter.

63. **Trivial (a small matter, no seriousness)** : 'Do not waste your time on *trivial* details.

64. **Trade (small or large scale buying selling; it can be within or out of the country)** : India has a long history of *trade* with (U.S.A.)

Commerce (on a large scale; generally with foreign countries) : They have made their fortune from industry and *commerce*.

65. **Empty (having nothing in it)** : The briefcase is *empty*.

Vacant (having some occupancy) : Only one berth is *vacant* in this compartment.

WORDS NEVER USED IN GOOD SENSE

Certain words and phrases are never used in good sense. To use these words where a good sense is meant will be ridiculous. It would be absurd to say ; 'He is a notorious scientist', or 'He concocted a good plan for the welfare of the poor'. Some of such words in common use are given hereunder .Students should learn these words well.

Accident	:	They met with an *accident*.
Accomplice	:	**Partner in some crime**: He was an *accomplice* in the theft.
Addicted	:	**To some bad habit;** drinking, gambling etc.
Adversary	:	**An opponent ; one who can cause harm.**
Airs	:	He should not give himself *airs* (conceited= airs).
Apprehensive	:	**Of some danger, loss or injury.**
Artisan	:	**One, who practises some art of inferior nature.**
Blunder	:	**A very serious mistake.**
Catastrophe	:	**A disastrous happening.**
Coalition	:	**Of men of divergent or opposite views** ; It refers a kind of partnership which is not homogeneous.
Commit	:	**To do something wrong** : *commit* suicide.
Concoct	:	**To make a plan for an evil purpose** : He *concocted* a false story to deceive her.
Counterfeit	:	**To imitate for unlawful purpose** : *Counterfeit* notes.
Concubine	:	**A woman having sexual relations with many persons.**
Cunning	:	**Doing things cleverly but in a deceiving manner.**

Credulity	:	**A simpleton** readiness to believe easily.
Dictator	:	**A despot ruler** , uses brutal force.
Despot	:	**A tyrannical kind of ruler**.
Demagogue	:	**An unprincipled leader or a ring leader**.
Effeminate	:	**Womanly** ('feminine' and 'womanly are used in good sense.) .
Fabricate	:	**To invent with a bad motive** : He *fabricated* a false story.
Fancy	:	**Imaginations, which are not guided by reason**.
Fine figure	:	He cuts *a fine figure* **(disgraceful or ridiculous figure)** (The phrase 'fine figure' is ironical.)
Fulsome	:	**Full or excess, so as to produce disgust, hatred.**
Glaring	:	**Conspicuous**, something evil : *glaring* error.
Hasty	:	**Quick to fault;** rash, easily excited; patienceless.
Inveterate	:	**Used for something bad** : 'an *inveterate* liar,' 'an *inveterate* enemy'.
Loiter	:	**To linger** at a time when greater haste is required.
Lonely	:	**Depressed** or **sad due to being alone.**
Minion	:	**An unworthy favourite.**
Notorious	:	**Evil reputation.**
Perpetrate	:	**Used only for crimes or offences.**
Plight	:	"She is in a sad *plight*."
Pocket	:	(i) **To put into one's pocket fraudulently** : "He *pocketed* the money fraudulently." (ii) **to submit patiently to an insult** : "He *pocketed* the insult patiently.
Prone	:	**To some vice or weakness**, as "He is *prone* to fever".
Sheer	:	Used as '*sheer* nonsense', '*sheer* folly'; we never say 'sheer virtue' but 'perfect or pure virtue.'
Shrewd	:	**Clever, but often in a sense implying some dishonesty or cunningness.**
To a degree	:	" He is insolent or dishonest *to a degree* (that is, **of high degree)**"; This phrase is usually applied to some **bad quality**.
Totally	:	**Always used for something bad**; as-'totally incompetent,' '*totally* blind'.
Trivial	:	**Things of little importance** : '*A trivial* or commonplace subject.'
Utter	:	'An *utter* fool, *an utter* failure'; **Always used for something bad.**

WORDS USED IN A GOOD SENSE

Some words and phrases are used in a good sense only , so students should learn the proper use of these words. Mere knowledge of Hindi meanings of these words is not suffice to use them in proper manner. Students must learn the *proper use of these words* :

Age	:	She is *of age* (= ***grown up***). She is *under age*(= a ***minor***).
Breed	:	He is a man of (*high*) breed (= ***a well-breed man***).
Bosom	:	He is my *bosom* (***fast friend***) friend.
Family	:	He is a man of (***high***) *family*.
Feeling	:	He is a man of (***tender and good***) *feelings*.
Famous	:	He is a *famous* artist.
Form	:	The boatman pulled together in *form* (= ***in good form*** **or** ***style***).
Order	:	Everything is in (***proper***) *order*.
Place	:	Everything was in *place* (= **in its *right place***).
Position	:	He is a man of (***good***) *position*.
Principle	:	He is a man of (***high***) *principles*.
Quality	:	He is a person of (***good* or *high***) *quality*; also-*quality* goods.
Renowned	:	Shakespeare was a *renowned* dramatist.
Rank	:	Man of (***high***) *rank*.
Taste	:	His remark was not in *taste* (= ***in good taste***).
Temper	:	He is out of *temper* (= ***ordinary* or *good temper***).(***But* 'in temper' or 'in a temper' means-'in *bad temper*'**; as– "She said all that in a *temper*, i.e., in a rage.")
Time	:	He arrived in *time* (= ***at the proper or right time***).

SOME RELATED PAIR OF WORDS

As bald as a badger.
As black as a gall.
As black as a coal.
As black as a crow.
As black as ink.
As black as midnight.
As black as pitch.
As blind as a bat.
As blind as a beetle.
As blind as a mole.
As blithe as a bee.
As hot as fire.
As hungry as a horse.
As innocent as a dove.
As light as a feather.
As loud as thunder.
As mad as a March hare.
As merry as a cricket.
As merry as a lark.
As mute as a fish.
As nimble as a bee.
As obstinate as a mule.

As blithe as a butterfly.
As blithe as a lark.
As bold as a lion.
As brave as a lion.
As bright as the day.
As bright as the light.
As bright as silver.
As brittle as glass.
As brown as a berry.
As busy as a bee.
As changeable as the moon.
As changeable as a weathercock.
As cheerful as a lark.
As clear as crystal.
As clear as day, noonday.
As cold as ice.
As cold as marble.
As cold as a cucumber.
As cold as a stone.
As cunning as a fox.
As dark as midnight.
As dark as pitch.
As dead as a door-nail.
As dead as a herring.
As deep as a well.
As drunk as a lord.
As drunk as a fiddler.
As dry as a bone.
As dry as dust.
As free as the air.
As fresh as a daisy.
As fresh as a rose.
As gay as a lark.
As faudy as a butterfly.
As gaudy as a peacock.
As gentle as a lamb.

...ld a hills.
As ... ghost.
As p... Job.
As play... butterfly.
...s plenti... quirrel or a kitten.
... poor as J... ckberries.
As proud as a ...
As quick as lightn...
As quiet as though...
As quiet as a lam...
As rapid as light...
As red as blood...
As red as a che...
As red as crim...
As red as ros...
As red as sca...
As regular a... work.
As rich as C...
As rich as a...
As dumb a... tue.
As fair as a...
As false as ... ot.
As fast as ... e.
As fat as ... Ben.
As fierce ... tiger.
As firm ... rock.
As flat ... board.
As flee ... a deer.
As sof ... butter wax.
Sound ... as a bell.
As steady as a rock.
As still as death.
As strong as the grave
As stupid as a statue.
As strong as a lion.

...d as gold
...aceful as a swan.
...grav as a judge.
...s greey as a dog.
As grec as glass.
As happ... a king.
As hard as ... marble.
As hard as ... e.
As harmless ... ove.
As heavy as ... and.
As hoarse as ... , a r...
As round as a ... r a gl...
As sharp as a n... , a r...
As silent as the ...
As silent as the gr... e.
As silent as the stars.
As silly as a goose
As silly as a sheep.
As slender as a gossamer.
As slender as a thread.
As smooth as a glass.
As smooth as velvet.

... as a donkey.
... as death.
...weet as honey, sugar.
...swift as an arrow.
...s swift as lightning.
As tall as a maypole.
As tall as a steeple.
As tame as a hare.
As timid as a hare.
As tricky as a monkey
As ugly as a scarecrow, a toad.
As vain as a peacock
As warm as wool.
As weak as a baby.
As white as a sheet.
As white as wool.
As white as snow
As wise as a serpent.
As wise as Solomon
As wise as Solomon.
As yellow as saffron.
As yielding as wax.